William Thomas Stead

**Truth About Russia**

William Thomas Stead
**Truth About Russia**
ISBN/EAN: 9783337299279
Printed in Europe, USA, Canada, Australia, Japan
Cover: Foto ©ninafisch / pixelio.de

More available books at **www.hansebooks.com**

# TRUTH ABOUT RUSSIA.

BY

## W. T. STEAD.

"The truths we least like to hear are those which it is most for our advantage to know."

CASSELL & COMPANY, Limited:
LONDON, PARIS, NEW YORK & MELBOURNE.
1888.
[ALL RIGHTS RESERVED.]

# CONTENTS.

## Book I.

| CHAPTER | FROM LONDON TO ST. PETERSBURG. | PAGE |
|---|---|---|
| I. | Why this Book is Written | 1 |
| II. | From the Standpoint of London | 4 |
| III. | From Paris after Seeing General Boulanger | 9 |
| IV. | In Belgium with M. de Laveleye | 21 |
| V. | The Capital of Prince Bismarck | 27 |
| VI. | In the Empire of the Tzar | 38 |

## Book II.

### WAR OR PEACE?

| | | |
|---|---|---|
| I. | At Count Tolstoi's, Yasnaia Poliana | 49 |
| II. | How England does not do her Duty | 56 |
| III. | Austria as Disturber of the Peace | 65 |
| IV. | Concerning Reptiles and Worms | 74 |
| V. | Bismarck the Peacemaker | 83 |
| VI. | Russia: What is Russia? | 90 |
| VII. | The Crux in Bulgaria | 98 |
| VIII. | Who is to Keep the Keys of the Tzar's House? | 107 |
| IX. | England's Real Danger in Central Asia | 113 |
| X. | The Tzar as Peace-keeper of Europe | 120 |

## Book III.

### NEW FIELDS FOR BRITISH ENTERPRISE.

| CHAPTER | | PAGE |
|---|---|---|
| I. | A Treaty of Commerce with Russia | 131 |
| II. | The Case for Reciprocity | 141 |
| III. | The Central Asian Railway | 148 |
| IV. | The Water-way to the Russian Australia | 159 |

## Book IV.

### THE TRIBUNE OF ALL THE RUSSIAS.

| I. | The Flock of Little Brown Sheep | 169 |
|---|---|---|
| II. | The Government of the Flock | 175 |
| III. | Shepherds and Shearers of the Flock | 186 |
| IV. | The Imperial Shepherd | 194 |
| V. | Eyes and Ears for the Tzar | 201 |
| VI. | A Plea for More Prisons | 223 |
| VII. | The Deputy Tzar of St. Petersburg | 246 |

## Book V.

### THE IDEAS OF GENERAL IGNATIEFF.

| I. | The Russian Mr. Gladstone | 259 |
|---|---|---|
| II. | General Ignatieff's Early Career | 270 |
| III. | From the Constantinople Conference to San Stefano | 276 |
| IV. | General Ignatieff's Policy in the East | 287 |
| V. | Minister of the Interior | 293 |
| VI. | General Ignatieff at Home | 298 |
| VII. | His Future | 306 |

## Book VI.

### THE SHADOW ON THE THRONE.

| CHAPTER | | PAGE |
|---|---|---|
| I. | CASTOR AND POLLUX, OR THE SIAMESE TWINS | 315 |
| II. | ARCHBISHOP LAUD REDIVIVUS | 322 |
| III. | THE EFFECT OF MONOPOLY | 329 |
| IV. | THE DOG IN THE MANGER | 339 |
| V. | THE STORY OF THE PASHKOFFSKI | 353 |
| VI. | EXILED UNHEARD | 363 |
| VII. | PERSECUTION NAKED AND UNASHAMED | 372 |
| VIII. | THE FUTILITY OF PERSECUTION | 380 |

## Book VII.

### COUNT TOLSTOI AND HIS GOSPEL.

| | | |
|---|---|---|
| I. | A WEEK AT YASNAIA POLIANA | 393 |
| II. | "RESIST NOT EVIL." | 404 |
| III. | "SELL ALL THAT THOU HAST AND GIVE TO THE POOR" | 420 |
| IV. | THE FIVE COMMANDMENTS OF THE KINGDOM OF HEAVEN | 426 |
| V. | THE TEACHER AND THE TEACHINGS OF COUNT TOLSTOI | 437 |

# TRUTH ABOUT RUSSIA.

## Book I.

### FROM LONDON TO ST. PETERSBURG.

#### CHAPTER I.

WHY THIS BOOK IS WRITTEN.

IN London in the spring of 1888 there existed a widespread feeling of uneasiness and of anxiety as to the possible outbreak of war in Europe. The Continent had just passed through the scare caused by the alleged concentration of Russian troops on the frontiers of Germany and Austria. Germany had enormously increased her armaments, Austria was preparing for war, and, to add to the general unrest, the rise of General Boulanger to notoriety in France seemed to menace with convulsion the disturbed quasi-tranquillity of the Continent. In military circles the talk was all of war. General Boulanger was going to overthrow the Republic, and then finding that he must do something to justify his ascendancy, it was gravely declared that he would probably attack England! London, with its incalculable wealth, lay at the mercy of a daring adventurer. Russia, it was added, was preparing to rush Constantinople, under pretext of an expedition to re-establish her lost ascendancy in Bulgaria. The air was full of premonitions of the panic which subsequently had a somewhat abortive issue in the columns of the *Daily Telegraph* and the speeches of the Duke of Cambridge and Lord Wolseley. The chief cause of this, no doubt, must be sought, first, in the abiding sense which rightly possesses the public mind as to the insufficiency of our armaments to stand the strain of serious war; and secondly, in the consciousness that Europe was entering upon a new era— the most conspicuous sign of which was the passing away of

B

the men who had made the history of the last quarter of a century. The reign of Frederick, whose death-bed was his only throne, marked the parting of the ways between the Old Europe and the New.

Before the new Emperor came to the throne of Germany, I thought it desirable to endeavour to ascertain as best I could, by means of a personal visit to the three northern capitals, what was the opinion of those in whose hands lay the destinies of the future as to the prospects of peace. Especially did it seem to me important to visit St. Petersburg in order to see the authorities who have it in their power either to keep the peace of Europe or to light up the flames of world-wide war. Whether for good or for evil, Russia holds in her hands the balance of power in Europe. The other states are either paralysed by internal dissensions, or foreign vendettas, or entangling alliances. Russia alone of the great military Powers is self-contained and self-sufficing, free alike from embarrassing alliances and paralysing antagonisms.

According to popular prejudice in England, the Tzar is the great disturber of the peace alike of Europe and of Asia. This is the root idea of the so-called traditional policy of the British Empire, and this largely influences the attitude of the Salisbury Government in its Continental policies.

Briefly stated, the Ministerial idea in foreign policy has been based upon the following conception of the situation. The disturbing forces in the European situation are France and Russia. France avowedly is in training for an attack upon Germany; Russia is her natural, her only ally. Russia, moreover, has designs of her own on the Balkan Peninsula and Constantinople, which render her of necessity a menace to the *status quo*. To keep the peace, it is necessary to form a League of Peace, of which Germany, from position and necessity, would form the nucleus. Germany and Austria made an alliance for defensive purposes, and to this alliance Italy was subsequently admitted. The idea of Lord Salisbury and his supporters was believed to be that England should also join this Peace League, at first as the ally of Italy. Signor Crispi publicly declared that Italy had concluded an alliance with England on the seas; and although Sir James Fergusson subsequently denied the existence of the alliance, Ministers are believed to have given the Italians some verbal assurances which, during Lord Salisbury's tenure of office, might compel the English fleet to undertake the defence of the Italian littoral against a French attack.

This is, however, only the extreme outgrowth of the underlying conviction about the Russian menace to the general peace which dominates the English Foreign Office and English society. If that conviction is erroneous, then the above attitude in relation to other Powers is more or less mistaken; and if so, the greatest service which any Englishman can render to his countrymen is to ascertain the truth about Russia. Is this great Empire which divides Asia with us a power which makes for peace, or which makes for war? In the New Europe upon which we are entering, must we regard the Tzar as peace-keeper or peace-breaker of the Continent? That is what I went to St. Petersburg to ascertain, and the results of my inquiries are chronicled in these pages. Events, of course, may utterly confound the conclusions at which I have arrived. Nothing, it is often said, ever happens except the unforeseen. I make no pretensions to the gift of political prophecy. I only claim that, having had opportunities which few Englishmen have enjoyed of ascertaining the actual aspirations of the men whose ideas and resolutions are the governing forces in Russian policy, I am fairly entitled to claim a hearing from those who care to form an intelligent judgment upon the governing factor in the great problem of peace or war.

Much of the matter of this volume has appeared in the *Pall Mall Gazette*. But the abiding interest of the subject has been held to justify its republication in a shape less evanescent than the columns of a daily newspaper, which "to-day is, and to-morrow is cast into the oven." If my conclusions are mistaken, of course there is no more to be said. But if they are sound, then the foreign policy of England should be revolutionised. A thesis which, if proved, carries with it so tremendous a corollary, needs to be considered as a whole, before its conclusion is either accepted or rejected.

As it is impossible to discuss Russia as a factor in international policy without taking into account the probable course of internal development, I have included in this volume, which deals primarily with Russia as the peace-keeper of Europe, chapters setting forth what seem to me the salient features of the domestic situation. Speculations of this nature, based, as they must be, upon a very rapid and cursory survey, cannot pretend to claim the same attention as the net result of a study of Russian foreign policy which has occupied my attention, with little intermission, ever since I entered journalism. Nevertheless, this side of Russia cannot be ignored. I have also added a chapter on Count Tolstoi, the novelist, under whose roof the chapters on "Peace or War?" were written, and whose personality excites more widespread interest, both in the Old World and the New, than that of any other subject of the Tzar.

## CHAPTER II.

### FROM THE STANDPOINT OF LONDON.

BEFORE leaving England, I made it my business to ascertain how things looked in the eyes of political leaders of all parties.

Ministers were not greatly preoccupied with foreign affairs. Their interests were firstly Irish, and secondly electoral and administrative. "Do you think," I was asked, "if we anticipated war, we should have reduced the navy estimates this year £800,000? Our only object is peace." The Ministerial view is that, if they have laid themselves open to the reproach of risking war, they have done so solely because they loved peace so well they were willing to risk war in order to maintain the Continental equilibrium. That they consciously desired war not even their worst enemies assert. But, in their exertions to maintain peace, the danger lay in the fact that they might be mistaken as to the Powers in whose support, in the interests of peace, they should cast the weight of English influence.

No Administration was ever bound over more heavily to abstain from unnecessary war.

Lord Salisbury is in office, and, barring accidents, there he is likely to remain. The only thing that would upset him would be the possibility that in his zeal for the maintenance of peace Lord Salisbury might commit the country to a war from which the nation recoiled. Lord Salisbury is strong by the strength of his weakness. He depends for his existence from day to day upon the support of the Liberal Unionists, headed by Lord Hartington, who would check, and check in time, any adventurous policy to which he might be inclined if he had a majority entirely of his own way of thinking. There is always a possibility that an English Tory majority may emulate the exploit of the swine of Gadara, and run violently down the steep slopes of Jingoism into the abyss of a war with Russia; but, fortunately for the prospects of his Cabinet, Lord Salisbury is warned off from this road to ruin by a double barrier. Lord Hartington and the Liberal Unionists are not Jingoes, and an unnecessary intervention in the affairs of Europe which involved the country in war would compel them to vote against the Government. Their antipathy to Home Rule, and their distrust of Mr. Gladstone, are too strong to be overcome by any lesser peril. For the sake of the Union with Ireland, and in order to keep Mr. Gladstone out, they will tolerate almost anything. The one thing which they will not tolerate is an avoidable war. Lord Salisbury has also to reckon upon the opposition of a formidable section of his own supporters. Lord Randolph Churchill, who was Chancellor of the Exchequer and Leader of the House of Commons when Lord Salisbury formed his Ministry, is now a supporter with views of his own, and as one of these views is an emphatic determination that England shall not be plunged into war for any purely Continental interests, Lord Salisbury could not go very far in a warlike direction without finding the wheels of his war chariot " spragged " by his own friends.

Whether from this or from any other cause, whatever they may have dreamed of once, the present attitude of Ministers is not that of men who are resolved to play a decisive or even a leading part in the European drama.

The coming man in the Conservative Cabinet, Mr. Balfour, Lord Salisbury's nephew, who has excited an extraordinary amount of enthusiasm among his own party by his courage and consistency, has a tolerably level head, and is not dominated in foreign politics by antiquated prejudices. He is a young man with a great career before him, able, upright, honest, and in private life as charming and attractive as in the House of Commons he seems to his opponents the reverse. When I called at the Irish Office, before leaving town, I was grieved to see that the harass and the worry of Irish administration were already bleaching the coal-black hair of the Chief Secretary. It was only here and there that the white hairs showed, but the process had begun. Mr. Balfour was as pleasant and as light-hearted as ever, for few Chief Secretaries—despite the tell-tale evidence of his hair—ever took their grave and responsible duties more easily. He was, however, too much engrossed in the work of his department to have much thought to spare for foreign complications. He made one remark, however, which is worth noting and quoting. I had remarked that the question of peace or war affected him perhaps more than anyone, because it was always England's troubles abroad which had given Irish Nationalists their opportunity at home; and if England were involved in war abroad the necessity of withdrawing the 30,000 soldiers now kept in Ireland would necessitate the concession of the Irish demands. Such at least, I said, has been the invariable course of Irish history. Such, I knew, was the deep-rooted conviction of at least one eminent member of the Conservative party. "I disagree," said Mr. Balfour; "I do not think that if England became involved in a foreign war it would necessitate any abandonment of the policy which we are pursuing. I think I see how this policy can be carried out resolutely for twenty years, whether we have peace or war, and those twenty years will solve the Irish question." Nevertheless, the more anxious the Conservatives are about achieving the success of their Irish policy, the more sedulously will they eschew the adoption of any adventurous policy elsewhere which might bring their Administration down with a run. They have given many hostages to fortune in Ireland, and the Union binds them over to keep the peace. The growing ascendancy of Mr. Balfour in the party cannot be regarded as otherwise than hopeful for the adoption of a pacific and intelligent policy abroad.

From the Irish Office to 10, James Street, is but a short walk, but between the occupant of No. 10 and the Irish Secretary there is a great gulf fixed. For No. 10, James Street—a pleasant little bye-street within a stone's throw of Buckingham Palace—was the town residence of Mr. Gladstone. I found him busily engaged writing in a snug study at the back of the house. He entered heart and soul into the problem which I wished to solve, and discussed the question with the keenest interest. Age has not dulled his interest in human affairs, nor have the disillusions of life deadened the enthusiastic faith with which he steps forth to meet the unknown future. One of his remarks was very characteristic. Speaking of the right of Bulgaria to independence, he exclaimed, referring to the differences between his point of view and that of those who take their stand on arrangements made at the Berlin Congress, "I believe in freedom. Yes, in freedom. F–R–E–E–D–O–M!" spelling it out letter by letter—"freedom in the plain, simple orthography of the word, and it is that which makes my standpoint so different from theirs." Mr. Gladstone has no belief in England being in danger of war from France or from Russia. He ridiculed the idea of a French invasion, and said that the arguments used against the Channel Tunnel made him blush to look a Frenchman in the face. "Not that I am so much for the Tunnel," he said, "as I am against those who are against it." Mr. Gladstone was careful to point out that he was not a "non-interference man," which is perfectly true. He has never been, and is not now, a non-interventionist. At the same time, he is a strenuous opponent of any alliances with any European Power. "It is," he declared with great emphasis, "not only desirable that we should be entirely free from entangling alliances for our own sake; I would go further, and assert that it is the indispensable condition of our being able at any time to intervene with advantage on behalf of the general peace." He was as much opposed to a league of pacific Powers, for the purpose of preventing war by force, as to any other kind of league. Even with the strongest case that could be made out in favour of such a league he would have nothing to do. To reconstitute the European concert on the basis of existing treaties, and to ally all the Powers against any one of their number who attempted to subvert the *status quo* by the sword, was entirely opposed to his ideas. It would involve an alliance with Germany to prevent Alsace and Lorraine ever reverting to France. That might be a good thing or a bad thing, but whether good or bad, it was not for Englishmen to settle. It was a matter primarily concerning the populations of those provinces, and after them the people of France and Germany. Englishmen had neither the knowledge to enable them to interfere in such a matter wisely, nor any responsibility for discharging such a duty. Suppose we put it the other way. "Shall you and I undertake to decide that because the populations of these provinces have become largely French in their habits of thought, language, &c., therefore they must be returned to France? That is not a question for us to decide. If we attempted to do so, the French and the Germans might, on their part, undertake to say whether or not we should grant Ireland Home Rule."

Mr. Gladstone expressed himself strongly in favour of a peaceable solution of the Bulgarian question. He would see with grave dissatisfaction any attempt on the part of any Power to interfere arbitrarily with Bulgarian freedom. He was full of praise of the capacity for self-government shown by the Southern Slavs. Leave them alone and they will do well. He still stands by the famous formula, "Hands off!" He had addressed it to Austria in 1880, and he thought that he had done good by so doing. I could see that he was equally ready to say, "Hands off!" to Russia, if in his opinion she should be encroaching upon the rights, the liberties, and the privileges of the Balkan Slavs.

There was, as might be expected, an entire absence of any predisposition to judge the policy of Russia or that of any other Power, excepting as he would wish his own policy to be judged. No man has a more singularly open mind, or is more generous in his judgment of others. Certain misapprehensions as to Russia's policy in the Penj-deh dispute which might have embittered other men, only made him anxious to ascertain whether or not he had been accurately informed in the matter, and no trace of prejudice could be discovered which would prevent him welcoming with all the goodwill in the world an *entente cordiale* between Russia and England.

Lord Randolph Churchill would not even allow Bulgarian freedom to stand in the way of a good understanding with Russia. Lord Derby remains true to his determination to maintain a policy of strict abstinence from Continental broils. He is, after Mr. Bright, the most thoroughgoing non-interventionist in the Empire. On the whole, so far as our statesmen are concerned, the danger of the adoption of a deliberately hostile policy to Russia seems to me of the slightest. The danger does not lie in that direction, but in a policy of drift above, with a constant liability to sudden gusts of popular passion and prejudice from below. The general note at present of the British

politician, whether in or out of office, towards foreign affairs, is
one of extraordinary and unintelligible indifference—unintelligible, that is, if statesmanship is to be henceforth anything
more than a mere game of finesse and intrigue, of bluster and of
bounce, with a horizon strictly limited by the date of the next
General Election. With that limitation, the prevailing apathy
is, alas! only too intelligible.

## CHAPTER III.

#### FROM PARIS AFTER SEEING GENERAL BOULANGER.

It was a splendid moonlight night, when the little two-funnelled
steamer *Samphire* left Dover Pier for Calais. Nearly four years
before, I had crossed the Channel at night on a hurried visit
to the King of the Belgians. But although the moonlight and
the straits were the same, how changed was all besides! On the
night before my audience at the Royal Palace at Brussels, the
Channel was as smooth as a mill-pond. Hardly a ripple moved
the waters across which the moonlight spread a long silver track
—a kind of celestial carpeting for the passage of Her Majesty's
mail. But this time the wind was up, and the steamer tossed
lightly as a cork upon the moonlit waves which thundered and
moaned and heaved under her bow. The night was lovely though
the wind was high, and the waves made the steamer heel and
roll until the bright lights of the Foreland—that double-eyed
Pharos which keeps watch and ward over the English Channel
from the brow of a ghostly range of white chalk cliffs—shone
sometimes above and sometimes below the boats which hung
from the davits at the side. There was something weird and
Spenserian in the great white cliffs with the blazing eyes of
flame gleaming sleepless over the tossing straits, while overhead
even the stars seemed to shift and wander as the vessel heaved
and rose and fell on the chopping sea.

I was not sorry the sea was rough. That little strip of
tumbling brine is worth to England, at the lowest computation,
the annual interest on a thousand millions sterling, and in the

present turbulent aspect of Europe there is comfort even in the *mal de mer* which haunts as a kind of local pestilence the waterway between the French and English shores.

Arriving in Paris on the morning of the day (April 27) on which General Boulanger was to make his long-expected manifesto, I found opinion much divided as to the prospects of his campaign; but on one point there was general agreement. That point is that General Boulanger is an honest man, a good fellow, unassuming and simple, the last man in the world who would be expected to play the part of a Louis Napoleon. He may have his Morny in Laguerre, and in his *entourage* there may be pestilent ruffians like the bloodsuckers whom the Third Napoleon gave *carte blanche* to drink from the veins of France, but he himself is no adventurer of the familiar type. His opponents ridicule him. He is nobody, they say. His friends idolise him, declaring you may trust him implicitly, but both agree in scouting the idea that he is capable, either for good or for evil, of playing the evil rôle of the Napoleons.

It may be a relief to some people to know that there was an equally universal agreement as to the absurdity of the conviction, seriously entertained in some influential quarters in London, that General Boulanger's accession to power would endanger the security of England. The suggestion was hailed with peals of incredulous laughter. " Attack England! What for? It is too absurd." And then everyone would laugh at the immensity of the joke. Two very decided views were expressed as to the grounds why such an idea should be summarily dismissed as entirely beyond the pale of possibility. The first was material. To invade England, the first essential is a fleet, and M. Ferry, by his colonial wars, destroyed the efficiency of the fleet. The wear and tear of the Chinese campaign played havoc with the material of the French navy, and so far from the French being in a position to undertake to command the Channel, and transport an army of 100,000 men to the coast of Kent, it is doubtful whether, if war were to break out with Italy, the French ironclads would be able to keep their ground in the Mediterranean. The second argument was moral; the French electors, it is said, have a mortal horror of war. It is doubtful whether they could be roused to fight for Alsace and Lorraine. It is certain that they would oppose any other war, and a war with England would be regarded, alike by the peace party, which includes all the industrious toilers in town and country, and all the war party, which is headed by the League of Patriots and the like, as being sheer lunacy. General Boulanger's popularity with the warlike section, as well as with the advocates of peace and progress, has arisen in no small measure from his unconcealed opposition to any policy which scattered the national forces, or diverted the attention of France from her own affairs. To suppose that he, of all men in the world, would suddenly place himself at the head of an army of invasion directed against England, is almost as wild a dream as to imagine Sir Wilfrid Lawson adopting a policy of free trade in drink as his programme, after being established in the Home Office, or to suppose that if Mr. Morley became Irish Secretary he would offer the whole of the Nationalists the historic alternative of " Hell or Connaught." " It is amazing, it is incredible," exclaimed one eminent diplomat, when I was endeavouring to explain the nature of the alarms which affect some eminent men in London, " it is marvellous to think that such a delusion could be entertained by anyone of regular brain." If General Boulanger's success means war at all, it will be war with Germany, and with Germany alone. But he strongly protests against the supposition that he is an advocate for war.

I had an appointment with the General at No. 73 at ten o'clock on the morning of April 28. I was there twenty minutes before time, and had to wait for half an hour after the time fixed. The corridor on the third story was filled with expectant visitors. All the seats were occupied, and men and women stood about the corridor waiting until the little curly-headed boy in buttons—a namesake and a compatriot of Joseph who was sold into Egypt—summoned them into the presence of the great man. It was a motley throng. One lady was reading the *Athenæum*, another wore the deepest mourning. A smart officer in full uniform strode in with his sword under his arm, seedy-looking veterans with Napoleonic moustaches lounged about patiently, like bullocks waiting for water; here and there an *ouvrier* in a blouse stood waiting, but the majority were well-dressed gentlemen. As a rule the interview accorded to each visitor did not exceed five minutes. The page-boy Joseph studied *L'Intransigeant* with the gravity of a philosopher in the intervals between the entry and the exit of the visitors. The corridor was like the antechamber of a Minister. Already it was full of those who were hastening to pay court to the rising sun.

The General's apartment was a pleasant, sunny room, with plenty of windows, a cheerful fire, and a pleasant greenery of shrubs at the opposite end. General Boulanger came forward to greet me. Nothing could be kinder and more cordial, more simple and unaffected, than General Boulanger's welcome. In appearance he reminds you of anything in the world excepting a fire-eater or an adventurer of any kind. He was simply dressed, and he might have been mistaken any day either for a German or an Englishman. A kindly, good-hearted creature he seemed, conscientiously bent upon doing his best, whatever he did, and by no means quite sure whither the destinies are driving him, but gradually acquiring a conviction that they have something great in store for him—that was General Boulanger as he seemed to me, and by no means a man for a *coup d'état*. But I am by no means sure whether he might not prove equal, if the occasion arose, to purging the Chamber—let us say of Jews, jobbers, and rascals—after the fashion of Colonel Pride. Of that, however, it is in vain at present to speculate.

After bidding me welcome and expressing the usual courteous compliments, General Boulanger explained that he feared he would not be able to answer my questions so fully as he would have wished to do, because he had put a lock on his lips which prevented him speaking. I had been told that he spoke English fluently. His mother is said to have been Welsh, and he was educated at Brighton. He explained that it was so many years since he had spoken English he could only use the language with difficulty. He understood it also very badly, and would prefer the conversation should take place in French. I said that if he could not speak freely to me, might I speak freely to him? "Certainly," he replied. I gladly availed myself of the permission :—

"In London," I began, "we look upon the situation with great interest, and we regard it as being serious."

"Moi aussi," said the General, "so do I; the situation is very serious."

"Generally speaking," I went on, "I think that I may say that in

England your movement is regarded as seriously threatening (1) the Republic, (2) the peace of Europe, and (3), although this is only in some quarters, the peace of England."

General Boulanger replied quietly, but decisively, "And all these suppositions are false."

"It may be so," I replied, "but that is the way in which the situation strikes the English mind. The popular English traditional idea of the French people is that, while they are very reasonable, industrious, and peaceable as a general rule, they are liable every now and then—say at intervals of from fifteen to eighteen years—to periodical fits of restlessness—almost madness—when they are apt to make trouble and rush into war, and the idea prevails among many of our people that such a period has now arrived."

General Boulanger nodded, to indicate that he followed the line of argument.

"The French people," I continued, "seem to be discontented with the Government and the system, which has disappointed their aspirations, and, being discontented, they usually fling themselves at the feet of someone. This someone happens to-day to be General Boulanger."

General Boulanger struck in—"Attendez. Much is said about my personal ambitions. The real truth is that I have striven to the best of my ability to serve my countrymen. The French people have seen this and recognised it. There lies the only secret of my strength. My strength is solely the strength of the feeling among the people that I have done this."

"No doubt," I replied; "it is not that we impute personal ambition to you. We merely note that France seems disposed to fling herself at your feet, and the danger is that the Republic may go under. Then if General Boulanger comes at the top, owing to the dissatisfaction felt at the shortcomings of the Republic, General Boulanger must do something to satisfy the restless cravings of the nation. If Russia will help, so they argue, he will go to war with Germany. But Russia will not help. Then, as he must do something, so they come to the conclusion that he will go to war with England."

General Boulanger, laughing, "But why?"

"Simply because they say you must do something, and as you cannot attack Germany single-handed with any chance of success, you will be driven to attack England."

General Boulanger listened attentively, and then replied, "What you say was true enough formerly, but it is not so now. At the present moment there are internal social questions which urgently demand solution. These questions must be solved. It is not war, but the solution of these questions, which is the business of the nation. War would postpone and aggravate them all."

I ventured to remind him that history abounded with examples of Governments going to war under these very circumstances, in order to evade or postpone internal difficulties.

"Yes," said the General, "that has no doubt been the case. But now in France the people have their minds set upon the solution of these internal questions, and they would tolerate no diversion which would distract their attention from them. As for the notion that I shall attack England, I have never dreamed of such a thing. Of course," he added, with a merry little laugh, "if England were to attack us, we should have to defend ourselves."

"England," I exclaimed, "attack you, with our little handful of an army!"

General Boulanger shrugged his shoulders, and we all laughed at the ridiculous idea.

The conversation then turned to the manifesto which he had launched the previous night. I remarked that I had been considerably surprised to read his declaration that he would be one of the first to vote for the suppression of the Presidency if it were proposed to abolish it in the Constituent Assembly summoned to revise the Constitution.

"It is quite true," said the General, gravely; "I am perfectly prepared to vote for its abolition."

"But," I asked with some abruptness, "what would become of you in that case? If there is no presidency, what would be your position?"

"Nous verrons," said General Boulanger; "we have a French proverb which says, 'There will always be water flowing under the bridge.'"

I did not quite see the point of the proverb, and he repeated it in English: "There is always water flowing under the bridge," and explained that, whatever happened, he did not fear that he would always find some opportunity in which to serve his country.

One of his friends subsequently told me that what General Boulanger would really like was not the Presidency, but the position of permanent Minister of War, an office from which he could watch over the welfare of the Army of the National Defence. This, however, is quite a different idea from that which he formerly favoured, which, as I reminded him, was to reconcile his candidature with the Republic by constituting him an American President:—

"*Peut-être*," said General Boulanger.

"But," I replied, "if there is no Presidency, what is there then left but dictatorship?"

"I have never dreamt of it," replied General Boulanger, with some emphasis: "*jamais, jamais!*"

The General then stretched out his hand. He shook my hand with a curious corkscrew-like twist, and then, retaining it in both of his, he said: —"My only idea has been to serve the people. It is for them that I have laboured, and my position is entirely due to their appreciation of my efforts for them."

"But is it not also," I said, "because they believe that you, best of all, will help them to regain the lost provinces of Alsace and Lorraine ?"

General Boulanger replied, "No doubt that may be the case. But mark my words. I shall never seek a pretext for making war against Germany; but, of course, if Germany attacks us, we shall do well to be prepared. France," said he, with more feeling than he had shown during the conversation, "can never forget her lost provinces. Never. But to attack Germany or to wish for war—that is another thing."

This brought me to the root of the question, and I attacked it without reserve.

"Tell me," said I, "do the French people still care as much as ever for Alsace and Lorraine ? Only yesterday I was assured that President Grévy had expressed a decided opinion to the contrary."

"M. le Président Grévy ?" asked the General.

"Yes," said I, "so I was told."

"Then, if so," said General Boulanger, "it is only a proof that M. Grévy is *un gâteux*. I mean," he explained, "that he has grown so infirm that his opinion has no longer the weight it had."

"But," I continued, "there are others of M. Grévy's opinion. I was assured yesterday by one who professed to be very confident on the subject, that there was not a single mother in Bordeaux, or Marseilles, or elsewhere, who would send her son to die for the sake of restoring Strasburg to France."

"We shall see, said the General, "who is right."

"And in the Nord also at the late election," I said, "the feeling of the people was decidedly adverse to war."

"And so am I adverse to war," said General Boulanger. "We do not desire war. We are for peace. But," he said, "my ideas as to peace are these—namely, that peace to be permanent must be honourable. It must not be a peace which has been imposed in the pride of conquest, and that has to be submitted to because the throat of the vanquished is under the heel of the conqueror."

I feared that this was only another way of saying that France would take the first good opportunity that offered to wrest back her ceded provinces, and I said so.

He replied with the stereotyped formula: "We shall not provoke a war, but we must be prepared against an attack."

We once more shook hands. "Au revoir," said the General, "when you return to Paris." And our place was taken by the next on the list. The stream of callers continues from half-past nine to half-past eleven every Tuesday, Thursday, and Saturday. General Boulanger may not be a great man, but he seems to have a remarkable gift in the knack of winning confidence and making friends. It reminded me, when I saw him welcoming successive visitors with such *empressement,* of a verse or two from the history of Israel in which it is written that—

"Absalom said, Oh, that I were made judge in the land, that every man which hath any suit or cause might come unto me, and I would do him justice! And it was so, that when any man came nigh to him to do him obeisance, he put forth his hands and took him and kissed him. . . . So Absalom stole the hearts of the men of Israel."

The net result of my conversations with the statesmen, the diplomats, and the journalists whom I met in the French capital is not difficult to sum up in a single sentence; they all say one thing and one thing only: France is for peace. If there is to be war in Europe, France will not make it. Neither will France upset the Republic. The French have not gone mad. They are a little restive and discontented, but their malaise is no more likely to result in war and revolution than a passing indigestion is likely to develop into delirium tremens. Whether General Boulanger comes to the front, or whether General Boulanger disappears, does not matter. If he were to put himself forward as the advocate for war, he would have no following, save M. Déroulède and the handful of enthusiasts who form the League of Patriots. If it depends on France there will be no war. France will neither attack Germany nor provoke war with Germany. France is for peace. So says the Prime Minister, so says General Boulanger, so says the Minister-maker, M. Clémenceau, and so say the representatives, journalistic and official, of other powers in Paris. I can hardly exaggerate the optimism that prevailed in all circles in the French capital as to the prospects of peace. "There will be no war; certainly France will make none. Nor do I think that Germany will make one either, so long at least as Bismarck lives," was the declaration made by one of the most influential men in France; and Ministers and diplomatists all say the same thing. As for the nightmare of a war with England, the suggestion is simply drowned in such shrieks of laughter that it is impossible to discuss the subject.

Everything, of course, may change, like the weather; but for the moment the political weatherglass in Paris points to "set fair."

I had a very pleasant and profitable time calling upon

Ministers and political and diplomatic personages, and I acknowledge with gratitude the ready courtesy and consideration with which I was everywhere received. My first visit was naturally paid to the Ministry of the Interior, now the official residence of the Prime Minister of France.

M. Carnot, the President of the Republic, being now on a tour in the South of France, there was no occasion to call at the Elysée, and as I had to leave Paris before the President's return, I contented myself with a view of his portrait at the Salon. M. Carnot, who, together with General Boulanger, M. Ferry, and Cardinal Lavigerie, figures among the more conspicuous portraits of the year, does not appear to be an impressive or an overpowering personality. A black-visaged gentleman with a certain wooden immobility of countenance, commonplace but obstinate, M. Carnot's portrait is a striking contrast to that of M. Ferry, whom he defeated in the contest for the Presidency. M. Ferry's deeply lined and somewhat gross countenance showed more character—not of the best sort—than could be discerned in M. Carnot, but both showed to a great disadvantage beside the honest, open, intelligent face of General Boulanger, whose excellent full-length portrait was almost as prominent in the Salon as the original is in French politics. But this is a digression. The Salon is at the Ministry of Fine Arts, and my first visit was paid to the Ministry of the Interior.

The French Home Office stands back from the Faubourg St. Honoré, almost opposite the British Embassy, where Lord Lytton displays in the hall the trophies which remind his visitors that the present occupant of the Embassy was at one time Viceroy of India. Unlike Mr. Matthews, whose windows look out upon a dismal quadrangle of stone, the French Minister of the Interior looks out on a garden; not a very large one, it is true, but its green grass triangle is a welcome relief to the eye. It is a famous place, is this centre of the centralised Government of France. Under the Empire here was the box-seat of the coachman to whom Napoleon entrusted the driving of France. From the comfortable and spacious chamber in which M. Floquet graciously gave me audience, and discussed the prospects of General Boulanger and of the peace of Europe, went forth the decrees which Imperial prefects in every department were ready to enforce.

C

The present occupant of the Ministry of the Interior, M. Floquet, is a man of singular rectitude, and of great civic courage. In his earlier days he was vehement and impulsive; and words and acts of his in those days of hot youth are still remembered in his favour even by those who differ from his sentiments. It is hardly fair to say that he has fought his way up step by step, for politics have never been to him the profession which they are to many Frenchmen. M. Floquet is a man of independent fortune, and he is in politics to serve his country, not to make himself a fortune. He was an honest man, and while M. Wilson was entrenched at the Elysée it was impossible for an honest man to make much headway in French politics. When M. Wilson fell, and it was resolved to make a determined attempt to cut out the gangrene of official corruption, M. Floquet naturally became Prime Minister of France.

The Ministry for Foreign Affairs stands on the other side of the Seine, near to the Chamber, and not very far from the Invalides, the gilded dome of which is one of the most familiar landmarks of Paris. Inside, the splendour of the Foreign Office throws the Ministry of the Interior entirely into the shade. M. Goblet, who is now Minister for Foreign Affairs, was no long time ago Prime Minister of France. Like M. Thiers, he is not tall. He reminded me at first—I don't exactly know why—of the portraits of Prince Gortschakoff, although in appearance he might easily be mistaken for an Englishman. He speaks with great precision and clearness. In the tribune and in former Ministries it is said he displayed some impetuosity of temper, and he is a Gallic cock that crows quite as loudly when defeated as when victorious. His room was business-like, and the great windows flooded the place with light. Immediately behind the comfortable and solid arm-chair in which the Minister transacts the foreign affairs of France hung several large maps, one I noticed particularly being by Kiepert, the German geographer.

After seeing Ministers it was necessary to see the Minister-maker, and I had a very pleasant talk with M. Clémenceau in the office of his paper, *La Justice*, close to the boulevard Montmartre. M. Clémenceau received me in his office, which is notable as having among its appurtenances a large cast of the Venus of Milo, a divinity not usually encountered in the editorial sanctum. M. Clémenceau, who was accompanied by his brilliant lieutenant, M. Camille Pelletan, looked pale and out of sorts. He had a hacking cough, but his spirits were high and his confidence both in peace and in the Republic was more emphatic than that of anyone I have met in Paris. His position with regard to the Floquet Ministry is somewhat equivalent to that occupied by Lord Hartington in relation to the Salisbury Cabinet. If at any time he were to withdraw his support, down would come M. Floquet and Cabinet and all. He is, however, going to continue to support the Government, preferring to do so from the outside for reasons which satisfied M. Floquet when M. Clémenceau alleged them as reasons for declining the portfolio that was placed at his disposal.

Quite as interesting as my interviews with the Ministers was the visit—my first—to the Salon, which was opened for private view. From the point of view of my mission I noted in passing that in this Salon there were comparatively few battle pictures, and hardly any of these related to the incidents of the Franco-German war. The most striking in its grim realism represented an incident in the taking of the Malakoff, when a French colonel salutes the colours which a French soldier has clasped in death. The foreground is a horrid compost of corpses, and the central figure of the dead soldier is only too vividly real. There was a confused battle-piece representing the battle of Borodino, and another called the battle of Waterloo. Here and there, there were pictures representing more recent events, but if the Salon walls afford any test, the French were not thinking much about revenge. They were thinking much more about what Matthew Arnold styled their great goddess Lubricity. The nudities in the Salon were very numerous and very naked, and very much not ashamed. Most of them were very ugly, as if mere absence of clothes atoned for all other defects.

By far the most striking painting in the Salon was M. Albert Maignan's magnificent picture of "The Voices of the Tocsin." It is a marvellous conception, executed by the hand of a master. It represents the ringing of the tocsin in time of war. Four men are pulling with desperate energy at the bell-ropes, straining every muscle with convulsive effort to make the great bell peal forth over the threatened land the dread alarum of war. Far on the distant horizon, the lurid glare of a burning hamlet flames blood-red against the sky, and overhead the great bell swings madly to and fro, and from its iron mouth pour forth in maddening rout the "Voices of the Tocsin." These are personified as creatures of the storm, entirely human, although fleeting down through the air like spirits, each with frenzied eyes, and a face of agonised alarm, crying aloud their message of terror and of dismay over a doomed land. It is a great picture, a wonderful realisation, full of the force, the fury, and the terror of the alarm of war.

How long, I wondered, as I stood before that painted canvas, will it be before "the voices of the tocsin" are let loose over Europe? how long before the journalists of the Continent are labouring like these tortured ringers to sound the alarm of war? Who knows? Not I, nor M. Floquet. Nor Prince Bismarck, nor the Tzar. If we could depend upon declarations, the tocsin will never be sounded by the French. Everywhere in France, in the highest quarters and in the lowest, there is only heard one word on the subject, and that word is peace. France will never declare war. France will never provoke war. If she is attacked she will defend herself with *élan*, and hurl back the invader with irresistible ardour, but to attack Germany—never! As for the supposition that, under any conceivable circumstances, France would attempt to invade England, that is treated as a joke worthy only of opéra-bouffe. The French, I heard everywhere, while ready to offer the most formidable resistance France has ever offered to an invading foe, were not prepared to undertake a war of conquest. Their army is a magnificent militia, so strong as to make France practically invulnerable. But it is neither organised nor instructed, nor capable of waging an offensive war beyond its borders. With one consent all Frenchmen whom I saw declared that, wherever there may be danger of war breaking out, the one Government which is absolutely certain never to declare war is the Government of France.

## CHAPTER IV.

### IN BELGIUM WITH M. DE LAVELEYE.

From Paris to Berlin, even an ordinary through train will take you first-class for five guineas in twenty-four hours. The attempt to make the journey in Imperial style in 1870 cost the Third Napoleon his throne, and France five milliards and two provinces, while the Germans, even with all their unprecedented victories, were more than eight weeks in covering the ground which in time of peace every traveller skims across in a single day. The road from Paris to Berlin lies through Belgium. In peace time the through train passes Namur, Liége, and Aix-la-Chapelle. In war time this through route is blocked by the neutrality of Belgium, a neutrality which it is erroneously supposed England is under treaty obligation to defend by force of arms. But the temptation to break through Belgium despite its neutrality will be almost overwhelming, if either Germany or France seriously desires to invade the other. For this reason: —ever since the great war the two Powers have been busily engaged in rendering their respective frontiers impassable, by constructing lines of fortresses against which an invading army from the other side will break its head in vain. France glares at Germany and Germany glares at France from behind a *chevaux de frise* of fortresses bristling with cannon and crammed with soldiers armed with repeating rifles beneath the hail of which no troops can live. But while the immediately adjacent frontiers are thus rendered inaccessible, immediately to the North lies the direct road—at present the open road—through Belgium, by which either combatant could march his forces into the enemy's country. My route lay directly along the line that would be taken by the invader. It was a line full of historic interest, crossing the cockpit of Europe. From Namur to Aachen how many armies have marched and countermarched, how many battles have been fought, how many fields fattened with the corpses of innumerable soldiers? As it has been, who can say how soon it may not be again, neutralities notwithstanding? May Day broke in peace and sunshine over the Belgian valleys, calling to labour the peaceful peasant and artisan, whom I watched busy in their fields and at their mines soon after five o'clock. It is a pretty, rugged country, the great rocks towering up picturesquely above the line, and the fresh, bright green of May beginning to make glad the woods and the valleys. Everything was peaceful and still. The first swallow I had seen this year darted overhead, the sparrows chirped by the wayside, flocks of pigeons lazily rose from the fields as the train hurtled past, the child on its way to the well with water-pails paused as we passed; the whole was an idyllic picture of rural life.

Right in the heart of the open road, through which the opposing hosts may rush, and which may become the arena of the great combat to the death, stands the ancient and famous town of Liége, on the river Meuse. It is famous, among other things in the past, as having been the birthplace of Charlemagne, whose equestrian statue is one of the most conspicuous monuments of the town. Liége was the seat of a prince-bishopric in old times, but it is more notable at present as the seat of a university which is attended by some 1,600 students, and which has the good fortune to have M. Émile de Laveleye as one of its leading professors.

It is a peculiar good fortune that so intelligent and observant a publicist should have been planted as it were in a watch-tower midway between the opposing Powers, and it was with great pleasure I accepted his invitation to break my journey at Liége on my way from Paris to Berlin.

"Not this year," said M. de Laveleye thoughtfully; "I don't think it will come this year. Prince Bismarck will not go to war, and in France, as you have found, they will not, in reality cannot, attack with any prospect of success. The deciding voice is at St. Petersburg. If Russia sends an army into Bulgaria, I fear that it will be almost impossible to avoid war with Austria. But even then I do not think the relations between France and Russia are so close as to lead France to attack Germany, even if Russia should be at war with Germany's ally in south-eastern Europe. I do not see how the war is to come about even in that case. And if there is no war in Bulgaria, there seems little chance of the peace being disturbed."

As we were walking through the streets from the station we

met many persons, women and artisans, carrying guns and gunbarrels in various stages of completion. Liége is a great centre of the gun trade, and business was looking up just then. The local makers had just executed an order for fifteen million cartridges for the Bulgarians—a fact of somewhat sinister significance. The Russian Minister at Brussels was not overpleased, but he could do nothing.

This is not the only connection between Liége and the Eastern Question. If Liége manufacturers fill the cartridge boxes of the Bulgarian conscripts, General de Brialmont, the Belgian master of the art of fortification, who is now building forts round Liége, has built a perfect network of impregnable fortresses round Bucharest. The Roumanian capital is now a fortress of the first class, and behind its steel-cased bulwarks the Roumanians could effectually check a Russian advance into the Balkan Peninsula. M. de Laveleye himself has done not a little to interest Western Europe in the affairs of the Southern Slavs. His was a potent voice in 1876-1878 in favour of the liberation of Bulgaria, and he is at this moment seeing through the press a second edition of his important work on "The Balkan Peninsula," in which he contends strongly that the only satisfactory solution of the Eastern Question is to be found in a federation of Roumania, Servia, Bulgaria, Turkey, and Greece, based on three principles—a Customs Union, a supreme federal tribunal for the settlement of differences, and reciprocal assistance in case of attack. M. de Laveleye has travelled in these regions, and he entertains a strong conviction as to the importance and the possibility of developing these nascent States into a powerful and pacific Federation.

General Brialmont, who is constructing simultaneously the fortifications designed to close the open gates through which Russia enters Turkey, and by which Germany and France can invade each other's territory, is a friend of M. de Laveleye, and, like most military men, he takes a more gloomy view of the prospects of peace than the politicians. He never ceases to lament that he received orders to fortify Belgium too late to have his fortresses ready before war will be declared. As he will have them completed in two years, it is evident General Brialmont does not regard the peace of Europe as likely to be of long duration. General Brialmont is also a specialist, and, like all specialists, is inclined to think that there is nothing like leather, or, in his case, nothing like steel-cased, turtle-backed forts. He is putting up twelve of them round Namur to block the rush of the French towards Germany, and eight of them round Liége to block the German advance towards France. They are odd little forts, hardly visible above the surface. In old times the castle was the most conspicuous object in the whole country side, and even the ruins of the old feudal keeps tower in grandeur above more modern buildings. But artillery is a great leveller. The earthwork rampart long ago replaced the castellated fortress, and now the great earthwork forts, such as those which made Metz and Mayence impregnable, are doomed. According to General Brialmont, the new explosives, of which both the opposing armies have ample store, will enable either of them to burst their way through all the so-called "impregnable" fortresses built a few years since. Of course, if this be so, the peril of Belgium is small, for in that case melinite will clear the way, and the battles will take place where they were fought in 1870-1. But General Brialmont probably exaggerates the destructive power of the new explosive, and under-estimates the toughness of earth and masonry. Even against melinite his fortresses are guaranteed to stand. They are in the first case planted like an island in the midst of a lake of concrete, which hardens into a solid rock against which shells will burst in vain. The fort itself is turtle-shaped, like the earlier ironclads in the American war, and the sloping roof is of the hardest steel. Each fort is armed with two immense guns revolving in a turret, exactly like the armament of our latest ironclads. It would, indeed, be difficult to describe General Brialmont's system better than by saying that he anchors round the position which he wishes to defend a flotilla of non-seagoing ironclads, fitted with turrets, protected by armour plates, and each manned by the ordinary fighting complement of a first-class man-of-war, after deducting those whose duty is to sail and not to fight. The largest Belgian fort will have a complement of 400 men; the smaller forts will be sufficiently manned by a garrison of 200. They will cost when finished four millions sterling, and, if adequately supported by a territorial army, will effectually bar the passage of any invading force. The Belgian door will be closed in 1889.

The question of supplying a field force sufficiently strong to support the forts engages much attention. The King is pressing hard for applying the principle of universal military service. His Ministers proposed it; the Liberals generally approved; but the Clericals, fearing loss of votes in the country, where the principle of compulsory military service is unpopular, opposed the Government, and the proposal was dropped. It will be revived again, however, and if the King can manage it the Belgians will before long be passed through the mill like the rest of the Continent. There seems to be some reason to believe—although the defence of Belgium is being conducted equally against both her neighbours—that the only enemy which is really feared is France. And they do not fear France very much. The French could only break through Belgium into Germany by exposing themselves to great danger of a flank attack, which the Germans are very conveniently placed to deliver. The Germans, on the other hand, would find Belgium, especially if fortified, a very convenient base from which to turn the French flank, and of course, in case of war, Belgium might see her way to enter into an arrangement by which she threw in her lot with Germany in exchange for an adequate *quid pro quo* of guaranteed security. If France were to triumph, the Belgians believe she would annex them without scruple. They have no such fear as to Germany. Nothing, of course, is known of any such understanding as is here alluded to. All that is known is that when the Belgians agitated themselves mightily for permission to make their own ordnance, reasons of State and Royal promises were invoked to send the orders for the new guns to Krupp.

M. de Laveleye talked much and well about the prospects in France, but it was evident that he could not assent to the contemptuous estimate of the forces behind General Boulanger that prevails in Ministerial quarters at Paris. Not that M. de Laveleye is a Boulangist—far from it. But he remembers the discomfiture of all the well-informed persons when Cavaignac went down before the Third Napoleon, and is loath to prophesy as to what is possible or is not possible in that "land of the unbeknown." General Boulanger, of course, has no name like that of Napoleon with which to conjure. But he represents a rallying-point for all the discontent; and if all the Monarchists, all the Bonapartists, and all the stupid people rally round him, he will be formidable indeed. The man who could command the suffrages of all the stupid would come in at the head of the poll everywhere. But even if General Boulanger achieved a momentary success with a negative programme, M. de Laveleye does not think that he could make war with Germany; while as to the possibility of a sudden descent upon England, that he regards as too ludicrous for discussion. "No doubt," said M. de Laveleye, "you are not strong enough in England, and if in the course of a long war your fleet were to be used up, or if the discovery of some new torpedo were to destroy your ironclads, the temptation to dash at London would be enormous. Why do you not adopt universal military service in England? Something between the Swiss and the German systems would enable you to enjoy a security which at present is impossible." I told M. de Laveleye that before we would ever listen to such an outrage on all the ideas most firmly held across the silver streak, we ought at least to try to provide such men as we have now in uniform with organisation, with improved weapons, with transport, with horses, and with artillery. When we cannot work up the half a million men—regulars, reserve, militia, and volunteers—out of a miscellaneous mob into an organised military force, it is absurd to suggest as a remedy for everything the addition of two or three millions of units to the uniformed crowd. It is not men we want so much as a guiding brain, a resolute will, and an unswerving purpose. But the fact that so intelligent an observer as M. de Laveleye, who knows England down to the ground, should believe that it would be well for us to adopt compulsory military service is an unpleasant fact which hardly harmonises with the optimism that hitherto has been universal. But it is always optimism limited. This year they say there will be no war. Nor possibly the next. But some time, possibly if Bismarck were to die—then! Bismarck is everywhere—in Paris, in Liége, in Berlin—regarded as the keystone of the arch of European peace. But, after Bismarck——?

## CHAPTER V.

### THE CAPITAL OF PRINCE BISMARCK.

Few pleasanter experiences ever befall a traveller than that which I enjoyed when I put foot on German soil. The train for Berlin did not leave Cologne for an hour and a half after the arrival of the train from Liége. It was after seven, and I thought all but an outside view of the great cathedral would be impossible. To my surprise the great Dom was open. A service was going on. About a thousand persons were listening to a sermon in praise of the Virgin Mary. The preacher was in a little pulpit decorated with the white flower of the Virgin, and his clear and resonant voice vibrated distinctly through the cathedral, as he denounced English Protestants for refusing to do honour to the Mother of God, and declared with great emphasis that what we are in the habit of calling Mariolatry was the very essence of the Christian religion. I did not mind his denunciations, and I was glad that, in however strange a fashion, woman should be reverenced. But after awhile he ceased; his vibrating accents, which, oddly enough, recalled reminiscences of Luther, although the preacher's face was spare and stern, died away, there was a movement towards the choir, and then from out the mists of night which rendered indistinct even the glories of the eastern windows, and filled the great cathedral with a sense of infinity, as of the firmament of heaven, there floated down upon the assembled worshippers a stream of exquisite melody. They were women's voices, limpid and sweet. What they sang I know not more than I know what the lark sings in mid-heaven; all that I know is that the voices of the unseen singers filled the great aisles of the cathedral with wondrous music, which floated upward to the vaulted roof, as if it bore on angels' wings the intense but inarticulate aspirations of the human heart. They ceased; the organ pealed, and the great congregation took up the refrain, singing heartily and well. In front of the choir stood the Mother Mary with her child in arms. Around her were arrayed a great wealth of shrubs and flowers, before her burned a multitude of candles, and again in front knelt a great company of boys and girls. Again the sweet voices of the choir thrilled through the great Dom; on each side of the nave worshippers were bowed in prayer. The great figure of St. Christopher bearing the Sacred Child on his shoulders, loomed huge over the crowd. The saints and sages who glowed with rich colour in the lower windows, the glory of the soaring arches, the proportions of the famous Dom, and, above all, the liquid beauty of the female voices and the sweetness of the sacred music, combined to produce one of those rare impressions which are the result of a union of the forces of romance, of art, of history, and of religion.

It was with difficulty I tore myself from the cathedral, took the train for Berlin, and fell asleep. I never woke till the conductor roused me with the statement that we were only half an hour from Berlin. I looked out. We were running through a flat, sandy country; the sun was shining brightly in the eastern sky; a canal glimmered in the sunbeams, and right in the centre of the scene, with a background of fir-trees, were two companies of Prussian soldiers at signal-drill. Part of them wore scarlet, the other part dark blue uniforms; and thus lit up the picture with a very bright spot of colour, full of suggestion as to the ceaseless watchfulness that is kept over the capital of the German realm.

I found Berlin more peaceful, if possible, than Paris, and if the only danger of war in Europe arose from the danger of an immediate collision between the French and the Germans, I would have returned to London at once. In 1870 the experienced permanent head of the Foreign Office congratulated Lord Granville on taking office at a time when the foreign horizon was unprecedentedly free from all menacing clouds. Within a fortnight the war broke out between France and Germany, and that contrast between pacific outlook and warlike realisation always recurs to the mind when the diplomatists are crying, "Peace, peace." Nevertheless, notwithstanding Lord Hammond's painful experience, I am inclined to risk the prediction that, so far as the two great antagonists are concerned, there has never been a time since peace was signed when there seemed less human probability of a renewal of hostilities. I found at Paris that the foremost politicians vied with each other in their protestations of their determination to abstain from provoking war. There is no reason to doubt the sincerity of these protestations. The French have not abandoned their desire to recover their lost provinces; but the very intensity of their desire makes them resolute not to sacrifice them for ever by making a premature plunge into a war in which they would have no allies and for which they are not prepared. France will not make the war of revenge this year, if for no other reason than this, that she is not ready, that she has no allies, and, what is much more serious, she has for offensive purposes practically no army. For defensive purposes she never was stronger. Her troops, carefully trained, well disciplined, and admirably armed, rest upon a chain of fortresses, which make France practically impregnable. But so far as attempting to cross the German frontier, to break through the German fortresses, and force their way to Berlin, there be dictate a peace which would restore Alsace and Lorraine, the French are no more prepared to attempt the operation than we are prepared to attempt the submission of the moon. The French army which started for Berlin in the summer of 1870 was at least furnished with maps of the territory through which it was proposed to make a promenade of victory, although it was but utterly unprovided with maps of the country in which the campaign actually was decided. But the French army under has no maps of Germany. Its officers know their own country; they know nothing about the land beyond the frontier. The fact is and it will be in enormous weight off the mind of every thoughtful man in Europe, the French have taken seventeen years to put themselves in a condition in which they can feel safe against a sudden onslaught from Germany. They will know to take extreme care not to they feel themselves strong enough to take the offensive evenhanded against their old colleagues. The war if ever it is to be begun on the initiative of France will come, perhaps, before the end of the century. It is even a true whether or not General Boulanger or some other unknown comes to the front. The French may no doubt, also as I begins, occasionally go mad, but the experience of 1870 have not been thrown away. The French have once for the Empire and never known—what it is to have ever served that an army in their own country—and whatever Bonaparte or Empire-Bonaparte may be in power, they will not lightly go to war.

through the great Dom; on each side of the nave worshippers were bowed in prayer. The great figure of St. Christopher, bearing the Sacred Child on his shoulders, loomed huge over the crowd. The saints and sages who glowed with rich colour in the lower windows, the glory of the soaring arches, the associations of the famous Dom, and, above all, the liquid beauty of the female voices and the sweetness of the sacred music, combined to produce one of those rare impressions which are the result of a union of the forces of romance, of art, of history, and of religion.

It was with difficulty I tore myself from the cathedral, took the train for Berlin, and fell asleep. I never woke till the conductor roused me with the statement that we were only half an hour from Berlin. I looked out. We were running through a flat, sandy country; the sun was shining brightly in the eastern sky; a canal glimmered in the sunbeams, and right in the centre of the scene, with a background of fir-trees, were two companies of Prussian soldiers at signal-drill. Part of them wore scarlet, the other part dark blue uniforms; and this lit up the picture with a very bright spot of colour, full of suggestion as to the ceaseless watchfulness that is kept over the capital of the German realm.

I found Berlin more peaceful, if possible, than Paris, and if the only danger of war in Europe arose from the danger of an immediate collision between the French and the Germans, I would have returned to London at once. In 1870 the experienced permanent head of the Foreign Office congratulated Lord Granville on taking office at a time when the foreign horizon was unprecedentedly free from all menacing clouds. Within a fortnight the war broke out between France and Germany, and that contrast between pacific outlook and warlike realisation always recurs to the mind when the diplomatists are crying, "Peace, peace." Nevertheless, notwithstanding Lord Hammond's painful experience, I am inclined to risk the prediction that, so far as the two great antagonists are concerned, there has never been a time since peace was signed when there seemed less human probability of a renewal of hostilities. I found at Paris that the foremost politicians vied with each other in their protestations of their determination to abstain from provoking war. There is no reason to doubt the sincerity of these protestations. The French have not abandoned their desire to recover their lost provinces; but the very intensity of their desire makes them resolute not to sacrifice them for ever by making a premature plunge into a war in which they would have no allies and for which they are not prepared. France will not make the war of revenge this year, if for no other reason than this, that she is not ready, that she has no allies, and, what is much more serious, she has for offensive purposes practically no army. For defensive purposes she never was stronger. Her troops, carefully trained, well disciplined, and admirably armed, rest upon a chain of fortresses, which make France practically impregnable. But as for attempting to cross the German frontier, to break through the German fortresses, and force their way to Berlin, there to dictate a peace which would restore Alsace and Lorraine, the French are no more prepared to attempt the operation than we are prepared to attempt the colonisation of the moon. The French army which started for Berlin in the summer of 1870 was at least furnished with maps of the territory through which it was proposed to make a promenade of victory, although it was left utterly unprovided with maps of the country in which the campaign actually was decided. But the French army to-day has no maps of Germany. Its officers know their own country; they know nothing about the land beyond the frontier. The fact is, and it will be an enormous weight off the mind of every thoughtful man to know it, the French have taken seventeen years to put themselves in a condition in which they can feel safe against a sudden onslaught from Germany. They will have to take seventeen more before they feel themselves strong enough to take the offensive single-handed against their old antagonist. The war of revenge, if it has to be begun on the initiative of France, will hardly begin, barring accidents, before the close of the century. And this is true whether or not General Boulanger or some other soldier comes to the front. The French may, no doubt, like the English, occasionally go mad, but the experiences of 1870-1 have not been thrown away. The French know what the English have never known—what it is to have war carried into the heart of their own country—and, whether General Boulanger or any other man be in power, they will not lightly go to war.

So at least they spoke in Paris, and the same opinions were

expressed still more strongly at Berlin. There will be no war in Europe if the Germans have to make it. I found diplomatists who are opposed on almost every other ground agree in this. Germany is for peace. Prince Bismarck's supreme object is peace. "Germany," said the representative of a Power with whom it is sometimes pretended that Germany is going to war, "Germany is in the position of a man who has had as good a dinner as he can swallow, and who only asks to be let alone." The apparent semblance of bellicose preparation is really due to the stress and strain of his overwhelming passion for peace. The opinion in best-informed circles in Berlin is that Prince Bismarck has practically secured an international guarantee of the *status quo*. There is no written agreement. England, for instance, has not signed any treaty promising to place her navy at the disposal of Germany in case France were to begin the war of revenge. But it is tacitly understood that all the Powers will use their utmost endeavours to prevent an outbreak of war. How far these endeavours will go is not exactly defined. But they will certainly go as far as possible without drawing the sword, and no one can say whether this diplomatic support may not, in some cases at least, develop into armed resistance. The relations between England and Germany, for instance, are now so much more friendly than they were a couple of years since, that it is now understood that if the dread entertained by some high authorities in England were realised, and the French were, in a gambling mood, to make a dash at London, the moment they developed their scheme it would be met by a declaration of war from Berlin. This would not have been so recently, but I am given to understand on very high authority that it would be so now.

The Germans are not in the least uneasy at the thought of a French attack. They are not expecting it, and they are prepared for it if it should come. I found at Berlin a very healthy and well-founded conviction that the French are not going to run their heads against a stone wall for the sake of Alsace and Lorraine. "There are only two men in France," said a foreign diplomatist who knows his Paris well, "who dream of war with Germany, and one of them is a woman. The other is a poet. Madame Adam and M. Paul Déroulède—behold the party of revenge! It is vehement and self-conscious, but it is hardly strong enough to upset the peace of Europe." As for General

Boulanger, it is not believed that he will be able to do anything; and he is ridiculed in comic songs. But Paris at Berlin stands for France, and the Germans have not yet realised the possibility of provincial France imposing its candidate upon the capital. General Saussier, who commands the garrison of Paris, would not hesitate to shoot General Boulanger or anyone else who attempted a *coup d'état;* but the danger of a Dictator in France does not come from the mob of Paris. It comes rather from the same forces which put Louis Napoleon over Cavaignac, and strengthened the arm of M. Thiers so as to enable him to crush the capital after a campaign directed from Versailles. General Boulanger, however, if he arrives as the choice of the provincials, will not have a mandate to go to war. He may regild the dome of the Invalides to amuse the public, which, by all Frenchmen, from Napoleon the First to Clémenceau the Minister-maker, is regarded more as a child to be amused than a rational adult to be consulted. There is another aspect of the question which it would not be honest if I ignored. There can hardly be two opinions outside France as to the immensity of the relief that would follow a final renunciation on the part of the French of the dream of revenge and the definite abandonment of the lost provinces. But at the same time it is possible that such a relief might be bought too dear if it involved the extinction of the last spark of idealism in the French character. And there is too much reason to fear that the dying away of interest in Alsace and Lorraine is due, not to the growth of an elevated morality, of Christian resignation, or even of philosophic complacency; it is due, I fear, chiefly to the supremacy of a vulgar and debasing materialism. The worship of the almighty dollar is the one faith that survives in France. So at least say those who live in the country, and who deplore the dwindling of all enthusiasms save the enthusiasm of making 10 per cent. "The Frenchman cares for nothing but the franc," said one shrewd Ambassador; "Alsace and Lorraine—pah! that does not pay!" And as the outward sign and symbol of the present condition of things, these melancholy moralists point to the ascendancy which has everywhere been obtained by the one race which is solely materialistic, which has no frontier, and whose Holy of Holies is the Bourse. France is eaten up by the Jews. "Rothschild is the real King of France. If the Comte de Paris were to ascend the throne, it would only be as the Viceroy of the Rothschilds," so I was told in Berlin; and whatever may be thought of this from other points of view, it cannot be said to impair the prospects of peace. If Rothschild be the Cæsar of the Third Republic, he is not likely to use his authority to plunge France into war for the sake of a disputed province. Peace, therefore, from good motives or from bad—peace will last between Germany and France: neither will attack the other for some time on its own initiative. If there be war, it will have to begin elsewhere.

The new Emperor seems as if he intended to make a change, but when I was in Berlin Prince Bismarck was Mayor of the Palace at Berlin, and a Mayor of the Palace who seemed likely to make his office hereditary. As an Amurath an Amurath succeeds, so when Prince Otto von Bismarck is gathered to his fathers, the present Count Herbert will step by legitimate heirship and the natural fitness of things into the vacant place. Count Herbert is a chip of the old block. He has been trained under a stern master, and he has followed his model sedulously, even in his *brusquerie* of manner, and when his turn comes he hopes to prove that a second Bismarck is as possible in Germany as a second Pitt in England. And unless Count Herbert is belied, he has his ambitions to hand down the Bismarck line with a mixture of English blood. They call him an Anglomaniac in Berlin, but they attribute his recent unusual journey to the Viceregal Court at Dublin in the depths of a wretched winter to a deeper and more romantic motive. Count Herbert is not married, at least not yet, and although his father during the war jested somewhat coarsely as to the advantages of a Semitic connection, his son is more likely to marry into England than into Israel. Prince Bismarck is hale and well. Every day he may be seen riding in the Thiergarten, and not even the grim and gruesome tale that is told about his favourite body physician—a tale recalling one of the stories of Herodotus—prevents him following his advice and profiting thereby. During his last great speech in the Reichstag, an English correspondent assures me that he counted him drink no fewer than eighteen glasses of some beverage, which his son and an assistant were kept busy concocting for him all the ninety minutes he was on his legs. Whether that beverage was the sherry and egg favoured by Mr. Gladstone, or some stronger liquor, is unknown; but, whatever it was, the Iron Chancellor needed a dram every five minutes that he was on his legs.

In Berlin no one counts for anything after the Emperor save the Chancellor and his son. In international politics the Bismarcks *père et fils* are as supreme as any Tzar. And, in the exercise of their autocracy, they are sometimes as rough as Peter the Great. Take, for instance, Prince Bismarck's intervention in the affair of the Princess Victoria's betrothal. Prince Bismarck, like the Tzar, thoroughly dislikes Prince Alexander of Battenberg. He may be cruelly maligned, this young man, but if so, he has none the less managed to convince the two most powerful men in Europe that he is a faithless, untrustworthy person, with whom the less honest men have to do the better. When the Emperor and Empress approved of the betrothal of their daughter to this Prince, Bismarck objected, and persisted in his objection. No one can complain of his doing so. He was therein true to the principle of Prussian State policy, which exacts sacrifices for the State equally from ruler and ruled. But that which was rude and brutal about the matter was the means taken by the Chancellor to strengthen his hand by letting the whole dispute get into the papers, or rather, unless he is much maligned, by taking direct means for putting the whole story into the papers. Sovereigns may be overruled by their Chancellors, without a murmur, but even a worm would turn if its Chancellor insisted upon vetoing its wishes with an accompaniment of bullying press criticisms. Prince Bismarck, however, cares for none of these things. If a press bludgeon lies ready to his hand, he will use it; nor does he weigh the possible pain to the vanquished against the advantage of strengthening by ever so little the chances of his vanquisher. The one thing needful in Prince Bismarck's eyes is " to mak' siccar " of attaining his end.

Tact, however, is not a pre-eminently Prussian virtue. Neither, to say the truth, does it seem to be held in the highest regard by the illustrious English lady with whom Prince Bismarck recently crossed swords. The Empress Victoria is a brilliant woman, full of " go," of enthusiasm and of indomitable courage. There is no saying what magnificent services she may yet render to her sex, and to civilisation, and refinement, and all the arts which beautify and sweeten life; but the very

D

pre-eminence of her position makes her a mark of jealousy and of suspicion. The Germans seem to have exhausted their regard for women in the days of Tacitus; they cannot tolerate the ascendency which this gifted and brilliant Englishwoman exercised over her husband and her immediate *entourage;* and she, on her part, perhaps not unnaturally, showed a reckless disregard of the prejudices and sentiments of her German subjects. The unceremonious fashion in which she bundled out all the sacred relics of Queen Louisa when she set a firm of Oxford Street tradesmen to furnish in English style the old palace where her Majesty was lodged during her recent visit to Berlin, made the German blood run cold. Sayings of hers also are repeated—witty and true, no doubt, but which sting all the more for their wit and their truth. But all admit that her devotion to her husband has been beyond praise. No mere *hausfrau* of them all could have excelled her patience, her assiduity, her tender care in the sick-room; but she is a woman, and for a woman to be so visibly in the foretop of the State is quite shocking to the serious German mind.

There is something very touching, and even ennobling, in the magnificent devotion of the Germans to their great Chancellor. I remember long ago asking Thomas Carlyle what practical advice he had to offer to those who, in this age of ballot-boxes and universal suffrage, nevertheless accepted his teachings, and only wished to know what practical immediate step to take first. Mr. Carlyle replied by telling me that those who saw the hollowness of the prevailing cant, those whose souls revolted against the mockery of supposing that supreme wisdom could be evolved out of the submissive consultation of the majority of fools, should hold themselves aloof and wait, possessing their souls in patience while things got worse and worse, until the supreme strong and capable man appeared, when they should step forward and acclaim him as their lord. He will appear, said Mr. Carlyle, if you are prepared for his coming. It did not sound very hopeful advice in England; but here in Germany they seem to have acted upon it with some considerable success. In the blunt Pomeranian squire they found their supremely able man. Although the Germans carry the right of private judgment to such lengths that there are at least six systems of philosophy, politics, and religion to be found wherever six Germans meet in a *bierhaus*, they have agreed to sink everything, bear everything, dare everything, to do his behests. It is very curious to see thus suddenly emerging from the chaos of principalities and of ballot-boxes this revived soul of the old kingship, as real, although not so picturesque, as when the ancestors of these same Germans raised some victorious chieftain upon his shield in the day of triumph, and swore him allegiance unto death.

Not, however, for war do these German tribes rally round Bismarck to-day, but for peace. They are a peaceful folk, these German men, and in Prince Bismarck they see the keystone of the arch of European peace. Behind his broad buckler they nestle secure, accepting whatever sacrifice he demands for the sake of peace; and after what I have heard in Paris and in Berlin, I cannot for a moment doubt that the German this time is right. Prince Bismarck's chief concern is peace. His methods are of the old order. If you wish for peace, prepare for war; but the preparations for war are not for conquest but for defence. That he is preparing for war, and that he has never ceased preparing for war, is true. All the way along the Polish frontier, which we skirted as I came to Russia—owing to the floods which had interrupted the traffic on the main-line through Königsberg—the Germans were making ready. They were doubling the line of rails, building landing platforms for cavalry and artillery, erecting sheds for horses—everywhere they were on the alert, to forestall attack—an attack which will not come. The three great Powers whose capitals I have visited are all in the same position. They can all hold their own in defensive war; but that is all. They are none of them strong enough to have any assured hope of conquering each other. Wars do not break out under these circumstances. Napoleon thought that he could march to Berlin: Prince Bismarck knew he could march to Paris. Hence a readiness for war on both sides in 1870 which does not exist to-day. Each knows the other to be too strong to offer much hope of victory. So the *status quo* will remain, and there will be no war.

All European interests were overshadowed in the German capital in May by the personal question of the Emperors—past, present, and to come. The shop windows were monopolised by the photographs and busts of the late Emperor, with views of his lying-in-state and of the procession to his last resting-place. In the streets the flower-sellers offered nothing but violets, the favourite flower of the Emperor who lay dying at Charlottenburg, and the portraits of the dying Kaiser and of the Crown Prince, who was so soon to ascend his grandfather's throne, were to be seen everywhere. It was, therefore, natural that as soon as possible after my arrival in Berlin I called upon Sir Morell Mackenzie.

Charlottenburg lies a mile or two out of Berlin, on the main line from the west. The rain was falling when I passed through the Thiergarten where Prince Bismarck takes his afternoon ride every day between five and six o'clock, on the other side of the chariot-crowned Brandenburg gate. There are no deer in the Thiergarten now, nor anything to distinguish it from any other suburban woodland, save the gilded statue that crowns the column of victory, and the numerous little wooden boxes affixed to the trees for the birds to nest in. As we drove westward a regiment of Prussian infantry passed us in the road, singing a cheerful marching song as they walked through the rain. The last regiment I had seen was in Paris, where some French infantry tramped along the Rue de Rivoli. What a contrast! The Prussians swung along with the precision and the impetus of a great machine. As they approached us swinging their left arms with measured regularity, the red band on the wrist cuff showed along the whole line like a red ribbon, the hundreds of arms making the same movement at the same moment. There was a solidity, a homogeneity about the column that was singularly impressive. How different it was in France! The infantry in the Rue de Rivoli were all shapes and sizes, a miscellaneous crowd in uniform, and carrying rifles, shambling along in a slipshod fashion which boded ill for the Republic if ever the great duel should be renewed between the Teuton and the Gaul.

Hardly had the blithe notes of the soldiers' song died away when the great dome of the Charlottenburg Palace appeared above the trees. As we approached it we could see the stalwart but youthful sentinels pacing to and fro before the gates, while a clump of soldiers clustered in what appeared to be a guard-room on the right of the Palace. We had an appointment with Sir Morell Mackenzie, and in a few moments we were being ushered along a long whitewashed corridor in the left wing of the Palace to the English doctor's room. Upon the door an envelope was pinned on which was written "Sir Morell Mackenzie." Our guide touched an electric bell, the door opened, and we found ourselves in the presence of the great specialist.

Sir Morell Mackenzie occupied a pleasant and well-lighted room adjoining the central portion of the Palace. We had hardly sat down when the bell began to ring. "It is the Emperor," said Dr. Mackenzie; "I must go," and he instantly left the room to attend his august patient.

Sir Morell Mackenzie looked slightly worn and anxious. His fine mobile features showed traces of the long vigil by the couch of the Emperor. Dr. Hovell, who had been up all night, had gone to bed. Sir Morell Mackenzie was now in charge, and was summoned from time to time, during our visit, to the bedside of the patient.

This is not the place to revive the painful controversy that raged round the dying Emperor, but I may mention that Sir Morell Mackenzie assured me that nothing could exceed the kindness and confidence which he had received from the first day of his arrival from the Emperor and the Empress. He was a stranger to them when he came to Berlin. He was accorded from first to last the most absolute confidence, and all his directions were implicitly obeyed. But, as erroneous impressions have gained ground on this point, owing to the bickerings of the doctors, and the attention paid to their differences by the press, it is well to say once for all that, however much controversy may have raged outside, in the sick-room Dr. Mackenzie's authority has been as supreme and undisputed as if the Emperor had been an ordinary patient in his own hospital.

As a patient, Dr. Mackenzie told me, the Emperor was all that could be desired, so far as temper, patience, and cheerfulness were concerned. He was as obedient and trustful as a fine-dispositioned child; he bore pain bravely, and he did not worry. The Emperor was in the habit of mind common to all sufferers from long-standing chronic diseases. In those cases patients alternate between a belief that they will live for a couple of years, when their minds are occupied with arranging plans for the future, and a fear that all will be over in a few days. In this case it was not over in a few days. But it was all over in a few weeks; and when I came back from Petersburg Berlin was draped in black, and William II. sat on the throne which Frederick III. had nominally occupied for exactly ninety days.

---

## CHAPTER VI.

### IN THE EMPIRE OF THE TZAR.

"Travelling in Russia is the most luxurious in Europe," said Lord Randolph Churchill to me shortly before I started. "The distances no doubt are great, but the carriages are so comfortable, the restaurants by the wayside so convenient and so well served, that there is no country more pleasant to travel in." His words often came back to my mind as, with aching head and weary limbs, I stood on the platform of the Schlaf-Wagen and watched for hour after hour the monotonous landscape of Eastern Prussia. At last we reached Eydtkuhnen, the last station on the German line. From thence the train goes on to Wirballen, the first station on the Russian side. Suddenly, as I was looking out of the window, I saw a little stream hardly deep enough for a duck to swim in, and on the other side of it, pacing leisurely along, a big burly fellow with long grey overcoat, something like the fleece of a sheep round his neck, and on his shoulder a rifle with a fixed bayonet. It was a Russian soldier mounting guard on the frontier of an Empire the other shore of which was washed by the Pacific Ocean and Behrings Straits. A picturesque figure he was—picturesque and significant. The train rolled on, leaving him behind. A moment more and we were in Wirballen. We were in a new world. The language, the manners, the appearance, everything had changed. Seldom have I seen so great a contrast in so short a time. At Eydtkuhnen everything was German. At Wirballen everything was Russian. The very characters of the alphabet were different, the uniform of the gendarmes, the shape of the locomotive, the talk of the people. It was as if Calais and Dover were suddenly brought within a hundred yards of each other, and you passed in a few minutes from England to France.

As if still further to mark the change, we had to deliver up our passports to a picturesque-looking gendarme in grey and red uniform, booted and spurred, with a sword by one side and a pistol at the other, but withal a humane-looking janitor of the Western railway gate of the Empire of the Tzar. On entering the airy and commodious restaurant was a bookstall in charge of a very pretty young girl. All the books and papers in her charge were Russian save one. The solitary exception was Zola's "L'Assommoir," which represented the contribution of Western genius and civilisation to the railway bookstall of Wirballen. Later in the year the stock of French books was increased, but in May "L'Assommoir" stood alone. Neither in May nor in June was there a single English book.

The Russian railway restaurant is infinitely superior to anything in France or Germany. Everything is delightfully clean and cool and airy. The chairs are of clean white wood. The display of viands is tempting, and the viands themselves are perfection. And then the tea! fragrant and refreshing as ambrosial nectar for the headachy, wearied traveller. In a short time my headache left me, and the rest of the journey was accomplished with comfort.

After dinner our passports were brought back, the bell rang, and we went out on to the platform. The train was waiting. And what a train! It was just as if we had suddenly been transported to America. There was the engine with the huge chimney, the tender piled high with wood. And the cars were all like those in Switzerland and in the States, without compartments and communicating, so that the train can be traversed when in motion from end to end. The engine fire is fed by two stokers, who are kept pretty busy heaving logs—short lath-wood we should call it in England—into the furnace. The maw of the steam fiend is capacious, and the woodpile on the tender diminishes amain. The smell of the burning wood is pleasant to the nostril; a faint piquant flavour of pine woods in springtime is liberated by the fire. At night the sparks fly fast from the funnel, but of black smoke there is none.

The second and third bell sound, and at last we are off, bowling along smoothly over a level sandy track through Poland towards St. Petersburg. The sun was sinking in the western sky, the ruddy flush on the horizon showing brightly red against the tops of the distant pines, but there was still an hour or two of daylight before we turned in for the night. How Irish the whole scene seemed! There were the Irish cabins, irregular and uneven, with the thatched roof, the peaty soil, splashing up black and miry on the walls; there were the patches of bog and the barefooted women, and there too was the inevitable pig, the "gintleman that pays the rent." But every rural district on the Continent is more Irish than English; for as Mill long ago remarked, Ireland is in the main stream of European life; whereas England is exceptional, and apart. But Russia on the threshold was more Irish than rural France, more Irish than rural Germany. There were, however, points of difference as well as of resemblance. The peasants were ploughing in the fields as late as eight o'clock. They wore sheepskins and high boots, and round their villages of thatched cottages stood more trees than are common in Ireland. Here and there, too, were oxen ploughing, which you never see in Ireland. Neither were there any of the extraordinary stone fences with which the finest peasantry in the world train the boldest hunters that ever followed fox. Neither hedge nor dyke breaks the expanse. Only here and there is a more or less dilapidated fence of unbarked saplings. And over and above all there was absent from the landscape the saddest, the dreariest, and most characteristic of all things Irish, the gable-ends of cottages which had been pulled down. It is not the round tower which is the distinctive Hibernian structure, but the rough triangular wedge of masonry left standing here, there, and everywhere in all parts of rural Ireland, marking the place where a family had gathered under the sheltering roof-tree of a humble home, but which now is but a desolation and a ruin, the rude tombstone of a perishing race. Alone among the peoples of Europe the numbers of the Irish dwindle in their own land. In Russia the population increases and multiplies amain, adding a million and more to its hundred millions every recurring year. Hence naturally the landscape is not scarred with the wreck of dismantled houses, nor is the eye pained by the perpetual reminder of the chronic civil war that rages across the Irish Sea between the evictors and the evicted.

The wayside stations in Russia are more picturesque than those of Western Europe. They seem all to be built of one pattern. They are of wood, of course. Russia is the country of wood, as distinguished from the countries of stone; just as it is the country of the plain as distinguished from the countries of the mountain. The wayside railway stations are one-story buildings, neatly and simply built. They are roofed with thin sheet-iron, painted a reddy brown. At first it is difficult to distinguish the iron from shingles. But when, as is sometimes the case, it is painted green to resemble verdigris, the iron is distinguishable. At every station there are three objects conspicuous in the front of the building: a clock, a bell, and a large thermometer. A station without the three would not be Russian; but if by any chance one were missing it would not be the thermometer. What stories of piercing cold and blazing heat the mere presence of that silent recorder of temperature tells! Of the climate of England many vile things have been said, but one thing may at least be said in its favour—it does not render a thermometer a necessity of life. In addition to the three stationary objects on the wall of the station, there is on the platform the gendarme, with his white stiff plume on his head, his spurs on his heel, his pistol under his right hand, his sword under his left. He stands almost as motionless as the water-butt from which travellers can descend to drink—a practice probably more common in summer than in early spring, for I never saw any passenger alight for that purpose. There is also the metallic gong on which the approach of the train is signalled from the previous station.

All night the train jogged smoothly on, and when morning broke we were running through a flat sandy country with here and there a lake. Then we entered a region more thickly wooded. The sun came out, and the landscape gave token of returning spring. All day long the train bowled along its smooth and uneventful course. At five o'clock we were at Gatschina, and at six we reached St. Petersburg.

I was in time to take part in the most characteristically Russian and Eastern Church ceremony in the whole year. Saturday was Easter Eve according to the Russian calendar. The long fast, practised here with an austerity almost incredible to easy-going Anglicans, was drawing to a close. The streets were gay with the white, blue, and red of the national flag. All the pastry-cooks' windows were full of red Easter eggs, and the white, sour-cream, raisin-speckled compound called the paska, which occupies the place of honour in the feast with which the good Orthodox broke their fast at an early hour on Sunday morning. As the night wore on, the streets became rather more instead of less crowded. The isvostchiks with their four-wheeled little droschkies were dashing about everywhere over the pavement, which is fanged with more murderous stones in St. Petersburg than ever I have bumped over in any other capital in Europe. Only on the Nevski Prospect—that splendid street which, with its electric lamps, stretches like a great beam of white light for three miles through the heart of the city—is the roadway passably smooth. The air was nipping cold. I had seen the snow-wreaths lying still unmelted by the railway side near Gatschina, and there was still a pinch of frost in the air. The sky was beautifully blue, with here and there a star. A few lights gleamed in the windows of the Anitchkoff Palace, whither the Tzar had returned that day from Gatschina: the dvorniks, or house-porters, swathed in huge fur overcoats, kept watch at the house doors. A great stream of people filled the sideways, while the roadway was as crowded as Regent Street at four o'clock. All was bustle, animation, palpitating life.

Passing the great Kazan Cathedral, which recalls visions of St. Peter's at Rome, and which was crowded to the doors three hours later by an immense crowd of worshippers, I made my way to the Cathedral of St. Isaac. There were officers in uniform, ladies in full dress, notables resplendent in decorations, all kept in order with difficulty, but with great good nature, by the soldiers and police. After a great crush, we got through the wicket gate. A moment more and we stood beneath the great dome, whose golden splendour forms one of the most conspicuous landmarks of St. Petersburg. From the gilded gates before the altar a carpet was spread down the centre of the nave. Exactly under the dome on a raised daïs or platform stood the table on which lay the full-length picture representing our Lord in the grave. On either side blazed an immense number of candles. Men and women of all classes advanced to the picture and reverently kissed it, crossing themselves the while, sometimes once, sometimes twice, and sometimes thrice. A few kissed the carpet at the foot of the table. All seemed reverent and devout. A clerk or some such functionary was reading the while from a desk behind, his voice sounding fitfully above the low hum and movement of the multitude. Conspicuous in the throng was the line of young guardsmen, handsome fellows in white uniform. The Cathedral was but imperfectly lighted; yet even by the flickering tapers you could discover the massive proportions of the great structure, and see something of the gorgeous splendour of its ornamentation. I had an excellent position, close to the daïs under the dome, fronting the altar. Immediately before me rose a colossal pillar, one of those supporting the dome, which from its mere immensity and solid grandeur seemed like an architectural reminiscence of the Roman Empire, looming up huge and strong from the misty past. The marble pavement was barely visible beneath the feet of the great company. But for the uniforms, which were Russian, the gathering might have been mistaken for an English congregation. The faces, the dresses—both of men and women—were much more English than any I had seen either in Paris or Berlin. Then after a while they began to light the candles which burn before the great pictures. The pillars of green malachite supporting the screen, the blue columns of lapis-lazuli on either side of the gilded gates that concealed the altar, formed an imposing frame for the singularly beautiful mosaic pictures of Jesus of Nazareth and His mother Mary with her child—both fortunately with no other halo than that of their intrinsic beauty. On either side were colossal mosaics of haloed saints—St. Isaac of Dalmatia, after whom the Cathedral is named, and St. Nicholas, favourite of Russian saints, on the left; on the right, St. Alexander Nevsky, the warrior King, and St. Catherine and her wheel. Above the gates was a group in silver, dimly visible, of our Lord and His angels; higher up, again, a picture of the Lord's Supper. All the while people were crowding into the Cathedral, until at last it seemed as if no more standing-room remained. Then suddenly the monotonous sound of the reader's voice was hushed in a great burst of song from the choir, which stood arrayed in blue and yellow vestments before the altar. The gates opened, and beyond a blaze of innumerable candles was visible above the altar the gigantic figure of our risen Lord in the great eastern window. After a time the gates closed again, but still the singing continued. Then came a procession of banners, preceded by a curious lamp and cross, which passed down the nave to the far end of the church. The procession is supposed to symbolise the disciples who came to our Lord's tomb. Then at last they come back to where the body lay on the daïs, and they ask, "Where is He?" And then comes the reply, "He is not here. He is risen!" After which the choir bursts forth into song, chanting the anthem of "The Resurrection."

What followed I cannot even attempt to describe. All that remains on my retina is a confused splendour of long-haired men in shining raiment, stiff with silver and gold, wearing wondrous headgear, crusted with jewels, chanting in an unknown tongue the praises of their God. First of all, the table with the picture of Christ in the grave was removed, and carried on the heads of two priests to the altar, the congregation crossing itself the while. Then came down a gorgeous procession of ecclesiastics, swinging censers of incense and carrying candles innumerable, who after various evolutions marched finally down the nave to the other end of the Cathedral. The choir assembled on the daïs. Before this, however, I should have mentioned what was perhaps the strangest sight of all—the lighting of the candles—and the most suggestive, dating as it does from a time when the early Christians met in catacombs and had to worship each by the light of his own lamp. Nearly every person in the Cathedral had a white taper. Before the procession started down the nave these tapers were lighted. Imagine St. Paul's at midnight filled with an immense concourse, and place in the hand of every other man and woman a lighted candle, and you may form some idea, but a very faint idea, of the scene in St. Isaac's. For St. Paul's in the interior is as bare as a barn compared with the splendours of the Russian Cathedral. When the whole human pavement of the Cathedral was thus illuminated, came the lighting of the great candelabra pendent from the roof. A long cotton thread hung down from each. It was lighted, and suddenly a red flame was seen running upwards to the candles. These candles are all connected by similar threads, and the light travelled from wick to wick lighting every candle. I did not see one missed, and the whole illumination was completed in almost as short a time as I have taken to tell it. But after the candelabra were all ablaze, the red flame from the burning thread continued to mount higher and higher into the vast and misty recesses of the great dome. Still it went upwards and upwards, climbing like a small red star to the infinite. Suddenly it stopped, and lo! from where it stopped a circle of living fire began to run along, until the dome was circled with a ring of flaming gas-jets which from the immense height seemed to flicker dim and small.

Then came back the procession. The long-haired men with shining garments of silver embroidery, with the jewelled crosses and strange enamelled head-gear, grouped themselves upon the daïs, and then the choir began to sing. They sang for nearly two hours with but brief interludes. The burden of their song was, "Christ is risen! Christ is risen!" And thereat there was much crossing and bowing in the great congregation, the movement of so many hands in the candlelight being indeed strange to see. The voices of the boys were sweet, the men were strong and deep—deeper, indeed, than can be heard anywhere outside a Russian church. It was a weird scene. Ever and anon the long-haired priests, habited in stiff and rustling vestments, would take a censer and march down to the altar swinging their censers the while, and then return, only to have the same ceremony repeated by another two, so on almost *ad infinitum*. Occasionally the choir would cease their singing, and in deep guttural tones a black-bearded priest would chant some verses, to which another would respond, and then again the choir would break out into the richest and loveliest song. For nearly an hour or more, I should think, the chief figure in the procession—who took the place of the Metropolitan, who was absent—stood in the centre of the daïs, making signs from time to time, but otherwise remaining motionless, save when he wiped his face, for his jewelled crown seemed to be very heavy, and the air of the Cathedral was thick with incense and warm with the heat of innumerable tapers. It seemed as if the singing would never end. The incense in the censers burned out, and they had to be replaced. It was no doubt all very beautiful and suggestive to those who understood it. To me, alas! being one of those whom the moujik describes as the niemetz, or the dumb, because they understand not Russian, it was utterly unintelligible. Melodious it was, no doubt, as the singing of birds at sunrise, but quaint and weird and unreal as a scene from another world. Only one thing stirred me, and that, oddly enough, by the same associations that were roused by the singing of a lark in a forest clearing which we had passed in the train. The associations were those of Borodino. In that fatal battle, when the cannon thunder ceased for a moment, the soldiers are said to have heard in the pause of the fight the glad trill of a lark's song raining down from the far blue sky. And now again in the crowded Cathedral, with its incense-laden air, and the twinkling of its lights, numerous as the stars of heaven, the only articulate sounds I could distinguish brought back reminiscences of the same grim fight. For all that I could make out in the maze of melodious sound were the words " Gospodi pomilioui (Lord have mercy upon us), Gospodi pomilioui, Gospodi pomilioui." It was these strange unfamiliar words that the French soldiers heard on the dawn of that fray when the grey-coated Russians knelt in prayer before they stood up to die for Russia and their Tzar. The walls of the massive Cathedral seemed to melt away, the lights grew dim and disappeared, the splendour of the high priests in their shining robes was forgotten. Only I seemed to hear the simple, earnest cry of the Russian peasant as he flung himself that day of doom across the path of the great Napoleon. " Gospodi pomilioui, Gospodi pomilioui "—" Lord, have mercy on us ! "

It was a salutary memory, checking into humiliation the momentary temptation to look down upon the faith which needed to find nutriment in ceremonial as of the theatre, in music as of the opera, and leaving only a bewildering consciousness of my incapacity of understanding, as of a missing sense. For, however strange and incredible it may be to those reared in the stern simplicity of English Nonconformity, that the souls of men can be stirred, their lives ennobled, and their deathbeds soothed, by what seem such fantastic combinations of spiritual truth and theatrical flummery, the fact remains. This Church, with all its pomp of ritual and melody of song, has at least taught the Russians how to die. Whether in spite of its rites and ceremonies, or because of them, it has made itself for centuries one of the most vital realities in all these Eastern lands. Even now, many Russians assert that Russia is not primarily a State ; Russia is primarily a Church. Great is the Tzar, but greater is the Orthodox Eastern Church, whose servant he is, and whose creed, which he must subscribe to before he is crowned, forms the only Constitution of his Empire. If this be difficult to understand, if it be strange for us Westerns to comprehend how this religion of ceremonial and outward rite is able to supply a hundred millions of fellow-creatures with the only draught of the water of life which will ever cross their lips in their pilgrimage from the cradle to the grave, it is no marvel. Think you, who have not even learned to decipher the Cyrillian alphabet so as to read the names of the stations and of the streets, that it is easier to penetrate at the first careless glance into the secret mysteries of the inner arcanum of the national life ?

About two o'clock the first part of the service was over. The procession marched down to the altar, the music ceased, and then the second service of mass began. I left the Cathedral, but outside the scene was almost as strange as within. For all round the sacred building, on all the steps, were displayed long rows of paskas and koolitchies, the heaps of clotted cream and currant cake adorned with paper flowers, and illuminated with tapers. The owners of the cakes sat behind their goods, waiting for them to be blessed by a priest. The lanes of light round the Cathedral, the bright-coloured decorations, the dense crowd, made a very vivid picture. Overhead a cross of brilliant gas flared outside the eastern window, and still higher, on the Cathedral towers, fires blazed in the brazen urns. And over all the stir and movement of the crowd, in the midst of which a gendarme's horse was prancing and curvetting restlessly, was audible a soft, deep, rich note of music as of a distant organ peal. It was the peal of the bells, far different from the riotous, jubilant music of our English bells, more solemn and soft and sad, like the undertone of mournful melody which is never absent from Turgenieff's novels.

# Book II.
## WAR OR PEACE?

### CHAPTER I.
AT COUNT TOLSTOI'S, YASNAIA POLIANA.*

WHEN I left London Lord Wolseley told me that my first duty would be to discover whether the Cossacks would be in Bucharest in May. May has come and gone, and never a Cossack has been moved towards the Roumanian frontier. I have spent three weeks in the capital of the Empire which in London seems to be regarded as the disturbing centre of European tranquillity, seeing every one who was likely to be able or willing to enlighten me as to the probable course of events. I have visited Moscow, and now I have retired to the country seat of Count Léon Tolstoi, far from the hubbub and turmoil of the great cities, to write at the desk of the author of "War and Peace" the net result of my observations as to the chances of War or Peace.

I have been exceptionally favoured in the opportunities afforded me alike of collecting information and of summing up the net result of my investigation. I am at a loss to express my sense of the cordial kindness with which I have been welcomed everywhere. From the highest to the lowest I have to acknowledge gratefully the same simple, hearty friendliness which has made my stay in this country a period of intense and almost unmingled enjoyment. And now, after living as it were in oxygen for a month in St. Petersburg and Moscow—after spending night and day in the midst of the immense stimulus that is afforded by a perpetual recurrence of new scenes and the incessant intercourse with the ablest and most interesting men and women who are gathered together in the capital of a great Empire—I have fled away into

* These chapters were written at Count Tolstoi's country seat in the Government of Toula in early June, 1888.

a secret place apart, to write down in the midst of the solitude and tranquillity of Nature, far from the hum and stir of cities, the judgment which I have formed on all I have seen and heard.

Here we are in the full splendour of the early summer. All day long the air is tremulous with the song of larks, and at night, when the stars begin to glisten and glitter in the beautiful blue of the sky after the gloaming, the nightingales fill the woods with plaintive music. The lilacs and the yellow acacia are in full bloom; the plantations are fragrant with the heavy scent of the lily of the valley, which grows everywhere wild among the trees. Great silver birches, with trembling leaves, bend and bow in the pleasant wind, and down the long avenue of elms you catch glimpses of the ponds, wherein the frogs keep up that curious chorus so strange to English ears. Everywhere the ground is covered with vegetation, green and rank. Nature overflows with verdure, and the bees in the acacias keep up a ceaseless and soothing murmur.

The silence at present is almost absolute. Only now and then the far-away notes of a lark invisible in mid-heaven can be heard, or the sharp twit-twit of the glancing swallow. It is still early morning. Later in the day the voices of children at play will sound fitfully in the distance, blending pleasantly with the bird's song, and the soughing of the wind in the trees, as natural and as beautiful as they.

I am writing in Count Tolstoi's little study. In the next room, separated only by a door that is ever ajar, lies his shoemaker's outfit—his awl, his knife, and his leather. On the wooden partition wall hangs the scythe with which a little later he will renew the pleasures of mowing which he has eulogised in "Anna Karénina"—pleasures which, however rapturous they appear in his pages, depend largely for their enjoyment upon the existence of a stouter back and sturdier loins than those possessed by gentlemen who first take to mowing in middle age.

In an hour or two the great novelist—perhaps the greatest living novelist—will appear in his moujik's garb, with the dark loose coat and leather girdle, and we shall sally forth together over field and forest, drinking-in the glad sunshine, and exulting in the beauty and glory and melody of spring. What a charm there is in these walks! One night we rambled for verst after verst through the woods, now stopping to drink at a rustic well, then exchanging greetings with pilgrims passing on their way to the shrines at Kieff or Troitsa, anon pausing on the hillside to catch the strain of music that floated up the vale from where the village maidens were trilling out in chorus a peasant's song. The sun sinking low on the western horizon lit up with golden radiance the zebra-like trunks of a great plantation of silver birches, filling them with a glow and a warmth that contrasted strangely with their appearance an hour later, when twilight had succeeded sunset, and their white bark glimmered pale and ghostly. The cuckoo's note rose and fell; a heavy-winged crow flapped his solitary homeward way overhead, and in the coppice the nightingale began with his first few broken notes to prepare his even-song. Before us in the moist glades of the forest the Count's daughters skipped from side to side, graceful as young deer, and as much at home in the woods as they. Further on, the workmen, finishing their evening meal, entered into friendly converse with the Count, while we warmed our hands at the fire on which water was boiling for their tea. What a change from the crowded streets of St. Petersburg, the Nevski, noisy with droschkies even at two and three in the morning, and all the artificialities of high society!

And now, after being here for two or three days, I begin to collect my ideas, and will attempt to present as clearly and as succinctly as I can the conclusions at which I have arrived as to the prospects of war or peace in Europe and in Asia, and more especially as to the future relations between England and Russia.

Before discussing what are the immediate prospects of peace or war in Europe, it is well to ask ourselves, What is this Peace which exists—what this War which men fear? Both are new phenomena in the world's history. We have a peace which is like no peace that has existed before. We stand face to face with a possible war like to none that in our time has ever desolated the world. It is worth while to look for a moment at these phenomena.

First, then, as to the peace. Peace implies rest, and in Europe there is no rest. Peace supposes security and confidence, but in Europe everywhere is insecurity and suspicion. Peace days the mustering of half a million of soldiers was regarded as a mighty feat. To-day Prince Bismarck adds to the ranks of the army of the Fatherland, with one stroke of his pen, 700,000 fathers of families, and not a single voice is raised even in passing protest. Germany in the centre of Europe fronts east and west with an available host of three million trained soldiers. France will have between two and three millions ready to hand. Russia before long will be able to put five millions into line. Austria and Italy we need not count. The blast of the trumpets that proclaims the beginning of war will summon the manhood of Europe to the work of slaughter.

Not only will the number of the combatants be far beyond those which were raised even in the days of the First Napoleon— the Grand Army with which he crossed the frontier on his march to Moscow only consisted of the same number of men that have been added this year to the German army—but the spirit in which it will be fought out will differ for the worse. Prince Bismarck has frankly told us what kind of war it will be. We shall fight, he said, if we do fight, until we are bled as white as veal. It will be a duel to the death—a war in which the avowed object of the combatants is the utter destruction of their adversary. "De saigner à blanc," to drain the very life-blood out of your enemy until you leave his carcase as white as that of the calf from which the butcher seeks to drain every ruddy drop of gore—that is the declared ideal of the foremost nations of the Continent in the year of grace 1888. The imagination refuses to picture what it means. All our recent wars were short. The longest was that of the Crimea, which was little more than the siege and the defence of a single fortress by professional soldiers. The Franco-Italian war was almost an affair of weeks. The Danish war was over almost before it began. The Austro-Prussian-Italian war lasted just six weeks. The Franco-German war was over in six months. The conquest of Turkey was completed in about the same time. But the next war will not be over in six weeks or in six months. To bleed each other white, when both combatants are pretty well matched, and when there are millions of men in reserve, is an affair of years. But when all business is suspended, and the reapers have been summoned from the farms to the battle-fields, it will be impossible to carry on war on this scale for years without utter collapse and ghastly famine. Hence the embattled millions will fight with the grim and desperate energy of men who know that, like Judas, what they do they must do quickly. They will strike terror. All the tourney rules of civilised war will be in danger of going by the board. It will be a contest of Titans waged with the ruthlessness of fiends. The next war will be in danger of degenerating into a nineteenth-century version of the horrors of the Thirty Years' War, on a scale far more gigantic, and therefore characterised by crimes far more colossal.

Apart from the certainty of horrors to which the burning of Bazeilles and even the sack of Magdeburg would be but as interludes in the infernal tragedy, there is another aspect of the struggle which is too often overlooked. The new style of warfare, in which battles are fought, not by a professional class set apart from the nation, governed by strict codes of military laws, and remaining apart from the activities of national existence, but by the nation itself, threatens to have most alarming results for humanity and civilisation. We are able to see something of what it involves in the criminal statistics of Germany since the war. The conquest of France was one of the most expeditious and in many respects one of the least objectionable wars ever waged. But it brutalised the Germans to an extent difficult to realise outside Germany. The citizen, plunged for six months into all the licence and savagery of war, acquired a taint from which he did not purge himself for years. War is the unloosing of all crimes, the sanctioning of all violence, the negation of the sanctity of property and of life. To accustom men to war is to accustom them to live in a world where the ordinary moral code is suspended. That code does not easily reestablish its authority when peace is concluded. The criminal statistics of Germany since 1871 show a terrible increase in all kinds of violent crime—murder, highway robbery, theft by violence, burglary, assaults on women and children—which after ten or fifteen years has only now begun to decline. The violence put in practice against the enemy in France left its poison in the blood of the Germans. What will be the effect upon civilisation and humanity of accustoming ten millions of citizens to make murder their daily passion throughout a long war, in which every evil dormant in the human animal would be given free rein, no one can foresee. One thing only is certain, that the consequences would be far more hideous and deadly than any one has yet ventured to conceive.

In face of such portentous possibilities it is difficult to find words adequate to condemn the amazing and reckless criminality of those who, in the press and elsewhere, are continually flinging the firebrands of taunts, and sneers, and recriminations between the nations. When the avalanches tremble overhead, even the fool might cease to whistle; but these gentry, with this measureless catastrophe impending, go shouting and hallooing like a very Tom of Bedlam escaped from his keepers. It is sport to the fool to do mischief, and the madman loves to scatter firebrands and death; but surely those journalists in London and elsewhere who "love to swell the warwhoop passionate for war" might at least reflect on the responsibilities of provoking a conflict which would have as its watchword " De saigner à blanc" all round.

## CHAPTER II.

### HOW ENGLAND DOES NOT DO HER DUTY.

I HAD just finished the last chapter and had gone out for a stroll with Count Tolstoi in the bright sunlight of the Sunday morning, when we saw a dense column of black smoke rising above the trees. Running down the avenue to the brow of the hill we saw that a fire had broken out in the village on the other side of the valley. The great column of smoke gave way to fierce crackling flames that, fanned by the southern wind, leapt ever and anon in vast sheets of dazzling fire towards the nearest cottage. We plunged down the valley, and before we climbed the hill on the other side the fire had seized the thatch of a peasant's house, and from it also were rising flames and smoke. Four other houses, timber-built and thatched, stood between the fire and the brow of the hill. Unless the wind changed, every one of them was doomed. And the wind did not change, but freshened rather, and the great flames, that roared and flapped and crackled in the breeze, as if they had been the standards of the Fire Fiend, leaped from house to house. We rushed from one to another, seeking what household goods could be saved. The cottages were untenanted. An empty cradle lay in one, from another I carried out a table. Count Tolstoi was nearly burnt alive in the rush: for the flames followed faster and faster, and before we could see where he was, the whole thatched roof was blazing overhead. The blinding smoke and the scorching heat of the burning houses drove all of us far away. Each burnt-out family gathered weeping and disconsolate round the slender remnant of their rescued possessions, and watched with streaming eyes the roof-tree go up in flame and smoke into the blue depths of the placid sky. How the flames roared, as if rejoicing over their prey! Each snug interior became a blazing fiery furnace, the ruddy glare showed red against the golden splendour of the noonday sun. It was a cruel sight. The savings of a lifetime, the carefully cherished homes, were eaten up ruthlessly in a moment; and there was no remedy. The nearest water was nearly half a mile off, and if it had been close at hand no fire brigade could have checked the fire when driven by such a wind. The cottages burned like dried brushwood, and in less than five minutes from the outbreak of the fire the whole row was ablaze from end to end.

Never shall I forget the piteous and tragic picture presented by that burning village. It was a brilliantly beautiful day. The blue sky flecked here and there with fleecy white clouds; the green meadow starred with spring flowers, in which within a hundred yards of the fire the young foals were sleeping stretched full length in the sun; the groups of peasant women and children, with their picturesque costume and comely, sun-burnt faces—formed the setting to the fiercely flaming destruction that blazed and smoked and devoured while we stood helpless by. A man who saw his life's work vanishing in smoke bent over his cart and sobbed aloud, unheeded, and here and there a woman kneeling on the grass wailed and wept, chanting amid her tears a weird and melancholy prayer. After a period of agonising suspense, when it was rumoured that two children, a boy of four and a twelve-months baby, had been burned alive in one of the huts, it was discovered that they were alive and well. Some of the little children wept aloud, wringing their hands; others sat wondering at the commotion, and one little lad seemed quite happy nursing a hairy little pig which had been saved from the last of the burning houses.

What a picture of desolation it seemed! how bitter the grief, how unavailing the efforts which the best intentioned could make to stem the onward rush of the fire as the wind flung the flames in fierce haste from roof to roof! It burned itself into my mind as, half-choking with smoke, I turned away from a sorrow which I could not alleviate and distress which I could not relieve. And as I hurried through the cool glades of the woods, where only the odour of the burning village could be dimly felt, and which soon hid even the whity-grey smoke which lay heavy on the hillside, I could not help feeling what a terribly vivid illustration the burning of these huts in Yasnaia Poliana had afforded at once of the incidents of war and of the perils of the European situation.

The fire had begun, it seemed, in a barn, where it was believed some boys had been playing with matches. The flame caught the straw, and in a moment five of the cottages were doomed. Had the wind been in the other direction twenty houses would have perished instead of five. But even as it was it was horrible enough. Five houses, insured perhaps to one-fifth of their value, were consumed; five families were homeless, and the fire made havoc of all their household gods.

The burning of villages—what is that but one of the ordinary and most familiar incidents of war? Not an army moves that does not leave in its wake devastation a thousand times more terrible than this. Those weeping peasants, those terrified children, those smouldering heaps of ashes where once stood homes and households, enable us, if multiplied a thousandfold, to image forth something of what war means. It is necessary for us to be reminded of the fact, for we English of all nations are most apt to forget the meaning of war. To us war is a thing to read about in the newspapers, as a kind of piquant sauce at breakfast, or, at the worst, to pay for in our income-tax. "War and bloodshed" are still to us, as in Coleridge's time, "animating sports, the which we pay for as a thing to talk of, spectators and not combatants." But to the others fire-visaged war is a grim presence whose hot dun breath is to Europe what the simoom is to the traveller in the desert. And this dread and terrible visitation can be let loose to scourge the world almost as easily as the barn in Yasnaia Poliana was fired by the match of a reckless boy.

And the boys with the matches—who are they? Alas! if the truth must be said, they are too often journalists, men of my own profession, who seem to imagine that the supreme duty of the editor is to exasperate national animosities and inflame prejudices that can only be slaked in blood. Said Baron de Jomini to me one day in St. Petersburg, in his pleasant way, "Peace! The Governments would have no difficulty in keeping peace if only the journalists were well hanged. It is the newspapers that excite the passions which hurry Governments against their will into acts of war." A wholesale holocaust of the editors of Europe might not be too dear a sacrifice as a peace-offering, but such a method of inaugurating the millennium is, for the present, beyond the pale of practical politics. I did, indeed, draw up a provisional list of the half a dozen most hangworthy of my *confrères*, with the assistance of a distinguished Ambassador, but the list is at present a mere counsel of perfection. We cannot string up our journalistic boys with matches; nay, we cannot even rap their knuckles; they must, if it please them, be free to strike as many lights as they please in the powder magazine of Europe. All that can be done is to implore them, from Mr. Buckle downwards, to remember their responsibility, and to endeavour to make them see the lurid glare of the peasant's burning homestead behind the glitter of their rhetorical incitations, and to hear the agonised wail of the homeless child as the echo of their bellicose rhetoric. We in England are apt to forget, snugly ensconced in our coign of vantage behind the silver streak, that others are more sensitive than ourselves, and that the small boy who halloos his comrades on to fight by alternate gibes and encouragement, while he stays out of harm's way up a tree, is not exactly the exemplar who should be followed by those who essay to speak in the name of England for civilisation and for peace.

When the fire was blazing at Yasnaia Poliana there were many inquiries as to where was the fire-engine, where were the pails, where the apparatus which, if ready at hand at the first, might have prevented the conflagration. The peasants said that the commune had paid the money for an engine some time ago, but the starosta, or village mayor, had pocketed it; and as the starshina, or mayor of the district, was his relative, nothing could be done. This, again, seemed to me an only too exact representation of the position of Europe. England, like the dishonest starosta, has received from Providence wealth, position, influence, everything that marks her out as bound in duty to play a great and useful *rôle* as the head of the Fire Brigade of the Continent. But, alas! like this cursed starosta, she pockets all and does nothing. Nay, she is even worse than he. His conduct was only negative. He was said to have employed the money given him for the fire-engine to improve his own house. To make the parallel exact he ought to have spent it in fireworks or lucifer matches, and endangered the safety of the village by the aid of the money given him to secure its safety.

In looking over the condition of Europe it is impossible not to be reminded of the *rôle* which England might play in securing the maintenance of peace. And in looking over Russia it is equally impossible not to be reminded of the *rôle* which England has played for the promotion of war. Eleven years ago this January the present Prime Minister saw his way to the prevention of a great and bloody war. So did Mr. Gladstone. So did the then Russian Emperor. If England had in January, 1877, risen superior to her ancient prejudices and decided that her deed must be as good as her word, the Turks would have bowed before the decision of Europe, and Bulgaria would have been freed without the sacrifice of a solitary soldier. It would not have cost England a single ship nor Russia a single regiment. All that was required was hearty, loyal co-operation between the two Empires. England had undertaken great responsibilities. Englishmen had made the world ring with their denunciation of the atrocities which had defiled the rose-gardens and corn-fields of Bulgaria with heaps of outraged dead. The English Government, making itself the mouthpiece of the offended conscience of Europe, had solemnly summoned the oppressor to liberate his victims and to redress their wrongs. England had assembled a great international court, and Lord Salisbury had found no difficulty in securing from united Europe the unanimous acceptance of his programme of reform. From no Power did England receive more hearty and more loyal support than from Russia. But when the crowning moment came, and the Turks waited to know whether England meant what she said, then, to our everlasting shame and dishonour, Lord Salisbury's master, whom we had placed in possession of the right to speak in the name and with the authority of England, thrust his tongue in his cheek, laid his finger on one side of his nose, and winked significantly at the Grand Turk. Instantly all that the Powers had done was undone. Sir Henry Elliot and Lord Beaconsfield neutralised the effect of Lord Salisbury's diplomacy, and instead of taking a great onward stride in the direction of peace and the federation of Europe the Continent was plunged into a long and horrible war. For all the blood shed in torrents at Plevna and the Balkans England was responsible. A single resolute movement of our fleet upon Constantinople, and Turkish resistance would instantly have collapsed. But that movement was not made. When the Turks were told by half our newspapers that if they stood firm England would hasten to their assistance, the die was cast. There is hardly a Russian village, from the Oural to the Vistula, from Archangel to the Crimea, but mourns to-day some son or brother who went but who returned not in the last great war. A hundred and twenty thousand Russians—brave, simple, kindly-hearted, as these good fellows whom I saw helping their burnt-out comrades, and giving of their scanty store of bread and kwas to those who had lost their all—died horrible deaths on the battle-field and in the hospital because Russia was left alone to do the work which Europe might have done without strain or danger if England had but been true. And this vast, frugal, industrious peasantry, whose only ambition is to be allowed to toil in peace from sunrise to sunset for 10d. a day, has been saddled with a war debt of a hundred millions sterling for the liberation of Bulgaria, not one penny of which would have needed to be spent but for England's crime.

The case is a signal illustration of the power of England for weal or for woe as the peacemaker of the world. For it so happens that if we had been indifferent enough to considerations of humanity and of liberty boldly to have ranged ourselves on the side of the Turks, and energetically organised for their defence, the peace might also have been preserved, although Bulgaria would not have been freed. We could have kept the peace with or without liberty for Bulgaria, whichever side we took, if we had only stuck to it. What we did was to stick to one side just long enough to make it impossible for Russia to draw back, and then to desert it just at the moment when our desertion rendered it impossible for Turkey to submit. If we had deliberately played our cards in order to expose Turkey to invasion, and to force the Russians to face the sacrifices of war, we could not, by the most malevolent ingenuity, have adopted a policy better adapted to secure that end.

If we can do no better than this, then a policy of absolute non-intervention is defensible, if only because it is better to be a corpse and a cipher than to be a madman and a fiend. But I am loath to believe that England is shut up to either of these alternatives. If *noblesse oblige*, then not less have position, wealth, tradition, and opportunity for usefulness, also their obligations. And do not let us deceive ourselves by dreaming of the impossible. Even if we wished it, there is no party in England, there are not fifty men in the House of Commons, who would deliberately and seriously propose to withdraw from the European Concert, and to abandon all claim to a voice in the settlement of international questions, in which at any moment we may take a deep and passionate interest. Mr. Labouchere may regret this, but he would not deny it. And as such is the case, all that remains to be done is to make the best of it, and to decide definitely upon using England's position in the counsels of Europe, not for any purposes of aggrandisement or of self-interest, but for the maintenance of the public peace.

Even if we were not called to this work by considerations of our own interests, we are bound at least to attempt it, if only to endeavour to repair, however tardily, the injuries which we have inflicted upon our neighbours. If there be such a thing as retribution for nations, as for individuals, then, indeed, we shall do well to make such atonement as may be possible for our manifold sins and offences—sins not committed from any deliberate criminality or desire to bring about war on our part, but chiefly from a reckless self-indulgence in the bellicose mood of the moment, without regard to the necessities of statesmanship or the responsibilities of our position. Coleridge's solemn and prophetic warning has seldom been absent from my mind since I left England on this journey:—

> Thankless too for peace
> (Peace long preserved by fleets and perilous seas)
> Secure from actual warfare, we have loved
> To swell the war-whoop passionate for war!
> Alas! for ages ignorant of all
> Its ghastlier workings (famine or blue plague,
> Battle or siege, or flight through wintry snows).
> . . . . Therefore Evil days
> Are coming on us, O my countrymen!
> And what if all-avenging Providence
> Strong and retributive should make us know
> The meaning of our words, force us to feel
> The desolation and the agony
> Of our fierce doings?

Not that of late we have been doing ourselves anything very fierce. We have not been doers of anything but mischief; all our fierceness has been in words that exposed us to no risk of broken bones, while they set our neighbours by the ears. We are in European politics very much like idle pleasure-seekers on the deck of a fragile craft that is threading its way through a narrow, crowded, and stormy sea. As the fancy seizes us, we rush from side to side, with supreme indifference to the effect which the sudden transfer of so much weight from larboard to starboard may have upon the steering or the stability of the vessel. If we were actually on board such a craft we should fortunately have all been drowned long ago, but the misfortune of our political situation is that we are, as it were, all supplied with patent safety life-belts, by which we can escape the fate to which our reckless plunging from side to side exposes our less fortunate fellow-passengers.

What then, must be the policy of England? That is the real question in discussing the problem of peace or war. All the other powers have their policy more or less marked out for them by circumstances. England holds the balance weight. England may not be able to put a single army corps into the field. But she can excite those who can put twenty army corps in motion, and she can at least refrain from encouraging, from provoking, from inciting, the masters of many legions to give the signal for war. It is not so much that England should at present learn to do well. The first thing is that she should learn to cease to do evil—to cease, that is, to excite, with hopes of ultimate support, the one State of Europe whose internal position and external designs constitute a peril to European peace.

If England undertakes the *rôle* of heading the fire-brigade of Europe for the prevention of war, she cannot act alone. Co-operation, not alliance, must be the key-note of her policy. The secret of our influence consists in our maintaining a position of independence. The moment we are allied with one Power we become instantly the more or less declared enemy of some other Power. Friends of all, allies of none, is our watchword, and it is fortunately one that is imposed upon us as imperatively by our party politics and our parliamentary system as by the obvious considerations of duty and interest. But the moment that England sets before herself the maintenance of peace based on the existing *status quo* she is practically driven to co-operate more or less closely with one set of Powers in order to restrain the actions of another set of Powers, who might, if unrestrained, bring about a war which would be of a magnitude and a nature so unprecedented and so ghastly as to justify the employment of almost any means to avert it.

And here let me observe, in passing, in order that I may not be misunderstood, that in defining the policy of England as the maintenance of peace on the basis of the *status quo*, I am fully mindful of the necessity which exists from time to time of modifying the *status quo*. No policy is so fatal to *status quo* as a dogged refusal to readjust it to altered conditions. Any such policy as that which we are discussing presupposes that the powers which agree to maintain peace will also agree to sanction and enforce such changes as are necessary to prevent the disturbance of peace. That is to say, all modifications in the existing *status quo* must be decided, not on the battlefield, but by the Concert of Europe; and Europe, when it has wisdom to decide what change should be made, must also have the resolution to enforce its decision.

## CHAPTER III.

### AUSTRIA AS DISTURBER OF THE PEACE.

THE development and strengthening of the principle of the European Concert is the true road along which civilisation must progress; but the question more immediately before us is, which are the Powers with whom it is possible to co-operate for the maintenance of peace, or, to reverse the order, which are the Powers whose avowed policy is to disturb the peace and violently to alter the *status quo* to their own advantage? These powers are two. France is obviously the first, Austria the second. France has no other foreign policy than one—the recovery of her lost provinces. France therefore stands avowed as the determined disturber of the peace at whatever moment may seem propitious. Any policy that has as its end the maintenance of peace must have as its first object the postponement indefinitely of that propitious moment. Without for a moment departing from the *entente cordiale* with France, and indeed acting really from a very sincere desire for the true interests of France, it ought to be a settled object of any effective peace policy to discourage any attack upon Germany for the purposes of revenge, and to prevent the formation of such groups on the Continent as might tempt France into a war for the lost provinces. Lead us not into temptation! When France says her Paternoster it is by such a policy that her prayer can best be answered.

There will of course be an outcry against this, on the ground that it seems to amount to a European guarantee of Elsass-Lothringen to Germany, and that it practically places England at the head of a Continental league against the French. Not against but rather in favour of the French. For, if those who make this objection were to take the trouble to ascertain the views of the French themselves, they would not be so confident in denouncing this peace policy as anti-French. The ablest and most influential Frenchmen to-day disclaim with unanimity any desire to attack Germany. Alsace and Lorraine, they say, will come back to France as certainly as the sun will rise to-morrow in the east, but apparently they expect them to come back by the operation of causes as much beyond their control as the revolution of the planets. Every reasonable Frenchman knows perfectly well that France has not at present the slightest chance of success in an offensive war against Germany, although they are quite well able to take care of themselves if they are attacked by Germany. Their policy is to wait upon Providence, watching the course of events, hoping much more from internal decomposition or disintegration in Germany than from any violent attack from without. When a politician of the standing of M. Clémenceau is not afraid to say that he would oppose a French attack upon Germany even if Germany had a Russian war on her hands, it is evident that France would not vehemently resent a policy which saved at once her *amour propre* and preserved the peace. France does not want to begin the next German war, like the last, under the malediction of the civilised world. She wants the approval of the moral sense of mankind, and she wants a certainty of success. She can secure neither if she is hurried into taking any premature step, and a policy that restrains her from yielding to the temptation of passion and the incitement of ignorance until at last her time has fully come will be the greatest benefit which Europe can confer upon the Republic.

There is another aspect of the question which should not be lost sight of. There may be—in Russia I am persistently assured that there has been—a possibility that the war on the Rhine may be begun by Germany. The possibility is, I think, remote. Germany asks only to be left alone. In 1875 there seems to be little doubt that the military party at Berlin had almost arranged for a renewal of the war, on the ground that France was recovering too rapidly, and in 1887 the Schnaebele incident might have brought matters to a crisis but for the menacing reserve of Russia. But, whether the initiative be taken by Germany or by France, the true peace policy is to seek to array an overwhelming preponderance of force against whatever Power is tempted to disturb the peace. If such an array be forthcoming there will be no war. Its mere existence will rob the situation of its venom.

The danger of war at this moment does not arise from the relations between France and Germany. The idea that the French may suddenly make a raid on London can only be entertained by those who are dominated by the traditions of the

Napoleonic Empire. As long as France was in the hands of an adventurer who depended for his power on the bayonets of his Prætorians, anything was possible. But if war is made to-day it will be made, not by mercenaries and professional soldiers, but by the manhood of France. And, so far as I can judge, the manhood of France is much more pacific than the manhood of England. Among no people, I regret to say, is there such readiness, if not to go to war, at least to talk about it, as among Englishmen. It is a dangerous thing for the peace of the world that the most loudly vocal person in the international market-place should be one who from his position is insured against ever being called upon to realise the consequences of his own words. The French electors have no such immunity and no such irresponsibility. They may elect General Boulanger or they may not, but if General Boulanger were to be demented enough to endeavour to launch them into war with England his fall would be as rapid as his rise. The strength of the French sentiment against war is curiously shown in the loathing that is excited by the name of M. Ferry. The French peasantry and artisans detest the author of the Tonkin campaign as much as the Gladstonians detested Lord Beaconsfield in 1880. If M. Ferry had been elected President, it is stoutly asserted by those who ought to know, that the streets of Paris would have run with blood before the capital submitted to the Presidency of the Tonkinois. The internal condition of France, therefore, instead of tending towards foreign war, operates in the opposite direction. For the present the Republic is peace, and peaceful it seems likely to remain whatever may be the fate which fortune has in store for General Boulanger.

It is far different with the other State whose policy menaces Europe with war. The one danger-point visible on the European horizon is not France, is not Russia, it is Austria. If there is a war in Europe in the next twelve months there is little doubt but that it will be provoked by Austria. Austria is the only danger. Austria is at this moment the only Power whose position is contrary to European treaties. Austria is the only Power which is pursuing a policy that may make war inevitable.

Austria is the only State that is making military preparations altogether in excess of its financial resources. And at the same time that Austria's foreign policy is so directly provocative of war, her internal condition is such that no one can predict what a day may bring forth. In the composite conglomerate of heterogeneous nationalities which make up the Austrian State there is only one compact and important element. There are only five million Magyars in Austria-Hungary, but they are more powerful than the thirty millions of their fellow-subjects. The Germans look to Berlin, the Slavs to St. Petersburg or to Moscow. The Magyars look to themselves. They are a brave and reckless race, full of martial fire, inspired by the memory of their past, and accustomed from of old to all the arts which give men power and place in political life. In Hungary there are but five millions of them out of fifteen and a half millions, but the five millions rule the ten ; nay, the ten hardly count against the five. They are in the position of an ascendant nationality, threatened with reduction to the level of the masses which at present are but as the pedestal of its power. The artificiality of their position makes them reckless. The memory of their disappointment in 1849, when the Russians crushed their rebellion, and restored the Hapsburg in the name of law, order, and the peace of Europe, has filled them with inextinguishable hatred of the Russian, whom they dread as much for what he may do in the future as they hate him for what he has done in the past. It is these Magyars who will make war if they can, and make it now. They are the only people in Europe who do not conceal their desire for war. They are animated at once by race-hatred and by the dread which ever haunts an oligarchy when it sees the stirring of the democratic depths beneath the whispers of the Northern wind. All this is true, it may be said, but it was not less true last year and the year before. Why are the Magyars more dangerous now than they were then? The answer is simple. The Magyars are more dangerous to-day because they believe that they are in a position in which they can force the hand of Germany, and secure for their attack upon Russia the support of the strongest military Power in Europe. That is a chance which does not occur every day.

The Magyars calculate that by throwing all their strength in one direction they may drag after them Austria, that Austria will drag Germany, and Germany Italy, and Italy perhaps England. It is something like the milkmaid's calculation as to the fortune she would make when she sold her milk, but nevertheless it dominates the imagination of the Magyars. It may be a delusion, but it is a delusion which they may act upon as if it were a reality. Nor are the Magyars greatly to blame for believing that for once they have at last got the whip-hand of the situation. The Germans have used them so long as bogeys with which to menace Russia that the bogeys feel inclined to do a little business on their own account. And then we must never leave out of account the reckless encouragement given to these gentry by the insensate folly of our English newspapers. Every one in London knows that if the Magyars attacked Russia Lord Salisbury would leave Austria to her fate with an imperturbable nonchalance tempered only by many crocodile tears of regret over the suicide of so high-spirited and chivalrous a State. But not a single ·blue-jacket would be risked for all the Magyars in Hungary. The Magyars, however, do not understand that, and the incitations of the *Times* and the *Standard*—*et hoc genus omne*—operate upon them like brandy. "Strike when the iron is hot," say they. "Now is our chance. We have the game in our own hands, for every one will have to help us if we can only by hook or by crook provoke Russia into war."

This line of argument is powerfully reinforced by the financial difficulties in which Austria-Hungary is placed. Under pressure from Germany she has been incurring fresh military expenditure, and ever fresh military expenditure, and all for what? A Power within an ace of bankruptcy does not spend extra millions on armaments without hoping at least to have something to show for its sacrifices. The King of France, who with twice ten thousand men marched up a hill and then marched down again, might do as he pleased, for he was King of France. But to move troops towards the frontier, to build great camps, to make all preparations for a struggle for life and death, merely in order to do nothing and sit still when all the money is spent—that is hardly possible for Austria-Hungary. The financial *malaise*, the longing to escape from suspense even by plunging into the deadly fever of war, all tell in the same evil direction as that in which the whole force of the Magyars is already impelling the State. Even if we do not look at the Balkans, but confine our attention to the interior of Austria-Hungary, we shall see enough to convince us that the danger point is to be found in Pesth.

Austria, like a drunken man, is in a state of unstable equilibrium, and the action of the Magyars may at any moment throw her off her balance unless she is held up and restrained by the iron hand of an international policeman.

The need for such restraint is shown very forcibly in the extent to which Austria has pushed herself already in the Balkan Peninsula. It is the fashion to speak in England of the Berlin Treaty as the charter of European peace. It was a great international compact imposed by Europe upon Russia, with the distinct and explicit declaration that its strict and literal fulfilment was indispensable to the tranquillity of the East. What has happened? Every provision in that treaty for the fulfilment of which Russia was responsible has been fulfilled. But the rest of the treaty? It practically does not exist. All the clauses which depend for their execution upon the Turks are of course null and void. The reforms stipulated for the protection of the Armenians have never been executed. The organic statute that was to have given contentment to Macedonia and the other Turkish provinces has been framed by an International Commission, and left exactly where it was, with the result that at any moment insurrections may break out in Macedonia or elsewhere with what is virtually a European certificate in advance of the justice of the insurgents' demands.

In this there is nothing new. Turkey has never kept a treaty or executed a reform. Her neglect to execute the provisions of the Berlin Treaty is therefore but consistent with her neglect to execute every treaty to which she has ever affixed her signature. Austria, however, is a civilised Power; Austria is supposed to be the *avant-garde* of German culture: Austria has a healing, an educational mission in these lands. Has Austria, then, shown herself any more regardful of the letter or the spirit of the Berlin Treaty than her barbarous neighbour?

By the Berlin Treaty Austria was authorised to occupy and administer for the restoration of order Bosnia and the Herzegovina, which were to remain Turkish provinces. I do not wish to labour this point, although it is one to which most Russians attach great importance. Austria, they say, according to the authority of her own officials, has restored order in Bosnia and the Herzegovina. Her mission is accomplished; her mandate has expired. Why does she not retire? Instead of retiring she is organising these provinces as if they were integral portions of the Dual Monarchy. She is filling them with soldiers and with Jesuits, and asserting on every occasion and in every way, direct and indirect, that in Bosnia she means to remain till the crack of doom. This may be natural; it may be politic, and it may be right; but is it in accordance with the spirit of the Berlin Treaty?

The whole history of Austria's connection with Bosnia and the Herzegovina is calculated to fill the observer with suspicion and distrust of Austrian policy. The Eastern Question was raised in 1875, not by Russia, but by Austria, not by the Russian propaganda in Bulgaria, but by the Austrian agents in the Herzegovina. Austria, which fomented the disturbance by which she hoped to profit, never lifted a finger to save her unfortunate *protégés* from being crushed by the Turks whom they had provoked. She contented herself with protesting before the world that she had nothing to do with the insurrection which she had excited, and had no designs upon the provinces, at the very time when she was negotiating with Russia by secret compacts for their appropriation. Again and again, in the most public and solemn fashion, Count Andrassy protested before the representatives of Austria-Hungary that he had never contemplated, and would never contemplate, the addition of Bosnia and the Herzegovina to the Empire Kingdom, at the same time that he had all but signed, sealed, and delivered to Prince Gortschakoff an agreement giving Russia a free hand in the Eastern Balkan in return for the promised occupation of Bosnia and the Herzegovina. Then when the time came, when Russia was compelled to submit her treaty with Turkey to be cut to pieces by a European Congress, Austria, which had sacrificed nothing, which had spent nothing, and which had done nothing—but lie —was furnished with a European mandate for the occupation and administration of the provinces which she had declared she would not accept as a gift, and which she no sooner occupied than she *de facto* annexed. Her action in the past is certainly not calculated to encourage confidence in the future in her protestations of disinterestedness or her assurances of good faith.

About the actual condition of things in Bosnia and the Herzegovina I cannot, of course, speak at first hand. I can only repeat what I heard in St. Petersburg from those who take a keen interest in the Slavs of the Balkan. Their story is always the same. The Bosniacs detest their new rulers, and only wait a signal from Russia to hurl the Austrians out of their province. "When the Turks got angry they occasionally cut off the head of one of us in each ten," said a Bosniac peasant: "but these Austrian fellows take the stomach and the heart of every single one." The Jesuit propaganda reacts against its Austrian patrons; and it is an article of faith held implicitly by every good Slavophil, that if Austria and Russia should ever come to blows, Russia can count upon the active assistance of every Slav in the occupied provinces. From a military point of view the occupation is likely to be equivalent to the paralysis of at least one *corps d'armée*.

For her position in Bosnia and the Herzegovina Austria has at least a quasi-sanction, although she has made permanent that which was temporary, and has converted an occupation for the restoration of order into a practical annexation. But in Servia she has not even the semblance of an international sanction for her encroachments. King Milan, by the Berlin Treaty, had to be king of an independent Servia. He is now merely the satrap of the Hapsburg. Francis Joseph has put Milan in his pocket. As Viennese policy is dictated from Berlin, so Belgrade politics are controlled from Vienna. I was emphatically assured by a diplomatist, who declared that he had himself a copy of the document, that Austria has concluded a military convention with Servia which places the Servian army on the footing of an Austrian army corps, and provides that in case of war the Servian troops shall be placed under the command of the Austrian Commander-in-Chief. If this story be true, Servia is not technically annexed. It is simply engulfed. The independence of a State which places its troops under the command of a neighbouring Sovereign whenever he pleases to go to war is a phrase rather than a fact. The fact is that in spite of the wishes of the population, which if not Russian is at least not Austrian, King Milan has practically annexed Servia to Austria-Hungary. The position is irregular. It may bring the Government into sharp collision with the people, and if the Servians should evict their King, there is too much reason to believe that he would attempt to return supported by Austrian bayonets. In that case it would be difficult to prevent war.

But bad as Austrian policy may be in Servia, it is in Bulgaria that the bad faith of the Dual Monarchy is most conspicuously displayed. Russia acquiesced—reluctantly, no doubt, but nevertheless loyally—in the surrender of Bosnia and the Herzegovina to Austrian ascendency. It was the price which she had to pay, and which she did pay, honestly though grudgingly, for the privilege of organising Bulgaria as an independent principality. Russia kept her part of the bargain. Austria did not keep hers. Russia has never raised a finger against Austria, even in Servia. But in Bulgaria Austria has interfered, and is interfering, to such an extent that she has practically established her own agent on the throne of Sophia. It is this which gives such deadly offence in Russia, and which at the present moment constitutes a live coal kept aglow in the midst of the Eastern tinder-box.

Ferdinand of Coburg is an officer in the Hungarian army. He is a German by birth, an Austrian by allegiance, and a Roman Catholic by conviction. He represents everything that is most inimical to Russia and her Slavonic Orthodox *protégés*. Yet he was allowed to go to Sophia, and is supported there to this hour by Austria. Russians believe that it was Austria that made war against Bulgaria through Servia when the Bulgarians, in defiance of Russian counsel, realised the Russian ideal of the union of the Bulgarians. And when the valour of the Bulgarians, the personal qualities of Prince Alexander, and the discipline which Russia had imparted to the Bulgarian levies, enabled them to triumph over the Servian invaders, it was an Austrian ultimatum and a direct threat of Austrian intervention which arrested the victorious Bulgarians in their triumphant progress towards Belgrade.

These matters belong to the domain of accomplished fact. If Austria has done all this already, it is easy to imagine how obvious to the Slavonic patriot appears the assumption that Austria is pressing or being pressed downwards to the Ægean, and that before long the Balkan peninsula, which Russia has watered with the blood of so many of her heroes, will have passed from under the sway of the Sultan to that of the Hapsburg.

Austria, therefore, is the one point of danger in the European horizon. She is dangerous because she is dominated by a reckless oligarchy passionate for war, and confident that they can force the hand of their allies if they fire but a single rifle across the Russian frontier. She is dangerous because her finances are so rickety and her political equilibrium so unsteady that she can with difficulty draw back from her present position after incurring so much expenditure without having anything to show for it. In her external policy she is dangerous because she has violated the spirit of the Berlin Treaty in Bosnia, has practically annexed Servia, has established her *protégé* on the throne of Bulgaria, and is pursuing a policy of *Drang nach Osten*, which will inevitably bring her into collision with Russia, who imposes an irrevocable veto on the Austrian advance to the Bosphorus. She is the one civilised power that has broken the Berlin Treaty, and which is obviously and avowedly moving eastwards on a mission of absorption, if not of conquest. What she has done may not result in war, but if she goes on war is inevitable. Hence the condition of peace is an imperative Halt! addressed to Austria.

## CHAPTER IV.

### CONCERNING REPTILES AND WORMS.

Mr. GLADSTONE said "Hands off!" but that imperative Halt! can best come from Berlin. This brings me to the policy of Germany—a theme full of interest not unmixed with mystery. What is the policy of Germany? It is the policy of Prince Bismarck. And what is Prince Bismarck? Is Prince Bismarck to be judged by his words or the words of his creatures on the press? If the former, then he is one of the most straightforward and honest of statesmen. If the latter, then he is a very Machiavelli under the mask of an honest broker. "The true Bismarck," said one who knows him well, "is the Bismarck who speaks in the Reichstag, not the Jews who write in the German papers." Unfortunately it is difficult to separate the one from the other. Judged by his public form as he appears in the German Parliament, the Great Chancellor seems almost an ideal politician. But when we turn from his speeches to his inspired papers, the eminent Dr. Jekyll disappears, and we have only the loathsome features of Mr. Hyde.

I am aware that most Englishmen will ridicule the idea of weighing the utterances of unknown and more or less disreputable journalistic hacks against the public speeches of the Chancellor. And these Englishmen would be right but for the fact that Prince Bismarck, who neglects nothing and presses everything into his service, has converted the German press into a vulgar and blatant speaking-trumpet of the German Administration. What with the Reptile fund for corruption and the immense power which the Administration has over the press for means of intimidation, the Chancellor has converted German journalism into the most effective and most disreputable of the instruments by which he governs Germany.

It is a new and horrible kind of State Church, the temporal power taking possession of the spiritual, and using it for its own ends. If all be true that I heard repeatedly from those who ought to know, as Queen Elizabeth used to tune her pulpits, so Prince Bismarck tunes his newspapers. He keeps them in good order by tips, by menaces, and by punishment. It would almost seem that the German journalists should all wear the *pickelhaube*, so absolutely are they under the thumb of the Administration. The clumsy nobbling of the press practised by less experienced statesmen has been by Prince Bismarck reduced to a system. Public opinion is an article manufactured to order. As a dyer will turn you out cloth red, green, or blue, to suit, so the great master at Varzin will produce a public opinion according to his needs. Prince Bismarck familiarised Europe with the phrase as to the importance of seizing the psychological moment. But it is only in Germany men understand that he not only seizes the psychological moment, he also manufactures it. And in the manufacture, I regret to hear it asserted on every side, lies seem to play almost as important a part as truth. Not, of course, that Prince Bismarck lies. But somehow or other, in the most persistent and systematic way, some convenient falsehood has the habit of getting into his papers when its circulation is calculated to facilitate his designs.

Where the lie comes from, no one, of course, knows. It is, perhaps, evolved in some mysterious manner from the depths of the inner consciousness of the fallen spirits who minister to him and do his pleasure. But whatever may be its genesis, it appears, and the Chancellor profits by it. "*Non olet*," he thinks. Why should he be squeamish?

The Reptile fund—so called because of Prince Bismarck's own phrase—consists of the confiscated fortune of the King of Hanover, together with an unknown grant from the war indemnity. Speaking of the attacks made upon the Government by the press, the Chancellor exclaimed on a memorable occasion that as his Administration was so exposed to malignant misrepresentations at the hands of its adversaries, he did not think it tolerable that he should be left unarmed against so powerful and so unscrupulous a foe. "I must have means," he said, "with which to hunt those reptiles to their holes and destroy them there." Hence the so-called Reptile fund, which is simply an indefinite amount of secret service money at the disposal of Prince Bismarck for controlling the press. With its aid, he is said to have organised a news service for the benefit of the German Government, the like of which exists nowhere out of the pages of the French novels which describe the spy system of Fouché. At its head stands Herr Holstein, the *âme damnée* of Prince Bismarck, who has at his command a disciplined host of confidential reporters, who enable him to follow unseen the movements of all his adversaries. The great Chancellor never neglects any foe, no matter how insignificant. The famous Third Section of the Russian police was mere child's play compared with the ubiquitous engine of observation which the Chancellor has established for the collection of information. "Power," said Lord Beaconsfield, "belongs to the best informed;" and there is no newspaper editor in Europe who organises so systematically the collection and tabulation of information as the German Chancellor.

What kind of information? All kinds of information, but chiefly that which concerns the doings and sayings, the movements and the writings, of those whom it may be necessary for him to crush. At the Chancellery of the Secret Intelligence Bureau at Berlin, under Herr Holstein, are kept the *dossiers* of every man or woman whom from time to time it thinks necessary to Prince Bismarck to watch with a view to ulterior developments. The minuteness of the information thus stored up for future use is very extraordinary, and suggests many uncomfortable reflections. A friend of mine resident in Germany once had an opportunity of seeing a copy of his own *dossier*. Therein he found set down all particulars of himself and his family and his relations. A list was given of all the people whom he was in the habit of receiving, and a detailed report as to all the correspondents to whom he was in the habit of writing. To this man, it was written, he sends letters every week, to the other every day, to a third he writes sometimes twice a week, and then ceases to write for a week or a month. The skeletons that we all try to keep concealed in the shadiest recesses of our secret chambers are thus kept as ready for mobilisation as a Prussian army corps. "Krieg, mobil," telegraphed Von Moltke along the wires from Ems in 1870, and instantly all the parts of the huge military machine fitted themselves together and descended upon France. So in case it is necessary to crush or to embarrass any opponent at home or abroad, Herr Holstein has but to press a button and the private records of that opponent's life are ready to hand, to be served up with such piquant sauce as may suit the public taste in any of the journals by which the inoculation of the public mind is arranged for in the interest of the Administration.

It is not stated that Prince Bismarck has abused the power which this collection of facts has given him. All that I say is that, unless universal report is a universal liar, he has grasped this power, and holds it like other thunderbolts in reserve. I need hardly point out that the man who sprung the Benedetti treaty upon the world at a critical moment is not likely to be too squeamish about employing the information accumulated by his police for the discrediting or for the destruction of his opponents.

But the possession of an indefinite amount of secret service money for purposes of corruption, and the accumulation from all the unseen channels of a ubiquitous secret police of a vast reservoir of information for use if required, are by no means the only instruments by which Prince Bismarck keeps his press in good order. "How is it done?" exclaimed a witty victim of the Chancellor's surveillance. "It is very simple. Some fine day all the editors of Berlin are summoned to the office of the oracle. They are told that the Government is in possession of such and such an important piece of information which is communicated to them, not for publication, but in confidence, in order that when the opportune moment arrives they may be well informed. A nod is as good as a wink to a blind horse, and before very long one or other of the editors discovers in some mysterious way that the time has arrived when the cat must be let out of the bag. He lets it out accordingly, and all his brethren follow suit, and the news, true or false, is launched in due form." "But what," I asked, "if an editor refuses to take the hint, and obstinately abstains from circulating the official *communiqué?*" "Then," was the reply, "it does not go well with that exceptional newspaper. Misfortunes always attend the journal which is foolhardy enough to ignore a hint from above." "What kind of misfortunes?" "Oh, all kinds of misfortune. Dormant lawsuits mysteriously reappear; official advertisements are withdrawn; privileges of sale or of display, which depend upon the goodwill of the Administration, are suspended. But perhaps the most efficient allies of the Chancellor and his myrmidons are the vendors of quack medicines for the cure of unmentionable diseases." "How, in the name of wonder, can that be?" "It is very simple. In the Fatherland the Government charges itself with watchful solicitude for the morals of its subjects. But as even Homer sometimes nods, so the most vigilant of Administrations sometimes fails to discover that the columns of German newspapers are defiled by the insertion of advertisements of immoral pills or by the addresses of unclean doctors. When, however, any newspaper continuously opposes itself to the will of the authorities, the custodian of public morals puts on his spectacles, and woe betide the unfortunate journal if in the obscurest corner of his badly-printed page there should be discovered lurking an allusion to the objectionable pill or the disreputable physician. The Administration is down upon him at once, and punishment is heaped on punishment until the editor consents to dance to the piping of Power. Then the custodian of public morals once more slumbers and sleeps, and the quack advertises his pills in peace."

Add to this that press prosecutions for press offences are as plentiful as blackberries, that editors are sent to gaol as felons for what would be regarded in England as perfectly justifiable criticisms upon the Chancellor, that half the cities in Germany are under a state of siege, and you can form some idea of the facilities which Prince Bismarck possesses for manipulating the journals of the Fatherland.

To him that hath shall be given, and from him that hath not shall be taken away even that which he seemeth to have. To a central Press Bureau thus subsidised, served, and terrorised, it is easy to see what strength will accrete quite naturally by the voluntary and unsuspecting co-operation of other journals. In the economy of Nature Darwin has taught us the important part which is played by the humble earthworm. All that it does is to eat dirt and to void the same, but to that operation we chiefly owe the creation of the mould of our earth. In the journalism of Europe it is the lot of some English correspondents abroad to fulfil with automatic and unfailing regularity the useful and, from Bismarck's point of view, the necessary functions of the earthworm. There are, for instance, some supreme types of the species on the *Times*, whose despatches, telegraphed daily to the leading newspaper of the world, are little more than ill-digested reproductions of the inventions and the calumnies of the Reptile press—their "news" is merely the secretion of the Reptile passed through the alimentary canal of the Worm. But it helps to form the compost on which public opinion is based, and thus from the great central bureau at Berlin are fed all the newspapers of the world.

When the Norse gods seized malignant Loki after he had slain the beautiful Balder, they bound him to a rock and fixed above him a poisonous snake, from whose jaws venom dripped constantly into Loki's face. When I listened to the descriptions of the working of the Reptile fund which I have reproduced above, Europe seemed to me to have taken the place of Loki, and Bismarck played the part of the vengeful gods.

The most marvellous example of the results which can be attained under the German system of press nobbling at home and of journalistic idiotcy abroad was the European scare produced by the alleged concentration of Russian troops on the German frontier. As a matter of fact, there was no such concentration. The Russian Government had moved 4,000 troops from Moscow to Warsaw. That was the solitary and slender substratum of fact, which was of course perfectly well known to the German War Office. But it so happened that at that time Prince Bismarck, for reasons best known to himself, was anxious to secure, with the moral sanction of Europe and the unanimous vote of the Reichstag, the addition of 700,000 men to the German army, and also to compel Austria to add several millions to her military expenditure. As Europe was in a condition of profound peace, the operation did not seem easy. To genius, however, all things are possible, especially to genius that has no scruples and that has a Reptile press. So it came to pass one fine day, nearly a month after the 4,000 troops had been moved up, that one of the Reptiles in some obscure corner of Germany discovered that the Russians were pouring troops westward towards the German frontier. Instantly all the other Reptiles discovered this menacing announcement, and reprinted it for the edification of the German public. The English correspondents of course telegraphed it to London. The news goes the round of the Continent, growing of course as it goes. To the excited imagination of nervous Europe the Russian frontier seems bursting with armed men. All day long the phlegmatic German seems to hear the rumble of batteries thundering up from unknown depths of Muscovy to concentrate on the frontier of Posen or the boundaries of Galicia. When the sun rose in the east its rays were obscured by the lances of Cossack hordes swarming to the plunder of the Fatherland. Every day brings news of fresh concentration, of the departure or arrival of new reinforcements for the frontier. Innocent bystanders imagine that all this thunder is real. Those behind the scenes know that it is produced by artifice, and is sheer illusion. But it is wonderfully realistic. Everything seems so natural, and of course so true. If it were not true, would a paternal Government, with all the facts at its finger-ends, allow such alarming statements to harrow up the soul of every Teuton? So every one said, and even the Russians, who knew that the only movement that had taken place was the despatch of 4,000 men from Moscow to Warsaw—4,000 out of 850,000—were not a little puzzled to understand what it could mean. The Bourses of Europe were disturbed. The rouble, which had been steadily going downward until it sank to exactly one-half of its nominal value, took a further plunge towards zero. Russian securities declined.

Business transactions all over Europe were checked, from dread of approaching war. Still was kept up the rolling of the German tomtoms, and a thousand sheets echoed the reverberations of the heavy tread of marching millions of menacing Muscovites.

At last the psychological moment had fully come. As in the opera the advent of the hero is heralded by long flourishes of premonitory music in which all the skill of the orchestra is employed in leading up to his entrance, so when the public mind was strained to the utmost, and all the Continent rang with the clangour of steel and the thud of the Cossacks' hoofs, Prince Bismarck appeared in the tribune and demanded the grant necessary to add 700,000 fathers of families to the effective strength of the German army. It was perhaps the most tremendous blood tax ever imposed in a single speech. But so marvellously had the *mise en scène* been managed, so dexterously had the great Reptilian orchestra played upon the nerves of the nations, that it seemed the most natural thing in the world. All the fractions of the German Parliament unanimously and enthusiastically acceded to his demand, and the press of Europe declared that the last inroad of militarism upon industrialism was forced upon the German Government by imperious necessity.

Great are the resources of a stage manager when he has an Empire for his theatre and all the newspapers as his *claque*; but was there ever a thaumaturgist so wonderful as the Chancellor of Germany? Who but he, with such slender materials to work upon, could have raised so gigantic a Brocken spectre on the German frontier? Four thousand men are moved from the former capital of Russia to the capital of the former kingdom of Poland, and a month later, when not a single soldier is being moved anywhere near the frontier, he so employs his magic art that a whole invading army of horse, foot, and artillery, seemed to be pouring down from Russia upon Europe. Like the secrets hidden in the mystic book which William of Deloraine bore from the tomb of Michael Scott, " All was illusion, nought was truth." But that illusion was real enough while it lasted to deceive almost every newspaper in Europe, to conjure millions from the closely-buttoned pocket of the German farmer and the German artisan, to add nearly three-quarters of a million of soldiers to the German standards, and to convulse almost to frenzy the excitable Magyars with visions of impending war.

And then when the money had been voted and the men added to the standards, the deception, having served its turn, was unceremoniously discarded, without even dropping the curtain to conceal the scene-shifters from the dupes of the great illusion. In the "Lady of the Lake," when Roderick Dhu waved his hand, the hillside, which had suddenly been covered with an armed and eager throng of martial mountaineers, as suddenly resumed its mountain solitude :—

> Short space he stood—then waved his hand.
> Down sunk the disappearing band;
> Each warrior vanished where he stood
> In broom or bracken, heath or wood;
> Sunk brand and spear and bended bow
> In osiers pale and copses low;
> It seemed as if their mother Earth
> Had swallowed up her warlike birth.
> The wind's last breath had tossed in air
> Pennon and plaid and plumage fair.—
> The next but swept a lone hill side,
> Where heath and fern were waving wide.

So was it with the Master at Berlin, and the mustering squadrons of Russian cavalry with which he has appalled the imagination of the Fatherland. The transformation was, of course, very easily effected, for Roderick had really raised his warriors from the bracken, but in Bismarck's case the array was merely an optical delusion, a cunning phantasmagoria which when it had served its purpose was allowed to disappear.

The incident, however, was not without its uses. It showed how completely the man who commands the newspapers commands the situation, and how impotent are the unorganised forces of truth when pitted against the tremendous park of journalistic artillery under Prince Bismarck's command. The Russian Government, after considerable delay, published an official statement showing how unfounded was the German alarm. It was too late. In journalism, as in catching a train, everything depends upon being in time. It was the case of the needle-gun against the muzzle-loader over again—a journalistic Sadowa in which Prince Bismarck and his new Model Reptile legion were victorious all along the line.

## CHAPTER V.

### BISMARCK THE PEACEMAKER.

EVEN to this day Europe, looking over a perfectly peaceful East, can, like Scott's hero in the " Lady of the Lake," scarce believe the witness that her sight receives as to the utter unreality of the great German scare :—

> Such apparition well might seem
> Delusion of a dreadful dream.

It is therefore small wonder that, with this incident before our eyes, we ask, How far can we rely upon Prince Bismarck as the keeper of the peace of Europe ? The episode sheds a disagreeable light upon various matters. A man capable of deliberately working up a misleading sensation on this gigantic scale is hardly worthy of our implicit confidence as an honest broker. If he can jockey public opinion in this cynical fashion, is he proof against the temptation of packing the cards when it suits his purpose in other directions? Take, for instance, the belief, which is almost universal, that he is constantly and strenuously thrusting Austria southward and eastward. The *Drang nach Osten* is regarded as distinctly Bismarck's policy, and his journals applaud every fresh development of Austrian activity in the Balkan peninsula. It is obvious that this is absolutely inconsistent with his public utterances. He poses before the world as the faithful friend of Russia who has been reluctantly driven to seek other alliances because of unfortunate misunderstandings at St. Petersburg. But such a *rôle* is utterly inconsistent with any active backing of Austria in her adventurous career in the East. Is he then provoking the caper which he seems to chide, and encouraging Austrian aggression at the same time that he is advocating the Russian alliance and professing to take his stand on the Treaty of Berlin ?

These questions are natural even to those who, like myself, have cheerfully recognised the justice of the German claim to the hegemony of Europe. How much more natural, then, must they seem to those who see their own interests threatened by the Austrian conquests ! Not until I had stayed some time in St.

Petersburg was I able to realise the extent to which the spectacle of the cynical Colossus at Berlin has impressed, and to a certain extent depraved, the public mind. It is only possible for Englishmen to form some idea of the effect by recalling the deep-rooted horror and dread with which Protestant children were imbued as to the infernal machinations and absolute ruthlessness of the Order of Loyola. Imagine Prince Bismarck a great personification of the Society of Jesus, as despotic, as unscrupulous, and as false as the Jesuits as pictured in the Orange Lodges, and you have some idea of the way in which the German Chancellor is regarded beyond his frontiers.

There is some excuse for this. Never outside the disciples of Loyola has despotism been so scientifically organised as in Germany. Russia, compared with her next-door neighbour, is a Republican anarchy. "How many Germans are there," recently asked Mr. Gladstone, "who believe in freedom?" They may believe in it, but if so they walk by faith and not by sight, for faith is the substance of things hoped for, the evidence of things not seen, and there is very little freedom to be seen in Germany to-day. The idea of the State omnipotent, omnipresent, and omniscient, has never been worked out so thoroughly. Germans have disappeared. Only Germany remains—a gigantic figure which has only one brain, and the grey matter of that brain is Prince Bismarck. To build up that Frankenstein the once independent, headstrong Germans have been mashed into a kind of bloater paste of humanity—the individual unit has disappeared, only the amalgam remains.

That which makes the German State so dread a portent in the eyes of its neighbours is that, rightly or wrongly, they conceive that in the evolution of its intelligence it has eliminated its conscience. Prince Bismarck recently boasted that the Germans feared God, but that they feared no one else. Excepting on his authority Europe would have been incredulous, for to other nations the Germans seem not to fear God so much as Prince Bismarck, and unless he is cruelly maligned there is very little fear of God before his eyes. What is said in many quarters is that the Man of Blood and Iron sticks at nothing in order to secure his ends. Falsehood, force, intrigue, treachery, war, are alike instruments in his hand, and are judged by him exclusively from the point of view of their relative efficiency. He will not lie if truth will serve him better, but if not, then for him, they say, falsehood is better than truth. It is painful even to repeat the kind of talk which goes on about Bismarck, and it is more painful because it is as often as not eulogistic rather than condemnatory. "Prince Bismarck," it was often said to me, "has no scruples. He sees his end, and he makes for it across every obstacle. Why not? The safety of the commonwealth is the supreme law. The Ten Commandments do not apply to States which are all founded on the negation of morality, and maintained by a systematic disregard of the prohibition of homicide. Why should he be squeamish? As Henri Quatre said that Paris was well worth a mass, do you think that the safety of Germany is not worth a lie? Empires cannot afford to have consciences, neither can statesmen. Strict veracity is a prejudice like consistency. Expediency is the only rule. So Prince Bismarck sees, and I only regret that in Russia we have no statesman so frankly, so cynically courageous as he."

The extent to which this conscienceless cynicism—that, rightly or wrongly, is attributed to Prince Bismarck—has impressed the public mind was brought home to me in very startling fashion when persons presumably sane, and certainly not under restraint, talked of "the poisoning of Skobeleff" as if it were as much the direct act of Prince Bismarck as the signing of the Treaty of Frankfort. The deaths of both Skobeleff and of Gambetta, the two chief antagonists of Prince Bismarck, unquestionably relieved Germany from much disquiet; but their decease was brought about not by the malignity of the Demon Omnipotens at Berlin, but by their own lamentable weakness. That, however, is ignored. Bismarck, it is stoutly asserted, had them both poisoned. And why not? they ask, as if it were the most natural thing in the world for Prince Bismarck to do. I do not wish it to be implied that this kind of talk is general in Russia. It is not; but that even a single individual should credit such a horrible suspicion, and that the feeling of foul play at German instigation should have been widespread in Moscow at the time of the death of Skobeleff, shows what bad fruit the cynical adoption of a policy of blood and iron has borne in the minds of men. The moralist may perhaps be puzzled to explain why it should be so much more heinous to remove a single enemy by poison than to cry havoc and let slip the dogs of war upon a whole nation, but the popular instinct brands the assassin and the poisoner with criminality so deep that I cannot for a moment even conceive the possibility of a European statesman resorting to the methods of Borgia or of Brinvilliers in order to dispose of his opponents. That such a thing should be believed to be possible is only a shade less revolting than that it should actually occur, and there are Russians who refuse to admit that in "the poisoning of Skobeleff" M. de Bismarck would see anything whatever inconsistent with his working theory of ethics. This is the shadow which the success of Blood and Iron has cast over the human heart.

Prince Bismarck, all agree, is at present working for peace. Is it, then, the first duty of all who work for peace to say ditto to Prince Bismarck? That is a practical question which Lord Salisbury seems for the moment to have answered in the affirmative. He is perhaps right if we can regard the peace of Germany as absolutely identical and conterminous with the peace of Europe and the peace of Asia. He is certainly wrong if the peace of Germany, so far from being identical with the peace of Europe and of Asia, should at any time happen to be inconsistent therewith.

I have no prejudices against Germany or its Chancellor. I have, I think, on the whole, been more constantly and consistently "German" in my views of our foreign policy than any English journalist or statesman. In season and out of season I have maintained that both for England and Russia the true watchword of their policy is, "Sine Germaniâ nulla salus." But although holding this view very strongly, I am unable to consider that the whole duty of England as a peace Power is fulfilled when our proxy is handed over to Prince Bismarck, and England's influence is simply so much plus to Germany's strength. Our position, to be useful, must be far other than that.

Prince Bismarck has never made the least secret about the sole principle of his policy. His one concern is the peace and security of Germany. So far as the peace and security of Germany can be secured by working for the peace and security of the world, to that extent, but no further, will he be willing to work for the peace and security of the world. But if the peace and security of Germany should be best served by sacrificing the peace and security of the rest of the world, then unquestionably he will sacrifice the rest of the world without scruple and without remorse. As we happen to be part of the rest of the world, we cannot exactly " go it blind " as the friend and ally of such a peacemaker as this. It may be argued of England that, as her commerce and her colonies are practically as wide as the world, the general peace is practically England's peace, and any Power that says ditto to England will be pretty sure that in serving England's interests it will be serving its own interests so far as they are peaceful. But this cannot be asserted of Germany. Wars could rage in three continents without materially affecting a single German interest other perhaps than beneficially. There are, therefore, contingencies in which it may be, and has been, Germany's interest to promote war rather than peace, and when her policy has been distinctly hostile to the general welfare, and especially hostile to the interests of England.

The first preoccupation of Germany is to prevent an attack upon her Rhine frontier by France, her second to prevent Russia attacking her on the Vistula, and the third, and very subsidiary, object of her policy is to keep Austria from attempting to avenge the catastrophe of Sadowa. The task is so difficult that Prince Bismarck, in his extreme solicitude for the Fatherland, has not hesitated to encourage almost any enterprise on the part of his neighbours which would divert their attention from the Fatherland. France has been encouraged to take Tunis, to seize Tonkin, to make war on China, to attempt to conquer Madagascar, in the hopes that colonial extension would drown the desire for revenge. I have no wish to blame Germany for our difficulties in Egypt, which were chiefly of our own making, but there will be no protest from Berlin if I say that Prince Bismarck smiled grimly when we settled ourselves at Cairo, reflecting with satisfaction upon the fact that England in Egypt diverted from the Germans in Alsace a certain measurable quantity of French hostility. To embroil France with Italy in Tunis, with England in Egypt, with China in Tonkin, all this appeared to Prince Bismarck excellent policy for Germany, as tending to the isolation and to the weakening of France ; and whether it was good policy for England, for Italy, or for China, that was not his look-out. German policy is self-regarding first and last.

In like manner, in Prince Bismarck's dealings with Russia, German policy has been by no means calculated to maintain the peace. When Lord Beaconsfield in 1877 refused to support the ultimatum of the Constantinople Conference by the coercive action of the fleet, Prince Bismarck encouraged him in a policy of abstention. When General Ignatieff visited him at Berlin just before war broke out, he found the Prince resolute to thrust Russia across the Danube. By every incitement and taunt he strove to force Russia single-handed into the Turkish war, instead of co-operating with the Russians in settling the question on a European basis. It suited Germany to let the Russian bear break his teeth on the bones of Turkey. The pressure of the Russian flood on the German dam was perceptibly lessened by cutting a sluice in the Eastern banks. When the war was over and there were 120,000 fewer Russian soldiers to count with, and £100,000,000 had been added to the Russian debt, and the whole Russian State had been strained and disorganised, Prince Bismarck saw in the result the justification of his policy. He could sleep easier of nights, knowing that Russia was so much weaker. Only when the war threatened to become general, and involve Germany, did he bestir himself in the interests of peace. After the war he has been true to the same general principle. To relieve Germany from Russian pressure he has gladly welcomed everything which diverted Russian attention to Central Asia and the East. "If you must quarrel with somebody, for heaven's sake quarrel with England, not with us," has been the note of his policy. It is natural enough under the circumstances, but its author can hardly be taken as a safe guide for the peace policy of Great Britain. The same characteristics distinguish his policy in Austria. He has thrust Austria southward, hanging round her neck the mill-stone of the Bosnian provinces, distracting the Magyar heart with dreams of vengeance, and the Austrians with visions of a new empire in the East. Everywhere and at all times he has been eager to help his neighbours to go anywhere, even to the devil, and to run into anything, even into his best friends, so long as they do not endanger the peace of Germany. War is dangerous, for no one knows how it may spread. Hence he is apt to deprecate war, excepting in Asia or Africa. But, if he can set his neighbours by the ears, so that without cutting each other's throats, they are absolutely unable to join hands, that appears to him an almost ideal policy.

This policy of setting everybody by the ears so that the German may rub his hands in peace over his own cup of coffee may be excellent from the exclusively German point of view, but from the English standpoint it can hardly be regarded as worthy of admiration, much less of blind acceptance. We have our own interests and our own duties, which we ought not to sacrifice even for the *beaux yeux* of Prince Bismarck, and the more resolutely we look after our affairs the more respect shall we command at Berlin. German policy is a resultant of many forces. Its objectionable features are as much due to the prejudices and the stupidity of its neighbours as to any inherent depravity on the part of Prince Bismarck. If the nature of any one of the forces with which Prince Bismarck has to deal were to be changed he would readjust his policy to the altered circumstances with alacrity. For Prince Bismarck is a real politician. He deals with actual forces as a chemist deals with gases or an engineer with steam. If he has played Russia off against England and England off against Russia, that is because Russia and England have led him into temptations which he was not strong enough to resist. He takes the line of least resistance, without arguing much as to its ethical fitness, and if we, by our insensate prejudices and traditional antipathies, play into his hands, we cannot wonder that he has made his game at our expense. That, however, in no way proves that he would not be very glad to change his play if we offered him a better and easier alternative. If we merely hold ourselves at his bidding, we shall receive as much consideration at his hands as an upper servant—no more and no less. If, on the other hand, we pursue a resolute, an independent, and a pacific policy of our own, we shall be able to depend upon his co-operation, which indeed is indispensable to any peace policy, without having to pay for it by acquiescing in the sacrifice of English interests to German security.

What, then, must be the policy, and what the understanding on which England must seek to secure the peace of the world? Leaving out of consideration the remoter developments due to the natural growth of such Empires as Russia and England, the peace of the world is only threatened at present by French designs on Alsace-Lorraine, by Austria's position and Austrian designs on the Balkan Peninsula. To keep the peace it is necessary to restrain both France and Austria within the limits of the *status quo*, and to impose an irresistible veto upon any appeal to the sword. These conditions, simple and precise, indicate clearly the lines along which we must work and the Powers with whom we must co-operate. Germany remains as at present the keystone of the arch of European peace. But in order to make that peace secure she must be supported by England on her right and Russia on her left. England, Germany, and Russia—if these three hold together, the peace of the world is secure.

## CHAPTER VI.

### RUSSIA: WHAT IS RUSSIA?

This brings me to the heart and kernel of my subject. Is it possible for England and Germany to enter into a hearty *entente* with Russia for the furtherance of the general interests and the maintenance of the general peace? That is a question upon which, after prolonged consideration and after exhaustive discussion with the directors of Russian policy, I have arrived at clear and definite conclusions. It is not often that the solution of a complicated political problem is so clear as that which lies before us in relation to Russia. Every consideration alike of duty and of interest points in one direction, and that direction would be taken to-morrow if English statesmen did not block the way. It is in London, not in St. Petersburg or in Berlin, where the difficulty lies. England is the chief obstacle to the establishment of those cordial relations between the three northern capitals which would enable Europe and Asia to remain at peace. England, and England alone, by persistence in an archaic anachronism which is neither a policy nor a principle, but only a moulting and mangy prejudice, perpetuates the antagonism and unrest which keep two continents trembling on the verge of war. I am not without hope that by placing the question of our policy *de novo* before the eyes of my countrymen I may lead to a reconsideration of their position and the adoption with open eyes of a policy more worthy of a Christian, a civilised, and a rational State than the practice of incessant bullyragging without sense, or aim, or object, which appears to be adopted by both parties as the only duty which we owe to the great Empire upon whose shoulders jointly with our own lies the responsibility of the civilisation of Asia. It may be that my conclusions will be rejected, and that my countrymen may decide upon a policy not of friendship, but of antagonism. If so, let them courageously face the consequences and prepare to carry out consistently, in a practical, business-like spirit, the policy which they determine to adopt, counting the cost before they embark upon it, and carrying it through when adopted with unfaltering will and steady purpose. But in any case, whether the decision be for peace or for war, I trust that henceforth we may at least recognise that we have to act like rational men face to face with a serious problem, instead of jabbering and spitting and snarling like a parcel of monkeys in a bamboo tope. The time has now arrived when we can take a new departure, and begin alike in Europe and in Asia to co-operate loyally to remove misunderstandings, to promote mutual intercourse, and to maintain the general peace.

Russia, what is Russia? Russia, in effect, replies the Russophobist, is the Devil. In the imagination of the disciples of David Urquhart, the man whose apostolate of hate and distrust has yielded a terrible harvest of death, Russia is incarnate Evil of all but irresistible strength, which with the intellect of a fiend and the appetite of an ogre is driven by the law of its being to torture and to oppress its subjects, to rend and to devour its neighbours. This abstraction, hideous as the loathliest phantom dreamed of by the poets of Hell, is for ever tramping with its hundred million pairs of legs towards two distant goals, and with a hundred million voices cries incessant "To India!" and "To Constantinople!" Conscience it has not, truth it knows not, mercy it recks not. Immeasurably huge, and ever growing huger with the years, it threatens Europe with an embrace of death, and it is stifling Asia. Confronted by so portentous a phenomenon is it not natural that they should fill the air with shrieks of alarm and call on all men to flee betimes from this terrific embodiment of the wrath to come?

So they ask, and to them I reply: "Shriek by all means; but, if you believe what you say, for Heaven's sake do something more than shriek, and whatever you do, at least desist from spitting in the monster's face, twitching stray hairs from his beard, and running little pins into his hide." If Europe is confronted with a menace as appalling as that which crushed the Byzantine Empire, the situation is one which calls for more active measures, more grimly serious work than the mere drawing of long noses and the putting out the tongue at the advancing Colossus. What! You ask us to believe that the greatest and most homogeneous mass of mobile humanity existing on this planet is bearing down like a tidal wave driven by the tempest upon our Empire and upon the Bosphorus, and you have nothing better to do than to relieve your feelings by calling it foul names and idly discussing the point at which at some future date, if your hypothesis be correct, you will be dashed into irremediable ruin!

It is time to cease this fooling, and to adjust your policy to your theories, or else consent to adjust your theories to the facts. If Russia be, as you suppose, the Devil incarnate of mundane politics, then as you hope for salvation prepare to meet her as befits brave and stalwart men. The only League of which England can then be the soul would be a League of War, the only work to which our Imperial resources could be dedicated would be the making of a crusade against Russia, and we should devote ourselves seriously and with fixed resolve, to create an army and a navy which would enable us to do battle on something like equal terms with our foe. This would involve us first in the conscription, secondly, in a permanent shilling income tax, and, thirdly, in the subordination of every domestic and Imperial consideration to the furtherance of the objects of the Anti-Russian league. There would have to be no cutting down of the Navy Estimates by £800,000 for fear of Lord Randolph Churchill, no blowing alternately hot and cold in the policy of the War Office. Our parliamentary system would have to be revolutionised in order to permit of the conclusion of secret alliances and the continuous prosecution of an undeviating policy.

Subsidies of millions would be required by the Turks, for all of whose misdeeds we should make ourselves responsible, and we should be at the mercy of every ally who chose to precipitate the war for which we had offered up our liberty, our wealth, our independence, and our Empire.

Still, if Russia be the infernal portent of Russophobist dreams, that policy with all its sacrifices, is inevitable. It is true that even if we did all that we could do we should not be much better off at the end. For in one respect Russia is really as formidable as her enemies pretend. She is indestructible. You may singe the Emperor of Russia's beard at Sebastopol and at the Baltic, but there will only be the smell of burning for a moment in the air, which the spring wind will carry away, while the Empire will live on.

You may even carve a red, corse-paven way, like Napoleon, to the heart of Russia, and just as the returning wave obliterates your footprints in the sand, so the tide of Russian life will silently sweep away all vestige of your victories, save perhaps where, as in the Temple of our Saviour at Moscow, the Russian himself erects a pious trophy on the scene of his deliverance, whose glittering cupolas flame resplendent in the noonday sun. The innumerable village republics which, united, make up the Empire of the Tzars, contain in every commune the heart and the head of Russia. Above all, the Russian cradle is never empty.

Compared with this all other facts are as if they were not. On the 31st December there will be at least a million more mortals lisping Russian than there were on the 1st of January. From a million to a million and a quarter is the annual excess of Russian births over Russian deaths. There are now nearly ten million more Russians in the world than there were when the present reign began. Against that increase all allies will fight in vain. That is the solid fact which dominates the situation.

When Lord Elgin was endeavouring to browbeat the mandarins in 1860 by threats of what the Western nations would do if the Emperor was obdurate, General Ignatieff told me he was much amused by the reply of a mandarin to the British representative. " How many soldiers," he asked, " will the Western Powers send to China ? " " Oh," said Lord Elgin, with heroic disregard of the possibilities of transport, "we will send 100,000 men." "All right," said the mandarin, "suppose they come, and each kills twenty Chinamen, what difference will it make? Two millions or three millions more or less; it is but as a bucket out of the sea, a handful of sand from the seashore, compared with the three hundred millions that will remain."

Whatever we do, Russia will remain, and Russians will continue to inhabit the whole of Northern Asia and Eastern Europe. That we cannot prevent, though we bleed ourselves like veal in endeavouring to slaughter them into impotence, and though we double our National Debt in the effort to ruin the Tzar.

What we can do is this. We can hammer this great human mass, as Napoleon hammered Prussia, into a really formidable weapon. We can give a force and a direction to this great glacier of humanity which it would otherwise never have acquired, and convert two hundred millions of men who might have been friends and customers into bitter, revengeful, and determined foes.

But what we are doing is to provoke resentment without taking any steps to defend ourselves against the irritation which we set ourselves to create. Mere bullyragging is not a policy worthy of a great Empire, even when it can be indulged in with safety. When bullyragging exposes us to an aggravation of every evil the thought of which set us snarling, it is not statesmanship; it is insanity. But, short of bullyragging, and insult, and an eager *schadenfreude* which seizes every opportunity for inflicting small inconveniences upon Russia, what is our policy to-day in relation to this Empire? If we do not prepare seriously to fight, we surely might in common decency try and keep a civil tongue in our heads.

Russia—what is Russia? I must guard myself against idealising the country where I have received so hospitable a welcome, and in which I have spent two of the happiest months in my life. There is a natural tendency for any one in my position to see things very much *couleur de rose*, but solid facts cannot be mistaken by either optimist or pessimist.

Russia is the nearest counterpart to the British Empire to be found in the world to-day. It is a world in itself, full of vast and unrealised potentialities of wealth and life. It contains a population of 120,000,000, increasing at the rate of 1,250,000 every year, in possession of the back-garden of Europe and of Asia. This population—for the most part ignorant, unsophisticated, and simple—is peaceful, laborious, and fraternal to an extent unrealised in the West. Since the Napoleonic Empire received its death-wound amid the flames of Moscow, the Russian people, as distinguished from the army and the Government, have never made war, excepting under the pressure of religious enthusiasm and humanitarian sympathy for their co-religionists in the Balkan.

Before 1876 the English did not understand this; but now we understand it. The normal temperature of a Russian peasant is that registered in England when Mr. Gladstone discoursed on Bulgarian atrocities at Blackheath and at St. James's Hall. At any moment that religious and humanitarian feeling may be roused so as to precipitate another war in the East; but, excepting as against Turkey, the Russian masses have no deep and passionate sentiments endangering peace. The Russian peasant, although one of the most excitable and enthusiastic, is the least bellicose human being extant, unless it be the Chinese. His one ambition is to cultivate his field in peace, to marry a wife, and to bring up his children. He is no politician, and the Government interferes but little in his life beyond levying taxes and enforcing the conscription. The life of Russia is not in the Senate, in the country house, or the barracks—the life of Russia is in the peasant's hut.

With this peasant-Russia England can have no quarrel, save in so far as she identifies herself with the misbelievers who defile the Holy Places and oppress the Orthodox brethren, in Europe and in Asia. Since 1878, when we signed the Berlin Treaty and extorted the Anglo-Turkish Convention from the Government of the Porte, England has accepted the standpoint of the moujik as to the necessity of rescuing the subject populations from the tender mercies of the Turks.

But out of the bosom of this population, which is pacific, kindly-affectioned, and contented beyond all the other populations of Europe, there is evolved by the dire enchantment of the conscription an army which in time of peace numbers 850,000 men, and in time of war can even now put 2,500,000 soldiers into the field. This vast body of men is the nearest approach to a definite organism on an Imperial scale that is to be found in Russia; but even this army is too widely scattered to have much cohesion or significance in a political sense. An army on a peace footing of 850,000 men sounds imposing, but when we compare the muster-roll with the acreage from which it is drawn, we discover that Russia has fewer soldiers per square mile than Great Britain and Ireland. The proportion to population is not half that which exists in Germany and in France. Nothing strikes you more on arriving in Russia, after passing through Paris and Berlin, than the absence of the military display which offends the eye at every town in France and Germany.

The sabre is always clanking in Berlin, and the soldiers meet you in every street in Paris; but in St. Petersburg it is quite different. *Militarismus* there must be, no doubt, in the barracks among the officers, but it does not flaunt itself abroad, even in the capital. At Moscow and at Toula it was as invisible as in Birmingham or in Sheffield. The barracks may be bursting with troops, but in the streets there is no display of martial pomp. Still, although Russia is agricultural and not military, the army, no doubt, must be reckoned with in estimating the Russia with which we have to deal.

The Central Asian advances were chiefly due to the military Russia—the Russia of the army. The officers there had everything their own way, and they used their opportunity, as officers will, to bring their frontier up to the line at which the control of affairs passed from the hands of the General Staff to that of the Foreign Office.

The army, so far as it is a political force at all, is like all armies—inclined to prefer active service to the piping times of peace; but I question whether the officers' quarters in St. Petersburg are more bellicose than our mess-rooms, or whether General Obrutcheff, at the headquarters of the General Staff, talks any more warlike nonsense than may be heard any day in the War Office or at the Horse Guards. So far as the army gives a bias to Russian policy, which it does not in ordinary times, it is a bias against Germany, as the most formidable, and therefore the most dreaded, antagonist beyond the frontier. In that matter all armies are alike; but I did not find any one, whether English, Russian, or German, who questioned the ability of the Emperor to hold his army in hand. In Central Asia the generals may have got out of hand, especially when they had behind them the inexorable forces that drove us from Calcutta to the Punjaub; but in Europe the army is in the hands of the Tzar. General Obrutcheff is powerful, no doubt, but the Tzar has but to sign a paper, and General Obrutcheff will disappear as General Tchernayeff and Loris Melikoff have disappeared before him. The army as an independent factor with an initiative and a policy of its own does not exist. When a policy has been initiated it gives it, no doubt, a forward impetus, and renders retreat difficult or impossible; but that is all. The Tzar will no more make war because his generals wish to measure their swords against the Germans than the British elector will vote for declaring war against France because Lord Wolseley thinks that the French may some fine day capture London with 100,000 men.

There remain besides the peasantry and the army, the two great permanent forces in Russia—the handful of cultivated and intelligent persons who take an interest in politics, and the official hierarchy that begins with the humblest tchinovnik and terminates at the throne. Of Russian newspapers I have not much to say. They are capable of being used to excite feeling for or against particular policies, but in themselves they hardly constitute an independent force in Russian polity. When we speak of public opinion in Russia I am reminded of the Church of Humanity in London, the members of which went down to worship in one cab, and in returning found their differences, but not their numbers, required the use of two.

There are so few who take an interest in politics in Russia, but these few there are in two camps. These are the Liberal Europeans and the National Russians or Panslavonic party. The former may be dismissed *sans cérémonie*. They are interesting and intelligent; but except so far as their ideas are shared by the Emperor, they do not count. The other, the Nationalists, are the only party in Russia, excepting for their most unfortunate religious intolerance, to which an Englishman could belong if he were Russian born. They are Russians before all, and they are not ashamed of it. Their policy, as defined to me by their leaders, is clear, consistent, and courageous. It is in

H

harmony with their traditions and the laws of their historical development, and in the long run it is tolerably certain to make itself felt in the direction of Russian policy. Of its main outlines I will speak hereafter. The important point to note is that although inclined to coquet with France in the belief that Germany has sold her sword to Austria, there is no antagonism to Germany as such. If Germany will be German, and not Austrian, Russian Nationalists will have no objection to the German alliance. Neither is there any antagonism between this party and England *per se*. On the contrary, there are many strong bonds of sympathy between them and ourselves. I will now proceed to examine in detail the questions at issue between us with the view of ascertaining whether or not it is reasonable to hope that a practical working *modus vivendi* can be arrived at.

## CHAPTER VII.

### THE CRUX IN BULGARIA.

DURING my stay in Russia I had frequent opportunities of ascertaining at first hand the views of the Russian Foreign Office. M. de Giers, M. Vlangali, Baron Jomini, and M. Zinovieff, all received me courteously; and the exceeding frankness of their conversation filled me only with one regret—that the etiquette of Ministries rendered interviewing impossible. A verbatim reproduction of the interesting discussions which I held with the directors of Russian foreign policy would be more useful for reassuring the public mind and convincing Europe that Russia is determinedly pacific than anything that I can say. But, alas! the "interview" is tabooed by M. de Giers as absolutely as by M. Floquet, and I must content myself, therefore, with a hearty expression of my indebtedness to those Ministers who so readily and so frankly consented to answer my questions on all branches of their foreign policy.

At the same time, I was given distinctly to understand that, although I was not at liberty to say "M. de Giers told me this" or "M. Vlangali replied as follows," I was at full liberty to embody in my articles, as the fruit of my observation and inquiry, the statements which they furnished me in reply to my questions; nor would any objection be raised, even if I textually reproduced any declarations that might be made to me as representing the views and objects of the Russian Government, so long as I did not offend against the inviolable law which forbids the reporting of private conversations. With this preface, therefore, I proceed to discuss seriatim the questions which are at issue between Russia and England.

The only point of difference now outstanding between Russia and England relates to Bulgaria. It was natural that the future of the Bulgarians should be the constant topic of conversation during my stay in St. Petersburg.

The Russians are very sore about Bulgaria, and not without cause. They spent 120,000 men and £100,000,000 of treasure in order to liberate a nationality which, ten years after its creation, is in the hands of an avowedly anti-Russian Administration. If we could bring ourselves to see a French prefect established at Cairo as the net result of Tel-el-Kebir and all our millions, we might form some idea as to the sentiment which the spectacle of "Mr. Ferdinand of Coburg" inspires in the Russian heart. That they have themselves largely to blame for the awkward turn which affairs have taken is an aggravation rather than an alleviation of the pain of the situation. It is never well to allow a nation to feel that it has been swindled. Russia feels that she has been choused out of her rightful position in the principality which she has created, and that Austria has run off with the oyster after Russia had opened the shell.

I do not propose here to enter into a discussion of the causes which brought about the present extraordinary eclipse of Russian influence in Bulgaria. Briefly stated, the ingratitude of the Bulgarians is nothing to be wondered at. Gratitude in politics is a lively sense of favours to come. If the Bulgarians had anything to expect from Russia in the future they would not have so speedily forgotten what they received from them in the past. But, apart from the operation of that invariable law, it was certain that unless Russia had driven Bulgaria with a very light hand the Bulgarians would turn restive. No British colony would stand much interference from London, and the Bulgarians, not even being Russians, were quick to resent orders from St. Petersburg. During the war it was said that "Russia had bought her Bulgar pigs, and that she intended to drive them." But the Bulgar pigs proved to be too much for their Russian driver. The English art of winning the loyalty of dependencies by letting them do exactly what they please is not suited to the meridian of St. Petersburg. The attempt to control the affairs of Bulgaria, not in the interests of the Emperor, but of the Russo-Jewish ring which had set its heart on the exploitation of the country, provoked the stubborn resistance of these Scotchmen of the East. Russia was somewhat unfortunate in the choice of her agents. Bulgaria was made the dumping-ground for Russian failures, and the result is what we see. England sent her Lanyons and her Shepstones to the Transvaal with similar results.

The situation was such that some disappointment on both sides was inevitable. But if Prince Alexander had been honest, straightforward, and free from complicity in financial affairs, and if Russia had been represented at Sophia by an agent wise enough to see that in order to secure the reality of power it is sometimes necessary to dispense with its semblance, the disappointment might have been minimised. As it was, with Prince Alexander's faults on one side and the shortcomings of the Russians on the other, the breach became so wide that no one could heal it. Prince Alexander disappeared, and in his place came an even more objectionable person in the shape of Prince Ferdinand of Coburg.

The English point of view is too well known for me to need to recapitulate it here. It will be more useful to set forth as clearly as possible what I was told by almost every Russian with whom I spoke. Russia is not going to Bulgaria. Russia has no intention of making Bulgaria a Russian province. Russia asks nothing from Bulgaria. She is quite willing to allow Bulgarians to manage their own affairs. Only, if Russia keeps her hands off, Austria must do the same. At present Bulgaria is in the hands of an Austrian agent. Prince Ferdinand of Coburg is an Austrian and a Roman Catholic. He is expressly excluded from occupying the Bulgarian throne by the Berlin Treaty, which declares that the Prince of Bulgaria must belong to the

Orthodox Eastern Church. Prince Ferdinand is not only an Austrian, but he is the agent of the Jesuit propaganda, the tool of the high personages who surround Francis Joseph. His position is illegal. He must go. As long as he remains at Sophia Russia cannot enter into any relations with Bulgaria.

But how, if Prince Ferdinand refuses to go? The Russian Government persists in denying the possibility of such obstinacy on his part. I was assured most emphatically that when the Powers were asked to declare collectively and jointly that Prince Ferdinand's position was illegal, and that it was his duty to disappear, he would have bowed at once to the joint collective Note of Europe, and made way for his successor. But, unfortunately for the peace and tranquillity of the East, Austria, backed by Lord Salisbury, refused to do jointly what every Government in Europe had already done separately ; and Prince Ferdinand, seeing that the Powers were not agreed, snapped his fingers in the face of Russia, of Germany, and of France, and continued to hold on to his precarious position at Sophia. The continuance of the open sore in Bulgaria is therefore due to Austria and to Lord Salisbury. But for this the only difficulty in the way of satisfying Russian *amour propre* would have vanished, and it is because we have refused the Emperor even the small satisfaction of one diplomatic success that the whole Balkan is kept simmering in unrest.

There is no axiom in diplomacy more elementary than that you should, whenever you can, oblige your opponent by conceding trifles. The more determined you are to oppose his demands in vital matters the more expedient is it to humour him in small affairs. Granting that Lord Salisbury is right in determining to oppose the establishment of the direct authority of Russia in Bulgaria, is it not his obvious policy to concede every point of form the better to enable him to resist in matters of substance? Never was there a more trivial matter of form than the modest Russian request to embody in a formal collective document six protests against an illegality which had already been presented in six separate representations. If England had been sincere in her protest she could not possibly have objected to uniting in a collective remonstrance against the breach of the Treaty. By refusing to do so, she not only exposed her previous protest to suspicion as to its lack of sincerity, she also took upon herself the grave responsibility of keeping the question open with all its vast possibilities of mischief.

The action of our Government shows, indeed, a sinister resemblance to the summary rejection of the Berlin Memorandum in 1876, which was the first act by which Lord Beaconsfield broke up the European Concert and rendered the subsequent war inevitable. As Lord Beaconsfield concurred in the Andrassy Note and dissented from the Berlin Memorandum, which was simply intended to make the former effective, so Lord Salisbury, while protesting independently against the illegality of the position of Prince Ferdinand, refused to follow up that independent protest by the collective action which alone could relieve Europe of a pressing difficulty. I only hope that the future may not continue the bodeful parallel between English Tory policy in Bulgaria in 1876 and 1888.

It is important to dwell upon the matter because the principle which it involves covers the whole of our future action in Bulgaria. Russia assures us in the most emphatic fashion, and without the slightest reservation, that she will not send an army into Bulgaria. If Austria will keep her hands off Bulgaria, not a Russian regiment will enter the principality. But Prince Ferdinand must disappear, and the Bulgarians must return to the way of legality and abide by the stipulations of the Berlin Treaty. Now, so long as the Russians do not occupy Bulgaria in force, we need not concern ourselves about the Bulgarians. These stubborn Scotchmen will take very good care of themselves, no matter who is on their throne and no matter what ascendency Russia exerts over their Government. Having secured from the Russians an absolute assurance that they will not employ military force to coerce the Bulgarians into obedience, it should be at once both our duty and our interest to heartily assist them in any minor satisfaction for their *amour propre* that they can suggest. Whether it is a collective protest against the Coburger or the acceptance of the candidate put forward by Russia as his successor, it is the same. So long as no Russian troops appear south of the Danube we can afford to help the Russians to whatever they ask for in Bulgaria, for in the absence of an army of occupation they can only get what they seek by consent of the Bulgarians, who, as experience has proved, are abundantly able to take care of themselves without our intervention. We have got to let Russia down quietly in the Balkan Peninsula. She is willing enough to get down if we will only enable her to do so with dignity. Why should we insist that she must also consent to be kicked downstairs in the presence of all her servants? Such insistence is the one thing that is likely to rouse a determination not to get down, but to force her way further up, even by military expeditions and the risk of war.

It seems to me that in this, as in most other things, we have to choose between securing the substance by helping Russia to the shadow, or sacrificing the substance for the sake of denying her the shadow also. The latter policy seems to be the present policy of England in Bulgaria. For the sake of everything which that policy was adopted in order to secure, I hope that it may be reversed before it is too late.

I have, however, strayed into a digression, and have interpolated a discussion of English policy in the midst of a statement of the Russian view of the Bulgarian question, which I will now resume. The Russian Ministers stoutly deny that the Bulgarians are hostile to Russia or in favour of the Coburg Prince. The Russian official view is that the Bulgarian population is tyrannised over by a usurping Camerilla. The junta at Sophia, over whom M. Stambouloff reigns supreme, control the army and the police, and through the army and the police terrorise the peasantry, who are beaten if they show their real proclivities, and who therefore stay away from the polls, giving the Camerilla a semblance of support which in reality they do not possess.

Russia, however, does not insist upon the disappearance of any one but Prince Ferdinand, and this she declares will be accomplished without difficulty the moment the Powers show themselves united in opposition to his stay in Bulgaria. What then? On this point the Russian idea seems to be that a Turkish and Russian Commissioner must proceed to Sophia to superintend the election of a new Sobranje that will be charged with the election of a Prince who will be acceptable to the great Powers. If the elections are free, the Russians profess the utmost confidence in the result. They may be mistaken, but they express unhesitating readiness to put their opinion to the test.

The Russians are putting forward no candidate for the throne at present. They suggested some time ago that the Prince of Mingrelia should be invited to succeed Prince Ferdinand. The nomination was, no doubt, an admirable one from the point of view of peace. The Mingrelski is a Parisian, with an unpresentable wife, who loathes war, knows nothing about armies, and, if he had been elected, would have been the bourgeois Prince of a peasant population. He has no ambitions, and would only take the place if ordered by the Tzar. That order, however, is not likely to be given. The more advanced party, who wish to see Bulgaria organised from a Russian military point of view, were so hostile to the candidature of the Mingrelski that it will not be revived. From a European point of view we might easily go farther and fare worse.

The Russians profess to be ready to accept any Prince who is Greek Orthodox, and who is not allied to any of the reigning families of Europe. These limitations are imposed by the Berlin Treaty, and they shut out the Duke of Edinburgh, whose wife is the Tzar's sister, and whose children might have founded a new dynasty representing both Empires, and springing directly from the Anglo-Russian *entente*. Russian subjects are not by treaty excluded from the Bulgarian throne, but a Russian General would probably fail to meet with unanimous acceptance. There might be other difficulties. A story is current in St. Petersburg that when the Tzar asked the Prince of Oldenburg to accept the post he begged to be excused. "In six months I should have to choose whether I broke faith with my subjects or violated my allegiance to your Majesty." Prince Alexander, of course, is tabooed; so is Prince Ferdinand. The talk among the diplomatists is of one of the princes of Sweden, who it is thought might be open to persuasion as to the respective merits of the Lutheran and Eastern Churches. It would seem an unfortunate thing to begin what might be only a temporary reign by an act of religious apostasy.

The candidate who most nearly complies with the necessities of the situation is Bozo Petrovitch, the first Montenegrin in the principality after the Prince. He is Slav, Orthodox, and a natural king of men. Of all the Balkan races, the Montenegrins alone preserved their independence during the centuries of Turkish domination. Everywhere else the Turks killed out the ruling families, or converted them, leaving a dead level of peasants to occupy the land. Hence there is, excepting in Montenegro, no vestige left of an aristocratic or monarchical stock. Nor are there any Orthodox Slavs in the Balkan outside the Black Mountain who have been accustomed to command. Prince Nicholas of Montenegro—whose daughters, stately mountaineers, with queenly presence, deep lustrous eyes, and magnificent physique, are now being educated in St. Petersburg—would perhaps be the best choice, but he has Montenegro to govern, and his selection would probably irritate Austria and alarm Servia. As a concession to Austrian prejudice, the choice of the Bulgarians and of the Powers might well fall upon Bozo Petrovitch, who is in some respects a better man for the post than Prince Nicholas. His selection would soothe Russian *amour propre*, it would probably be acceptable to the Emperor, and when the Montenegrin Prince found himself in the saddle, his independence and capacity would secure Europe more effectively than any treaty arrangement against any attempt to exploit Bulgaria either in the interest of Russia or of Austria. If, therefore, as is not improbable, any attempt be made to put forward Bozo Petrovitch as the successor of Prince Ferdinand, I sincerely hope that England will raise no objection. Suitable candidates are too few to justify a veto upon any competent person merely because it may suit Austria to declare that "no Montenegrin need apply." Austria has made enough trouble in Bulgaria already, without attempting to enforce a veto which would sacrifice Bulgarian interests to Austrian susceptibilities.

What, then, does Russia want in Bulgaria? First and foremost, she wants to see Prince Ferdinand sent about his business. Secondly, she wants free elections for a new Sobranje, by which a prince could be chosen. Thirdly, she would like to see a Montenegrin on the throne. Fourthly, she wishes the union of the Bulgarias legalised by the assent of Europe. That is all. Considering what Russia has spent and suffered for the creation of Bulgaria, who can say that she is exigent in her demands? Which of these proposals conflicts with English interests or in any way sacrifices the freedom or the independence of Bulgaria to Russian ambition? Yet it is precisely because we haggle and higgle and keep thrusting our finger into Russia's eye over this paltry business, that the chief, if not the only, immediate difficulty arises to the establishment of an *entente* between ourselves and Russia. Prince Bismarck has to all appearance energetically, and certainly in public, supported the Russian proposals; and although the Montenegrin nomination has never come before Europe, the Chancellor is not likely to hesitate about a personal question of that kind, if by its concession he can smooth the ruffled dignity of Russia and definitely banish the possibility of a Russian occupation of Bulgaria.

I heard some talk—not in official quarters—of establishing a military convention between the Bulgarian Government and Russia, similar to that which is said to exist between the Servian Government and Austria. If the Servian Convention be a reality, and it passes without protest, no exception need be taken to a similar Bulgarian Convention, although technically, of course, King Milan, being independent, is more free to conclude military conventions with his neighbours than the vassal Prince of Bulgaria, whose territory is not even conterminous with Russia. Fact is, however, often at variance with diplomatic fiction. The fatal Convention by which Prince Alexander bound himself to employ the Bulgarian army as a Turkish contingent was diplomatically correct enough; but in reality it was such an outrage on the fundamental principle of Bulgarian existence as to render his deposition inevitable. A military Convention with Russia on the other hand, while totally inconsistent with diplomatic fiction, might on the whole not be out of harmony with the necessities of the situation.

"Russia," said one of her Ministers to me, "refuses to be angry with the Bulgarians. We regard them as naughty children, who need only to be left severely alone for a time in order to secure their return in penitence. When that happens, Russia will astonish the world by her forbearance and by her forgiveness. Till that happens Russia will wait. Time is on her side, for the situation is so false that it cannot last."

"But," I asked, "how long will your patience last? Is it eternal?"

To which he replied, with a smile, "It will last longer than the duration of the Coburg."

## CHAPTER VIII.

### WHO IS TO KEEP THE KEYS OF THE TZAR'S HOUSE?

THE Bulgarian question is the only matter in dispute between Russia and England; but it would be a mistake to imagine that a stable *entente* can be built up on a temporary compromise as to the selection of an occupant for the Bulgarian throne. That is possible, but if there be an *arrière pensée* on either side the *entente* is as far off as ever. For the moment there is—outside Bulgaria—a temporary lull in the East. The outbreak in Roumania, at first attributed to the malignant agency of the Russian rouble, is now better understood to have been agrarian in its origin. Absentee landlordism provokes agrarian discontent elsewhere than in Ireland, and the liberality with which Russia dealt with her peasants in the matter of land is a more powerful stimulant to agrarian agitation on her borders than any secret funds which may be at the service of M. Hitrovo. Every Roumanian peasant, I am told, received under the Roumanian Land Act as much land per family as every Russian peasant on the other side of the frontier received per head. Hence the moment that the pressure of population on the means of subsistence became severe, there arose a demand on the part of the Roumanians for Russian terms. It is many years since Cavour observed that "the equal right to the soil given by the Russians to all their peasants was more dangerous to Western Europe than all the armies of Muscovy." It is only to-day that people are beginning to discover how prescient was the remark of the Italian statesman.

Roumania, however, is neither here nor there. No one in Russia, so far as I can discover, proposes to lay a finger upon King Karl. His subjects may upset him some fine day, in which case Prince Bibesco might succeed to the throne. But as long as the military effects of the upset are confined within the limits of Roumania, it will not disturb the general peace. War on a great scale would only ensue if Austria on the one hand, or Russia on the other, were to occupy, on any pretext whatever, any one of these principalities. Macedonia is the most serious danger-point in Turkish territory. A rising in Macedonia, with consequent massacres or contingent complications in Eastern Roumelia, might task to the uttermost the energies of the European fire brigade, and give the Great Powers bitter cause to regret that they had allowed Turkey to violate with impunity the twenty-third clause of the Berlin Treaty.

Behind all Balkan questions, however, there ever arises the one question which dominates the whole situation—Constantinople and the Bosphorus. Who is to hold the keys of the Straits? who is to keep the keys of the Tzar's "house"? Unless an agreement can be arrived at on that point, the antagonism between England and Russia is likely to continue, and even to grow more acute. Is such an agreement possible? I venture to believe that it is, and for this reason.

The question is not a pressing one. It is nearly a hundred years since the Tzar and the First Napoleon discussed whether or not Russia could be trusted with "the keys of her own house," and still the Grand Turk slumbers by the Golden Horn. It is nearly fifty years since the Tzar Nicholas in his frank straightforward way told Sir Hamilton Seymour that we had a Sick Man on our hands who might die at any moment; but Nicholas and Sir Hamilton are dead, and the Sick Man still lives. "Those old empires," as M. Thiers said to Nassau Senior, "are very tough. They creak and creak as if they were going to pieces next minute, but although they may lose a limb now and then, or shed a province, they contrive to exist." The Sick Man seemed nigh unto death in 1878, when the Russian armies were streaming through the Balkan passes, and Skobeleff stood sword in hand before the lines of Stamboul. But the crisis passed, and the Sick Man survived and survives.

That is why an agreement is possible between Russia and England. If the Sick Man were suddenly to give up the ghost to-morrow, the chances of an arrangement would be very slight; but if the Sick Man lingers long enough to enable us to realise how disadvantageous the *status quo* is to us, an agreement will not be difficult. Every day the Sultan continues to reign on the Bosphorus tells in favour of an understanding between England and Russia as to the future custody of the Straits, because it increases the odds in favour of Russia and tends to make England regard with continually diminishing favour the *status quo*. There can only be one settlement of the question of the Bosphorus.

Russia will some day own the keys of her own house. If she may not grasp them when she is 120 millions strong, or when she is 150 millions, she will take them when she is 200 millions. It is only a question of time. Hence, as there can only be one settlement, it is important to consider what England should do when that inevitable settlement arrives.

Time, which increases the strength by multiplying the subjects of Russia, operates in the opposite direction on the strength and the resources of Turkey. Of these two States, one must increase, the other decrease; and the greater the disproportion between the greater and the less, the more certainly will the less be drawn submissively into the orbit of the greater. This suits Russia very well. Russia has not at present the slightest intention of bringing about the general overturn in the East by making a descent upon Constantinople. Her policy is to preserve the Sick Man as carefully as the Prince of Wales preserves his game at Sandringham until close-time expires, and the birds are ready for the gun. Russia is not ready to bag the Bosphorus, and until she can do so safely she naturally prefers to maintain the *status quo*. And for this reason: next to being herself in custody of the Straits, she prefers a custodian who is practically in her pocket. The Turks are the custodians of the Straits; but if we ask, Quis custodiet custodes? the answer is the Tzar.

One of the oddest customs in St. Petersburg is that of keeping a dvornik or hall-porter to watch or to sleep, as the case may be, outside the door of every important building in the city. Pass along the Nevski Prospect at any hour of the night or early morning and you will see these dvorniks sitting outside the doors of the respective mansions, wrapped in their sheepskins, keeping watch in deep slumber over the house. Now, the *status quo* at Constantinople is simply a political adaptation of this Russian custom. The Sultan is the Tzar's dvornik; or, as we should say in England, the Turk is Russia's hall-porter. That is an arrangement that suits Russia well enough; but just because it suits Russia, it does not suit England, if, as some say, our interests are necessarily antagonistic to those of Russia. For what does it mean? It means that Russia has all the convenience of having the key of the Straits in her own pocket, while all the inconveniences and the responsibility are thrown upon the Turk. When England was threatening to go to war with Russia about

Penj-deh, the Turk intimated that he would close the Black Sea against the entry of an English fleet. Had he done so then, we should have had to make war upon a neutral Power or consent to be shut out of the only field of offensive operations against Russia.

The Black Sea is the Achilles' heel of the Russian Empire. If we are to regard ourselves as hereditary and eternal foes, it is a matter of absolute necessity that we should be able to get into that sea whenever we are in strained relations with Russia. But in order to enjoy that liberty of ingress and of egress, it is indispensable that the doorkeeper on the Bosphorus should not be so much under the thumb of our enemy that when the critical moment comes he may be compelled to bar the gate in our face. That is what he threatened to do in 1885; it is what he will be driven to do at the next crisis. For Russia has means of exerting pressure upon Turkey—financial, political, military, and naval—which tend to render the Sultan more and more the subservient puppet of the Tzar. Under cover of the Turkish mask the Russians will be more secure than if they themselves held Constantinople. At Constantinople they would, at least, be open to attack and to blockade. With the Turks doing their work for them, we should be powerless.

This situation will become more and more clearly manifest every year; every year the Russians will be growing stronger and more numerous; every year the Turks will be growing weaker and more dependent. For the moment the real facts of the situation are somewhat veiled by the presence at Constantinople as our representative of "the English Ignatieff" in the form of Sir William White, while Russia has her Sir Henry Elliot in the person of M. Nelidoff. But no personal ascendency on the part of the English Ambassador can obscure more than temporarily the relative positions of Russia and Turkey. The Russians know that well enough, and they do not propose to alter the *status quo*. When I tried to discuss it with those high in authority, their replies showed clearly enough that for them the question of the Straits was far beyond the range of practical politics. "Why speak about it?" I was asked. "There is no such question before us."

But sooner or later the question will be raised, and the chief hope of a pacific settlement lies in the fact that the slow and steady operation of natural forces tends to make the Turkish ownership of Constantinople far more disagreeable to England than it has hitherto been to Russia. It is possible that it may not be Russia, but England, which will make the first move towards putting the guardianship of the Bosphorus into other hands than those of the Turk.

This contingency, as yet but dimly perceived by the few, will before long become obvious to all. When that time comes, the question of the Straits will be ripe for settlement, and the long-expected demise of the Sick Man will leave the ground clear for his successor. However remote that succession may be, it is well to consider it before it arrives, in order that it may not take us unawares, and that we may be prepared with a solution that will harmonise our respective interests. The first thing to know is what the Russians want, and as to that there is no concealment. When their Turkish dvornik dies, Russia will take the keys of her own gate into her own keeping. That is to say, as we have our Gibraltar at the entrance to the Mediterranean, and our Aden and Perim at the exit from the Red Sea, so Russia will insist upon having her fortress gates on the entrance to the Black Sea. The Russians do not care about Constantinople so much. Its importance is traditional and legendary rather than actual and political. They disclaim any designs on the Balkan Peninsula or in Asia Minor. " Hands off" all round is their demand, but a Russian lock and key on the entrance to the Black Sea.

When I asked them why they were so anxious to have the keys of the Bosphorus in their own hands, they replied by saying that the possession of the Straits would make for them the difference of 200,000 men; 10,000 troops in a couple of forts on either side of the Bosphorus would enable them to leave the Black Sea coast as undefended as the shores of the Caspian. It would cover their one vulnerable point, and enable them for the first time to feel safe in the Black Sea.

" That is all very well," I replied, " but do you want the keys of the Bosphorus in order to exclude the Black Sea from the arena of war, or do you want to shut us out in order to convert the Black Sea into an immense arsenal, from which, at a given moment, a new Armada might issue forth and join hands with the French to sweep the British flag from the Mediterranean? "

Nothing of that, I was always assured, was dreamed of by the Russians. Defence, not offence, was their ideal. They were much more likely to dismantle the Black Sea fleet if they held the keys of the Bosphorus than to fill the Euxine with preparations for naval war. "If so," I asked, "would you have any objection to our having a lock at the other end of the corridor? If Russia had her forts on the Bosphorus, might England have her forts on the Dardanelles?"

"Yes," was the reply, "if you want war in six months or six weeks. Otherwise not. Surely it would be the very acme of madness to plant a Russian General on the Bosphorus and an English General on the Dardanelles, with all the Turks and Levantines in Constantinople between them. Every one knows what would happen. The Russian General on one side, and the English General on the other, would be perpetually stirring up the Turks with a long pole. There would be encroachments, intrigues, violations of understandings, trespasses on frontiers, and what not, until even war would be a relief. In principle we have no objection to the counter-check in the Dardanelles, but as a matter of practical politics it is out of the question. Constantinople may be a free city or not, as you please. The forts of the Dardanelles may be dismantled, and the navigation of the Straits inter-nationalised and neutralised, as you internationalise the Suez Canal. The only *sine quâ non* upon which we shall insist, when the Turk goes, is the establishment of Russian forts on the Bosphorus, which will enable us to shut out hostile fleets from the Black Sea."

There is force in this objection. The near proximity of Russian and English garrisons, with such a Devil's Caldron as Stamboul lying between them, would not be a solution for peace. For England I should deplore so fatal an extension of our responsibilities as that of garrisoning the Dardanelles, involving as it would do the holding of territory with land frontiers both in Europe and in Asia. When we have cast big guns sufficient to supply the fortifications of our own seaports, we may begin to dream of establishing a new Gibraltar at Gallipoli. But this is a matter of opinion. What is more to the point is the fact that when the break-up comes, Russia will not accept as a possible solution of the question of the Straits any settlement which establishes an English bolt and bar upon the outside gate of the Black Sea. Regulations might be made for navigation; the waterway up to Constantinople might be freed from forts, and a British naval station might be established at Mitylene—all that might be arranged. But England at Gallipoli—never!

It is well to know where we stand, to know what is possible and what is not. Certain solutions may be preferred by us to other solutions, provided they can be obtained without disproportionate sacrifices. If, however, the difference between the English occupation of Mitylene and the English occupation of Gallipoli involves the difference, not only between war and peace with Russia in the remote future when the Sick Man dies, but, what to us who are living now is much more important, the difference between cordial and strained relations with Russia in the immediate present, then indeed there are very few who would not decide for Mitylene. Mitylene is possible; Gallipoli is not. But, as Mitylene would serve us better and cost us less, the Russians do us good service by putting an imperative veto betimes upon the suggested alternative of a British fort on the Dardanelles. With Egypt, English, and a naval station within a few hours' steam from the mouth of the Dardanelles, we can await with composure the inevitable moment when the Russian Emperor takes over from his dvornik the keys of his own house.

## CHAPTER IX.

### ENGLAND'S REAL DANGER IN CENTRAL ASIA.

THERE remains one last question to be disposed of—the question of Central Asia and of Afghanistan. The idea that the Russians, either as a people or as a Government, contemplate the design of the invasion and conquest of India is one of those delusions which are to nations what evil spirits were to individuals in the days of "possession." The Russians no more contemplate the conquest of India than our Jingoes contemplate the conquest of Poland; but both Russians and Jingoes agree in believing that, if necessity should arise, they can make a good deal of trouble each for the other—the one in India, the other in Poland. The more clearly it is recognised that there is no more question of an invasion of India in force by the Russian army than there is of the entry of Lord Wolseley into Warsaw at the head of a British army corps, the more likely is it that we shall see where our real danger lies; for that there is real danger of some kind from the proximity of Russia and England in Asia is indubitable. It is hopeless attempting to face the real danger until we have definitely dismissed the imaginary peril from our minds.

What is the real danger? The real danger is largely self-created, but still it exists. It consists in the idea, with which our own writers and officials have so diligently inoculated the Asiatic mind, that every advance of Russia in the direction of Afghanistan endangers our position in India. The strength of the Russians for mischief is not material but moral. It is based, not upon the proximity of their cannons, but upon the ubiquity of our alarmists. Lord Lytton was probably the most effective agent who ever served the Russians in Asia. He and his troupe of panic-mongers could not have done the Tzar's work better if they had been salaried with roubles as advertising agents of Muscovy. By their fuss and their fidget and their reckless expenditure of life and money in order to conjure away the mere shadow of a Cossack on the far side of Afghanistan they convinced our fellow-subjects in India that Russia possessed a capacity for upsetting our Empire, which in reality she lacks. While the Germans and the Jews between them have been steadily co-operating in Europe to depreciate the rouble and impair Russian credit, our Jingoes and Anglo-Indians have in the most reckless fashion set themselves to raise Russian credit as much above par in Asia as the rouble is below par in Europe. Lord Salisbury once remarked to General Ignatieff that, unless rumour lied, Russia had many agents in India. "Thousands of agents," coolly replied the ablest Russian in the diplomatic service—"we have literally thousands of most useful agents in India." "What do you mean?" asked Lord Salisbury, in some amazement at the cynical avowal. "Our agents," replied General Ignatieff, "are headed by your own Viceroy, and they include almost every official in your service and every newspaper writer in India. They occupy themselves constantly in doing, far more effectively than any one else could do it, the kind of work for which we are supposed to employ agents in other countries. They disquiet the minds of the well-disposed by spreading fears of a Russian advance; they encourage the hopes of the ill-disposed by simulating alarm at our approach; they fill the bazaars with stories of our irresistible prowess, and, in short, they do everything that we could wish to magnify our reputation, and prepare every *mauvais sujet*, every native who is discontented with your Government, to turn with longing and hopeful gaze towards the great white Tzar." General Ignatieff was right. There is no room for Russian agents in Russian pay in India. The ground is covered, from the Himalayas to Ceylon, with far more effective auxiliaries who draw British pay, but do the Russian's work.

Now that the actual Russian has come alongside the Afghan frontier, it is to be hoped that this reckless "bulling" of Russian prestige in Asia will be abandoned by our people. But it is too late to undo the mischief which fifty years of hysterical and morbid alarmism have worked in India. It has given the Russians a vantage ground which all their artillery could not have secured them; and it is a vantage ground which they would be more than human if they did not use to their profit and to our inconvenience. Their railway enables them to deliver troops on the Afghan frontier a couple of days after they are landed from their base on the Caspian. Although this single line of railway drawn across the desert is of little use for the transport of an invading army, it is all that is required to furnish the semblance of danger. The delusion, although as unreal as Pepper's Ghost, is quite as startling to those who do not know the trick. Unless there is a complete change in our relations with the Russians, unless cordiality succeeds distrust, and loyal co-operation in Asia and in Europe replaces the present tension of hostility and intrigue, the Russians have us at an immense disadvantage on the Afghan border, not because they are in a position to do us any injury whatever, but because they can so practise on our idiotic, self-created fears as to drive us almost to the verge of Imperial suicide. They cannot do us any harm, but they can make us do immense harm to ourselves.

Up to the present moment no Russian soldier has ever come within range of our Indian outposts. But the presence in Afghanistan of a wandering Polish adventurer in 1840, and the arrival of a Russian envoy at Cabul in 1878, provoked spasms of delirium, which cost us tens of thousands of brave men and tens of millions of treasure. Every penny squandered on the Afghan campaigns, every life sacrificed in those dreadful defiles, was sacrificed to exorcise a phantom conjured up by our own nervousness. It did not exorcise the phantom; it weakened India, it intensified the hatred with which we are regarded in Afghanistan, and above all it taught the Russians the enormous value of that kind of phantasmagoria in the great game of Central Asian politics. As we continued to make ourselves disagreeable in Eastern Europe, the Russians determined, and very wisely determined from their own point of view, to exploit our fears in the direction of Afghanistan. The extension of their frontier beyond Merv, the construction of the railway, and the whole of their recent policy in those regions, indicate with absolute unreserve their intention to profit by our folly.

If that folly is not succeeded by sober sense, I confess I look forward with some alarm to the future of India. If the present craze continues, the Tzar has only to stretch his finger in menacing fashion in the direction of Herat to plunge the Indian finances into confusion, and to secure the disorganisation of the whole Indian military system, by compelling a concentration of troops at Pishin and Quetta. He has but to order the Russian drums to beat in the neighbourhood of Zulfikar, or to suggest that a company of Cossacks should pursue some bandits across the border near Maruchak, for the Indian Government to stop furloughs, to telegraph for reinforcements, and to prepare to plunge headlong for a third time into the death-trap of Afghanistan. That is an advantage which as an English patriot I grudge to my Russian friends.

There is, however, some hope that the very awkwardness of the position into which we have forced our way may lead to a tardy discovery that the Russians can, after all, make it worth our while to be on friendly terms. When Russia acquired the mouth of the Amoor and her Pacific ports, Lord Elgin asked the Russian plenipotentiary why Russia was so anxious for a naval base in the Pacific. His reply was frank and characteristic, "We do not want them for their own sake, but chiefly in order that we may be in a position to compel the English to recognise that it is worth their while being friends with us rather than foes." Precisely the same reason dominated the acquisition of strategical points on the Afghan border. But for the necessity of being able to convince England that her real interests are not inextricably bound up with the maintenance of Turkish power in Europe, the Central Asian fleece would not, as Skobeleff remarked, have been worth the tanning. This is useful for England. The fatal sense of being "in the air," of being able to do what we pleased without exposing ourselves to reprisals, has been responsible for much of the criminality of our policy in relation to Russia. We would never have dared to act in any such fashion to France, with whom we made the *entente cordiale* quite as much from fear as from love. So it may be that the *entente* with Russia, which we have scouted with scorn as long as Russia was too far off to make us realise the consequences of our own acts, may be brought about, not by the prompting of morality, but simply under the pressure of the sordid but permanent forces of interest and fear.

The position in which we have by our alarmist propaganda and our Afghan superstition voluntarily placed Russia is as follows:—

We have drawn a frontier line across the north of Afghanistan, beyond which the Russians admit that they have no interest at present, and up to which we may, if we choose, with their hearty goodwill advance our frontier. On the north of that frontier line the Russians are at home. They have garrisons stationed there connected by railway within a couple of days of their base on the Caspian. They answer for order, they police their frontier, and they are by telegraph within a few hours of St. Petersburg. On the other side of that frontier line we are not at home. Our nearest outpost is nearly 600 miles off on the road to Pishin. A territory as large as France, as mountainous as Switzerland, as poor as the highlands of Scotland, and inhabited by fierce and fanatical tribes, stretches between our furthest point and the Russian lines. We have no warden of the marches at Zulfikar or at Maruchak. We have no Englishmen in all Afghanistan to tell us what is going on, to say nothing of undertaking to keep the peace of the border. We cannot answer for order on our side, neither can we undertake that the surges of the civil war that are chronic in Afghan may never dash over the clearly-marked line that has been drawn from the Oxus to the Murghab.

What is more, we cannot even attempt to exercise any effective control of the Afghan borderers without thrusting an army through their country, thereby rousing the deadly animosity of the Afghan tribes.

What is the natural and necessary result of such a condition of affairs when it is superimposed upon a kind of nervous frenzy among our own people, which causes them to rush into Afghanistan, as the bull plunges at the cloak of a matador, whenever a Cossack lance shows itself on the Afghan frontier? This. The moment the Russians think that we are worrying them unnecessarily in Europe, they will discover ways and means of worrying us in Asia. Their power to do this depends not on their strength, but on our nervousness, and they need not move a man, or fire a rifle. They will discover that some tribes just within the Afghan frontier have raided some tribes within Russian territory. They will ask us to punish the marauders. As we are 600 miles off, and have not even agents who could tell us so much as whether there had been any such raid on Russian territory, we can do nothing but promise to make representations at Cabul. Before these representations can reach the Ameer, we shall hear by telegraph that the raids have been repeated, and that Colonel Alikhanoff has been ordered up to the scene of the foray "with instructions." What these instructions are will depend upon the extent of pressure which it is necessary to employ to convince Lord Salisbury that the British Empire is after all of more value than Austrian interests in Bulgaria. If we were sensible and not nervous, we should sit still and let Alikhanoff deal with the marauders as best he could, following them, if need be, across the frontier, and defiling the sacred soil of the Ameer with the hoof of the Infidel. As we are not sensible, but are very nervous, we shall fly into a rage, bluster about making the infraction of Afghan territory a *casus belli*, order troops out to India, and begin to prepare for a countermove in Afghanistan. Meanwhile the wily Muscovite will rub his hands and chortle in his joy to see how admirably the charm works, and how completely the shadow of an advance across the Afghan frontier convulses England with preparations for war. That is not a position which is endurable by sensible people. The Russians do not want to conquer Afghanistan. But if we are hostile they will do their level best to tempt us into it; and if we are no wiser in the future than we have been in the past, we shall inevitably fall into the snare which has been set before our eyes.

What, then, is our true policy in Afghanistan? Obviously, in the first place, to cultivate friendly relations with Russia, and, in the second, not to be too fidgetty about infractions of the frontier. We have no right to expect any frontier to be kept sacro-sanct and intact which we refuse to police. If we will not or cannot shoot the rascals who raid the Russian's cows, the Russian will shoot them himself, not caring whether to do so he has or has not to cross the boundary line which Sir Peter Lumsden has marked out. If he is wise, he will for his own sake return to his own side when the robbers have been disposed of; but if, as is probable, he is not wise, and tries to annex Afghan territory, so much the worse for him and the better for us. The first Infidel who enters Afghanistan makes his opponent a present of the alliance of all the Afghan tribes, for the Afghans are ever the friends of the second comer. If England and Russia are to be enemies, then the first move in the game of each is to lure the other into the defiles of the Afghan mountains. The Russians understand that perfectly, and will act upon it. If they advance they will not go further than Herat, and the watershed of the Heri-Rud. Unfortunately the English have no other idea as to Afghanistan than that of keeping the Russians out—the very thing that suits them best and us least.

There remains the question of the civil war which will ensue when the present Ameer dies. A civil war is the Afghan mode of conducting a general election, and the best thing for every one would be to let the various candidates fight it out among themselves. But unless the *entente* is established, there will be a Russian candidate—strictly unofficial, of course—at Herat, and a British candidate, not unofficial, at Cabul. It will be almost miraculous if we escape being dragged into the vortex of Afghan feuds if the Ameer should die before we have arranged matters amicably with the Russians. The Russians disclaim all intention of interfering in Afghanistan. They desire nothing more than that we should take possession of the whole country, and govern it as we govern the Punjaub. The Emperor has repeatedly expressed himself in the strongest terms in this sense. But if we have to fight the Russian bear, the British lion had better not begin by filling his belly with that bag of stones. For the Russians an English conquest of Afghanistan would be quite the most convenient arrangement that could be devised. But to make India bankrupt, and to intern an army of 50,000 men in the Switzerland of Asia, merely in order to give the Russians the advantage of meeting us a thousand miles from our base, with millions of fanatical highlanders in our rear, that is a sacrifice which, with all my desire to oblige my Russian friends, I must respectfully decline to make. In Asia, the alarmists say, everything depends upon the issue of the first battle. If so, I prefer to choose my own ground near my own base, which I can fortify at my leisure, and where the population surrounding my camp, and from which I have to draw my supplies, would not be as hostile as the Russian invader.

If we have to fight Russia in Asia we must resolutely make up our minds that it is better for us and worse for them that we should fight them on the Indian not on the Russian side of Afghanistan. Every mile we advance to meet them from our present base weakens us and strengthens them. Every mile which they advance to meet us weakens them and strengthens us. If we but realised that, and acted on it steadily and without flinching, Russia's capacity to injure us in Asia would disappear. But as we shall do no such thing, the very reality of the danger to which Russia can expose us by playing upon our fears affords a solid hope for the establishment of future peace.

## CHAPTER X.

### THE TZAR AS PEACE-KEEPER OF EUROPE.

I HAVE now passed in review almost all the questions of foreign politics which would have to be considered in any serious attempt to establish good relations between England and Russia. I hope that in my survey of the situation, although it is made from the meridian of St. Petersburg, there is nothing that cannot be accepted by observers in the latitude of Downing Street. What will be said doubtless is that the great question is not this or that or the other possible solution of specific details in dispute between the two countries, but whether there is any reasonable prospect of making any arrangement with Russia that will be permanent. Is the ground solid enough on the Russian side of the stream on which to rear the solid piers on which such a bridge between the nations would have to rest? On this point I have only to say that I wish I were as sure of the solidity and stability of the foundation on the English side as I am of that on the Russian, and I would feel more safe in answering for the resolution and good faith of the Emperor than I would for continuity of purpose and straightforward integrity on the part of the shifting and shifty party politicians of my own country.

In making such an agreement with Russia, everything of course depends upon the Emperor. When there was a Nesselrode or a Gortschakoff at the Foreign Office this might not have been the case, for the personal convictions of the Emperor were liable to be swayed by the strongly entrenched authority of an experienced Chancellor. But that is not the case to-day. Alexander III. is his own Foreign Minister. When I remarked to M. de Giers that his policy had inspired even the English with confidence in the honesty and sincerity of his desire for peace and good relations, he hastened to interrupt me in order to declare that in everything he had done he only represented the Emperor. Hence the immense importance which attaches to the personality of the Tzar. As long as he reigns, it will be his convictions, his ideas, which will influence the course of Russian foreign policy; and it is with him that we have to do.

"Of all the Russians," said to me M. Suvorine, the editor of the *Novoe Vremya*, "the Emperor is by far the most distinctively Russian." "That is interesting," I replied; "because of all the Russians he seems to me most to resemble an English gentleman." Alexander III., from the point of view of the *entente* between England and Russia, is almost an ideal Emperor. If you could imagine a human being who was au fond Lord Hartington, and at the same time imbued with the religious temperament of Mr. Bright, and the intense domesticity of Lord Granville, you would conjure up a conception which is as nearly as possible the English equivalent of the Russian Emperor. There is in him a deep natural piety, such as that which forms the background of the Quaker soul; he is devoted to his wife and children, but his intellectual type most closely resembles that of Lord Hartington. That is to say, his is a mind not viewy—not given to speculation—a mind solid and sure, practical and sound—which brings to the consideration of every question when it arises, but not before, the business-like common-sense and strict integrity of purpose which characterise the leader of our Liberal Unionists. It is the mind of a man who is capable both of inspiring and of reposing confidence—an honest man, who endeavours to see things from the standpoint of justice, and then who automatically *sans phrase* tries to do right.

In the Russian Windsor at Gatschina, by the seaside at Peterhof, or in the Danish home at Copenhagen, the Emperor delights for a time to forget the cares of State in the society of his wife and children. He is perfectly idolised by his family, and all those who serve him in any way are overflowing in praise of his kindly unassuming disposition. A devoted husband, whom not even his worst enemies have ever accused of a single fault against his wife, he is a most affectionate father, the companion and friend of his boys. Few more pleasant scenes were described to me during my stay in Russia than that of the Tzar of All the Russias officiating as master of the children's revels in the happy family party that assembled last autumn at Copenhagen, superintending all their games and participating in all the boyish sport. There was no romp so great as he. There were the English children, and the Greeks, and his own; and a Royal time they seem to have had of it. To these Princes and Princesses his Imperial Majesty was merely "Uncle Sasha," and it was "Uncle Sasha! Uncle Sasha!" all over the place. Sometimes he would stand up in the midst of the merry throng and challenge the youngsters to pull him down. One after another, and then altogether, the bevy of Princes and Princesses, grand-children of the King of Denmark, would wrestle with the Tzar and try to throw him over. But although the struggle lasted until the whole party streamed with perspiration, and the gardens rang with merry laughter, the Emperor never was thrown. The Greek Princes are as sons of Anak, but the Tzar is as Hercules for strength and muscle, and "Uncle Sasha" always stood his ground.

And as it was in the pleasant playground in Denmark, so it is in the great affairs of State in Russia. Alexander III. stands his ground. All agree in declaring that although he is slow to move, deliberate in the extreme in making up his mind, when his resolution is once taken, and his foot is once put down, no consideration on earth will induce him to take it up. Only on one condition will he re-consider a decision once formed. If it can be proved to him that he has been misinformed, if he is convinced that what he believed to be a fact, and which was allowed to influence his policy as such, was no fact, but a fiction, then, with the honesty and sense of justice which are his pre-eminent characteristics, he will frankly and publicly own himself in the wrong. Of this the most signal illustration was afforded the world last year, when Prince Bismarck convinced him that he had been deceived by the forged despatches from Bulgaria. It was rather a painful confession, which a weak man would have made grudgingly, and after which he would have modified as little as possible the policy based upon his mistake. Not so Alexander III. He felt that he had unwittingly been unjust to Prince Bismarck, and he acknowledged it, and frankly re-adjusted his policy in favour of Germany. The full extent to which this re-adjustment has gone is only beginning to be perceived in Europe.

The Emperor is a strong man who takes short views. He sees what he believes to be his duty from day to day, and he does it honestly to the best of his ability, in the spirit of the maxim that "sufficient to the day is the evil thereof," and in the faith that strength sufficient for the day will be given him from on High. It is a different feeling from that which prompted Metternich's saying, "*Après moi le déluge*," for the Emperor feels that he and his are in the hands of God—who alone sees the end from the beginning, and will find tools to carry on His work when the day comes for that work to be done. That deep, silent, but abiding conviction has grown much upon the Emperor of late years. In his youth, when he never expected to ascend the throne, for which his elder brother, to whom he was passionately attached, was carefully trained and educated, while his own education was comparatively neglected, he was full of high and buoyant spirits, headstrong and vehement. But since his brother's death, and the shadows of the great responsibilities which overhang the throne darkened over him, he has become more and more deeply impressed with a sense of the invisible and eternal world into which at any moment he may be hurled. Europe has watched with admiration and sympathy by the bedside of the Emperor at Charlottenburg, where a ruler in the visible presence of Death, whose grisly hand was already clutching his throat, calmly and manfully did his appointed task from day to day, and left the rest in the hands of God. But Europe has forgotten that other Emperor who was summoned to the throne by dynamite, and also lives and reigns in the constant shadow of the fate which overtook his beloved father. People do not speak about it, but the shadow is there, and the Emperor knows it, but he goes about his daily work cheerful and unperturbed. When last year the Nihilist attempt of March 13 came within a hair's-breadth of success, the Emperor displayed the most absolute self-command. The whole Imperial family was to have been blown up on their way to the fortress of St. Peter and Paul. When they went to the service in commemoration of the death of Alexander II., it was at the station that the Emperor was informed that he had just escaped by the skin of his teeth from a catastrophe similar to that which had destroyed his father. He went down to Gatschina with his wife and children, laughing and talking in the carriage as if nothing had happened. Not until the children had left for the Palace, and the Emperor and his wife were driving alone through the Park, did he break the news to the Empress. She, poor thing, of less iron nerve than her husband, broke down utterly and wept. Small wonder that a woman to whom thus suddenly has been revealed the charged mine over which she has so lightly passed, shuddered with horror. Not so her husband. "I am ready," he said simply; "I will do my duty at any cost."

The Emperor does not seem bowed down or crushed beneath the Imperial load, the full weight of which neither he nor any one can adequately realise. He stands erect and joyous; cheerful, without bravado, with the simple open face of a man who has preserved amid all the affairs of State the heart of a little child. Those who know him well say that he is totally free from that worrying fretfulness, that wearing anxiety, which is incompatible with sincere faith in the providence of God. Not by his own will or of his own choice was he called to this perilous post, from which he can only be relieved by death. Until he is relieved he will hold it, often painfully conscious of his own shortcomings, but nevertheless doing his duty as best he can, according to his lights, and leaving the rest to God. As for Nihilist plots and foreign intrigues, and all the endless coil of Imperial business, it is all in the day's work, which he discharges, so far as he can see it is his to do, with the composure of a philosopher and the serenity of a Christian.

The Emperor has a horror of war. He commanded, as Tzarewitch, the army of the Lom in the Bulgarian campaign, and he saw enough of the realities of campaigning to recoil with his whole soul from the thought of war. The kindly human affections of a good *père de famille*, which are so strong in him, intensify the repugnance with which he contemplates any and every disturbance of the peace. It is his ambition, one of his Ministers remarked to me, not to be a great Sovereign, but to be the Sovereign of a great people, whose reign was unstained by a single war. He is not for peace at any price, but for peace at almost any price compatible with national honour and the defence of the interests of Russia, which have been committed to his care. Since he came to the throne, his voice, his influence, his authority have constantly been directed to prevent war. He is the natural ally, alike by constitution and by conviction, of any Power that honestly seeks to maintain the peace.

Hence the Emperor's desire for a good understanding with the two Powers in Europe which have everything to lose by war and nothing to gain. At the very beginning of his reign he met the German Emperor at Skiernewieze, to renew those ties which had for nearly a hundred years bound Germany and Russia in a natural but informal alliance. By that understanding he remained until the forged "proofs" of Bismarck's duplicity alienated him from his German friends. But after the demonstration of the forgery, the Emperor has gladly sought to renew the former intimacy with his next-door neighbour, and to link Russian with German influence in the maintenance of the *status quo*. His hope is that Russia and Germany may get back to the position in which they stood at the Skiernewieze interview; and unless Bismarck is more hopelessly committed to the Austrian alliance than is probable, considering his shrewdness, the Russian-German *entente* ought not to be far off.

The Emperor is notoriously desirous of coming to a good understanding and a hearty working agreement with England. Russia, Germany, and England—if these three hold together, they will, he is convinced, maintain the peace of the world. Whether these three Powers will hold together depends of course primarily upon England. If England were to make friends with Russia, Germany would probably follow suit, for the recent policy of Bismarck has been based upon his calculations as to his ability to keep Russia played off against England, and England played off against Russia. The force of such a peace league would be enormous. Austria dare not stir without Germany. France is impotent without Russia. A triple league, in which both Germany and Russia united with England for the maintenance of the peace, would render war impossible. That is the object of the Emperor. Whether he will succeed or not depends not upon him, but upon us.

There is one danger arising out of the character of the Emperor which it is necessary to state frankly and recognise without reserve. At present, notwithstanding the policy which England has pursued both in Central Asia and in Bulgaria, he has not lost faith in the possibility of coming to terms with us. Open hostility, frank and resolute opposition, he can understand; but trickiness, bad faith, and falsehood, with these he has no patience. Once let him be convinced that England's word is false as a dicer's oath, and that England is capable of accepting, let us say, the ideal of the Cyprus Convention and living up to it, and he will sorrowfully but resolutely turn his back upon the hope of an English *entente*. When once this takes place, wild horses will not bring him back to his present position. When the Emperor is satisfied that he has been wilfully deceived, he is done with the deceiver once for all. No considerations, even of Imperial interests, can induce him to palliate a lie, or to condone a fraud. Whatever we have to do with this man, it will be well to deal with him straightforwardly, speaking the truth, and acting honestly and above-board, as he will certainly deal with us. Otherwise we shall make shipwreck of everything.

This is, however, by the way. The Emperor is too familiar with the trouble caused to central governments by the licence of distant subordinates to cherish any ill-will against England for the scurvy part which we played in attempting to steal a march upon Russia in thrusting the Afghans forward to Penj-deh. At St. Petersburg there is only one opinion on the subject, which, of course, the Emperor fully shares—namely, that our Commissioners wished to bring about war. Captain Yate, I was told, had frankly confessed this to Russian officers, and whether it is true or false, it is an article of faith in Russia. There is little doubt that the Emperor had not the least desire to go to war with England about Penj-deh, and nothing but the most hopeless perversity on the part of our Commissioners, both in what they did and in what they did not do, brought us so near to the verge of war. The Emperor thought war was being forced upon him, and he made ready for it, deciding, it was said at the time, that he would, if need be, surrender the whole private fortune of his family to relieve the finances, as an example to his subjects; but no one was better pleased than he when the difficulty was arranged and the frontier delimited. How Mr. Gladstone, of all men, could ever have forced him so near to a collision is one of those abysmal mysteries which are beyond the plumb-line of the Russian mind.

More serious is the difficulty about Bulgaria. The Emperor's action in relation to Prince Alexander is so striking an illustration of the idiosyncrasy of his strongly-marked character as to justify my referring to it, even after what I have said of Russian policy in Bulgaria. The Emperor's breach with Prince Alexander was due to two causes, either of which was fatal. He is convinced that the Battenberg lied to him, lied deliberately and of set purpose to deceive. From his childhood the Emperor, like his sister the Duchess of Edinburgh, has had an almost physical horror of a lie. When he detects any of his Ministers in deceit, that man ceases to be Minister, and no ability or genius is allowed to atone for that one cardinal crime. When Prince Alexander, who had already excited prejudice against himself by placing Nihilists in office, was caught out in a lie, the Emperor would have no more to do with him. Over and over again Russians have told me how much they regretted this exceeding severity on the part of their Tzar. Why could he not make terms with Alexander when he grovelled at his feet? they ask, and then they say, with a sigh: "We would have done it at once, and it would have been a good thing for every one, but of course it was no use thinking of such a thing with our Emperor. When once a man has deceived him he never trusts him again." The fact is that the Emperor regards such conduct as Prince Alexander's as men in society regard cheating at cards, a kind of sin against the Holy Ghost, which, once committed, can never be forgiven or atoned for, either in this world or in that which is to come.

Apart, however, from this revolt at the duplicity of the Prince, the Emperor felt that his conduct in condoning the revolution of Philippopolis, which united Eastern Roumelia and Bulgaria, touched his honour. There is something almost Quixotic in the Emperor's sentiment of honour. He wished, like every Russian, to see Eastern Roumelia united to the Principality; but he had undertaken that there should be no alteration in the *status quo* in the Balkan. Suddenly the *status quo* is revolutionised in the direction of his wishes, and the revolution is approved by the Prince whom Russia placed on the throne. Instantly in Vienna and Pesth voices were heard accusing the Emperor of bad faith, of connivance in the insurrectionary movement. These accusations fell upon the Emperor like a sword-cut. If there is one thing more than any other to which he attaches supreme importance, it is the maintenance of an absolute truthfulness; if there is one point on which he is sensitive, it is a reflection upon his honour. Prince Alexander's conduct in accepting the union of the Bulgarias gave colour to the doubt cast upon his word and the suspicions of his good faith to his neighbours. That was decisive, and, to wipe off this reproach, the Emperor painfully set himself to oppose the very political consummation which he most desired, and broke irrevocably with the Prince whose conduct had exposed him to suspicion.

This action of Alexander the Third in opposing the union of the Bulgarians because to have approved of it would have implied acquiescence in a breach of faith is very characteristic of the just man who sweareth to his own hurt and changeth not. As he acted in this question, so he will act in others. He will sacrifice his interests to his honour, and oppose the realisation of a cherished object of Russian policy rather than consent to it at the price of a stain upon his fair fame as a man of honour and a gentleman. It is Quixotic if you please; but to the Emperor it is simple duty. He distrusts long views. He is dominated ever by the practical duty which lies ready to his hand. When any particular act seems to him clearly wrong he will not do it, be it never so convenient. The conscience of the Emperor, and his conviction that the future is in the hand of God, who will set him his task and show him His will from day to day, are factors of the first importance in estimating the future course of European politics.

The Emperor is eminently a healthy man. He is the *mens sana in corpore sano*. " He has a good head," I remarked to an Ambassador in St. Petersburg. "And what is of even more importance," was the reply, " he has got a good stomach." He is not nervous, and does not get into fidgets. All his habits are regular. In the morning he reads his letters and meets his Ministers—M. de Giers on Tuesday, Count Tolstoi on Thursday, M. Wischnegradsky on Friday. At one he lunches with his wife and children. Then at four or half-past, after transacting other business, he goes out for a stroll in the woods with his boys. Sometimes he fells trees, but, unlike Mr. Gladstone, he equally enjoys sawing them into lengths. In winter-time he helps in clearing away snow from the ice-hills. In the evening he dines. No one in all Russia leads a simpler, healthier, more natural life.

And this is the man whom our newspapers vie with each other in representing as if he were the embodiment of every vice but one! He is a level-headed, conscientious, sure-footed Sovereign, conscious of such responsibilities as he has realised, and only afraid of doing that which seems to him to be wrong. For the good relations of England and Russia, and for the peace of the world, it is simply of inestimable importance that a monarch so steady and self-possessed should be directing the policy of Russia. If only a hand as strong and a head as cool directed the policy of England, the *entente* between the two empires would no longer be a thing to wish for, it would be an accomplished fact.

# Book III.
## NEW FIELDS FOR BRITISH ENTERPRISE.

### CHAPTER I.
#### A TREATY OF COMMERCE WITH RUSSIA.

"Good relations between England and Russia?" said General Ignatieff to me one day; "there is nothing which I desire more heartily; and not only good relations political and diplomatic, but commercial and industrial. Why, for instance, should we not have a treaty of commerce with England, based on intelligible principles?" I pricked up my ears. "For the last ten years," he continued, "I have never ceased to advocate the alteration of our commercial treaties on a basis which would have tended directly to draw us closer to England." I said at once that I was naturally all attention, and that the great precedent of Cobden's commercial treaty with France illustrated the fact that nothing tended more to establish a good political *entente* than improved business relations. But what hope was there that with Russia anything of the kind was possible?

"Not only possible, but easy," he said, "provided that you once grasp the right principle, and that we are friends instead of foes. The wrong principle is that of the most-favoured-nation clause, which finds a place in all our commercial treaties, and which secures to every nation, regardless of its commercial policy in relation to us, the maximum advantages secured to the nation which from motives of policy or of trade we wish to favour most. As President of the Society of Trade and Commerce I have repeatedly protested against this. The right principle is the principle of discrimination, by which we should treat those nations well which treat us well, and *vice versâ*."

The idea which General Ignatieff thus let fall in the course of a long conversation seemed to me to promise to bear excellent fruit. I discussed it everywhere; I found that in the very highest quarters it was regarded with favour. The Minister of

Finance, M. Wischnegradsky, even discovered in General Ignatieff's suggestion an original idea of his own. M. Wischnegradsky is a very smart man, who somewhat resembles in appearance a mixture of Mr. Waddy and Mr. Bright. The Minister told me that his opinion was dead against the most-favoured-nation clause, as in his view every treaty ought to be specially drawn to suit the special circumstances of the trade of the negotiating country. He had been, he said, for some time engaged in conducting an exhaustive study of the whole question of the existing commercial treaties, and he expected that his Report would be ready in four or five months—that is to say, about the time when the Government Departments in St. Petersburg resume activity after their summer hibernation, to perpetrate a bull. When that Report was complete, a decision would be come to as to the direction in which action would be taken, and M. Wischnegradsky assured me most emphatically that he was entirely in favour of the idea of discrimination, and was most anxious to do everything in his power to promote the development of closer commercial relations between England and Russia.

I also met a very intelligent member of the Finance Administration. He said at once that the idea in theory was excellent, but the difficulties of its application were considerable. The whole question, he pointed out, was dominated by the political relations of the different Powers. "The adoption of General Ignatieff's policy might be possible, provided that we were friends with England; but not otherwise. For what would it practically come to if it were adopted? We should have to denounce all our existing treaties and begin, *de novo*, to construct a new commercial system, which would, broadly speaking, admit English goods into Russia at a lower rate of duty than that levied on imports from Germany. Now, I do not want to say anything hostile to anybody, but if you think that such a change would not be very keenly resented at Berlin you must have studied with very little advantage the history of the last fifteen years of German politico-commercial policy. To put it bluntly, it would put a strain on our relations with Germany, and that we cannot afford to do unless we are assured beforehand of a stable working *entente* with England. It would be very pleasant, no doubt; but it is well to be on with the new love before you are off with the old, and unless you can get your dear countrymen to adopt a less antagonistic policy to Russia I fear you may whistle for your commercial treaty."

Therein I think my friend spoke the simple truth. We are, by our insane and insensate indulgence in the cult of an archaic and obsolete prejudice, deliberately barring against ourselves the gates of what might be our best market in Europe. Said a foreign resident in Russia with whom I discussed the question, "You are perfectly right; the commercial question is dominated by the political. You in England have to choose whether you prefer to be doing good business with the Russian or to be perpetually sticking pins into his hide. You can do either one or the other; you cannot do both. The more I see of this country the more I am lost in amazement and indignation at the spectacle which it presents. With Siberia and the Caucasus it is almost as vast a mine of undeveloped wealth as the United States of America. It literally teems with all the raw material, the undeveloped potentialities, of wealth. Its population is barely sufficient to till the soil, but it can produce grain enough to feed all Europe. The country, however, has at present neither the men nor the money for the development of its enormous resources. England is bursting with capital seeking in vain for profitable employment, and every profession is overrun with men who might find ample opportunity for employing their energies in opening up Russia. The two empires supplement each other. Each has everything the other wants. But because of this cursed habit of snapping and snarling at each other's heels, this religious or irreligious cult of the devil of national prejudice and animosity, the relations between them dwindle, and they are gradually drifting into an attitude of increasing isolation. The Russian peasant cannot feed the London artisan, nor can the Sheffield cutlers sell their knives to the Russian peasant, because why? Because a set of God-forsaken wretches with pens in their hands in Petersburg and in London keep on day after day gibing at each other, maligning each other, and imputing all manner of evil against England or against Russia, until on each side it begins to be believed that their first duty to each other is not to exchange products for manufactures, and establish good relations based upon mutual interchange of surplus commodities, but to exchange insults and to prepare to interchange shots. If Jomini would hang all the editors in the interests of peace, I would offer them all up as a burnt offering upon the altar of Trade."

But, I have been asked, must there be a political *quid* for the commercial *quo?* What concession must we make to Russia politically in order to secure lower tariffs on British goods? I do not think that any idea of any such bargain has entered the Russian mind. Russia wants nothing, particularly from England; only friendship must be substituted for enmity, and a loyal desire to help each other take the place of a persistent and pertinacious policy of nagging and playing at cross purposes, which is the distinguishing note of our traditional policy in relation to Russia. We have taken so little by it. Our gain, to perpetrate another bull, has been all loss. Why, then, can we not re-consider our position? There is no country in the world, except the United States, where we could do a bigger business than with Russia. It would be mutually advantageous, and that which blocks the way is the demented determination which prevails in Downing Street to be more Austrian than Prince Bismarck himself. Our relations with Russia, thanks largely to the fact that we have the good fortune to have at Petersburg an Ambassador who has his head screwed straight on his shoulders, and who clearly sees the altered condition of European policy, have seldom been better. But not even the presence of Sir Robert Morier at the British Embassy can quite counterbalance Lord Salisbury's persistence in supporting a Bulgarian policy which is condemned by Prince Bismarck quite as much as by M. de Giers. If we would do to Russia in Bulgaria as we would that Russia should do to us in Egypt, a change would come over the relations of the two countries which would open the way for a modification of tariffs that might have the same happy results which followed the conclusion of the Anglo-French Treaty of Commerce in 1860.

The more I reflect upon what I heard and saw in Russia the more convinced I am of the immense opening there is for British manufactures in Russia. That great continent is almost undeveloped. At present it is practically stationary. It is one of those periods of hibernation which precede a sudden access of unusual activity. There is some reason to believe that the slumber stage is passing. Everywhere in Russia I heard, especially from English manufacturers and merchants, that this is a year that promises to be of unequalled prosperity. First and foremost, the harvest, especially in the south, is far above the average. Never in the memory of man has there been such a hay crop as that of this year in the southern provinces. And then wheat and rye and oats and barley promise to make the Russian's barns burst out with plenty. Prices are low, it is true, but food is plentiful, and the prospect of a bumper harvest is stimulating business all over the Empire. Everywhere, especially in the South, there is lamentation for want of roads, for want of coal, for want of machines to garner and to move the crops.

Up to May this year the exports of grain were double those of the first five months of 1887. The *Novoe Vremya* calculates that Russia may send abroad forty millions' worth of corn, as against twenty-one millions exported last year; and although this is an extreme estimate, it serves to indicate the expectations which prevail in Russia as to the nature of this year's harvest; and on the harvest everything depends in Russia. The Tzar's dominions are little more than one vast farm. The difference between a poor harvest and a rich one is the difference between comfort and poverty over three-fourths of Russia.

The prospect of the harvest has had a wonderful effect upon business of all kinds. Mills are running night and day, without being able to overtake their orders. A cotton manufacturer told me that he had orders to keep him going till Christmas, and that all his neighbours were in a like condition. Woollen mills are as busy as cotton, and iron works are enjoying a period of great prosperity.

Peace is now regarded as secure, and business of all kinds is expanding in consequence. One of the first results of this revival of business will be the demand for fresh railways. Russia in the matter of railway communication has practically retrograded in the present reign. She has not built on an average more than 300 miles of railway per annum since 1880. She had 14,073 in 1880; she had only 15,934 in 1885. Yet in these six years her population has increased seven millions. What a contrast this presents to the United States! Russia in Europe has two million square miles, with a population of forty-two to the square mile, and one mile of railway to every 5,000 persons. The United States, with a population of 50,000,000, an area of nearly three million square miles, has a mile of railway for every 400 inhabitants. The Americans have little more than half the population and eight times as many miles of railway. They had 92,971 miles open in 1880, and 123,320 in 1885. That is to say, the Americans added to their railway system in these six years twice the whole railway system of Russia!

The imports of rails have fallen off, and that of engines and machinery is not one-third of what it was. Partly this may be due to her protective tariff, which has fostered Russian iron and steel works; but if Russia were to waken up to any serious extent, and set about railway building on any large scale, she would have to buy abroad, and if we are wise we shall take care that the Russian orders come to the English firms. We can buy more of their grain than any other nation, and we can supply them more cheaply than any other with the manufactured articles which they require.

The foreign trade of Russia is comparatively small. A former Minister of Ways and Communications told me that he estimated her internal trade as fifty times as great as the external. Russia is in this respect like the United States. Both are worlds in themselves; the only difference being that the United States has free trade within its own boundaries, whereas Russia imposes a Customs duty on imports from Finland, which is an integral part of the Empire. Nothing would please Moscow manufacturers better than to see the Finnish precedent extended to Poland, and the possibility that such a result might follow the concession of Home Rule to Poland might create a sentiment on the part of the Muscovite manufacturers in favour of conceding some measure of autonomy to the ancient kingdom.

Of the foreign trade of Russia nearly one-third is done with England. It is almost hopeless attempting to reconcile the discrepancies between the official figures published in St. Petersburg and London, but both agree in showing that the exports to the United Kingdom amount to at least 30 per cent. of the total exports from Russia. The percentage of imports is not so high, but it amounts to 25 per cent. of the total. Germany is our only important rival. She sells more goods to Russia than we do, but she takes fewer Russian goods in exchange. The comparison of the figures of imports and exports into European Russia of the two countries brings out the fact that whereas Germany has exported to Russia on an average goods worth £20,000,000 per annum for the last ten years, the annual average of British imports into Russia was £12,500,000. The two countries account for £32,500,000 out of a total of 47 millions. Of exports from Russia England has taken an annual average of about £17,000,000, while Germany has only taken £16,500,000, making a total of £31,500,000 out of 53 millions total. The figures as given in our Statistical Abstract are as follows:—

| | TOTAL IMPORTS. | | |
|---|---|---|---|
| | From England. | From Germany. | To Russia in Europe. |
| 1877 | 9,281,000 | 14,847,000 | 29,146,000 |
| 1878 | 16,156,000 | 26,313,000 | 55,771,000 |
| 1879 | 14,629,000 | 26,686,000 | 54,821,000 |
| 1880 | 15,485,000 | 27,426,000 | 57,833,000 |
| 1881 | 10,844,000 | 21,990,000 | 47,613,000 |
| 1882 | 12,467,000 | 21,418,000 | 51,836,000 |
| 1883 | 13,359,000 | 16,866,000 | 51,370,000 |
| 1884 | 12,311,000 | 17,583,000 | 48,625,000 |
| 1885 | 9,459,000 | 14,391,000 | 38,140,000 |
| 1886 | 10,800,000 | 13,516,000 | 37,391,000 |
| Total for 10 years | 124,791,000 | 201,036,000 | £472,546,000 |
| Average | 12,479,100 | 20,103,600 | £47,254,600 |

| | TOTAL EXPORTS. | | |
|---|---|---|---|
| | To England. | To Germany. | From Russia in Europe. |
| 1877 | 14,845,000 | 19,613,000 | 50,828,000 |
| 1878 | 19,110,000 | 17,536,000 | 59,654,000 |
| 1879 | 18,436,000 | 18,665,000 | 60,641,000 |
| 1880 | 14,829,000 | 13,812,000 | 47,636,000 |
| 1881 | 15,579,000 | 14,881,000 | 48,136,000 |
| 1882 | 21,009,000 | 17,801,000 | 59,072,000 |
| 1883 | 21,012,000 | 18,884,000 | 60,778,000 |
| 1884 | 15,211,000 | 18,291,000 | 55,050,000 |
| 1885 | 15,399,000 | 14,225,000 | 49,794,000 |
| 1886 | 13,993,000 | 11,859,000 | 43,651,000 |
| Total for 10 years | 169,423,000 | 165,627,000 | £535,240,000 |
| Average per annum | 16,942,300 | 16,562,700 | £53,524,000 |

We are therefore Russia's best customer, and our trade is much more important to her than her trade is to us. Russia does not take more than 5 per cent. of our exports. We take over 30 per cent. of hers. We export to Russia 25 per cent. of the goods she receives from abroad. What she exports to us is not quite 6 per cent. of our total imports.

Here are some other statistics illustrating the same point:—

| | EXPORTS. | | |
|---|---|---|---|
| | To England. | To Germany. | Total Exports from Russia. |
| 1861 | 7,632,000 | 2,524,000 | £15,986,000 |
| 1871 | 17,177,000 | 7,491,000 | £35,275,000 |
| 1881 | 15,579,000 | 14,888,000 | £48,136,000 |
| 1887 | 18,234,000 | 15,170,000 | £56,851,000 |

| | IMPORTS. | | |
|---|---|---|---|
| | From England. | From Germany. | Total Imports. |
| 1861 | 4,773,000 | 3,790,000 | £14,275,000 |
| 1871 | 9,728,000 | 16,271,000 | £35,622,000 |
| 1881 | 10,844,000 | 21,990,000 | £49,903,000 |
| 1887 | 9,164,000 | 4,251,000 | £33,324,000 |

These figures, which were supplied to me by the Minister of Finance, are by no means satisfactory from the point of view of English trade. If exports from Russia to England had kept pace since 1861 with the total exports from Russia we should have taken 27 millions worth of Russian goods in 1887, instead of 18¼ millions, while the Germans would only have taken 9 millions instead of 15 millions. Germany has multiplied her purchase of Russian goods sixfold in 26 years: we have not multiplied ours threefold. If we turn to Russian imports from England the case is the same. We have not doubled our imports, which are actually lower than they were sixteen years ago. The Germans have multiplied their imports threefold. The only consolatory feature is that the exports to England were higher in 1887 than they were in 1881, and show an increase of nearly five millions sterling over the imports of 1886. The exports of 1888 will probably show an even greater increase. The increase of Russia's foreign trade cannot, however, be regarded as satisfactory. There was a leap upwards after the emancipation of the serfs; but after 1871 the rate of progress was not maintained, and in the present reign the volume of trade has dwindled. At the same time the population has increased, so that, while there are more potential customers for English manufactured goods by many millions, the quantity of goods actually sold to the Russians has not increased, but diminished.

In all these statistics allowance must be made for the fluctuations of the rouble. In 1871 the rouble was worth half as much again as it is now; but in the above statistics the rouble is taken as if it were never more nor less than two shillings.

I had a long and interesting conversation with M. Wischnegradsky in the Ministry of Finance on the subject. He professed himself to be very sanguine as to the development of Russian trade. He disclaimed most emphatically any idea that he was opposed to the widest possible influx of English capital. The jealousy of foreigners which is sometimes expressed in the papers he repudiated. The edict against the employment of Germans in the western provinces was, he remarked, solely a retaliatory measure consequent upon the expulsion of Russian subjects from Germany. No restriction had been placed upon the introduction of English skill or English capital or English labour. The English manufacturers and men of business whom I saw in St. Petersburg and Moscow unanimously agreed that there was no jealousy on the part of the people. They get on well with their workpeople; and the English-managed factories are models to the Russian.

The effect of the high tariff has been to induce foreigners to establish their works inside the Russian frontier, sometimes just within it, in order to enjoy the protection ensured to the Russian manufacturer in the Russian market. Germans and German Jews have chiefly profited by this arrangement, but as employers the Germans are by no means so popular as the English. They are, however, more enterprising and more on the alert. The Germans, for instance, have practically cut us out of the petroleum-carrying trade by their quicker perception that the old style of petroleum ship must give place to the tank steamer, and the French have forestalled us in raising the three millions capital required to construct the great pipe by which the oil that flows to waste on the shores of the Caspian will be conveyed to the ports of the Euxine. English managers earn substantial salaries in Russian mills, and if English capitalists were not so scared by the periodical alarms raised by interested parties, a much greater proportion of Russian business would pass into our hands.

The prevalent idea among many British merchants at home is that Russia is always either on the verge of a revolution or on the brink of a ruinous war. As a matter of fact she is neither. From time to time large British firms, finding themselves excluded from Russia by the tariff, have meditated seriously the establishment of branches inside the Russian tariff wall. Those that have done so have not had any reason to regret it. But most of those who have talked of it still hang back. There is a general distrust, a vague uneasiness, which, coupled with political antagonism, practically close Russia as a field of investment to English capital. The reputation of English goods stands high in Russia, and the English factories more than hold their own by the enterprise, the energy, and the intelligence by which they are directed. Of course they chafe a little at the Russian laws and Constitution, but on the whole, they are doing very well.

The Russian system cannot be regarded as calculated to encourage the development of their industrial resources. The principle that no one is to be allowed to do anything until he receives special permissson, which is the exact reverse of the English principle that every one is free to do everything that is not specially forbidden, leads to endless delays, and opens doors to all kinds of corruption. The delay that took place in issuing the concession to Spratt's Russian branch was enough to deter any but the most sanguine speculators; and if Russian wealth is ever to be adequately realised all these narrow and antiquated restrictions and limitations must disappear. It is not a hundred years ago since no one was allowed to build a mansion in any part of Russia until his plans had been passed by some office in St. Petersburg. Things are not so bad as that now, but a great deal has to be relaxed before the men who have got capital and intelligence can make the most of the illimitable resources of the Russian Empire.

## CHAPTER II.

### THE CASE FOR RECIPROCITY.

RUSSIA is a country with a high protective tariff. We raise it is true, £20,000,000 a year by import duties, against only six or seven millions levied in Russia; but her Customs revenue is equivalent to 16 per cent. *ad valorem* upon her total imports, while our Customs revenue is only 5½ per cent. upon our imports. Even when compared with protectionist France and protectionist Germany, the Russian *ad valorem* rate is high. The proportion of Customs revenue to imports in France is about 6½ per cent. In Germany not quite so much. There is therefore a deal of room for improvement without even remotely approaching a policy of absolute free trade.

Although England levies £20,000,000 per annum at her Custom-houses, none of this falls upon Russian goods. We do not even impose a *metage* duty upon the wheat, the oats, the linseed, the tallow, and the timber, which we receive from Russia. Russia, on the other hand, taxes our imports unmercifully, and the tendency during the present reign has been to raise rather than to reduce the import duties.

If Russian statesmen contemplate the adoption of a policy of reciprocity with differential duties discriminating between those nations which treat Russia well and those which impose obstacles to her goods, she has plenty of shots in her locker in the shape of duties which she can reduce. England, on the other hand, has none. We have abolished all the taxes we used to levy on Russian goods, and we can do no more. At present Russia does not discriminate between nations which favour her with open ports and those which oppose to her exports the hostile wall of a protectionist tariff. This she is bound to do owing to the most favoured nation clause in her commercial treaties, which secures trade for all the Powers with which she has treaties the best terms which she concedes to any one of their number. Hence she is tied, while other nations are free, and she can only strike at her enemies in a war of tariffs by striking at her friends at the same time. This is especially brought home to the Russian mind by the fiscal policy of Germany.

The staple product of Russia is grain. Out of a total export valued at from 43 to 60 millions sterling, the value of the grain export has varied from 21 millions to 36 millions sterling. It is with wheat and rye and oats and barley that the Russian pays his bills abroad, and it is duties upon these cereals which chiefly disturb his equanimity. From this point of view the policy of England is all that could be desired. Grain from Russia is admitted as freely into our ports as grain from India, Australia, and Canada. We have adopted free trade in grain for forty years and more, and even the shilling registration duty has been abandoned long ago. Germany, however, has taken the other road. Prince Bismarck has shown himself no friend of the Russian farmer. Pressed by the Conservative squires of Prussia to protect their staple product, he has clapped heavy duties upon Russian corn, raising the import duty nearly five-fold in six years. Germany, therefore, has shown Russian commerce no mercy. Even now she is not content. The German Junkers are clamouring for more protection, and when I was in Russia the arrival of some waggons of Russian grain on the Russian frontier led the German press to threaten a still further increase of duties on Russian grain. As we do not export grain to Germany, we are not affected by the increase in the German tariff. But it hits Russia hard, and it is not surprising that there should be a widespread feeling in favour of discriminating between the imports from England and from Germany. In a war of tariffs such as that which Russia wages with Germany, Russia needs a free hand. It is impossible for her to make the most of her position when she is compelled by her treaties to treat friend and foe with absolute impartiality.

It may be argued that it is impossible that Russia would ever find it politically sound policy to strain her relations with Germany merely to confer advantages on English traders, for not even the most extravagantly optimist believer in the possibility of an *entente* between England and Russia could hope to see that *entente* so deeply rooted as to make it worth Russia's while for our sake to alienate her German ally. To this the answer is that, while Russia will not make any advances towards us if we are hostile or Austrian—for the two words are synonymous, she will be very glad to deal with us as friends, even if Germany should object. Germany, even when professing the greatest friendship for Russia, has repeatedly hampered Russian commerce, injured Russian credit, and depreciated the Russian rouble. Professor Martens, in his interesting preface to the last published volume of the Collection of Russian Treaties, points out that when the Emperor Nicholas and the King of Prussia were vowing eternal friendship, and were united in the closest alliance, the Court of Berlin constantly displayed the greatest hostility to the development of Russian commerce. "What can the West think," asked Nicholas once, " of the close alliance of the Conservative Powers, when it sees us at open war in the region of our commercial interests?" The precedent may be invoked at St. Petersburg when it is necessary to reply to a threatened increase of the German tariff by the imposition of an extra ten per cent. on all goods entering Russia from the German frontier.

Germany is in alliance with Austria, but the two Powers do not find their political relations impaired by sharp commercial rivalry. Nay, Austria and Hungary, although under one Crown, like Finland and Russia, find Imperial unity not incompatible with fiscal quarrels, and Russia may find her German neighbour all the more reasonable because she can play off the Saxon against the Teuton in the field of commercial competition.

The precise mode in which Russia will find it best to discriminate in favour of the Powers which treat her well is a point for experts to settle. But a reduction of from 10 to 20 per cent. on all goods imported from a country which admits Russian goods free of duty would be a step in the right direction, and would give the English manufacturer a considerable advantage over his German rival. There is one consideration that must never be forgotten : Russian stock is held largely in Germany. The interest on that stock is largely paid for with Russian grain. Of Russian bonds, the amount held in Germany has been much reduced in the last two years. I was told when at the Ministry of Finance that the total held in German hands was now not more than £43,000,000.

In the last twelve months £10,000,000 has been transferred to France and Holland, and some £30,000,000 had returned to Russia. But if England did a larger trade with Russia than she does, Russian stock would pass into English hands, and Russian dependence upon the Berlin Bourse would disappear. In any case we need not disturb ourselves about the distribution of Russian bonds. That will readjust itself easily enough without our care.

The attitude of the Russian Government to Germany in fiscal matters is very simple, and very straightforward. It was laid down to me with great clearness by a Russian Minister:— "We have no prejudice against Germany. Quite the contrary. We admire German culture, and we admit without hesitation that Germany has done a great deal for us Russians, chiefly in the way of education and discipline. But that is no reason why, out of sheer gratitude, we should allow Germany to monopolise advantages which Russia might share. Germany is needful to Russia, and helpful. But the relations between the two countries in commerce, as in politics, must not be unilateral. At present Germany is absorbing our foreign trade. Everything reaches us through Germany. Even oranges, not one of which can grow on German soil, come to us from Hamburg. Germany is flooding us with cheap and nasty manufactures. In Siberia bad German knives marked as English are ousting all others from our markets. That is not what we wish. We wish to develop our commerce with England. It would be all for our interest to do so. Why not?"

Why not, indeed?

When I was in St. Petersburg General Annenkoff remarked to me that no two countries had more need of each other than England and Russia, or less risk of rivalry in the commercial world. It is different with Germany; over and over again I was told during my stay in St. Petersburg that the new development of German competition would sooner or later compel England to open her eyes to the fact that the German, instead of being her staunchest ally, is now her most formidable competitor. "In the last dozen years," said General Ignatieff, "Germany has taken a new departure. You have no longer to do with the old Germany, which was largely agricultural, free-trading, and pacific. You are face to face with a new Germany, militant, aggressive, and colonising, which confronts you in every market in Europe, in every continent in the old world and the new, and which is undermining your industrial and commercial supremacy. Germany aspires to be a great colonial and a great commercial Power. If she succeeds it will be at the expense of England. You will wake up too late to discover the truth of what I tell you." There is truth in what the Russians say. Russia can never compete with us in the foreign market. Russian colonisation can never threaten our colonial empire. Russia has got enough land of her own for an infinite expansion. Germany has not. Russia besides is, after all, a mass of 120 millions of human beings, each one of whom is capable of consuming British manufactured goods, whereas Germany has welded its forty millions of Germans into a gigantic entity, which is directed in everything, both as to the goods it buys from abroad and the business it does with its neighbours, by the all-pervading activity of Prince Bismarck.

Englishmen who do not travel or who do not trade abroad have no idea of the strenuous fashion in which Prince Bismarck uses the power and the prestige of the German Empire to push the interests of all the Germans and German Jews who sell corn brandy, potato spirit, or shoddy cloth, to the non-German-speaking world. In the Balkans every Austrian and every German Consul and Vice-Consul, I was told, is little better than a bagman for the Austrian and German firms, who are driving English trade out of the Principalities. But it is not only Consuls and Vice-Consuls who act as commercial travellers for German speculators. German Ministers, German Ambassadors, strain their influence to browbeat or to corrupt the Governments to which they are accredited to induce them to place their orders with German rather than with English firms. To Englishmen this prostitution of diplomacy to the mere cadging after orders is very disreputable. Prince Bismarck does not see things in that light. If he can get a big order for Krupp by a judicious distribution of decorations among expectant ministerial underlings, or if he can oblige a group of financiers from Berlin or Frankfort by bringing pressure to bear upon the Chinese Government for the concession of a loan, it seems to him quite right and proper. His finger is in everything. He nobbles newspapers, pushes rivals out of the field in business, and rigs the market. No one imputes to Prince Bismarck for a moment any personally interested motive in all this. It is not for himself, but for his country, for the greater honour and glory

K

and profit of Germany, that this is done. We have no right to throw stones, although we are nowadays so virtuous. The Power which made the opium war, and which has opened so many markets at the cannon's mouth, has no right to play the Pharisee in reproving Prince Bismarck. All that I wish to insist upon is that whereas we have ceased to do that kind of thing, the Germans have just taken it up, and are carrying it out with characteristic thoroughness wherever they get an opportunity.

There is not a British Consul in any part of the world who will not tell you that it is the German who is our most formidable competitor. There are more German commercial travellers on the road in Finland than British tourists, and there is not a village in the Transvaal where you will not come across the trail of the ubiquitous Teuton bagman. They go wherever we go, and then, if they can, they shut us out wherever they have got the upper-hand. They crushed our mission stations in the Cameroons, and snapped up Northern New Guinea under our very noses. Their newspapers indignantly protest against any attempt on our part at self-defence. Poor little Servia affords a melancholy illustration of the extent to which a commercial policy of this uncompromising kind can be used to crush the independence of a State. It is rather odd, but it is by no means incredible, that the cruelty to which the unfortunate Queen Nathalie has been subjected might in all probability have been averted if the Servians had but established many years ago a great ham and bacon factory at Belgrade. The connection between pork-butchering and a Royal divorce is much closer than appears at first sight. Servia economically depends for its existence upon the export of its pigs. These pigs find their chief market in Austria-Hungary, and whenever the Belgrade politicians do not dance to the piping of Vienna the statesmen of the Empire-Kingdom discover that the Servian pigs suffer from some infectious or contagious disease which necessitates the immediate prohibition of their importation. The Servian, shut up with his swine, is starved into obedience, and thus King Milan is compelled to recognise Francis Joseph as his swineherd, for Servia is economically at the mercy of Austria. Against the slavish acceptance of the dependent position, Queen Nathalie, as a Russian, naturally revolted. *Hinc illæ lachrymæ*, none of which need have flowed if a factory had existed which would have enabled the Servians to export their pigs in a shape to which even Austrian susceptibility could take no objection.

The art of making your right hand serve your left is carried to great lengths in Germany. An Austrian officer bitterly complained that all the sensational alarms of the concentration of Russian troops on the frontier were got up in the Berlin War Office in order to facilitate certain transactions on the Berlin Bourse. The result of these manœuvres he said, bitterly, "is that Austrian securities are depressed far below their real value. The Germans buy them up at their lowest, and when they have made their purchases, then Prince Bismarck reassures every one. Europe breathes freely, Austrian stock goes up with a bound, and the German Jews make their fortunes." This is exaggerated, no doubt, but it is idle to pretend that Prince Bismarck, who neglects no means of power, ignores the Stock Exchange in the preparation of the psychological moment. A judicious depreciation of certain stocks is as useful as the organised *claque* of the Reptile Press, and he has ways and means of rigging the market beyond those enjoyed by any other mortal. He can veto loans, create a panic, and "bull" and "bear" to an extent impossible to any other mortal, even to the Rothschilds themselves. It is the same principle that he applies to journalism applied to finance. The State as an entity interferes in everything, influences everything, controls everything. We have not to contend merely with the German trader. We have to reckon everywhere with the German trader *plus* Bismarck. That is to say, we have to do with a keen, intelligent, pushing, hardy, parsimonious rival who has the German Empire behind him to push him through every door which we open, and to double-lock behind him every door which he opens himself.

## CHAPTER III.

#### THE CENTRAL ASIAN RAILWAY.

I HAD expected to meet General Annenkoff at the terminus of the Central Asian Railway, which he had just constructed to Samarcand. Business to which even a rendezvous in the heart of Central Asia must yield, detained me in St. Petersburg. It was therefore not in Central Asia, but on the Neva, in his own house on the quay, that I had the pleasure of meeting the most famous railway engineer of Europe. General Annenkoff had just returned from the ceremony which marked the completion of his latest enterprise, and his room was littered with carpets, silks, and other trophies from Central Asia. It is a large, pleasant room, approached by a staircase of white marble, and looking out upon the Neva, that magnificent stream which is at once the glory and the soul of St. Petersburg. The most conspicuous objects in the spacious apartment were two large-size portraits in oil of his wife and her sister, singularly beautiful ladies, admirably painted. The workroom was strewn with files of Russian, French, and German periodicals. The *Graphic* was the only English publication that caught my eye.

General Annenkoff is very like Lord Wolseley in size, age, and personal appearance. He speaks English very well, interlarding it now and then with French. He wore his general's uniform, spurs included, which must be a bore to an active engineer. All the gendarmes who do duty as police at the railway stations wear spurs in Russia, an arrangement that was probably devised as a melancholy satire upon the speed (!) of the Russian railways, while, oddly enough, the Cossacks wear no spurs. General Annenkoff is a man of energy and decision, a kind of Napoleon of railway making. There are not many men of his initial velocity in the world, and in Russia there are hardly any. General Ignatieff is in politics what General Annenkoff is in engineering.

"So you opened your railway on the right day," said I, "notwithstanding the rain, which was said to have washed away part of the line?"

"When I fix a day," said General Annenkoff, "for opening a line, it is opened on that day, come rain or storm. But all these stories of the damage to the line were untrue. They are not unnatural, for they emanate from those who, having declared the line could never be made for the money, endeavour to save their own reputation by destroying that of the railway. I made the railway for half the sum estimated as indispensable. My estimate for the Siberian Railway also is just half other people's figure. They say sixty million roubles. I have fixed the price at thirty millions. The difference of thirty millions is quite sufficient to account for the circulation of many reports detrimental to the railway made fifty per cent. under the other estimate."

"Then you are satisfied with your line?"

"Perfectly: it was made cheaply, but well. Labour is very cheap in those regions. And what workmen they are! No initiative, it is true, but admirable imitators. Show them anything you like, set them to do it, and they will reproduce everything to a marvel. Skilled workmen who in Russia could earn two roubles a day there are content with thirty copecks, the cost of living is so cheap. I rented a palace in Samarcand for my family at thirty-five roubles a month."

"What about the Anglo-Russian Junction Railway?"

"Oh, that depends upon you, and the construction of a line through Candahar. We could make a branch from Merv to Herat without difficulty, if you would run your railway on from Pishin to Candahar to meet our line in Herat. If that were done I would undertake to deliver your reliefs, officers, and men, for India at Candahar in nine days after leaving London. Not at present, of course. There are links in the line of railway communication to be completed, and, what is still more important, the speed on the Russian railways needs to be increased. But if we bring it up to forty-five versts, or thirty miles an hour—the German average—and that which the express already attains on the Petersburg-Moscow Railway, I could deliver your troops in Candahar in nine days from London."

I mildly suggested that the Russian railways would take a good deal of stirring up before they could realise an average of thirty miles an hour. General Annenkoff replied—

"My railways always do fifty versts, or thirty-three miles an hour; but I am not slow. I cannot tolerate the sluggish rate of our trains. The Russians, I regret to say, are slow. They have not yet learned that time is money. In Asia they are still further behind. When a chief says gallop he seldom goes faster than a slow trot. In Bokhara I led them a pretty dance. Wherever I go I quicken the pace."

I said I feared that the cost of transit would render the relief of the British garrison in India viâ St. Petersburg too expensive a luxury save in war time, when it might be impossible.

"Oh," said he, "in that case your route would be the Canadian Pacific or the Cape, not viâ Suez. But why should there be war? I am the best friend that England has, I assure you. Our interests in Central Asia are exactly the same, and the more business there is done the better. There is no opposition of interests between us. For we are so different."

"But," said General Annenkoff to me with emphasis, "we must partition Afghanistan. Of that there is no doubt. I had Captain Yate and Mr. Peacock staying with me at Tchardjui for some days, and we discussed the question thoroughly. We all came to the same conclusion. There is no other way out of it. You must take one part and we will take the other, by amicable arrangement, of course; a quarrel is out of the question."

"No, thanks," said I; "personally I have no objection if you take the whole, but I object very much to take any for ourselves. At London they object equally to allow you to take it or to take it themselves."

"But why not?"

"Because we have been twice in Afghanistan, and each time we were glad to get out. We have no wish to go a third time. Once bit twice shy; we have been twice bit."

"But that is all nonsense. You will have to go, whether you like it or not. And why not? You are already in Beloochistan; it is all the same. You have your railway at Quetta. You push it on to Pishin. You will soon have to make it run to Candahar. It is all simple and easy. Then from Candahar to the Russian frontier there will be only two stages. I can make the branch to Herat from Merv. You will join us there with your line coming from Candahar, and the thing is done. And when the railway is made there will be no more quarrels between England and Russia in Central Asia."

"Russia," said I, "has many railway junctions with Austrian railways, but the junctions do not preclude differences between Vienna and St. Petersburg."

"Because between Austria and Russia there are the questions of the Balkan outstanding to divide the Governments; but what is there in Asia between England and Russia? Nothing. There are no questions left when once the railway is made. That abolishes the only difficulties; those of a frontier defended by Asiatics, not by Europeans. Believe me, the railway is the tie that will link the two empires in friendship."

"For you it would be convenient; but for us I do not see the advantage."

General Annenkoff continued briskly: "It will come, it will come. Why object to our making the line to Herat? It is quite simple, and you will come and join us there. See," said he, handing me several photographs of the works in progress along the Pishin-Sibi line, "these were taken on the spot by my friend, a Russian, who is there examining the progress you are making."

"With the knowledge of our authorities?"

"Certainly. Why not? When we were on the Tedjent—that is the same river which at Herat is called the Heri Rud—Captain Yate, Mr. Peacock, and I dined with the Colonel in command of the Russian garrison there. We found him a most intelligent man; a soldier, every inch of him, and in full command of his men. Who do you think he was? It was the Turkoman chief who commanded the Tekkes against Skobeleff at Geok-Tepe. There he was, as Russian as myself, and a Colonel in command of a regiment of Russians. There is no man more loyal to us in all Asia."

"But he was only nominally in command. Had he not a Russian adjoint?"

"Certainly, he had an adjoint; but he was so completely in command of purely Russian soldiers that the other day he placed his adjoint under arrest and sent him off to headquarters. Captain Yate was immensely impressed with this. All the time you have been in India you dare not trust your native officers with such a command as we give to this Tekke chief within a year or two after he was in arms against us. Colonel Alikhanoff also, he was a Daghestani. Believe me, we are able to make these people serve us, and can trust them more than you seem to be able to trust your natives. So, at least, your officers tell me."

I admitted the justice of the claim. Tommy Atkins would not like to be led into battle by a Malay or a Goorkha. And as for allowing " a d—d nigger " to arrest an English Colonel—imagine the wrath of the Horse Guards!

I asked General Annenkoff if he was going to make the Siberian Railway.

"Oh," said he, "that is as yet only a project. But remember, Lord Hartington called me a foolish fellow in 1881 because I advocated the construction of the railway across Afghanistan. That railway has already gone further than Merv: it stretches to Bokhara and Samarcand. The other will come true still, despite Lord Hartington and his sneers at 'foolish persons.'"

General Annenkoff is a man of mark, a man of energy. He has evidently made up his mind that Russia will be asked to make the railway to Herat, a fact which logically will carry with it her ascendency in Afghan Turkestan.

The opening of the Central Asian Railway took place on Sunday, May 27th, or, as the Russian calendar has it, on May 15th. It is a great feat, of which the Russians have good reason to be proud, whether regarded from the point of view of the statesman or the engineer. It seems but the other day that the tract of territory through which the railway passes was haunted by as fierce and intractable a set of man-stealers and murderers as ever plagued the world. For centuries the borderland between Persia and Turkestan had been the unhappy hunting ground of wild tribes whose occupation was rapine, and who swept off the victims of their forays to be sold like cattle in the great slave mart of Merv. Even so recently as

1881, when Mr. Gladstone was imprisoning Mr. Parnell, and Mr. Forster was wrestling with the Land League, the Russians found their way barred from the Caspian to Samarcand by the famous fortress of Geok-Tepe, round which the Tekke Turcomans rallied for their last stand against the troops of the Great White Tzar. To-day the trains come and go with almost as much regularity between Geok-Tepe and Merv, and proceed from Merv to Samarcand, as between Wimbledon and Waterloo, and the through train for Bokhara starts from the Caspian with as little to-do as the Scotch express leaves Euston for Edinburgh. For a thousand miles right into the heart of the mysterious Central Asian regions the Russian military engineer has thrust his wonder-working parallel rails; and it is possible at this moment to reach the tomb of Tamerlane, in the heart of Southern Tartary, nine days after leaving St. Petersburg.

Every facility was offered me to visit Samarcand, including free transit over the whole of the Central Asian line. The Foreign Office and the War Department vied with each other in the courtesy with which they offered to remove every obstacle in my way, but unfortunately circumstances prevented my accepting the hospitality of the Governor-General of Turkestan. From St. Petersburg to Samarcand the traveller has a choice of routes. If he wishes to travel comfortably and leisurely, he goes from Moscow to Saratoff, on the Volga, and floats rapidly down that great stream in one of the river steamers to Astrakhan, from whence he takes the boat to Krasnovodsk or Ossoun Ada, on the Asiatic shore of the Caspian. As the railway was to be opened on the 27th May, and I could not possibly leave before the 17th, the longer and pleasanter route by the Volga was out of the question. I had therefore planned out the following itinerary, which may be useful to those who may wish to take the overland route to the Afghan frontier, and visit Penj-deh or Herat *viâ* St. Petersburg. From London to St. Petersburg, even before the summer acceleration of service between the Russian capital and the German frontier has taken place, can be easily performed in three days. Leaving the London train on its arrival at six, you have time to dine before you leave by the courier express, which starts for Moscow at half-past eight. Suppose that you left London on Friday night, the 11th of May; on Monday evening you arrive at St. Petersburg. The following will be your dates:—

| | | |
|---|---|---|
| Monday night, | May 14, 8.30 P.M., leave St. Petersburg for Moscow. | |
| Tuesday morning, | ,, 15, 12.0 noon, leave Moscow for Riazan. | |
| Tuesday evening, | ,, 15, 7.0 P.M,, leave Riazan for Kozloff. | |
| Wednesday morning, | ,, 16, 4.0 A.M., leave Kozloff for Rostoff. | |
| Thursday morning, | ,, 17, 12.0 noon, leave Rostoff for Vladikavkas. | |
| Friday morning, | ,, 18, 4.30 P.M., arrive at Vladikavkas. | |

At Vladikavkas your further progress by rail is barred by the Caucasus, across which the engineer has not yet carried the train. Between you and the nearest station on the other side of the great range of mountains stretches a distance of about 150 miles, which you cross by a post road in eighteen hours. It is a magnificent road through the mountains, climbing over a pass 8,000 feet high—2,000 feet higher than the St. Gothard and the Simplon—and then descending by a slope more ghastly than any down which you drive in Switzerland. You would leave Vladikavkas about six at night, and driving all night post, you would arrive at Tiflis at noon on Saturday. From Tiflis you would take the train to Baku, where you would arrive on Sunday afternoon, the 20th inst., at four o'clock. From Baku a steamer leaves for Ossoun Ada, crossing the Caspian in twelve hours.* At Ossoun Ada, which you would reach on Monday morning, the 21st inst., you could take the train for Samarcand. The distance is slightly under 1,000 miles, and you cover it in two days. You would thus be able to reach Samarcand on Wednesday morning, May 23rd —supposing, of course, that you missed no connections and were able to keep your time—twelve days from London to Samarcand, *viâ* Russia, that may be regarded as being attained. To reach Samarcand *viâ* India would take almost as many weeks, if, indeed, it could be accomplished at all, for the Afghans are grim warders of the roadway, and from Pishin to Penj-deh is not a tract of country easily traversed by the European.

The cost of this journey is about as follows for travelling

---

* Since I left Russia it has been decided that Krasnovodsk is a better terminus than Ossoun Ada.

expenses only, not reckoning food and other charges, and reckoning the rouble at 2s. :—

| | | |
|---|---|---:|
| Fare from London to St. Petersburg | | £17 |
| „ „ St. Petersburg to Vladikavkas | | 9 |
| „ Mail cart across the Caucasus | | 2 |
| „ Tiflis to Baku | | 3 |
| „ Steamer from Baku to Ossoun Ada | | 1 |
| | | £32 |

Fare to Samarcand from the Caspian at present I do not know.

Fifteen years ago M. de Lesseps wrote to General Ignatieff calling attention to the necessity under which civilisation lay of uniting Europe and Asia by rail. By his Suez Canal he had united the Mediterranean and the Red Sea; by the Panama Canal he proposed to make a water-way between the Atlantic and the Pacific; but, as not even M. de Lesseps could propose to make a canal across Afghanistan, he suggested to General Ignatieff the advisability of doing the work by a railway. Mr. Gladstone was then in office in England, and Mr. Gladstone disapproved of the project. Mr. Gladstone has since repented him in sackcloth and ashes of his refusal to countenance the Russo-Indian-Afghan Grand Trunk Line, and so acute is his remorse that it even drives him to the form of self-reproach which for him is before all others the most humiliating—namely, the reflection that if the proposal had been made to Lord Beaconsfield it would probably have met a different fate. The Russian Government, however, in those days thought as little of the scheme as did Mr. Gladstone. A special Ministerial Council was called to consider the scheme, and the project was condemned. M. de Lesseps' idea was that Russia should make a railway from Orenberg to Samarcand, while England should construct the line from Peshawur to Samarcand. The course of events has not justified the wisdom of the great French projector. In 1873 he pointed out that the route from Calais to Calcutta overland was 7,370 miles long. From Calais it was possible to travel by rail to Orenberg, and from Calcutta to Peshawur, so that 5,100 miles were covered. A gap of 2,270 miles remained, of which 1,470 miles lay in Turkestan and 800 in Afghanistan. Since then the railway has grown apace, but not along the line suggested by M. de Lesseps—not through

Peshawur and the Khyber Pass, but through the Bolan to Quetta and on to Pishin. The Indian railway stretches now into Afghanistan, while the Russian railway to Samarcand started, not from Orenberg, but from Ossoun Ada on the shores of the Caspian. Between the two termini of the railway systems which start at Calais and Calcutta there is now but a gap of 600 miles.

The Russians have done their share, and the new railway brings them into direct communication with the northern frontiers of Afghanistan. I had an opportunity of talking the matter over with Mr. Mestcherin, the engineer who has superintended from St. Petersburg the construction of the new line.

"It is quite simple," said Mr. Mestcherin, "quite simple. The line is made for a thousand miles. All is peaceful, and, what is not less important, it already pays its working expenses."

"But," said I, "the line was not originally projected as a commercial enterprise?"

"By no means," said Mr. Mestcherin; "it was *ab initio* a war railway. It has been constructed by the military department. The actual work of laying the rails was performed by soldiers, in order that soldiers might use the line."

"When was it begun?"

"It was first projected by General Annenkoff after the opening of the campaign against the Akhal Tekkes in 1877. It was begun in 1881, in order to facilitate the operations conducted by General Skobeleff for the reduction of the Tekkes in 1881. Originally it was only intended to carry it as far as Kizil Arvat, the first Tekke fort captured by the Russians, which is distant 217 versts, or nearly 150 miles, from the Caspian."

"What led you to decide to carry it further east?"

"The threatened war on the Murghab in 1885, which you call the Penj-deh dispute. When it seemed as if the differences about the boundary of Afghanistan would result in war, the order was given to carry the line eastward to Samarcand. This was April, 1885."

It was the old story of civilisation getting a lift on the powder cart. Because the Afghans seized Penj-deh and were brushed out of it roughly by Colonel Komaroff, it is now possible to travel for a thousand miles in a first-class railway carriage into the heart of Central Asia, and to make the pilgrimage by rail to the tomb of Tamerlane. The Central Asian Railway seems to be the one solid, useful fruit that resulted from that idiotic dispute. But it seemed strange to me that a railway so extended could be constructed so rapidly through a country so recently subdued, with apparently so little peril from the fierce marauders of whose utter subjugation it was the outward and visible sign. So I asked Mr. Mestcherin whether they had not had great difficulty in preventing the Tekkes from destroying the line as fast as it was made.

"Destroying the line!" said he. "Certainly not. Why, it was they who made it. The whole of the earthwork, &c.—everything, in short, that could be done by unskilled labour—was done by the Tekkes and the Persians. They were delighted at the opportunity the line afforded them of earning regular wages, and we have never had the slightest trouble with them."

"How many were employed in the construction of the line?"

"The technical work was done by two battalions—railway battalions—of our soldiers, or say 1,000 men, trained in the art of railway-making. The labourers numbered 5,000. They were almost exclusively natives of the country through which the railway passes. Instead of fighting against us and making slaves of their neighbours, they have worked cheerfully for very small wages in making the line. It would have been difficult to have constructed it at all without their help. The heat in those parts is something terrible, touching 58 degrees Réaumur, which is about 160 degrees Fahrenheit. Not only are the natives better accustomed to the climate, but their labour is very cheap."

"About what price?"

"When the railway was begun the wage for a native labourer averaged 15 cop., or say 3d., a day. Now the demand for labour has doubled the daily wages of the Tekkes. Sixpence a day is now the minimum, with a tendency to rise to 7d."

"Were there any serious engineering difficulties?"

"Next to none. To begin with, we have an admirable landlocked bay in which, no matter how stormy the weather, we can disembark passengers and merchandise with ease and safety. Then the gradients are very easy. The steepest ascent is 1 in 125. We have very few cuttings or tunnels. The line runs for the most part over level steppe. We had to bridge three rivers, the Murghab at Merv, the Tedjent, and the Amou Daria. We have one bridge a mile and a quarter long, which we put up in 103 days. It is of wood. They are all of wood, of the same construction as the bridges across the Neva."

"But had you not great difficulties with the sands? I have heard that some eminent authorities maintain that the desert winds will destroy your permanent way or overwhelm it with shifting sand."

"It was feared at one time that such would be the case. The line on approaching Merv passes for 200 miles across a sandy plain, and as the sleepers are laid on nothing but sand thrown up from the desert, there was danger that the wind would carry it away. This, however, was prevented very simply, by remembering the truth that it is the first step which costs."

"How?"

"If," said he, "the line were left as if it were an ordinary earthwork, as soon as the wind began to blow, it would eat into the corners of the embankment, on whichever side the wind was blowing, spreading the sand over the steppe, until the railway would be destroyed. For the sand will not bind."

"Well, how did you manage to prevent this?"

"Very simply. All that is necessary to do is to keep the wind from taking the first bite, so to say, of the sand-work. That is to say, if we can but put a solid edge on the shoulder of the embankment the thing is done. We made many experiments, and at last discovered that by erecting a little seven-inch rampart of clay, on the edge of each shoulder of the permanent way, we could effectually prevent its denudation under the wind. Hence we secured the safety of the embankment simply enough. Seven inches of clay is too tough a plating for the wind to eat through, and beneath the armoured edge the whole embankment is secure."

"How is the line constructed?"

"Very well, and very simply. We have not metalled the permanent way; the sleepers are merely laid in the sand or earth, with the exception of a short stretch in which the sleepers rest on 12-inch cubes of asphalte, for the making of which there is plenty of bitumen. The sleepers are of wood; the rails of steel, manufactured partly in the Puhloff Works, St. Petersburg, and partly in the south of Russia by the Siemens-Martin process. The south Russian rails are supplied by the new Russian company, of which an Englishman, Mr. Hughes, of Millwall, is chairman. The stone for the construction of the stations and other necessary masonry was found along the line. A very good sandstone is met with near Kizil Arvat."

"Has it been an expensive line?"

"One of the cheapest we have ever made. It costs us, without rolling stock and rails, which are supplied by the Government, 19,000 roubles a verst, or £2,850 per mile, as against an average of 22,000 to 35,000 roubles per verst in Russia. If you add the cost of the rolling stock and the rails you have an average of 35,000 roubles per verst in Central Asia, as against from 38,000 to 51,000 roubles per verst in Russia."

"What rolling stock is there on the Transcaspian?"

"About 90 locomotives, 1,200 waggons, and 600 open cars. Of passenger carriages there are not many, only sufficient to keep going a train daily each way. The locomotives all consume petroleum, of which there is a small supply on the line, but which abounds in inexhaustible quantities at Baku. You have not adequately appreciated the enormous saving that petroleum effects as compared with coal. It takes, roughly speaking, 50,000 tons of petroleum to work our traffic on the Transcaspian. The efficiency of oil is double that of coal. That is to say, we can generate twice as much steam per pood by petroleum as by coal. But that is by no means the only difference. A pood of petroleum costs 9 copecks; a pood of coal from the Donetz basin, 40 copecks. Thus, you see, we work our traffic in Central Asia at a cost of £27,000 for fuel in oil. If we had to use coal, it would cost us—how much do you think? Just £240,000. The fuel that is twice as efficient is, weight for weight, more than four times as cheap."

"What kind of traffic do you expect to carry?"

"The traffic that we are carrying now. From Asia we bring to Russia cotton, wool, silk, fruits, and furs. To Asia we carry manufactures of all kinds. The value of the stuffs moved each way is about the same. In 1886 we estimated it at 15,000,000 roubles cash—that is to say, a total movement of £3,000,000 sterling. The majority of these goods being light, they bear a comparatively heavy freight. The receipts already balance the working expenses."

"Do you intend to carry the line on to Tashkend?"

"No; the engineering difficulties are greater than the commercial and political advantages that such a line would secure."

"Then you don't intend to run a branch to Herat?"

"Certainly not; it would not pay. Herat is a long way off our main line. If you choose to make a line through Afghanistan, that is another matter. At present the nearest point at which we touch Afghanistan is not by rail, but by river. The railway crosses the Amou Daria at Tchardjui. From that point we have steamers which ply southward as far as Kilif, in the direction of Afghanistan. Northward they go with the stream as far as the Aral Sea. These steamers are 22 feet broad, 150 feet long, and 500 horse-power. They are of very light draught, and will do 25 versts, or 16 miles an hour, in smooth water. The Amou Daria, however, flows with a current like the Neva, of seven versts per hour, and this must be taken into account in reckoning what these boats can do. Each of these steamers is navigated by 30 men, and can carry 300 soldiers and 20 officers. They were built in sections in St. Petersburg, taken by rail to the Volga, and thence so onward to Tchardjui."

So much for Mr. Mestcherin about General Annenkoff's railway. It is an enterprise which, however daring it seemed when projected, has encountered no difficulties in its execution. It has been a great pacifier, and its success fills me with vain regrets that our projected railway from Suakin to Berber was never constructed. The Hadendowas and the Bishareens would probably have been as amenable to the temptation of regular daily wage as the Akhal Tekkes and the Turkomans. But the Russians did what we only talked of doing, and the result is that the railway to Samarcand now runs with safety and regularity through a territory but lately the terror and the despair of civilised man.

## CHAPTER IV.

### THE WATER-WAY TO THE RUSSIAN AUSTRALIA.

ONE of the chronic delusions of our time, as I suppose of all times, is that the old times were more romantic, more adventurous, more heroic, than those in which we earn our daily bread. I never could see things in that light. The Victorian age is as adventurous as the Elizabethan, and there are as many weird and magic marvels in the prosaic workaday world of the nineteenth century as in the romantic verse of Spenser's "Faërie Queen." Of which facts I have been reminded very forcibly by an interview which I have had with Captain Wiggins, of Sunderland, a North Countryman worthy to be named beside Hawkins or Frobisher, or any sturdy mariner of all those who three hundred years ago sailed the Spanish Main, and built up by sturdy seamanship and English valour the maritime supremacy of England. Captain Wiggins is the man who has found the lost key of the water-gate which leads to Russia's Land of Gold in Siberia, and the story of his difficulties in endeavouring to force his way to the door reminds one of the magic spells by which in the romances of chivalry heroes were warded off from hidden treasures. Certainly no hoard, not even that of Monte Cristo, ever approached in value the store of treasure which Nature has laid up for Russia in the gold mountains of Siberia; and no magician ever reared by his evil arts more subtle and provoking barriers in the path of the bold explorer than the icebergs and other obstacles in Siberia and St. Petersburg have placed in the way of Captain Wiggins and of the Phœnix Company.

The story of Captain Wiggins' repeated efforts to open up a water-way to the heart of Russia's inland Australia is one of the most interesting chapters in the history of maritime adventure. Within the heart of the immense domain which Russia possesses in Northern Asia there are practically inexhaustible resources from which the world can draw supplies of the two things it most desires—wheat and gold. But at present the wheat-land is left untilled because its crops cannot be brought to market, and the gold remains imprisoned in its native quartz because it is impossible to carry to the heart of Siberia the heavy machinery necessary for its extraction. To liberate these two vast stores of food and of wealth it is absolutely necessary that there should be a waterway between them and the outer world. There is such a waterway, although it is locked by ice for nine months out of every twelve, and it is of simply incalculable importance to the future of Siberia that during the only three months that the water-gate is open, no artificial impediment in the shape of red-tape barriers, official circumlocution, &c., should be allowed to close it.

Siberia is an Australia lying in the latitude of Canada. Like Russia when Peter the Great came to the throne, the first necessity for its growth is access to the sea. No foreign foes need now to be fought and conquered before the new Russia can clear a way for its commerce to the world's highway. It is the foreigner, indeed, who is in the present case the indispensable ally without whom Siberia would remain landlocked for another generation. Captain Wiggins has unlocked the gate which is to Siberia what the Neva was to Russia of the eighteenth century. It was difficult, almost impossible, but to courage and perseverance all things are possible, and Captain Wiggins has before this impressed even the blind into his service. During his last journey up the great Siberian river he met an old Samoyed chieftain, whose acquaintance he had made eleven years before. The old native had gone blind, but he recognised the Englishman instantly by his voice, and assisted, blind as he was, in piloting the *Phœnix* up the stream. There are two great rivers, the Ob and the Yenissei, by which the trade of the world can penetrate three thousand miles into the heart of Asia, piercing the richest undeveloped country in the world, and tapping the immense market of Northern China. But until the other day it was believed that all access to these rivers was impenetrably barred by the ice-pack which was believed to stretch from the Iron Gates to the North Pole. It is true that some hundreds of years ago Russian traders coasting round the Siberian shore discovered that it was possible to make their way into the estuary of the Ob, but their knowledge died with them, and it was not till 1874, when Captain Wiggins, in the steam yacht *Diana*, went on a voyage of discovery, in the course of which he picked up the Weyprecht Expedition, he rediscovered that it was possible to pass the Iron Gates or the Kara Straits, and to take a ship right into the water-way of the Ob.

Nova Zembla, which stretches like a bow to oppose the navigation of these waters, is really pierced by three straits, all navigable, the middle being known as the Iron Gates. Admiral Lutke, who surveyed the Siberian coast for the Russian Government, maintained that the Iron Gates were impassable, and even after Captain Wiggins passed them it remained an article of faith with many experts that Admiral Lutke was right and Captain Wiggins wrong.

Professor Nordenskjöld, in pursuit of scientific objects, and haunted by the idea of a North-Eastern Passage and the open water-way to the Pole, succeeded in entering the Yenissei a year after Captain Wiggins had shown that the navigation was open.

The following report of an interview in Petersburg in June last gives Captain Wiggins' own version of his enterprise:—

"Well, Captain Wiggins," said I, as I seated myself at the table in the Hôtel d'Angleterre, St. Petersburg, opposite St. Isaac's Cathedral, where the sturdy North-country mariner was breakfasting with Major Gaskell, "and where is your ship lying?"

"Oh, the *Phœnix*," he replied; "she is at Yenisseisk, two thousand miles up the Yenissei, in the heart of the gold region of Eastern Siberia. I took her out there last summer, and left her there with her crew to be ready to go down the river with cargo to meet us at the mouth of the river, whither we hope to arrive in August. I left the Tyne August 5 last year, and anchored at the mouth of the Yenissei on September 1. The *Phœnix* is a slow boat, of 273 tons register, carrying about 400 tons cargo and coals, with a crew of eleven men all told and one passenger—Mr. Sullivan, the Managing Director of the Phœnix Company, to whom the ship belongs, and who made the voyage in order to ascertain by personal observation the exact commercial conditions of the country. She is of sixty horse power nominal, and we never got more than nine knots an hour out of her. On our way out we had very rough weather in rounding the North Cape. In ordinary circumstances we would make Vardo in ten days. From Vardo to Golchika, at the mouth of the Yenissei, took eight days. So that we may reckon that between Newcastle and the mouth of the Yenissei a slow boat can ply in three weeks. Allowing a fortnight for loading and discharging, the voyage out and home can be made in a couple of months. When I made the journey in 1878 to the mouth of the Ob I was exactly two months going and coming. I left on August 1 and returned on October 1."

"But this time you did not return."

"No, because my object was to prove that it was possible to take the *Phœnix* into the heart of Siberia. So leaving Golchika we steamed up the stream for a whole month, stopping at Touroukhansk to leave part of

L

our cargo of salt, to be stored for the use of the great fish-curers who have their establishments on the Lower Yenissei. The current of the river ran full five knots an hour against us, reducing our speed to four knots an hour over the ground, or little more than walking speed. Nevertheless, we toiled on day after day, always anchoring at night, until at last, on October 9, we took up our winter quarters at Yenisseisk, where my men are now making ready to collect cargo to descend the river to meet us when we arrive at Golchika."

"What ship are you going out in?"

"We have bought the *Labrador*, an Arctic vessel of 500 tons. We shall also take with us a tender to deliver cargo at the mouth of the Ob and to take in the goods that will be brought down by the river steamers. Then we shall go on to the Yenissei and deliver the rest of the cargo to the *Phœnix* for transport up the river."

"Tell me, did not the last attempt to open up trade with Siberia by this route fail disastrously?"

"Most disastrously, but not more disastrously than it deserved to fail. Never was an enterprise more certainly doomed to failure from the outset than was the despatch of the little fleet of merchantmen which left England for the Ob in 1879. Five large sea-going steamers of deep draught, and about as capable of standing the nip of an ice-pack as so many match-boxes, were chartered at large freights to go to Nadim, on the Ob. They started a month too soon, in defiance of the strongest warnings. Five thousand tons of Siberian goods were purchased in the interior and sent down to meet them at Nadim; but none of them ever reached their destination—and for the very best of all reasons. It was impossible. Cavalry could as soon ride across the Channel as these big eggshells of steamers could have delivered their cargoes at Nadim. For eighty or a hundred miles north of Nadim there stretches shoal-water stormy enough to be impassable by river steamers. It is this bar of shallow sea which constitutes the greatest obstacle to the navigation of the Ob, and that is the obstacle which we have to overcome. We have to lift the lame dog over the last step in the stile; but these speculators in 1879 knew nothing of the conditions of the navigation. They ignored the advice of those who did, and so the whole enterprise came to a most ignominious collapse. They did not even get to the outer edge of the Ob shore. They cruised about in fog surrounded by floating ice for a month, without ever making their way through the Iron Gates, and at last growing thoroughly alarmed, they gave up the attempt, and brought their cargoes home again. The 5,000 tons of Siberian produce sent down for shipment was wasted, and so both in England and in Siberia the project of opening up a new trade route became utterly discredited; but nothing happened in 1879 which I did not predict before the ships left port, and therefore there is nothing whatever in the experience of that year to discourage us to-day."

"Then you have no doubt as to the success of your enterprise?"

"Not the least in the world, if the Russian Government will but give us facilities. The conditions are so simple."

"What are these conditions?"

"A practically illimitable territory, producing the finest wheat in the world, and gold-mines of a quite uncalculated richness, whose inhabitants must be supplied with salt, oil, and manufactures from Europe. The only route by which they receive these necessaries is that overland from Russia. The freight is for these necessaries therefore enormous. By the Ob and the Yenissei we can deliver the same goods for less than half or one-third the freight. How, then, can we fail to do an immense business, even although the ice only allows us to enter the rivers two months in the year? But we have difficulties to contend against. We ask, among other privileges, permission to employ for the delivery of the cargoes ordered by Siberians the only vessel on the River Yenissei which can load and discharge such cargoes. That vessel is the *Phœnix*. It happens to be a foreign ship, but we ask for no monopoly in her favour. We only ask that, as she happens to be the solitary steamer capable of delivering the goods Russia's subjects want, the Russian Government should not employ its authority to prohibit her employment."

"Are there any other steamers on the Yenissei?"

"There are—five paddle steamers, passenger boats, and floating bazaars, none of them cargo boats, and none of them fitted for carrying the boilers and heavy machinery that will be required for the development of the Siberian quartz goldfields. One of these river steamers is quite a curiosity in its way. It was built on the river by Mr. Guadaloff, of Ural iron, with Swedish boilers and machinery, which were brought over the Ural at immense cost, and constructed by him with hardly any of the machinery which is regarded as indispensable in our ship-building yards. It is a palace of a boat, 200 ft. long, capable of steaming nine knots an hour, and must have cost its patriotic constructor £40,000. These great river boats are floating bazaars. They ply up and down the river, anchoring opposite every village, whose inhabitants come on board to inspect the goods displayed on the various stalls on deck, and to make their purchases; but these light river craft could not receive or deliver the heavy castings which we have to carry for the gold-miners. Pray don't mistake us. We have not the least desire to monopolise or even to share the river traffic. Only, as we cannot get our goods up the river at all unless we carry them in our own steamer, it is a *sine quâ non* that our steamer shall be permitted to do the work until such time as the Russians are prepared to buy and to take delivery of our cargoes at the mouths of their rivers. When that day comes we shall withdraw at once from the up-river work, and stick to the ocean transit, which we regard as our legitimate business."

"What about the steamers on the Ob?"

"The Ob is better supplied with steamers than the Yenissei, and we do not ask for any privileges of plying up that river."

"Do you ask for any privileges for your goods?"

"Only two—first, that we should be allowed to import certain goods free of duty; secondly, that at the mouth of each of these rivers there should be established what we call a port of franc—that is to say, a port of entry, with Custom House and depôts. These, however, are secondary to the absolute necessity of being allowed to deliver our cargoes to the Russian subjects who are wanting to buy them, and to receive the goods which Russian subjects are wanting to sell. If you knock even a single link out of the middle of a chain, you might as well destroy it altogether, and unless we can be guaranteed that the goods which we bring to the mouths of the two great rivers will find river-craft capable of taking them inland we had very much better stay at home, as we should only have our trouble for our pains."

"You have often been in Siberia, Captain Wiggins?"

"Yes, I know it pretty well, so far as the river basins are concerned. My first voyage was made in the *Diana* in 1874, when I spent eight weeks in the Kara Sea, steamed one hundred miles up the Gulf of Ob, and proved that there was open water to the mouth of the Yenissei. In 1875, in the cutter *Whim*, I simply sailed through the Iron Gates to prove that they were open.

"In 1876 I went up the Yenissei for 1,000 miles in the steam yacht *Thames*, a vessel of 150 tons. There I wintered, but sledged home 4,000 miles across country to try to get some people with faith enough to try to open up trade with the Yenissei. In 1877 I went back overland, and finding that no one would listen to my calculation as to the trade that might be done there, I sold the *Thames* to the mayor of Yenisseisk. In 1878 I took the *Warkworth* out to the Ob and back. I took a general cargo out and brought wheat home, and did the voyage in two months. In 1879 the speculators rushed in and spoiled the business so utterly that it was not till last year I returned to the scene of my former enterprise. Last year I took the *Phœnix* up to Yenisseisk, and came home overland. In August I hope to start with the *Labrador* for the mouth of the Yenissei, and load up from the *Phœnix*."

"What kind of business do you expect will be done with Siberia?"

"General cargo of manufactured articles, and machinery for the development of their gold-fields. Hitherto the only gold-mining in Siberia has been alluvial washings. They have simply not been able to transport to the gold-fields the heavy machinery needed for crushing quartz. One mine-owner succeeded some time ago in bringing a miserable, second-hand, worn-out stamping mill and rolling machinery from the Amoor. He has made a fortune, and every one is naturally anxious to put down similar or better machinery. If that machinery is to get to Siberia, it will have to go by the Yenissei, and it will have to be delivered by the *Phœnix*, for there is no other route and no other vessel by which such heavy machinery can be taken out."

"You believe in Siberia?"

"Immensely. The wheat region is a vast belt of black soil capable of producing the finest grain for flour-making purposes in the world. The cargo I brought in the *Warkworth* was proved on analysis to be even better than the Indian wheat. This virgin soil has not yet been tilled, for there is no means of disposing of the surplus crop. But the great future of

Siberia lies in the gold-mines. There are literally mountains full of auriferous quartz which no one has yet been able to touch. Once bring in the machinery, and you will see Australian development equalled by that of Siberia. Ports will be created at the mouths of the great rivers, towns will spring up around every mine, populations will assemble, and all this means business. There is a new market opening up before the world, and we hope to be the first in the field."

"What a land God has given the Russians!" exclaimed one of Nordenskjöld's seamen, as he gazed with envious admiration on the fertile prairie land of Northern Siberia. A great land indeed the Tzar has as his back-garden—a land used hitherto but as the prison for exiles from Muscovy, but now destined to become a leading factor in the trade of the world. Our Ambassador at St. Petersburg has secured the concession of privileges as to trade and Customs duties which open up this immense territory to British enterprise. The concession of five years' free imports in the Yenissei, and one year in the Ob, together with one year's permission to navigate the Yenissei with a British vessel, seems but a small thing; but it is, as Sir Robert Morier says, "potential with commercial revolutions, the importance of which can hardly be exaggerated, and which, by opening up new channels on a vast scale for British imports and exports, is capable in the course of time of the largest results." This concession comes opportunely as an illustration of the possibility of doing good business with Russia if only we substitute friendship for bullyragging, and treat Russia as a neighbour with whom we wish to be on good terms, instead of a kind of omnipotent devil with whom all relations other than those of execration and hostility are impossible. "A colossal fortune," wrote Mr. Seebohm long ago, "awaits the adventurer who is backed by sufficient capital and a properly organised staff, to carry on a trade between this country and Siberia, viâ the Kara Sea." It is this road which at last is open, and goods can be taken with only once breaking bulk from the warehouses of London and Newcastle to the consumers in the heart of the Siberian gold-field on the northern frontier of China.

Mr. Sullivan, the managing director of the Phœnix Company, has called special attention "to the friendly and liberal feeling displayed by his Imperial Majesty the Tzar, and by the Russian Ministers, in thus assisting British commercial enterprise;" and this little incident illustrates the desire that exists in Russia to welcome any indication of a saner feeling on our part as to the mutual relations of the two countries. In this the Russians are true to their traditions. Ivan the Terrible gave concessions to English traders in Russia far more favourable than those conceded to traders of any other nation. Peter the Great filled the Russian service with Scotchmen, and nearly all the Tzars have shown a marked predilection for Britons as agents in the development, industrial and commercial, of their immense and undeveloped Empire. If England were to pursue a more neighbourly policy in her dealing with Russia, the present Emperor would be willing to go a long way in the direction of commercial concessions. This concession of free imports to the adventurous pioneers who have opened the Kara Sea to commerce is a sign of good things to come, if we have the courage to press forward on the right road.

The future of Siberia is so incalculable that it is unnecessary to do more than merely allude to the practically undeveloped gold-reefs which await the arrival of heavy machinery in order to yield their riches to the world. Siberia is said to produce some five millions sterling of gold per annum. This is obtained by the mere scratching of the surface. No machinery such as is set up at once in every accessible gold-field in America, Africa, or Australia, has been available in Siberia. The fortunes that have been made in that country—and the Siberian millionaire may vie with the Silver Kings of Nevada—have been picked up with the most primitive appliances, owing to the impossibility of carrying heavy machinery over the Urals to regions where railways were unknown, and where it was believed eternal frost barred all access from the sea. The genius and perseverance of Captain Wiggins enabled him to open up a water-way available for the transport of merchandise for three months in every year. The shrewd instinct of Sir Robert Morier, a Cobdenite of the larger sort, with a passion for facilitating the commercial intercourse of the peoples, saw at once what an opportunity this afforded for mutual accommodation on the part of the two nations, and he threw himself heart and soul, with all his exuberant energy, into the negotiations which, after many delays and disappointments, were finally crowned by success.

The possibility of an immense development of the latent wealth of Siberia was forcibly pointed out by Mme. Novikoff in the useful volume "Russia and England," which was published as far back as 1880. Whether the introduction of stamping mills, and all the appliances required for extracting gold from the auriferous rocks of Siberia, will lead to multiplying the output of gold tenfold, as some confidently anticipate, is a question the solution of which must be left to the next few years.

An unfortunate accident to the *Phœnix*, which was stranded in the Yenissei on her way down to meet the *Labrador*, has postponed the realisation of Captain Wiggins' dream until next year. The *Labrador* was detained at Vardo waiting for the arrival of a river steamer to replace the *Phœnix*. When her consort arrived, her crew were frightened by the ice, which presented no real difficulty, and returned. There was nothing for Captain Wiggins to do but to return to Vardo, and to look forward to renewing the voyage in good time next summer.

## Book IV.
## THE TRIBUNE OF ALL THE RUSSIAS.

### CHAPTER I.
#### THE FLOCK OF LITTLE BROWN SHEEP.

THE familiar story of the dashing reviewer who qualified himself for reviewing a book by cutting open a few pages and then smelling the paper-knife is a fitting parallel to my presumption in venturing to say anything about the political problems which demand solution in Russia to-day. I have only been two months in the country. I cannot speak six words of the language of the people. The whole of my previous training, political, religious, and social, has been such as to render it difficult to occupy the standpoint from which all such problems must be judged—the standpoint, that is, of the Russians themselves. As an Englishman, a Radical, and a Nonconformist, it is difficult for me to look at questions with the eyes of a Muscovite, who believes in the Tzar and in the Greek Orthodox State Church. The arrogance of the West, which is as much constitutional as intellectual, is almost fatal to an appreciation of the difficulties of the East. Only by the door of humility can one enter into the house of understanding.

To put yourself in his place is the first condition of forming a just judgment, and it applies equally to all sorts and conditions of men. It is idle to judge either Tzar or Cossack from the standpoint of English or American democracy. But the gift of sympathetic imagination by which a foreigner, alien in race, religion, language, and manners can divest himself of his national and sectarian prejudices, and see with the eyes of a stranger whose language he cannot speak, and to whose country he is paying a hurried visit for the first time, is one of the rarest and yet one of the most indispensable pre-requisites for the task before me. One thing, however, I may claim. The heart sees further than the head in most things, and I do honestly and sincerely love the Russian people. This partiality of mine does not blind me to their faults. Even the most devoted of lovers can hardly ignore his mistress's squint and freckles when all her acquaintances enjoy nothing so much as caricaturing her personal defects. His very affection makes him more keenly alive to her imperfections, more tremblingly sensitive to her mistakes. But sympathy is ever the surest guide to the solution of political problems, and before it is possible to arrive at a solution. we must at least know the factors with which we have to deal.

In thus frankly expressing the partiality and friendly feeling with which I regard this great people whom we have so wantonly injured, I make no limitations or distinction. It is the fashion in some quarters to profess sympathy with the Russian people and to express detestation of its government.. I make no such distinction. All governments are imperfect, the Russian at least as much as any other. If we are never to sympathise with anything that is imperfect we must confine our sympathies to archangels, and the Government of the Kingdom of Heaven. The Russian Government is related to the Russian people fully as much as Lord Salisbury's Administration is related to the English people, with this difference : If Lord Salisbury were to take a *plébiscite* he would either be beaten at the polls or have a very small majority, whereas the Russian people would vote by a majority of at least ten to one in favour of the Tzar. This may be a mistake on the part of the Russians, but as long as they are of this way of thinking it is absurd to profess great admiration for them and nothing but detestation for the political system which they not merely tolerate but support. Like master like man ; you cannot separate the nation from the autocracy. This in no way precludes me from seeing many things that to an English Radical seem hopelessly wrong and politically unsound, but it at least is a safeguard against that most utterly barren of all phases of thought, the pharisaic attitude of intolerant contempt.

I have no fear that while honestly setting down what seems to me the truth, I shall offend those who during my visit extended to me such exceeding kindness. "See my police stations with your own eyes," said General Gresser, the chief of the

Petersburg police, "note whatever you think is wrong, and don't only praise what is good. Tell me frankly what is amiss, so that I may mend it," and the same sensible and courageous spirit animated the Tzar and his advisers. Blunders I shall make no doubt, errors in detail are unavoidable, which must appear very ludicrous to those who are better informed; but I hope that no Russian will read what I have to say without recognising that whatever misconceptions there may be owing to the difference of political environment and national idiosyncrasy, I have at least set down nought in malice, but have sincerely set forth that which seems to me the truth about his country.

I had not been in Russia half an hour before there flashed upon me a conception of the country and its people that has never left me. Subsequent experience deepened the first impression, and the idea thus formed has been to me the key and the clue to all my observations about Russia. We had left Wirballen behind us, and were coursing along with that peculiar heavy pulsating movement familiar to travellers on Russian railways across a level and uninteresting country. The sun was going down the western sky; it had been raining, and the ground was wet and boggy. Here and there a peasant was ploughing in the fields, and at every crossing or block station a barefooted woman stood clasping a folded flag with both hands, the guardian angel of the railway. As village after village came into view on either side the conviction grew that here was the real Russia. Not St. Petersburg, not even Moscow, nor the cities on the Volga, nor the shambling country towns and seats of Governments—these are not Russia. Of the 120,000,000 of the subjects of Alexander the Third not twenty millions live in towns. The hundred millions live in villages, each of which is a microcosm of the Russian Empire. That village there on the brow of that sloping hill, or that one nearer at hand in the sheltered valley, is the true Russia, the organic unit or nerve-cell of the great Colossus of Eastern Europe. Over these humble little collections of one-storied cottages in clay, or brick, or timber, with their thatched or shingled roofs, there is reared a more or less imposing and substantial superstructure of empire, with all the appurtenances thereof, looming large against the Eastern sky.

But it is neither among the palaces of St. Petersburg nor amid the glories of the Kremlin, that you find the real Russia. Army, navy, diplomacy, Grand Dukes and courts, all make a brave show and glitter from afar, attracting, nay monopolising, the gaze of the outside world. But it is not in the army, or the navy, or the cities, or the court, that Russia exists. They are excrescences, or legitimate and necessary outgrowths, which you please, but the real Russia is in the village. That is the characteristic, the essential, the unchanging type, repeated again and again wherever you travel in the dominions of the Tzar. The Russian is a villager, and Russia is a vast conglomeration of villages.

A Russian village is neither as picturesque as an English village nor as squalid as an Irish one. It consists of an indefinite and ever-varying number of one-storied cottages, planted more or less irregularly in the centre of the fields owned and tilled by the villagers, the whole forming a little world, almost self-contained, self-supporting, and largely self-governing. To my English eyes, if I may perpetrate an Irish bull, the most conspicuous feature of these villages was what wasn't there at all. As the train proceeded mile after mile, and village after village was left behind, I marvelled at the constant uniformity of type; and when I left Russia after my two months' sojourn I was as much as ever impressed with the same fact. All the cottages were one-storied, nor was there in one village out of ten any building larger than a cottage. The eye ranged in vain for anything corresponding to the squire's country-seat, the substantial farmer's conspicuous farmstead. Neither was there any steeple pointing skyward, nor anything corresponding to the snug vicarage of our English parishes. Now and then, at long intervals, the green or blue cupola of a church would stand out against the sky, and the white walls of the main building gleamed bright against surrounding browns and greens, but that was the exception. As a rule, village after village presented the same features, and only the same features. There was no great building, towering its aristocratic front above its humbler neighbours. All the cottages were of the same elevation; all the cottagers were on the same level. Here at last in the Empire of the Tzars is realised that ideal of absolute democratic equality for which, outside some of the Swiss communes, you may search in vain in Western Europe.

The idea possessed me more and more: Here is Russia, the

real Russia, the Russia of the hundred millions of peasants: and what is it? What are these villages but so many flocks of little brown sheep nestling on the great pasture lands of the Tzar? Just like sheep, all lowly, all of one size, all of one colour, all gregarious, crowding together for company, instead of standing apart each on its own patch. The whole of the dominions of the Tzar seem but as one vast grazing ground or meadow, in which, broken up into innumerable little flocks, are scattered one hundred millions of his Russian sheep. Far away in the fat valleys of Siberia, in the dense forests of the north, and in the fertile steppes of the south, you find the same little flocks, varying only in colour and in numbers, but in other respects the same. All equal, all democratic, all owners of the land they till. And far away, at an immeasurable distance, at Gatschina, stands the Head Shepherd, high over all.

Given 100,000,000 of Russians, scattered in half a million villages over a territory larger than all the rest of Europe—how to create the best government suited to their needs? That is the problem which the Russians have solved after their fashion, much to the scandal of the West; but the moment you approach it with the idea of the village firmly grasped as the central and dominating factor of the whole, you discover how difficult it is, and how vastly the problem differs from those with which we have to deal in the densely-peopled West, and how idle it is to prescribe as an infallible specific the application of the Western machinery of constitutional apparatus.

To begin with, it is but the other day that these peasants were as saleable as if they had actually been sheep. It is not thirty years since, in Whittier's grandiloquent phrase, the late emperor, "with the pencil of the Northern Star wrote freedom o'er his land." The Decree of Emancipation was dated 1861. Many of the adults, therefore, who are ploughing the fields and mowing the hay in Russia, were actually born in serfdom, as much the property of their landlords as the fields they tilled and the cattle they tended. To them, therefore, cling of necessity some of the vices of slavery; its shiftlessness, its lack of forethought, its indifference to truth, and all the easy-going, happy-go-lucky style of life that is natural to those who, having no prospect save that of dying as they have lived, in servitude, can conceive no higher ideal of existence than to take things as easily as they can, and throw the responsibility on anybody rather than shoulder it themselves.

Then, again, the peasants know nothing, or next to nothing, of politics. How many men in that collection of shanties takes in a newspaper—I do not ask daily, but even weekly? How many of the men—I say nothing of the women—could read, even if the papers were supplied gratis? Supposing the whole village were burnt out, and all the contents of all the huts were piled in a heap in the fields, how many books would there be discovered? I saw the loot of the five burnt houses in Yasnaia Poliana, and I did not see a single book among the spoil. There were a few of the Tolstoi tracts, which the Count had recently distributed, and there were sacred pictures, rescued reverently from the raging flames. But of books proper there was not a trace. In most Western villages the school-house is the most conspicuous feature; in all Russia there are not 30,000 schools, and the number of scholars receiving instruction in 1883 was 2,440,000. At the Prussian rate of attendance to population, the number of scholars in Russia, instead of being under two and a half millions should be at least fifteen millions; even at the English rate it should be twelve millions. And of all the 60,000,000 women and girls in Russia, there were in 1882 barely 300,000 in public elementary schools. The proportion in the old days before emancipation was still worse, so that of the adults the number who can read and write is very small. Every year there are 4,000,000 children born in Russia, nearly double the whole number of scholars in her schools. The statistics of the percentage of illiteracy among army recruits does not bring this out clearly enough, for all the conscripts of late years were born since the emancipation. But the figures are bad enough. In 1882 the average percentage of recruits able to read and write was only 19 per cent. In 1883 it was 23 per cent., a slight but considerable improvement. The percentage among the women is of course much lower. It is therefore probably above the mark to say that out of every ten Russian males in each village two might be able to read, and out of every ten Russian women hardly one.

How, then, are these flocks of illiterates governed—who are the shepherds of these sheep and who their shearers? What, in other words, are the means by which the business of government gets itself transacted amongst a population so uninstructed, and in which, according to Western ideas, the very rudiments necessary for political institutions hardly exist? In order to answer this question simply, and to exhibit as it were a section of one of the flocks, which form the organic fundamental units of Russia, I will try to show at what point and how a Russian peasant touches the adminstrative machine.

## CHAPTER II.

### THE GOVERNMENT OF THE FLOCK.

THE first thing that strikes an Englishman is the absolutely republican, democratic character of the government of these Russian villages. There is nothing like it in England, nor does the Local Government Act passed this year venture to propose any such radical concession to the sovereignty of the village as is enjoyed as a matter of right by each of the little brown flocks of sheep which pasture on the broad lands of the Tzar. The Folkmote, or assembly of all the householders, has died out in the West. It still flourishes in Russia. On the night of the fire at Yasnaia Poliana it was decided to hold a skotka, or meeting of the Mir, to discuss the question of prohibiting the use of tobacco as a preventive measure against future fires. The gathering took place in the open air, outside the house of one of the better-to-do villagers. Count Tolstoi sat under the shade of a rough verandah; the men and boys crowded round him, standing. Now and then a woman stopped to look on and listen as she passed. There were no set speeches, but a general good-humoured talk went on, and in the conversation the matter was freely discussed. Some, following the Count's lead, approved of the prohibition. Others opposed it. One strong point urged by the anti-tobacconists was that small boys were taking to smoking, and that it was necessary to put a check upon their reckless inexperience. To this it was triumphantly replied by the smokers that if the small boy were forbidden to smoke at all he would merely evade the edict and smoke surreptitiously, and that, for practical purposes, would mean that instead of smoking in the open he would smoke in barns and byres. That is to say, the prohibitory law proposed to prevent fires would drive the small boy from smoking in the open air, where he could smoke safely, to smoking in the very places where it is almost as dangerous to strike a match as in a powder magazine. Notwithstanding this, the majority was in favour of prohibition, and, if Count Tolstoi had not been present, it would, without more ado, have passed a law there and then ordering that every member of the Mir caught smoking after the enactment of this interdict should be fined one rouble, or do three days' work for the community. Count Tolstoi is against compulsion even in the cause of asceticism, and he succeeded in getting the Mir to substitute for the proposed law a voluntary pledge, signed by each of the anti-tobacconists, by which they undertook to pay a rouble or to do three days' work if they broke their pledge.

The curious thing about the Mir is that its decisions are almost always unanimous. The minority has such a strong sense of the necessity for the solidarity of the Mir that when it has clearly ascertained that it is the minority it votes with the majority. At Yasnaia Poliana, the smokers, finding themselves outnumbered, were going to vote the prohibitory law to a man, and would have done so had not Count Tolstoi interposed with his *ria media*. Only the anti-tobacconists signed his pledge. Both smokers and non-smokers would have voted the law.

Every member of the Russian village seems to regard it as his natural right as a member of the Mir to exercise all the prerogatives of legislation and of sovereignty.

At Yasnaia Poliana they were about to prohibit smoking. In other communes they have banished vodka shops. In others they have imposed fines upon those who break the Sunday rest by working in the fields. There seems to be absolutely no limit to the authority of the Mir over its own members. If it pleased, it could proscribe the eating of meat, the use of paraffin oil, or the wearing of an unpopular dress. From the decisions of the Mir an appeal lies to the administration of the Zemstvo; but, as a matter of fact, the decisions of the Mir are usually acquiesced in. The sense of the importance of unity, and the much greater hold which the Russian mind has of the ideas of cohesion and solidarity than of the ideas of individualism and independence, which lead to the absence of divisions in the villagers' Parliament, prevent many appeals to the superior authorities.

To these intermediaries the peasant does not take kindly. The Tzar he understands, and his Mir. But the Assembly of the *noblesse*, and the Zemstvo, and all the other artificial creations which have been invented to stand between the two aboriginal authorities of Muscovy, are more or less exotic, without deep root in the soil.

I remember when I was in Ireland two years since being twitted by an Irish peer for carrying my devotion to Russia to such a length as to see no means of helping Ireland through her present difficulties save by the establishment of some modification of the Russian Mir in every Irish village. I thought of Russia when in Ireland, and I thought of Ireland when I was in Russia. My conclusion was the same. Here in Russia we have the true peasant Republic, the most democratic and socialistic of any institution now existing in all Europe, which may yet supply to a world wearying of unrest, of individualism and of universal competition on the principle of the "devil take the hindmost," a clue to the solution of many of our most pressing difficulties.*

* In thus describing the Russian village republic, I am aware that I shall be accused by those whose one idea of Russia is despotism, of allowing myself to be biassed by sympathy with the autocratic system under which such decentralisation is possible. I may, therefore, quote, for the confounding of this class of critic, the following passage from "Stepniak's" sketch of the "Moujiks at Home." "Stepniak," an avowed Nihilist, cannot be accused of sympathy with the autocracy. But he is a Russian, and knows the Mir. He says, "Up to the present time the law has allowed the Mir a considerable amount of self-government. They are free to manage all their economical concerns in common—the land, the forests, the census, the public-houses, &c. They distribute among themselves, as they choose, the taxes. They elect the rural executive administration. They elect the judges of the volost, or district. The jurisdiction of the peasants' tribunal is very extensive, all the civil and a good many criminal offences, in which one of the parties at least is a peasant of the district, are amenable to it. They are not bound to abide by the official code of law. They administer justice according to the customary laws and traditions of the local peasants. The women are in all respects dealt with on an equal footing with the men. Labour, not kinship, is

M

I looked at the little throng of men and lads as they clustered about the porch where Count Tolstoi sat, and listened to their laughter and their murmured talk, and somehow or other the scene recalled reminiscences of Homer and the simple out-of-door life of our race in the world's prime. The westering sun had sunk low on the horizon. A few swallows were hawking overhead for belated flies; here and there on the green among the houses young foals ran timidly after their mothers; while within the neighbouring sheds cows and sheep settled themselves down to rest. At the doorstep of the wooden cottage, or at the window-sills, sat perched the women and girls of the village, picturesque in their simple costume of red and white, and some bright with the beauty of a sun-browned peach.

It was a bit of old-world life that seemed to revive memories of heroic times long since gone down into the abyss of the past, and yet it was intensely real and alive. This simple assembly, which was carrying on its business in unceremonious democratic fashion, has survived while dynasties and constitutions have gone to wreck, and has triumphed alike over the silent decay of time and the violent assaults of enemies and rivals. All over Europe this ancient primeval institution has perished. Here it survives, the apparently one indestructible institution in the country besides the autocracy and the Church. It is the primitive cell, the water-tight, iron-bound compartment which keeps the Russian State afloat. This is the only Government of which the majority of Russians have any experience. For the peasants this is *the*

always recognised as giving an indefeasible right to property. The Mir recognises no restraint on its autonomy. It embraces all domains and branches of peasant life. In olden times the Mir elected the parson. Sometimes the Mir decides that the whole village shall abandon Orthodoxy and become evangelical. To the Russian peasant it seems the most natural thing in the world that the Mir should do this whenever it chooses. The Mir forms indeed a microcosm, a small world of its own. With the Russian Mir the law is nowhere, the conscience everywhere. Not merely criminal offences, but every disputed point is settled according to the individual justice of the case, no regard being paid to the category of crime to which it may chance to belong. The Mir recognises no permanent laws restricting or guiding its decisions. It is the personification of the living law speaking through the collective voice of the community." —"The Russian Peasantry," vol. i., p. 139.

Government. It is like themselves. It is not scientific, it is popular. It is the simplest form of democracy, and it has all the defects of democracies when they are ignorant, impulsive, and left without the guidance of the cultured class. But it has accustomed the uncultured class to the practice and the principle of association, it has saddled every adult with responsibility, and it has, under the outward semblance of the most absolute despotism, preserved in activity the nearest practical realisation of the ideal of the Paris Commune on a Christian basis. That ideal—wild, unpractical, visionary, and largely antagonistic to Christianity—went up in flames in May, 1871. The Russian ideal, realised long ages since as a practical necessity of the peasant's life, has weathered the storms of centuries; it has emerged uninjured from the Tartar conquest, from the enslavement of the people, from the revolution of Peter, and the reforms of successions of Tchinovniks.

As it was, so it is; the one hope of the Russian peasant, the one institution to which he has clung in evil and in good report, the one solid basis upon which in Russia the reformer can plant his foot.

To the unlettered peasant the world is at once immensely large and extremely small. The small world is that in which he lives, and which he knows. The great world is that of which he knows nothing, which lies beyond the boundaries of his fields. This immense unknown and invisible world includes in its scope and compass all things: God and His saints, heaven and hell, Petersburg and the Tzar, ironclads and newspapers, Parliaments and Courts—all more or less unreal and shadowy, and conceivable in a dim way by the rustic imagination. As for directing the policy of the Empire and voting for this or that Minister, the villager would just as soon dream of asking to be allowed to reform the hierarchy of the angels, or to decide by his vote the revolution of the planets. These things are beyond him. They come into his life as disease comes, and the sunshine and the tempest, but with their ordering he has nothing to do, nor does it occur to him that his voice or vote could possibly under any circumstances have any more power over them than it has over the rising and the setting of the sun. But in his own little world, the village, the common, the fields, there he is among realities, among his equals. Being allowed to govern the world in which he lives, he does not concern himself about that which is unseen and far away.

The legislative functions of the little peasant republic I have already described. It has also judicial and administrative powers which practically include the whole of the peasant's life. Every three years each commune elects its starosta. If an elder, he becomes the village mayor, salaried during his term of office, and he discharges the functions of chief magistrate. He is an elective judge who has power to try all petty offences, and all minor civil actions rising out of landed disputes. Here we have, therefore, for nine out of ten cases which come before a law court, an elective peasant magistracy which secures to an extent beyond the dreams of a London workman the great principle of trial by your peers, without a jury. When more serious cases have to be dealt with, the whole Commune comes together. At such an assembly members can be expelled from the Commune, sentences of flogging passed, and even decrees made out for the banishment of any of its members to Siberia. This power of banishment is about to be circumscribed. It is too deeply rooted in the Russian Constitution to be abolished. All that the Administration dare propose is that in future, as Siberia is to be practically abolished as a penal colony, the Commune shall only be allowed to banish their members to Asia on condition of their raising the money to pay for their transport. Formerly, if the Commune passed such a sentence, the Imperial Government undertook the responsibility and defrayed the cost of its execution. By altering this, and throwing the cost upon the Commune, it is hoped to curtail in practice the exercise of a right which in principle is inseparable from every Mir.

But by far the most important, and, from the Western point of view, the most suggestive function of the Mir, is that by virtue of which from day to day, in rough and ready fashion, it endeavours to realise the ideal of our Socialists. When I was talking about attempting to naturalise the Mir in Ireland Count Tolstoi somewhat impatiently asked if I did not think it more important to endeavour to naturalise the spirit of Christian brotherhood, of which the Mir was only the outward and visible expression, and without which no mere machinery would work. There was some force in his objection. For until you have people imbued with the idea that it is their duty to adjust the means of subsistence to the needs of those who want rather than to the will of those who have, the Socialist side of the Mir is not likely to come into existence.

When the Count and I were walking one evening, an old peasant and his wife came to complain of the action of the Mir in the village where he lived. He was an old man, and he had lived and worked in his fields all his life. But his daughter had now got married, and the commune had taken away from him one-half of his land. This he considered unfair, and he came to the Count to complain. The Count heard his tale and his wife's walking to and fro under the trees, and had little trouble in convincing the old man that the Mir had acted justly. He had no longer the same need for so much land; he had neither so many mouths to feed nor so many hands to till it. He was, besides, getting old, and the Mir might justly have taken all his land to hand it over to younger hands, giving him bread for the rest of his days. The Mir, therefore, had acted mercifully and justly, and he must go back and be content. The old pair professed themselves quite satisfied with the decision of the Count, whom they had consulted as an *amicus curiæ*, and departed.

These re-partitions of land are of constant occurrence. If a family increases, more land is given to it. If a family diminishes, the land is reduced in proportion. This is not carried out with mathematical accuracy or strict punctuality. There is always a wide margin allowed in Russia, both as to time and space. But the principle is never questioned. The reason is simple. The commune is in reality a joint-stock co-operative association, jointly possessed of a landed estate, for which it is collectively responsible to the Central Government for the due payment of taxes, repayments of purchase-money, and the like. To maintain the efficiency of the association, and to enable it to make its payments to the State with the necessary regularity, all its members must be solvent, each must be able to do justice to the land, and at the same time have sufficient land on which to employ his labour. Hence the continual redistribution of fields, which although sometimes carried to excess, is nevertheless indispensable for the efficient working of the co-operative scheme. The adoption of an arbitrary policy is checked by the necessity of supporting those who are deprived of land, and the discouragement to industry that ensues if a peasant is harshly deprived of the increment of his own labour.

There are many enemies of the Mir who contend that it hinders the growth of individualism, that it leads to the domination of the vodka seller and wire-puller, and that thousands of communes are at this moment over head and ears in debt. All that may be true, and in a great measure is true. But the Russian peasant is not primarily an individual, but a brother; and as all the rest of the world has gone in for individualism, why should we grudge him his experiment in fraternity? Vodka is not the exclusive malady of Russian Mirs, and as for the debts of the co-operative land-owners, they are no greater, if indeed they are so great, as those of private land-owners all over the world. Agricultural depression, like death, with equal foot visits the dwellings of all who make their living from the land.

As education progresses, and as the principle of co-operation is better understood, the simple organisation of the Mir affords opportunities of which the Russian, with his trained associative instinct, will not fail to make much greater use than he has hitherto done.

It was not a Russian, but Mazzini, an Italian, who proclaimed that the epoch of individualism was exhausted, and that the era of association had begun. If he was right, then the Russian moujik is likely at last to march in the van in the onward march of human progress.

The author of "Home Colonisation" might do worse than spend a month in Russian villages. There is something very refreshing in this sudden and complete reversion to a primitive type. Between London and a Russian village the antithesis is the most complete imaginable. One is the most artificial, the other the most natural community imaginable. London, if snowed up or otherwise cut off from the outside world, would die of starvation in a week. Every Russian village is self-sustained and victualled, as it were, for chronic siege. There is something very fascinating about the spectacle of communities thus planted out apart, and able to produce almost all that they consume, and consume almost all that they produce. Sir Robert Hamilton, just before he left Ireland for Van Diemen's Land, remarked that the best hope for the solution of some of our most pressing social difficulties was the creation of natural, organic, self-contained rural communities which would not be liable to the violent and unnatural oscillations which are experienced by the artificial communities of a more complex civilisation. Here in Russia we have such communities by the hundred thousand. They are backward, rude, objectionable in many ways, but they possess a rough and vigorous vitality that enables Russia to weather many storms which would have proved fatal to a more delicately organised system.

Take, for instance, the depreciation of the rouble. This has hit Russia hard, no doubt, but the drop of the value from 38d. to 19d. has hardly been felt by the peasant, whose simple wants are almost all satisfied from his own fields. For the surplus of his crops, which he sells abroad, he receives less money, and he has to pay dearer for all that he buys from abroad; but in the staple articles of his existence the difference is little felt. These changes, the result of foreign competition, and over-production, and the depreciation of silver, and financial crisis, affect only the fringes of his existence, instead of convulsing it from the centre to the circumference.

There are, of course, certain articles which the peasant must buy from without. It is beyond the resources of the most ingenious and self-sufficing rural community to smelt and forge iron, to make salt, to produce petroleum, or to coin roubles with which to pay their taxes. Neither can they grow cotton or spin it into shirts and calico dresses. For all these things they must sell a certain proportion of their crops, or dispose of a certain proportion of their labour. But excepting for iron, and salt, and petroleum, and cotton, and taxes, they do not go beyond the boundary of their own village. The Russian peasant is for the most part a vegetarian—not on principle, but of necessity. Cabbage soup and black bread form the staple of his diet. Occasionally he treats himself, when he can afford it, to a glass of tea, nibbling as he drinks it at a piece of sugar, which is purposely made almost as hard as granite, in order that he may not find it crumble too easily in his mouth. On still rarer occasions he tastes the luxury of meat. But his normal diet is that of an anchorite. Cabbage, and buckwheat, and rye, together with milk from his cows and eggs from his hens, suffice for his temporal needs, with the indispensable kwas, a kind of cross between barley-water and small beer, which he manufactures for himself out of rye.

At the corner of every field the good-wife has reserved a patch for the flax which she reaps and spins into a coarse kind of towelling in the long winter. The fleece of his sheep, sometimes woven into wool and sometimes worn *au naturel*, supplies the peasant with a warm winter coat, and the hides of his cattle are available for the characteristic national boot. His wife and daughters draw the water from the well. Firing he finds in the nearest wood. Even if snowed up and cut off from all communication with the outside world, the little village would contrive to exist. It contains within itself all the necessities save salt. The iron implements do not need to be constantly renewed. If the petroleum gives out, they can fall back upon their old blazing birch-bark strip; and the homespun linen and woollen will serve if the calicoes from the mills are not to hand. Horses and oxen, cows and pigs, sheep and poultry, are seldom lacking, and almost every homestead has its guardian watch-dog as a four-footed sentinel against the wandering thief or the prowling wolf.

The interior of a Russian hut is not very inviting from the æsthetic point of view. It differs from an Irish cabin in being smaller and warmer, and in having usually a more or less uneven flooring of wood.

The great stove, which forms the central and solid nucleus round which the house is built, and on and around which the household sleep, is a necessity in Russia, where life would become extinct if they had no other means of warmth but the open peat fire of the Irish cabin. The furniture is scanty. A London pawnbroker would hesitate at advancing twenty shillings on all the plenishings of many a peasant's home. A holy picture is almost the only ornament on the walls, but that is never absent.

The humans do not resent the visits of their live stock, attracted by the warmth from the outside cold, and a friendly sociability unites man and beast in one family. Yet the peasants are in their persons cleaner than our people. Once a week every villager has his parboiling in the bath or in his oven, an ordeal to which many of our poor would not willingly subject themselves. The country people that I saw were generally clean, and most of them seemed healthy and robust. The ordinary prejudice in the English mind about the dirtiness of the Russian is not borne out by the personal appearance of the moujiks and their wives. How they keep themselves so clean in houses so small, so overcrowded, and often so dirty, is a mystery I did not solve.

The villager is innocent of drains, for he has abundance of the great deodoriser all around. Epidemics sometimes make sad havoc among the little brown huts, but he is free from sewer-gas and the plague of the plumber.

The women can as a rule neither read nor write, but they can bake, and they can brew, and they can milk and spin, and in short have the faculty of using their hands, which is dying out among the English servant-girls, every one of whom can read the *Family Herald*, and even write letters to the editor.

Emerson, in one of his essays, remarks that the ideal life is that which enables man to have the detachment and the individuality which is only possible in the country, with the intellectual stimulus which is only possible in the town. The conditions have not produced these ideal results in Russia, but they are there. A Victorian Minister who travelled from Vladivostock to Warsaw in the course of a tour round the world, told me that nothing struck him more than the contrast between the conditions of rural life in Russia and in Victoria. The Russian is a social fraternal soul. He will not plant his farm-house in the centre of his farm, as far as possible from his neighbours. All the little brown huts are pitched together like tents in a camp. In Australia and in America the settler squats out apart. Each man, in the centre of his 160-acre lot, leads a lonely life. When you are nearly a mile from your next-door neighbour, farming is not much better than solitary confinement for life, with no prospect of escape. Mr. Grant Allen once declared that the result of the American system was that the men committed suicide or fled to the town, while the women went mad. From these evils the Russian peasants have escaped by the resolute tenacity with which they have persisted in living together. No demonstration of the economic advantages of further scattering availed anything.

To all such arguments the one conclusive answer was, that it was too dull. Dulness they could not endure, and so they have preserved their simple family life, and continue to live in villages where every man knows his neighbour, where all are equal before the law and in the Mir, and where, in a sense now unknown to the Western world, every man is his brother's keeper. It has its drawbacks, this life; there are many things in it that are bad and black and disheartening.

But, on the whole, it is not only Mr. Ruskin who would say that the life of a Russian peasant is more natural and human, and therefore has greater opportunities for attaining to the ideal and the divine than the life of a resident in our London slums.

## CHAPTER III.

#### SHEPHERDS AND SHEARERS OF THE FLOCK.

The better to understand how true it is that, to the immense majority of Russians, Russia is a self-governed community, with extremely democratic and even socialist institutions, it may be well to examine how often the peasant's life is interfered with by an authority over which he has no control.

First, there is the Conscription. In this, no doubt, the hand of the central power is heavily felt by the peasant. It is also true that the peasants have no voice in deciding what number of troops are required for the safety of the Empire. The German peasant and the French small proprietor have that right theoretically. In practice, they have about as much to do with it as the Russian peasant. It is a question settled by military experts in consultation with financial authorities. The Russian peasant has compensations for his theoretical deprivation in two particulars. First, the blood tax is levied more sparingly by the Emperor than by either Constitutional Germany or Republican France; and, secondly, while the peasant has no voice in fixing the number of men required, he has authority in selecting those persons who have to serve. The starosta, and the Mir, do not know what number of regiments the Tzar must needs maintain to keep the Turks in order and the Austrians in check. But they do know better than any one else whether

Ivan Ivanovitch, who is the chief support of his widowed mother, or Peter Alexandrovitch, who is a wild and useless youth, can best be spared for the service of the State. And although this liberty of deciding who shall go may be and is no doubt abused, still it is a recognition of the right of the people to manage their own affairs, and to decide which of their number can best be spared for military service.

There is a primitive simplicity, a rude clumsiness, about the working of these rural institutions. Until the Russian has for three years reported himself when the day of Conscription comes round, he must never stray so far from home as not to be able to return to his original commune when the recruits are chosen. He may have got work hundreds of miles off, but back he must tramp to stand his chance when the day comes round. It is a great burden, that weighs grievously on the more independent and enterprising youth, who have to lose their employment and walk half across Russia merely to report themselves in case they should be wanted. But unless each man was actually in person present at his appointed place on the stated day, the whole Cosmos would no doubt seem to the official mind to have gone to wreck.

It is not for me to say a word in defence of universal military service, but it is worth while pointing out that the army is to the Russian a more useful school than it is to the more advanced Western nations. Military training may make a man of Hodge, when it would be mere waste of time and degradation to a University professor. The army in Russia is a disciplinary institution inculcating habits of order, of precision, of which the peasant stands as a rule sadly in need. When stout Radicals in France are found supporting General Boulanger, because the training of a soldier is so much more practical than that of a politician, we cannot marvel if there are those who feel that the passing of Russian youth through the military mill may not be without its compensations. If only it taught the Russians that time is money, that punctuality is a virtue, and that it is possible to measure time more exactly than by an easy-going guess at the position of the sun—when there is a sun, which there is not for half the time—the Conscription would pay its cost in the course of a single generation.

The army also, more than any of their institutions, excepting the pilgrimages, knits federated little peasant Republics into an organic whole. It is not needed so much in France, it is not needed at all in England or America. When the whole nation is constantly reading about what is going on within its borders, you do not need to resort to the coarse mechanical expedient of actually laying hold of the material bodies of men, and compelling them to march in certain companies, to live in certain barracks, and to associate at certain hours. But in Russia, where the outlook of the peasant is limited, this expedient may be at any rate better than none.

Then again, the army is in Russia an educational institution. Only 23 per cent. of the recruits who are taken can read or write —in Poland only 14 per cent. But before they complete their five years' service the soldiers all learn these necessary arts. If they pass their required examinations they can obtain their discharge two years sooner. The men also in the army are taught other, and in some respects higher, ideals of life than they would have acquired in their villages. They travel, they see new lands, and have the stimulus of fresh minds. In Russia, therefore, the army is less a mere incubus upon the national life, and more of a university for the poor, than it is in any other country in Europe.

Military service is still far from popular in the villages. The Russian peasant usually marries young, and although he does not indulge much in the ecstacy of romantic love, he finds it a very unwelcome exchange to be hurried off to the distant barracks just when he had expected to have started housekeeping in his own village. But the weeping and the wailing with which the villagers used to mark their sense of the fate that awaited the unlucky conscript in the old days have disappeared. Military service is shorter, the soldier is treated more humanely —corporal punishment was abolished in the whole of the army during Alexander the Second's reign—and although the recruit would gladly remain at home, he is no longer lamented as a lost man.

The second great interference of the Central Government in the affairs of the peasant is in the imposition of the taxes. The chief tax is the repayment of the purchase money advanced for the purpose of setting the serfs up in business as co-operative proprietors of their lands. This, in any case, would be imposed by a Central Government, and the Emperor probably made quite as good terms for the peasant as would have been made by any Parliament in the world. But here again, although the Central Government fixed the amount to be paid by the local community, the community itself assesses the quota for each of its members. Mr. Goschen, who has such aspirations for extending the octopus grip of the Tchinovniks of Somerset House over the whole income-tax-paying community, might perhaps with advantage observe the care with which the Central Government of Russia maintains a local popular body between itself and the individual taxpayer.

When at St. Petersburg M. Wischnegradsky was kind enough to say that he would furnish me with any information I desired concerning the financial position of the peasants. In reply to my inquiry he gave me the following summary of the extent to which the peasants are affected by taxation:—

The total sum of direct taxes annually paid by the peasants of the Russian Empire to the State Treasury amounts to 118·8 millions of roubles (comprising 41 million roubles for the repayment of debt for purchase of land), which makes about 1¼ roubles per head of rural population (both sexes), or about 5 roubles per head of adult male population.

The outstanding arrears on the 1st January, 1888, amounted to 55 millions of roubles.

The taxes imposed on peasants by local authorities amount, according to the last inquiries in European Russia, excluding Poland, to 50·3 million roubles, or about 2½ roubles per head of adult male population.

The last-named sum (50·3 million roubles) comprises 18·1 millions of roubles of the taxes for general local needs, and 32·2 millions of roubles for needs administered by special functionaries elected by peasant communities.

All the taxes paid by peasants are collected by functionaries elected by the peasant communities out of their members, and acting under the control of the Imperial Administration. The total sum advanced by the State to peasants for purchase of land amounted on the 1st January of 1888 to 872 millions of roubles. The amount of sums advanced up to the end of each year 1862-1886, the annuities, which were computed in the beginning of the operation at 6 per cent. of the sum advanced and then diminished, according to the law of the 28th December, 1881, to the amount of nearly 12 millions of roubles, the sums really paid by peasants for percentages and normal extinction, and for anticipated extinction of debt, and the outstanding arrears, are shown on the table at foot.\*

The diminution of outstanding arrears in the years 1884 and 1885 is mainly due to the annihilation of a considerable sum of these arrears by virtue of the Ukaz of 15th March, 1883, given on the occasion of the crowning of his Majesty the Emperor.

The total sum of the debt for purchase of land extinguished by regular and anticipated payments, and by alleviation, amounts to nearly 179 millions, or about 30 per cent. (in the mean) of the

\* In this connection it may be worth while to give the figures relating to the Land Purchase Law, by which, in 1862, the peasants were made owners of their holdings. This information, like the foregoing, was supplied by the Minister of Finance.

| Years. | Total sum advanced by the State from the beginning of operation to the end of corresponding year. | Annuities corresponding to the state of the debt at the end of corresponding year. | Sums really paid by peasants for percentages and normal extinction of debt. | Sums paid by peasants for anticipated extinction. | Outstanding arrears at the end of corresponding year. |
|---|---|---|---|---|---|
| | Roubles. | Roubles. | Roubles. | Roubles. | Roubles. |
| 1862 | 4,684,865 | 281,092 | 79,242 | 1,254 | |
| 1863 | 47,697,957 | 2,860,677 | 1,367,089 | 7,641 | 229,676 |
| 1864 | 132,170,854 | 7,930,251 | 5,291,263 | 22,196 | 1,759,281 |
| 1865 | 228,938,006 | 13,736,280 | 11,756,923 | 45,897 | 4,435,915 |
| 1866 | 342,289,227 | 20,537,354 | 17,185,051 | 112,081 | 6,469,645 |
| 1867 | 425,878,245 | 25,552,695 | 23,481,080 | 154,244 | 9,826,980 |
| 1868 | 512,453,723 | 30,747,223 | 25,642,250 | 305,112 | 11,983,648 |
| 1869 | 539,404,101 | 32,124,246 | 35,588,408 | 925,408 | 17,120,621 |
| 1870 | 556,602,770 | 32,028,040 | 32,494,268 | 535,367 | 15,696,601 |
| 1871 | 589,133,094 | 35,073,581 | 36,019,114 | 573,872 | 20,596,792 |
| 1872 | 623,095,176 | 38,086,686 | 37,501,301 | 485,377 | 19,164,059 |
| 1873 | 646,906,534 | 39,469,416 | 40,312,513 | 494,120 | 18,718,737 |
| 1874 | 665,308,673 | 40,095,765 | 40,285,699 | 528,975 | 15,938,718 |
| 1875 | 681,409,922 | 40,713,524 | 40,562,059 | 418,128 | 15,140,781 |
| 1876 | 692,443,919 | 41,045,619 | 39,077,418 | 592,165 | 15,120,784 |
| 1877 | 708,321,818 | 41,832,341 | 40,670,998 | 547,810 | 17,014,022 |
| 1878 | 721,364,817 | 43,211,115 | 43,841,110 | 595,166 | 18,381,024 |
| 1879 | 733,641,550 | 43,462,306 | 43,552,788 | 713,222 | 17,641,141 |
| 1880 | 747,226,431 | 44,142,428 | 40,599,735 | 1,021,396 | 17,371,826 |
| 1881 | 761,631,179 | 44,968,944 | 41,204,310 | 1,362,464 | 20,180,074 |
| 1882 | 781,106,114 | 43,201,498 | 39,797,745 | 587,565 | 23,649,584 |
| 1883 | 826,893,566 | 45,858,276 | 41,991,316 | 646,656 | 26,830,326 |
| 1884 | 846,068,368 | 38,734,406 | 39,251,931 | 679,228 | 18,826,114 |
| 1885 | 856,062,542 | 40,474,689 | 34,807,683 | 1,109,095 | 15,767,069 |
| 1886 | 868,193,879 | 41,028,679 | 37,942,886 | 600,141 | 18,270,789 |

total sum advanced, but this percentage varies for different communities, mainly according to the date on which the advance was made and to the amount of alleviation received.

The Central Government, which demands military service from the peasant, and which mulcts him in direct taxes to the extent of five roubles per adult male, leaves him otherwise very much alone. The pisser, or secretary, who is a low-class Tchinovnik, elected by the Mirs, and paid out of the local rates, is the pivot of the local administration. Inadequately paid, imperfectly educated, and of indifferent honesty, the secretary exercises much more power than he is always able to make good use of. He has to make out documents, to fill up the papers due to the Bureaucracy, and to act as the official nexus between the Volost or union of Mirs and the Imperial Administration. But he is a local officer, locally elected, locally controlled, and locally paid.

The only serious interference with the peasant other than that of conscription and taxation is that of the police. The ispravnik, or chief constable, the uriadnik, or rural constable, are appointed and controlled by the Ministry of the Interior. There is not, however, one constable to every village. The number of the uriadniks is between 5,000 or 6,000 for the whole Empire, or less than half the strength of the police of London.

There are serious complaints as to the abuse of power by these rural constables, and it is possible that they are often well founded. The only violence I saw during my stay in Russia on the part of any one was on the part of the policeman who came up to Yasnaia Poliana when the village was blazing. He bustled about, bullying and kicking the peasants as he ordered them to assist in saving timber from the fire, in a fashion which would have justified them in knocking him down. If he would do this in the presence of Count Tolstoi, he would probably be even less particular when there was no one present but the rustics. Granting, however, that all the police maintained directly by the Central Government abuse their power when they have the opportunity—a tolerably safe proposition whether in England or in Russia—the fact remains that there is not one policeman to every village—sometimes not more than one to a district as large as an English county.

The fourth point of contact between the peasants and the

Imperial Administration is in the Courts of Justice. The most of their local litigation is transacted in their own local courts; but more serious crime brings them into the presence of two Imperial officials, the Juge d'Instruction, or Public Prosecutor, and the Justice of the Peace—a stipendiary magistrate who exercises jurisdiction over several volosts. Both these officials are appointed by and responsible to the Minister of Justice in St. Petersburg. In every state this function is vested in the hands of the Central Government; and I was glad to hear even in Liberal quarters that the judicial bench was on the whole incorrupt, and gave general satisfaction. The Justices of the Peace are upright men, more practical if less idealistic than their predecessors, but acting in a fashion which inspires general confidence. Trial by jury, although frequently threatened, and at present seriously threatened, has, on the whole, worked well, although on this point there is a conflict of testimony. The Russian juries, trained in the practical common-sense methods of the Mir, never hesitate to suspend the operation of the law when, in their opinion, it would work injustice. This is partly due to the stiff and indefensible nature of the Russian code, which does not allow the same wide and liberal margin for the judges to adjust punishment according to the circumstances of the case. English judges repeatedly order merely a nominal punishment in cases where the prisoner, although technically guilty, is morally innocent. Russian judges have not that option. If a jury finds a man guilty of manslaughter, even although his action was meritorious, he receives the prescribed penalty just the same as if he were a criminal in intent as well as in fact. Under these circumstances Russian juries exercise the wise and humane discretion which English juries used to exercise when our Criminal Code was a disgrace to mankind: they return verdicts of "Not Guilty" even when the facts are beyond dispute. It is asserted, on the other hand, that the extreme leniency of the jury leaves the country unprotected, and that the innocent are sacrificed. Hence the pedants and sticklers for the letter of the law talk loudly about suspending trial by jury. I hope, however, that so retrograde a step will not be taken under the present Tzar. To get juries to convict, sentences must be made more elastic, and the prisons enlarged, so as to render imprisonment less terrible than it is in the present state of overcrowding.

The district *maréchal de noblesse* superintends the schools with the aid of the clergy and occasional Government inspection; but there are so few schools, unfortunately, that this does not amount to much to the average peasant.

The peasant does not concern himself much with the Zemstvo, or local Governing Council, elected by the peasants, the *noblesse*, and the towns, which exists side by side with the Assembly of the *Noblesse*. The Zemstvo collects the taxes, levies the rates, and superintends the local administration. If the Zemstvo fails in its duty, the Governor can bring it before the Courts. If they appeal, the matter is relegated to the First Department of the Senate, which is a kind of Judicial Committee of the Privy Council, and the Council of the Empire.

In addition to all these regular and permanent points at which the Central Administration touches or may touch the life of the peasant, there is the arbitrary action of the Government. If the Tzar willed it, any one of these peasants might be banished or imprisoned for life. The power exists; but practically it is not exercised. The peasants themselves send more men to Siberia by the free vote of their own Mirs than all those exiled for political propaganda or by the administrative process. In 1885 3,751 were banished thither by the Mir, while only 368 were exiled by executive order. In 1887 there were only 165 political exiles sent to Siberia. These figures are worth while remembering, if only as a proof how few the harsher side of Russian despotism affects. Mr. Forster the Liberal and Mr. Balfour the Conservative lock up 1,000 political prisoners in a single year out of 5,000,000 of the Irish, and all our Unionists declare that the hardship is inconsiderable. Even after making ample allowance for the difference between Kilmainham and Siberia, the contrast between from 200 to 400 political exiles out of a population of 90,000,000 in Russia, and 1,000 suspects or political criminals out of a population of 5,000,000 in Ireland, is sufficiently marked to carry its own moral; and of the 165 political exiles sent to Siberia in 1887, it is probable not five were peasants.

N

## CHAPTER IV.

#### THE IMPERIAL SHEPHERD.

Over all these scattered flocks of little brown sheep, whose internal economy I have attempted briefly to describe, is the great shepherd, still in the popular estimation the good shepherd, the Tzar.

The dual character of the Emperor is seldom appreciated in the West. The dispute between the two knights as to the shield in the fable may be paralleled by the controversy which rages between those who see only the Tzar-Tyrant and the others who only see the Tzar Tribune. It is, however, only in the West that the latter character of the Emperor is entirely ignored. No Russian, not even the bitterest Nihilist, ignores the popular conception of the Tzar as the good shepherd. Of this a very remarkable illustration is afforded in the last chapter of Stepniak's latest book, "The Russian Peasantry." It is an offence to many Russians even to name " Stepniak," who they say is a well-known murderer; but that fact makes his testimony as to this aspect of the question all the more valuable.

After surveying the condition of his countrymen from the advanced Nihilist standpoint, "Stepniak" concludes that the "Tragedy of Russian History" is—what? "The fatal superstition," as he calls it, " in the Tzar Tribune as the Champion of the people." "Stepniak" says "the worse the officials, and the more impossible the access to the Tzar, the stronger grew the people's conviction that he would redress their wrongs if he only knew them." The Tzar, he points out, is a glorified personal Mir. "The Tzar is the common Father of the country, its Protector, and the supreme dispenser of impartial justice to all, defending the weaker members of the community from the stronger. The Tzar "pities" everybody like the Mir. The whole of the nation's riches "belong to the Tzar" exactly in the same sense as the land and meadows and forests within the boundaries of the commune belong to the Mir. The most important function the peasant's imagination imposes on the

Tzar is that of universal leveller—not, however, of movable property. The Tzar is in duty bound to step in and to equitably redistribute the natural riches of the country, especially the land, whenever this is needed in the common interest. "The people repose implicit confidence in the Tzar's wisdom and justice. He is absolute master of the life and property of every man within his dominions, and no exception may be taken to his orders. The occasional blunders made by the Tzar, however heavy they may be, must be borne with patience, as they can be only temporary; the Tzar will redress the evil as soon as he is better informed on the matter."

No one can for a moment accuse "Stepniak" of partiality to the Tzardom. No more prejudiced witness could be brought forward to certify to facts the existence of which no one deplores more bitterly than he. We may therefore accept as beyond dispute the reality of the peasant's faith in his Imperial Shepherd.

It is easy to point out the many everyday objections to this popular belief, just as it is easy to describe the disadvantages which Russia suffers from the absence of the mountain ranges to which Western Europe owes its distinctive characteristics of climate and character. But the Russian autocracy, like the Russian plain, exists. Without them the Russian Empire would not be, and they must both be taken into account as fundamental factors. There are no Alps in Russia, neither is there Constitutionalism. It might be better for Russia if Mont Blanc stood where Moscow stands, just as it might be better if the peasants all believed in Parliamentary institutions. But the facts being otherwise, it is well to recognise the facts, and try to make the best of them.

The faith of the Russian peasants in the Tzar has its counterpart in the faith of the Emperor in the Tzardom. Often faith lingers among the rustics when it has died out in the objects of their devotion. In Russia the Tzars believe in the Tzardom, the present Emperor at least as much as any of his predecessors. Not that Alexander III. is an optimist. It is somewhat difficult to be an optimist on a throne to which you have been called by the bomb of the assassin. A saying of his is repeated in St. Petersburg which sheds a ray of somewhat sombre light upon his character. One of his brothers was talking to him once about the inextricable tangle of human affairs, and expressed very emphatically a similar opinion to that which made Alphonso of Arragon famous. If he were Ruler of the Universe, for instance, he would alter many things, and, in short, reconstruct the affairs of this world on an altogether new and improved pattern. The Emperor listened to him for a time, and then said, " I do not think so. As God made it otherwise, He must know best. But for my part, if He should end it all tomorrow I should be very glad."

Not a particularly cheerful observation to fall from a Vicegerent of the *bon Dieu*, but characteristic of the serious-minded ruler who is daily confronted with the insoluble problems of this confused and confusing world. He has not the fierce, frenzied faith of Peter, a Titan re-incarnate, who not merely saw the need of remaking the world, but felt sure he was called to do the work. But he has a great seriousness of mind, a deep conviction as to the responsibilities of his position, and a steady determination to do his duty as he sees it from day to day, leaving the rest to the Higher Power in whose hands an Emperor is but as a Moujik, and the affairs of the greatest of the kingdoms of the world are but as the waves of the sea which He holds in the hollow of His hand.

The Emperor believes firmly in his Tribunitial character. It is the theory of the Tzardom that every Russian, without distinction of rank or station, has a right of formal appeal to the Emperor direct. There is not a criminal who has not the right of formal appeal to the Emperor direct. There is not a criminal who has not a right to telegraph to the Tzar, nor a Moujik who is not free to write to the autocrat. Of this a curious instance was brought to my knowledge which occurred immediately before my visit to St. Petersburg. A rich rascal in the farthest east of Siberia, having murdered several poor men in order to seize a treasure which they were escorting, was condemned to death. From the condemned cell he telegraphed to the Emperor pleading for a reprieve. The Tzar received it, and sent for the Governor of Eastern Siberia, who was at that time in St. Petersburg. He went into the circumstances of the case with him, and decided to let the law take its course. Baron Korff, the governor in question, told the story to a Russian friend of mine, who exclaimed, " How could a criminal such as that obtain direct access to the Emperor?" Baron Korff replied with some astonishment, "Are you so ignorant of the constitution of your country as not to know that every Russian subject has always the right of personal appeal to the Emperor?"

This, it may be said, is the theory, but is it the practice? The Emperor regards the theory as essential to the Tzardom. All letters addressed to him pass directly into his hands. Some months ago Count Dmitry Tolstoi, the reactionary Minister of the interior, who must not be confounded with Count Léon Tolstoi the novelist, ventured to suggest to the Emperor that as the daily budget of correspondence and telegrams addressed personally to him constituted a heavy tax upon his Majesty's time, would his Majesty graciously deign to allow him, as Minister of the Interior, to go through his letters—to subedit his correspondence—in short, in order to weed out such as were obviously from madmen, whereby his Majesty's time might be economised. The Emperor's face grew dark. "You forget," he said, "that I am Emperor. How dare you propose to stand between me and my subjects?" So the unedited letters come direct to the Emperor every morning, and are dealt with by him.

Nothing could more clearly indicate the conception which Alexander the Third entertains as to his duty to his subjects, and of their rights in relation to himself. He is the shepherd of the flock. Every member of that flock has a right of direct appeal to him, and woe be to the hireling who ventures to stand between the shepherd and the sheep. In Eastern countries the Caliph used to sit under a palm tree dispensing justice, and listening to the complaints of all the aggrieved. Nihilist plots render it impossible for the Tzar to sit at the doorway of the Anitchkoff Palace to receive the petitions of his subjects, but the principle is the same. Every post-office is open. Every mail train will bear the petition to the Emperor's council-chamber. When General Gordon was at Khartoum he placed a box for petitions outside his head-quarters, the key of which he kept in his own possession. Into this box all those aggrieved by the conduct of his officers, all complainants of every rank, could place statements of their cases, confident that it would pass without any intermediary directly into the hands of the Governor-General of the Soudan. The Emperor has the same idea, and carries it out as best he can under certain conditions.*

It is this conception on the part of the Emperor which seems to me to encourage the hope that the Emperor may not be indisposed to take the steps necessary to enable him to realise his own ideal, and to give practical effect to the theory on which he is at present acting.

The Emperor Alexander the Third is, in many respects, a model autocrat, in disposition and in ideal. He has two great qualifications for the discharge of the difficult duties of his post —steadiness and courage. He is emphatically not a flighty man. He is sober, sensible, and sedate. He is not rash or precipitate. He is slow in forming a resolution, but when he has mastered a subject, and has the facts at his command, his decision is made once for all. His one anxiety is to do right, and when he has come to a conclusion that a certain course is right, he acts upon it regardless of danger. "Our Emperor," said one who knows him well, "is somewhat of an *enfant terrible*. When he sees what he thinks he ought to do, he goes to his object like a bullet from a gun. He does not ask what is in the way. Public opinion, censures of the press, all these things are nothing to him more than the croaking of frogs in the pond. Pressure, as you understand it, will never make him swerve a hair's breadth from his course. If you want him to change, you must not bring pressure to bear; you must persuade him. Once convince him that anything is right and he will do it. Otherwise he will not, no, not though all the voices in Europe, in the world, were denouncing him!"

The contrast between that type and that of the climbing

---

* As may be imagined, the curiosities of the Imperial letter-bag are numerous. I was shown one letter written to "Alexander Romanoff" by a blunt Yorkshirewoman in Normanton, who had taken upon herself to address the Tzar. She had a son—a boy of twelve—whom she intended to send into the army as a soldier of the Queen. She expected he would go to India, and there she thought he might encounter the Russians. Hence her letter to the Tzar. "I don't know what you want with India," she wrote. "I think you have land enough for any one man already; but if, as they say, you are going to India, I hope when you get there you will look out for my boy, and be kind to him!" The Emperor was much amused at the good woman's application, and gave the letter to an English friend of mine, in whose possession I saw it.

politician in constitutional countries is sufficiently marked, nor is the comparison altogether to the advantage of the West. The Emperor gave a signal illustration of his determination on the day of his coronation. Most monarchs at such a time would have attempted to give at least a semblance of popular concession to their first exercise of power. But Alexander III. deemed otherwise. The time seemed to him to call not for concession but for repression. Hence at the immense banquet at Moscow, when the representatives of all Russia were gathered together to celebrate his coronation, the Tzar addressed the elders from the provinces in words which Lord Wolseley, who was present, told me were received in awe-struck silence. "You have heard," said the Emperor, "that there was going to be a new partition of land. It is not true. There will be no addition to your lands. Go home and tell the peasants this. I intend to rule as my father ruled. Learn you to obey as your fathers obeyed." In Victor Hugo's "Ninety-Three," the Marquis proved his quality by shooting the sailor who had just saved the ship from the consequences of his own blunder. And an Emperor who could thus on his Coronation Day put his foot down upon the most ardently cherished expectations of his subjects, has at least sufficient iron in him to dare to do whatever may be necessary for the good of the State which is entrusted to his care. What, then, is necessary should be done in order to make the Emperor to realise his ideal, and to make him a more efficient and beneficent shepherd of his sheep? That is a question which must often have occurred to the Emperor, and any light upon that subject, from whatever source, cannot but be welcome.

The Emperor is head of the Executive power, and Tribune of the people. These are two functions equally necessary and indispensable. The Government must go on, and there is no power but the Emperor's will to make it march. He is the source of all power. There is not a Tchinovnik in the land who does not derive the authority which he uses or abuses from the Tzar. He must, therefore, be in constant and systematised relations with the heads of the bureaucracy. The great machine of government, the Executive in all its branches, has the autocracy as its central principle and initial force. There is no doubt much to be done in bringing the various departments of the State into harmonious and regular working, even to realise the ideal of the Executive Autocracy. "Where is the autocracy?" asked one day a brilliant and audacious Minister. "I see no autocracy; I see only administrative anarchy. Each department usurps some of the autocratic power. Ministries make alliances for offence and defence; they make war upon each other, or make peace. All that I see; but the autocracy—where is that?" M. Leroy-Beaulieu, in "L'Empire des Tzars et les Russes," far the most interesting and trustworthy account of Modern Russia published in recent years, points out this feature of the Russian Government in forcible terms. But, after all, that is not the chief defect of the Muscovite system, and it is not without its advantages in the absence of any real safeguards for popular rights and liberties.

The Emperor is the Tribune of his people. But this function, which represents the popular as opposed to the administrative aspect of the Tzardom, has largely fallen into the shade. It was inevitable that it should be so. The executive functions of the Tzar are sufficient to exhaust the energies of any mortal. The demands of administrative routine are all-engrossing. In our own Administration we see the tendency of mere red-tape and routine to absorb all the time and faculties of administrators. Our admirals, for instance, who sit as sea-lords on the Board of Admiralty, are kept so busy with mere office routine that they have no time to think out the great questions of naval policy. There is high authority for the dictum that a man cannot serve two masters, and it is obvious that if he tries, the master who is near at hand and whose demands are constantly repeated will obtain more of his service than the master who is far off and whose demands are either inaudible or intermittent. In the case of the Tzar, while there is necessarily constant and close connection between the autocracy and the bureaucracy, there has been a gradual but steady diminution of the points of contact between the autocracy and the democracy. In other words, the Tzar constantly tends to become more and more the first Tchinovnik in the Administration, and less and less the popular Tribune of the peasant's imagination. Emperors may strive against this tendency as they please; as long as it is only their own fitful will, no matter how imperious and resolute it may be, that is pitted against the steady, automatic, irresistible encroachment of the great administrative machine, so long will the latter tend to become supreme, and when it becomes supreme its doom will be sealed. For the saving principle of Russian autocracy is not the concentration of all power in the hands of the bureaucratic agents of one despot, but in the establishment of the champion of the popular rights, the tribune of the people's wrongs, as the master of the whole Administration of the Empire. When the Tzar ceases to be Tribune, he will cease to be Tzar.

The instinct of self-preservation combines with the sense of duty to press upon the Emperor the adoption of some means by which he can give to the Tribunitial side of his imperial position something of that backing in organised institutions which the executive side of his authority so amply possesses. The practice of government and the distribution of human energy are governed by the great law which impels matter to take the line of least resistance. In Russia as in England, it is the imperious clamant demand, insisted upon persistently, which is attended to. The great silent aspirations for justice and right which cannot make themselves a nuisance to the ruler are ignored. Every one does that which he must, rather than that which he would, and no human will is an adequate counterpoise to the dead weight of the pressure, all-pervading as that of the atmosphere, of the business demands of great Administrations. In England we have systematised the pressure of popular discontent in the House of Commons. In Constantinople, where it is quite unorganised, a conflagration is the only means by which the populace can warn the Sultan of the existence of wide-spread dissatisfaction. In Russia the bureaucracy, being constantly *en évidence*, and always able to present sufficient claim for the attention of the Tzar, will inevitably annex the Emperor and absorb the Autocracy. The Tribunitial power, not being backed up by any substitute for the House of Commons, is being driven to the wall. All that remains of it is the Emperor's letter-bag.

The necessity for something being done in this direction has been recognised by successive Ministers. The late Emperor had drawn up and signed, some days before his assassination, a decree summoning a National Assembly, elected by the provincial assemblies and the town councils, which would have been consulted concerning all legislative proposals. The Nihilists blew that tentative scheme into a thousand fragments when they killed Alexander II. But even under his successor, both General Melikoff and General Ignatieff put forth schemes for the summoning of a consultative assembly representing all Russia, which would have given to the Tribunitial side of the Emperor's position something of that reinforcement which it needs. Unfortunately neither of the Ministers was able to carry his scheme, and the Tzar has gone on from year to year without any attempt to give more substance to his Tribunitial power.

For it must never be forgotten that, by the law of its being, the bureaucracy regards the popular side of the Tzardom as its natural enemy. The natural law of the Tchinovnik is to convert the Tzar into a mere Tchinovnik, and to regard any attempt to exercise the Tribunitial power as an attack upon the fundamentals of the State. Every Tchinovnik likes to feel that he is clothed in all the majesty of the imperial power, and the very conception of the possibility that the Tzar may use his power to punish the Tchinovnik is a nightmare to the official mind.

The constant struggle of the bureaucracy is to compel the Tzar to see through their eyes, to hear with their ears, and to speak through their lips. In this enterprise they have been singularly assisted by the men who profess more than any others to represent the popular aspiration after liberty and justice. The Nihilists, by necessitating the constant protection of the person of the Emperor from the dynamite or the poison of the assassin, have practically shut him up in the secret chamber of the Tchinovnik. An Emperor who made constant progresses through his dominions, and who was accessible to all his subjects, might still play the tribune to some purpose. But these opportunities are limited to a man who is constantly dogged by the assassin.

The Tzar, although personally fearless, has hitherto been hindered in his efforts to realise the great ideal of the Tzar-Tribune by the very men who are driven wild by non-exercise of his Tribunitial power. The Nihilists have been the most potent allies of the Tchinovniks. Between them they have done much to destroy the only check which exists upon oppression, injustice, and corruption. The precautions which until recently had to be taken to protect the passage of the Imperial train were enough to make any one despair of any return to the methods of Haroun al Raschid. When last year the Emperor passed southward, the line was guarded in certain districts by soldiers with loaded rifles. A soldier stood at every fifty yards, with instructions to shoot any one who persisted in approaching the line. Several peasants were shot dead, some because they were too drunk to hear the challenge of the sentry, others because they did not understand it. Navvies working on the line were compelled to withdraw for a quarter of a mile, and for six or eight hours no one was allowed to cross the rails. The inconvenience thereby occasioned can better be imagined than described. The worst of it was that until this year no one could truthfully assert that such precautions were unnecessary.

Now, however, there seems to have dawned for Russia a better and a brighter day. The terrible catastrophe which destroyed the Imperial train at Borki, as the Tzar was returning from the Caucasus, seems to have broken the spell under which Russia had lain so long. The overwhelming outburst of enthusiasm evoked by the miraculous escape of the Emperor and his family afforded universal and unmistakable testimony to the loyalty and affection with which the whole nation regard their Sovereign. Restrictive and precautionary measures which were indispensable when Russia was honeycombed with conspiracies against the life of the Tzar would be obviously odious and insulting if they were persisted in after such a magnificent demonstration of the passionate devotion of the nation to the Emperor. Even Russians do not wear furs in summer, and after the thanksgiving service in the Kazan Cathedral a relaxation of the severity that followed the attempts of the Nihilists is inevitable.

Even in the inner circle of the Nihilist conspiracy, signs are not wanting that the long-looked-for change is at hand. The very remarkable confession of M. Tikhomiroff—one of the ablest of the Revolutionaries, who, after devoting years of his life to the service of the Revolution, has now abandoned Nihilism, and prays only for forgiveness from the Emperor whose Government he had so determinedly opposed—indicates that the period of despair is drwing to a close : that hope is beginning to shed its beneficent rays upon the darkest hearts. The generous response which Madame Novikoff has publicly made to M. Tikhomiroff is a not less gratifying indication of the approach of an era of reconciliation and of peace.

The stories current about the precautions taken to protect the Tzar before the fortunate sequel to the accident at Borki were grossly exaggerated. The Emperor went in and out among his people without any more appearance of protection than that which is extended to Mr. Balfour. At Peterhof, when the German Emperor visited him, he strolled about freely among the crowds who attended the Imperial fête, and he has just returned from an extended tour to the Caucasus. But even when all deductions have been made, the fact remains that the Emperor leads a very secluded life, receives very few people, and is the very reverse of a hard-riding Sultan. How, then, is it possible to make this earthly omnipotence omniscient? How can he be furnished with eyes and ears other than those of the bureaucracy? In what way can he be brought into close and confidential intercourse with his people, so that they can communicate to him their grievances, and he can impart to them his guidance?

## CHAPTER V.

### EYES AND EARS FOR THE TZAR.

WITHOUT presuming to dogmatise, and without venturing to anticipate what will be more fully dealt with in the next chapter, I may perhaps be permitted to indicate two points in which, to the sympathetic eye of a stranger, it seems possible to make a change for the better without any breaking of autocratic crockery. The first is the need of allowing greater liberty of initiative to the individual and to the locality. The second, the importance of pressing all the capable subjects of the Tzar into the service of the State.

The safety and the strength of Russia are largely due to the thoroughness with which the principle of decentralisation has been carried out in its local administration. The peasants may be unlettered, superstitious, and ignorant, but they are on the spot, they know the facts, they feel where the shoe pinches them, and a fool can often manage his own affairs better than the wisest of men can manage those of his neighbours. The interference of the Central Government no doubt is often necessary, and indeed inevitable. But that interference can never be other than mischievous when it stifles local initiative, subordinates the action of those who suffer evils which ought to be removed to the authority of officials at a distance, to whom these evils are more or less inconceivable, except as materials for despatches, and makes even the most necessary acts of self-preservation, which to be effective must be immediate, await the pleasure of remote and more or less indifferent administrators who have a thousand other things to distract their attention.

Ireland has been repeatedly brought to the verge of revolution simply because Westminster was twelve months too late in recognising the facts of the Irish situation. If that is so in a small country in close and constant communication with the capital, with a free press, and a representative from every Irish county at Westminster, how can it be otherwise in Russia, where there is no such close intercommunication between the centres and the extremities, where there is no Parliament, and where the press is gagged?

The Tzar must of course feel this more than any man living. The burden of responsibility which rests upon that monarch would crush any one who realised it, we do not say entirely, but even to the extent of ten per cent. Yet it is quite possible that he feels as if it were, to a certain extent, a flinching from his duty to seek to lessen it. The Tzar will never run away from his autocracy, as some Englishmen have run away from the task of maintaining the Union, not from any conviction in favour of Home Rule, but from sheer weariness and cowardice.

Not to save himself would Alexander III. lessen by a single iota the weight of his Imperial crown. But if he should once see that the assertion of a minute and embarrassing responsibility for all the details of the affairs of daily administration tends to injure the nation over which he rules, he would not hesitate for a moment in removing the injury, even although it lessened his responsibility.

To the eye of one accustomed to the growth of free communities in England and English-speaking lands, Russia seems as if she were choked in the swaddling clothes of infancy. No doubt there is not that individual initiative in the Russian that there is in the Englishman and American. No doubt the Tzar will often have to take the lead; even were his subjects Americans, there would be need for his intervention. But that only increases the importance of refraining from any action which seems calculated to cripple such initiative as the Russian people themselves possess. Hence, if my readers were to ask me what of all things seems most necessary in Russia, I would not say a parliament—I would not even say a free press—I would say that the first thing needful is to reverse the principle which dominates the Russian Administration. Instead of as at present holding that nearly everything is forbidden, excepting that which has been specifically permitted, why not let everything be permitted, except that which has been specifically forbidden? The change in phrase seems but slight. If it were carried out it would go far to relieve the Tzar and his Ministers of many of these difficulties to-day, and give an impetus to enterprise and industrial, social, and religious activity, which would in a short time work wonders. At present a man cannot even endow a bed in a hospital in Vladivostock without getting permission from St. Petersburg. Individual initiative is not so superabundant in Russia that there need be a specific legalisation for every fresh manifestation of its existence. If the *onus probandi* were thrown upon those who wish to restrict individual or associated activity, instead of upon those who wish to move, a blow would be given at many of the worst evils from which Russia suffers. It would give the nation more chance to grow.

"Hands off!" is a great formula, a formula to conjure with in the Balkan Peninsula. It might prove not less efficacious if used in another sense in Russia itself. If the Centralised Government at St. Petersburg would but keep its hands off the various tentative efforts of Russians to improve their institutions and to discuss their own affairs and to develop their own resources, what a blessing it would be! The St. Petersburg Departments may be very wise, but that is no reason why they should act as a perpetual extinguisher upon all manifestations of local and provincial independence. A nation of a hundred millions cannot be kept for ever in leading-strings of red tape, especially when, as is often the case, that red tape is held by a highly respectable collection of mediocrities. What is most needful, surely, is to give Russia her head.

No one can ignore the fact that in Russia progress has hitherto come chiefly from above. No one would propose to abate by a single jot or tittle the reforming and progressive authority of the Tzar. All that I ask is that the Government, in its zeal for reform and progress should not insist upon having a monopoly of those good things too exclusively in its own hands. The Imperial power may often be invaluable as an incentive where private enterprise fails. But that is no reason why it should be exerted to drive private enterprise out of the field.

The second great desideratum in Russia seemed to me so clear as to be almost an axiom. The Emperor ought to be able to avail himself of the talents of all his subjects in the arduous task of governing his immense dominions. To place any artificial barriers in the way of the utilisation of all the natural capacities of his subjects in the work of maintaining, defending, and governing the Empire is surely a great mistake. In one sense it is true that in Russia the career is open to all talents, but this is not exactly the same thing as securing for the State the service of all the capacities. To begin with, five-sixths of his subjects never have the chance—the very elementary chance—of learning to read and write. There ought to be twelve million children at school; there are only two and a half millions on the school register. Five-sixths of the available natural capacity born into Russia is therefore allowed to run to waste. The one-sixth that remains forms too small a proportion to undertake safely the very large order of governing so great an Empire. Still, if they were all available, something could be done; but unfortunately they are not. While Russia admits men of all religions to office, provided they have a distinctive religion of their own, she has no room in her service for men who, born Orthodox, have seen cause to leave the National Church, or who hesitate at taking the Sacrament as a qualification for office. Thus, so far from being able to harness to the service of the State all the men and women competent to help the Tzar in governing his Empire, he is unfortunately compelled to rely upon the services of only a fraction of that sixth of his subjects which alone is taught to read and write. Now, the work of ruling a great realm that stretches from the Vistula to Behring's Straits, and from the Arctic Circle to the borders of Persia, is not such child's play that those entrusted with it can afford to dispense with any of the natural talents with which its inhabitants may be endowed. The result of trying to do so is before us. Russia is at a standstill in almost everything except the increase of population. Instead of having all the best of the brain and conscience of the Russians heartily co-operating in the State's service, the conditions are so arbitrary and the disqualifications so numerous, that the Tzar is deprived of the services of many of the most intelligent and the most conscientious of his subjects. Hence the importance of giving every citizen a chance of being useful in the State service by making education universal and compulsory, at least in European Russia, and by flinging down all the barriers, whether of ecclesiasticism or of politics, which at present practically deprive the Tzar of many of the most independent and the most conscientious of the educated minority.

The Emperor's Letter Bag is almost the only means by which the mass of his subjects can make known to the man who is their natural and appointed Tribune, their grievances or their complaints. The department of the Imperial Chancery which attends to this Tribunitial side of the Emperor's daily work is presided over by General de Richter, one of the best men in Russia. General Richter is from the Baltic provinces, a Lutheran and a sincerely pious and devoted Christian. He commanded in Sebastopol during the Russo-Turkish war, as a general in the artillery. Few men whom I met in Russia impressed me more favourably. An honester and more straightforward man never breathed, or one more full of all the better and nobler aspirations of humanity. He has an office under him which is concerned with answering petitions and attending to applicants for the Imperial intervention. To him the Emperor refers the 100 petitions per day which arrive on an average every twenty-four hours, and to him come, in long queue, the petitioners who seek to bring their troubles before the Emperor. He is as it were the Tzar's secretary, and no better man could be found for the place. A high-minded man of stern integrity, his selection for the responsible post which he occupies in the Imperial *entourage* and the confidence which the Emperor places in him is an indication that Alexander the Third is a better judge of men than some of his critics are disposed to admit.

"That portfolio of General Richter," said a dashing young officer whom I met on my way to Gatschina, "should be made of waterproof, for it is watered with tears of the suppliants of a whole nation." General Richter is the Sandalphon of the Empire. He listens to the sounds that ascend from below:—

> "From the spirits on earth that adore
> From the souls that entreat and implore
> In the fervour and passion of prayer,
> From the hearts that are broken with losses
> And weary with dragging of crosses
> Too heavy for mortals to bear."

He is the door-keeper of the Earthly Providence whom men call the Tzar. He has to read the petitions, to receive the petitioners, to be the ear and the voice of the Emperor. It is heart-breaking work; for after all, the extent to which a Sovereign, even when he is an autocrat, can intervene between mortals and adverse fortune is very limited; and yet, as Titus said, no man should approach the person of Cæsar and go away unsatisfied.

It was this aspect of the Imperial responsibility which made me feel so keenly the analogy there is between General Richter in Russia and the editor of a newspaper in England. There is probably no mortal in England who receives so many petitions from the aggrieved, or is so constantly invoked as a *deus ex machina* by the suffering and the oppressed, as a newspaper editor. In our free democracy, the editor is the keeper of the ear of King Demos. "If you will but take up my case," so runs the familiar and constantly repeated formula, "public opinion will be roused, and I shall get my rights. If you will but show up this injustice, let the light in upon that abuse, call attention to some scandal"—"If, if." Alas! for the delusions of popular superstition. Public Opinion, our great Tzar, can interfere but fitfully and more or less at haphazard in the redress of individual grievances. All the petitions in General Richter's portfolio, what are they to the endless stream of complaints, of protests, of petitions of all kinds with which our press teems? And our

o

Public Opinion, omnipotent as it is when it is fairly roused, cannot concern itself about all these things at once. Now and then it will bestir itself, and some particular sufferer is snatched from ruin by its intervention, or some measure is forced through Parliament by its potent voice; but as a whole, Public Opinion is a somewhat inert force which only occasionally interferes directly in the righting of wrongs. And therein Public Opinion resembles the Emperor. The great machine of the State goes on automatically; the Law Courts meet and administer justice, the taxes are collected, the railway trains start, the tramcars run through the streets, and all the world and his wife get breakfast every morning without much interference from Governments, whether set in motion by Tzars or by Public Opinion. And the great collective joys and sorrows of humanity, births and marriages and deaths, disappointed love, broken health, pestilence, famine, blighted ambition, bankruptcy and insanity, all the great matters which make up the warp and woof of our lives, are beyond the control of the most puissant of Emperors. He is but a fly on the rim of the teacup in which the waves of our feverish existence make their mimic storm.

Nevertheless, although this minimising estimate of the Emperor's position may be strictly correct, there are undoubtedly many things in which he can interfere, and interfere with effect. If he does not interfere, no one interferes; for the Tzar as Tribune is the only authority who can be invoked to prevent the injustice that is done by those who act in the name of the Tzar, the chief of the Executive power. He is the Russian House of Commons—the representative of the Common people. I was very much impressed by the remark made to me by a Moscow Liberal who was arguing in favour of a limited franchise for the election of a National Assembly. I objected that any such system would of necessity leave all the peasants without a single representative. "Oh," replied my Liberal, "they need no representative in any assembly, for the Emperor represents them." But for the due fulfilment of his *rôle* as House of Commons, it is necessary that he should have eyes and ears and tongue independent of the Administration of which he is at once the supreme head and the only check.

How can that be done? He who can solve that question, solves everything. The ordinary solution which is suggested by the working of systems of representative government in the West is that of summoning a representative assembly. The Zemskie Sobory, or consultative assembly, which Russians always invoke when they are pressed on this subject, would no doubt enable the Tzar to take counsel with his people, and form some better idea than he can at present of the wants of his subjects. But for the present that scheme is in abeyance, and it is perhaps too long a stride to take at once. "You are summoning a States General," was the answer to General Ignatieff's proposal to assemble an immense concourse of three thousand delegates in the Temple of the Saviour at Moscow; and it is easy to understand that an autocrat would hesitate before consenting to the establishment of anything resembling a Parliament within his dominions. Since then Russia has been receding rather than advancing in the path of progress, and that which would have been a daring stride when General Ignatieff fell, must appear a reckless leap in the dark to the men who now surround the throne. Besides, the Tzar does not see the advantage of summoning an elected assembly. He sees its dangers and its drawbacks. But he fears, not unnaturally, that its tendency would be— especially if, as many reformers propose, it were elected by a more or less limited constituency of the intelligent classes—not to give eyes and ears to the Tzar to enable him the more efficiently to exercise his high prerogatives, but rather to set up a rival and conflicting authority within the Empire, which would paralyse the autocracy. This may appear desirable to those who hate the autocracy, but the autocrat can hardly see things in that light. And as the first condition of any change in Russia is to convince the ruler of Russia that it is useful and necessary, it is no use harking back perpetually to the Zemskie Sobory, or to any Parliamentary apparatus whatever. The time for that may come hereafter; it has not arrived to-day.

The Russians do not seem to take kindly to representative institutions. The City Councils of Moscow and St. Petersburg are the nearest approach to Parliaments to be found in Russia. It is very difficult to secure the attendance of the members; and frequently in Moscow, I was told, no business can be transacted because they cannot get together a quorum.

The Zemstvoes, or rural assemblies, can hardly be said to have justified the expectations with which their establishment was hailed. The peasants have never taken kindly to these institutions, which, while intended to be a link between the people and the Tzar, have come to be a barrier between them. The peasants are compelled, on pain of a legal penalty, to send delegates; otherwise they would, in many cases, ignore the Zemstvo altogether. These delegates are compelled to attend—a provision which excites great dissatisfaction. In "Anna Karenina" Count Tolstoi satirises the futility of the Zemstvoes; and in this the novelist represents faithfully the views of the peasants whom he reveres. A landowner who had held high office in the Imperial Ministry assured me that if the franchise were limited to those who cared for it, hardly any peasants would vote in the elections for the Zemstvo. The Russian peasant is very much of the opinion of the Chinese who, hearing some Europeans eagerly discussing a political question, asked with wondering amazement why they gave themselves so much trouble about such matters. "Were not the Mandarins paid to settle them?" It is silly to keep a dog and then to bark yourself; so the Moujik does not see the sense of having a government, and then having to do, or rather to pretend to do, the governing himself, at a great loss of time and expense. The rival candidates bully, cajole, and corrupt the village starostas, and then secure the support of the delegates by keeping them alive and supplying them with vodka.

This apathy or hostility on the part of the peasants to the Zemstvo has been actively seconded in its destructive influence by the jealousy of the Tchinovnik. The dominant idea of the dominant party in Russia at present is to reduce the status, to destroy the initiative, and to control the deliberations of the Zemstvo. To increase the power of the *maréchal de noblesse* and the rural gentry on one side, and on the other to saddle every Zemstvo with an official representing the Central Government, without whose leave nothing can be discussed, and by whom anything can be vetoed, are ideas which may commend themselves to a blind and timorous bureaucracy, but they do not conduce to the development of the spirit of self-government beyond the confines of the Mir.

What, then, must be done? I am not sanguine enough to believe that any one, much less a foreigner who has only paid a flying visit to the country, can possibly do more than merely throw out a suggestion for the solution of the crucial problem before Russia and her ruler to-day. But in the absence of all other suggestions that seem to promise any exit from the present *impasse*, I venture, with all diffidence, to put forward what seems to me a very simple and natural suggestion, which has at least the merit of making no pretence to originality, but is merely the logical and natural development of what already exists, and which has the immense advantage of being capable of being tried as an experiment without endangering for a moment the stability or the prestige of the Autocracy.

Eleven years ago, in Madame Novikoff's *salon* in Brook Street, I remember hearing Mr. Gladstone assure his hostess that in his opinion the freedom of the press in England had done more to rid our Administration of corruption, and the public service of scandal, than had been effected by all the debates of all the Parliaments in which he had served. Immediately before leaving for Russia in the spring of this year, I recalled the remark to Mr. Gladstone's remembrance, and asked him if anything had occurred to modify his conviction. "On the contrary," he said, "I am more than ever impressed by the immense services which the press has rendered to the purity and efficiency of our public service. It is the constant flood of light which the press pours in upon all the dark places in which corruption lurks which is the best safeguard against these evils, against which every Government has to contend. In our administrations abroad we have usually introduced a free press prior to the establishment of Parliamentary institutions." Mr. Gladstone would not commit himself offhand to a definite opinion that this was always the best mode of progress—the subject required exhaustive examination—but it was evident that his mind inclined in that direction.

The natural and simplest mode by which Governments in the West are kept informed of what is going on is by conceding to the press a liberty which, although it may verge upon licence, is nevertheless invaluable as the eyes and ears of the Administration. The State does not concern itself with the collection or distribution of news—that is a business undertaken by private individuals as a speculation, and the competition of the rival newsmongers suffices on the whole to keep the rulers tolerably well informed of the wishes, the sufferings, and the grievances of the ruled. In the German Empire, where the Administration takes a far more comprehensive grasp of all the details of the life of its subjects, Prince Bismarck has organised an Intelligence Bureau, infinitely superior in the minuteness and the precision of its information to that possessed by any German newspaper. Every German official can be utilised as a news-collector, and the high standard and trained intelligence of the German bureaucracy enables Prince Bismarck to rely upon it for this service.

Germany, however, possesses both a Parliament and a press which supply a constant supplement to the facts collected by the Intelligence Bureau. Russia has neither an Intelligence Bureau, nor a Parliament, nor a free press. The result is that the Tzar is often in the dark. He has the slenderest means of knowing what is going on in his extended dominions. He has, of course, the ordinary official reports, but he has no regular systematised means ready to hand whereby he can check these reports, or on which he can rely for an exposure of the misdeeds of the officials. Suppose—unfortunately no impossible supposition—that by some gross job of the Minister of the Interior a corrupt and oppressive governor is appointed to some province. What means are there other than a letter or petition by which the corruption and oppression of that governor can be brought to the knowledge of the Tzar? The *prestige* of the Tzar's authority is used to blindfold the Tzar. The consequence is that the most hideous wrongs may be perpetrated—and must, from the nature of things, be sometimes perpetrated—wherever a corrupt and unscrupulous official finds himself in the midst of a submissive population. There is little or no check upon his misdeeds. The State has repeatedly been plundered in the most scandalous fashion, and no one has dared to expose the theft. If the Emperor knew, he would no doubt make short work of all these knaves. But he does not know; he cannot know; and so the evil work goes on for years unchecked.

The newspapers which are still suffered to exist are all under the thumb of the Minister of the Interior, who tends more and more to obscure the Tzar from the eyes of his subjects. The things which it is most important for the State that a newspaper should say, are the things which the Minister of the Interior most resents their saying. Imagine what would have happened in London if the Metropolitan Board of Works had been armed with powers to suppress the *Financial News* when it began its exposure of the corruption of its officials. No one accuses the members of the Board of Works with being personally corrupt; they simply followed the natural instincts of governing bodies, and resented attacks upon their officials as if they were obviously unjust. Fortunately, the Board of Works had no such power. The press continued its attacks, and at last a Commission was appointed, whose inquiries revealed a state of corruption of which even the assailants of the Board had no adequate conception.

I had a long and most interesting talk on this subject with M. Suvorin, the editor of the *Novoe Vremya*, now the most widely circulated and most influential newspaper in St. Petersburg. Speaking of the difficulties under which the press laboured in the discharge of its duty in Russia, M. Suvorin remarked that his position was a very critical one. By the Russian press law any newspaper after a third warning could only be published under the preventive censure, which, in the case of a daily newspaper, was equivalent to suppressing it altogether. The *Novoe Vremya* had already received two warnings. A single mistake on the part of any reporter or sub-editor might bring down upon him a third warning, which would practically destroy the greatest newspaper in the Empire. Under these circumstances, it is easy to see how cautiously an editor must move when dealing with the most flagrant abuses in which either the Minister of the Interior or any of his relations or officials might possibly be interested. But I said to M. Suvorin, " A warning would never be issued for mere resentment at an unguarded expression? So grave a step could only be taken to punish some flagrant outrage upon good faith, or some scandalous attack upon the Government." M. Suvorin shrugged his shoulders. " I will tell you the story of my two previous warnings, and you may judge for yourself. The first I received more than ten years ago." " But that was before the present reign began." " Quite true; and so was the second. But no amnesty is allowed for press offences; no lapse of time is allowed to annul the fatal record. My first offence was committed when M. Makoff was Minister—Makoff who subsequently committed suicide. I was away from the office. My *locum tenens* wrote a New Year's article of the usual kind, restrospective and speculative. He wound it up by a flourish, in which he expressed a hope that the New Year would bring Russia good things in its train—peace, prosperity, and a little liberty. For that innocent aspiration the *Novoe Vremya* received its first warning." "Merely for hoping the New Year would bring Russia a little liberty?" "Precisely; that was the only offence. The second was even more extraordinary. You may remember during General Loris Melikoff's Ministry, General Greig, then Finance Minister, made a provincial tour in which he made some curious speeches." "I remember it perfectly." "Well, General Greig was utterly wrong in these speeches, and the *Novoe Vremya* pointed out in one or two trenchant articles that the Minister's figures did not correspond to the facts, and that he was obviously unfit for his place." "That was rather strong, was it not?" "Yes, but it was perfectly true, and the proof of that was that in a few days General Greig was compelled to resign." "Then why were you warned?" "Oh! that was in order that Loris Melikoff might clear himself from the suspicion of having inspired the articles. Loris Melikoff notoriously wanted to get rid of General Greig, and therein he was quite right. But he did not wish people to say that he had set on the *Novoe Vremya* to attack his colleague, and so he issued the second *avertissement*." "But that was absurd. Surely, when General Greig fell, and the justice of your criticism received the strongest possible confirmation, the warning was withdrawn?" "By no means; it is still on record against me. And any day I may receive a notice that, owing to some paragraph or other which offends some one in the Ministry of the Interior, my third warning has been issued, and my property is ruined."

I pondered over this, and then remembering the Tribunitial power of the Tzar, and the right which every Russian has to write to him, I asked why M. Suvorin did not write to the Emperor, pointing out the flagrant injustice of reckoning these old warnings against the *Novoe Vremya*, and appealing to him to wipe the slate. I was answered, "He could write to the Emperor, no doubt; but what would be the result? The Emperor would naturally and of necessity lay his complaint before the Minister of the Interior. The more entirely the Emperor took M. Suvorin's side, the more indignant would be the Minister that the matter had been taken over his head to the Emperor. If the Emperor was determined, his immediate petition might be gained, but he would probably be marked down for vengeance at the first opportunity. The Minister would bide his time, but he would take good care that anyone suffered for my temerity in appealing to the Emperor against his department."

Under these circumstances what exit is there from the *impasse?* The Minister of the Interior's power is practically absolute; it is exercised secretly. The subject of his vengeance has no opportunity of making his defence; he is at the mercy of the official whose misconduct it may at any time be his duty to expose. When I exclaimed against this monstrous regimen of injustice, Russians used to reply by saying that their editors "were such third-rate men they could not be trusted with the liberties which, for instance, journalists like yourself enjoy in London"—for they were very flattering. To which I used to reply by asking how any but sixteenth-rate men could continue to edit a newspaper in Russia under Count Dmitry Tolstoi. If by any chance I were to edit a Russian newspaper, I should certainly receive my three warnings in the first week of publication, and would probably be packed off to Siberia in a fortnight.

It is true that considerable licence is allowed to the press in certain directions; but this is due to the administrative anarchy which prevails in the Russian Government. "As soon as General Ignatieff became Minister of the Interior," I was told by one who ought to know, "a deputation of editors waited upon him to know how many of his Ministerial colleagues he left them free to attack. General Loris Melikoff, they said, drew up a list for their guidance. So many Ministers had not to be criticised—so many others were fair game for the press." When I was in Russia the papers were allowed to attack the Foreign Office as much as they pleased. The one department in which the press, according to Mr. Gladstone, is almost entirely mischievous, was open to them; while the one department in which its influence is almost entirely good was closed. The regulation of the press belongs to the Ministry of the Interior. Hence home affairs had not to be meddled with; but between M. de Giers and Count Dmitry Tolstoi there was no love lost. Therefore "my poor *ministerium*," as Baron Jomini ruefully remarked, was left to be the target for all the journalistic missiles of the Russian press.

If the Tzar is to be an earthly Omnipotence, then he must

first seek to acquire an omniscience corresponding to the magnitude of his power. Great is Jove, the Father of Gods and Men; but imagine a blind Jove! To be the Tribune of all the Russias the Tzar must be accessible to all the Russians; to be head shepherd of all the flocks of the Russian sheepfold, his eyes must be on all his sheep, and his ears open to the plaintive cry of the weakest lamb.

But, alas! excepting for what he may learn from the Tchinovniks, upon whose abuse of authority his power is the only check, the Tzar is often left in the dark. At two feet or so he can read small print; at two hundred feet he can discern the features of his fellows; beyond that range he must depend upon others, and those others the very men whose misconduct may be driving his subjects to despair. Neither can he hear further than other men. Heimdall, the warder of the Norse gods, heard the grass growing in the fields and the wool on the sheep's backs, but Alexander III. can hear no human voice at the distance of two hundred yards; and much that he ought to hear—the groanings of the typhus-smitten captive in the overcrowded prisons of Tomsk and Tiumen, for instance—is thousands of miles away. How, then, can he be made to see and to hear?

It is the condition of the efficiency, even of the existence of the Tzardom. The solution of this problem is the Riddle of the Sphinx that confronts the Emperor and his advisers. Humbly, and with all diffidence, I venture to mention some methods by which it seems possible, in the absence of any more practical proposals, the Tribunitial power of the autocracy might be made more potent for the benefit of the Russian people.

1. The Tzar could lay down certain broad general principles for restraining the abuse of his delegated authority by the Tchinovniks. This would be practically the Tzar's Bill of Rights to his people, and while in no way limiting his absolute autocracy would secure that his high and singular power should only be used to override these general principles by his own personal act. I have not the presumption to attempt to draw up such a Bill of Rights. One article, however, may be suggested—an article which might be as useful for the Tzar as for his people:—

"No one shall be committed to prison without being furnished with particulars of the charge against him within one week of his arrest. No one shall be detained in prison without being brought to trial longer than six months after his arrest, and every one who is imprisoned beyond that time shall, on appealing to the Emperor, be at once released, unless the Emperor shall personally declare, in a document signed by his Imperial Majesty, that the continued imprisonment without trial of that individual is necessary for the welfare of the State."

This surely is no immoderate proposal. If it had been acted upon in the last reign, Alexander II. might have been living to this day. It was the bitterness engendered by arbitrary imprisonment without trial which helped to explode the dynamite that slew the Tzar. Of the justice of the proposal there can hardly be two opinions. It leaves absolutely intact the absolute right of the Tzar to imprison for ever any one without trial, providing he does so on his own direct personal responsibility. But so vast a power is not one that can be delegated to any Tchinovnik.

2. The Tzar could select say ten, twenty, or fifty of the most trustworthy Russians, and commission each of them to act as the *alter ego* of the Tzar Tribune in a specified circuit or district. Each would have the duty of being eyes and ears for the Tzar, on his circuit. While they would, in some respects, resemble the Chinese censors, they would correspond more nearly to the *Justiciarii errantes* of our old Norman kings, who would ride in circuit independently of the official administration. They would hold the Tzar's Courts in all cases of appeal against the misconduct of officials; by them all prisoners would be released who were unjustly imprisoned; they would be the visible, palpable, popular, accessible representation of the Tribunitial power. Each, after going circuit, would return to the Tzar, and report directly to him. He would thus be able to inform himself of the needs and aspirations of his subjects.

3. The third thing which the Tzar might do to realise more fully the ideal of a Tribune is to create for himself an organ by means of which he can communicate constantly with his people, and by means of which they can communicate with him. There are many good Russians devoted to the autocracy who would assert that the only means by which such free and constant intercommunication can be effected is by resorting in some form to the principle of representative institutions. Whether it is the

Zemskie Sobory or some other constitutional apparatus, no one proposes that the suggested assembly should have other than consultative functions, the sovereignty of the Tzar being left unimpaired. I have of course nothing whatever to say against any such organised method of bringing the ruler and the ruled into closer communication for counsel and encouragement. But the first fact to be taken into account is that the Tzar, for reasons good or ill—it matters not—will not establish a representative assembly, and regards even the modest proposal to summon the Zemskie Sobory as equivalent to a suggestion to create a States-General. In face of that *non possumus*, what can be done to attain an end which is admittedly very much to be desired? At present the Tzar has very scanty means of ascertaining the wishes of his subjects or of hearing their complaints; for whenever these wishes and these complaints are opposed to the interests of the officials, they can use his authority to blindfold his eyes and stop his ears. In other words, his subjects cannot speak to the Tzar on those occasions when it is most important in the interest of the Tzar himself that they should speak. There is no more right of public meeting, when it suits a Tchinovnik to forbid any public assemblage, than there is in any open space or highway in London except by the grace of the Home Secretary. Deputations occasionally are sent to St. Petersburg, but there is no right of public petition, there is no right of free press. All the doors by which in other States the monarch and his subjects are able to communicate with each other are carefully bolted and barred and guarded by vigilant sentries of Tchinovniks, who can usually keep the Emperor in a state of ignorance.

If the Tribunitial power is to become a reality, some means will have to be contrived to open up channels of communication between the Tzar and his people. I frankly confess that I see no other way comparable for safety and efficiency to that of the establishment of an Imperial Newspaper, in which his subjects would have the right of setting forth their grievances. In this era of the printing press, it is not necessary to assemble men in a deliberative chamber in order to secure public expression of their wishes. The chief efficacy of the House of Commons as a redresser of grievances is the privilege of publicity which it enjoys. That publicity depends chiefly for its efficiency upon the reports of the proceedings in Parliament which appear in the public press. There is no need for such a roundabout method of securing publicity in Russia. If the Emperor were to establish a journal, as other monarchs have established a Parliament, as a rostrum from which their subjects can set forth their views, he would secure a much more effective guarantee against abuses being hushed up and oppression perpetuated than by any other means compatible with the existing interdict on the ordinary safeguards of constitutional States.

Government by journalism may yet have a great future in Russia. At present there is not a journal in Russia that possesses any influence worth speaking of. The field, therefore, is clear for a journal that will be a tolerable substitute for a free press and a popular parliament. But such a paper must be the Emperor's paper, in the same sense that the army is the Emperor's army, and the navy the Emperor's navy. No one would dream of proposing that the Tzar should himself turn editor, any more than that he should take command of his own fleet. But as he has his Admiral, so he would have his Editor, whom he would authorise to publish the truths which Tchinovniks wish to hide. In such a newspaper, the right to print a petition of grievance might be conceded by the Emperor to certain categories of representative persons throughout the country. If, for instance, one thousand persons, the mayors of the chief towns, the presidents of the Zemstvoes, the heads of the various religious bodies, the chiefs of the various professions, the spokesmen of mercantile and manufacturing classes, and representative peasants, had a right to set forth at reasonable length, in the columns of the Imperial paper, their petitions for the redress of grievances, a safety valve would be opened the value of which no one would profit so much by as the Emperor. All such petitions would appear as of right, unless the Emperor personally ordered the suppression of any particular petition, in which the fact of such suppression would be publicly announced as the direct act of the Emperor.

It would be a mistake, however, to convert the Imperial newspaper—which would be quite as important an institution as the Council of the Empire, or the Senate, or the Army, or the Navy—into a mere gazette for the publication of petitions of grievances. It would be equally important as a means of diffusing throughout the whole empire the wishes, the ideas, and the information of the Emperor and the ablest men in his service. Other Emperors have endowed universities for the culture of a handful of the youth of their subjects, and have founded libraries visited by the learned. It will be a greater glory for the Tzar Tribune to allocate a portion of his revenues for the founding of a newspaper which would be the popular university of the whole empire, and would bring every week to the door of every peasant the wisest thoughts, the ripest culture, and the most useful information bearing upon the events of the day that could be collected by the ablest writers in Russia. In what other way can the Head Shepherd at Gatschina minister so well to the daily mental and spiritual wants of those sheep which look to him as to an earthly omniscience for guidance and for counsel?

The idea, fantastic as it may appear to those who have not yet learned that when autocracy survives in an age of democracies and printing presses it must use the latter to instruct the former, if it would continue to exist, is not strange to the present Emperor. One of the most hopeful constructive efforts of his reign has been the founding of a little weekly paper, the *Rural Messenger*, one copy of which is sent every week into every Volost in the Empire. When General Ignatieff was Minister of the Interior, it gave promise of becoming a real means whereby the Tzar and people could communicate with each other. After General Ignatieff's fall, it continued indeed to exist, but it lost its promise. But it still circulates, and although its editor is a feeble creature enough, the paper contains in itself the germ of an institution which yet may bring saving health and strength to the Russian Empire. If the Emperor were to grasp the idea of utilising the press as a means at once of popular education, popular guidance, and popular representation, and were to instal as first Imperial Editor, let us say, a statesman of the standing and experience, of the genius and courage, of General Ignatieff, with a competent staff, who would be responsible solely to the Tzar for the contents of their sheet, it would be as if he had found a new sceptre, while to Russia it would be as if the nation had suddenly found its voice.

Government by the representatives of voting majorities, which may be ignorant, passionate, or prejudiced, is not in favour in Russia.

But the true alternative is not the Government of Tchinovniks, each trading upon the delegated authority of the Tzar. It is the Government of the Tzar constantly in communication not with the elected but with the elect of his subjects. To winnow out these elect, to discover in each Volost, in each Mir, who is the capable, the honest, and the public-spirited person who is best fitted to be Correspondent to the Emperor, that would naturally be one of the first functions of the Imperial Editor. It is work that can be done. If it were done, even if very imperfectly, what a check it would place upon corruption, what a stimulus to public enterprise, what sure means of discovering those abuses which eat into the vitals of the State! It would give the Emperor the hundred eyes of Argus in every province in his Empire, while every reader would be as an additional arm of the Imperial Briareus, who would at last wage war with the abuses of the Tchinovnik with some possibility of success. Until the Tzar can rely upon the intelligent and systematised support of his people he will be more or less reduced to the status of the first Tchinovnik of his realm. But if he can secure and command that support, he may yet surpass all the glories of his predecessors and rise to the height reserved for the Tzar Tribune.

## CHAPTER VI.

### A PLEA FOR MORE PRISONS.

ONE of the most urgent necessities of Russia is more prisons. If the head shepherd at Gatschina had a million sterling available for improving the weak places in the fold, the first claim would be that of the prisons. Russia has outgrown her prisons, just as a thriving boy outgrows his small clothes. The result is that there is great overcrowding in most of her gaols, and overcrowding in a gaol is often only a polite mode of describing death by slow torture.

Exception may be taken to the doctrine that the criminals of Russia have the first claim upon the revenues available for internal reform. But the objection is not well founded.

The criminal convict has the first claim not because of his crime, but because of his absolute dependence upon the State for existence. When Society—for whatever cause—locks up a man in gaol, it becomes solely responsible for his welfare. As long as he is at large he may look after himself, but when he is in gaol the State must look after him or he will perish. All who are thus deprived of liberty by the State become foundlings of the State, adult children to whom the State stands *in loco parentis*, and for whom it is bound to provide, despite their criminality, as if they were more peculiarly the children of the State than the honest men who are still at large. No one who has any practical acquaintance with the ruling men in Russia, from the Emperor downwards, will for a moment deny that they are as benevolently disposed towards their prisoners as any member of the Howard Association. In the very infancy of the humanitarian movement, Howard was welcomed to Russia by Catherine the Great, and the first draft of prison reform in Russia was inspired by the writings of that indefatigable philanthropist, who perished in Russia a victim to the typhus of her gaols.

Early in this century, the Emperor Alexander I. reformed his prisons on the basis of a scheme drawn up by an English Quaker, Mr. Venning, and the present Emperor yields to none of his predecessors in the sincerity of his desire for the wellbeing of his prisoners. M. Galkin-Wratzky, who is, as we should say, President of the Prison Board of the Empire, is a humane and intelligent Administrator, who, at the beginning of the reign, spent two years in making a personal inspection of all the prisons in Siberia. He has just become a member of the Howard Association, and invitations are now going out for an International Russian Congress for penal reform which will be held at St. Petersburg in 1890. Educated Russians wince much more at the thought of inflicting cruelty directly by means of the cat-o'-nine-tails than do educated Englishmen, and although they have recently established capital punishment in certain circumstances by the introduction of martial law, the execution even of the worst criminal is regarded by Russian society as a slur upon the national character. This squeamishness exists side by side with a most extraordinary indifference to what seem to Englishmen much worse evils. Those who have not been in prison—and it is one of the faults of our social organisation that almost all the regulations for the treatment of prisoners are made by men who have never been in prison, and who are therefore necessarily without that personal experience which is indispensable for wise action—cannot realise how easily a prisoner may be tortured without the use of the knout. You have only to let the heating apparatus get out of order in winter-time to cause prisoners far more acute and prolonged agony than the worst pain inflicted by a birching; and in summer-time an overcrowded, unventilated dungeon inflicts upon a certain percentage of its inmates a more terrible sentence of death than any that is inflicted by the gallows or the guillotine. From the point of view of pure humanitarianism I would much rather that the Russians used the knout, and built fresh, healthy prisons, than that they continued to drag on with their present overcrowded gaols, from which they plume themselves the knout has been banished.

The subject is one on which Englishmen can speak freely without exposing themselves to a charge of pharisaism. The revelations made this year by an official committee of the abominations to which untried prisoners are compelled to submit in our police cells and assize courts suffice to clear us from any accusation of attempting to pose as immaculate in this matter of prison reform. We have so much to do at home, that we cannot be censorious in complaining of the shortcomings of the Russian system. It is more scandalous that the wealthiest cities in England should grudge the money necessary to provide the ordinary decencies of life for untried prisoners than that convicts should be overcrowded at a receiving house in Siberia. But as we ruthlessly expose our own shortcomings, we may call attention to the weak places in the Russian prison system.

Broadly speaking, these weak places are two. The first is that the prisons are too few and too small, which leads to their overcrowding; the second that the Empire is so huge and the cities so far apart that it is impossible for the administration to exercise over them anything approaching to the close, steady, constant supervision which exists in smaller and more densely peopled countries. The immensity of its spaces secures to the local officials who have charge of the thousand prisons which are scattered over the two continents which acknowledge the sceptre of the Tzar a practical immunity from effective control. Uniformity which we found impossible to obtain until Home Office inspection was developed into direct Home Office control is an unattainable ideal in Russia, and, whatever is done, there will always be many abuses and great irregularities. The ordinary English idea of the autocracy as a terrestrial omnipotence, capable of securing immediate and absolute obedience in all parts of the Russian dominions, is curiously contrary to fact. It is one thing to decree a law at St Petersburg, it is another thing to get it enforced on the Volga or in the Caucasus. A remark made by a provincial recently when on a visit to Petersburg struck me as very significant. "Do you think we care for Petersburg—we at Saratoff or Orenburg? You can make what laws you please by writing words on paper in your Petersburg office, but as for us we have our own customs; what is Petersburg to us?" Of course in a great thing, when obedience is absolutely necessary, the Central Government can enforce its will. But in small things it is practically powerless. Said an English manufacturer to me, who had the control of large mills in South-Eastern Russia, "The first thing the Russians whom I have to do with ask themselves whenever a new law is issued from Petersburg is, How can we evade its provisions, and go our own way, without regard to the interference of the Government?" A very healthy sentiment this in many things, but it is not one which conduces to the regularity of the official machine. The Central Government, like a great dynamo-electric machine, may generate force and light at the centre which should illuminate and purify all Russia; but the conductors are so imperfect, the distances are so great, and the resistance set up is so stubborn, that what ought to have been a hundred-candle arc, at Taganrog or at Tiflis barely flickers with the radiance of a farthing rushlight. This difficulty is insurmountable except by an improvement of the means of communication and the encouragement of all those who will shed a glare of publicity upon the shortcomings of the prison administration in the provinces.

It is otherwise with the building of new prisons. If the Emperor personally spent an hour in an overcrowded prison, such as those which Mr. George Kennan described at Tiumen or Tomsk, I do not believe that a month would pass before he ordered the building of a new prison, with as little regard for the difficulties of the Finance Minister as if he were ordering the construction of a military railway during a campaign. The existence of such a plague spot as the gaol at Tiumen, at the very threshold of Siberia, through which exiles, whether innocent or guilty, must pass—and 25 per cent. of those who enter its walls are innocent women and children voluntarily accompanying their husbands and fathers into exile—is a scandal, which if it were once adequately realised by the Emperor, would be abated with the same energy and decision that he would insist upon the repulse of an attack upon a Russian outpost by a hostile invader. Some things need to be done without counting the cost, and the provision of adequate accommodation for the men whom you lock up in gaol is one of them. Take for instance the case of Tiumen.

"The Tiumen prison," writes Mr. Kennan, "was originally built to hold 500 prisoners, but was subsequently enlarged by means of detached barracks, so that it could accommodate 800. On the day of our visit it contained 1,741.* In going through the prison, the warder showed them cells that contained four times the number of prisoners that it was intended they should hold. Mr. Kennan says:—

"The air in the corridors and cells was indescribably and unimaginably foul. Every cubic foot of it had apparently been respired over and over again until it did not contain an atom of oxygen; it was laden with fever germs from the unventilated hospital wards; fetid odours from diseased human lungs and unclean human bodies, and the stench arising from unemptied excrement buckets at the ends of the corridors. I breathed as little as I could, but every respiration seemed to pollute me to the very soul, and I became faint from nausea and lack of oxygen. It was like trying to breathe in an underground hospital drain."

Small wonder that 28 per cent. of the men so confined were passed into the hospital. That hospital Mr. Kennan describes as follows:—

"The hospital wards were wholly unventilated; no disinfectants apparently were used in them, and the air was polluted to the last possible degree. It did not seem to me that a well man could live there a week without becoming infected with disease, and that a sick man should ever recover in that awful atmosphere was inconceivable. The patients, both

---

* "Plains and Prisons of Western Siberia," by George Kennan *The Century*, June, 1888, p. 171.

men and women, seemed to be not only desperately sick, but hopeless and heart-broken. I could not wonder at it. As I breathed that heavy, stifling atmosphere, poisoned with the breaths of syphilitic and fever-stricken patients, loaded and saturated with the odour of excrements, disease germs, exhalations from unclean human bodies, and foulness inconceivable, it seemed to me that over the hospital doors should be written—'All hope abandon ye who enter here.' About 300 persons die in the hospital every year. There is an epidemic of typhus almost every fall."

Clearly this is not a state of things which the Emperor would allow to continue, provided that he once adequately realised it in all its horror.

But how can the shepherd at Gatschina realise these things? He has appointed Mr. Galkin-Wratzky, a benevolent, humane, and intelligent man, to look after the prisons, and there, so far as he is concerned, the matter rests. But Mr. Galkin-Wratzky is but one among a number of other administrators, each with an army of Tchinovniks beneath them, all crying like the horse-leech, " Give! give!" and how can it be wondered at, if his claims for the millions of roubles required to build new gaols are passed over when the Finance Minister adjusts his budget? "I asked M. Ignatof," says Mr. Kennan, "if the Central Government in St. Petersburg was aware of the condition of the Tiumen forwarding prison, and of the sickness and misery in which it resulted. He replied in the affirmative. The local authorities, the prison committee, and the Inspector of Exile Transportation for Western Siberia, had reported upon the condition of the Tiumen prison every year, but the case of that prison was by no means an exceptional one. New prisons were needed all over European Russia as well as Siberia, and the Government did not yet feel able financially to make sweeping prison reforms, or to spend perhaps ten million roubles in the erection of new prison buildings. The condition of the Tiumen prison was, he admitted, extremely bad, and he himself had resigned his place as a member of the prison committee because the Government would not authorise the erection of a new building for use as a hospital. The prison committee had seemingly recommended it, and when the Government disapproved the recommendation he resigned."

Tiumen prison is one of the most important in the Empire. It is the doorstep of Siberia. All the 17,000 exiles who are passed into Siberia every year go through Tiumen. If such a state of things prevails there, what is likely to be the condition of prisons in more remote districts? Surely this is one of those matters in which the Tzar Tribune might directly interfere?

Bad as the case of Tiumen is, that of Tomsk is still worse. The description which Mr. Kennan gives of it is enough to give one the nightmare. Built to accommodate at the utmost not more than 1,900 prisoners, it is packed with from 3,000 to 5,000 every year. Typhus fever prevails there constantly, and the sick lie in their wards uncared for. The following statement of the prison surgeon rivals anything that Howard described in the lazarettoes of last century:—

> You can hardly imagine the state of affairs that existed here in November. We had 2,400 cases of sickness in the course of the year, and 450 patients in the hospital at one time, with beds for only 150. Three hundred men and women dangerously sick lay on the floor in rows, most of them without pillows or bed-clothing, and in order to find even floor space for them we had to put them so close together that I could not walk between them, and a patient could not cough or vomit without coughing or vomiting into the face of the man lying beside him. The atmosphere in the wards became so terribly polluted that I fainted repeatedly upon coming into the hospital in the morning. In order to change and purify the air, we were forced to keep the windows open; and as winter had set in, this so chilled the rooms that we could not maintain on the floor where the sick lay a temperature higher than 5 or 6 deg. Réaumur above the freezing point. More than 25 per cent. of the whole prison population were constantly sick, and more than 10 per cent. of the sick died.
>
> "How long," I inquired, "has this awful state of things existed?"
>
> "I have been here fifteen years," replied Dr. Orzheshko, "and it has been so more or less ever since I came."
>
> "And is the Government at St. Petersburg aware of it?"
>
> "It has been reported upon every year. I have recommended that the hospital of the Tomsk forwarding prison be burned to the ground. It is so saturated with contagious disease that it is unfit for use. We have been called upon by the prison department to forward plans for a new hospital, and we have forwarded them. They have been returned for modification, and we have modified them, but nothing has been done."

I make no apology for quoting so largely from Mr. Kennan's admirable papers, although they are occasionally disfigured by a blunder which causes the enemy to blaspheme, such, for instance, as the alleged hostility of the Government to the Siberian University, which the Government has opened and endowed. His story of the Tomsk prison hospital is typical of so much. It may be regarded as the supreme type of the whole system by which local necessities are controlled by the well-meaning but distant and ill-informed central power. I say ill-informed, because to inform the mind it is not necessary merely to confront the eye with precise and accurate printed statement of the facts. Government offices, alike in London and in St. Petersburg, usually have paper information enough. Dr. Orzheshko's reports no doubt are all stored away in Mr. Galkin-Wratzky's pigeon-holes. But suppose that Mr. Galkin-Wratzky, instead of reading the report and docketing it by rote, had actually spent one single night in the midst of this pest-house of a hospital by which the Administration inoculates with infection the stream of colonists which is peopling Siberia, does any one imagine that fifteen years would pass and nothing would be done? Distance itself deadens sensibility.

It would cost men less to kill a Mandarin in China if they could do it by pressing a button which dealt death at a range of 10,000 miles than to kill a fly in their own parlour. That is the argument for Home Rule all the world over. We have had scores of illustrations in Ireland and in our own colonies of the ghastly mischief that is done by the Central Government persisting in keeping the control in detail of distant affairs in its own hands. The same evil reappears in Russia, and this disease-saturated hospital is but an emblem of the mischief that results from over-centralisation. It is impossible to realise what you cannot see, and the Tzar's Ministers at St. Petersburg cannot in the nature of things be as keenly alive to the horrors of Tomsk and Tiumen as the people on the spot. So these horrors continue and will continue.

There is no one but the Tzar who can mend the matter, and how is he to know with a realising knowledge what are the facts? There is no newspaper in Russia which dare publish these things. The Censor carefully cuts out all the articles of Mr. Kennan from the *Century* before it is delivered to any but the numerous privileged persons in the Empire. Possibly this volume may be forbidden to cross the frontier for even quoting the official statements reported by Mr. Kennan. And yet what chance is there of getting things mended unless light can be shed upon them, unless the attention of the Tzar and his people can be called to them? The people who suffer are dumb. The

people who administer are powerless because they have not got
the funds. And the keeper and distributor of the funds, he is
kept as much as possible in the dark. He cannot make personal
visits of inspection to all the prisons of the Empire, and he has
no *adlatus*, no Imperial *alter ego*, altogether independent of the
official hierarchy, who can be continually on the road seeing for
the Tzar, hearing for the Tzar all that is done and said in the
great prison world. How under such circumstances can the
Tzar be a real Tribune?

There are admirable prisons in Russia. What is wanted is
to level up the bad to the level of the good. Mr. Galkin-Wratzky
is doing it as fast as he can with the funds at his disposal. If
more funds are allocated to the work of prison building, no one
will be better pleased than he. I had a long and very interesting conversation with him when I was in St. Petersburg, and he
seemed to me quite as earnest about prison reform and the
humane treatment of prisoners as any English Home Secretary
whom I have ever seen. But our Home Secretaries are perpetually flooded with questions by inquisitive Members of
Parliament, and goaded from behind by the objurgations of a
press, one of whose chief functions is to worry the Home
Office. The Home Secretary is, with us, kept up to the mark
by a constant pressure from without, for the like of which Mr.
Galkin-Wratzky must often sigh in vain. There is no press
with its Argus eyes to discover the abuses which prevail in the
darkest corner of the Empire; and there are no M.P.s to back
him up in his demands for the necessary millions needed for new
prisons. It is only by convincing the Tzar that anything can
be done; but alas! the Tzar has many things to do, and how
can his eyes be in every place? Mr. Lansdell, no doubt, has
been accorded liberty to inspect Russian prisons, and his account
is calculated to encourage the Government to continue that progress in reform of which he speaks with such enthusiasm. But
Mr. Kennan, whose testimony is at least as valuable, is practically precluded from enlightening the Tzar and Russian society
as to the actual condition of the prisons of Siberia. It would be
more in accordance with the best traditions of the Empire if Mr.
Kennan were invited to Gatschina, and entrusted with a special
mission to inquire into and report upon the prisons of the
Empire. Alexander III. is not a man who is afraid of learning

the truth; but of course such an audacious innovation could only come direct from the Imperial initiative.

When I was in St. Petersburg I naturally wished to visit the prisons, in order to see for myself the condition in which, in the capital at least, prisoners passed their lives. I do not think that any Englishman ever made such an application who was animated by more friendly sympathy with the Russian Government. For many years past I had exposed myself to no little obloquy and misunderstanding by steadily refusing to heap denunciations on the Russian prison system, and by constantly reminding a somewhat angry and indignant public of the facts which might fairly be pleaded in mitigation of the worst abuses alleged against the Russian administration. But when I asked to be allowed to visit the fortress prison of Schlüsselburg, in which the political prisoners are confined, the permission was refused. Of course I cannot complain of this refusal. Our Government would probably have equally refused to allow the most sympathetic Russian editor to visit the Fenians who were locked up in the Libby prison, or even Mr. Balfour's captives in Kilmainham and Tullamore. The obstacles that have been placed in the way of Russians who desired to visit English prisons no doubt justify reprisals. Our Home Office was actually absurd enough on one occasion to refuse to allow a Russian visitor to inspect any gaol but the model prison at Wormwood Scrubs. The older prisons could not be visited! The Tzar might possibly have been very willing that an independent inspection should have been made of Schlüsselburg. He has never been there himself. He has never received any statements from those who are confined there. He must, of necessity, trust solely to his officials. I was assured that those who had visited the prison were well satisfied with the treatment of the prisoners, and I would be very glad to believe it. In that case, the refusal to allow me to visit and to converse with the prisoners sacrificed an opportunity for dispelling a widely-spread prejudice which prevails to the detriment of the authorities, and gives colour to the assertions of the Nihilists, who maintain that the impenetrable mystery under which Schlüsselburg is shrouded is due to the fact that its unhappy inmates are subjected to treatment on which it is not safe the light of day should ever be thrown. The unknown is always horrible, and my failure to obtain permission to inspect the imprisoned

Nihilists will deepen the uneasy impression which the Nihilists have created, that their imprisoned comrades are treated even worse than Michael Davitt was at Portland, or O'Donovan Rossa by the Irish gaolers who drove him to the verge of insanity.

My experience of Russian prisons was necessarily very superficial and fragmentary. When it was proposed that I should write some account of Russian prisons I at once decided to get locked up for experimental purposes, if it were possible in the conditions of time. But a few inquiries soon convinced me that although I might without difficulty pass a night in one of the St. Petersburg police stations, it would be practically impossible to get myself committed on a short term of imprisonment to a Russian gaol without my identity being discovered. And of course, for practical purposes, the only advantage of such an experimental sojourn in one of his Imperial Majesty's prisons would vanish if it were known to the authorities that I was an English editor endeavouring to do "the Amateur Casual" on Russian soil. One resource remained. I might be committed by administrative order as a political prisoner for three days, provided that the Russian Government would enter into the spirit of the thing, and really commit me without passing the word to the gaol authorities. Of course this would be but a *pis aller*, for the sceptics would never believe, if I were well treated, that the Ministers had not passed the word to their subordinates, and the value of my testimony would therefore be diminished. Nevertheless, as it seemed the only thing to do, I made application to one of the most influential Ministers of the Emperor, for the privilege of an experimental imprisonment. The request, however, was refused. I had some difficulty in making the Minister believe that I meant it seriously, but nothing that I could say would induce him to lock me up. I made a similar application to the Secretary of the Prison Commission, with the same result. As a last resource, I begged the governor of the great new prison on the other side of the Neva to lock me up for at least one night. Even as a voluntary prisoner you get a much better idea of how the prison machine goes than a visitor. It was in vain. It was contrary to the Gesetz.

Failing the experimental method, there only remained the

ordinary resource of an official inspection. That inspection I made early in May under the guidance of Mr. Saloman, Secretary of the Prison Board, who was kindly deputed to accompany me by Mr. Galkin-Wratzky, President of the Prison Board. Mr. Saloman was an admirable guide. Although still a young man, he has inspected the prisons of England and many other European countries, and a valuable and lucid report on the history of prison reform in Russia from his pen is now lying before me as I write. He speaks English, French, and German fluently and well, and is full of enthusiasm for his work in particular and humanitarian progress in general, but especially along the line of morals and religion. He holds the position of Secrétaire du Conseil des Prisons, or, as we should say, Secretary to the Prison Commission, or Prison Board, under which are placed all the prisons of the Empire, excepting those reserved for political offenders, which are retained under the direct control of the Minister of the Interior. With these latter, as I have explained, I have had nothing to do. My visits were confined to the three typical Petersburg prisons in ordinary use for ordinary offenders. The first which I visited was the House of Correction in the Offitserskaye Oulitza. Externally the building is not imposing. But for a round tower at one angle it might easily be mistaken for an ordinary building. It was surrounded by no grim and lofty wall such as that which frowns down upon all those who dwell in the shadow of our English gaols. We went into the chancellerie of the prison, and were introduced to Mr. Greschner, Councillor of State, who is the governor of the gaol. Visions of the kindly old governor at Holloway flitted before me as I shook hands with Mr. Greschner, who, although a younger man and a civilian, had something of the same *bonhomie* and sedate good nature which characterise Colonel Milman. He stated that he had under his care about five hundred prisoners. In the female wing, which is separated from the rest of the prison by a high wall, were about one hundred and fifty women, under a separate staff of matrons. Under him were about forty warders, or one to each dozen prisoners. The average duration of each prisoner's sojourn in the House of Correction was about three years. They are all employed in various handicrafts, and I was invited to go over the prison. I gladly consented. In appearance there is wonderfully little to choose between different sets of men. The physiologist would find it difficult to distinguish between criminals and members of Parliament, and in Russia also there were as beautiful and as interesting faces inside the gaol as any of those which you meet in the Nevski Prospect. The points of similarity between all men are so great that even the greatest differences of station and of training seldom do more than temporarily obscure the unity of the family. As for the criminals, if we knew all about them, we should probably find that morally we have little to boast about. I always feel that if I had been in their place I should probably have been worse than they. Certainly no consciousness of superiority ever excludes me from the most absolute sympathetic identity with the most unfortunate of the poor fellows whom society finds it necessary to keep fast under lock and key.

The prison, although dating from the close of the eighteenth century, has been reconstructed internally in the last four years. Insanitary buildings have been cleared away, light and air have been let in, and better provision made for supervision and inspection. The old scandals of card-playing and drunkenness, to say nothing of the abuses inseparable from the proximity of prisoners of both sexes, have been suppressed, and the gaol, as it now is, although structurally antiquated, and objectionable owing to the lack of separate sleeping accommodation, is, with those allowances, in excellent order. Everything was clean and neat. The prisoners seemed comfortable, as prisoners go. The turnkeys were men much like our turnkeys, only somewhat smaller in stature and better armed. Each one carried a short sword on one side and on the other a loaded revolver. As we entered each workroom the whistle sounded, and all the prisoners stood to attention. Another whistle, and they resumed their work. We found them busy joinering in a room in which, save for the uniform of the warder, there was nothing to indicate that the prisoners were not ordinary carpenters in an ordinary workshop. Their dress is not so distinctive as ours. There is no Russian equivalent to the broad arrow that disfigures English prison clothes, and the only visible difference between the men in their busy hive of industry and their brothers in a similar workshop outside, was that the inmates of the House of Correction were cleaner than their free brethren. The prisoners are taught carpentry by a skilled craftsman, and some of their work was excellent. As far as possible, the prisoners do work for the State, but a certain proportion of their work goes into the open market. In the smith's shop I found them busy filing locks and keys for the new prison which is being built on the other side of the Neva. There was a forge and lathe, and all the usual apparatus of an engineer's workshop. The prisoners seemed to be busy, and therefore apparently contented. Labour is the great solace of mortals; for, as Mrs. Browning puts it, " God in cursing gives us better gifts than men in blessing." We visited the shoemakers' room, where the work of bootmaking in all its departments was in full swing. It was in this place that this year one of the prisoners contrived to fasten to the sole of his foot the long, sharp, flat knife-blade by which the leather is cut. He stuck it on with cobbler's wax, and boldly marched out into the corridor, where the prisoners are searched on their return to their cells. I witnessed the operation of searching. The prisoner strips to his shirt and drawers: every article is felt by the warder, who then passes his hand all over the body. The sole of the foot is, however, not examined. When the prisoner with the knife approached the ordeal, he diverted the attention of the officer by letting a small stamp drop on the floor. It was picked up and taken away. The adroit convict was passed. Unfortunately for him, and his fellows in the ward, the knife was discovered, and it is now in the governor's drawer. The whole of the men in the ward were regarded as guilty, and sentenced to be birched. As there were seven of them, this has brought up the total of cases of corporal punishment inflicted for breaches of prison discipline to thirteen this year already. Last year in the whole prison there were only twelve cases.

We passed through the rooms of the weavers and of the bookbinders, and of the folders of cigarette papers, and found the men always busy and apparently contented. After the workrooms I was shown two or three cells in each of which there were about half a dozen prisoners picking oakum. One of them came to the door and begged to be given other work to do. His request was refused. In one of these cells was a man who might have been mistaken for Mr. Hyndman. He had one half of the side of his head shaved. I questioned him through Mr. Saloman and found him a genuine Russian. He had been in for something—he did not say what—somewhere; when he came out his papers were missing, and after working for some time on the railway, he was arrested, and was now in for two years. In Russia, if any man is not able or willing to give a correct account of himself and prove his identity, it is usually found that he is an escaped convict from Siberia, and he is incontinently clapped into gaol for four years—which seems to our notions rather heavy punishment for attempting to travel *incognito*.

We then passed into the dormitories. They are large rooms in which the prisoners sleep on trestle beds ranged side by side. The largest room contains thirty-four beds—the smallest seven. No talking is allowed after evening prayers, which are said in each dormitory under the direction of a warder. Morning prayer is also said in the same way. A hymn is sung before and after dinner. Service only takes place in the prison chapels on Sundays and on Saturday nights. Of these chapels there are three. The largest, which is pleasantly ablaze with colour, and gorgeous with pictured saints, was naturally that of the Orthodox Church. There is a choir of prisoners, but, of course, no instrumental music; for the Eastern Church has the prejudice of the old school of Presbyterians against the "kistfu' o' whustles." The Liturgy is said or sung on the Sunday mornings. On Sunday evening there is preaching. The Lutheran and the Roman Catholic chapels are smaller, and much less ornate. I fear that many a prisoner whose eye hungers for colour would find the superior brilliancy of the Orthodox chapel a more seducing argument in favour of Greek orthodoxy than any which it wields outside. After you have been a certain time in the midst of the deadly monotonies of gaol walls, the eye hungers and thirsts for brightness and colour.

After the chapels the schoolroom. Here sixty prisoners can be seated at once, and, as 120 receive instruction each day, the school is worked in two shifts. The proportion of illiterates among the prisoners is very high. About 75 per cent. can neither read nor write. The proportion of illiterates among female prisoners is even higher. School lasts for one and a half hours each shift. It is here where the letters are written which prisoners can send to their friends once a fortnight. One visit is permitted for one half-hour per month for each prisoner. The visits take place under much the same conditions as in England. The visiting-room, with its wire grille, is, however, more airy and convenient than the dark little pen in which prisoners communicate with their friends in Holloway.

We went to the kitchen, where the dinner was being got ready. The smell of the soup was fragrant and appetising. Great bowls of boiled buckwheat stood ready to be served, and the reservoir of soup was piping hot. I tasted both. Buckwheat is an acquired taste, but the soup was capital. It is served out in wooden bowls, each containing a portion for five, who sit round the bowl with wooden spoons, helping themselves. In the bakery we found the great loaves of rye-bread all hot from the oven. In appearance rye-bread is like a dull gingerbread, but in taste it has an acidity not pleasing to the unaccustomed palate. The Russians all eat it when at large, and the prison bread is quite as good as that you get in private houses. I asked about the dietary scale. I was assured by Mr. Saloman and the governor that no restriction is placed upon the amount of food prisoners may consume. They had as much bread as they cared to eat at breakfast, at dinner, and at supper. As a rule, the daily consumption of bread did not exceed two pounds per man. There was no skilly. Kvass, a kind of thin beer, was supplied them, and this again without limit as to quantity. Of the soup each man could have as much as he pleased; also buckwheat. The only article which was weighed out was meat. Every man received a quarter of a pound of meat per day. I thought of our poor heroes of Trafalgar Square, with their meagre, stinted allowance of stirabout and skilly, and heartily wished for their sake that they could have enjoyed the dietary scale of the Russian dungeons instead of the statutory allowance doled out under the supervision of Sir Edmund Du Cane and Mr. Matthews. Many of these men must fare far better in gaol than they do out of it. How many Russian peasants and landless people in the great towns can command every day a quarter of a pound of meat, limitless soup, ditto kvass, ditto buckwheat, and two pounds of excellent bread? Mr. Saloman's righteous soul is stirred within him by this reflection, and he meditates no end of changes in the English direction. Before he succeeds in getting his changes adopted, I sincerely hope he may enjoy the privilege of a brief incarceration in one of our prisons. A week's imprisonment in Pentonville—say for an attempt to address a meeting in Trafalgar Square—would probably enable him to appreciate better than he can at present the arguments in favour of the more liberal Russian diet. They do not weigh their prisoners in Russia on entering and on leaving gaol. That is a practice which they might introduce with advantage. There is no argument so crushing to the assailants of the cruelty of prison treatment as the evidence of avoirdupois, the statistics of the increase of weight which has accompanied the alleged privation and torture. And as they do not weigh their prisoners, neither do they photograph them; neither do they take impressions of their thumbs, as is done in some French prisons. In this direction something remains to be done.

After we had gone through the main building, "Now," said I, "for your torture chambers. Where are your punishment cells?" I was conducted downstairs to a corridor. Here were the "black holes" of the House of Correction. There were six of them, standing side by side. One of them was filled with oakum; the rest were empty. They were simply cells with a brick flooring, and, so far as I could see, no means of warmth. They were absolutely empty. The prisoner must either walk, or stand, or sit down on the brick floors. Although called dark cells, they are not quite dark. A square orifice above the door makes darkness visible. Here prisoners are confined for breaches against prison discipline for a maximum of two days on bread and water. The punishment is not excessive according to English ideas of prison discipline, but its severity would of course be enormously increased if the cell were left without heat in the depth of winter. When I was in gaol I never qualified for the dark cell. I very nearly did so when I was seized with an almost irresistible impulse to throw my hymn-book at the chaplain's head on account of some atrocious sentiment he was uttering, but I resisted the temptation, and lost the opportunity of making experimental acquaintance with solitary confinement in our punishment cells. "What other punishment have you?" I asked. "Where is your triangle and the cat-of-nine-tails?" They assured me they had neither, and Mr. Saloman, who is quite an enthusiastic humanitarian, seemed to think that I was quite capable of asking to see a gallows or a guillotine. "But you flogged the men who stole the knife; what did you flog them with?" "Oh, that was birching," he explained. When corporal punishment was abolished in Russia, as a penalty that could be inflicted by a court, it was still retained as a disciplinary measure in the prisons. When a prisoner has been so obstreperous as to have committed an offence which cannot be adequately punished either by low diet, by oakum picking, or by solitary confinement, or even by two days in the punishment cells, he is liable to receive thirty strokes with a birch rod, which may be increased up to one hundred by an order of the Administration. The birching is administered by warders in the presence of the Governor. The prisoner is stretched flat on the ground, and if he is obstinate his hands and feet are held. The blows are then administered on his back. The birch in use—one of which I brought home with me—is a slight affair, much lighter than that in use at English public schools.

Apropos of diet, I omitted to mention one feature in the Russian prison dietary which I hope will be introduced into English prisons when the next Royal Commission reports on the reforms necessary to improve the treatment of prisoners. That feature is the unspeakable charity and mercy of allowing the prisoners to procure tea every day if they care to pay for tea and sugar out of their earnings in gaol. Only those who have known what it is to go on day after day with no vision of any beverage more inspiring than skilly can appreciate the enormous boon which this simple Russian rule would confer upon the English prisoner. If Mr. Saloman in his zeal for severity *à l'Anglaise* should take to abolishing the prisoners' tea, then upon his head and those of his children after him be maledictions unutterable.

The exercise ground, in which each prisoner has a right to a tramp round in the open air in the morning and afternoon, is not a cheerful place, but it is more cheerful than the dismal trench in which Mr. Parnell and his fellow-captives took their constitutionals during the days when they were in Kilmainham. But the most distinctively Russian adjunct of the gaol was the bath. The Russians have no full-length baths like those in our gaols. They have taps, where the prisoners wash. They have shower baths and they have vapour baths. Imagine a room in one corner of which stands a furnace in which blazing wood heats a great heap of large stones red hot; erect on the same side of the room as this stone-heating furnace a small grand stand of half a dozen tiers of seats, rising one above the other. Fill your grand stand full of Russian prisoners, and then fling buckets of water upon the red-hot stone heap.

Mr. Saloman has translated Dante into Russian verse, and he, no doubt, can do justice to the scene which follows, when the heated steam, rising in ever-increasing volumes, fills the prison chamber, and all the prisoners enjoy their weekly parboiling. The salamanders like the seats next the furnace. Ordinary human beings take their places at the other end. By the time the steam has ceased to rise, the prisoners are as white as scalded pigs. This, also, is an institution which might not be without its uses in Pentonville and Millbank.

After glancing at the warders' quarters, I had now pretty well exhausted the male side of the House of Correction. There was less to call for remark in the female wing. The women were neatly attired with white hoods, and were employed in laundry-work, in needle-work, and in other labour. There were very few young women—120 out of the 150 were over twenty-two—most of them a long way on the other side. There were one or two beds fitted with mattresses—a luxury which the matron grudged to those serving their first imprisonment. The women's beds for the most part were mattresses stretched on three rough planks, supported on a trestle. They also had their teapots, their sugar basins, and their Easter eggs. In this prison neither men nor women are provided with Bibles and prayer-books by the State.* If they want these luxuries they must buy them, as they buy tea and sugar, out of their own earnings. Here, as on the men's side, the dormitories contain many beds. A prisoner is never alone, which must be hard to bear. If, as every one knows, the society of saints and sages occasionally palls, how much less tolerable must be the perpetual company of thieves and burglars and murderers! I spoke to one poor woman who would have been very glad to have had

* This Mr. Galkin-Wratzky denies, but the statement was made to me by the officials of the prison, and the prisoners said the same thing.

Q

sometimes a secret place apart. She said she had plenty to eat, and was quite warm, and that all the officials were very kind, and that she was quite contented—a remark which seemed to irritate the matron, quite unnecessarily, I thought. But she went on to say she came from the Baltic provinces, she could only speak Russian imperfectly, and her fellow-prisoners teased her and plagued her on account of her mistakes in pronunciation and grammar, which she said emphatically is a very un-Christian thing of them to do. Poor woman! Very un-Christian, indeed, but common enough outside the gaol as well as inside. The mischief of being inside, however, is that you cannot get away from your tormentors. There were not many pretty faces among the women. There was one—a young girl with mournful grey eyes and a face of sweet and tender beauty that haunts me still. She came from Novgorod, and was in on a charge of theft. Poor thing! she looked more like a saint than a thief. "I don't like these pretty ones," said my guide. "Nor have I any pity for them. They are far the worst." A dictum at which, despite his authority, my soul rebels, and I keep wondering, as I write, what will become of that poor child.

The hospital we did not visit. The sanitary arrangements seemed to be very good. The closets were, perhaps, rather few, but they were clean. On the whole, I left the House of Correction with pleasant reminiscences of active and, on the whole, contented industry, well fed, healthily housed, warmly clad, and profitably employed.

"Now," said Mr. Saloman, "I am going to take you to a prison that is still unreformed, and, which is a black spot in our prison system." So saying we rattled off to Demidoff Pereoulok, where we stopped at a low, insignificant building, at the door of which a small crowd assembled. A shrine of our Lord was displayed outside before which the devout crossed themselves. Inside were some five hundred of the least of these His brethren, to whom all service rendered is accepted as if done for Him. "This prison," said my guide, "is doomed. We only began our last prison reform in Russia in 1879, and in St. Petersburg in 1884. We have reconstructed the interior, but it is too small, and we are going to replace it as soon as we can." The prison was clean. It consisted of a series of large rooms, down the centre of which ran a sloping wooden platform, on which the prisoners slept side by side like sardines. In English prisons you have at least your own plank bed; here there was not a plank bed apiece. The prisoners at night-time lay down without undressing altogether on the long wooden platform. I believe a pillow of some kind was provided for them. They had neither mattress nor blankets. There were, so far as I could see, about 60 in each room.

The prison was shockingly overcrowded. It was constructed to hold 200 prisoners; on the day on which I was there it held 500. The Governor, Colonel Venkievitch, a pleasant, genial officer, who had constructed a curious little summer garden on the roof of the crowded little prison, was very apologetic. He did his best, "but what could you do when you had twice as many prisoners as the gaol ought to hold?" "But why had you so many prisoners?" The answer was that General Gresser, who rules Petersburg with an iron hand, now sent out of the city 20,000 persons every year. Formerly the annual ejectments by will of the police only amounted to 8,000 a year. The number of prisoners, therefore, who were temporarily detained at this House of Transfer had nearly trebled, while the accommodation remained stationary. Hence the overcrowding. This surely was a scandal to occur in the very heart of the capital. They seldom stay long here, it was explained. Parties are made up twice or thrice a week, and despatched to their destination. It is from this gaol that all the exiles from the Government of Petersburg depart on their long journey for Siberia. I stood under the measuring stand in the corridor by which every exile is measured before he starts for Siberia.

What skulls teeming with despairing thoughts that little wooden arm had lightly rested on! What stories it could tell if, when it touched the crown of the head, it could read what was fermenting below! Few things that I saw that day impressed me more than that silent witness of so many pitiful and tragic scenes:

For so overcrowded a building the House of Transfer smelt sweet and clean. The prisoners, however, had nothing to do; nothing to read. They were simply herded together, innocent and guilty alike, to talk and dawdle and snooze, in a state of enforced idleness in which evil communications would have ample opportunity to corrupt good manners. At night such as could not find a place on the wooden platform slept on the floor. None, it was said, remained there more than two weeks, but this is doubtful. When a friend of mine called to inquire after the fate of a servant who had been locked up, he was told that he might remain there for two months. Possibly two weeks is the average. The right of banishment by order of the police is very extensively used. Any loafer, vagabond, or suspected person, without visible means of subsistence, is liable to be banished the city without notice or trial. He has no business there, and he is sent back to his native Government. This is the theory, but in practice the expelled person constantly returns and is re-expelled—a practice which swells the numbers of the victims of police banishment. Hence many people find themselves in the House of Transfer who have been guilty of no crime. They are simply obnoxious to the heads of the police, or they have lost their papers, or for some other cause are ordered to change their place of residence. For the two weeks during which they remain in enforced indolence they may have to sleep side by side with the worst criminals, and to spend every hour in the twenty-four in the same degrading companionship. Here also they have nothing to read, not even a Gospel or a prayer book.

Mr. Saloman was very glad to hurry me away from this overcrowded den to the stately prison which is rising on the other side of the Neva. This is indeed a splendid structure. When it is completed it will accommodate 1,050 prisoners. At present the building is sufficiently far advanced to accommodate 480. It was begun three years ago, and its construction will cost £100,000. It embodies all the latest and most approved notions of prison reformers, and when finished will be one of the most perfect prisons in Europe. It is constructed on the cellular principle, and is lit throughout with the electric light. Each cell costs on an average 1,000 roubles, or say £100. About thirty political prisoners were accommodated in one of the livings, but their existence was not known to my guide, and I only heard about it after I had left. Each cell was fitted up with apparatus for industrial employment. One of the cells contained a loom of considerable dimensions. Each was furnished with Bible, massbook, and educational works. They were better lighted than the cells in Coldbath Fields, and all the fittings seemed very good.

Colonel Sabo, the Governor, was very courteous, but he refused to lock me up all night. He consented, however, to furnish me with a complete suit of prison clothing, and locked me up in a cell while I made my toilet. When I had put the suit on I found that, compared with the English prison dress, the Russian is made of slightly stiffer material, and there is no stock. The shirt also is somewhat coarser, but the difference is very slight. It was here that I first discovered the curious Russian substitute for stockings. In place of stockings, they supplied me with light towellings, which I in vain tried to wrap round my feet. The peasants, it is said, prefer these wraps to worsted stockings. I do not. The dress was warm and comfortable. The cell was clean and bright. I could climb up and look out of the window. A prisoner was taking solitary exercise round a grass plot. He was a first-class misdemeanant, a Prussian, imprisoned for propagating Nihilism and entitled to be exercised alone.

We visited the hospital. It was very clean and airy. The young doctor, who was in the dispensary attached, was very polite. So far as any one could see, everything in the new prison was in excellent order, and I think on the whole I would rather serve my time in the new cellular prison on the Neva than in Pentonville or Millbank.

The fortress of Peter and Paul is not used at present as a political prison. Prisoners who are coming before the courts are kept there, as the situation is convenient. Mr. Galkin-Wratzky was very anxious that I should see the prison in the Litainia. Unfortunately I was not able to comply with his request.

## CHAPTER VII.

#### THE DEPUTY TZAR OF ST. PETERSBURG.

ONE of the most interesting and, after the Emperor, one of the most powerful men in Petersburg is General Gresser. Alexander III. is the Tzar of Russia, and General Gresser is the Tzar of Petersburg. He is one of the three energetic men of Russia whom I met, General Ignatieff and General Annenkoff being the other two. From head-quarters opposite the Admiralty he directs the government of the city with a restless vigour that is the admiration and the despair of his subjects. There is a municipality in Petersburg, with a Mayor and a Town Council, but the man on horseback is General Gresser. He is from the Baltic provinces, and his untiring energy and resolute will would have made him first favourite with Peter the Great, had he lived when that weariless Titan was still in the midst of his superhuman labour. The police, the fire brigade, the Sanitary Commission are all under his orders.

He received me at nine o'clock in the morning.

At the prefecture of the police there was a long *queue* of men and women with petitions waiting their turn for an audience. In an inner hall, the antechamber to the General's sanctum, I met his staff. The head of the detective department, the chief of the political police, the head of the Sanitary Commission, with other leading officials, were assembled with their reports. At the door was the head of the *queue* of petitioners—ladies, workmen, servant girls, tradespeople, each with a grievance, a petition, or a memorial. An officer at the door received each in turn, and despatched them with civility, referring their memorials to the official whose department it concerned. There was a curiously oriental air about it all. General Gresser sat like the famous Cadi under the palm tree, dispensing justice as seemed right in his own eyes. Every one is free to come in person before the Governor, who, according to universal repute, does his level best to administer justice with equity and despatch. All manner of disputes, some of them trumpery enough, are brought to him for his decision. When I was there one housewife came to complain that the police to whom she had complained about the adulteration of milk had compelled her to pay for the sample which had been taken to the analyst. Other suppliants have much more serious business in hand. For General Gresser has absolute power to banish from the limits of his jurisdiction any one whose presence in the capital seems undesirable. He can also impose fines and pass sentences of imprisonment, nor are his powers sparingly used.

General Gresser speaks no English, and I interviewed him by the aid of a friend who acted as interpreter. He was exceedingly cordial, and talked with the utmost freedom about his duties and responsibilities. I naturally asked him about the progress of his campaign against the Nihilists. He spoke of them without bitterness. He had all their leaders, he said, in exile or under lock and key. The rank and file were very quiet, but it would be a mistake to regard the conspiracy as extinct. It was spreading underground among students and workmen. There was absolutely no trace of it among the peasants. In dealing with the Nihilists he had always pursued a policy of prevention. Some of his predecessors when they knew that a plot was being hatched, deliberately, and as a matter of policy, allowed it to ripen, and then, when everything was ready, stepped in at the last moment and swept the conspirators off to gaol. He proceeded on exactly opposite lines. The moment he knew of a plot, or the germ of a plot, he crushed it before it made any progress. I asked him whether he shared in the popular view as to the close connection between the Jews and the Nihilists. He said that he had the best reasons for knowing that the Nihilist disorders in the University were all the work of the Jewish students. They were stopped, he said, very simply. He sent for the three leading Jews in Petersburg— men of enormous wealth and influence in the city. When they arrived at his office he told them that he had ascertained beyond all doubt that the Jewish students were the originators of the Nihilist disturbances in the University. As they were the heads of the Jewish community, he had sent for them to ask them to use their influence to restrain the young Jews from sedition. He added, " If after this I hear of any Nihilist manifestations whatever in the University, I warn you that I shall immediately expel every Jewish student from Petersburg." The threat was efficacious. From that day there has not even been an audible whisper in the University against the authorities. We talked of Ireland and of Trafalgar Square. I could not resist the temptation of telling him of the brutalities which the metropolitan police had inflicted upon their captives after they had them helpless in the black-hole of Scotland Yard and in the cells of the police station.

"What!" cried General Gresser incredulously. "Do you mean to say that your police struck prisoners in custody when they were actually in the station?"

"Certainly!" I replied. "They beat them over the head with their truncheons, blacked their eyes, and maltreated them abominably. There is no doubt about the fact. The statements of the victims were taken down and published, but neither Sir Charles Warren nor Mr. Matthews nor the Unionist majority in Parliament would allow us even so much as an inquiry into the subject. Not a single policeman was so much as reprimanded."

General Gresser sprang to his feet. "Abominable!" he cried, with refreshing emphasis. "What! A policeman strike a prisoner in the cells! What an outrage! If ever my men were to do such a thing, nay, if they were even to strike a prisoner if he resisted being taken into custody, they would be severely punished. My orders are most peremptory, and they dare not disobey them."

"But," I objected, "if a prisoner will not come, and assaults the police?"

"They have no authority to strike him. They must hold him till assistance comes, and then carry him to the station. None of my men are allowed to use anything but a pencil and paper. They must report; they must not strike."

I doubted that this could be so, but after considerable inquiry outside I found General Gresser's statement confirmed. The Petersburg police have no truncheons. The Russians usually obey a policeman without much trouble. Drink makes the Russian stupid or jolly; it does not seem to infuriate him. If a policeman finds an awkward customer, he summons the dvorniks to his aid, and they carry him to the station. So far as my own brief experience went, I never saw any policeman in

Petersburg using violence, although in Easter week there was any quantity of drink going, and the streets were crowded with holiday folks.

I only regretted Mr. Matthews could not hear the scornful indignation with which General Gresser repudiated the suggestion that under any provocation his men could act with the brutality of our metropolitan police last November.

General Gresser asked me to inspect his police stations. "I will give orders," he said, "that you shall see everything you wish. Go everywhere; speak to every one; ask to see what you please. Everything under my orders will be open to you. You had better inspect the fire brigade, and go through the cells; then come back here and tell me what you find wrong, that I may put it right."

I thanked him, and, as his ante-room was full of people waiting to see him, I took my leave.

I had not time to visit all the police stations of St. Petersburg. I preferred to make an exhaustive inspection of one which was also noteworthy as being the headquarters of the *police des mœurs* of the Capital. It is situate in the Piske, and is a fairly typical station, but larger and more completely furnished than others. In addition to being a police station, it is also a police court, and attached to it are the premises of a division of the fire brigade, a small hospital, the examining rooms of the *police des mœurs*, and the cells in which prisoners are confined for periods varying from one day to three months. I had as an interpreter an exceedingly amiable and intelligent physician, Dr. Duncan, the head of the Sanitary Commission of the City and former chief of the *police des mœurs*.

General Gresser had given orders that I was to see everything, and I went over the whole premises from garret to basement, and wound up the inspection by ringing the fire-bell, and turning the whole division of the fire brigade out into the streets, to the no small amazement of the inhabitants.

The police station was clean—much cleaner than the abominably dark and dirty dens which serve as police stations in London. The court did not differ much from that we use in England, but business was over when I visited it. The officers in charge were exceedingly courteous, and everything was in good order.

The cells were large, airy, and commodious. There were several prisoners in the larger cells, confined for various terms of imprisonment for minor offences. In two of the smaller cells there was a policeman locked up for some misdemeanour. That was to me a pleasant sight. We shall never have humane laws, humanely administered, until it is obligatory upon all who are concerned in their making or administration to serve some term, however short, of the imprisonment which they inflict upon others. If I had my way, no judge should ever pass a sentence until he had actually been imprisoned in gaol; and pending the realisation 'of that ideal, I always rejoice to see limbs of the law themselves fast in its clutches. It will help them to put themselves in the place of their prisoners, and to be touched with a fellow-feeling for the sufferings which they may hereafter have to inflict.

We asked all the prisoners how they were, whether they were warm enough, whether they got enough food, and whether they had anything to complain of. They all answered that they were well satisfied in every respect but one. Could we not procure for them the favour of having some books? They had been locked up some of them for weeks—some would remain there three months—and during all that time they had nothing to do, and nothing to read. They had neither Bible nor Testament, nor Prayer Book. It was a cruel shame. If General Gresser or Mr. Galkin-Wratzky were locked up for three months in a bare room, without pictures, papers, books, or without anything whatever to do, I think they would go mad. Certainly, if they emerged in possession of their faculties, they would see to it that every police cell was furnished at least with Bible and Prayer Book. Unfortunately these excellent officials have never been locked up. And so the scandal continues, just as the London police cells continue to be a disgrace to the good name of England, because the Middlesex and Surrey magistrates are never compelled to learn by actual experience the miseries which they inflict upon the untried prisoners who await trial in their courts.

The women were in cells on one side of the corridor, the men on the other. Adjoining the cells were the police barracks. The night duty men were sleeping. The place seemed none too large, but not uncomfortable. The barracks of the fire brigade men were somewhat better. The kitchens below were clean.

The little hospital had a cheery, homely appearance. Altogether my reminiscences of the station were not unpleasant. Of the horrible chambers of the *police des mœurs*, and the examining surgeons, the police spies, and all the sad, revolting paraphernalia of the institution which seems to me the supreme negation of God, I had better not speak. It also was clean enough.

A woman was in attendance at each room, and so far as so essentially brutal a thing can be made tolerable by strict regulation against cruelty or abuse, everything was done. But women were brought there, often on suspicion, often without cause, and compelled to submit without remedy, and without redress, to the last nameless outrage which man, in the wantonness of power, inflicts upon the helpless and the weak. The doctor was a polite and smooth-spoken official. But it was as if I was standing in the vestibule of Hell.

The official, whose rank appeared to correspond to that of our superintendent, told me, in answer to my questions, that St. Petersburg was divided into forty-two police districts. The population in the district of the Piske was 24,000. "Look," said he; "here are all their papers." These papers, describing the identity, age, occupation, antecedents, and character of them, were filed alphabetically, in a closet at one end of the Court. The papers were of various colours. Those persons who were suspected of crime had papers of a different colour from the rest. Those suspected of political disaffection had also papers distinguished in the same way. There were a good many of both kinds. The owners of these papers were living under the special surveillance of the police. On remarking upon their number, the official called my attention to another small closet, in which were two files of a still different coloured paper. "These," said he, "are the descriptions of the worst of all—men and women whom we must arrest the moment we can discover them." Of these extra dangerous characters there were, I should say, 2,000. In every police station in the Empire copies of these papers are filed. But their very number is a safeguard. How can any ordinary policeman remember the names and descriptions of the 2,000 men and women who are "wanted"?

The salary of each chief of a police district is about £240 per annum, reckoning the rouble at 2s. Each chief has under him two assistants, seven under officers, and thirty-six constables, which brings up the police force to about 2,000 men, assuming that the numbers at that station were a fair average. Each constable is paid 25 roubles, or 50s., a month, and is lodged free in the barracks. They are equipped with a side-sword and a revolver. The latter is carried unloaded, and there are said to have been only one or two instances in which it has ever been known to be fired. The St. Petersburg police are young men for the most part, who are inferior in height and physique to our English constables.

The fire-brigade men, who were turned out ready for action in two minutes and a quarter after I rang the fire-alarm, are well got up, and the horses were in good condition and capital goers. The procession of a Russian fire brigade is a sight to be seen. First there prances in front a brass-helmeted cavalier, who is supposed to clear the way; behind him come the manuals, hose-pipes, ladders, and all the other impedimenta of the fire brigade carried on carts crowded with firemen, each drawn by galloping steeds, uniform in size and colour. Each division has horses of different colour, so that when there is a general muster at a fire the colours of the horses enable you to tell in a moment from which division they have come. Some of the firemen's chariots are drawn by four and five horses abreast, the two outsiders almost at right angles to their companions in the shafts. The art of thus galloping sidewards would puzzle English horses. The whole cavalcade, with its banner, its fore-rider, and its brass-helmeted firemen, makes a very pretty spectacle in broad daylight. At night-time the effect is even greater, judging from the procession which rattled past me one night in Moscow on its way to some distant fire.

There are plenty of soldiers always walking about St. Petersburg, but you seldom meet them on the march. They are, however, available in case of disturbance, and when force is to be used, it is the Cossacks, not the police, who administer the blows. An Englishman, long resident in Russia, gave me a very vivid account of the vigour with which General Gresser acted in suppressing a riot in the suburbs of the city. The workmen of a well-known English firm had struck. The strike seems to have been an aimless affair; the men did not know why they struck, except that some people had told them they would get something if they did. Their wages, they admitted, were as high as those paid in any of the neighbouring mills; they had no complaint against the management; but they stopped work, smashed the windows of the mill, and barricaded themselves in their barracks. My informant went to the police station to see what was to be done. Suddenly the bell of the telephone rung out clear and shrill. The officer in charge instantly saluted the telephone. "'Tis the General ! he is a devil of a man ; he never gives us any rest," said he, as he went to the instrument, and saluting again said, " Yes, your excellency." Bystanders can only hear what is spoken into the telephone, and General Gresser's orders were only heard by the man at the instrument. " Certainly, your excellency," said he, and the instrument was rung off. " Did you ever see such a man ? " said the officer, ruefully, looking furtively at the telephone as if he feared it would carry his words to his chief. " He says I must take all my men, proceed to the quarters of the rioters, and arrest the ringleaders ! There is not one of us who would come back alive. They are barricaded upstairs. But what can we do? The General says it must be done ! " The attempt was made and failed. Next morning General Gresser himself arrived on the scene, and with him came 1,000 Cossacks. He went direct to the quarters of the strikers and asked them what they wanted. They howled and hooted ; they wanted to strike. There was a great crowd of some 2,000 to 3,000 workmen. They were in a very excited state ; still General Gresser persevered. He tried to make himself heard above the din, urging the strikers to return to work. " Disorder," he said, " I cannot allow. Settle your disputes quietly, and I will do what I can to bring about an amicable settlement. But riot, violence, destruction of property, that cannot be allowed. I call upon you to disperse." A wild roar of defiance broke out from the angry mob, and a brickbat hurled at General Gresser's head warned him that his persuasion fell on deaf ears. He stepped back and gave the word of command to the Cossacks. They rode forward at the charge, swinging their heavy whips in the air, and crashed in a moment into the mob—through the mob—smiting right and left as they rode until they got to the further side. Then they wheeled round and rode back through the remnants of the crowd. In three minutes there was not a man left in the place, save those ridden over by the horses or felled by the Cossack whips. The poor strikers had got something indeed—more than they bargained for. No one was killed, but a great number were considerably knocked about. The strike was over in a moment. The workmen went back to the mill, the machinery started, and since that time there have been no more labour riots in that region. General Gresser, it is admitted, risked his own life in trying to persuade the rioters to desist from violence. He did not appeal to force until it was evident reason was of no avail. Then he moved; and the dash of that avalanche of Cossacks upon the rioters was a sight which those who saw it will never forget.

The heavy hand falls like a thunderbolt when authority is worked in Russia. How much, however, we can do with batons and bayonets and prancing horses, without absolutely shooting, was not understood till November, 1887, and admirers of Mr. Matthews see nothing to censure in the brutality displayed on Bloody Sunday. If that temper prevails with us, where liberty is the first principle of the State, it is easy to understand how heavily Power deems itself justified in striking in Russia, whose institutions are based not on liberty but on authority.

Far be it from me for a moment to excuse, much less to justify, the brutal exercise of force, with which the Russian authorities sometimes trample out all resistance to their will. But it may at least be said on their behalf that all States which are organised from above, all autocracies, are more or less in the position of an inverted pyramid, and in their case the instinct of self-preservation prompts to much more violent measures against resistance to authority than is dreamed of in a popular democracy. "A democracy," said Wendell Phillips long ago, "is a raft, a monarchy is a ship. You cannot sink the former. The waves which wash over it excite no alarm, and occasion a mere passing discomfort. But if in a despotically governed state disorder prevails, it is as if the ship had sprung a leak. It must be stopped at all hazards, or the vessel will founder." In Russia, in the eyes of the Administration, power is something sacred in itself. Respect for power is with Russians as essential as respect for law, respect for liberty is with us. He who strikes at Power, or even proposes to modify the method of its exercise, in their opinion imperils the foundations of Society, and may therefore be hunted down like a mad dog. A political school which proposes to abolish the autocracy is not in their eyes a thing to be reasoned with but to be stamped out like rinderpest. Thence arise frightful instances of individual hardship and of cruel injustice, which in their turn breed savage revenge. Power, with its dungeon, is confronted by Despair with its dynamite.

It is strange to reconcile the excessive humanitarianism of Russians in many things with their inability to understand our indignation at arbitrary imprisonment, exile by administrative order, and all the prison horrors to which their political criminals are submitted. Said an English resident to me when discussing this paradox, " I can only explain it by comparing the Russian attitude to their political suspects to our attitude in relation to fish. If you think of it for a moment, what can be more paradoxical than the contrast between our conduct to each other and our conduct to a salmon? For our amusement we practise the most cunning deceptions upon the great fish. We entice him with dainty morsels to swallow our hook, we play with him for an hour, enjoying the fierce agony of his battle for life, then we land him with the gaff and beat in his skull with a mallet, never thinking even for a moment of the life which we are destroying, of the treachery we have practised, and of the pain we have occasioned. It is our right. We are anglers, the salmon is only our prey, and the most humanitarian of men, like John Bright the Quaker, feel no qualms of conscience, but rather exult over the dying agonies of the finny victim of their rod and their line. The fish has no rights. Neither have the political suspects *vis à vis* with the Russian Government. They are only as so many salmon."

The analogy would probably be closer if for salmon we substituted sharks. For no fisherman hates a salmon, whereas the Russian Government does unfeignedly detest all who conspire against authority. But the explanation is more terrible than the fact itself. That man never ceases to be man, or sacrifices the right of man to justice and humane treatment, no matter what may be his offences real or suspected, is a fundamental principle of civilisation. To forget it even for a moment is a crime against humanity which all governments are in danger of committing, and the more authoritative the government the greater its temptation.

Hence arise many abuses. For every official who is guilty of malpractices can almost always crush the witnesses of his guilt by branding them as suspect of offences against those terrible articles in the Penal Code which doom to penal servitude and loss of civil rights not only all those who plot against the Government, but even those who combine for the purpose of attempting to alter the form of Government at any future time, and those also who refrain from denouncing to the authorities a friend, a father, or a lover who may belong to such a combination. In our own Empire in India the wary and experienced native will tell you that it is never wise to complain of an official, no matter how flagrant may be the official's misconduct; better suffer in silence than expose yourself to his resentment. Hence the natural and constant check upon the malpractices of officials fails, and as a result corruption flourishes. Take the case of General Trepoff. That official was not serving this State honestly. It was clearly to the Emperor's interest that his corruption should be exposed. But the Emperor's authority would have been invoked to lock up or banish any citizen who dared to denounce his unfaithful servant. At last, Vera Sassulitch shot him. A Russian jury decided that she had done right. But it is an anomalous state of things when gross offenders such as General Trepoff can only be exposed by the revolver, at the imminent risk of the life of the exposer.

What makes this all the more unfortunate is that the rate of pay of most Russian officials is out of all proportion to the needs of their social position. In England we have frankly recognised the fact that men will steal if they can steal safely, unless they are placed out of the temptation to steal by liberal salaries. In Russia the official is miserably underpaid, while his opportunities of plunder are limited solely by his conscience. Take as an illustration the official salary of the chief of the Sanitary Commission of St. Petersburg. This officer has supreme control over the health of the city. He has to see to the registration and isolation of all cases of infectious and contagious disease; he superintends all the sanitary laws, unwholesome buildings, and, in short, he oversees the sanitation of St. Petersburg. Next to the office of the Chief of the Police, his office affords the widest field for making a fortune, not by any abuse of power, but simply by turning a blind eye to breaches of the law.

Builders, manufacturers, householders—all now and then would find it paid them well to square the chief medical officer not to look too closely into their affairs. In the City of London, a small area with a population of less than a third that of St. Petersburg, we pay our chief medical officer a salary of £2,000 per annum. In St. Petersburg the chief medical officer receives from all sources, including allowances, an annual income of £300 per annum. His salary is made up as follows:— Official salary £120; allowance for office rent £50; allowance for cabs £50; table money £80.—Total £300. His offices cost him £150 per annum, so that his net annual income is actually but £150 per annum, little more than the earnings of a skilled artisan. Dr. Duncan is a Scotchman, who has old-fashioned Puritanical notions about honesty, and he is content with his pittance. If he were like most men he might be amassing a fortune. He has control of a staff of thirty medical inspectors, each of whom receives a salary of £160. He, their chief, has £150 net. To expect officials to be honest on such salaries is like placing a starving man in charge of a cook-shop and then expressing indignation if he should help himself to a crust of bread.

The sum and substance of the above matter is that Russia has outgrown her administrative apparatus. She is continuing to pay her officials salaries, and to accommodate her prisoners in gaols, which might have done very well in the reign of Peter, but which, even if we make allowance for greater simplicity of life in Russia than in England, are ridiculously out of proportion to the actual necessities of the Russian nation to-day. What is needed is the re-adjustment of her institutions to the altered circumstances of the times, and to the necessities of her immense growth, both material and intellectual. This requires money, and a broad and statesman-like survey of the situation. As England's policy in 1877-8 cost Russia £100,000,000 sterling, it does not become an Englishman to upbraid her for the enforced delay of costly reforms. Neither can we altogether free ourselves from blame for the reluctance of Russia to persevere in the path of Liberal progress. Lord Russell's absurd and cruel patronage of the Poles in 1863 gave an impetus to the re-action from which Russia still suffers; and our traditional policy has certainly not been such as to encourage the Russians to regard with sympathy the political ideas which England represents. I hope that we are entering upon a new era in which the influence of the two Empires upon each other will not be mischievous and destructive, but may be mutually helpful. The past cannot be recalled. But we may learn from its experience, and profit by its lessons.

# Book V.
## THE IDEAS OF GENERAL IGNATIEFF.

### CHAPTER I.
#### THE RUSSIAN MR. GLADSTONE.

ONE Saturday evening in St. Petersburg, I was talking in my room at the Hôtel de l'Europe with a Russian visitor. It was still in May, and it was dark at night in the Northern capital. In June there is no night in St. Petersburg. I have read the newspaper in the streets at midnight, and have gone to bed in almost broad daylight at one o'clock in the morning. The ruddy flush of sunset never leaves the western sky until it glows into the splendour of sunrise; but in May it is dark about ten, and my room had darkened during a conversation which I did not like to interrupt by lighting candles. Hence after a time the familiar features of my visitor gradually became less distinguishable through the gloom; but as he talked, I could almost imagine myself in the presence of the most famous of English statesmen. I seemed to be having a *tête-à-tête* with Mr. Gladstone in the uniform of a Russian general. There was the same boundless vivacity, the same eager intelligence, the same marvellous store of reminiscence and of anecdote, the same keen and penetrating subtlety of thought, the same ecclesiastical cast of mind. My visitor was none other than General Ignatieff. It was neither my first interview with him nor my last; but never before had I been so deeply impressed with the extraordinary similarity between the late Prime Minister of England and the late Minister of the Interior of Russia. General Ignatieff is the Russian Mr. Gladstone. He is a younger man, no doubt; Mr. Gladstone is nearly eighty—General Ignatieff is only fifty-six. They bear both of them the distinctive marks of the difference in their respective careers. Mr. Gladstone is a Parliamentarian, bred and born; General Ignatieff is a diplomatist. But making allowance for the difference of environment, the resemblance between the two statesmen is greater than that which exists between any other statesmen in Europe.

Many Russians who idealise Mr. Gladstone somewhat resented a comparison which suggested that Mr. Gladstone could for a moment be compared to any mundane statesman—especially to an ex-Minister who has been out of office for nearly six years. But having seen Mr. Gladstone more closely than his devout worshippers in St. Petersburg, I could not avoid being impressed with the resemblance between the author of the Treaty of San Stefano and the author of the pamphlet on "The Bulgarian Horrors." General Ignatieff has much of the courage, the energy, the subtlety, the exuberant vitality, of Mr. Gladstone. I know no other who can be compared to the English statesman for the ingenuity of intellect which never leaves the conscience at a loss for a plausible formula, and the wealth of recollection which never fails to supply the most apposite precedent or the most telling anecdote at the very moment they are required. General Ignatieff is perhaps in some things a man of somewhat broader view than Mr. Gladstone, but he pays for this by possessing less than Mr. Gladstone the faculty of concentration. Even in the defects of their great qualities they are curiously alike. Both are continually exposed to the taunt that they are "too clever by half," which is, no doubt, quite true in the mouths who abuse even the immense privilege of stupidity conceded without a murmur to most of the human race; and General Ignatieff, not less than Mr. Gladstone, continually suffers in reputation for accuracy of statement, because of an extraordinary vividness of historic and ethical imagination, which, like a powerful magnifying-glass, makes constantly visible to him all the minute details both of principle and of fact invisible to ordinary men. They both sometimes fail to see the forest for the trees. This, however, is a less venal offence in the eyes of their critics than the wonderful adroitness with which they can always extricate themselves from the tightest of tight places, in which they seem to be fast. The extreme nimbleness of mind which makes Mr. Gladstone the despair of those who seek to corner him in debate, is paralleled in General Ignatieff by a mental agility which makes it as difficult to catch him as to shoot a swallow on the wing.

Even in small details they are wonderfully alike. They were both brilliantly successful in their youthful studies; both astonished all their friends by striking out for themselves an entirely different career from that for which they had been trained, and both enjoy in private life the highest and most irreproachable of reputations. Except perhaps Mrs. Gladstone, I know of no wife more absolutely devoted to her husband, and so perfectly satisfied with his success in attaining the ideal perfection of the husband, as Countess Ignatieff. Both have numerous families; but it must be admitted that General Ignatieff can boast a credential to character which Mr. Gladstone does not possess. He has lived for twenty-six years in the same house with his mother-in-law, the Princess Galitzin; and even Petersburg gossip, reckless as it is, never ventures to assert that in all these years the domestic felicity of the Ignatieff *ménage* has been marred by a single squall. And lastly, like Mr. Gladstone, General Ignatieff is an eminent Christian of the highest ecclesiastical type. If he does not read the lessons in the Orthodox church on his estate at Kieff, it is only because the custom of allowing statesmen to officiate at the reading-desk is English rather than Russian. But he is as keenly interested in the affairs of the Church as Mr. Gladstone. Together with his family he sings in the choir in his parish church near Kieff, and no one is more punctual than he in discharging all the functions of a Greek Orthodox. I do not know that General Ignatieff would ever go so far as to attend church thrice on the very Sunday in which he was busy constituting a new Administration—an exploit which probably Mr. Gladstone alone has ever accomplished. Neither has General Ignatieff ever disestablished and disendowed a Church. But he has left his impress on the Church in a not less remarkable fashion, as his name is closely associated with the crisis in the Bulgarian Church which dissevered it from its dependence on the Greek Patriarch of Constantinople, and was the first step towards establishing the independence of the Bulgarian nationality.

These, however, are but details of personal idiosyncrasy, or of the accidents of history. The more important points of resemblance, which must impress any one who is familiar with them both, are political. General Ignatieff, like Mr. Gladstone, believes almost equally in God, in the People, and in Himself. And as Mr. Gladstone believes in the House of Commons, so General Ignatieff believes in the Autocracy. And in all these things neither of these men believes by halves. They have all the strength and the energy that comes of their confidence in the Invisible God, in the visible People, and the Ego created by the former to serve the latter, and which is eager to make its calling and election sure.

Although General Ignatieff was trained to be a soldier, and has spent the prime of his life in diplomacy, he is almost as fanatical a believer in the importance of commercial questions as Mr. Gladstone. It was when he was discoursing of the advantage of a new commercial treaty in my darkening room that I first discovered that General Ignatieff was Mr. Gladstone's Muscovite double. Almost alone among Russians, General Ignatieff is an orator who, but for the rare opportunities afforded for the display of eloquence in Russia, might have had a considerable reputation. Like Mr. Gladstone, he is a prodigious worker—enormously interested in details, and sparing himself no labour in order to do his work. Both are a little too sanguine, but that is a fault on virtue's side. And lastly, both are agreed almost in every particular as to the proper policy to pursue in the East—a policy whose watchword is "Hands off all round;" and both are convinced that this true policy can only be efficiently executed if England and Russia go hand-in-hand towards its accomplishment.

But at the same time that I was impressed with the resemblance between General Ignatieff and Mr. Gladstone, I was conscious that the younger man possessed traits of character which recalled Mr. Labouchere rather than Mr. Labouchere's leader.

Mr. Gladstone is capable of an ideal devotion to a cause; General Ignatieff's mind is not cast in quite so heroic a mould. Take out from Mr. Gladstone that element that appears when he is in his more exalted moods, fill up the void with Mr. Labouchere, and you have General Ignatieff complete. It is a curious combination, but those who know Mr. Gladstone and know Mr. Labouchere will be at no loss to understand General

Ignatieff. Their only difficulty in dealing with him is to decide accurately where Mr. Gladstone leaves off and where Mr. Labouchere begins.

General Ignatieff naturally impresses all those who meet him with his ability. Almost alone among the politicians whom I met in St. Petersburg, he combines political insight, personal disinterestedness, and indomitable energy. It was an immense relief to talk with a man of such luminous ideas, so full of *élan*, and so buoyantly conscious of his own initial velocity.

General Ignatieff, discredited in certain quarters on account of his passionate nationalism and his extreme devotion to the Russian cause, is yet thoroughly imbued with modern ideas, and his mind is open to all the higher inspirations of the democratic movement of the nineteenth century; for therein Count Ignatieff differs greatly from some of the ablest of his countrymen. Some are European, and not Russian; others are Russian, and not European. He is both Russian and European.

But before surrendering myself to the charm of General Ignatieff I fenced myself round with a very *chevaux de frise* of misgivings and suspicious questionings. At bottom all these disquietudes sprang from one root, which, broadly speaking, was the doubt in the veracity of one who had borne for so many years the unenviable sobriquet of the " Father of Lies." " If General Ignatieff be false, and the truth is not in him," so I reasoned with myself, " of what avail are his brilliant gifts? Without truth, the most talented politician is but as tinkling brass and a sounding cymbal. Especially are they of no avail under the present Tzar. General Ignatieff may be as able as the Evil One, and in character as spotless as an angel from heaven; but if he cannot be trusted to speak the truth, he is impossible."

So it seemed to me; although I admit that if an equally severe rule were to be applied to rule out politicians from public life in England, it would have gone hard with all our statesmen. Without going back to Lord Palmerston's falsification of the Afghan correspondence, it is safe to say that, if their political opponents may be believed, our three last Prime Ministers have all committed the sin that is a sin unto political death. Mr. Chamberlain, in the days when he was a Radical, distinguished himself on one occasion by saying that Lord Beaconsfield seemed to have such a constitutional gift for inaccuracy that he only spoke the truth inadvertently and by accident; and this was but a strong way of saying what the whole of the Gladstonians constantly asserted during the closing years of Lord Beaconsfield's Administration. As for Mr. Gladstone, who can recall the controversies connected with General Gordon and with Home Rule without calling to mind the vehement and persistent accusations brought against the Liberal leader by the Tories and Unionists, which, if they had been well-founded, would certainly entitle him to share with General Ignatieff the sobriquet of Mentir Pasha? And Lord Salisbury! Who does not remember his famous repudiation of the Schouvaloff Memorandum, and other similar prevarications, which at one time led to the use of the phrase "a Salisbury" as a political pseudonym for an assertion in which the truth was not? I do not recall these things in order to raise controversies; I only refer to them to illustrate the caution with which statements circulated as to the falsehoods of Ministers should be accepted as conclusive evidence against their fitness to return to power.

I must say that I found the current report about General Ignatieff's veracity very closely resemble the habitual talk which passes among Unionists as to the liberties which Mr. Gladstone is alleged to take with truth. Russians who idealise Mr. Gladstone, of course were dreadfully shocked when I told them that there are men suffered to prolong their baneful existence in this planet, who can speak and write of Mr. Gladstone exactly as they suffer themselves to write and speak about General Ignatieff; but of course to Englishmen that is no news. But whereas all Mr. Gladstone's enemies agree in their explanation of "how Mr. Gladstone lies," there are great differences of opinion as to how General Ignatieff takes liberties with truth. Mr. Gladstone, we know, is only held to deceive others after he has first of all most absolutely deceived himself; and the marvellous convolutions of a brain which his foes describe as Jesuitical and sophistical are held to account for all the inconsistencies which they sometimes profess to observe between the fact and Mr. Gladstone's record of the fact. Of General Ignatieff some Russians say much the same thing, while others say that he has far too lively an imagination, and too short a memory. When writing these lines two visitors called upon me—one a Russian doctor of medicine, the other an English doctor of divinity. Both were equally sure that General Ignatieff deserved his sobriquet, but while the first was quite sure that he never made a false statement on public affairs, and only fibbed in private, the other was equally certain that in private life no one could be more strictly truthful, while it was on public affairs that he gave free rein to his fertile imagination. This did not help me much.

So acting upon the principle which I invariably apply whenever it is possible—that the best thing to do when in doubt is to apply to the fountain-head—I took occasion, in the course of one of my many conversations with the General, to inquire how it was that he had acquired so evil a reputation.

As usual, General Ignatieff rose to the occasion. One of his friends said once that if you woke him up in the dead of the night, from the midst of a sound sleep, and stated to him a case demanding instant decision, he would within two minutes after hearing the facts be prepared to give a clear, a shrewd, and an intelligent answer—so collected is he, and so ready at command stand all the mental faculties of this remarkable man.

"I will tell you all about it," said he pleasantly. "First of all, let us take the 'Father of Lies.' This is the way in which that name was applied to me. Many years ago, just after I had been appointed Ambassador at the Porte, a certain German Jew who had been employed as an agent of the Third Section of the town police thought that he could make a little addition to his income by publishing a book about people in St. Petersburg Society. When the book was passing through the press, he wrote to me a letter, in which he informed me that he had included me in his sketches, and that he had seen fit to describe me as bearing the name of the 'Father of Lies.' It was his title for me, and he intimated that if I would transmit to him at once the trifling little sum of 2,000 gulden, he would desist from giving me this pleasant appellation; if, on the other hand, I refused to send him the money, his book would shortly appear at Vienna, and I should find myself branded all over Europe as a liar and the 'Father of Lies.' I declined to pay him the money, and he made good his threat. *Voilà tout!*"

"But," I said, "that may explain how the name was invented, but how came it to stick?"

"Chiefly," said he with sublime audacity, "because I have always spoken the truth. There is nothing that people believe so little, that seems so incredible to them, as the truth. A dozen years before the last war, I told Midhat Pasha that at the first opportunity I would establish an independent Bulgaria. He laughed; but in 1877 he exclaimed, 'You told us—you told us, but we would not believe. Then, again, you must allow a good deal for the stupidity of people who think everything is false that is strange, or the like of which they have never seen; and for the malignity of others who seize hold of any and every report that may damage one of whom they are jealous, and whom they dread. But," said he seriously, "I tell you that I have made a point never in all my life to say anything that is not true. I admit that on some occasions I have not said all the truth when speaking to opponents or to enemies who would have used the information I withheld to damage the cause of my country. That I admit, that is allowable, and for that no one can blame me, for I have done no more than what every diplomatist must do. But when people tell you that I lie, and that I am the 'Father of Lies,' ask them, would you, to mention a single instance in which they ever knew me to have spoken falsely on any matter of serious importance?"

One who had had business with General Ignatieff during the whole time of his stay at Constantinople, and who had known him intimately ever since, said, "I have had to do with him in the most intimate political and diplomatic and personal business for twenty years, and I never once knew him to say anything that was not strictly true. I always trusted him implicitly, and he never deceived me—never! Nor do I know any man who in public business is more to be trusted when he says anything than General Ignatieff." That was somewhat emphatic testimony. I asked a clever lady, who for years had been up to the eyes in all the diplomatic affairs of the East. "Is it true," I asked, "that the Eastern peoples with whom General Ignatieff had to do all these years never discovered that he was untrustworthy?" "Quite true," she said; "no man ever had a greater prestige among these peoples." "Then how, in the name of wonder, did he acquire his reputation?" "Oh! that is simple enough. It suits many people to give him a bad name; and then, although in public affairs and in the transaction of business he is very exact, he is a man of lively imagination, a famous *raconteur*, in private life. All his stories, if not true, are at least *ben trovato*.

This gives people a handle against him. But, after all, what does it amount to? He talks much, and talks well. If he only talked half as much, and twice as stupidly, none would remark anything."

Some of the "falsehoods" of Ignatieff which were repeated to me were manifestly humorous exaggerations after the style of the Americans. Sydney Smith's famous remark that "the only way to get a joke into the head of a Scotchman was by means of a surgical operation" might justly be applied to many a worthy Russian. Then, again, some of Ignatieff's "yarns" were, it seemed to me, although strange, by no means necessarily false. A man who has travelled and negotiated from Pekin to the cataracts of the Nile must necessarily have seen many things which to the stay-at-home Petersburgers naturally seem incredible. As the Eastern king beheaded as a liar the man who said that in the North water became solid enough in cold weather to bear armies, so General Ignatieff's reputation for veracity has suffered because of the inability of men who have never seen Asiatic tribes to understand their condition of life and thought.

Other statements brought to me as indicative of his failing could not properly be regarded in that light. An Ambassador may, for instance, make in perfect good faith an erroneous report as to the condition or the intentions of the Power to whose Court he is accredited. But that in itself is no proof of his lack of veracity, although it may convict him of want of accurate information, and a failure adequately to grasp the facts of the situation. For instance, it is alleged that it was General Ignatieff's reports as to the weakness of the Turkish army in 1876 which led the Russians so to under-estimate the resistance with which they had to deal in 1877. It may be so; and, if true, it would show that Ignatieff, like other men, under-estimated the extent to which the preparatory fighting with Servia and Montenegro in 1876 had helped to rally the old martial spirit of the Ottoman Turks. There were very few men who in 1876 could foresee that the Power that had made such a poor show in the campaign against Servia, would in the very next year display a resistance that for months baffled the utmost efforts of the Russian Empire. I do not know what were Ignatieff's reports, but not even his worst enemy dares to suggest that in that matter he ever wrote a line which he did not believe to be absolutely true.

A popular delusion is that General Ignatieff deceived Lord Salisbury at the Conference of Constantinople. For this I have never been able to discover any foundation, or even any semblance of a foundation. General Ignatieff's conduct throughout the whole of that Conference, as it seemed to me, looking at it from a distance, was transparently loyal and straightforward. I am familiar with the whole of the Protocols of that famous gathering, and it was simply impossible for the plenipotentiary of one Power to be supported more energetically by the plenipotentiary of another than Lord Salisbury was at that time by General Ignatieff. If there was treachery, if there was perfidy, if any one played false to Lord Salisbury, then it was not General Ignatieff, it was his own colleague, Sir Henry Elliott, and his own chief, Lord Beaconsfield.

The nearest approach to any apparently authentic statements of his that do not accord with fact was capable of a perfectly satisfactory explanation. When General Ignatieff was at Livadia, immediately before the Conference, he repeatedly lamented the fact that the Russian Government had, as its manner was in those days, left him practically without any instructions on the eve of the most critical period in the Emperor's reign. But a member of the Administration stated most positively that he had seen with his own eyes the most detailed instructions that any man could desire, which had been handed to Ignatieff. It was remarked, when the story was told me, that the conflict of authority between General Ignatieff and an anonymous member of the Administration by no means necessarily proved that it was General Ignatieff who misstated the truth. But when I mentioned the difficulty to the General himself he solved the matter at once. "I had no instructions," he said; "it is quite true. I said so then, and I say so now. But it is equally true that very detailed instructions were drawn up, and to these the member of the Ministry no doubt alluded; but these instructions were not adopted by the Government; they simply embodied the views of a skilful scribe in the Foreign Office in the form of a Memorandum, upon which I was not allowed to act, and on which, as a matter of fact, I did not act. So when you see both sides of the shield, how easy it is to reconcile the apparent contradiction."

The net result of my inquiries was to convince me more than

ever that General Ignatieff was often very like Mr. Labouchere. His keen eye for a good story leads him to invent an anecdote rather than spoil a joke ; and General Ignatieff himself would find it sometimes difficult to be quite sure how much is memory and how much is imagination. There is a natural prejudice in Society against a man who can always cap your best stories, and a natural suspicion as to the source from which such an inexhaustible supply of apposite anecdotes is drawn. There is also in him an extraordinary faculty of appropriation, by which he confuses the part which he played (which may have been that of the humblest second fiddle) with that of the chief performer in the great orchestra. "They do say," maliciously remarked one of his relatives, "that sometimes he thinks he created the world!"—so genially does he confuse his own work with that of others. He is facile and accommodating, and in talking to political opponents his language sometimes dangerously recalls the discourses of Mr. Facing-both-Ways. This may be due to an excessive desire to please, and a disposition always to say what his hearers would like best to hear ; but it is rather confusing, and results in a confusing impression. No doubt every question has two sides, but if you hold forth exclusively on one side to one set of men, and on the other to another set, it is not surprising if, on comparing notes, both sides should feel somewhat at a loss to understand your real convictions. Whatever may be the cause, I found the opinion very general that General Ignatieff could never come back, and the only reason for this was the deep-rooted distrust which somehow or other he seems to have inspired in his contemporaries and colleagues as to the reliance that could be placed on his word. Be this as it may, it is not a question for me to settle. Considering that during the years when General Ignatieff's name was most familiar to Europe, England was represented by Sir Austen Layard at Constantinople, and by Lord Lytton in India, while Lord Beaconsfield was Prime Minister of the Queen, it hardly becomes an Englishman to prosecute this inquiry further, although it would have been absurd, when writing upon General Ignatieff, not to refer to the one accusation which is said to have deprived Russia of the services of her ablest statesman.

## CHAPTER II.

### GENERAL IGNATIEFF'S EARLY CAREER.

GENERAL IGNATIEFF's career has been from first to last full of honourable achievements and of honest hard work. In talking to me, it was always General Ignatieff's proudest boast, "I am a labouring man;" and he never had a higher eulogy to bestow upon any one than to describe him as "one who works." He is what they call a "German-Russian"—not because he has a trace of German blood in his veins, but because he unites the German habits of industry and application to his Russian genius. General Ignatieff is a Muscovite of pure blood; he himself was born at St. Petersburg.

He was educated at the Corps of Pages, where he distinguished himself by passing brilliant examinations; and on leaving college he carried off the gold medal. He was educated for the army at the Military Academy and the Staff College; and as the Crimean War had then broken out, he began his career as a soldier.

He was attached to the staff of General Berg, who commanded the Russian army entrusted with the defence of the Baltic coast; and it was perhaps symbolic of the old era, which I hope and trust is now drawing to a close, that the young officer first smelt powder and had his baptism of fire from the mouths of the English cannon. Our admirals ranged up and down the Russian coast, burning a few tar-barrels here and there, and wasting a little powder; but the attack was singularly ineffective. Although young Ignatieff was shifted about from point to point along the coast, he never had an opportunity of taking part in any serious action.

After the war was over, he was sent to London as military attaché, and subsequently rendered good service to Russia in helping to save Bolgrad at the Paris Conference. That was his first distinguishing achievement, and his success marked him out for a diplomatic career. The Russian Foreign Office sent him on a tour of inspection in Egypt and in the East. He got as far as the cataracts of the Nile, when he was summoned home to undertake the first Russian mission to Khiva in the year 1857.

At that time, eighteen years before poor Burnaby's famous ride, Khiva was a kind of unknown land of horrors. The Khan reigned apart in the midst of the desert in the Khivan oasis, jealously forbidding all access to strangers, who he rightly surmised would be the pioneers of an invading army. When General Ignatieff accepted the mission, and started with only twenty Cossacks to ride to the Oxus, he was assured by many that he was certain to be killed, and that he might count himself lucky if he escaped impalement. The young soldier-diplomat turned a deaf ear to these Cassandras, and started on his mission. He emerged alive, but not without experiences which no man would lightly face.

He was nearly overwhelmed by a sand-storm, and very narrowly escaped utter destruction at the hands of the marauders who hung upon the heels of his tiny company. Thirst, privation, and heat as of Gehenna, made that first Central Asian journey long memorable to him. Ignatieff, however, did his work. He concluded the first commercial treaty with Khiva, and thereby opened the door which civilisation entered, mounted on its powder-cart, eighteen years later. From Khiva he was ordered to proceed on a similar mission still further East, to the Khan of Bokhara. It was on this journey that their famous escape by fireworks occurred, which General Ignatieff narrated to Sir J. West Ridgway during his stay in St. Petersburg, with his usual spirit.

"I had only some score Cossacks with me," said General Ignatieff, "and a man in charge of the fireworks which were to be handed over as part of the gift to the Khan. It was very difficult and dangerous in those days getting to Bokhara. Now you can reach it by rail—but then! It was different indeed. Well, one night when, worn out with a long and fatiguing march, we had halted in a valley, we noticed with alarm that we were surrounded by some hundreds of the Turkomans, apparently bent on making an attack. As they outnumbered us by ten times, we prepared to make what seemed in all likelihood to be our last fight. Just as the action was about to begin, the man in charge of the fireworks came up and asked if he might be allowed to see what he could do with his fireworks, of which he was very proud. The chances seemed heavy that none of us could survive, and in that case, of course, the fireworks would be lost. So, not hoping much from the experiment, I gave him a sick soldier to help to discharge the fireworks, and in a few moments the Turkomans were startled by a rocket hissing and leaping and plunging along the ground among their horses. Another followed, and then another, and soon they had a more brilliant pyrotechnical display than ever had been seen in Central Asia before. The effect was marvellous. The Turkomans abandoned their intended attack, and sent messengers to crave our forgiveness. They said they thought we were merchants, and they had intended to plunder our caravan. Now that they discovered we were sent from the Government, and had the Devil's fire, they asked only to submit. I insisted that they should send as hostages the sons of their chief. These were given, and they were marched in front of our company, with revolvers at their heads, until we were far beyond the danger of a possible attack. The soldier whose ready wit saved my life was subsequently promoted to a commission by special order of the Emperor."

General Ignatieff, having returned alive from many hair-breadth escapes in Central Asia, was marked out as a rising man in his profession. A difficulty arising with China, he was despatched as special Envoy to the Chinese Court. He arrived there at a critical moment. The Chinese-Russian difficulty was thrown into the shade by the crisis that led to war between China and England and France. In the negotiations that followed the capture of the Summer Palace, General Ignatieff played a conspicuous part. His position was extremely delicate and dangerous. Russia was not at war with China, but he recognised from the first that the interests of European nations were *solidaires* as against those of China. He furnished the allies with maps, and used his utmost efforts to bring the negotiations to a satisfactory close. It was his first attempt to play the *rôle* of an honest broker, and he appears to have done his part with courage and success. As soon as the treaty with the French and English was signed, General Ignatieff resumed his own negotiations, and succeeded in obtaining from the Chinese the cession of the Ussouri province, a region as large as Austria, drained by a river larger than the Danube, with sea-ports on the Pacific, and limitless possibilities of development inland. No more distinguished diplomatic success was ever achieved by a single man; for General Ignatieff might say with reason, " Alone I did it." No doubt the Fates favoured him, and the circumstances were extraordinarily favourable; but a man with less courage and prompt decisiveness of character would have failed where General Ignatieff achieved an unexampled success.

After his return to St. Petersburg, General Ignatieff, then but about thirty, became one of the lions of Russian Society. He was young, brave, accomplished, and fascinating. He married a beauty and heiress, the daughter of the Prince Galitzin, and was appointed Chief of the Asiatic Department of the Foreign Office — a post now held by M. Zinovieff. There he remained until, a vacancy occurring at Constantinople, he was sent in 1864 to fill the most difficult and important post in the diplomatic service of Russia. There is no need for me to recapitulate the story of his ascendency at Constantinople. He was the youngest, but far the ablest, of the diplomatic corps, and he speedily established a position which resembled that enjoyed during the Crimean War by the Great Eltchi, with this difference : Lord Stratford de Redcliffe had influence with the Sultan alone, General Ignatieff possessed at the same time the confidence both of the Grand Turk and of his Christian subjects. To ride two horses at the same time, when they are going in opposite directions, is one of the most difficult feats of diplomatic horsemanship ; but General Ignatieff accomplished it. He retained the confidence of Abdul Aziz to the last, and to this day there is no name which is so much esteemed as his among the Christian races of the East.

It is idle to say that such a position could only be obtained and maintained by systematic and wholesale deception and double-dealing. Even if it had been obtained, it could not have been retained for thirteen years by such discreditable means. No one can go on trading year after year on a capital of falsehood, or float for ever on flash notes on the Bank of Confidence. General Ignatieff's *rôle* was, after all, not very difficult. It was one that only required frankness and courage. To the Sultan he spoke from the first with all the brutality of truth. Russia had no wish to disturb him in possession of his dominions; but he was keeper of the entrance into Russia's house. He said to Abdul Aziz, " You are the doorkeeper of the corridor to Russia's house; be a friendly doorkeeper, be our doorkeeper, and we will be friends and support you. Be unfriendly, become the doorkeeper of England, of Austria, or of Germany, and you will compel me to crush you." He used the same language to all the Pashas. Abdul Aziz, the unfortunate who was suicided with scissors, trusted him to the last. It was, indeed, largely because he leant so implicitly on General Ignatieff that he was deposed. In that conspiracy Russians believe that England had almost as much to do as Lord Salisbury believes that Russian gold had to do in the deposition of Prince Alexander. The Sultan used to say that General Ignatieff was friendly as a friend and frank as a foe, and a curiously-illuminated specimen of Arabic handiwork, the gift of Abdul Aziz, is one of the most conspicuous ornaments on the walls of General Ignatieff's study on the Moyka.

In dealing with the Pashas and the Grand Viziers, General Ignatieff soon discovered the enormous importance of having the *dossiers* of his enemies pigeon-holed ready for use. Most of the Pashas had been guilty of offences against the State. This man had been corrupt, that man had received bribes, the third had swindled the Treasury, the fourth had done all three, and more besides. Whenever these gentry opposed his demands, he used to invite them to a confidential interview. There he would point out in his charmingly ingenuous fashion that he had noticed with regret the opposition they were offering to the just and reasonable demands of Russia. It was necessary that these demands should be conceded, especially in the interests of the Ottoman Empire; and if they persisted in their opposition, he would find it necessary to appeal to the Sultan. "In that case," continued their host, " it is as well that you should have an opportunity of reading these papers," and therewith he handed the luckless Pasha a tolerably comprehensive statement of the frauds which he had practised upon the Treasury, and the breaches of trust of which he had been guilty. "I have no wish to speak about these things," he resumed, "only, in case your opposition continues, after so many days I shall have no option but to bring the matter before the Sultan." The Grand Vizier usually collapsed. "Why do you not oppose him?" once asked a foreigner of a Pasha. "Because if I did I should be finished," was the reply; and this power of "finishing," this reserved prerogative of the bow-string, which lay *perdu* in Ignatieff's pigeon-holes, enabled him to keep an almost unbroken ascendency at Constantinople.

With the Christians—Greek and Slav—he had as little difficulty. He supported their claims energetically, but told them frankly that he was not in favour of precipitating the *culbute générale*. He even deprecated the insurrection in the Herzegovina, foreseeing that Prince Bismarck alone would profit by kindling an insurrection in a province which Austria would snap up. But before all the Eastern races he kept aglow the ideal of an emancipated East. To the Turks, as to the Christians, he boasted openly that it was his intention to make an independent Bulgaria as far back as 1864, and he was as good as his word.

Prince Gortschakoff soon began to regard with jealousy and suspicion the rising star of his rival in the East. This showed itself in many ways; among others, in a cowardly evasion of responsibility. The whole responsibility was thrown upon Ignatieff. If he failed, he bore the blame; if he succeeded, his success redounded to the honour and glory of Prince Gortschakoff. It is difficult accurately to appraise the extent to which the interests of Russia suffered by the jealousy with which the old Chancellor regarded the young Ambassador. Many deplorable disasters might have been averted if the late Emperor could have made up his mind to the superannuation of Prince Gortschakoff, instead of allowing him to influence and to deflect the foreign policy of Russia long after his conduct in private life showed only too painfully evidence of decaying powers and of a disordered mind. There is much to be said against the French system of changing Foreign Ministers every six months; but to continue to entrust the control of the foreign affairs of a great empire to an octogenarian, after he has lost all control over himself, is an extreme quite as dangerous in the opposite direction.

## CHAPTER III.

### FROM THE CONSTANTINOPLE CONFERENCE TO SAN STEFANO.

AFTER the marriage of the Duchess of Edinburgh, a suggestion was made, it is reported, by the Prince of Wales that Count Ignatieff would be a *persona grata* as the Russian Ambassador in London. The suggestion was not carried out, and Ignatieff remained on the Bosphorus. It is difficult to say how far the course of recent history might have been changed had Count Schouvaloff exchanged posts with General Ignatieff. The influence of Ambassadors is one of those things which the great public constantly forgets; but it is a real force which varies indefinitely according to the character of the Ambassador, and the power, moral and material, with which he is backed. "An Ambassador," said Ignatieff to the late Emperor on one occasion, "is not a mere machine for transmitting notes and writing despatches; any clerk can do that. What an Ambassador has to do is to labour for his country so as to bring her interests into accord with the interests of the country to which he is accredited. He ought to be able to wield in peace an influence equal to a force of 50,000 men. If an Ambassador is not worth 50,000 men, I would dismiss him." If Ignatieff had been, not at Constantinople, but in London, he might have saved Russia not only 50,000 men, but twice that number. It was, however, ordered otherwise, and we do not well to pry with our speculations into the mysteries of what might have been.

General Ignatieff had already had some brief experience of English life. He lodged, when military attaché, in a house opposite the Carlton Club, and he seems to have had the free run of most of the Service Clubs during his sojourn on the Thames. He made many acquaintances in London; among others, that of Lord Palmerston. "In England," said General Ignatieff, "you must act straightly. So I spoke everywhere openly about the blunders which Lord Palmerston had committed in Afghanistan, where, mistaking Vitkevitch, a Polish refugee, for a Russian agent, England had plunged into a disastrous war. He met me in the train, going down to the Isle of Wight, and we had a long talk. I told him that the world was quite big enough for both of us, and that unless England interfered with us we should never encroach on England. I think he rather liked my plain speaking"—which is no doubt probable enough. Lord Palmerston was not the only Englishman with whom Count Ignatieff was acquainted. Lord Elgin he met and liked much in China, and he had long and interesting discussions with General Gordon, who came to see him at Constantinople. Gordon seemed to Ignatieff a man remarkable for his dislike of official routine, and for his understanding of the characters of the Moslem and of the Chinese.

I should like to have overheard the conversation at the Russian Embassy when General Gordon dined with General Ignatieff, and spent the night in discussing Chinese philosophy; but of that discussion not even a note remains. General Ignatieff knew Lord Lyons and Sir Henry Bulwer. I do not think there can be a doubt that if he had come to England in 1874 he would speedily have become a favourite in London Society.

The most remarkable illustration of his capacity for winning the confidence of those opposed to him was afforded at the Constantinople Conference of 1876-7, when he made friends with Lord Salisbury. There is no incident in his career to which he more constantly refers. He speaks of his association with Lord Salisbury with genuine pride—by no means without cause; for Lord Salisbury went out to Constantinople primed with every kind of suspicion of General Ignatieff. For months before his departure nearly every English paper had been stuffed with the most violent denunciations of the Russian Ambassador. Lord Salisbury had been taught to regard Ignatieff as a very Machiavelli, who would be his chief antagonist at the Conference. But no sooner did he reach Constantinople, and see Ignatieff as he actually was, than he threw his suspicions to the winds, and entered into the most cordial relations with the man against whom he had come prepared to work with all his power.

According to General Ignatieff, the change was brought about very simply, and in the most natural way. He met Lord Salisbury at dinner soon after his arrival, and in the course of conversation the English plenipotentiary remarked to his Russian vis-à-vis, "I am told that you are a terrible man, and that you have so many spies and agents all over the East."

Ignatieff replied, "It is quite true that I have many helpers." "But who are they?" "I wish you would go into the provinces and see for yourself about my agents. Paid agents I have not; not one rouble do I need to pay for help. But you will find that every one who fights for his country, who fights for his faith, who struggles for freedom in all these lands is my friend, is my agent, is my helper. I have thousands of these—yes, twenty thousands—and they are my strength. But you are the support of the savagery and tyranny of the Turks." Lord Salisbury did not relish the remark; but the truth of it seems to have gone home. When they met again, General Ignatieff found him still suspicious and antagonistic. "But," said he, "Lord Salisbury is a labouring man, and I am a labouring man. When I saw that he was in earnest to know the truth, I put all my papers at his disposal, and gave him all the help I could in every way. 'Do not believe anything I tell you,' I said to him, 'until you have verified it for yourself, and then you will see if I tell you the truth.'" Lord Salisbury accepted the challenge, and was satisfied with the result. General Ignatieff had given him a Memorandum upon the Turkish Constitution. Lord Salisbury read it, and told him that he was satisfied as to his correctness, and that the Turks had really been lying.

Hence he was not indisposed to meet General Ignatieff loyally when the latter said to him in his simple direct fashion, "Now you must make up your mind whether you are a good Christian or a good Turk. If you have decided to be a good Christian, and to support the amelioration of the lot of the Christians, then I will take your programme as my own, and support you loyally throughout; but if you are for Turkish tyranny, then I will take the Russian programme, and press it with all my force. That will certainly make it much worse for the Turks." "Lord Salisbury," said the General to me, "was a good Christian; so was Lady Salisbury. That was where I met them. I knew very well both his qualities and his defects. He is impulsive and vehement. I made play to have these qualities on my side rather than to have them against me, and I succeeded. But I did so only by doing exactly as I said—by supporting him faithfully and loyally. I did not mix him," said he, using a curious phrase—"indeed I did not. I spoke the truth and acted straightly. If you look in the Protocols of the Conference, you will see that I always supported him. No one could be more moderate, more pacific, than I. It was Sir Henry Elliott, and Lord Beaconsfield, and Prince Bismarck who made that Conference to fail, not either Lord Salisbury or myself."

One of General Ignatieff's reminiscences had naturally a very deep interest for me on account of its bearing on an episode in my own career in 1885. "Lord Salisbury," said Ignatieff, "came to me one day saying that Sir Henry Elliott had point-blank denied my statements that the Turks sold Christian slaves in the bazaar of Constantinople. I replied at once to him and to Lady Salisbury, who was present, 'I will prove that I spoke true. Give me your money, and I will send to the bazaar with any one whom you please to appoint, and there I will buy for Lady Salisbury a Christian girl, a Christian child, a Christian slave.' Thus challenged, Lord Salisbury did not flinch. The money was produced, and I sent off a man with their man to the bazaar. In a short time they came back with the news that with the money they could buy a Christian girl of sixteen, who was held by her owner at the disposal of Lady Salisbury. It was quite true; but of course the girl was not bought. All that was necessary was to prove the fact. Lord Salisbury was very indignant."

I could not help regretting that the purchase was not completed. The presence of a comely Christian girl of sixteen in Arlington Street or Hatfield, as a brand plucked from the burning, would have been a useful object-lesson for London Society. But she was left to her doom, and was probably bought up by some of the Pashas whom Lord Beaconsfield was supporting against his own plenipotentiary.

When the Conference was proceeding, a vigorous attempt was made to confine the area which was to be endowed with autonomous institutions to the north of the Balkans. General Ignatieff went at once to Lord Salisbury and said to him, "What will they say in England, where the Conference originated, in response to Mr. Gladstone's agitation against atrocities committed south of the Balkans, if the Conference only protects the Bulgarians north of the Balkans, who have not suffered, and leaves unprotected those on whom the atrocities were committed?" Lord Salisbury at once admitted the justice of this objection, and he insisted at the Conference on the extension of the autonomous institutions to all the territory inhabited by the Bulgarians. What is called "the Big Bulgaria of San Stefano" was thus in reality nothing but the precise and more scientific definition of the area which had already been marked out as Bulgarian by Lord Salisbury at the Conference. Lord Salisbury is the joint author with General Ignatieff of the Great Bulgaria, to destroy which, a year later, Lord Salisbury nearly plunged England into a Russian war.

The friendship between General Ignatieff and Lord Salisbury continued unbroken until the Conference dispersed. Neither did it appear to have undergone any strain when General Ignatieff visited England a month or two later, in order to secure the adhesion of the Powers to the Protocol which was intended to prevent the outbreak of war. Why Lord Salisbury subsequently turned against General Ignatieff, is one of those mysteries which will be solved when we discover how it was that he came to regard Lord Beaconsfield with reverence, instead of the loathing with which that Semitic hero at one time inspired him. Many explanations are current in St. Petersburg; but that most generally received is that Count Schouvaloff, who was then the intimate friend of Lord and Lady Derby, did not hesitate to play his colleague a trick in order to play into the hands of his friend in the English Cabinet. The antagonism between Lord Derby and Lord Salisbury, who were both playing for the reversion of the Conservative leadership, was very sharp, and it was intensified by a still stronger current of opposing sentiment on the part of their respective wives. Count Schouvaloff, who had allied himself with Lord and Lady Derby, drinking wine with the one and talking evangelical religion with the other, had always been hostile to General Ignatieff. He was not a little dismayed at the alliance struck up between Lord Salisbury and the Russian Ambassador, which, if it had been successful, would have practically secured the reversion of the Conservative leadership to Lord Salisbury, and established Count Ignatieff as heir-presumptive to Prince Gortschakoff. So it is asserted that by every insidious method of sap and mine he set to work to damage his rival's prestige, finding ready helpers in his allies at the English Foreign Office. Whether or not it be true, as I was told, that Count Schouvaloff hinted to Lady Derby that Lord Salisbury had been hoaxed by General Ignatieff, and whether or not Lord Derby and the opponents of an energetic policy against the Porte eagerly availed themselves of the story in order to hold Lord Salisbury up to ridicule, I cannot say. All that is known is that the story was told. Lord Salisbury was laughed at and described as the gullible dupe of an accomplished deceiver, and with characteristic impulsiveness he tried to rehabilitate his reputation by opposing General Ignatieff as vehemently as he formerly supported him. The phenomenon is by no means unusual.

General Ignatieff told me that he was opposed to making any war in the East. War, as he once told the late Emperor, was a public misfortune which injured every one; and, in his opinion, the chief function of diplomacy was to prevent international questions reaching such a condition of entanglement as to necessitate their severance by the sword. He was especially opposed to the war that was on the point of breaking out between Russia and Turkey. From the first outbreak of the insurrection in the Herzegovina he had written to Prince Gortschakoff, pointing out that the movement seemed to him the opening of the game which Prince Bismarck was playing in the Balkan Peninsula. The chief object of that game was to thrust Austria forward in the East, so as to render impossible the achievement of the chief object of Russian diplomacy—the establishment of a *modus vivendi* between Petersburg and Vienna, which would render possible an amicable solution of the Eastern Question when the Sick Man died. Prince Bismarck's calculation seemed to him to be that as soon as Christian blood was made to flow in the East, all the good people—in other words, all the excitable Orthodox Russians—would insist upon rushing to the rescue of their co-religionists, without regard to the exigencies of Russian finance, the condition of the Russian army, or the difficulties of the international position. Bloodshed, in short, would liberate one of the great uncontrollable forces of Europe, and hurl it against the Turk in such fashion as to weaken Russia, and give Austria an opportunity for seizing territory which would effectually bar the door to any hope of an Austro-Russian *entente*. This suited Germany, but it did not suit Russia.

At the same time General Ignatieff would have been much

less averse to the threatened war if it had been made in 1876, at a time when the Turks had not rallied their forces for the defence of the Balkans. If, when the attack was made by the Turks on Servia, the Russians had been ready to reply by a counter-attack upon the Danube, the Turkish lines of defence could have been forced, and the Russians might have arrived at Constantinople before Lord Salisbury. Unfortunately, however, the Russian forces were by no means ready to take the field, and diplomatic difficulties were still to be unravelled. All that was done was to muster an army at Kishineff, which stood at ease all the winter, while the Turks bought Peabody rifles and Krupp cannon, threw up earthworks, drilled and armed thousands of recruits, and fashioned under the very eyes of the impatient Ignatieff the panoply of steel against which the Russians shattered the army with which they had hoped they would be able to liberate Bulgaria.

During the Conference, the day after the Turks had proclaimed their new Constitution, General Ignatieff met Sir W. White, who had been summoned to Constantinople from Belgrade to consult with Lord Salisbury. "Have you read the Constitution?" asked Ignatieff. "No," said the Englishman. "What does it matter? It is not serious?" "But," said Ignatieff, "you must really read one Article." And so saying, he pointed to the Article which set forth that, all provisions to the contrary notwithstanding, the Sultan was to retain an absolute right to banish from the capital any person whose presence might seem objectionable to him. "Mark my words," said Ignatieff; "the first man to be exiled under that clause will be Midhat Pasha, the author of the Constitution."

The prediction was fulfilled to the letter. Meeting Ignatieff some time after, Sir W. White recalled the prophecy and its fulfilment. "Oh! yes," said the General carelessly, "I arranged that." "But you had left Constantinople before Midhat's exile!" "Certainly, but I arranged it just before I left." "How?" "It was very simple. The weather was stormy in the Black Sea, and I could not leave for some days after the departure of my colleagues. I went on board my steamer, and anchored exactly opposite the Sultan's palace. I did not go and bid him farewell, but waited. In a day or two, as I anticipated, there came an aide-de-camp from the Sultan to express his regret and surprise that I, whom he had known better than any of the Ambassadors, should be departing without paying him a farewell visit. I replied that, of course, I should have been delighted to have paid my respects to his Majesty, but that it was no longer necessary. I had paid my farewell visit to Midhat Pasha, as, under the Constitution, it was to him, not the Sultan, that such an act of respect was due. Almost immediately after arriving in Russia I heard of the exile of Midhat. My parting shot had secured his downfall." Neither of these stories was told me by General Ignatieff; they are current in Constantinople, and they are apt illustrations of his insight into the Turkish character.

After his return to Russia, General Ignatieff had an opportunity of knowing how little the Government was prepared for a great campaign. Contrary to his urgent warnings, the War Office had allowed the Turks to forestall them in the purchase of arms of precision. He had seen the Turkish preparations, and he foresaw that war in 1877 would be a far grimmer thing than the campaign might have been in 1876. So when it was determined to make a supreme effort to avert war, General Ignatieff was chosen as the Envoy to Europe to secure the assent of the Powers to the Protocol which was to have afforded Russia opportunity to retreat from the *impasse* into which she had been forced by the machinations of Germany acting upon the impulsive enthusiasm of Muscovy. There is a curious parallel, and at the same time a marked contrast, between this hurried European tour of the Russian diplomatist seeking to secure allies for the prevention of war, and the equally hurried European tour of M. Thiers six years before in search of allies to make war on Germany. Both tours were failures; and in both cases the failure resulted from causes entirely beyond the Envoys' control. When General Ignatieff came to Berlin, he spent three days in almost uninterrupted discussion with Prince Bismarck. He found his worst fears confirmed as to the object of the German Chancellor. When he pointed out that the Bulgarian Question was properly European, and that the decisions of a European Conference could not be set at naught by the Turks with impunity, Prince Bismarck replied by declaring that Bulgaria was a Russian question, that Russia's honour was at stake, and that if Russia felt bound to vindicate her honour, Germany would certainly not lift a finger to prevent her acting as the self-appointed *mandataire* of Europe. Ignatieff replied that Russia knew how to defend her own honour, that it was an international question, and ought to be dealt with in an international way; but it was no use. It was hardly reasonable to expect that Prince Bismarck would refuse to reap the crops which he had ripened, now that the time of harvest had fully come.

In Austria, General Ignatieff saw the Emperor-King. "Why cannot we arrange matters in a friendly way?" said Francis Joseph. "If," replied General Ignatieff, "you had any really Austrian statesmen, matters could be arranged in twenty-four hours; but you have always as your Foreign Minister either a Magyar or a Pole, and Magyars and Poles have always *arrières pensées* in dealing with Russia, so nothing can be done." At that time General Ignatieff knew nothing of the intention on the part of Prince Gortschakoff to concede the occupation of Bosnia and the Herzegovina to Austria. At Reichstadt the three Empires had only made an agreement to do nothing in the East without mutual consultation—an agreement which seemed to him stupid, for the Eastern Question is either Russian or European, and never an *affaire à trois*. Subsequently at Vienna a Convention was signed, by which Austria was permitted to incorporate Turkish Croatia in the Empire-Kingdom. To this no objection need be taken. But the private Convention which Prince Gortschakoff signed with Count Andrassy, acquiescing in the occupation of Bosnia and the Herzegovina, was kept secret, nor did most Russians know of its existence until the bargain was fulfilled.

When General Ignatieff came to London, he was received in friendly fashion by Lord Salisbury, and he had an opportunity of meeting both Mr. Gladstone and Lord Beaconsfield. For the former he conceived, not unnaturally, an immense regard; and a beautiful plate of Mr. Millais's portrait is the only portrait of a non-Russian which hangs on the walls of General Ignatieff's study. It is significant of the Gladstone cult in Russia that Mr. Katkoff gave similar distinction to the same portrait in the office of the *Moscow Gazette*. German visitors sometimes resent the unique position occupied by Mr. Gladstone's portrait; but to their expostulations General Ignatieff replies by declaring his respect for Mr. Gladstone as a true Christian and an enlightened statesman. Of Lord Beaconsfield, as is but natural, he speaks with less enthusiasm. The only thing which impressed him about the then Prime Minister was his hankering after Turkish islands. He talked even then, more than twelve months before the Anglo-Turkish Convention was signed, about occupying Cyprus; and in conversation he suggested to General Ignatieff the possibility of an understanding with Russia on the subject of the Bosphorus, provided that England were in occupation of Mitylene. General Ignatieff did not encourage the idea; Mitylene, he said, was too near; it was only two hours' steam from the mouth of the Dardanelles. Lord Beaconsfield did not press the discussion. The negotiation for the Protocol failed, the Turks began to attack Montenegro, and the war began.

When it was drawing to a close, General Ignatieff was sent for by the Emperor. "What do you propose now?" said his Majesty. "I propose," said General Ignatieff, "as soon as the Russian armies are within sight of Constantinople to summon the Conference which dispersed in January, and take up the work exactly where it was left off. To the Powers I would say, 'You failed at the beginning of the year because there was no force with which to beat down the Turkish resistance. Now Russia has done your work. The Turkish resistance is crushed, and 100,000 Russian soldiers are within call to execute your will.' What a splendid position we should have had! Europe would have undertaken the responsibility, but Russia would visibly and manifestly have been her *mandataire*, and Russia would have enforced whatever the Conference decided. With 100,000 Russian soldiers south of the Balkans, there would be no unnecessary delays, and a European sanction would be at once given to the work achieved by the sacrifices of Russia." "It is perfect," said the Emperor, and for a time General Ignatieff quite understood it would be adopted.

Unfortunately however for Europe, for Russia, and for the East, the senile jealousies of Prince Gortschakoff once more intervened to balk the execution of this excellent scheme. Prince Gortschakoff wished to sign the treaty which concluded the war. If the original Conference met, he would not be Russia's plenipotentiary, and the signature would not be his, but

Ignatieff's. "Some men," said Ignatieff once, in describing his own methods, "have only one object, and one road thither. I have one object, but to it I have many roads. If one is blocked, I take another. To me, object is everything; means are nothing." He therefore promptly devised a plan for enabling his original proposal to be carried out, with the addition of Prince Gortschakoff's signature. "Let the Conference be summoned at Constantinople, just as if nothing had happened since last it assembled, and then let it at once adjourn to Odessa, on the ground that in Constantinople, situated between the opposing armies, it could not deliberate in security. Then when the adjourned meeting was held in Odessa, Prince Gortschakoff could take the position of Russian plenipotentiary."

It was of no avail. The hot-heads who were against consulting Europe insisted upon the conclusion of a treaty of peace between Russia and Turkey. General Ignatieff was ordered to draw up a draft of the proposed instrument. He sat down, and in twenty-four hours in his study in St. Petersburg he had written out the Treaty of San Stefano from first clause to last clause. He took it down to the Foreign Office, and read it over to the Ministers. They marvelled at his despatch, but unanimously approved of his proposals. "*Hélas, le pauvre Turque!*" said M. Onou; but his sympathies were Platonic, nor were they shared by the heads of the Foreign Office. As General Ignatieff had drawn up the treaty, so it was agreed the treaty should be.

General Ignatieff went to San Stefano with the treaty in his pocket, and in due time the signatures of the Turkish Commissioners were appended to the document. Russia stumbled blindly onwards to the humiliations of the Berlin Congress—humiliations which might have been softened, if not altogether avoided, had his advice been taken in time.

## CHAPTER IV.

### GENERAL IGNATIEFF'S POLICY IN THE EAST.

OF the Berlin Treaty, General Ignatieff is of the same opinion that he was of the Treaty of Frankfort. When the telegram appeared saying that Germany had wrested Alsace and Lorraine from France, General Ignatieff, who was then at Constantinople, hastened to the German Embassy. " Permit me to congratulate you," said he, with the irony of truth, to his German colleague, Count Kaiserling, "and to thank you. For you it is a prodigious mistake; but on Russia you have conferred the greatest possible boon." To him it seemed that Germany had wantonly incurred a perpetual blood-feud with France, and had thereby practically placed herself *hors de combat* in any future quarrel in which Russia might be interested. Better have taken more money and left the territory. That was fatal—a paralysis in advance of the independence of Germany.

Of the Berlin Treaty, General Ignatieff held equally strong opinions. "It is a treaty, not for peace, but for war!" he exclaimed as he read it. "My treaty was not for war, but for peace." He had more reason for saying that than he has for asserting, as he persistently does, that in framing his treaty he had the preservation of Turkey more at heart than had the Congress of Berlin. The Berlin Treaty took more territory from the Porte than he, for he left it Bosnia; but it restored Macedonia to Turkey—a crime against civilisation for which Lord Salisbury has yet to atone.

General Ignatieff is of opinion that the practical conversion by Austria of her occupation of the Turkish provinces into annexation is equivalent to the nullification of the Berlin Treaty. He holds, therefore, that the Treaty of San Stefano ought to revive the day after the Austrians refuse to retire from Bosnia. As the chief effect of this would be the re-appearance of the Big Bulgaria, it may be well to repeat what General Ignatieff said to me on the subject. "The Bulgaria of San Stefano is only the Bulgaria of the Constantinople Conference with rectifications necessitated by closer knowledge of the ethnographical and geographical details. In the Treaty of San Stefano I proposed to construct a Bulgaria that would be homogeneous as regards nationality and religion. I proposed that a mixed Commission of Greeks, Servians, Bulgarians, presided over by Russia, should, as a family question, decide what should and what should not be Bulgaria. If a village was Greek, it should go to the Greeks; if it was Bulgarian, to Bulgaria; if Servian, to the Servians. That was for peace and permanence, to bring the frontiers into accord with the ethnological facts. What has been done? Macedonia has been created, and with the strife of race has come also the strife of religion. The dispute will now never end. The Greeks refuse to recognise the authority of the Bulgarian Exarch outside the limits of Bulgaria; the Bulgarians refuse to submit to any other authority but the Bulgarian; they will never agree. The Greeks deny nationality to the Bulgarian Church outside the Berlin Bulgaria. So the strife goes on."

"Well," said I, "although it will hardly make peace to object to Austria remaining in Bosnia and the Herzegovina, what would you do with these provinces?"

"That is easily settled. Turkish Croatia would go to Dalmatia, as was arranged by the Convention of Vienna. The rest of Bosnia would go to Servia, and Herzegovina would go to Montenegro. That is what I proposed long ago. The people wish not for Austria."

"And the true policy in the Balkan?"

"Hands off all round! I have always opposed any annexation in the Balkan. When Mr. Gladstone said 'Hands off!' to Austria, I applauded him. I had said it years before in my despatches, not only about Austria, but also about Russia. I have no rostrum, no Parliament, like Mr. Gladstone, to defend myself and explain my policy. But I say not less emphatically, 'Hands off all round!' Of course, this cannot be applied to Russia if it is not applied to Austria. Russia, for instance, never will permit Bulgaria to be converted into a weapon in the hands of Austria and of Rome, to be used by them against the Slavs and Orthodox. But you need be under no alarm as to Russian military intervention in Bulgaria. Never would I consent to send Russian soldiers to fight against their fellow-Slavs. The Russian standard has never been unfurled in the Balkan, save for the liberation of the Christians. That flag must never be the symbol of conquest, nor must we march under it against our brother-Slavs."

General Ignatieff shares the conviction of the Government—that in due time the Bulgarians will rid the principality of the Coburger. I asked him what he would do to put things straight. He replied—

"The Grand Duke Nicholas once asked me that question, and I replied, 'For eight years I have never been asked my advice, until it seems as if there were no more blunders left to be made.' It is not easy now for any one to say what should be done. Besides, although practical men may know what they would do, but they never say it until the time arrives; for the right action depends always upon the combination of circumstances. Literary men may discuss what should be done. Practical men never. I know what I would do; but I will not say it now."

General Ignatieff is less reticent about what he would have done at the beginning if it had fallen to his lot instead of to that of Prince Dondonkoff-Korsakoff to draw up the Bulgarian Constitution.

"The Bulgarians had had the Turk and the *Phanar* (Greek) on their back for centuries. The moment they were taken off you expected them instantly to enjoy the latest and most improved Liberal constitution! It was absurd. Peoples like children need to be trained to walk before they run. It was nonsense to give the Bulgarians just freed from bondage the most advanced constitution of the most enlightened and experienced nations."

"What then," I asked, "would you have done?"

He replied—"The Bulgarian is very well able to govern himself in small areas. The local district was an area in which he should have had local self-government; but at first no Parliament and no Prince! No Prince, I said, and for that I was accused of being a Republican. I only wished the Principality to escape the expense of a Prince and a Court. What had they to do with a Court? What I proposed was this:—I would have nominated eight or nine—whose names I submitted—most respectable men who would have had provisional charge of the various departments of State. These I would have called Consuls, and they would have deliberated together in College. As President I proposed the Bulgarian Exarch, thereby following

T

the precedent of Montenegro, where the Exarch always presided over the Council of Ministers before the Prince was elected. After two or three years, when the local *Zemstroes* were at work, and the Consuls had got hold of the work of administration, they could, if they pleased, have formulated some improved Constitution. They could have summoned from each district two or three of the most respectable inhabitants to a Sobor or Skuptchina, which would have sat two or three weeks, and which, being composed of really respectable industrious people, would have been able to speak and act for Bulgaria. Instead of that, what did they do? They supplied a brand new Constitution, under which the lawyers got all the power, and which had no relation whatever to the history and traditions of the people. What was the result? Men who could not govern ten men were set to govern a province, and all has gone wrong."

General Ignatieff feels very acutely the injustice of the censures heaped upon him for the disappointment and disillusionment of Russia in the Principality which he created. It does, on the face of it, seem absurd that he who had all Bulgaria to look after for years should never once have been consulted as to what should be done after it came into existence. He himself sums up the situation thus:—"I sometimes have said I was like a *chef-de-cuisine* who had made all his preparations for a dinner. He puts all his little pieces ready, when suddenly he is removed, and another cook comes, who puts the forcemeat into the sweets, and the sugar into the soup, and then the poor *chef-de-cuisine* is abused for the bad dinner; but it is not his fault that the ingredients were wrongly mixed by the blunderer who came after him."

I have already mentioned that General Ignatieff objected to the establishment of a British Sentry Box at Mitylene, and of course still more strongly to the occupation of Gallipoli. He was, however, not obdurate about Mitylene. He suggested Lemnos, and had no objection whatever to make to our position in Egypt, even if it were made permanent. He spoke very strongly about 'the inconvenience to which Russia was subjected by the arbitrary action of the Porte, in closing the Black Sea to the outer Russian trade, whenever there was sufficient alarm of fever, or small-pox, or cholera to afford the Pashas an excuse for subjecting all ships to quarantine. The possession of the Straits also gave the Turks opportunity to blockade the Black Sea littoral in time of war, even although without the possession of the Straits it was quite beyond their power to make that blockade effective.

"We must have our way to the sea clear from obstruction. Surely that is no exorbitant demand for a nation of 120 millions!"

If Russia got her double-barrelled Gibraltar in the Bosphorus, she would forswear all further annexation; so at least says General Ignatieff. He is very emphatic on that point. We must have our way to the sea free from hindrance. If we cannot get it by the direct route, we shall be driven to take a detour. What does that mean? It simply means that if the Straits are closed or only opened intermittently by sufferance Russia will drive down to the sea through Asia Minor, through Persia or anywhere else to have her unimpeded water-way from her own ports to the open sea.

Empires grow towards the sea as the roots of trees stretch towards the spring. There is an irresistible power of attraction about water, which governs Russia's growth by making her gravitate to the sea.

Granting the open straits freed from Turkish bolt or bar, and according to General Ignatieff the gravitation to the southern seas would cease. Persia, I ventured to suggest, would blossom as a garden if Russia were to establish a suitable port in the Shah's dominions. "No, thank you," said General Ignatieff, "we have no ambition for any such gardens; we have too many of the same kind already, and if we have one outlet by the natural short cut to the Mediterranean, why should we go so far off to get to the sea? Of course if that is closed we must go anywhere, everywhere, in order to get to the sea."

Speaking of Asia Minor brought Armenia to the front. General Ignatieff's views of Armenian policy are, that the establishment of an Armenian nationality will not be realised for fifty years to come. At present all that can be done is to establish some kind of local autonomy similar to that which exists in the Lebanon, but not quite so drastic. He would give the Armenians power to elect their sub-prefect, and he would reform the police. There are too many Kurds to render the experiment of self-government safe except perhaps in Kararmenia next the sea, where something might be done. " But above all, whatever you do," General Ignatieff impressed upon me, " don't try to do too much at once. Europe has too much oppressed the Turks with imposing upon them the execution of too great reforms, with the result that nothing has been done."

I told General Ignatieff of Mr. Bright's summary counsel to the Armenian delegates who came to London to invoke the assistance of the English Government. " Go to St. Petersburg, gentlemen, and see the Tzar. He is your only friend; he can help you and no one else either will or can." He remarked that Russia had already 700,000 Armenian subjects, and did not wish to add to their number.

" No," said he emphatically, " I do not wish to see another yard of land added to the Russian Empire, either in Asia or in Europe. We have got too much already, to want any more. What we need is to develop our own resources, to look after our own business, and to let time do the rest." Once more I seemed to hear the voice of Mr. Gladstone crying in the wilderness against extension of Empire and annexations, and pleading only to be allowed to stay at home and mind his own affairs. But when I remembered the annexations made by Mr. Gladstone, I could not but feel that however sincerely General Ignatieff might deprecate the addition of territory to the Russian Empire, the law of gravitation will prove irresistible.

No one protested more vehemently against our going to Egypt than Mr. Gladstone, and yet it was Mr. Gladstone who sent Lord Wolseley to Tel-el-Kebir, and it was by his order that Lord Alcester opened fire on the Alexandrian forts. General Ignatieff's wishes are one thing; what General Ignatieff, if he ever returned to office, might be driven to do is another. Of one thing we may be quite sure. As he demurred to making any pledges about Khiva, knowing that no promises can be absolute, he will, if ever he should return to power, refuse to make any promises, which from the experience of the past he knows that circumstances may render it impossible for him to perform.

## CHAPTER V.

MINISTER OF THE INTERIOR.

WITH the signature of the Treaty of San Stefano General Ignatieff's diplomatic career has terminated—at least for the time. He was spared the indignity of being sent to Berlin to assist in the undoing of the work of the war, and the establishment of the Austrian *avant poste* in the Balkan Peninsula. For some time after that great eclipse General Ignatieff remained *en retraite*. In this he resembled the country which he had served so faithfully. The cloud which cast its shadow over the Russian Empire naturally enveloped the Count in its darkest folds.

After the signature of the Berlin treaty the internal *malaise* of the Russian people found expression in the innumerable plots of the Nihilist Camorra. In Germany, after the French war, the general unloosing of the obligations of morality, which is the first condition of foreign war, produced a terrible harvest of private crime. In Russia, the indifference to human life and suffering engendered by the siege of Plevna and the passage of the Balkans bore fruit in political assassination. Vera Sassoulitch tried to kill the Prefect of Police of Petersburg. General Menzentsoff was killed. So was Prince Krapotkin. At last an attempt was made by Solovieff on the life of the Emperor in April, 1879. This roused the Government to energetic measures, and when men of energy were called for, General Ignatieff was to the front. A state of siege was proclaimed, and in each of the great provincial centres the ablest and most energetic men were placed in supreme command. Among these military governors General Ignatieff was appointed, and the great commercial centre of Nijni Novgorod was named as the place where he must answer for order.

Nijni—the scene of the greatest fair in the world—is perhaps the most important city in Russia after St. Petersburg and Moscow. It is now the seat of General Baranoff, who was transferred thither from the capital. When General Ignatieff was appointed, there were those who declared that at last the hour of his enemies had come. The post was one for which he had no previous training, and it was hoped that it would infallibly break his reputation. How could a diplomatist who had spent almost all his life abroad, and who knew absolutely nothing of commerce, govern Nijni Novgorod? Even his friends felt some misgivings. But General Ignatieff signally vindicated the confidence of the Emperor. Good common sense, great capacity for taking pains, and genial good humour, made him in a short time one of the most popular of provincial governors. He applied himself zealously to promote the public peace and the general well-being. He never enforced any of the exceptional prerogatives with which he was armed, and although he had in his pocket a letter from the Emperor authorising him to annex, if he thought fit, two or three large Governments to the area of his authority, he never produced the letter but contented himself with his original limited jurisdiction.

He was content to keep Nijni in profound peace, to give no man cause to regret his existence, and to make all the working and commercial classes feel that he was a man who understood their interests, and who recognised that it was the first duty of the Government to promote their welfare. Never before had the great gathering of the merchants been at once so orderly and so contented, and when half the term of office for which he had been appointed expired there was only one opinion in the place as to the success of his administration.

Instead therefore of breaking him, the arduous duties of civil administration at Nijni only started the Count on a new career. He was appointed a second time to the governorship of Nijni in September, 1880, but at the beginning of the new reign he was asked to undertake the duties of Minister of the Domains. It was but a temporary appointment, which he vacated in a very short time, when on the fall of General Loris Melikoff, General Ignatieff became Minister of the Interior.

This was the most important post in the service of the Emperor, and the fact that it had been bestowed upon General Ignatieff, whose experience of civil administration was but of yesterday, was a remarkable tribute to the prestige of his name and the success which he had achieved at Nijni Novgorod.

He began his administration characteristically. After his appointment, he made ready to go to the Cathedral, where for the first time as Minister of the Interior he was to take part in public worship. To his surprise he found that the

Prefect of Police had a company of Cossacks at the door to escort him to and from the Cathedral. "I do not want these men," said he quietly, "I can go without an escort." The police expostulated. "It is not safe. Your predecessor never went without an escort. Remember the fate of the Emperor, and do not imperil your life and expose the State to the danger by a reckless disregard of necessary precautions." General Ignatieff replied, "I refuse your escort. At the beginning of my career, when I rode to Khiva, everyone said I was sure to be impaled. If I did not fear the impalement in Khiva, why should I dread assassination in St. Petersburg?" And so saying, he dismissed the Cossacks, and drove unattended to the Cathedral, where his arrival alone and in safety created a profound impression. Lord Carnarvon acted with similar intrepidity when he succeeded Lord Spencer as Viceroy of Ireland, and with equally satisfactory results. The danger in St. Petersburg was greater, but General Ignatieff never found any inconvenience result from dispensing with a military escort.

At the Interior General Ignatieff remained for thirteen months, and for those thirteen months the history of his department is the history of Russia. I can only glance briefly at its salient characteristics. It was distinguished above the administrations which had preceded it and still from that by which it was succeeded by extreme activity. General Ignatieff worked fifteen hours a day with an energy which seemed actually inexhaustible, receiving all sorts and conditions of men with an amiability which nothing could ruffle and a patience and courtesy too rare in official circles. He would in a single day receive personally some two or three hundred persons, and whether they were governors of provinces or simple peasants, he was never inaccessible. He was aware that he had to learn his business, for the greater part of his life had been spent abroad, and he was a comparative stranger to the internal administration of the Empire. He made mistakes, no doubt. He overestimated his own strength. He was but one man in the midst of a great centralised administration. Under his order were no fewer than 36,000 officials, most of them sluggish, inert, and indisposed to be driven, even by a Minister of the Interior, one step faster than their ancient jog-trot. But for the wonderfully sanguine spirit of the man, he must have sometimes felt inside his department almost as powerless as a brisk blue-bottle fly in the interior of the drum of a threshing-machine. His buoyancy of spirits saved him from despair, and he worked on, hoping to learn from his very failures as Peter the Great was taught the art of war by successive defeats.

First and foremost he decided that something must be done to check the corruption which eats into the efficiency of the Russian administration. Those who remember how Mr. Childers in 1869 wrecked his health by an attempt to bring honesty and efficiency into the comparatively small department of the Admiralty administration can form some idea of the fury excited against General Ignatieff when it became known that he intended to deal with the ancient and well-established rule of allowing officials to supplement their insufficient salaries by benevolences—*anglicé*, tips—and douceurs from the public. General Ignatieff was seized with the idea that there were too many officials, and that if every tchinovnik did a good day's work, one half their number might be dispensed with. In that case the remainder might receive sufficient salaries to make them independent of bribes. Therein he resembled many a Radical reformer at home whose name stinks in the nostrils of our Civil Service. Government clerks who come to office late and who leave early cannot naturally be expected to love an administrator who works himself fifteen hours a day and thinks that they should all do likewise, solely in order to cut down their number by fifty per cent. My own impression is that in Russia, as in England, the extent to which an increase of salary can be secured by a diminution of the staff is easily exaggerated; but the error, if it be an error, into which General Ignatieff fell is another point of resemblance between him and Mr. Gladstone. Lord Randolph Churchill also will keenly sympathise with the Russian statesman, and will fully appreciate the intensity of the animosity which such a programme excited.

That General Ignatieff did not mean to rest content with cutting down the numbers and increasing the work of the minor tchinovniks was soon made clear by the drastic method in which he dealt with the great scandal of the Bashkir lands. It was discovered that the governor of the province of Orenburg, in which they were situated, had been making his friends comfortable by alienating the Crown property for their benefit. He dismissed the governor, punished his subordinates, and procured an alteration of the law so that in future not an acre of Crown land can be alienated without the express sanction of the Council of the Empire.

So much for his attempt to reform the administration over which he was placed. The great public questions with which he tried to deal were (1) the reform, or rather the restriction, of the sale of drink : (2) the Jewish Question : (3) the migration of peasants. It was in facing these questions that he hit upon the happy expedient of calling in the aid of the first Commissions of Experts. The plan resembled very much our method of preparing for legislation by the appointment of a Royal Commission of Inquiry. A small deliberative committee of the officials and of the general public was constituted for the purpose of taking evidence, and of making recommendations for the amendment of the law. It was an admirable expedient, and as the sittings of the Liquor Commission were public it familiarised the Russians, almost for the first time, with the public discussion by serious practical men of grave questions of public interest.

These three questions, of the liquor trade, of the Jews, and of the migration of peasants, go to the root of the local well-being of the Russian people. The Jewish question was forced upon the attention of the Government by the despairing wrath of the peasantry exploited by the Jewish traders. The liquor question was one of those questions which it was necessary for the administrator to raise in order to check the demoralisation of the people. The liquor commission reported in favour of increasing the duty on vodka, and of restricting the number of the places at which it can be sold. The Jewish commission had not completed its report when General Ignatieff fell, and the same thing may be said of the migration of the peasants. General Ignatieff's fall took place too soon to enable Russia to profit by the result of his new departure. Similar commissions still sit to deal with other questions, but they sit with closed doors, and the choice of their members leaves much to be desired.

Taken together, the Commissions of Experts and the establishment of a peasants' organ for the statement and the discussion of difficulties, offered ground of hope for the adaptation of the autocratic system to popular necessities, which constituted a hopeful augury for the new reign.

Another measure by which General Ignatieff honourably distinguished himself was by the wisdom and liberality with which he dealt with the Old Believers, Russian nonconformists whose adherence to the old ritual had exposed them for two hundred years to ostracism and neglect. He also energetically supported any and every scheme which seemed to tend in the direction of commercial and industrial improvement; and in whatever way he could he laboured to stimulate the life of the nation. He was never afraid of a new idea. Old fossilised tichnovniks looked upon him as the victim of a kind of demoniac possession, from the legion of ideas which filled his active brain. To their somnolent and timid minds, these ideas in number and activity resembled the bees which swarm around the hive on a summer day, and resembled them also in this, that each idea like the bee had its smarting sting.

Above all, he sought to bring the Emperor into personal and frequent contact with his people. The Tzar was the Emperor of the common people, and General Ignatieff was never so happy as when introducing deputations of peasants or of merchants to the Emperor. It was in pursuance of this same idea that he projected his striking and daring scheme for the re-assembling of the Zemskie Sobory, or consultative assembly of the Russian people—an old institution which had worked well in the past, but which had not been summoned for many generations—the ultimate rejection of which was the signal for his retirement from office.

## CHAPTER VI.

### GENERAL IGNATIEFF AT HOME.

GENERAL IGNATIEFF's study in his house on the Moyka Canal, one of the three which give St. Petersburg a semblance to Rotterdam or Venice, is one of the pleasantest and most interesting rooms in the Russian capital. It is on the third storey, and is lighted by three windows. When I was there a splendid bearskin was stretched in front of his writing-desk; at the opposite side of the room a tiger skin lay in front of a settee, above which, on one side hung a life-size portrait of Countess Ignatieff, while the wall immediately behind it was ornamented with a singularly effective trophy of arms, not so large, but much more picturesquely displayed than that which Lord Wolseley has over the mantlepiece of his room in the War Office.

Every one of these weapons or pieces of armour had its history, and it was pleasant to hear their owner's stories of his relics. The helmet and mailclad shirt of the Crusaders, in the centre, was brought from Abyssinia by the adventurous Ashimoff Cossack, who has been prospecting Abyssinia in the interests of the Orthodox Church and of Holy Russia. Conspicuous among other weapons is the dagger or short sword, with gilt belt and scabbard, which was a gift to General Ignatieff from Schamyl, the famous patriot of the Caucasus. Schamyl, whose name still lingers in our memory as having been a kind of Circassian Kosciusko or Garibaldi, was interned at Constantinople after the subjugation of his mountaineers. There he lived under the surveillance of the Russian Embassy, and when, in his declining years, he wished to make the pilgrimage to Mecca, he did so by favour and grace of General Ignatieff. As a pilgrim he had to leave his arms behind at Jeddah, and from there he sent this dagger to General Ignatieff, as the weapon with which for twenty-five years he had fought against Russia. A pair of pistols, inlaid with coral, were the gift of another famous political proscript. They belonged to an Albanian, the last descendant of Iskander Beg. He was a Catholic, who had been imprisoned a long time in Constantinople. As neither France nor Italy would help him, he turned to General Ignatieff, who smuggled him on board a ship bound to Italy, in a sailor's costume. As he could neither read nor write, it was agreed that if he reached his destination safely he should send these pistols to the Embassy at once, as a sign of his deliverance, and as a token of his gratitude. Here also are the famous Peabody rifles, samples of an armament which General Ignatieff endeavoured to secure for Russia before the war of 1877, but which was ultimately snapped up by Turkey, together with all manner of weapons old and new, from the crossbow to the revolver, which he had collected in the course of his wanderings throughout the East.

A photograph of the house in which the Treaty of San Stefano was signed hangs as a perpetual reminder of the crowning diplomatic achievement of his life. Mr. Gladstone's portrait hangs near; all the other portraits are those of Russians.

General Ignatieff does not look older than his years, and his physique is not quite so spare as might have been expected in so energetic a worker. He neither smokes nor drinks; and the cigarette which is so constant an accompaniment to conversation in Russia, is conspicuous by its absence from the lips of all the Ignatieffs. He wears the ordinary dark blue uniform of a Russian general, with white cords and tassels, and the usual gold and silver lettered shoulder straps. The only decoration I ever saw him wear was the simple cross at the throat. I suppose that he could cover his breast with crosses and medals and orders if he chose to wear the trinkets to which many people attach so much importance, but he is singularly indifferent to these gewgaws. He confuses one with another, so little does he care for them. Talking of decorations reminds me of the advice which General Ignatieff once gave to the Emperor on the subject of Central Asia: "If you want to have peace on the Afghan Frontier, the remedy is simple. Let both Governments, England and Russia, agree that no decoration or promotion shall be given to any frontier officer who ever gets into difficulties in Central Asia. At present the temptation is irresistible to make difficulties to gain distinction. An officer goes from Petersburg to some miserable outpost on the Afghan frontier. He is forgotten unless he can do something. If he can do something, that is, if he has to fight or diplomatise or get into or out of some scrape important enough to make people turn their eyes towards him, he is honoured and decorated. Stop the issue of all crosses, and we should have peace." It might be an improvement on this suggestion that it might be well to issue crosses to those who serve their term without ever doing anything to cause their existence to be remembered by their countrymen.

Like many Russians who know their Turkomans, General Ignatieff is dubious about the advantage of the new Afghan frontier. Drawing a frontier line through wastes tenanted by nomads is something like drawing a frontier line across the sea, and expecting it to be respected by the fish. Tribes which range backwards and forwards over distances of hundreds of versts seeking pasturage for their cows, reck little of stone pillars set up by Boundary Commissioners, and the divided allegiance between the Russians and the Ameer can hardly fail to cause trouble. Not that General Ignatieff cares one copeck about Sarik or Salor or Jemshidi of them all. He declares that the whole of the territory in dispute, which in 1885 nearly brought England and Russia to war, is not worth, in coin of the realm, if put up to auction, a single silver rouble. His sovereign specific for the prevention of any wars arising out of frontier questions in Central Asia, would be to pack off all the diplomatists and ministers who have to settle the question to the place of dispute. There he would intern them for six months, and if they did not die they would agree to some arrangement without a war. In view of the possible death of the Ameer, he advocates a friendly understanding with Russia in favour of maintaining the territorial *status quo*, without which he thinks the proximity of the Russian outposts may lead to Afghan alarms, costing our Indian treasury a very pretty penny. Our subsidies to the Ameer are looked upon with scant favour in St. Petersburg, where they tell me roundly that Abdul Rahman is simply exploiting our nervousness for his own ends. As long as the amount of the subsidy depends upon the degree of tension that prevails between England and Russia, so long the wily savage at Cabul will take good care to do nothing to facilitate an *entente* which might be as inconvenient for him as an understanding between Russia and Austria might be for Prince Bismarck. *Divide et impera* is not exactly the Afghan motto. At Cabul they wish not to govern, but to make money out of the differences of their neighbours. "Where you make your mistake," said General Ignatieff, "is in thinking that there is only one Afghanistan. There are several. The best policy is to let them all stew in their own juice; do not bring the frontiers too close together, and remember that the Afghans, like the Germans, have their own game to play in keeping us at cross purposes."

General Ignatieff was very unwilling to be interviewed. "I do not like your interviews and conversations," he said. "But every one knows my ideas. Why do you care to ask me?" He was ready enough to talk; but to make declarations which may be regarded as putting forth his own views, that he absolutely refused. His attitude in relation to the Government was strictly loyal. In order to avoid any possibility of being accused of opposing the Government or intriguing against it, he says, he has not written a political letter for three years. At the same time General Ignatieff speaks out quite fearlessly and frankly to those whom he meets in Society or elsewhere, if any one asks him his opinions. As the number of such persons is necessarily very limited, I have taken upon myself the responsibility of collecting together the notes of our numerous conversations, which were in no sense confidential, and giving them to the world. There is no sense in limiting the circulation of the ideas of an Ignatieff to the handful of men and women whom he may meet in Petersburg Society.

General Ignatieff is in no sense a Parliamentarian. He is, like all Russians, a believer in the Autocracy; and his only regret is that in Russia there is not Autocracy enough, for the Autocrat is the only resource of the people against the Tchinovnik. At the same time he sees that the Autocracy would be enormously strengthened, both against the anarchist and the Tchinovnik, if the Emperor could be brought more visibly into direct contact with his people. Hence his advocacy of the Zemskie Sobory—a project of which I can say nothing here beyond remarking that I found it most severely criticised by middle-class Liberals and constitutionalists, who complained that it was much too democratic. Their ideal was the representation of the Cultivated *Intelligentia*—his, the representation of the whole people. And their objection to his scheme was precisely this—that if the peasants were directly represented, all other classes would be swamped, and the only result of assembling the Zemskie would be to strengthen at once the prestige and popularity of the Tzar, without in any way increasing the hold of the middle classes on the government of the country.

One advantage which the Parliamentary system undoubtedly has in General Ignatieff's eyes is that its free and open debate in the House of Commons affords a Minister who is accused an unequalled opportunity of vindicating his character against his assailants. "Some day, when I am dead," he remarked, "but not before, my papers will show the truth about the things about which so many *mensonges* have been spoken of me. With us the accused has no defence. He must be silent while the calumnies are repeated on every side, until at last they are accepted as incontrovertible truth." I confess I should like to hear General Ignatieff replying to M. de Giers in a debate on foreign policy, or to listen to him treat M. Wischnegradsky as Mr. Gladstone was wont to polish off Mr. Disraeli when the latter ventured into the field of finance. The dumbness of the Russian system is a great drawback. The Russian common people call all foreigners "*nemtzy*," or "the dumb;" but in the political field it is the Russians who are the *nemtzy*. "Why can you not at least publish a Blue Book now and then?" I asked at the Russian Foreign Office. "Because," was the reply, "the Emperor would not tolerate the publication of mutilated and mangled and misleading despatches. That is possible in England. It is not possible here. So we publish nothing"—and suffer severely for their reticence. But our own diplomatists are aware that all is not clover even under the English system, and many an Ambassador must have writhed with indignation at the semblance of publicity afforded him by a Blue Book or a debate which left the public more hopelessly than ever in the dark as to his objects and his difficulties.

General Ignatieff talked very freely about the press. When Minister of the Interior he had to administer the law as it existed, and on one occasion I was told by the editor of the *Novoe Vremya* he issued, obviously under orders from above, a circular absolutely forbidding the publication of articles, even in support of a scheme to which he was deeply attached. Instead of leaving the press to the uncovenanted mercies of a secret department of the Home Office, he would constitute a special court, where all charges against newspapers—whether brought by the Administration or by private individuals—could be heard publicly, and dealt with on some intelligible principle. I cannot vouch for the details of his scheme. All that I know is that it was based upon the principle that in dealing with newspapers, as with everything else, publicity and responsibility are the best safe-guards against injustice.

Of his views on liberty of conscience it is only necessary to say that he combines the breadth of view of the cultured man of the world with the Christian tolerance which has so honourably distinguished the Eastern Church, excepting where it has been converted into a mere political institution. One of the minor incidents of his Administration was the release of three bishops of the Old Believers, who had been kept imprisoned at Sousdal ever since the Crimean War for some theologico-political offence.

We talked about Poland. All the difficulty with Poland, in his opinion, arose from the Poles themselves. Russia was at present face to face with the Polish demand for the western provinces. Let the Poles but definitely and publicly withdraw their preposterous claims to provinces which are as Russian as Moscow, and at once the Poles could share in all the privileges and local institutions enjoyed by the Russians. Poland at present is treated, like Ireland, as an integral part of the Empire, but it is denied equality of rights. In English Acts of Parliament the word "man" is held to include woman whenever it imposes a penalty, but to exclude woman when it confers a franchise. Russia treats Poland much in the same way. The Poles suffer exceptional disabilities, but are denied the ordinary privileges of Russians. The result is that although Poland is perhaps at this moment the most flourishing part of the Russian Empire, from a manufacturing point of view, the open sore of Polish animosity is not healed. A short time ago a Russian officer was paying a visit to the house of a Polish friend. One of the little girls had been misbehaving, and the ladies were discussing how it should be punished, not knowing that their guest understood Polish. The aunt recommended, as the severest disgrace that could be inflicted, that the little girl for a whole day should be called a "Russian!" Still, the Poles prefer the Russians to the Prussians; and I was told, when in Moscow, that during the recent alarm about a possible war Polish manufacturers doing business had planted all their factories on the Russian bank of the Vistula, fearing that all west of that might be annexed to Germany as the result of the threatened war. Russia can claim that in Poland she can show two results superior to any that England can produce in Ireland. She has steadily been the friend of the peasant, as against the landlord, and under her sway the industries of Poland have been developed beyond those of Russia itself. In Ireland England supported the landlord against the peasant, and Irish manufactures were deliberately destroyed in the interests of their English competitors. Russia also has an excuse for her restrictive measures in Poland, in the claim which the Poles obstinately maintain to purely Russian provinces. It is as if Ireland, as a condition of acquiescence in Home Rule, were to insist that Wales and Lancashire were to be considered an integral part of Ireland.

The political question is complicated by the religious. Who says " Pole " says " Catholic," and the Pope unfortunately has not been able to disassociate the Catholic Church in Russia from its exclusively Polish character. General Ignatieff urged upon the Pope that he should appoint Slavonic bishops in Russia from other nationalities than the Polish. But the Poles object to anything which would prevent them exploiting the Catholic religion in the interest of their hopeless nationality.

The Jewish question naturally came up for discussion.

Count Ignatieff vigorously disclaimed any desire to expel the Jews from Russia. He had some Jews on his estate, he said, where they were allowed to settle, provided that they would work in the fields like the other peasants. But the Jew is indisposed to agriculture. The Jewess does not like to go out into the fields. The Jew prefers to trade. The Russian peasant is very simple, and the astute sons of Israel find little difficulty in making their book at his expense. General Ignatieff had frequent visits from the Rabbis when he was Minister of the Interior, and in his interviews with the deputations he displayed his wonted ready wit. He told them that when they had revised the Talmud, and cleansed it of passages which taught the Jews that no faith need be kept with the Gentile, they might come back and ask to be allowed to share the privileges of Gentiles. "We are groaning under a bondage as of Egypt," said the Rabbis. "But," retorted Ignatieff, "if so, why do you not make an Exodus? Where is your Moses? I shall only be too glad to give him full powers to take all your people off to the land of Canaan. Pharaoh would not let you go; I, on the contrary, will be delighted to give you every facility for your departure." From this arose the story that General Ignatieff was preparing to expel the whole Semitic population from Russian territory.

But so colossal a displacement of millions is an enterprise from which even General Ignatieff would shrink dismayed. The difficulty, however, is not solved, nor does it appear to be soluble. We have already made the discovery in London that

U

the presence of a colony of Russian Jews is an all but intolerable nuisance. We can sympathise better now than of old with the unfortunate Russians, who have five millions of the poorest Jews in Europe encamped within their frontiers.

Lastly, I often talked with General Ignatieff of the Heathen Chinee. He regards the Chinese menace as real both for Russia and for England. The Chinese may yet devastate Russia worse than the Mongols. He lamented that Europe should be inoculating a peaceful people, devoted solely to trade and agriculture, with the fever of war. The West might have something better to do than to teach the 300,000,000 of Chinese the use of the latest weapons of European civilisation. The peril, however, is not from the march of some millions of Celestials; it is to be found rather in the steady influx at every point along the Asiatic frontier of the migrating Chinese. What will be the ultimate effect of this portentous factor on the development of humanity, science has not yet begun even to speculate.

## CHAPTER VII.

### HIS FUTURE.

SINCE his retirement, General Ignatieff has held no public office under the Emperor. In Russia the opportunities for active public service outside the official ranks are unfortunately few. But there are two societies, both of considerable importance, which carry on a kind of quasi-political existence, ever under the shadow of Russian officialism. One is the Society for the Promotion of Trade and Commerce; the other, the famous Slavonic Benevolent Society. The commercial association is the nearest Russian analogue to our Associated Chambers of Commerce. It has more than two thousand members in all parts of Russia, and it devotes itself to the consideration and discussion of all matters affecting the development of industry and commerce in Russia. General Ignatieff is president of this society, and in that capacity is in direct touch with the leading business men of Russia. The Slavonic Society needs no introduction to

English readers; it represents the men who in 1876 organised Russian enthusiasm into a weapon which gave the death-blow to the Ottoman Empire in Europe, and it still flourishes on the prestige which it gained from that unique exploit. Mr. Aksakoff, who was its inspiring soul, is dead. I made a pilgrimage of sympathy and of reverence to the grave at Troitsa Monastery, in which, beneath a cross-crowned granite boulder, lies all that is mortal of the good and great man in whom in that memorable crisis Russia found her voice. But though Mr. Aksakoff is dead, the Slavonic Society lives on. I attended one of its meetings in the Town Hall of St. Petersburg; it was quite like Exeter Hall. There was an imposing array of bishops and of the higher clergy on the platform, supported by a fair show of generals and officers in uniform. The audience was numerous and eminently respectable, with quite an English proportion of ladies and clergy. There was a choir, which sang Russian religious music with considerable feeling and power; and there were various papers read from the platform. The meeting had been intended as a demonstration in favour of General Ignatieff, who at the previous meeting of the Council had been unanimously elected as its president. He had a bad bronchial attack, and did not attend. Had he been present it is probable that he would have been the subject of a great outburst. Russian meetings, they tell me, although usually sober enough, are apt to get out of hand with excess of uncontrollable enthusiasm when once the deeps are broken up. I regret that it was not my good fortune to witness any such an expression of feeling which General Ignatieff would probably have been able to evoke.

General Ignatieff is no wild visionary about Panslavism. He once told Count Andrassy that Panslavism was distinctly the creation of Austrians. All the early Panslavist writers were Austrian subjects. Panslavism is only a principle which is developed out of the oppression of the Slavs. It is the cry for fraternal help against intolerable oppression. Austria and Turkey are the two great generators of Panslavonic enthusiasm. It is their injustice, their oppression, of the Slavs which, by forcing their subjects to cast a despairing look around for help, led to the invention of the Panslavonic bogey. The worse Austria treats her Slavs, the more terrible will be the picture which will be drawn of the avenging Slavonic idea. To kill Panslavism in the simplest way is to treat the Slavs justly. Their own national idiosyncrasies are quite sufficiently distinctive to render it impossible for them to unite except under pressure of external danger or persecution. It is only when the pressure from without is sufficiently strong to lead them to subordinate everything to the consideration of defence, that a Panslavonic agitation is possible. As for really establishing a gigantic Slavonic Empire, including all the Slavonic peoples, under one sceptre, that is a dream, and not a particularly lovely dream. What the Slavonic enthusiasts hope for is exactly the same as that for which English enthusiasts long when they talk of the union of the English-speaking peoples. We do not dream of conquering the United States, or of compelling every English settlement to obey laws passed by the House of Commons. All that we hope for is that on all the world's broad surface no English-speaking race shall be domineered over and oppressed by any other race, that all differences between the various English families shall be adjusted by arbitration rather than by war, and that there should be a general league or brotherly union for defensive purposes, whereby all English-speaking men should make common cause against any one who might attempt to crush the weakest member of the fraternal league. That is our ideal. It is also the ideal of the Slavonic Society—a society to which, if they were Russians, most Englishmen would of course belong. So far from regarding the Slavonic Society with alarm, it seems to me that the only reason for regret is that an association with aims so legitimate and so inspiring should not receive much more general support from all classes. According to English ideas, the Emperor would be the natural patron of such an association, just as the Queen is the natural patron of our Anti-Slavery Society. Slavery is a domestic institution of many of her Majesty's neighbours, just as the oppression of Slavs is practised by some of his Imperial Majesty's imperial allies. But to a Russian Sovereign the oppression of Slavs can no more be regarded as a normal and natural and permanent condition of things than the institution of slavery can be so regarded by our Queen.

What is to be the future of General Ignatieff? There are many who say that he has no future. "Russia, however," as one of our Ambassadors in Southern Europe remarked the other day, "is not so over-stocked with able men that she can afford to put her ablest permanently on the shelf." He has been Ambassador at Constantinople, Governor of Nijni Novgorod, Minister of the Domains, Minister of the Interior. Will he ever be Minister again?

Possibly not, and yet, without being Minister, there is one post, not yet created, for which he seems to be pre-eminently fitted. In a previous chapter I have ventured to set forth some considerations which lead me to believe that the next step which could and ought to be taken in Russia in order to give more force and effect to the Tribunitial side of the Autocracy is the establishment of an Imperial newspaper, in the columns of which all *bona fide* representatives of the Russian people would have a right to expose their grievances and plead for redress, and through which the Emperor could place himself in direct and constant communication with his people. If the Emperor should determine to take that step, there is no one in all Russia so well qualified to fill the post of first editor of the organ of the Tzar-Tribune as General Ignatieff.

He has energy, initiative, and an all-round survey of affairs both at home and abroad. The functions of such a newspaper would be almost exclusively domestic, and its editor would necessarily be in personal communication with representative men in all parts of the Empire. General Ignatieff is the only man I know in Russia who, if entrusted with the duty of the Tzar has sufficient standing and official experience to be able to take up with adequate authority the position of spokesman and representative of the Tribunitial side of the Autocracy. He would be a terror to all officials who neglected their duties, and he would take a positive pleasure in bringing the voice of the people to bear upon all slothful or corrupt Tchinovniks. His industry is unrivalled. He is full of ideas, and the position of Imperial Editor is one for which he might have been specially created. The air of publicity in which he would live would at once suit his genius and secure the prompt exposure and correction of any of the defects of his qualities.

It is indicative of the confidence which General Ignatieff succeeds in inspiring in most of those who have to do with him seriously, and not as a mere person in Society, that people wish to see him in office in the department in which they are most interested. I have just explained my view as to his natural calling for the position of Imperial editor. Others would like to see him back at his old post of Minister of the Interior. The men with whom he works in the Society for the Promotion of Commerce are quite sure that he would be the Heaven-sent Minister of Finance and of Commerce. The whole of the Slavophils, and all those who are keenly interested in the prosecution of a strong national foreign policy, are quite indignant at the suggestion that General Ignatieff could possibly be placed anywhere but at the Foreign Office.

The most sceptical critic of General Ignatieff cannot deny that he has this extraordinary consensus of different and even antagonist opinions in his favour, and that in this respect he stands entirely alone. There may be other men whom sections of Russian opinion would prefer to see holding this, that, or the other portfolio; but there is no man among all the Russian Ministers—past, present, and to come—whom with common consent a large body of interested and intelligent public opinion designates simultaneously, not for one portfolio, but for three, as being not only a good man, but as being quite the best man that is available for each.

This, no doubt, is, in the eyes of some who call themselves the friends of the Autocracy, General Ignatieff's worst offence. He is popular, they say; as if popularity, no matter how it is acquired, were in itself a crime. For them, no doubt, that is a convenient doctrine. It is not a crime with which they are ever likely to be charged. But the Autocracy is far too strong for any Tzar to regard the popularity of his Ministers as a possible danger, but at the same time it sacrifices its efficiency when it is compelled to work through Ministers who do not inspire confidence, and who cannot command the hearty co-operation of the people.

In the midst of the dead level, as of an immense steppe, General Ignatieff towers head and shoulders above his contemporaries and rivals. What wonder, then, that the peasant and the trader, and the practical men of Russia, look to him with an almost touching confidence? He has his ideas, and he does not hesitate to speak and act in their support, being neither afraid of the Autocracy nor of the people, so that the thing be right. He once said, "I am the opponent of those who make difficulties, the friend of those who want to get things done."

The man who is not afraid—that, indeed, is the man for the situation in Russia to-day. But those who fear, and their name is legion, naturally will not welcome the return of General Ignatieff to the service of the State.

The slothful man saith, there is a lion in the way, a lion is in the streets; and as the door turneth upon his hinges, so doth the slothful upon his bed. There are many of the slothful tribe in Russia to-day, and it is from them and from their kindred that the cry goes up when the name of Ignatieff is mentioned, that there is a lion in the way—nay, a whole Daniel's den full of lions—ready to devour unfortunate Russia, if the Emperor ventures to avail himself of the General's services.

First and foremost, there is the declaration that the Emperor will not tolerate him—a declaration which, if true, would of course settle everything. But the Emperor will do what he sees to be best for his country; and if the Emperor sees that it is necessary to pursue a more active and courageous policy, no personal prejudice, supposing for a moment that any such existed, will stand in the way of his commanding the services of one of the most active and courageous of his subjects. Whether there is any such prejudice is a matter on which I do not feel competent to speak. Of course, in discussing the question, I presuppose as a *sine qua non* that the Emperor, after his seven years' experience, desires to resume the progress which was suspended owing to the war and the internal troubles which cost his father his life. If so, he will rely of necessity on statesmen imbued with progressive ideas, among whom General Ignatieff stands first. If, on the other hand, he is reluctant to rouse himself to the exertion necessary for a more vigorous policy, but prefers to let Count Dmitry Tolstoi potter on in the present inane fashion, then unquestionably General Ignatieff will remain at Kieff, or in his pleasant home on the Moyka. There will be no place for him in the Imperial Councils, no portfolio for him in the Administration of the Empire. His employment pre-supposes the adoption of a policy in which the Emperor will strenuously endeavour to realise the ideal of the Tzar-Tribune.

But, say some, the Ministers are against General Ignatieff. But if the Emperor be for him, what do the Ministers count? If the Emperor be against him, of course that ends the matter;

but if the Emperor decides that Russia has need of his services, which of all the mediocrities in office would not hasten to pay court to the rising sun? or which of them, if he took the other course, would even count as an appreciable minus to the strength of a patriotic Minister backed by a resolute Emperor? It is, however, no doubt true that the present administrative anarchy which exists under the mask of the Autocracy is very hostile to the development of men of General Ignatieff's calibre. Russia at present is a great Empire, but she has no great man. The moment any man of originality and independence appears, all the mediocrities in office abandon for the moment the internecine feuds which they are carrying on with each other, in order to crush the man who offends them by his superiority. Their opposition is, however, less formidable than that of the official class of which they form the departmental chiefs. Russia is a great bureaucracy, the Tchinovnik is ubiquitous, and the Tchinovnik is against General Ignatieff. Were it not that Nicholas Pavlovitch is a man who feels that obstacles exist only in order to be overcome, his heart might well sink within him at the thought of the banded ranks of the officials whose numbers he wishes to reduce in order that he may improve their organisation, increase their efficiency, and pay them sufficient to place them beyond the temptation of corruption. The opposition of the Tchinovniks will be crushed as between the upper and the nether millstones, if they venture to oppose a Minister supported on the one hand by a determined Emperor, and on the other by the popular masses.

I have left to the last the absolutely amazing objection that it would never do to employ General Ignatieff, because Bismarck or Austria or Lord Salisbury might not like it. I confess I marvel at the abjectness of spirit which can lead men thus meekly to admit their readiness to subordinate the interests and the welfare of their own country to the prejudices or the interests of their neighbours. General Ignatieff on this astounding theory may be the ablest and most supremely gifted of Russian statesmen; but if Prince Bismarck should prefer that Russia should be in the hands of blockheads, in order that she may be weakened, and in order that he may have her at a disadvantage in the haggling of the Continental market-place, his will must be accepted as law. You must not offend Bismarck; you must be ready to sacrifice the interests of Russia to the susceptibilities of Austria. So runs the argument.

It seems to an Englishman, or indeed to any citizen of a self-governed country, that the attempt to proscribe the employment of the services of any statesman by rival Powers is one of the strongest possible reasons in favour of placing him in office. So far as their interests are antagonistic to Russia, so far must their hostility to any Russian statesman be the most practical testimonial which they can offer in his favour.

["MENTIR PASHA, indeed! who is such a Mentir Pasha as yourself?" said Madame Novikoff, after reading the proofs of "The Shadow on the Throne." This I print in justice to that vehement and enthusiastic lady who introduced me to M. Pobedonostzeff in order to enable her to express her total and absolute dissent from all the views herein expressed on the Greek Orthodox Church and the relations between Church and State in Russia. She would be simply horrified, she tells me, to be thought for a moment to be *solidaire* with my views on Religion and Russia. As she could not be more horrified than I should be if it was thought that I was *solidaire* with the persecuting reactionary policy that unfortunately prevails in Russia on religious matters, this frank expression of her opinion serves as a useful preface to explain how it is that I could not honestly keep silence. For I am a Nonconformist, and the son of a Nonconformist; trained from childhood to regard the intervention of the State in affairs of religion as not only impolitic for the State and dangerous to religion, but as distinctly anti-Christian. I am an Englishman to whom religious liberty is the most vital of all liberties, and who finds it absolutely impossible to conceive of liberty of religion that does not include as its essence liberty of propagandism. My opinions may be altogether mistaken, but in this matter I must speak as I believe. The standpoint of Madame Novikoff and her friends is not mine; and from my standpoint it is as impossible to arrive at any other conclusions than those which are here expressed, as it would be for me, having formed this judgment, to abstain from frankly stating what seems to be the truth]

# Book VI.

## THE SHADOW ON THE THRONE.

### CHAPTER I.

CASTOR AND POLLUX; OR THE SIAMESE TWINS.

AMONG all the myths of Hellas and the legends of old Rome there is no more poetic and inspiring conception than that of the Great Twin Brethren, offspring of the Immortals, who at important crises in the affairs of men were wont to appear radiant in celestial glory, and decide the issues of the fight in favour of the cause beloved of the gods. It forms the subject of one of Macaulay's most spirited lays, and his glowing verse has familiarised every schoolboy with the ideal of the Great Twin Brethren who fought so well for Rome.

Who is there who does not recall the thrill with which he first read of how as Aulus the Dictator was girthing Black Auster—

> "He was aware of a princely pair
> That rode at his right hand.
> So like they were, no mortal
> Might one from other know:
> White as snow their armour was;
> Their steeds were white as snow.
> Never on earthly anvil
> Did such rare armour gleam;
> And never did such gallant steeds
> Drink of an earthly stream."
>
> "And all who saw them trembled,
> And pale grew every cheek."

And when asked their name and abiding-place, they replied—

> "By many names men call us;
> In many lands we dwell:
>
> \*   \*   \*   \*   \*
>
> And for the right we come to fight
> Before the ranks of Rome."

The human mind has outgrown the nursery lore of the world, but the truths which the dreamers of old enshrined in mystic legends remain, unaffected by the lapse of time or the progress of civilisation, as part of the indestructible foundation on which our life is reared. No longer, it is true, do simple mortals see the radiant shapes of the goddess-born, who rode before Black Auster at the battle of Lake Regillus, amid the ranks of the cavalry and infantry of modern war; nor do even the most fervent of the Faithful behold the angelic contingent whose flails, flashing fire at every stroke, routed the enemies of Mohammed at the battle of Al Bedr. But though the glory and the poetry of the legend have faded, like the glow of sunrise in the morning air, mankind still relies with unshaken faith on the invisible but potent Abstractions which, whether they are called Ideals or Principles, do more to nerve the arm and strengthen the heart of man than all the Dioscuri of whom the ancients dreamed.

Whenever the Russian peasant raises his eyes from the clods from which his daily task is to extract by the alchemy of labour nourishment for man and beast, and contemplates for a moment the eddying fortunes of the "fight by truth and freedom ever waged with wrong," he sees some dim and shadowy vision of two great Principles, whose aid he unconsciously invokes, as the Roman sighed for the apparition of the sons of Zeus. These principles are the ideals of Authority and of Religion, incarnated for him in the Tzar and in the Church.

These great Ideals are to him what Castor and Pollux were to the Romans, as the gods who live for ever who fought so well for Rome.

"These be the Great Twin Brethren
To whom the Dorians pray."

Wherever wrong is done, wherever injustice is committed, there he thinks it would be put right if the Tzar would exert his strength; and as the Tzar is far off and has other things to attend to, the Church is there with its admonitions to reprove the guilty, and its consolations to comfort the sufferer. The peasant would find it difficult to formulate in words the inarticulate longings of his heart; but deep down in his secret heart this faith in God and His saints and the Church, in which He is revealed and worshipped, and the faith in the Emperor the vicegerent of God, the incarnate personification of Authority, help him to live, to labour, and to die with placid serenity of soul.

Things may be going wrong now—are, in fact, always going wrong—but the Tzar with his omnipotent power will put it right some day, and in the meantime there is the Church with her consolations and her promises of life eternal and the judgment that cannot err. Through the dark and hazy mental atmosphere of the peasant's mind these two ideals of Authority and of Religion float like the angels of God, nor does he ever separate the two. It is God and the Tzar always, and the Orthodox Church is to him inseparable, even in thought, from the State which it saved. Not even the Moujik lives by bread alone, and ennobling conceptions of truth, glimpses of the Divine, however fitful and distorted, are as heavenly manna to his soul.

All this explains and excuses much of the confusion of mind which has led the present advisers of the Emperor to adopt a policy that to the dispassionate eye of a sympathetic observer seems to be about as perfect an example of the *corruptio optimi* to be witnessed anywhere in the world. More than anything else, more even than the shattered body of the murdered Emperor, it seems to me to testify to the terrible force of the Nihilist explosive. Of all the trophies of the Nihilist *camorra* that of which they have most reason to be proud is the persecuting policy of M. Pobedonestzeff—a policy the popular excuse for which is the terror they have inspired.

It is comparatively easy to blow to pieces the body of a mere mortal, even if he be an Emperor; but it is more difficult to shatter by material means the ideals of life, and to destroy by explosives the faith of a nation. This, however, has been done so thoroughly that the most saddening unbelief seems to have taken possession of the Ministers who stand nearest the Tzar. They profess more loudly than ever to believe in the Autocracy and to believe in the Church, but their actions seem to speak more clearly than their words, and proclaim that they have lost faith in both.

The underlying idea of their policy seems to be that faith in God will perish, unless enforced by the pains and penalties of the Tzar; and that the Tzardom will disappear, unless men are forbidden to speak to their fellows what they believe about God. In other words, it seems to be assumed that in Russia neither Tzar nor Church will survive, unless they form a sort of Austro-German alliance against liberty.

What a conception is this which is offered to the Russian people in place of the ennobling vision of the sister-angels of Authority and Religion! As of all the ancient legends few are so inspiring as that of the Dioscuri, so of all modern facts few were more hideous than the existence of the Siamese Twins. These unfortunates, linked together by an unnatural ligament which hampered their every movement and made them a source of mutual misery instead of mutual help, were towards the end of their days tormented by a horrible fear of approaching death. Could one survive the other? What would happen if an accident befell either? Such fears made life a torture, and paralysed even such opportunity for happiness and usefulness which they might have possessed, by concentrating all their failing energies in the nervous attempt to ward off their approaching dissolution. What has been done in Russia substitutes for the radiant conception of Authority and Religion as the Great Twin Brethren of the Russian State (each independent and strong and comely), ever present for the succour of the oppressed and the encouragement of the disconsolate, a gigantic Imperial simulacrum of the Siamese Twins, in which the Autocracy and the Orthodox Church, linked together in unnatural fetters, conscious only of their mutual weakness, are so much concerned about their own preservation against destruction as to have neither time nor thought nor energy to spare for the wants of men. Cæsar must take care of God, and on the principle of *do et des* it is expected God will take care of Cæsar. It is a kind of mutual insurance society maintained at the expense of the religious liberty of the Russian people.

A Russian historian of last century quaintly described the evil fate of his country in the past when he said that for generations Muscovy was hidden from Europe by two gaunt and grisly spectres which overshadowed it before and behind —the Mongols in the East, the Poles in the West. History repeats itself. Russia, the true Russia, is once more concealed from the West by spectres which overshadow its government with their baleful presence. These spectres somewhat resemble the Mongols and the Poles. The spectres of to-day are Laziness and Fear. The former based upon the indifferentism and fatalism of the East, the latter displaying itself in the intolerance hitherto peculiar to the West.

At bottom both of these curses are due to want of faith. What does it matter ? Why should we exert ourselves ?—everything will go on pretty much the same whether we do anything or not. Perhaps something may turn up, who knows ? And so from want of clearly seeing definite objects to be attained, and of unhesitating faith in their value when attained, energy is paralysed, and nothing is done. The Russian is ever ready to fall back upon a kind of transcendental mysticism when he recoils from any effort which is distasteful. Give him sufficient spur, and he will do anything ; but unless spurred hard he is apt to fold his hands and trust to Providence. Peter the Great must often have been driven fairly wild by the nonchalance and apathy of his subjects. To this day they will only exert themselves vigorously under immense pressure. Even in their campaigns they never put forth their full strength at first. It needs a series of disasters like those of Plevna to rouse them to the full measure of their capacity. Then everything goes down before them; but until then they let things slide.

"It is the climate," said one Russian. "Impossible," said another, "for in Russia we have all climates." "But," added a third, "we have many climates, but not one good one." There are no mountains, and everything in Russia suffers from that lack. Perhaps the Caucasus may rear men of more energetic type. Except in the Caucasus, and perhaps in the Oural, the Russians are all men of the plain. No one can say that the Russian is a lazy man. In spring and summer the peasants are up at sunrise, and they labour to sunset, and on the whole they get through a fair day's work every day in the year. But the intense cold, the long nights, and the hybernation which winter enforces do not tend to the development of that sustained energy which is characteristic of men of more temperate clime.

The fierce heat of summer is only less enervating than the bitter cold which drives the peasant to the warmth of his stove; and the æstivation of Russian Administration is almost as remarkable a feature of Russian life as the hybernation that takes place in winter. From June to October, government is almost suspended in St. Petersburg; every one is in the country, or at watering-places, or at the seaside. It is only when you witness the temporary suspension of administrative activity that you begin to understand how sane men can dream, like Count Tolstoi, of dispensing altogether with a central government. If Russia can do without St. Petersburg from June to October, why not from October to June?

The precise mode in which the climate operates in producing the *vis inertiæ* which is the despair of the reformer in Russia has never been scientifically examined; but it may be that human nature which is constantly exposed to extremes of heat and cold becomes impervious to any but the most violent incentives to activity. A horse that is constantly ridden with a severe spur cannot be roused by a mere touch of the heel; and so the Russians, alternately scourged by blazing heat and

Arctic cold, may find insufficient any but the severest stimulus to sustained exertion.

"It is laziness," said a Russian to me, who had long enjoyed close acquaintance with the interior *penetralia* of the Administration—"it is a laziness which is our national weakness and the secret of all that is going wrong. None of us, from the highest to the lowest, likes to do anything that he can possibly avoid doing. We never do to-day what we can possibly put off till to-morrow. In all our Administrations, how many work with a will? Here and there an Ignatieff or an Annenkoff, but the majority only seek to take things easily. Go into our Government offices and see the clerks 'at work.' What are they doing? Some smoking cigarettes, others playing at cards; others, again, gossiping; but no one works if he can avoid it. Why is it that necessary changes are not made? Why dare we not establish the Zemskie Soborz? Because it will take trouble, and we all hate trouble. Anything for an easy life; that is our motto all round. Every one is glad to throw responsibility on some one else, and ultimately it all falls upon the Emperor. If he is a Peter the Great, that may work; but there has only been one Peter the Great, and our Emperors seldom realise that they are the mainspring of everything."

The mainspring of everything! What a responsibility! But what if the mainspring itself be oppressed with a constitutional *vis inertiæ?* Then, indeed, there would be no hope visible, for in Russia everything depends upon the Emperor. If he has not enough internal fire to generate the necessary steam, the train will stick in the mud, and his Ministers will be only too delighted to sprag the wheels.

Lazy fits Russia has always had, and by fits and starts she has overcome her laziness. Far more serious, to my thinking—because more unnatural and contrary to her national traditions—is the Timidity which is the prevailing note of part of the Administration. Whatever Russians may be accused of, they are not cowards; they are the bravest of the brave, both as a nation and as individuals. But in dealing with those who differ from the Orthodox Church, M. Pobedonestzeff has substituted fear for faith as the principle of action. There is nothing so cruel as fear, nor, as a rule, anything so blind. There is, of course, much excuse for men who have passed through the Nihilist terror. Ministers whose Sovereign has been blown to pieces in the streets of his capital may be excused if they take stringent precautions against a repetition of such a crime; but seven years have elapsed since the Emperor was killed, and still M. Pobedonostzeff seems to have panic in his soul.

When I was at Troitsa Monastery, that which interested me most was the hole in the door through which a Polish cannon-ball had torn its way into the very innermost sanctuary of the saint. Two hundred years ago the Poles had besieged the monastery, and the round hole in the gate still remained to testify to the rude impact of the Catholic Poles on the tough fabric of Russian Orthodoxy. Through that hole is visible a vista of history too often forgotten in the West, which explains much otherwise inexplicable in the present. But it seemed to me that the Polish cannon-ball symbolised not inaptly the violence which is being done to the best and the holiest traditions of the Eastern Orthodox Church by the intolerance of the present *régime*. Although M. Pobedonostzeff is the most Orthodox of Greek Churchmen, he is the means by which an intolerance worthy of Rome is forcing its way into the inner sanctuary of Holy Russia. Fortunately the hole is not very big.

## CHAPTER II.

### ARCHBISHOP LAUD REDIVIVUS.

THE contrast between the tolerance which has heretofore been the distinctive note of the Eastern Orthodox and the intolerance of the Roman Catholic Church has often been remarked; it was signally illustrated by an incident which occurred at the close of the Chinese War of 1860. The French and English forces had broken down the resistance of China, and were dictating peace at the sword's point. In order to settle the conditions of peace British Envoys were sent to the headquarters of the Chinese, and were by them most foully murdered in flagrant violation of all the laws of war. The next day General Ignatieff, then a young officer of twenty-eight, went alone, in full uniform, into the Chinese camp, and succeeded in securing the bodies of our unfortunate officers. Arrangements were made to give them the last honours of a military funeral. In Pekin there were only two Christian cemeteries—one belonging to the French, the other to the Russians. As our murdered officers had gone to negotiate terms on behalf of the allies (French and English), it was naturally assumed that the French graveyard would receive their remains. This assumption, however natural and human, omitted to take into account the intolerance of the Roman Church. The English officers who had fallen in the discharge of their duty, although forming part of the allied army and acting jointly for France and England, were Protestants, and therefore heretics; for them there could be no resting-place in a Catholic cemetery. The moment General Ignatieff heard of it he sent word to the British commander that the Russians would regard it as an honour to be allowed to bury the English officers in the Orthodox cemetery. The offer was cordially accepted, and the whole Russian colony, General Ignatieff at their head, attended at the obsequies of the Protestant victims of Chinese treachery—obsequies conducted by English Protestants, according to the rites of their Church, in the burial-ground set apart for the use of members of the Greek Orthodox Church. The episode is worth while recalling just now, when an attempt is being made to graft the intolerant spirit of the Roman Church upon the reasonable and Christian tolerance that in the East has generally distinguished the Orthodox Communion.

M. Pobedonostzeff, the *procureur* of the Holy Synod, is one of the most interesting and commanding figures in Russia to-day. His influence for the last seven years has, in the opinion of many well calculated to judge, overshadowed the throne. He had a share in the education of the Emperor, and exercises over his mind an ascendency which constitutes one of the darkest shadows of the new reign. Far be it from me to speak evil of M. Pobedonostzeff. By almost universal repute he is a good and honest man. He is a lawyer of integrity and erudition, he is an omnivorous reader, and he is a very faithful son of the Greek Church. If after exercising such great power for so many years he should have succumbed to the temptations of personal ambition, or if he should have been somewhat nepotist in his patronage, or a little unscrupulous in misrepresenting his opponents for the sake of the Orthodox cause, these are the worst offences which even scandal has ever laid at his door. The Emperor is said to have implicit confidence in his honesty of purpose and singleness of aim; and of the existing Ministers, nearly one-half are said to owe their nomination more or less directly to the influence of M. Pobedonestzeff. M. Pobedonestzeff is a diligent student and enthusiastic disciple of Mr. Carlyle's; and few men in Petersburg are more familiar with English literature than he. His wife speaks English admirably, but his acquaintance with our language is literary rather than colloquial. Our literature seems to have affected him rather oddly; for as he is the best-read in English of any Russian Minister, he is the centre and rallying-point for all ideas most distinctively opposed to the Liberal and progressive principles of our English polity.

M. Pobedonestzeff, according to those who know him well, is a lawyer rather than an ecclesiastic; but in his religious exercises he is very devout, and in his fervour he sometimes displays an emotion not frequently manifested by Ministers of States. He is also notable as havng translated Thomas à Kempis into Russian. He is a Russian Archbishop Laud, and possesses many both of the qualities and of the shortcomings of the ill-fated adviser of Charles Stuart. In his face he reminded me of the late Mr. Fawcett and Lord Edmond Fitzmaurice, if you can mix two such incongruous personalities. He is of middle height, spare, and somewhat professorial in his appearance. A good narrow man, quite convinced that he is doing his duty, and capable of impressing that conviction on the minds of others—that is M. Pobedonestzeff, who considers that he has been called of God to save Russia from the "splittering" which has filled Europe with rival creeds.

M. Pobedonestzeff is perhaps more mediæval than Archbishop Laud. I used to say in St. Petersburg that it was like meeting a man who had been asleep for 600 years and had suddenly roused himself and walked about the streets clad in the spiritual and political raiment of the thirteenth century. Unless he is greatly belied, he holds the appliances of modern civilisation in scant esteem. His objections to a proposed concession for a new railway might have been inspired by a perusal of Carlyle's Latter-day pamphlet on the proposed statue to Hudson.

There is much that is imposing in the ideal of M. Pobedonestzeff; it is the ideal of a Hildebrand adapted to the policy of Russia. To him Russia is a Church rather than a State; she is primarily a Religious Communion, and only secondarily a secular community. The Church saved Russia in the past; the sacred duty which history has bequeathed to the Russian Government as the first of all its duties is to safeguard the Church against anything which could menace its security and unity to-day.

There is no need for me to trouble English readers with a description of this doctrine. Imagine every sophism with which the Anglicans did battle for the Test and Corporation Acts, by which they opposed Catholic Emancipation, by which they persisted in closing the Universities to Dissenters, and rallied all the forces of intolerance in defence of Church Rates and the monopoly of the graveyard; collect every argument which for the last fifty years had been used, and used in vain, to repel the victorious advance of the cause of religious liberty; condense them down into human shape, give them a suit of clothes and a pair of spectacles, and you have M. Pobedonestzeff. He is the supreme State Churchman of our epoch. If he is right, then the whole course of modern civilisation is mistaken; and of all men and nations in the world, England and Mr. Gladstone are the most utterly wrong in their estimate of the functions of the State in relation to Religion.

Of course I shall be told that I am presumptuous in thus speaking of M. Pobedonestzeff, and that Russia is not subject to the same conditions as those which prevail in the West. M. Pobedonestzeff is, of course, not answerable to me, nor have I any right to sit in judgment upon any one; only as I am writing for Englishmen who, without distinction of party, have learned to recognise that the infliction of disabilities for religious opinions is both unstatesmanlike and anti-Christian, I may be permitted to assume, as water boils at 212° and freezes at freezing-point in St. Petersburg as well as in London, so the general principles of religious toleration and the right of man to full religious liberty are truths which do not depend for their application upon parallels of latitude, and which therefore must ultimately prove fatal to the system now in vogue in Russia.

One of the most extraordinary delusions by which this able and conscientious man endeavours to conceal from himself the fact that the stars in their courses are fighting against him is the distinction which he endeavours to draw between liberty of conscience and liberty of propaganda. He is willing, of his infinite grace, to allow his fellow-man to think what he pleases in his conscience, because, after all, that is a matter which is beyond the reach even of the Grand Inquisitor of Muscovy; but if you should make any attempt to communicate the faith that is in you to a brother or a friend, if you should endeavour to cheer the lives of those you love best by imparting to them the conviction that has made you braver to face temptation, and stronger to bear the burdens of life, then he descends upon you in wrath with all the pains and penalties of administrative decrees. If you try to convert a man, no matter how godless and indifferent he may be, to any form of religion save that of the Orthodox Greek Church, you are liable to be banished to the Caucasus or to Siberia; or if you are a foreigner, to be sent out of the country. I put the matter as clearly as possible to one of the Ministers. "Suppose," I said, "that I settle in Russia, and that I derive from my religion a strength and a consolation which my dearest friend, who is nominally a Greek Orthodox, but in reality is of no religion, does not possess—if I try to make him share the faith which blesses me——" "I will put you in prison," said the Minister.

That seems to be the principle and the practice of the new firm now in the ascendant in Russia—the firm of Diocletian, Torquemada, Pobedonestzeff, and Co., Limited.

There is, I am glad to admit, even in M. Pobedonestzeff a rudimentary sense of the injustice of religious persecution. It does not prevent him from persecuting; it only prompts him to make excuses for persecution. The excuses, if accepted in the cases for which they are invented, leave his worst offences without defence.

Mr. Gladstone remarked very justly, in the course of a conversation which I had with him before I left London, that it would be unfair to regard the action of the Russian Government against the Roman Catholic Church in Poland as prompted solely, or even at all, by a spirit of religious persecution. The religious question, he pointed out, was in Poland so inextricably bound up with the political question that a measure of political self-defence might easily be mistaken for religious intolerance. M. Pobedonestzeff lays great stress on the same point, and declares that Catholicism is identified in Russia with Polonism, and that it would be difficult to find in any corner of Russia a Catholic whose first preoccupation was not the severance from Russia of her western provinces.

I think there is little doubt but that this is greatly exaggerated; nevertheless, let us rule out of the account against M. Pobedonestzeff all the complaints entered by the Catholics. As we hanged, drew, and quartered Catholics under Elizabeth, not as Catholics, but as traitors, let us admit that when the Russian Government punishes Catholics, it punishes them not as Catholics, but as Poles.

I am even disposed to make a similar liberal assumption in the case of the persecution of the Lutheran Churches in the Baltic provinces. The Lutheran pastors in the Baltic provinces occupy a position not dissimilar to that occupied by the Protestant clergy of the Irish Church; they are the chaplains of the Protestant landlords, encamped in the midst of a native population for whose welfare they have cared little, and which has grown up either heathen or Greek Orthodox. Russia in the Baltic provinces has backed the peasants against the landlords; and in the prosecution of her policy of breaking down the German domination, she has come into collision with the Lutheran pastors. M. Pobedonestzeff declares that the German landlords boycott such of the natives as turn Orthodox. He therefore banishes all Lutheran clergymen who make proselytes from Orthodoxy, and passes a law which places every Lutheran vicar at the mercy of the Administration. At the present moment there are three Lutheran ministers in Siberia who were sent there for no other crime than that of having dissuaded members of their own flocks from becoming Greek Orthodox, or for having attempted to convert a Greek Orthodox to Protestantism. The law which placed the benefices of the Lutheran clergy at the mercy of the Governors of the provinces, who can sequestrate them on suspicion by their own will and pleasure, was condemned by the Council of the Empire—a consultative body, nominated by the Emperor, which meets once a week to consider business laid before it; but its condemnation was ignored. The Emperor sanctioned the law, which is now in force. It is obvious what an engine of tyranny this law created. Any scoundrelly Lett who chooses to denounce a Lutheran minister to the Governor of the province may secure the sequestration of his living without public trial or without any other authority but the will of the Governor. Nevertheless, I am willing to excuse all this, for the sake of argument, and for the time being, in order to leave no pretext for saying that I do not make allowance for the peculiar political complications which embarrass the Russian Government in its dealings with the other Churches. Let it be granted that Lutherans do not deserve to have the ordinary securities against injustice because they are Germans, as I have already conceded the right to persecute the Catholics because they are Poles; there still remains enough to justify the condemnation which civilisation will pronounce upon those who in Russia to-day employ the sword of the civil power to outrage the inviolable liberty of the human conscience.

The Western Churches, according to M. Pobedonestzeff, are eager to attack, not only the power, but even the unity of Russia. That may be true of the Poles, it may be true of the Lutherans, but it is not true of the English Protestants; neither is it true of the Stundists, Molokani, and other Evangelical sects which, in defiance of M. Pobedonestzeff's interdicts multiply and increase in Southern Russia. Yet of all these we are proudly told, "Never will Russia allow the liberty of their propaganda, never will she allow them to take away from the Orthodox Church her children," and she appeals to Supreme Justice with the same assurance with which Torquemada justified the *auto da fé* in Madrid.

When I visited the prisons of St. Petersburg, I have already described the overcrowding that I found in the small prison which is a kind of Clearing House for the transfer of prisoners from one place to another, and for their temporary accommodation pending their despatch to Siberia or to their own native province. Shortly afterwards I went to inspect a charitable institution on the northern bank of the Neva. When there I was told that the gardener of the establishment, a Russian from Smolensk, who had lived for fourteen years in the capital, bearing an irreproachable character, had held a little prayer-meeting in his own house. He was what is called in Petersburg a Pashkoffetz—that is to say, he was an Evangelical Christian of the school of Lord Radstock, given to the singing of Sankey's hymns, and to the inculcation of the familiar doctrines of English Evangelicalism. He was arrested, with his wife and child, carried off to this overcrowded old prison, and thrust in with the rest. When his friends came to inquire, they were told that he might have to stay in the prison two months, or he might be sent away in two days. Fortunately for him his time came before the week was over; but he was sent off with his family to Smolensk, nor was he suffered to return to the home and situation in which he had spent the last fourteen years of his life. When I remembered the condition of that overcrowded prison, and thought of the offence for which the poor gardener had been first thrust in among criminals, and then banished from the place where he was making a living, I felt that there was only a difference in degree between the various members of the firm of Diocletian, Torquemada, Pobedonestzeff, and Co., Limited, and that the sole surviving partner is a worthy representative of the Roman Emperor and the Papal Inquisitor.

## CHAPTER III.

### THE EFFECT OF MONOPOLY.

I REMEMBER once being told by Cardinal Manning that the real Reformation of the Church was that which took place at the Council of Trent. I replied that it might be so, but that there would have been very little Reformation in the Council of Trent —if, indeed, there had been a Council of Trent at all—if there had not been a good roaring Protestant Reformation going on outside. I was forcibly reminded of the truth of this remark at every turn in Russia. Everywhere you are confronted with the mischief that results from the establishment of a monopoly. The Russian State has protected many native industries, but none have been "favoured" with such heavy bounties or have enjoyed a monopoly secured by such a prohibitive tariff as the Greek Orthodox Church. And the result has been exactly the same for the Church as it is for manufactures; the protected industry languishes, the consumers suffer.

Last July the Russians celebrated at Kieff the nine hundredth anniversary of the introduction of Christianity into Russia. For nine centuries Russia has been nominally Christian; for half of that time (excluding the period of Tartar domination and Polish wars) the Eastern Church has enjoyed as complete a monopoly as power could secure it; and what is the result?

"The first dogma of the Christian religion," said Count Tolstoi to me as we walked along the *chaussée* that leads from Toula to Kieff, "is the doctrine of the Trinity. For 900 years our Church has had the peasantry absolutely in her own hands, and how many of the peasants do you think have any notion of what the Trinity is?" I did not venture to guess. The Eastern Church lays great stress upon the dogma of the Trinity—a difference of opinion as to the precise origin of the third person of the Trinity being an insurmountable obstacle in the way of the re-union of Christendom. If the Church had been a living, teaching force, instead of being a more or less automatic performer of ceremonies, the doctrine of the Trinity would have been mastered by every peasant; for it is the special boast of the dominant school that there are no *confessionslose* people in Russia. Every Orthodox must take the Communion at least once a year. No one can get married without going to Confession and to Mass. Judge, then, my surprise when Count Tolstoi continued, "Not one peasant in ten—I sometimes think, nor one in a hundred—has the least idea of what the Church's doctrine of the Trinity is. I have asked them over and over again, and they usually give very extraordinary answers. I must have questioned some hundreds of pilgrims as to their idea of the doctrine of the Trinity, and of these hundreds I do not remember six who could even name the persons of the Trinity. As a rule, they say that the Trinity consists of Jesus, the Virgin, and St. Nicholas. But we will ask the next pilgrim whom we meet, and you shall hear for yourself."

We had not long to wait. Seated on a little knoll by the side of the road there were three or four pilgrims. Two of them seemed mere tramps, but a mother and son were much above the average, and to her Count Tolstoi addressed himself. She said she was on the road to Kieff; her son had fallen into the river, and had been rescued from drowning. In gratitude to God she had vowed to make a pilgrimage to Kieff with her boy, and she was on her way thither. She was therefore a good pilgrim—not a mere tramp, but one who was fulfilling a religious duty. But when asked about the Trinity she replied, "Oh yes, I know all about the Trinity; there were three brothers who were thrust into a cave and set on fire, and in the fire Jesus came and walked with them. I have read all about it in the Gospel;" and she was going off into fresh detail when the Count stopped her. "There," said he, "you have a fair sample; she thinks the three Hebrew children were the Trinity. That is the net result of nine hundred years of dogmatic teaching by a Church which has had exclusive possession of the field."

I do not wish to lay much stress upon this argument, for it is possible to find very devout Christians who have not the ghost of an idea as to who are the persons of the Trinity. The dominant party, however, regard such dogmas as vital, and I commend to them the question how far a Church which leaves its members in such blank ignorance of its vital dogma can be regarded as justifying the policy of protection which has been pursued for centuries. The Old Believers, or Raskolniki, may be mistaken in their views. It is no doubt most lamentable that they should make the sign of the Cross with two fingers instead of with three; but it is admitted that, notwithstanding this and similar deplorable heresies, they have often a better knowledge of their religious doctrines than the members of the State-protected State-favoured Orthodox Church. The Russian Nonconformists number millions; they have been subjected for two centuries to proscription and discouragement; but they have held fast the faith, and persecution has taught them to know it better than protection has helped their more favoured fellow-countrymen.

In a small village in the province of Novgorod a pious lady was reading the Bible to some of her peasants. It was a simple service, but the written Word seemed to produce a deep impression on some who were present; one old peasant, who sat in a nook apart, was observed to be weeping as he listened. "I am aggrieved," said the simple fellow through his tears, "in my soul. How is it that we have never heard anything of this before? We know the names of some of the Saints, because on their days we have our fairs; but we never even heard that Christ had come upon earth, or we never understood what it meant. We are born in darkness, we live in darkness, and we die in darkness, and nobody cares."

The bitter cry of the aggrieved peasant might be echoed by millions. "Nobody cares!" It is the epitaph that might be inscribed on the tomb of a dead Church.

Far be it from me to say that the Russian Church is dead. With all its shortcomings, it is still an institution by which men and women seek to gain clearer glimpses of the ideal than is possible to poor mortals in this work-a-day world; but I may at least point out that, M. Pobedonestzeff himself being judge, the condition of the Church, despite all its State-protection and monopoly, in many districts is deplorable indeed. In all Russia how many village priests are there who are capable of preaching—I do not say once a week, but once a month—a sermon in which they could give their flocks the simplest ethical guidance, or the most elementary outline of doctrine? It is, of course, possible to say that, whatever it may have pleased God to do by the foolishness of preaching in the days of the Apostles, Russians want no preaching, and are content with their liturgies and Gospel. But M. Pobedonestzeff cannot say that, for he takes credit to himself for stimulating preaching, and extending the rare practice of delivering sermons. Neither can any intelligent man who looks at the Church as a teaching organisation, and as a spiritual instructor, deny that a Church whose clergy are too ignorant to be trusted to preach even a fifteen-minutes' discourse without the Bishop's sanction, is not a Church of which its chiefs have much reason to be proud.

"The practice of preaching is spreading," said a Minister to me. "How far?" I asked. "What percentage of your clergy preach to-day?" "In the North I could not say; in the South perhaps one in ten; the proportion would not be great in the North." One in ten! And this is the result of monopoly. Surely the "splittering" of which M. Pobedonestzeff stands in such dread could hardly have more lamentable results than this. The apathy of the Clergy, the impossibility of relying upon the average priest to perform the ordinary functions of the clergyman in England or in Ireland, the formality which is almost universal—all these things Russians admit and deplore. The utmost that they can allege in deprecation of hostile criticism is that they are making efforts to mend matters, of which assuredly they stand in need. But the great stimulus to activity, that of unrestricted competition, is expressly excluded by law, with the natural and necessary result. Establish a monopoly, and every one goes to sleep. It is the Protestant competition which has kept the Roman Church up to the mark; and its standard is never so high as where Protestantism is vigorous, and never so low as where Protestantism practically does not exist. In Sicily and in Southern Italy, in the Azores, and in other places where it has a monopoly, things are as bad with the Roman Catholics as they are with the Eastern Church in Russia. It is the Nonconformist and Wesleyan competition which has roused the Anglican Church into activity, and has transformed the whole spirit of the English parsonage. In Russia competition is excluded, and the prevailing spiritual torpor is the natural—nay, the necessary —result.

The best thing that could happen to Russia—better even than the sudden determination of the Emperor to shake off the trammels of his *entourage*, and to appear among his subjects as a hard-riding Tzar, determined to see with his own eyes, and hear with his own ears, all that is going on in his dominions —would be a great spiritual revival within the Eastern Church. Here and there the earnest voice of an eloquent priest is heard, amid the monotonous chant of the unending liturgies, pleading for a religious life that will be other than merely formal; but for the most part these voices find no echo, and sometimes, if the accent is at all strange, the preacher is silenced altogether. The Church, with its ecclesiastics, does not, as a rule, concern itself about the mundane affairs of this life. The Service of Man (save as an immortal spirit whose blessedness hereafter can best be secured by the recitation of a certain number of creeds, and the performance of ceremonies) is a matter which it regards too often as beneath its notice. I do not say—it would be a monstrous and wicked exaggeration to say—that a great spiritual apparatus designed to furnish these millions with the Water of Life has gone utterly to rust and ruin; it has reared, and still rears, saints holy and noble as are to be found in any Church; but regarded solely from a mundane point of view, and looked at with the eye of a purely secular person who can only judge of religious systems by the extent to which they minister to the wants, stimulate the consciences, and satisfy the intellectual needs of men, the Russian Church stands sorely in need of whatever impetus can be given to it from without. I do not suppose that any foreign Church can ever make much headway in Russia; the national spirit is too strong; the instinct and traditions of centuries are too deeply rooted. Neither can any one wish to see the Eastern Church torn by divisions such as those which have rent the Western Church in twain. But until Russia has a priest in every village who is intelligent, pious, and sober, and a Church which recognises that its duty is to minister to the daily wants and daily needs of humanity, and not merely to say Masses for our souls hereafter, is it not suicidal folly to close the door to the widest possible influx of other forms of Christian faith? Instead of vetoing propaganda, even of mistaken creeds, would it not be better to welcome it as the most efficacious way by which the Orthodox can be roused to make a counter-propaganda? Better schism than sleep; better divisions than death. And the best and simplest remedy against somnolence and paralysis in religion, as in business, is free and open competition.

In my conversations with Ministers and others in Russia on this subject I never made any reserve as to my convictions on the subject of religious propaganda. They were always very courteous, but our views were hopelessly opposed. Russia, they used to tell me, concedes full liberty of conscience to all residents within the Empire. The Ministry for Foreign *Cultes* has no fewer than fifteen different religions to look after. In the Nevski, as I was shown with pride, stand Catholic, Protestant, and Armenian Churches, all open for divine service. Any man or woman may worship God as he or she pleases, according to the rites of the Church in which they happened to be born; but no one born a Greek Orthodox is free to join their Communion. You may be born in Russia, Turk, Jew, or Papist, but if you are born again in the dominions of the Tzar, you must only be born again as a Greek Orthodox. The *naïveté* and childishness of the idea is very amusing when you hear it for the first time. "The Eastern Church," I was told, "is much opposed to propaganda;" to which I replied that it was lucky for the Eastern Church that the Apostles were not of the same opinion, otherwise there never would have been any Eastern Church. "Oh! but the Apostles," was the reply, "were united in one faith; they had no divisions to distract them, and they had all lived in personal contact with Jesus Christ." Even admitting this— and it is a great admission—that cannot be said of the Saints to whom the conversion of Northern Europe is really due. Cyril and Methodius in Russia, the apostles who converted Germany, Augustine and Columba in England, all were propagandists, and it is to their propaganda that European Christendom owes its existence; yet none of them had seen our Lord, and they differed widely from each other on fundamental points of faith and ritual. To this my host replied that I was a European and a Western; that, therefore, I could not understand Russian views on the matter—Russia was not European, but Asiatic. To which the obvious answer was that the Apostles, to a man, were not European, but Asiatic; and that Russia was really following, not the Asiatic apostles of Galilee and Tarsus, but such European persecutors as Decius and Alva.

There is a curious similarity between the Russian and the Irish character, especially in the simplicity which leads them to suppose that there is something so unique about their respective nationalities as to be quite beyond the comprehension of foreigners. I have never made the experiment, but I am inclined to believe that if you cornered either a Russian or an Irishman in a mistake in an arithmetical sum, he would try to get out of it by saying that two and two might make four elsewhere, but that they sometimes made five in Petersburg or Dublin. Certainly, the Multiplication Table is not more absolute than the doctrine that Christianity owes its existence to propaganda conducted in opposition to the interdicts of Governments, and that, in placing a veto upon propaganda, the Russian Government is in the true line of succession, not to the men who said "Woe is me if I preach not the Gospel!" but to the heathen Emperors who cried "*Christianos ad leones!*" But here were cultivated men, professedly Christian, calmly arguing as if one of the most obvious credentials of the orthodoxy of the Russian

Church was its antipathy to that principle which is the first law of Christendom. "To go into the world and preach the Gospel to all nations" was one of the most positive precepts given by Christ to His Disciples.

To do M. Pobedonostzeff justice, he is in this, as in many things, superior to his followers, in that he is not opposed to propaganda, provided it is the propaganda of the Church to which he himself belongs. So far from objecting to it, he would even give the Eastern Church the monopoly of propaganda; and the result is that the Eastern Church, being at ease in Zion, settles upon her lees, and refuses to bestir herself. In vain does the worthy Procurator use his utmost efforts to induce the sluggish and inert Communion to rise to its feet and set about the fulfilment of its divine commission. The Church as a whole—for there are always exceptions to every rule—does not care for any of these things; it chants its appointed services in the ears of its own children, and allows the rest of the world to go to the Devil in its own way—notwithstanding all the exhortations of M. Pobedonostzeff. This is very natural, and most excellent in the eyes of the Freethinkers and indifferentists who, from the days of Catherine, have had a leading share in the Government of Russia; but to any one who really believes in the importance of the Christian faith, and who sincerely holds the conviction that the Oriental Church is the divinely-appointed depository of Truth, it is very painful.

The repetition of services, no matter how ornate and elaborate, even if multiplied a thousand-fold, cannot weigh for a moment as evidence of sincere conviction against the callous indifference to the propagation of what they profess to believe is the only saving faith throughout the world. Churches will be zealous for propagandism exactly in so far as they are conscious of the reality and the importance of their belief. Judged by this standard, the Russian Church can hardly be said to have a very robust faith. This M. Pobedonostzeff feels, and he is doing his best to galvanise the Church into a spasmodic display of propagandist zeal. But not even the mounting of the Orthodox propagandist on the back of the Russian police can tempt the stolidly indifferent Orthodox to bestir themselves about extending what they regard as the true Orthodox faith. When in a farmyard the groom exhausts all other means to induce his lazy steed to rise from its straw, he has always one unfailing resource—he sets fire to the straw. If M. Pobedonostzeff really wishes to rouse the Church into activity, and to set it about its proper business, he also will have to fire the straw of monopoly and protection on which it lies supine. Not until the Church is energised by the free current of spiritual life which impels other Communions to seek to make proselytes for their faith will it vigorously set about fulfilling its divine commission.

The real strength of the opposition to propaganda in Russia lies, not in men like M. Pobedonostzeff, but in those who regard him and all earnest believers as more or less benighted fanatics. There are many who believe with Gibbon that all religions are to the people equally true, to the philosopher equally false, and to the Government equally useful, and they resent as a possible source of indefinite trouble the introduction of religious propagandism into Russia. Before a man can change his creed, even to become an Orthodox, he must have his conversion registered at St. Petersburg in a Government bureau. The ideal of the official is immobility, and there is nothing so motionless as a corpse.

Every fresh influx of spiritual life into Russian Christianity seems from this point of view pure evil; it makes trouble, it exposes to new dangers. Who knows whither it may not lead? So they maintain a whole hierarchy of officials whose duty is to extinguish with Government authority any light that might perchance kindle a flame even in the darkest places of Russia. It is simply inconceivable to Westerns that grown men can take so much pains merely to prevent any light shining in Russia excepting through the regulation windowpane, which is all crusted over with the dust and cobwebs of centuries; but so it seems. Millions may be wrapped in the death of ignorance, of vice, and of indifference, and the official mind cares nothing. But if in the ears of these sleeping millions any earnest man or woman ventures to sound an awakening blast upon a trumpet that is not exactly of the official shape and pattern, then what a commotion! Russian officialdom is moved to its depths. Conclave sits after conclave, and at last, after infinite consideration, the official veto is pronounced, and all is silence once more. What a triumph! The trumpet of irregular pattern is heard no more. But the sleepers? Let them sleep; as dead men tell no tales, sleeping men make no trouble.

What a picture we have here presented! In the far East along the Volga Moslem propagandism, defying the edicts of the Government, wins village after village from Christianity to the faith of Islam. Among the educated classes scepticism and atheism eat their way silently but surely, making easy havoc of those who believe, from all that they see and hear, that the Church only stands by support of the civil power, and that Christianity could not maintain itself for a day without the prop of Cæsar's sword.

Everywhere in Russia, as in all countries, ignorance, squalid poverty, gross superstition, and revolting vice, are preying upon the millions of the people. All the good people, all the believing souls (whatever their *nuance*, however they lisp their Shibboleth), are all too few to make head against the hosts of evil. But not a soul may speak, not a pen may write, not a voice be raised to do combat with the enemy, if they are suspected of heresy by those who wear the official uniform. And those who are in uniform, and who are in the ranks, where are they? Alas! too many are asleep at their posts while the wolves ravage the flock, and the hungry sheep look up and are not fed.

In a country-place in Northern Russia the peasants were gathered together in a little cottage to listen to the reading of the Gospel. When the reader had finished, one of the peasant women stood up, and with a curious light in her eyes began to speak. "I have been a wicked woman," she said; "you all know that I have been a very wicked woman" (a murmur of assent went round the wondering rustics)—"I have been very bad," she continued, "but who is to blame? I have never been taught that there is a Living God over me, who cares whether I am bad or good." Immediately opposite the cottage was the house of the priest. To him, after the little meeting dispersed, the reader communicated the woman's indignant plaint. Alas!" said the poor priest, "what can one do? I have my hay to get in, and my land to attend to, and such long services to perform, and my dues to collect, how have I time to teach such as she?"

No time, perhaps, but the Government might at least have kept its hands off those who were able and willing to teach "such as she." It might have, but it did not; for the little Bible-reading was suppressed by order of the police, and the peasants are left to this day without other ministrations than those of the priest whose hay, whose dues, and whose services, left him no time to attend to the instruction of his flock.

## CHAPTER IV.
### THE DOG IN THE MANGER.

THESE, it may be said, are general statements. What proof is there that they are true? What facts are there to show that the spirit of intolerance is more rampant now than it was under Alexander the Second? I can best answer such an objection by telling the story of a very humble attempt to do something, not in the way of sectarian propaganda, but merely to teach morality, the details of which were told me on authority which is incontestable. It is but a small affair, quite insignificant no doubt, were it not so typical. You do not need to drink a hogshead of brine to be satisfied that sea-water is not fresh; and you can only analyse great cargoes by the close scrutiny of small samples. The very insignificance of the example is the best security that it represents the normal attitude of the Russian Government of to-day when brought face to face with any kind of teaching which does not absolutely coincide in all particulars with the views or prejudices of the ecclesiastical authorities. The incident is minute, almost trivial; but the principles which it illustrates are not trivial, but vital.

The *Russki Rabotchi*, or the *Russian Workman*, is a little monthly eight-page paper which has been published in St. Petersburg for some years past by a young lady for the purpose of disseminating cheap and instructive reading among the people. The little paper is entirely unsectarian, non-political, and not in the least polemical. The woodcuts she borrowed from the Religious Tract Society of London, the letterpress she wrote for the most part herself. It was originally started by her mother as far back as 1875, and carried on by her until her death in 1881. One year later its publication was re-commenced by the daughter, and carried on by her in filial devotion to her mother's memory as an attempt to discharge some part of her own duty to her fellow-men. In 1882 its circulation was very limited—not more than 200 copies being printed. It was disposed of almost exclusively to subscribers, who paid one rouble per annum for the twelve numbers post free. Dreading any interference on the part of the authorities, she made no attempt to increase the circulation of the *Russki Rabotchi* by distribution through colporteurs or through newsagents. When the sale increased, as it did steadily until it reached 3,000 copies monthly, more than 2,000 were sent out through the post; the rest were sent out by hand, for the most part in St. Petersburg. The young lady did everything herself but set the type. She designed, wrote, sub-edited, and despatched the little magazine all by herself. The cost of paper rendered its sale unremunerative, but she gladly defrayed the expense, as she gladly incurred the labour of producing the little monthly messenger for the sake of the service which it enabled her to render to thousands of unknown friends in all parts of the Russian Empire. A great correspondence sprang up between her and her readers, and her heart rejoiced at the many grateful tributes which reached her from all kinds of people who had found help and encouragement in her writings. One day a priest would write and say how useful he had found her paper in the preparation of his sermons; another day a monk sent saying, "All our brotherhood prays God for you, and thanks God that He put it into your heart to publish it." Many humble people wrote thankfully; and all—whether Orthodox, Lutherans, or Stundists—learned to welcome the little monthly *Rabotchi* as a fresh and genial reminder of the moral and religious side of life. "The beautiful English pictures," as the woodcuts were styled, being superior to anything produced at the same price in Russia, added to the popularity of the publication; and if the Government had not interfered, the *Rabotchi* would have been probably circulating 5,000 or 6,000 numbers every month, and encouraging many times that number of readers all over Russia to think seriously of life and of its opportunities, to care for the welfare of their neighbours, and to cultivate in the daily round of daily life the kindly spirit and sweet reasonableness of Jesus of Nazareth.

To English readers, accustomed to papers with circulations of quarters of millions, this humble little Russian monthly may seem but a small thing. But with journalism in Russia it is the day of small things; and the history of the little magazine enables us to understand, as well as the history of the most important newspaper, the kind of difficulties which the Russian authorities, under the present *régime*, place in the way of those who try to use the press for the benefit of their fellows. The struggle made by the editress of the *Russki Rabotchi* against the obstacles placed in her path by the Government affords a useful illustration of the ways of the Russian censorship, and the arbitrary and irrational intolerance which now prevails in the Russian Government.

When she had written her copy and sent it to the printer's, the printer's first duty was to send proofs to the Civil Censorship, which is a branch of the Chief Administration of the Press in St. Petersburg. There they lay for two or three days, during which time the Government Censor was supposed to be scrutinising every line for lurking traces of any doctrine inimical to the existing constitution in Church and State. If in the articles he found so much as a single text or allusion to Scripture, or anything which bore any semblance to religious teaching, the articles had to be sent on to the Ecclesiastical Censor. This office is held by an Archimandrite, who is under the direction of the Synod. Here two or three days more were consumed, and then, if all was right, the articles were passed for the press. As soon as the first copies of the completed issue were printed they must be sent to the Censor to see that there had been no change made in the proofs since they were passed. Then, but not till then, the journal could make its appearance to the world.

The *Rabotchi* was not circulated by colportage. Had this been done, every copy would have had to be subjected to the censorship of every provincial Governor before permission would be given for its sale; and every police-officer in every town would also have had power to interdict its distribution—so many are the bolts and the bars which a paternal Government interposes between its children and the printed page.

For a few years all went fairly well with the *Russki Rabotchi*. The Civil Censor never found fault with it, and the Archimandrite of the Ecclesiastical Censorship was not unreasonable. So blameless was the publication that in 1884 the *Official Messenger*, the recognised organ of the Government, printed a notice of the *Russki Rabotchi*, which it recommended to its readers as one of the best publications for the people, praising its pictures and its cheapness, and specially commending its letterpress as containing profitable and intelligible reading for the common people. Nor was this all. The Society for Promoting the Circulation of Useful Books (whose headquarters are at Moscow, and which is as Orthodox and respectable as it is possible for Episcopal patronage to make it) reprinted no fewer than ten of the stories published in the *Rabotchi*, printing off 12,000 copies of each, and sending them forth for general circulation among the peasantry.

But in 1885 a change came over the spirit of the Government. The Civil Censor continued to be civil, but the Ecclesiastical Censor became suddenly most exacting; it seemed impossible to please him. His nose detected latent heresies, not merely in what was said, but in what was omitted to be said. An appeal to all men orphaned by sin to seek fellowship with God was objected to on the ground that it was not coupled with a statement that it was in the Church and through the Church alone that the reconciliation could be effected. On one occasion she had quoted a passage from a discourse by St. Macarius concerning the woman who was healed who had an issue of blood. "I cannot pass that," said the Censor, notwithstanding the authority of the Saint; "it is too much like the doctrine of the Stundists." On another occasion he vetoed the use of an extract—not garbled, but given textually as written—from the works of St. Tichon Zadonski, a Bishop of Voronège, whose recent canonisation did not spare him from censure. In order to avoid the interference of the Ecclesiastical Censor, she once wrote the story of "Paul and Silas" in such a way as to avoid a single quotation from the Testament, or even a distant allusion to its Biblical origin. Again and again she would get her proofs back with all the best passages struck out with a red pencil. She had to set to work to re-write the eviscerated passages in such a way as to turn the objections. Again and again she tried and failed, until at last some wretched colourless, spiritless compromise would be arrived at, from which all the life and glow and warmth had departed. There was a long trouble over the "Prodigal Son," for it is really rather difficult to make that parable harmonise with the exclusive claims of the Church. Nevertheless, although with a sinking heart, she persevered, altering, re-writing, and always in the end getting her little paper passed by both sets of Censors. One day, however, she received a private hint that trouble was brewing. A priest or a bishop in the South had found a copy of the paper on the table of one of his parishioners, and he had sent it up to the Committee of the Synod, in order that it might be reported on. What the Committee of the Synod found objectionable in a paper which both Censors had passed for the press is not known; all that is known is that the *Church Messenger* shortly afterwards denounced the poor little *Russki Rabotchi* as a most pernicious paper, spreading the most dangerous heresy among the people (specially among the people of the South), and gibbeting its amiable editress as a very harmful person. Considering that not a single copy of the paper had appeared until every line had been examined and approved by two sets of Government functionaries, the absurdity and the injustice of this calumny are apparent. The Civil Censor, when appealed to, said that he had refused to suppress the paper—it was a good paper, a useful paper, that spoke against all kinds of evil. Beyond this officious condemnation in the official paper of the Synod, couched entirely *in generalibus*, of the *Russki Rabotchi*, its editress received no official notification that the Committee of the Synod had decided to crush her paper. She was advised to call upon two or three priests who were members of the Committee, who might perhaps tell her wherein she had offended, or what were the articles to which exception had been taken. The priests could tell her nothing; they said they really did not know. The Committee preserved a sombre silence. All that she knew was that the Ecclesiastical Censor had received a strict order to pass nothing whatever that was sent to him for publication in the *Russki Rabotchi*; he was not even to open the envelope containing the proofs, for the Synod had ordered peremptorily that the paper must be stopped. Shortly afterwards the *Official Messenger*, which two years before had eulogised the paper, now declared that its circulation was forbidden; and the police in some localities actually went about from house to house collecting back numbers in order that they might be destroyed.

From that day to this no information, official or otherwise, has been vouchsafed as to why the Synod crushed the paper. Two years have elapsed, and still not even the courtesy of an intimation as to how or in what article she had brought down on her head the wrath of the Government has been afforded her. Neither of the Censors, Civil or Ecclesiastical, would or could throw any light on the subject. She was simply crushed by the arbitrary decision of a secret conclave, and remedy for such a wrong there is none in Russia. Her little paper was suppressed, not by the frank brutality of an Imperial ukase, but by the secret assassination of an ecclesiastical *camorra*. It is odd how ingeniously Churchmen contrive to do their evil work. Western Churchmen never shed blood; they only delivered the heretics over to the secular arm, which burnt them alive. Eastern Churchmen do not suppress papers like the *Russki Rabotchi*; they simply strangle them in silence by a decree, for which they offer no defence, set forth no explanation, and justify by no consideration of law or of public policy.

As a pendant to this instructive little episode there is the not less suggestive incident of the expulsion of the Hiltons. The suppression of the *Russki Rabotchi* illustrates the ruthless fashion in which persecuting administrators will extinguish every farthing rushlight that gleams amid the vast darkness that overhangs their country, if it is not ensconced in an official candlestick. The expulsion of the Hiltons shows the same spirit working in another sphere. It displays an equal indifference to the material interests of the country, and to the claims of resident Englishmen to be treated with ordinary justice.

When I saw M. Wischnegradsky, the Minister of Finance, he assured me, with great emphasis, that there was nothing which the Russian Government desired more than to see capable Englishmen settling in the Empire, and employing their enterprise in developing its manufactures, and their capital in opening up its latent resources. There is no doubt that the influx of moneyed and energetic Englishmen to act as captains of industry would be one of the greatest advantages which could accrue to the Russians. The experience of the Hiltons is, however, not very encouraging for Englishmen to accept M. Wischnegradsky's invitation.

Mr. Edward Hilton was a capable and conscientious Englishman, who came to Russia in 1849, and twenty years later was entrusted with the management of extensive copper mines and works on the Ural range in the Government of Ufa. For fifteen years he discharged his duties to the satisfaction of his employer and the content of his workmen. His relations with the local authorities were excellent. So far from allowing his own religious opinions to influence him in opposition to the religious views of the people among whom he lived, he personally collected funds with which to repair the Orthodox Church, and readjusted the business of his office so as to set the people free to attend to their religious duties. For the first ten years of his management his relations with the local priest were excellent. In 1878, however, this priest died, and with the appointment of his successor, a narrow and bigoted man, the trouble began. Mr. Hilton, as representative of his employer, Colonel Pashkoff, had charge of the schools which the latter erected and maintained on his estate. The new priest insisted on closing the school at Bogoyavlensky on certain church festivals not included in the official list of holidays. Mr. Hilton allowed the children to attend service, but opened the school after the service was over. The other schools outside this priest's jurisdiction were not even closed during the hours of service, although Mr. Hilton had left the local priests free to do as they pleased. It was a trifle. Mr. Hilton may have been wrong, or he may have been right. The affair is too trumpery to be discussed. Such friction is inevitable whenever men work together; a passing difference of opinion which, if the parties are left alone, without any chance of invoking the strong arm of power on their behalf, never stands long in the way of the establishment of a satisfactory *modus vivendi*.

Mr. Hilton shortly after had occasion to dismiss the teacher for insubordination, and temporarily closed the school. While the school was closed the priest lost his allowance for religious instruction, a circumstance which seems to have led him to invoke the assistance of the civil power to destroy his adversary. Mr. Hilton was a foreigner, an Englishman, and a Protestant. He had expressed the universal opinion of every Englishman— and every practical man of any experience—that there are too many holidays in Russia for the effective carrying on of business. He had opened the school in the afternoon of a day when the priest had ordered it to be closed, and he had indirectly by closing a school deprived the priest of a modicum of his salary.

Added to this he had on several occasions distributed Bibles, Testaments, and tracts through the authorities to the peasants and workmen, and, to crown the edifice of his iniquities, he had remarked that the priest in question had assumed an authority that did not belong to him, and was very keen in looking after his own interests. Therefore, in the priest's mind, it was decided that Mr. Hilton must go.

Of course, under any ordinary system of Government, it would have been impossible for any priest, were his grievances tenfold those of the priest of Bogoyavlensky, to have avenged himself in any such manner. Mr. Hilton was doing good work for his workmen, for the district, for his employer, and for the Government. He had been repeatedly thanked by the Governor of Ufa, both publicly and privately, for the excellent relations which he had established between the people and the office; the result of which was that, compared with other districts, the magistrates had very little to do in his district. Besides directing the extensive industrial operations of Colonel Pashkoff, and superintending his schools, he had established a Free Library, open to all the people of Bogoyavlensky. From the secular, material, and moral point of view, nothing could be more satisfactory for Russia than to have such a man discharging such functions in such a district. All this, however, seems to have counted as nothing against the offended pride of a single priest, who knew how to make use of the evil spirit of religious intolerance which is unfortunately at present supreme in St. Petersburg. The story of how this was done sheds such clear light upon the methods of the mediaevalists who now bear sway in Russia, that I do not hesitate to set it forth in some detail. Edward Hilton was a British subject. He was well-to-do, occupying an influential position as the manager of a wealthy noble in a region far removed from the seat of Government, where his benevolence, his tact, and his good sense, kept everything in peace and order. He could invoke the interference of the British Ambassador, and his employer had friends who were highly placed at Court. If with all these securities for at least a semblance of fair treatment, Edward Hilton was sacrificed without mercy or scruple, à fortiori there is little reason to believe that the friendless and insignificant Liberal or Nonconformist who falls under the displeasure of priest or tchinovnik can expect fair play or justice from the powers that be.

On March 30, 1884, Edward Hilton received a summons from the Ispravnik, or head of the police, requesting his immediate attendance. Thinking that there had been some disturbance somewhere on the estate, he went over to the Ispravnik's house to hear what was the matter. He was astounded when he received peremptory orders, issued by the Minister of the Interior, Count Tolstoi, M. Pobedonostzeff's shadow, to leave Russia in forty-eight hours. He was accused of no crime. He was afforded no opportunity of repelling any charge. He was simply ordered to bundle up his baggage and depart. The only document which he received was an official note of the route to be followed. By this he was forbidden to pass through either Moscow or St. Petersburg. The delay of forty-eight hours was subsequently extended to a week. On April 6th Hilton started for Orenburg. The winter frost was breaking up. The hill streams were swollen with melting snow and broken ice until they became rushing torrents. They had to be crossed at all hazards. Describing his journey afterwards in a letter to his brother, he wrote :—

> I had to walk across one of the rivers—the Bela—at a place where it is some 200 feet wide, and where the ice still remained, though just a little higher up, and also a little lower down the stream, great gaps were to be seen. And even where I crossed the ice was discoloured, and for the most part covered with water. I had to walk upon poles about seventeen feet long and three inches thick, loosely laid end to end in rows of three abreast. Many of the workmen accompanied me to the river-side, but only two ventured to cross over with me. The others shrank from the risk, knowing that at any moment, especially considering the friction from the tossing blocks higher up, the ice might break up, in which case the chances of saving one's life would be but slight.

On arriving at Orenburg he obtained permission to go to St. Petersburg. All this time he had no idea why he was thus summarily expelled. The only clue which he had to this arbitrary decree was afforded him by a hint from the Ispravnik to the effect that it was due to his difference with the priest, to which allusion has already been made. When he got to St. Petersburg, however, he received further information.

Sir Edward Thornton was then our ambassador at St.

Petersburg. In his mild and ineffective way he appealed to M. de Giers, inquiring why a British subject should be thus harshly treated. To which M. de Giers replied on the authority of M. Pobedonostzeff that "Edward Hilton is a fervent adherent of a religious sectarian, and notwithstanding repeated warnings, persists in propagating doctrines forbidden by the dominant Church." M. Pobedonostzeff himself wrote to state that Edward Hilton was a Communist, and a disturbing element who could not be allowed to remain in Russia.

The assertion to which M. Pobedonostzeff gave currency was not only false but ludicrously absurd. A sturdy English Nonconformist who had invested all his savings in Russian industrial enterprises, and who for the last fifteen years had managed the estate of one of the wealthiest of Russian nobles, was not exactly the man to be a Communist and a disturber of the peace. But it is well that we have this typical instance on record as an illustration of the facility with which even State Churchmen personally honest and even pious will bear false witness when appealed to in the interest of intolerance. Of course M. Pobedonostzeff knew nothing personally of Edward Hilton, whose life was passed a thousand miles away from the residence of the Procurator of the Holy Synod. But on the authority of some obscure and unnamed *delator*, who might, for aught he knew, be animated by the most unworthy motives, the Procurator of the Synod of the Orthodox Church did not hesitate first to brand with a cruel and utterly false accusation a British subject, whom he gave no opportunity of being heard in his own defence, and then to pass sentence upon him as guilty, without apparently taking any trouble to test the accuracy of the information on which he acted. The whole proceeding was an outrage on the most elementary principles of human justice. To call a man a Communist and a disturber of the peace in Russia is like raising the cry of mad dog after an unfortunate cur whose destruction you desire to accomplish. Give a dog a bad name and hang him is summary procedure, but it can hardly be accepted as an ideal method of meting out justice to human beings.

Edward Hilton replied at once and with much natural indignation to the accusations. No man was less of a Communist than he. Neither had he ever been a disturbing element in a district which, thanks mainly to his influence, was remarkably tranquil. As for the accusation that he had propagated doctrines forbidden by the dominant Church despite of repeated warnings, he met that also by a flat denial, challenging his accusers to specify a single warning, public or private, that he had ever received, or a single act of his which could be described as that of propagandism. In passing, it is worth while to note the accusation which the Russian Government by its excuse brings against itself. To justify the expulsion of a foreign resident on the allegation that he propagated doctrines forbidden by the dominant Church reveals a mediævalism of thought that makes credible almost any extreme of intolerance. A dominant Church with a right to forbid the propagation of doctrines is an unlovely spectre indeed to be affronting the light of day in the last quarter of the nineteenth century. Still, granting the right of this baleful survival to exist, that is no reason why its intolerant prerogatives should not be exercised in accordance with truth and justice. Even an unjust law can be administered fairly. Unfortunately, in the present case the unfairness of its administration seems to have kept step with the injustice of the law.

Mr. Hilton was accused of propaganda of doctrines forbidden by the Church. The only colourable pretext for this accusation was the fact that he had distributed copies of religious books in his district. He replied that not one of these books was given by him directly to the people. In every case they were distributed through the representatives of the Russian Government, or of the Orthodox Church. He gave them to the commander of the troops, to the priests, and to the schoolmasters. If there was any distribution among the people, it was done by their agency. There was not a single copy of any religious work issued by him which had not first been certified as unobjectionable by the Holy Synod (of which M. Pobedonestzeff is the procurator), and stamped with approval by the official censors. Nay, more; before distributing them to the schoolmaster, Mr. Hilton had taken the precaution of submitting them for approval to the District Inspector of Schools. That official returned them with the following note:—

"The books are all approved by the Censors, and some of them I knew before to be approved by the Minister of Public

Instruction. All of them are good and useful, and some of them especially so, being both full of instruction and very simple in form. It is, of course, superfluous to speak of the benefit of such books as the New Testament of our Lord Jesus Christ and of the Psalms. The diffusion among the people of these sacred books is particularly desirable."

Mr. Hilton further noted in his defence that during his thirty-five years' sojourn in Russia his conduct had never been subject of complaints, and that he had never even been accused of violating any law of the Empire.

Representations so cogent, backed by the influence of the British ambassador and the presence of the highly-placed friends of Col. Pashkoff, produced a semblance of yielding on the part of the Government. Count Tolstoi declared on June 5th—" I will allow Mr. Hilton to return to his home at Bogoyavlensky, and will give orders for the whole affair to be investigated on the spot." Back Mr. Hilton posted to Bogoyavlensky. On his arrival he was told that two months were allotted to him in which to arrange Colonel Pashkoff's business. At the end of two months he must leave. " But," said he, " the whole affair is to be inquired into." To that the Ispravnik could say nothing. Mr. Hilton waited for the summons to present himself before the tribunal which Count Tolstoi had promised would inquire into the whole affair on the spot. Week passed after week, and no summons arrived. At last, when six weeks had gone by, he grew alarmed, and applied to the Governor of Ufa. That official received him courteously, but stated that he had received no instructions whatever to have the affair investigated; his only orders were to see that Mr. Hilton left the country in two months. " It is quite evident," he said, " that the Government is determined you shall leave Russia. I therefore advise you to go." Another respite of twenty days was granted, but Count Tolstoi's promise was cynically violated. When Mr. Hilton came to Petersburg to remonstrate with the Chief of the Third Section of Police for this breach of the Ministerial word, he was told—" We need no investigation or trial in order to send a foreigner out of Russia. The Government have made up their mind that you shall leave Russia—I advise you to do so."

In the course of these negotiations, Count Tolstoi had written to Sir Ed. Thornton with a new series of charges against Mr. Hilton. These were—

(1) That he had publicly said there were 5 per cent. too many holidays kept by the Orthodox Church.

(2) That he had insulted the Clergy by saying that holidays were instituted by them for their own gain.

(3) That he had used his influence as manager in Colonel Pashkoff's schools.

Mr. Hilton rebutted these charges; but it is obvious that if Englishmen are to be expelled from Russia for saying that there are too many holidays, Englishmen had better give the Empire a wide berth. Every Englishman who sets his foot in Russia says so. The truth is so obvious, and if Mr. Hilton estimates the number of superfluous holidays at only 5 per cent., he put it lower than any other Englishman I ever met. Personally, I should be inclined to multiply the 5 per cent. at least by five. It is obvious that the manager of an estate who represents the absentee patron of the schools must necessarily exercise influence in their management; but in no single instance, Mr. Hilton stated, did he interfere with the course of instruction, whether religious or secular, or interfere in any way with the internal working of the school. All that he did was to see that the children attended school on all days not marked as holidays in the official list.

"The charges," Mr. Hilton said, "are false. I should be glad to face my accusers." But this satisfaction was denied him. Accused by an anonymous enemy, condemned unheard, he was banished without a trial.

"The expulsion of my brother," wrote Mr. William Hilton, "can neither be justified by the law of the land, nor on the ground of the public weal. The summary proceedings against him have deprived him of an honourable and lucrative position. His removal from the country will expose him to the loss of his hard earnings, which have been invested in a paper-mill near St. Petersburg. We hope that he may be allowed at least to remain in this city, especially as he is now out of Colonel Pashkoff's employ."

Even this was refused him—so vindictive and unrelenting is the genius of religious persecution. Sir Edward Thornton said to him as he bade him farewell—" Well, Mr. Hilton, I have done all I can for you. It is a sad case. You have been treated shamefully. But what can I do? I do not say it is just, but they have the right to send foreigners out of the country if they feel so inclined."

Mr. Edward Hilton was succeeded by his brother—an Englishman, and a Nonconformist, like himself. For a year or two all went well. But then upon him also, as upon his predecessor, the vulture of persecution swooped. He was accused of having given a New Testament to a workman. For this grave and heinous offence he also was sentenced to banishment. But this time fortunately there was at the British Embassy an Englishman whose strong and vehement nature could not easily brook the perpetration of acts of flagrant injustice upon his countrymen. Brushing on one side official etiquette Sir Robert Morier wrote to M. Pobedonestzeff a letter in which he appealed to him in the name of common justice between man and man, to look into the case himself, and to prevent the execution of what seemed to Sir Robert a decreeof injustice. M. Pobedonestzeff, who is an honest man although narrow-minded and bigoted, was roused by the vigorous and manly appeal of the British Ambassador. He answered that he would look into the case. He did look into it, and he found that Sir Robert Morier was right. The arbitrary decree of expulsion was unjust, and he annulled it. But the tardy reversal of the unjust decree came too late. The second Hilton left the country, declaring that no consideration would induce him to remain under a Government where such intolerable vexation could be wantonly inflicted upon honest men.*

* The expulsion of the second Hilton—Mr. Henry Hilton—which M. Pobedonestzeff was honest enough to admit to have been unjust, was the occasion of a very spirited protest addressed by Colonel Pashkoff to Count Tolstoi, which made the latter Minister exceedingly angry, and, let us hope, correspondingly uncomfortable. It is not often that in Russia a Minister of the Interior is addressed with such uncompromising candour.

"The expulsion of Hilton and his numerous family without any reason, only in consequence of some unfounded accusation, which he was not given an opportunity to refute, depriving him of a lucrative employment, which provided for the future, breaking up his home, seems to be an act of such intense unfairness that it shocks every sense of justice. Involuntarily one asks oneself how long such acts of arbitrary administration will be tolerated here. It lies in your power, Count Tolstoi, to allow this man, who is suffering unjustly, to vindicate the truth. Will you really deny him this? Is it credible that you will oblige him to leave Russia and

Neither of the Hiltons was ever accused of any disloyalty to the Empire. Neither of them ever took the slightest interest in the internal politics of Russia. Both were upright, conscientious, God-fearing men, doing good work in responsible positions. But the demon of intolerance could not let them rest. False accusations were brought against them by anonymous assailants, and on the strength of slanders put in currency by malice they were driven from the country as ruined men. If that fate could overtake such men, so influentially protected, and so free from any compromising surroundings, what chance have the others of having even a fair administration of an arbitrary law? As I heard the story of the Hiltons—my own countrymen and co-religionists—my scepticism as to the complaints of the Nihilists was gradually undermined. If they do these things in the green tree, what will they not do in the dry? Such incidents as the above go far to sap one's confidence in the existence of a conception of justice in the minds of M. Pobedonestzeff and Count Tolstoi.

## CHAPTER V.

### THE STORY OF THE PASHKOFFSKI.

IN order that the public may understand the kind of treatment which it is thought not unfitting to extend to those who are guilty of the great and heinous offence of deserting the Greek Orthodox Church, I will set forth briefly the story of the persecution of the Pashkoffski. It is a useful object-lesson. It is an illustration of the way in which religious liberty is understood by the Procurator of the Holy Synod, and it affords a melancholy and suggestive picture of the extent to which the world still stands in need of the teaching of Milton's "Areopagitica" and Locke's "Religious Toleration." Nor can I disguise from myself that if such things can be done and defended by M.

publish abroad how impossible it is to get justice or a fair trial? . . . Will you, in conclusion, allow me to turn your attention to your responsibility before God in this iniquitous proceeding, for which you may possibly soon have to give an account."

X

Pobedonostzeff in full light of day when dealing with a harmless and inoffensive sect, there is no saying what enormities might be considered justifiable by men of the same cast of mind if they were confronted by a really formidable conspiracy directed against the existence of the State.

I am very reluctant to have to make this admission, but I should fail in my first duty to my countrymen if, in telling them " Truth about Russia," I did not inform them how and in what sense liberty of conscience is interpreted by the Minister whose influence is for the moment supreme in the ecclesiastical administration of the Russian Empire.

I cannot forget when first I met Lord Radstock, the founder of the Pashkoffski. It was eight years ago. He had just returned from St. Petersburg, and I waited upon him to obtain some information as to the progress of his evangelistic mission in the Russian capital. I stated my errand, and waited for a reply. At last Lord Radstock said solemnly, " The Lord knows! " " Yes," I said, " I know He knows; but I want to know: can you not tell me?" Again, Lord Radstock ejaculated in an absent-minded way, " The Lord knows! " " Yes," again I said, " but cannot you give me some facts which you know?" Lord Radstock looked at me, and then said, " You had better go to St. Petersburg and see for yourself." " I should be delighted," I replied, " but as I want the information for to-morrow's paper, and as the only means of getting it is for you to tell me, will you not give me some information?" Whereupon Lord Radstock said it was the Lord's work, and that He knew; more than that I could not extract from him. I could have shaken him for sheer disgust, and I left. Yet this was the man whose propaganda so alarmed M. Pobedonestzeff, that to check it he has not hesitated to discredit Russia in the eyes of the civilised world.

Every one remembers the familiar story of the man who was sent to Rome in the Middle Ages, in the hope that the sight of the corruption of the Papacy would rid him of his faith in Christianity, and who returned a more fervent believer than before. Nothing but a Divine religion, he said, could have survived the abuses which abounded in Rome. Something like the same train of thought was suggested by the alarm which Lord Radstock excited in the mind of the Procurator of the

Holy Synod. When a battery of artillery opens fire apparently at a cock-sparrow, there must be something behind that cock-sparrow; and unless there had been something behind Lord Radstock he never could have excited such animosity in the Russian Government.

"He was but the telegraph wire," said a Russian General in high position; "through him came the spark from on high." There was certainly nothing in Lord Radstock himself to account for the effect which his preaching produced. A clever Countess, who attended his first services, described to me with much gusto, and a keen sense of the ridiculous, the early meetings held by Lord Radstock among the fine ladies of St. Petersburg society. His imperfect French—his evangelical discourse—the English habit of kneeling with the head in the opposite direction to the speaker—above all, the invitation to those who wished "to find Christ" to call upon Lord Radstock next day at one—all combined to indispose the worldly but cultivated Russians to accept his message. Nevertheless, somehow or other, no one has yet explained how his message was eagerly welcomed by many as a fresh revelation of Christian truth.

Most of those who joined the Pashkoffski at first were ladies of society, who were able to speak English as fluently as their own native tongue. There were, however, some gentlemen, among others a Count Korff, who shared with M. Pashkoff the dangerous honour of being conspicuous among the leaders of the new movement. At first the new movement showed no signs of hardening into a sect. Its members went to church as much as they did before, but they held Bible-readings in their own houses, to which they invited their friends and their servants. There was at this early stage no intention of any collision with the Church. The deepened and quickened note of spiritual life ran in a much more profitable direction than towards the creation of a new sect. A new sense of Christian brotherhood seemed to be developed in St. Petersburg. Fine ladies began to go "slumming," not as a mere pastime, but in real earnest. The great ethical ideal of Christianity, that of personal service to "the least of these my brethren," once more exerted its power over the lives of men. District-visiting among the poor was organised; Bible-women were engaged; ladies took turns in visiting the prisons, in reading to patients in the hospitals. It was no uncommon sight to see a great lady, to whom all the salons of St. Petersburg were open, skurrying through the streets on a humble droshky, to read and to pray by the bedside of some dying girl in the foul ward of the lock hospital. No infection deterred them from the discharge of their self-imposed duties; no place was too dark for them to refuse to illumine it with the radiance of their presence. The world wondered and passed on, but the work grew.

The Bible-readings in the larger houses led by degrees to Bible-readings in the humbler homes. The priests began to take alarm. Nothing could have been simpler than these services. A portion of the Bible was read and explained; the usual fervent exhortation followed, a hymn was sung, prayer was offered up for Divine guidance, and the meeting dispersed after friendly and fraternal greetings had been exchanged. Simple and unpretending though the Bible-readings were, they exercised a great attraction upon those who had never been presented with a conception of a religious service other than the sustained splendour of the ecclesiastical ceremonial of the Greek Church. There is nothing mysterious about this; it is the same phenomenon with which every Englishman is familiar in every branch of English Nonconformity.

The real story of the remarkable religious movement which goes by the name of M. Pashkoff may some day be told in full. I cannot profess to do more than merely to outline the salient features of one of the most curious religious awakenings of our time.

Never had a spiritual movement an odder beginning. Nearly twenty years ago, as a young and beautiful Russian lady was reading a novel in a railway carriage on a Swiss railway, she was startled by the unceremonious action of her fellow-traveller, a grey-haired English gentleman, who, without a word of apology or of introduction, snatched the novel out of her hand and flung it out of the window. She was beginning indignantly to expostulate with him when he stopped her by asking her, in a voice full of deep and tender feeling, whether she ever prayed for her country. "Pray for my country?" she said—"of course; in church we pray over and over again for our country; but besides that, no." "Why not?" he said, kindly; "why not pray for your country?" And then, in very loving and patient fashion, he began to tell her of how, for many years past, he had it specially borne in upon his mind that he must pray for Russia, and get other people to pray for her. "Look here," said he: and producing a well-thumbed pocket Bible he turned to the first two pages. The lady saw, to her astonishment, the pages filled with Russian signatures, many of which she recognised as those of her friends in St. Petersburg. "Every one of them," continued the strange Englishman, "has signed his or her name in this Bible, promising that for the rest of their life they will every morning and evening pray for their country. Whenever I see a Russian I always ask him to make me that promise, and I beg of you to do the same." The lady was much impressed with the sincerity and quaintness of the request, and added her name to the others. Her travelling companion then read to her the prophecies of Isaiah, with which, like many other fine ladies, she had till then been totally unacquainted. When that journey was over the two who had so strangely met parted, never to meet again. But the conversation of the old Englishman, whose heart was consumed within him by reason of his ardent longing for the welfare of Russia, dwelt in her memory, and led to a complete change of life.

This lady shortly afterwards came over to England, and when in London, together with other Russian ladies, she made the acquaintance of Lord Radstock and other fervent Evangelicals of the Plymouth Brother type. The experience which she gained of their religious life led her to desire to see something done to realise the prayer which she and her companions were offering up night and morning for the welfare and the salvation of Russia. It was from that incentive that there came the first visit which Lord Radstock paid to St. Petersburg in 1874.

He created considerable sensation. He was an English peer who preached in the American chapel. He was simple, earnest, and obviously sincere. He spoke in English and in a French which was far below the standard of St. Petersburg society—the most cultivated polyglot community in the world. But his direct appeals to the hearts and consciences of his hearers, his simple expositions of the Bible, and his evident conviction of the reality of his own salvation, impressed Russian society.

Then he began to hold drawing-room meetings, and very soon drawing-room meetings became the rage in St. Petersburg. Lord Radstock had two or three appointments every day. His note-book was filled with engagements. Three or four well-known people openly professed to have "found salvation."

Among these converts the most conspicuous for his wealth and position was M. Pashkoff, whose name has been applied to all those who follow Lord Radstock in their adhesion to what we should call in England simple Bible Christianity. M. Pashkoff is an extensive landowner. He owns estates in the provinces of Nijni, Tamboff, Moscow, and Orenburg. In the latter province also he has extensive mines. The Pashkoff mansion, which stands on the Quay of the Neva, a little beyond the British Embassy, became the head-quarters of the new movement. At first people thought it would pass like any other fashionable craze, after it had had its day. But when Lord Radstock returned in 1876, it was evident that "the new religion" had taken firm root in Russian soil. To M. Pobedonostzeff, however, there seemed something terrible and dangerous in this spectacle of Russians actually worshipping God in an informal fashion, not sanctioned by the Orthodox Church. He attended some of the meetings, and then did his best to procure the intervention of the authorities, so as to prevent the holding of any more meetings. He failed, fortunately. His hour had not yet come. The late Emperor was indisposed to persecution, and the ascendancy of M. Pobedonostzeff had not yet been established.

The movement began to spread in the country. When the Pashkoffski went in summer to their estates, they gathered their servants and their country people about them, and told them, in their familiar phrase, what the Lord had done for their souls. Many of these simple folk heard the Word gladly. The alarm of the priests increased. It is persistently asserted that some of the Pashkoffski, in their new-born zeal for spiritual religion, smashed their icons, or sacred pictures. This is denied as vehemently, but I hardly think the point material. Here and there in every such movement there is almost certain to be some vigorous zealot who longs to give visible practical demonstration of the change of his opinions. The image-breaker is one of the most familiar figures in the history of religions. All the best kings of Israel destroyed the graven images ; our own Reformers and Puritans made a clean sweep of all such things; and so long as a man only smashes images which are his own property, I cannot for the life of me see why any one should interfere. Nevertheless, it is always well to abstain from doing anything which might shock the sensitive consciences of one's neighbours, and the Pashkoffski stoutly maintain that although they may have dismantled some of the icons, having no further use for them, there are no instances of wholesale image-smashing on record against them. Any isolated case that could be discovered or invented was exaggerated a hundredfold, until those who heard the outcry of the Orthodox might have pardonably believed that Lord Radstock and M. Pashkoff, at the head of an army of St. Petersburg iconoclasts, were marching, axe in hand, through Russia, smashing icons wherever they found them.

There seems to be no doubt, so far as I can ascertain, that the first acts of aggression came, as usual, from the Established Clergy. It is always the men in possession who presume upon the strength of their position, in order to force the weak into an unwilling conformity. The story as told to me was that when it was known that any poor man had been attending Bible-readings, he was waited upon by a priest, who told him that he must be either one thing or the other. He could not be both ; he must choose. He must give up his Bible-reading and his hymn-singing, or be refused the Communion. It was the imposition of a new Test, not less pernicious because it was sanctioned neither by the will of the Emperor nor the councils of the Church. This action on the part of the priests led to unwise polemics on the part of those whom they assailed, and a condition of mutual irritation was set up, which augured ill for the peaceful development of the new movement.

The times were stormy. The Nihilists, in pursuance of the campaign of terrorism which culminated in the murder of the Emperor, had succeeded in destroying the nerves of the Russian Ministers. With a diabolical ingenuity they seized all the scanty means available for the dissemination of literature for the propagation of their doctrines. New Testaments were scattered far and wide in which only the first few pages bore the Gospel according to St. Matthew, and all the rest was the Gospel according to Dynamite! The tracts of the Society for Promoting Religious Literature were abused in the same fashion. Nihilism and the Nihilist propaganda seemed to confront the Administration at every turn. In a fever a patient will strike at the doctor or the nurse. Russia, delirious with the suppressed fever of Nihilism, could hardly be blamed if she struck wildly at any and every person whose shadow irritated her shattered nerves. Lord Radstock was such a person. He was forbidden to return to Russia, and he obeyed the interdict; but the work went on, and goes on to this day.

The earlier years of M. Pobedonostzeff's ascendancy were marked by a gradual increase of the ferocity with which the new movement was treated by the authorities. The priests preached against it, which was, of course, well within their right, and if they had contented themselves with preaching no one could have complained. But the Spiritual power in Russia had unfortunately not sufficient faith in its teaching to rely upon the spoken word without invoking the sword of the Temporal power. Threats were freely used to induce the simple folk to abstain from Bible-reading. Police were put on observation on houses where the Bible was known to have been read. The singing of hymns even in private houses was regarded as a sign of the spirit of schism. It was admitted by high police officials that in quarters where the Bible-readings prevailed they had much less to do, but now the police were employed to suppress these meetings. The Pashkoffski complain that the police picketed them, browbeat those who attended the meetings, and tried to extort from them a promise that they would never read the Bible in the presence of three or four of their fellow-men.

The propaganda of the Pashkoffski, accompanied as it was by a great deal of active philanthropy, led as usual to the exploiting of the humanitarian by the knave and the hypocrite. Lazy scamps, who were much more conscious of their possession of a stomach than of a soul, used to attend the meetings and apply for relief, and their success led to the preposterous rumour that M. Pashkoff was paying Isvostchiks three roubles a head to listen to his discourses. In the country he was accused of paying the Moujiks as much for listening to one of his discourses as they could earn in labour from sunrise to sunset; and I actually heard the wife of a high official in the province where M. Pashkoff preached, discussing the matter seriously from the point of view of the displacement in the labour market that would ensue if landlords took to paying labourers for listening to their Evangelical eloquence instead of keeping them employed in the fields! The prejudice which makes the Catholics of Ireland so furious against the "soupers" of the Protestant propaganda in the poorer districts is rampant in Russia, and the jealous and timorous priesthood raised a cry of alarm at the prospect of seeing the children of Mother Church converted to Pashkoflism at so many roubles per head.

I listened to the story of the way in which M. Pobedonestzeff and the police, with the hearty assent and consent of Count Dmitry Tolstoi, harried these unfortunate Christians, with feelings of indignation and shame. As if there were so many people anxious to take trouble to help their fellow-creatures in Russia or anywhere else in the world, that any State can afford to be intolerant as to accepting or rejecting the services of those who offer to help! And to think that this Government, which hunts down Bible-readings, establishes brothels under official regulation, and supplies a regular staff of official doctors to make vice "safe!" It is simply too horrible for words. One poor scullery-maid from the country, who had been attending a Bible-reading in a General's house, found one day the meeting stopped by order of the police. She burst out into a wailing cry. "All the places where we are ruined are left open and no one cries to close them; but the one place where they wanted to save us is closed." It made no difference that the meeting was held at times when there was no service in the Church, that nothing was said against the Church, or that the priest of the parish had wished to take part in the gathering. It was to read the Bible, to sing, and to pray; that was enough. Away with it! away with it, in the name of God and the Tzar, and by order of M. Pobedonestzeff!

Said a factory hand when the police informed him that they could not allow him to go to Bible-readings in the evening —" Why did you never interfere with me when I went every night to the public-house to drink—why do you only interfere when I begin to read the Bible?" The answer is not recorded. It would probably have been similar to that which the Jewish rabble would have given in explanation of their choice,

"Not this man, but Barabbas." The Church all this time offered, with few and rare exceptions, no substitute for the meetings which it suppressed. It was simply playing the part of the dog in the manger. Instead of rousing itself to outdo in good works and in spiritual activity the followers of Lord Radstock, it was chiefly concerned to stamp with heavy heel upon every manifestation of quickened spiritual life and humanitarian enthusiasm. Instead of refusing to quench the smoking flax or break the bruised reed, it ordered out the police to extinguish the smouldering fire, and to trample out the first glimmering of reviving life.

Here I must for a moment interrupt my narrative of the progress of the Pashkoffski, to bestow a passing glance upon the still more remarkable religious phenomenon which goes by the name of Stundism in the Southern provinces of Russia. In St. Petersburg the Evangelical movement, although it sprang directly from the fervent desire of eccentric Englishmen to rouse Russians to a more strenuous and sustained aspiration for the welfare of their country, was from the first misrepresented as if it had not been national. The Pashkoffski, it is said, were distinctively English, and as such could never be regarded as true Russians: not even if they took more pains and spent more money in endeavouring to help Russians than any similar number of the Orthodox. But in the South the Evangelical movement could not be exposed to that reproach. Its origin was not English, but Russian. It began in the reading of a Russian Testament issued by M. Pashkoff, but approved by the Censor. It was carried on by the son of a Russian priest, who had lived in America, and who, when he returned to his native land, began to hold prayer-meetings lasting about an hour, American fashion, among the villagers. The fame of these Hour-meetings spread far and near. Deputations were sent to see and to report. The essential features of the Hour-meeting were those of the Bible-reading. There was the same appeal to the Scriptures, the natural impromptu prayer, and the singing of hymns. *Stundism*, as it was called from the fact that the meetings lasted an hour (*ein Stund*), spreads fast among the Southerns for the same reason that Dissent spreads in parishes where the Anglican Church is purely formal and there is no real spiritual life or healthy humanitarian activity in connection with the Establishment. Men and women, weary of formalities and ceremonial, troop off to other folds, where earnest men speak to seeking souls of the eternal truth, which alone can minister to the wants of the human heart. The Molokani, or Milk-drinkers, form another dissenting sect which is strong in the South, and, together with the Stundists, they maintain in many an isolated village, and in many a remote province, a flame kindled from the Lamp of Life which no persecution has yet been able to extinguish.

## CHAPTER VI.

### EXILED UNHEARD.

It was in the year 1884 that the two movements, that of the Stundists in the South and that of the Pashkoffski in the North, first joined hands. Nothing could be more simple or more natural. Evangelical Christians, united by the bond of a common faith, and still further united by the bond of a common persecution, naturally wished to join hands in brotherly fellowship. Hence deputations came to St. Petersburg from the Stundists, the Molokani, and the Baptists.

The circular letter summoning the sectarians of the South to a Conference in St. Petersburg, was signed by Colonel Pashkoff and Count Korff. It addressed them as beloved brethren, and began by setting forth that the earnest last prayer of Christ for the unity of all who believed in Him, had not yet been carried out. " Does it not seem to you," said the writers of this epistle, "that the hour is come to carry out the testament of the Head of the Church ? " To bring about the unity of the Church by compacting together the sects who had revolted from Orthodoxy seemed to them all they could do to contribute towards the realisation of the last prayer of Christ. They therefore, having in view this idea, proposed to each Church that " one person from among those whom the Holy Ghost has placed among you to be presbyters of the flock " should be sent to St. Petersburg " to seek together with us before the Lord His ways, which He Himself has appointed for the perfect unity of the Church of Christ."

Very interesting accounts of that first Conference of the Russian Evangelicals lie before me, in the shape of the diary of a Baptist from Tiflis, and a report prepared at the close of the sittings. About 100 met in the house of the Princess Lieven, where they had prayers and the breaking of bread. " As the greatest part of those present were not baptised according to the faith," says the uncompromising Anabaptist, " we did not partake with them "—not a very hopeful beginning for the attempt to restore unity to the Church of Christ. There were present representatives from all parts of the South, as far as Tiflis in the East, and Bulgaria in the West, including German brethren from Odessa, and an American missionary. Altogether there were 25 Russians, and about 45 Swedes, Germans, and English. The meetings were very simple and informal. When they met they sang a hymn, then all knelt, and those prayed who felt moved so to do. Then anyone who felt prompted to speak to the brethren did so, usually speaking from a text out of the Bible. In the afternoon they discussed the points of the proposed programme; in the evening they dined. Men and women, nobles and peasants, all spoke and prayed in Him. The delegates had, according to their own account, a very good time. They carried, after some considerable discussion, the first clause of the programme, viz. :—

"That to the body or Church of Christ belong all those who have in Jesus Christ redemption (exclusively) through His blood, and the forgiveness of sins. The body of Christ consists of living members born from the Holy Ghost through the Word."

But when they came to the second clause, which dealt with baptism, they were utterly unable to agree. After a long sitting it was with a feeling as if a great stone were lifted off their hearts that they unanimously agreed to withdraw all the other articles of the programme, and confine themselves solely to insisting on love and good works.

The Conference lasted from the 1st of April to the 6th, and was productive of the best results in quickened zeal, the consciousness of mutual support, and the enthusiasm that such meetings naturally engendered. Anything that was wanting to create a deep impression was supplied by the action of the Government.

On the 20th of March, a fortnight before the sectarian delegates assembled at St. Petersburg, Colonel Pashkoff and Count Korff were summoned to appear before General Orjevsky, who managed the political police under the Minister of the Interior. General Orjevsky asked them to sign a paper promising (1) Not to preach the Gospel; (2) Not to circulate tracts; and (3) Not to receive the sectarians who were coming from the South. They immediately and decisively refused. They were then ordered to leave Russia in a fortnight, and forbidden to correspond with the Southern sect. If they disobeyed, General Orjevsky threatened that they would be deprived of the management of their estates. The Princess Lieven was at the same time forbidden, in the name of the Tzar, to receive the sectarians in her house. With astonishing courage these official intimations were treated as non-existent. The Conference was held as if no interdict had been pronounced. The delegates met in Princess Lieven's house. Colonel Pashkoff and Count Korff preached, tracts were distributed, and arrangements were made for a more frequent intercommunication between the brethren, exactly as if the interview with General Orjevsky had never taken place.

It was, therefore, hardly a surprise to the promoters of the gathering when, on the morning of the 6th of April, a note arrived from M. Zaharoff, one of the delegates from the Southern Churches, announcing that he and all the other Russian delegates —Baptists, Molokani, and Stundists—had been seized by the police the previous day, and clapped into gaol. Colonel Pashkoff and Count Korff posted off to General Gresser to ascertain what was the matter. They were not allowed to see their guests, now the captives of the police, but they soon ascertained how the trouble had arisen. The Orthodox priests in the villages from which the delegates had come, imagining that the sectarians had gone to St. Petersburg to petition the Tzar concerning religious liberty, sent word to the authorities at the capital as to their suspicions. The authorities, as their manner is, arrested the whole of the suspected sectarians, and subjected them to a police inquiry. They remained under arrest over Saturday night and Sunday morning; then they were liberated—the police finding no harm in them. There was a great rejoicing when they reappeared at the Princess Lieven's, and, in the simple words of the narrator, "love, joy, and peace reigned during the meeting," which continued till eleven o'clock.

On the delegates returning to their hotel, they found the police waiting for them, and they were again marched off to prison.

The cause of this second arrest was somewhat peculiar. When the police arrested them the first time, it seems that some men —presumably Nihilists—who owned some type, were living in the same hotel. When they saw the police arrive to arrest the sectarians, they feared for themselves, and emptied their cases of type down a drain. As ill-luck would have it, the type choked the pipe. A plumber was called in, and promptly communicated the cause of the stoppage to the police. The police instantly—after the usual fashion of the force—put two and two together, and re-arrested the sectarians, on suspicion of complicity with the owners of the secret printing press.

Sunday night found Stundists, Molokani, and Baptists in one prison, and they confessed afterwards that nothing ever contributed so much to the unification of the various branches of the Evangelicals as that common imprisonment, which taught them in grim practical earnest that they were united by the same sufferings as well as by the same cares and the same hope.

Next day the police conducted them from prison to the railway station, and packed them off to their respective homes. So ended the famous Conference which first brought the Evangelicals of the South and the North into union.

But the mischief, in the eyes of the authorities, had been done. A junction had been effected between the two poles of the Evangelical schism. The North had grasped hands with the South, and Orthodoxy trembled at the thought of the portentous results which might follow so alarming a re-union. Authority felt itself threatened, and determined upon reprisals. In this M. Pobedonostzeff argued exactly as do the Nihilists, without their excuse. For, as an ex-professor of jurisprudence and the procurator of the Christian Church, he, of all men, should not have forgotten, even in the midst of a panic excited by the hobnobbing of a few peasants from the South with a few people in Society in the North, the allegiance that was due to the sublime abstractions of Law and of Justice. All the forces of the State were at his disposal. The Courts were open, and the exchequer of an Empire was available for retaining the services of the most eminent counsel to arraign the conduct of those who might have offended against a law which had been fashioned ready to the hand of the persecutor. On so grave an occasion, when issues so vital to the welfare of the community were at stake, and when action was being taken by a Government in the sacred name of religion, it might be assumed that every formality would be observed that the most scrupulous could demand, that the guilty persons would be arraigned in full light of the day, and that their condemnation, if decided on, would be pronounced by the highest judicial authorities under circumstances that precluded even so much as a suspicion of partiality or prejudice. All this is the merest truism familiar to even the junior student in the school of jurisprudence in which M. Pobedonostzeff had been a distinguished professor. We shall now see how far M. Pobedonostzeff bore these maxims in mind in dealing with what seemed to him the formidable coalition between the forces of Evangelical heresy in Northern and Southern Russia.

Of all the institutions in Russia, that which is at once the most peculiar to the country, and the most deeply rooted in the national esteem, is the Autocracy. The great ideal of a Secular omnipotence anointed by God for the dispensation of justice on this earth, is one heritage of the Russian mind which has survived all the abuses of power, and has been proof against the sap and mine of destructive criticism. But, as the fate of the late Emperor showed, there were not wanting even in Russia men to whom no divinity hedged round a king, and the explosion which summoned the Emperor to the throne was a solemn and unmistakable indication that the Autocracy itself, in the minds of some of its subjects, had been weighed in the balance and was found wanting. Under these circumstances, it might have been supposed that any Minister loyal to the Autocracy would have shrunk with instinctive horror from any unnecessary appeal to the great prerogatives which are vested in a Russian Emperor, and have refrained, even at great personal risk and inconvenience, from using the august sceptre of the Tzar as a weapon for striking down a personal or a polemical opponent. In politics as in poetry it is a sound rule, *Nec Deus intersit nisi dignus vindice nodus*. It may be convenient to invoke the will of the Vicegerent of Heaven, as is sometimes done in the East, to settle a dispute as to a basket of figs or the ownership of a lame ass; but in Europe, even so far East as St. Petersburg, there is some sense of the proportion of things as well as some regard for the dignity of an Emperor whose word is obeyed as law by a hundred and twenty millions of human beings. This consideration, if no other, might have deterred any Minister, not anxious to discredit the Autocracy, from invoking the personal intervention of the Emperor in any matter which could possibly be left to the jurisdiction of the ordinary tribunals of the Empire.

But there were other considerations which might have deterred M. Pobedonostzeff from resorting to the rough-and-ready expedient of invoking the arbitrary exercise of the Imperial power as a means of ridding him of his adversaries, M. Pashkoff and Count Korff. Chief among those was the fact, well known to M. Pobedonostzeff, and not less well known to all concerned, that in transferring the adjudication of the case of the accused schismatics from the ordinary tribunals to the personal decision of the Emperor, he was appealing from a Court which was certainly judicial and presumably impartial, to a tribunal which was arbitrary, and which was notoriously prejudiced strongly against the accused. The Emperor has never made any secret of his personal feeling against some at least of the practices of the Pashkoffski. He could no more be impartial in sitting in judgment upon a layman who ventured to administer the sacrament, and who was believed to have destroyed a sacred image, than a sporting squire could be impartial in trying a poacher, or a brewer in dealing with the obstruction caused by a Temperance procession. No matter how earnestly the Emperor might try to rid himself of prejudice, it was inseparable from his religious convictions; and even if by some impossibility he succeeded, no one would believe that the miracle had been accomplished. In any judge, much more in a supreme judge, whose throne is the fount of justice, it is not enough to be impartial; you must not even be suspected of partiality. Even the shadow of a suspicion soils the ermine; how much more must it besmirch the stainless purity of the Imperial, the Supreme, Court of Final Appeal? Yet, knowing that to relegate the question to the Emperor, transferring it from the regular judicial tribunals, would expose his Sovereign unnecessarily to the imputation of sitting as judge in a case where the very strength of his religious convictions rendered it impossible to be impartial, M. Pobedonostzeff decided that the fate of M. Pashkoff and of Count Korff should be decided by the personal fiat of the Emperor.

The lack of impartiality in the judge selected by M. Pobedonostzeff to hear the case of Self v. M. Pashkoff, however objectionable from the point of view of the Autocracy, was comparatively trivial compared with the objections that must be taken to such a course from the point of view of the jurist. For the procedure of denunciation before the Emperor is deficient in every particular in those safeguards which even jurists of the School of St. Petersburg admit to be indispensable for the proper administration of justice. It is accepted by men of all creeds, of all schools, of all parties, and of all nations, that when any one is accused, even of the most trivial offence, he has a right to demand that his accuser, after being put upon his oath, shall make his accusation publicly in the hearing of the accused. It is further accepted as an elementary maxim of jurisprudence that the accused, after being furnished with the full text of the accusations against him, is entitled to be heard in his own defence. Thirdly, it is equally a truism of the Courts that he is entitled to cross-examine the witnesses called to prove his guilt; and further, that he shall be afforded time and opportunity for calling rebutting evidence to substantiate his innocence. In addition to these four great safeguards, with which jurists in all ages have sought to secure the liberty of individuals from the injustice of arbitrary judicial decisions, we in England have always regarded the trial of the accused by a jury of his equals as one of the most important guarantees for justice that can be provided by law, and only second to that is the publicity which is the light of justice.

Every one of these principles, whether they be the four universally accepted among all civilised men, or the two which form an essential part of English jurisprudence, was violated by the decision for which M. Pobedonostzeff and Count Tolstoi were

Y

jointly responsible, of submitting the decision of the question of guilt and of the punishment of the leaders of the Pashkoffski to the personal adjudication of the Emperor.

(1) M. Pashkoff and Count Korff were accused not on oath; they knew not by what accusers.

(2) After being accused secretly by anonymous witnesses, none of whom were present to give their evidence *in propria persona*, M. Pashkoff and Count Korff were neither asked nor permitted to make any answer. As they were secretly accused, so they were condemned unheard.

(3) The evidence against them was subjected to no cross-examination. It may have been all true. If so, there was the less reason for refusing to test it by the simple but searching ordeal of the witness-box.

(4) Neither were they permitted to call witnesses to rebut false accusations or to substantiate their plea of innocence.

So much for the four great principles of jurisprudence, every one of which M. Pobedonostzeff, himself a professor of jurisprudence, set at naught when, for the sake of a more swift and arbitrary punishment of his adversary, he submitted the consideration of their case to the personal adjudication of the Emperor. As to the right of trial by jury of their equals, and the publicity which is the safeguard of justice, of these I need not speak.

The Emperor listened to M. Pobedonostzeff. He accepted his voluminous *dossier* of accumulated accusations as sufficient proof of the guilt of the accused. He never called upon them to speak in their own behalf, for, indeed, it is not regarded as consistent with the Imperial dignity to conduct such an inquiry. He never permitted them to cross-examine witnesses, nor did he even insist upon their appearance before him. Neither did he ask the accused whether they had any witnesses to call to vindicate their innocence.

The Emperor listened in secret. He decided in secret. But he published his decision openly. M. Pashkoff and Count Korff were exiled from Russia.

M. Pobedonestzeff triumphed; but at what a price! In face of Russia, still seething with the fierce unrest of a revolutionary fever which ridiculed the restraints of the written law, appealed solely to arbitrary means, and openly vindicated personal reprisals as a legitimate method of political warfare, he had exhibited the spectacle of Authority itself dispensing with the ordinary securities for a fair trial, resorting to arbitrary methods, and introducing personal reprisals into the arena of administrative action! And he had done even worse than this. For he had made his Emperor unjust!

A decree of exile pronounced after an *ex parte* hearing of the second-hand and unsworn hearsay, that was the method relied upon by M. Pobedonostzeff for restoring unity to the Church and of crushing the Evangelical revival. For the sake of the principle at stake on both sides it would perhaps have been better if, instead of exile, the recusants had been sentenced to be burned alive in the Nevski Prospect. The additional severity of the punishment would not in the least have affected the question of the justice or the injustice of the sentence, but it would have compelled both the Emperor and the world to reflect upon the real significance of the arbitrary employment of autocratic power for the suppression of religious liberty. Unfortunately for the sake of the cause with which they were identified, the flame of their burning did not shed a lurid light upon the policy of M. Pobedonostzeff. M. Pashkoff and Count Korff were ordered to leave the country at once, and policemen were sent to see that the decree was executed.

M. Pobedonostzeff, however, was not quite so destitute of the subtlety of the ecclesiastic as to leave with his opponents the advantage of saying that they had been banished without even the semblance of an option to remain. The two men who had been secretly accused, and condemned unheard, were sent for and informed that if they would sign a paper, a copy of which was given them, they would be permitted to remain in the country of their birth.

This paper set forth a pledge that they would never again take part in any Bible-readings small or great, and that they would never, under any pretext, hold any communication with their fellow-subjects and fellow-Christians the Stundists and the Molokani of the south.

Of course they refused to sign this pledge, which seems to justify the inference that in M. Pobedonostzeff's opinion Bible-readings are more dangerous to Russia than habitual drunkenness, reckless gambling, habitual lying, and shameless adultery.

Against none of these has a pledge ever been exacted by the Procurator of the Holy Synod. M. Pashkoff, who has large estates, asked for leave to visit them to put his affairs in order. His request was refused. At last fourteen days' grace were reluctantly extended him. Count Korff's wife lay ill; he pleaded that for her sake the execution of the decree might be postponed. His request was refused. M. Pashkoff and Count Korff were then cast out from Russia as too dangerous to be permitted to live within the dominions of the Tzar.

## CHAPTER VII.

### PERSECUTION NAKED AND UNASHAMED.

So far my narrative of the Pashkoffski. Now I give place to M. Pobedonestzeff. Nothing that the most indignant commentator can say in condemnation of the treatment to which the unfortunate Evangelicals were subjected can compare for severity with the effect which M. Pobedonestzeff's own account of his action must produce on the mind of any civilised man. Here, in his own official documents, we have persecution naked and unashamed. There are some slight mistakes in these official memoranda, but, on the whole, I should be well content to have the case between M. Pobedonestzeff and M. Pashkoff decided upon the *ex parte* statement of the former. The official indictment of M. Pashkoff is to any Western reader an unanswerable condemnation of M. Pobedonestzeff. The self-portraiture of the intolerant persecutor who brands as criminal the preaching of God's Word because the preacher is not licensed by the authorities, leaves nothing to be desired on the score of completeness and fidelity. It is sufficient to read these to understand M. Pobedonestzeff, and to understand also that while his ascendancy continues, Russia, in matters of religious liberty, must be regarded as a mediæval and barbarous Power rather than a civilised State of the nineteenth century.

A Humble Memorandum of the Chief Procurator of the Most Holy Synod to His Imperial Majesty in May, 1880.

After the departure of Lord Radstock, who during his long stay here preached and held prayer-meetings among the upper classes, which, I regret to say, he did without being hindered, his follower M. Pashkoff began to preach in the Russian language. He has now been preaching for two years, and this he has done without permission, the Government laying no restraint upon him—in contravention of the law (Article No. 126 of the Statute for the Prevention of Crimes) which forbids the holding of any meetings in the capital unknown to and without the approval of the Authorities.

At first M. Pashkoff confined himself to preaching in the circle of his friends—ladies and gentlemen of the upper classes; but he soon proceeded to address the common people. He frequented the cabmen's lodgings and other similar meeting-places of the working people. The Russian people, who are generally very fond of hearing anything of a religious nature, assembled in great numbers to hear these sermons. M. Pashkoff distributed among the people books (tracts) translated from foreign languages, or written in the narrow spirit of the Radstock sect.

During the present year the meetings at M. Pashkoff's house have increased in numbers, and are increasing from week to week. Besides visiting the cabmen's lodgings, M. Pashkoff throws open the splendid halls of his mansion for prayer-meetings, to which all who like may come, from ladies of the upper classes down to the lowest workmen. These halls already prove to be too small for these meetings. Last Sunday more than 1,500 persons were present, representing every grade of society. Many went out of curiosity; others—mostly persons of the common stamp—in order to hear something about religion. Many persons, particularly those in the higher walks of life, are fanatically attached to those meetings, and hope to find in them some new revelation of faith. M. Pashkoff has now introduced a peculiar order of prayer according to the Protestant fashion. Everywhere you find laid out hymn-books, translations into coarse Russian verses of extracts from a collection of well-known English hymns. M. Pashkoff ascends the pulpit, gives out the number of the hymn in the hymn-book, his family accompanying him on the harmonium, and a hymn is sung by the choir, joined by the voices of those assembled who follow the text in the book. Then a sermon is preached by M. Pashkoff, after which another hymn is sung. M. Pashkoff in his sermons, which are extremely one-sided, brings prominently forward Lord Radstock's teaching, viz., love Christ,\* do not trouble yourself about good works, no good work will save you, Christ has already saved us once for all, and nothing further is needed. This doctrine, laid down in the one-sided and narrow way in which M. Pashkoff repeats it, is extremely dangerous. The effect of such teaching

---

\* This, of course, is an obvious and familiar misrepresentation of the Evangelical doctrine. Good works were always preached, and what is more, were practised as a result of salvation, but salvation itself was declared in the words of the Apostle Paul to be by faith and not by works.

on the masses will be to create an indifference to sin, and to form an empty and fantastic faith and a love to Christ at once chimerical and presumptuous. But what is still more important is the fact, that although M. Pashkoff repudiates being a sectarian, he in fact shuns the Orthodox Church and repudiates it. He preaches without having received the blessing of the Church (to say nothing of permission from the civil authorities), and puts himself on a Protestant footing, orders his prayer-meetings after the Protestant fashion, and carefully avoids saying anything in reference to the Most Holy Virgin Mother of God, or to the Saints—thus putting aside the doctrines of the Orthodox Church. We have been informed that out of these meetings preachers have sprung up who openly forbid the worship of and deny the Most Holy Virgin, the Saints, and the Holy Images. We have been given to understand that some cabmen and workmen have turned preachers, and address the common people. It is said that M. Pashkoff himself, when on his estate of Nijni-Novgorod during the summer season, preaches in a more decided tone. Count A. P. Bobriusky preaches in the same spirit on his estate in the Government of Toula (last year he spent at Lausanne, but is now returned home). In Petersburg one of the most ardent admirers of Lord Radstock, Julia Zasetsky, the daughter of the partizan Davidoff, has been working in the same spirit for many years and with great zeal, having under her care the night houses in the suburbs of St. Petersburg; she goes to these places to preach and hold prayer-meetings, in which she avoids mentioning the Virgin Mary and the saints. I am sorry to have to state that the authorities have been treating this movement with indifference, though it has been going on under the very eyes of every one, and has greatly shocked all those who are devoted to the Church. If persons in the Government mentioned it at all it was only to ridicule the movement; but in such matter there is nothing to laugh at. The movement is far more important and dangerous than it may seem at first sight, and it is visibly gaining ground. These preachers are all of small capacities, of narrow-minded dispositions—but such men are the most dangerous as founders of sects, for their stupidity makes them all the more persevering, obstinate, and concentrated, and these are the very things calculated to work upon the masses of the people. By way of illustration we may point to the dissemination of new socialistic hallucinations, the instruments of which are these very men, stupid and narrow-minded. The alienation of our upper classes from their own Church and her institutions, and their ignorance of the Church and people, fully account for the numerous instances of secession to the Romish Church during the first quarter of this century. To this same cause we may trace the enthusiasm for Lord Radstock and M. Pashkoff shown by the ladies and even by gentlemen of the upper classes in St. Petersburg. On the other hand, many from among the common people may be taken by this schism just as they are entrapped by various other schisms which are continually springing up into existence. In the popular mind, along with a deep sense of religion, there exists a belief in the mysterious sense of the letter of the Holy Scripture—this is the reason why all Russian sects have for foundation of their faith some one text of Holy Scripture misunderstood or perverted. A man who believes in some peculiar interpretation of a passage in Holy Scripture becomes its obstinate defender, and a fanatic follower of the sect based upon it. The Church alone possesses the full, clear, catholic interpretation of the whole text in the sense of a catholic belief, and every one who separates himself from the Church, or sets himself up for a preacher, becomes a sectarian. M. Pashkoff is just such a self-called preacher, and he tries to catch people by isolated passages of Holy Writ, which he repeats in various ways, obstinately and perversely, without taking any notice of the teaching of the Church, setting aside this her teaching altogether. He is dangerous, because he calls into existence a new sect which, rising in the north, from the capital, and from among the upper classes of society, threatens to coalesce with the *Stunda* which sprung among the peasants of the south-west of Russia. He is dangerous because the people listen to his addresses, at first unconsciously, without taking into consideration how this teaching stands to the Church, and then after they have listened for some time, and drink in that which has been spoken to them backed by texts, they suddenly become a sect separated from the Mother Church and hostile to her. Therefore, before it be too late, it seems necessary without delay to put a stop to Pashkoff's meetings, and to others of the same kind, and to try to prevent the spreading of the new sect, in reference to which the Church and the State, which have been undivided in Russia, cannot remain unconcerned.

It is necessary—

(1) Without any further delay to recur to the measure foreseen in the 126th Clause of the Statute concerning the Prevention of Crimes, viz., to forbid the Pashkoffs' self-appointed prayer-meetings and sermons.

(2) In consequence of the evident enthusiasm of M. Pashkoff about the exclusive nature of his teaching, and his love of propaganda, it is necessary to send M. Pashkoff away from Russia, if only for a time.

(3) To take active measures against similar meetings and sermons in St. Petersburg and other parts of Russia, if such should take place.

(4) To forbid Lord Radstock to visit Russia.

(5) In order to gratify the religious want which drew the people to M. Pashkoff's meetings, it is necessary to call similar meetings and have prayers in the spirit of the Orthodox Church, with the assistance of the ablest and most zealous priests. This must be the care of the Church authorities in the capital as well as in the various dioceses.

AN EXTRACT FROM A CONFIDENTIAL REPORT OF THE CHIEF PROCURATOR OF THE MOST HOLY SYNOD TO THE MINISTER FOR THE HOME DEPARTMENT, DATED 22ND APRIL, 1882. UNDER NO. 81.

In May, 1880, with the consent of the Minister for the Home Department, and of Count Loris Melikoff, I presented to the late Emperor a memorandum concerning the activity of M. Pashkoff; of which I now enclose a copy.

This investigation was owing to the arrest, in Ostroff, of an inhabitant named Zypkine, in consequence of an information laid against him, that he preached a doctrine hostile to the Church, and persuaded people to burn the Holy Images. It was ascertained that this man had been detained in a prison * where M. Pashkoff used to preach; that he resided for some time in Geneva and became a Calvinist, and that M. Pashkoff sent him to preach. There was found on Zypkine a letter from M. Pashkoff, in which M. Pashkoff called him brother in Jesu, and encouraged him to preach. Then on the 9th of May, 1880, I received from Loris Melikoff a communication under No. 403, stating that he, acknowledging the urgent necessity, for the sake of order in the State and social peace, to put a stop to the prayer-meetings at M. Pashkoff's house, and to other of the same kind, as also to prevent the further spreading among the people of this false religious doctrine, had presented to the Emperor a report in which he proposed to charge a Special Commission with the deliberation and working out of the necessary measures. In consequence of this, it pleased His Imperial Majesty to order a Special Commission, under the direction of Count Valouieff, consisting of the following persons :—The Chief Procurator of the Most Holy Synod, the Minister for the Home Department, the Chief Commander of the 2nd Section of His Imperial Majesty's Chancery, the State Secretary Kakhanoff, and Count Loris Melikoff.

The conference took place on the 10th of May, 1880, and they were unanimously of opinion that it was necessary to take immediate steps to put a stop to the obnoxious propaganda of M. Pashkoff, about which an official report was drawn and signed by all the members. These suggestions were honoured by the approval of the Emperor, in consequence of which, on the 25th May, 1880, under No. 475, an order was issued by Loris Melikoff to the Governor in charge of the capital, to the following effect :—

In the year 1878, in St. Petersburg, at Colonel Pashkoff's, prayer-meetings began to be held, which at the time drew the attention of the Government, in consequence of which, in accordance with the Imperial wishes, the Metropolitan Police received orders not to allow such meetings, prohibited by the law, to take place ; but, notwithstanding this, such meetings not only did not cease, but in the current year assumed still greater dimensions—being thrown open to all men of every station in life and to persons of every age, thus giving birth to imitators among the followers of the doctrine preached by M. Pashkoff. Taking into consideration that by the law (Clause 79d. 126) all meetings unknown to and disallowed by Government are prohibited, and that, by Canonical Rules, preaching the Word of God is not allowed to persons who are not duly appointed to do so by the Church authority, I, upon the ground of the Imperial order given to me, and after having obtained the consent of the Minister for the Home Department, ask your Honour to see that in future no prayer-meetings be permitted to be held either at M. Pashkoff's or

---

* This was incorrect ; Zypkine had never been in prison. The Procurator confused him with another man.

at the abodes of his followers without being known and allowed by the authorities of St. Petersburg; and that the person shall not preach God's Word in private lodgings and apartments. In case any persons break the above-mentioned regulation, you must let me know without delay, in order that I may give further orders. In reference to this I received from Count Loris Melikoff the information under No. 485, countersigned for Loris Melikoff by P. Besobrasoff; and at the same time, in accordance with the suggestion of the Council, the Emperor ordered M. Pashkoff to leave for a time St. Petersburg and Russia.

After the announcement of the Imperial order the meetings ceased for a time, and M. Pashkoff left to go abroad.

Meanwhile, the Police authorities were changed in St. Petersburg, and the former strict orders were, as it seems, forgotten. Taking advantage of this, last year M. Pashkoff renewed his obnoxious activity, and in the current year he increased and extended his operations, having acquired new fellow-workers, of whom the chief is the ex-Minister of Ways and Roads, Count A. P. Bobrinsky, who now preaches openly in St. Petersburg.

Before the commencement of Lent, Lord Radstock reappeared in St. Petersburg, and opened his meetings with the assistance of his lady admirers, known to your Excellency, and belonging to the highest classes of society, I am ashamed to state. At this time I gave verbal communication concerning this to your Excellency and to the Head Police Master of St. Petersburg, and asked that Lord Radstock might be sent away without delay, pointing to the above-mentioned suggestion of the Council—Lord Radstock being the chief cause of the mischief.

I now consider it my duty to draw the attention of your Excellency to the increasing activity of M. Pashkoff, coupled with the remarkable boldness, about which I receive from all quarters, not only from the Most Holy Synod, but also from private individuals, information and bitter complaints.

This activity is particularly obnoxious, because it receives fanatical tendency, and goes on in the spirit of Jesuitism and intolerance. So early as 1880 I was told* that M. Pashkoff and his agents persuaded the working people on the foundry to throw away their crucifixes, backing their persuasions by presents and help in need. When I personally reproached M. Pashkoff with this, he did not deny this fact. Now, M. Pashkoff, availing himself of his wealth, tries to allure to his doctrine the common and poor people; and as for his doctrine, I am sorry to say it advocates alienation from the Orthodox Church, creating enmity towards her, her institutions, and ministers, with the flat denial of the worshipping of God's Mother and the adoration of the Holy Images. M. Pashkoff has opened here† a free eating-house, to which people are admitted under

---

\* If so, I am assured that the Procurator was told a lie, as many better men have been before him. There is not one word of truth in this second-hand libel. M. Pashkoff has always denied it, and has in vain challenged any one to prove it.

† This also is incorrect. The eating-house was "free" to all who paid for their meals, but in no other sense.

the condition of listening to the sermons preached by M. Pashkoff and Count Bobrinsky. He and Count Bobrinsky have opened an asylum in which the poor are admitted under the same conditions. In many families discord has already been created between the members who have accepted M. Pashkoff's teaching and those who have not; this discord is the keener because the followers of M. Pashkoff accept his hostile feeling against the Orthodox Church.

M. Pashkoff's activity is not limited to the capital. His agents, recruited from among all classes of society, and not unfrequently from ex-prisoners, who pretend to be converted by him to the true faith, in the capacity of missionaries further his principles in the different parts of Russia where his teaching has already taken root. Now in the clerical department is collected in all dioceses information about different sects. From some dioceses comes positive information about the formation of a new sect, which has received the name of Pashkoffski or Evangelicals. Thus, lately I received from the Bishop of Astrakan information of the spreading of the sect of Evangelicals in the Zareff's district; the centre of which is in the village of Pryshyb. The followers of this doctrine already number about 1,500 men. It is openly asserted that this sect is being advanced by M. Pashkoff's agents, who distribute among the people peculiar\* editions of the New Testament with underlined texts, hymn-books translated from the German and the English, and peculiar pamphlets of M. Pashkoff's editing—pamphlets, I am sorry to say, allowed to be printed by the Civil Censor without the knowledge of the Clerical Censor; about which circumstance we corresponded with the Chief Department of Censorship. Among others there is edited Mr. John Bunyan's "Pilgrim's Progress," with remarks of peculiar tendency. I am sorry to say that this book was published without passing under the Censor's eye, and allowed by the Government without asking the Clerical Censor, although its contents are religious, dogmatic, and purely Protestant. All the above circumstances compel me to beg your Excellency to direct your attention to the activity of M. Pashkoff, and to give orders to carry out the Imperial edict of 1880. I think that Lord Radstock ought to be sent away at once from Russia, and strictly forbidden to return, and M. Pashkoff and Count Bobrinsky must be invited to leave for foreign parts.

To these documents I only add one remark. A trustworthy Russian assures me that he knows personally two servants who received costly "presents and help in need" from some members of the Pashkoffski, on condition that they would abstain from going to church. I should like to cross-examine these servants as to the nature of this contract, which would seem to argue more imbecility and extravagance on the part of the Pashkoffski

---

\* There were no "Peculiar" Editions. The only version issued was that authorised by the Synod.

than falls to the lot of ordinary mortals; but granting, for the sake of argument, that I choose to pay a man to leave his church, that is surely less heinous than to pay a woman to consent to the commission of a deadly sin. But no one proposes to expel from Russia those by whose payments the houses of ill fame are maintained. A Russian boldly countered this argument by saying that the payments of the patrons of the *maisons tolerées* only concerned the body, whereas those who purchased apostasy from the Church sinned against the soul! Occupants of such different standpoints naturally find argument difficult and agreement impossible.

In addition to the official memorandum of M. Pobedonestzeff I may quote the following extract from the communication of the Bishop of Moghileff, dated the 27th of March, 1884. The Governor of Moghileff had urged the Emperor to take measures against the Stundists, the Emperor had referred the matter to the Synod, and the Synod instructed the Bishop of Moghileff to report on the subject. Of course he concurred. He wrote—

> Stundism, in its further development, may greatly shake the foundations of the true religious belief of the common people, and spread among them a mistrust of the lawful authorities.

Which is no doubt true when the lawful authorities ignore the elementary rights of the human conscience. The Bishop deplores the obstinacy of the Stundists, much in the same way that Laud deplored the wilfulness of the Presbyterians, when Jenny Geddes flung her famous stool at him and his prelatical tippets:—

> They not only will not give up their errors, but even scoff at all the admonitions tending to bring them back to the true path.

Wherefore, concludes this logical Bishop:—

> Taking into consideration all these facts, we cannot but recognise the justice of the measures proposed by the Governor of Moghileff concerning the extermination of Stundism, by restraining the liberty of action and of disposal of property by the local leaders, and by putting them under serveillance. Particularly is this so with respect to the chief heretics. This measure is quite expedient, and in accordance with the meaning of the 41st clause of the statute concerning the prevention

of crime, and the necessity of this measure is such that without putting it into practice, without withdrawing all the external supports of Stundism, all the exhortations of the clergy might prove powerless to bring back the erring ones into the bosom of the Orthodox Church, and to prevent the further spreading of Stundism.

Seldom has the impotence of the Church unless it can command the help of Cæsar been more frankly admitted by a representative of the spiritual power.

## CHAPTER VIII.

### THE FUTILITY OF PERSECUTION.

THERE are, I fear, comparatively few incidents in the Muscovite annals that impress the Western imagination. Yet there is a period in Russian history which is as full of the highest human and spiritual interest as the long struggle which the English and Scotch Puritans waged with the Stuarts. The difference between the two is simple. We got rid of our Stuarts at last, whereas in Russia the Nonconformists got the worst of it. The great religious revolt of the Raskolniks, or Old Believers, against the innovations introduced by the patriarch Nikon in 1659, gave rise to a fierce persecution. It is true that the immediate causes of that revolt were but trifling. The question whether you make the sign of the cross with three fingers or with two, whether you spell Jesus with the "e" or without it as "Jsus," whether you stamp the wafers with a cross which has four equal beams or which has the upright larger than the cross-beams, whether you sing Hallelujah twice or thrice, whether you use five instead of seven wafers in celebrating the mass, and whether you march in procession westward or eastward round the church—all these things seem to the Western mightily unimportant. But these questions, absurdly trivial though they seem to us, gave rise to a bitter persecution which more than anything else justifies the confidence which we repose in the conscientious integrity and grim tenacity of conviction which characterises the Russian people. For the last two hundred years the true life of the Russian people has been religious, not political. In things political the Russian is often a mere pawn moved hither and thither in uniform as it seems good to the Tzar; it is in matters religious that he has lived an active life. It is in this channel the Russian's thought has run, and in this channel it runs to this day. There are no political parties in Russia, but the whole land is honeycombed with religious sects. That is equivalent to saying that the peasants think about religion; they don't think about politics. Where parties do not exist, political life is dead; where there is thought there must be division, for no too human minds are cast in the same mould. On all subjects outside the exact sciences, the more thought, the more diversity of opinion; it is only those who never think who never differ.

The attempt which M. Pobedonestzeff is making is but the repetition of an experiment which failed so disastrously two hundred years ago as to fill us with good hope as to the issue of the present persecution. It was the persecution by the dominant Orthodox in the seventeenth century which gave to the Old Believers, who clung to the ancient unreformed rite, that vigour and vitality which they have never lost. There has seldom been a more striking illustration of the futility of persecution. If the Government could but have left the Old Believers alone the schism might have died out. But with the fatuity natural to Governments which meddle in spiritual affairs, the authorities would not leave them alone. Angry at being opposed by a pack of ignorant Moujiks, the Russian Government of that day decided that it would make short work of the Raskol, with the result that to this day a dozen millions of the best Russians under the Tzar's sceptre are devoted adherents of the Old Rite. No Englishman or American reading the story of the persecution of the Old Believers can help being impressed by the extraordinary resemblance between it and the persecution of the Puritans.

As America was colonised by the refugees from the Laudian persecution, so the great backlands of Muscovy owed their peopling to the flight of those who sought amid the wolves and the bears of the trackless forest, or in the vast expanses of the steppe, freedom to worship God. There are scores of Russian Massachusetts planted out in the wilderness, communities founded by exiles for conscience' sake, who were pursued year after year with relentless animosity by rulers whose realm contained no better or more valuable subjects. As the persecution of the Covenanters supplies the heroic element in the history of the Lowland Scotch, so the persecution of the Raskol from 1682—1712 supplies to the Russian mind an awful background in which all the sublimer human virtues are seen in a state of heroic development. Nor can any one, no matter how far removed he may be in race or in religion from these sturdy peasants, fail to feel some human pride at the thought of the magnificent endurance of these simple men and women in withstanding during the lifetime of a whole generation the terrible vengeance of a ruthless Government.

The persecution was fiercest in the reign of the Empress Sophia Tzarevna. The Raskol, she decreed, was to be exterminated. Any not attending Church were to be interrogated—if necessary, under torture—to ascertain whether they were dissenters, and who had perverted them from the Orthodox faith. Any Raskolnik who was discovered was knouted until he recanted. If he was obdurate, he was burned alive.* Baptists were burnt alive without permission to save their lives by recantation. The Orthodox who did not heartily join in the Raskol hunt were knouted and fined. Then, as Charles Kingsley would have said, began "a slaughter great and grim." Thousands are said to have been done to death, amid all circumstances of horror. They were to be exterminated. The knout, the stake, the dungeon, did their work. The heroism, the constancy, the splendid daring of these poor peasants and unlettered women, were a baptism of blood to the slowly awakening intelligence of Russia. Minds previously impervious to the teachings of the Old Believers were smitten with conviction when they heard the doctrines of the Raskol proclaimed between the blows of the knout or chanted amid the smoke and flame of the martyr's fire. In vain the Government redoubled its severity, organising Raskol hunts and threatening with death all who did not co-operate in exterminating this abominable heresy. The Russian Nonconformists laughed at their vengeance; and as if in fierce defiance of the persecutor's stake, invented the awful doctrine of "the baptism of fire," by which they burnt themselves voluntarily to death in great holocausts of hundreds at a time. In the thirty years it

* Kostomaroff: "Historical Monographs," vol. xii. "History of the Raskol," p. 374. Also article by Abramoff in "Memoirs of the Country" (1884), p. 96.

is estimated that no fewer than 10,000 men and women burnt themselves to death in the north of Russia alone.*

On two occasions as many as 1,500 perished in one great conflagration. Against such people what could all the troops and all the hangmen of all the Tzars effect? At last, after scores of thousands had perished, Peter, although denounced by them as the actual incarnation of Antichrist, left them to live in peace, on condition they paid a double poll tax. They continue under disabilities down even to the present day. But their numbers have increased instead of diminishing, and now, besides the original Raskolniks, there are as many new Sectarians, all representing dissent from the lifeless formalism of the Orthodox Church,† and all subject more or less to the displeasure of the Procurator of the Holy Synod.

In May, 1883, thanks to the influence of General Ignatieff, who was then Minister of the Interior, some concessions were made to the Old Believers in a law which constitutes the charter of their liberties.

Its limitations are somewhat considerable. Starshinas who are Sectarians are not allowed to take any part in the business of the commune. Sectarians must have the ratification of the authorities, if they wish to fulfil any civic duties. Sectarians may repair their meeting-houses if they can obtain the permission of the authorities, but there is to be no change made in the external appearance of such places of worship. The opening of a meeting-house can only be permitted by special order of the Minister of the Interior, after communicating with the

* Abramoff: "Memoirs of the Country" (1884). pp. 111, 112.

† See Haxthausen's "Russian Empire," vol. i., p. 278. "It appears clear that if the Eastern Church does not, and soon, throw off subjection to outward forms, develop her theology, and give that instruction to the people of which she is undoubtedly capable, she will inevitably lose her influence, opposed as they are by the speculative tendencies of the present time, which are set forth and manifested in these sects, and deep wounds will be inflicted on her." So wrote Baron Haxthausen as far back as 1843. Yet when Lieutenant-General Alexander Kirèeff, one of the most orthodox of the Orthodox, this year proposed that, with a view to the promotion of a spiritiual revival in the Eastern Church, an Œcumenical Council of the Orthodox Churches should be summoned in Russia, the Censor exercised his authority to prevent for several months the subject being discussed in the Russian press.

Procurator of the Holy Synod. Even then the ceremony must be performed without any solemnity. They are not allowed to open monasteries and hermitages; no Sectarian meeting-house is to be allowed to assume the external appearance of an Orthodox temple, neither may they be allowed to have bells. No Sectarians may publicly show themselves in procession or in vestments. Neither are they allowed to carry holy images through the streets, except in case of a funeral, when one holy image may be borne before the bier. Neither are they allowed to sing in the streets or in public places. How wretched must have been their condition, when such a charter as this was hailed with enthusiasm as a vast stride in the direction of religious liberty!

The Tzar has no more faithful subjects than his Raskolniks. Like all dissenters, their position of protest leads them to examine more closely than those who go with the stream, the grounds of the faith that is in them. They are more sober, and, they tell me, as a rule more intelligent. In doctrine the majority do not differ very much from the Orthodox; but because of their two-fingered sign of the cross, their omission of "e" in Jesus, and other trivialities, this competent and trustworthy class of citizens is practically disfranchised, and treated as if they were beyond the pale of the Empire, except so far as they suffer its disabilities and bear its burdens.

The new sects, which represent the rise of a more intelligent faith, will naturally command more sympathy in the West than the Old Believers. Yet they too were persecuted at the outset with almost as much fierceness—allowing for the difference of century—as were the Raskolniks by the Tzarevna Sophia. The Molokani, or milk-eaters, who owe their name to the fact that they drink milk on fast-days, trace their origin to a tailor who, at the close of the eighteenth century, was arrested, knouted, and banished to Siberia.

The accession of Nicholas was marked by a revival of the persecution of this inoffensive sect of Protestant Evangelicals. At Saratoff, two of their leaders were publicly knouted to death.* The spectacle, instead of breaking the spirit of their followers, multiplied their numbers, and to this day the Molokani have more than held their own against official persecution. Like our

---

* Kostomaroff: "Historical Monographs," vol. xii., pp. 442, 443.

Quakers, they refuse to swear and refuse to fight. When taken by the Conscription they are enrolled without the oath, and are employed among the non-combatants. That which the knout and the stake failed to effect is not likely to be achieved by the fussy worrying of the present régime. The Stundists, who are the most powerful of the Protestant sects of the South, have had to share the ordeal which is usually allotted to the leaders of a spiritual revival. It is the appointed way of all successful propagandists. Christianity itself would have perished in Jerusalem but for the persecution that drove the apostles out into the larger world. The Stundists made converts chiefly because of the advertisement afforded them by persecution. When Michael Ratusbury was put on his trial a second time and accused of spreading Stundism in Ekaterinasloff, he made a reply which contains in a nutshell the secret of the growth of religion all the world over. He said:—

"I had not the time to propagate the Stunda all over Kherim. But when the police came from the town to arrest me, and assembled the people, the priest came also, and when the people talked to him on Scriptural matters he could prove nothing from the Scripture. Then it was that the people began to doubt whether he was well versed in the Scriptures himself. When I was cast into prison all knew that I was locked up because I had read the Gospel. They wondered exceedingly, and all who could read procured the Gospel, and began to read for themselves. When I was locked up for the second time people wondered again, and began to search after the Gospel with greater zeal, to read it. That is how our doctrines have spread, and not as some people think, through my having propagated it. *

The real cause of the religious revival in Russia is the dissemination of the Bible. Imagine the effect—the natural and inevitable effect—of placing in the hands of the enthusiastic and imaginative peasant the Gospels and the Old Testament, and enabling him to contrast the ideal of the spiritual life as conceived by Isaiah and Paul, and the formalism and apathy of the Orthodox clergy. "The foundation and strength of Stundists," said an Orthodox priest, "are to be sought in the spread of popular education among the people." Dissent is rooted in reading the Bible. It is so in this country—it is so in Russia.

Sixty years ago the Emperor Nicholas suppressed the

* The Russian Peasantry, vol. ii., p. 570.

Russian branch of the Bible Society. To-day M. Pobedonestzoff still allows the Bible to be circulated, but if he is logical he will have to follow in the footsteps of the men of 1826. The Minister of Public Instruction of that day saw in the Bible Society "a revolutionary association, whose sole objects were to shake the foundations of religion, to spread unbelief among the faithful, to kindle civil war and foster rebellion in Russia."

Against such a system of oppression as Admiral Sheshkoff represented, the Bible is the most dangerous of all weapons. If M. Pobedonestzeff has not yet prohibited the circulation of the Bible in Russia, he has suppressed the Society for the Encouragement of Moral and Religious Reading. This admirable and inoffensive Society was founded in 1876, with the approval of the Synod of the Government. All books and pamphlets issued by the Society were placed under the care of both censors, civil and ecclesiastical, the police, Governors, and the Minister of the Interior. Notwithstanding all this apparatus for securing the orthodoxy of these publications, the priests and bishops kept up an intermittent agitation against the Society, as disseminating Protestant doctrines of faith and morals. Especially was the Holy Synod exercised by the care taken to distribute far and wide in Russia the works of a certain Mr. John Bunyan, whose "Holy War" and "Pilgrim's Progress" were regarded with special favour by the Evangelicals in the diocese of Astrakhan. The result was that the Society was suppressed, and its tracts confiscated. The latter, however, were subsequently restored after considerable trouble.

It is not my intention, even if it were within my power, to tell in detail the story of the persecution which has gone on intermittently ever since, and which I am assured is going on to this day, in all parts of Russia. Every now and then decent, respectable, law-abiding citizens are swooped down upon by the police, and banished to the Caucasus or elsewhere, for no other sin than that of worshipping God according to their conscience. I have already described how Englishmen in the service of Colonel Pashkoff were treated. Russians appear to have been even less mercifully dealt with. One Almanovsky, cashier on Colonel Pashkoff's Tamboff estate, was thrown into gaol for three months, and only released on signing an agreement never again to enter the Colonel's service. His offence was that he had given away New Testaments, printed by the Holy Synod, distributed tracts authorised for distribution by the Censor, and had spoken to some of his neighbours about Christ. Another employé, M. Kirpitchnikoff, head forester on the same estate, was accused by some peasants, whom he had a short time before punished for stealing wood, of having spoken blasphemously about the icons, or sacred pictures. He denied it absolutely, but against a heretic any accusation seems to be readily believed. Kirpitchnikoff was condemned on this tainted testimony, and sentenced to transportation to Siberia. Even if the offence—such as it is—had been proved, such a sentence grates horribly upon a civilised ear. To speak irreverently about a fetish is no doubt dangerous among savages, but free criticism of sacred pictures in a civilised state is not usually regarded as a crime deserving transportation. Kirpitchnikoff was chained hand and foot, and compelled to proceed thousands of miles from Tamboff to the province of Yeneseisk, walking part of the way in company with murderers, robbers, and ruffians of the deepest dye. All attempts to procure a re-hearing of his case failed.

I was assured—for, of course, I cannot possibly pretend to know these things otherwise than on the testimony of those who seemed to me honest and truthful witnesses—that similar hardships are inflicted upon the Evangelicals in all parts of Russia. Men are compelled to give up their situations, families are expelled from the cities where they have established their homes; others are deprived of their business. Others again are either interned in their own villages, or banished to distant provinces. Their offence is in most cases the same. They give away a Testament, or hold a prayer-meeting, or invite their neighbours to a Bible reading. In listening to the recital of these sufferings inflicted upon the possessors of a living faith by the professors of a dominant Orthodoxy, I felt as if I had suddenly been transported to the period when Prynne was pilloried, and the Puritans crossed the Atlantic in the *Mayflower*.

The constant pressure of the clergy to choke off competition by the arbitrary use of the sword of Cæsar is occasionally varied by exceedingly interesting attempts to hold public disputations for the conversion of the heretics. As many as 6,000 persons have been gathered together to listen to debates between missionary priests on the one side, and the spokesmen of the Sectarians on the other. Unfortunately the leaders of the latter are exiled, and their followers have a natural dread of being condemned to the same fate if they are too bold to take the lead in public controversy. Hence the challenges and the insults of the missionary priests usually fail in eliciting adequate response; and if unlettered men, learned in the Bible, stand up to confute the errors of the Orthodox, they are apt to be overwhelmed with clamour and threatened with violence. On one occasion at St. Petersburg a charwoman, who was pointed out to me as an object of interest, astonished an immense concourse by replying with perfect self-composure to the denunciations of the priest. From the Sectarian's point of view these Conferences were unmixed good. They stirred up the minds of the people; they afforded a platform at the expense of the Government, where the spiritual members of the proscribed sect could at least testify to the earnestness with which they clung to their faith, and the sincerity and reverence with which they approach the Scriptures; and they too often led to those displays of unfairness by which it seems to be the fate of an intolerant majority to create prejudice against the faith which resorts to such ignoble weapons.

These Conferences were not confined to St. Petersburg. The *Novoe Vremya* published some years ago an interesting narrative of Conferences held at Vladikavzkaz, in the Caucasus, between the Baptists and the Orthodox. The passage from the letter of a correspondent, who was evidently no partisan of either party in the dispute, may be accepted as a fairly impartial account by an onlooker of one phase of the controversy. He writes :—

"Powerful and dangerous opponents of the Established Church have appeared in the numerous Russian sects which have found here a rich ground for their propaganda. Of these the most troublesome are the Baptists. They are strong by reason of their sincere attachment to religious principles, and by the exemplary life which they lead; and they naturally became an eyesore to the Orthodox clergy. They were officially recognised as 'not dangerous,' and they circulated their tracts everywhere. The priests seized the tracts, but, to their great annoyance, the police refused to confiscate them. The clergy thereupon finding it necessary to have recourse to other means, decided to hold the usual

Conference. On the first occasion they were greatly defeated. The Baptist orators cleverly contrived matters so as to place the dispute on safe ground for themselves. 'Compare,' said they, 'your lives and ours.' This was not convenient for the established clergy, and they decided to entrust it to an outsider. After some trouble they secured a missionary preacher, who held forth at great length to an immense concourse. The effect of his discourse was, however, destroyed when the police identified him as a lay brother who had been turned out of two monasteries for immoral conduct."

Clearly with such representatives the Orthodox could make but little headway against the Baptists. It was therefore necessary to fall back upon the civil power in order to rid the Caucasus of the Anabaptist heresy. Hence it need surprise no one that in March last year three prominent Evangelicals of Tiflis were suddenly banished to Orenburg by order of the Governor-General, Prince Dondoukoff-Korsakoff. By way of reconciling them to this banishment they were first cast into prison without trial. They were then removed to Orenburg, where, according to my latest information, they still remain. Their alleged crime was Baptist propaganda. With characteristic blundering, one of the three turned out to be not a Baptist but a Lutheran. The discovery of that mistake, however, made no difference in his punishment.

The spectacle which is thus presented to us of the authorities, animated as it were by some strange suicidal mania, spending their time, thought, and energy, in harrying and destroying those who, as all experience has proved, would be the most trustworthy and loyal subjects of the Emperor if they were but allowed to obey their conscience in the matter of religion, is melancholy indeed. The task of governing the enormous expanse of territory which owns the authority of the Tzar is so immense that it would strain the intellectual and moral resources of any nation adequately to discharge it even when every moral and intelligent man and woman was pressed into hearty co-operation with the Government. Political life in Russia, in our sense of the word, is practically extinct. The religious life of the country is much more important. For one who thinks about constitutions and autocracies, there are a score who ponder deeply the things belonging to the Kingdom of Heaven. The genius of the nation has been forced into theological grooves, where, if allowed free scope to luxuriate, it would immensely facilitate the work of government by contributing to create those good citizens without whom no state can be permanently strong or great. But, by a strange fatuity, the evil genius who now darkens the throne of the Tzar as by the shadow of an eclipse, has set itself to harass, to persecute, and to drive into antagonism, the element in Russia which is full of hope and full of promise both for the future of the nation and the stability of the throne.

Against the Catholic Poles, against the German Lutherans, M. Pobedonestzeff may wage war with some plausible semblance of justification. But against the Stundists, against the Molokani, against the Pashkoffski, against the Evangelicals of every shade, only the incorrigible perversity of the persecutor can find a pretext for prosecuting a campaign of extermination. This is a matter far more serious for the Power that persecutes than it is for the remnant who are persecuted. Now, as of old, the blood of the martyrs is the seed of the Church. To-day, as yesterday, suffering alone gives the true faith—the key by which it can unlock the hearts of man. It must needs that offences come, but it is woe unto those by whom they come. When Colonel Pashkoff and Count Korff were exiled they addressed a letter to the Emperor, in which this truth is set forth with much fidelity. They say :—

"The Lord's work in Russia will not be hindered or stopped by our exile. What are in such a work two persons like us? The Lord has many servants who willingly follow His commands, and who are endowed more than we with power and authority from Him. We are punished innocently, but the Kingdom of God will grow with still more power than before, for your good, Sire, and for the good of our dear country. Our undeserved exile will serve to consolidate this work. Such an order from your Government has afflicted all the followers of Christ, but it has also stimulated their zeal. The persecution not only of us but also of books written with the sole object of giving men to understand the love of Christ which passes our understanding—books which are permitted by the Censure, and by Pobedonestzeff himself allowed to be spread abroad, when, in the year 1880, they were seized in Nijni by Count Ignatieff—such a persecution puts upon all the servants of the Lord the duty of propagating orally the knowledge of Christ more than they did before.

"They try to persuade your Imperial Majesty that the so-called Evangelical Sectarians and Baptists are apostates who deny their native land and people, who separate themselves from everything Russian, who are rebels against the supreme authority, and are advocates of the universal levelling of ranks. Allow me, Sire, to tell you positively that such an opinion about them is unjust. They are as much children of Russia as the Orthodox ones, they love you as much as those do; they submit to the Tzar not from fear but from conscience sake and from the desire to fulfil the will of God. Sire, allow me, your loyal subject, who loves you with the love of Christ, and who prays for you and for Russia, to implore you, in the name of Christ. Grant to Russia the supreme good which is in your power, make it lawful for every one to profess openly and without hindrance the hope in the Lord; recognise for us the right to believe as our conscience directs us; blot out all the punishments which are inflicted, equally with thieves and murderers, upon us who, being guided by the Spirit of God, confess Christ, or those who, for conscience sake, leave the Orthodox Church; and then the blessing of the Lord, which is the most precious thing in the world, will be poured upon you, Sire, upon your Imperial family, and upon all Russia."

To that prayer no answer has yet been returned. The Orthodox seem to be in fear for the Church of the Living God if the Ispravnik is not ready with pains and penalties for those who, for conscience sake, leave the Orthodox Church.

For all such timorous ones, alike those who persecute from fear, and those who dread lest that persecution may extinguish "the spark of God" in the Russian Empire, I will conclude with a little apologue of Count Tolstoi's—

" When I hear," said he, " that the Church is perishing, or going to perish, because of this, that, or the other, that is being done by men in power, it reminds me of the story of the boy and the eagle. A little boy rushed one day into the parlour to his father, crying, excitedly, ' Father, an eagle, an eagle in the kitchen! Come quickly and rescue it, for the woman cook will not let it go.' And the father said, ' Peace, my boy. If it were really an eagle it would fly away, nor could a woman cook stand for a moment in its way. Believe me, it is only a hen.' And when I hear that the Church of Christ, which, if it exists at all, is real, eternal, spiritual, and Divine, is going to perish because of what the Government is doing, I think of that eagle caged in the kitchen by the woman cook, and I say to myself, ' Peace, peace; it is no eagle, it is only a hen!' "

# Book VII.
## COUNT TOLSTOI AND HIS GOSPEL.

### CHAPTER I.
#### A WEEK AT YASNAIA POLIANA.

IN Russia and out of Russia, I have found people more interested in the personality of Count Leo Tolstoi, the novelist, than in that of any other living Russian. He is the first man of letters in contemporary Russia, but that alone would not account for the widespread interest in his character. He is a great original, an independent thinker, a religious teacher, and the founder of a something that is midway between a Church, a school, and a socio-political organisation. He not only thinks strange things, and says them with rugged force and vivid utterance—he does strange things; and what is more, he induces others to do the same. A man of genius who spends his time in planting potatoes and cobbling shoes, a great literary artist who has founded a propaganda of Christian anarchy, an aristocrat who spends his life as a peasant—such a man in any country would command attention. In Russia he monopolises it, and the fame of his originalities has spread abroad so far until it is probable that there are more people anxious to "hear about Tolstoi" in Boston and San Francisco than there are even in Petersburg and Moscow.

When I visited Yasnaia Poliana it was in the last week in May. The prolonged winter had been finally shaken off, and the time of the singing of birds was fully come. At Petersburg the snow was still falling fitfully. But in the night spent on the rail between the two capitals the train seemed to have transported us from Iceland to Italy. The glad surprise of the sunbeams glimmering through the bright green leaves of the trees in the early morning, when the last rays of the setting sun had fallen on snow-wreathed and leafless branches of the great forest, was one of the pleasantest experiences I ever enjoyed in travel. After a day at Moscow, and another in pilgrimage with Countess Ignatieff and her party to the famous Troitsa Monastery, I started for Toula by the Southern Railway. Long after all else in Moscow had faded out of sight, the great cupolas of the temple reared to celebrate the retreat of Napoleon flamed like the glory of the Shekinah above the city which is the Holy of Holies of Orthodox Russia. Five or six hours by rail in the comfortable Russian carriages, with convenient stations well supplied with excellent viands, soon pass, and Toula is reached. Toula is not the nearest station to Yasnaia Poliana, the country seat of Count Tolstoi, but it is the nearest station where conveyances can be obtained. From the roadside stations you have to walk; and if you have a portmanteau, it is better to drive twelve miles than walk two. Driving is cheap in Russia. The vehicle at Toula was not a very imposing equipage, being in appearance something like a dirty, overgrown Bath-chair, but it was comfortable enough. The horse jogged along at a steady trot, and the driver did not charge a couple of roubles for the journey. Toula, the Sheffield of Russia, is as clean as the English Sheffield is dirty. The road to Yasnaia Poliana skirts the suburbs of the town, but you could see the great white churches, which in Hallamshire would have been black with grime in a month. There is a wonderful lack of compactness about Russian towns. They straggle " promiscuous like " over an expanse of country, just as the Russian roads meander cheerfully across the whole width of a field. At every turn you are reminded that the Russians have ample elbow-room. The ruts on the cross road that led from the station to the chaussée were somewhat alarming, but the horse took them as a matter of course, and the springs did not give way. Here, at last, I saw children again. In Moscow and Petersburg the children do not show much in the streets; but in the outskirts of Toula the little urchins were playing on the green as happy and as dirty as any English children fresh from the mystery of mud-pies could wish to be.

Leaving the town behind us, we passed a file of prisoners on the march, with a couple of armed guards, and reached an open common, on which some troops were doing skirmishing drill. The sky was gloriously blue. The larks were singing overhead. The emerald green of the fresh spring grass and growing corn, the dainty verdure of the trees, the bright yellow patches of weeds in the fallow—how fresh and springlike they seemed after the cold grey granite quays of the ice-cold Neva, which I had left only three days before. The road was good and well metalled. It passed through an undulating country, well cultivated, amply but not densely wooded, but certainly not crowded with population. From time to time long strings of little country carts drawn by small ponies would pass laden with hay or corn. The Russian country cart is fearfully and wonderfully made, and combines the maximum amount of dead-weight with the minimum quantity of freight. If we regard an American buggy as representing the ideal of serviceable lightness, the Russian country carts stand at the other extreme of clumsy heaviness. They resemble low wedge-shaped crates, built up on a complicated labyrinth of timber resting on four wheels. The horses are very quiet, and for the most part dispense with the bit. At every verst mile-posts marked the distance traversed, and when we were about one mile distant from Yasnaia Poliana I saw on the right hand of the road in the fields a group regarding me curiously. On coming nearer I recognised two of them as acquaintances I had made in Petersburg; and jumping from my vehicle I found myself in the presence of Count Tolstoi, his two daughters, a niece, and a disciple, the two latter having preceded me on a visit to the Count.

Count Tolstoi is very like his portraits. He is a man of sixty, with iron-grey hair, sun-burned countenance, plentifully furnished with grey beard and moustache. His hair is parted down the middle, and is thick and full. His brow, furrowed with the ploughshare of thought, is broad and massive; his eyes, small and piercing, gleam out beneath bushy brows. His nose, large and prominent, has full and expressive nostrils. The features are so strongly marked that once seen they cannot be soon forgotten. The countenance is one of earnest gravity, with a background suggestive of sad and sombre thought. There is sometimes a childlike sparkle of joyousness in his eye—there is always a kindly accent in his voice; but sometimes the furnace, usually banked up within, blazes forth; the face becomes as black and lowering as a thundercloud, and the whole man trembles and quivers with overmastering passion. He is rather above the average height, and his threescore years have not bowed his stature; but he is no longer as robust as he was. He looked somewhat shrunken and worn, as if time and the ever-burning fire within were making inroads on what was once a stout and stalwart form.

Count Tolstoi dresses *à la moujik*, but not as a nobleman. He wears a coarse dark blouse buttoned up to the breast, and fastened round the waist with a leathern girdle. Collars, cuffs, and such frippery, he eschews. On his head he wore a soft, weather-beaten, brimless hat, and whenever he walked abroad he carried a stout staff. The costume of the disciple was like to that of his master. Simplicity in dress is a distinctive note of the Tolstoian gospel—one among the many points in which it resembles that of the Quakers. The disciple—a young man of culture—had forsaken all in order to propagate the new doctrine. He was in charge of the library of the propaganda at Petersburg, where he had given me samples of all the tracts which they circulated and the pictures by which they instil the Gospel according to Tolstoi through the eyes of the illiterate peasants, so far as it is permitted by the censors.

The daughters of the Count, who were walking with their cousin, a judge's daughter from Petersburg, had just come to the country from their winter home in Moscow. The Count had come by himself some weeks before—walking "a pilgrimage," as he put it, along two and three hundred miles of country roads, sleeping at night in the peasants' huts, and faring as best he could through the day. The Countess, a good, sensible, motherly wife, but for whom the sharp edge of ragged circumstance would make sad havoc of the air castles of the Count, was sorely grieved at the risk he ran; but a wilful man must have his way, and, although the spring had barely begun to soften the chilly breath of lingering winter, Count Tolstoi persisted in shouldering his knapsack, and trudging along the two hundred miles of muddy roads which lay between Moscow and Yasnaia Poliana. The Countess remained behind to be confined of her thirteenth child—a tiny little morsel of humanity, which was just six weeks old at the time of my arrival. She had arrived from Moscow with her family only a day or two before I came. The house, therefore, was in some confusion. The books were not unpacked, and the furniture had hardly recovered from its winter rest.

Of the large family of the Count there are now nine living. The second son is married and settled. The other eight are at home. One was finishing his university course at Moscow. Him I did not see. The eldest son, like his sisters and younger brothers—bright, lively little lads—spoke English very well. The little Alexandrine, who was small enough to sit on the floor and play with her dolls, was the only member of the household who could not speak English, and she was beginning to learn—an English governess having just arrived to take her in charge. There was also a Swiss tutor, who taught the boys French; so that the household was somewhat polyglot.

But this is anticipating. One of the girls took my place in the trap, while I walked through the fields with Count Tolstoi. There was at first an impression of gentleness about his talk, mingled with a frank eagerness as that of a clever child, which contrasted somewhat oddly with his rugged exterior, his beetling brows, and piercing eyes. He spoke English well, although not so fluently as his daughters, who told me that they could not speak Russian as well as they spoke English. Although he never had any difficulty in making himself understood, sometimes when in vehement, earnest conversation, he seemed to grapple half angrily with the unfamiliar tongue, so as to compel it to adapt itself to his meaning. Sometimes, too, he would break out into Russian, and ask his daughter to interpret; but this was slow work, and he always fell back into English, which he spoke very correctly, although with a strongly marked foreign accent.

Climbing over a fence and scrambling across a ditch, we found ourselves in the Count's grounds. They were extensive, but everything was as far removed as possible from the trim propriety of an English park. Everywhere, under the trees, along the walks, in the orchard, and up to the very steps of the house, there was a luxuriant herbage. I suppose an English gardener would have regarded them as weeds, and have broken his heart in despair over them; but here they grew so rankly everywhere that they no more seemed like weeds than do buttercups in a meadow. A couple of comely nut-brown maidens, in the picturesque peasant's dress of Turkey red, were at work in the garden. Here and there a man had mown down the rank overgrowth, but the net impression was one of luxuriant wildness.

The house did not stand in the midst of a trim oasis reclaimed from wild nature, but was planted right in the midst of nature itself, with all its lavish magnificence of verdure. After all, you can hardly wonder at a liking for a free growth which fills the plantations with the fragrance of the lilies of the valley, great bunches of which the little ones used to make it their duty to gather every morning.

The house of Yasnaia Poliana is barely visible through the trees from the highway, from which it stands at a distance of about a mile. The ground slopes downwards to a little stream, and rises again in a slight acclivity, close to the summit of which, at the end of a lordly avenue, stands the white country house of Count Tolstoi. The roof, like all Russian roofs, is of painted sheet-iron; in front of the house stands a raised platform of stone. On the first floor there is a balcony with a verandah. The trees overshadow the house at one end. At the other there is a small flower garden and an open space where the boys played at croquet, and where we had royal fun in trying to teach the household cricket. It was rather difficult, to be sure, with an improvised bat and a soft ball; but we managed famously, the cook promising to become quite an expert, although his habit of always striking twice at the ball, once forward and once backward, was rather bewildering at first. Behind the house stood an open space, in the centre of which was an aged tree, with maimed branches. Under this tree the pilgrims stood in picturesque groups waiting the appearance of the Count, who obeys literally the Scriptural command, " Give to him that asketh of thee, and from him that would borrow of thee turn thou not away." When the Count appeared at the door they would step forward and salute him. He would exchange greetings, and then they entered into conversation. It was here where the Count conducted his inquiries into the theological belief of the pilgrims, and satisfied himself that while they have imbibed the spirit, they know next to nothing of the doctrines of the Christian creed. At the close of the conversation the Count presents them with twopence, or two five-copeck pieces, with which they seemed to depart well satisfied. A very pretty picture it was to see these pilgrims, with their staffs and listed shoon, and clean bright faces, standing under the tree talking to the great novelist, as the sun was slanting westward, and the milkmaids were making their way to the byre.

The kitchen garden and a very extensive orchard lay behind the house. In the front, to the east, stood a summer-house, clean, airy, and comfortable, in the midst of trees and shrubs. At the end of another small avenue leading to the village, which lay on the rising ground on the other side of the stream, was the country villa of a Petersburg judge, who married Countess Tolstoi's sister. Further on again was the farmyard, with the cows, the poultry, and the horses. Some of the poultry were very good; there were any number of cows, and about half a dozen horses, serviceable, useful animals, but none of them so showy as you would find in a similar establishment in England. In front of the house lay the ponds, of which there were three—one large pond, where people bathed and the villagers washed their clothes; two smaller ones, in which the bull-frogs kept up an incessant chorus. No one in England has the faintest notion of the vocal capacity of the Russian frog. He warbles all day and all night —not exactly like a nightingale, but with a variety of note quite incredible to those accustomed to the monotonous croak of the English frog. The larger pond is very pretty, surrounded as it is with great trees, in the shade of which nestle one or two picturesque cottages. The walk round one of the smaller ponds was the favourite resort of Count Tolstoi's mother, and much frequented by him for her sake. All round the house spread woods, crossed by bridle-paths in the most embarrassing confusion. Nothing seemed easier than to find your way from the village to the house; but happening once to take a wrong turning, I wandered a full hour among the trees before I could find my way out. Count Tolstoi at one period in his career had a great passion for tree-planting, and I am really afraid to say how many trees he planted in and around his residence. They are all coming on bravely now, and it was very pleasant under the blazing noonday sun to wander through the endless shady glades of his plantations.

About two or three miles from the house stands the church, which with its cupolas forms a conspicuous object in the landscape. It is at the further end of the second village on the estate. The village near at hand is that where the fire took place, which I have described in a preceding chapter. In the midst of these villagers Count Tolstoi leads a curious patriarchal existence. His pride is to be one of them, and yet he is not one of them. They look up to him with curiosity and affection, not unmixed with respect. No amount of similarity in dress can bridge the chasm that yawns between the baron and the peasant. Count Tolstoi thinks that they understand him. It is all simple to them: he wears their dress to "save his soul." I suspect, however, that the peasant is not quite satisfied with this formula as a complete explanation of the Count's conduct. Nothing could seem to be more idyllic than the relations between Count Tolstoi and the peasant folk. They come to him from miles around to take his opinion, to submit their differences for his adjudication, or to hear his views upon the questions of the day. Before his family came back from Moscow he used to spend his evenings with the peasants, discussing with them the great problems of the time, and doing his best to learn from them what they had to teach those who pride themselves upon their superior culture and greater civilisation. If he can ever be induced to put on record these debates in the nights of that early spring, he will do more for his cause than by the hoeing of many a field of potatoes.

On arriving at the house, Count Tolstoi showed me into a little room on the right-hand side of the entrance. "There," said he, "you can occupy that—sleeping in the little library among the books, and you can dress in the adjoining room, where I dress." The dressing-room was also the sitting-room and work-room of the Count. In the recess by the window lay the shoe-making tools with which he used to employ himself; near the door was a wash-stand and mirror.

"Perhaps you would like to wash now," said he, opening the wash-stand. "You can wash here. When you are done you can empty the water out so," and, suiting the action to the word, the Count stepped outside on the raised terrace in front of the house and flung the dirty water out into the garden. This was done so naturally, and with such an evident unconscious confidence that it was the right thing to do, that you could not feel more than a momentary impression as to the incongruity of the novelist, philosopher, and nobleman, emptying his dirty water for the convenience of his guest. I had been told, moreover, that the Count's simplicity was more theatrical than real —that he posed as a peasant and "did" his hair with a silver comb, and so forth. I saw nothing of this. There was certainly no silver plate or luxurious plenishing in the Count's living-rooms. Everything was severely plain, and in harmony with the desire of its occupant to simplify his life.

At the same time the Tolstoi *ménage* is not that of a peasant. The dreams of the idealist are seldom capable of translation into the prose of actual life, especially when your idealist happens to be married and the father of a large family. Against this law the idealist chafes and frets. But on the whole it is a good thing for the idealist that the wife acts as a guardian angel to break the sudden transition from heaven to earth by shielding the seer from the consequences of too abruptly attempting to realise his dreams. If Count Tolstoi had been celibate, and had been free to carry out his theories to the full, there would now have been no Count Tolstoi. Even the attempts to come within hailing distance of his ideals has injured his health. If he were now, at the age of sixty, to attempt to live solely upon what he could earn as a moujik, he would speedily succumb. It is impossible for men past the prime of life suddenly to adapt themselves to the hardships and privations of the sturdy labourer. From this fate he has been saved by the sound common-sense of the inestimable lady who is the mother of his children, and the head and heart and soul of his household.

Countess Tolstoi, the daughter of a Moscow physician, married the Count nearly thirty years ago, when she was very young. She has borne him thirteen children, and was this year nursing the youngest, as she had nursed all its predecessors. Upon her rests the whole burden of the management of the household at Moscow and at Yasnaia Poliana. She controls, directs, manages everything. To the Count the possession of a house superior to that of a peasant is a sin. In his eyes his family lives in culpable luxury, because they have servants to clean their boots and a cook to prepare their food. He lives in their house, as it were, under protest. The Countess has done all that she could to meet his views. They have simplified their existence. The merry summer parties, when Yasnaia Poliana was crowded with gay and joyous guests, for whose amusement the days were passed in music, dance, and song, and amateur theatricals, have been given up. The young ladies dress simply. Wine has almost disappeared from their table. There has been a minimising of the pomps and vanities of this wicked world. But when it came to be a question of abandoning everything, and going forth to fare as the peasants, the Countess drew the line. She could not do it. For her children's sake, if not for her own, it must not be. The Countess was not unsympathetic to the ideas of her husband. In addition to all her household cares, she has ever taken the keenest interest in the development of his ideas, and has worked laboriously as a copyist and a translator. Count Tolstoi's handwriting is illegible to most mortals. All his MSS. is therefore copied for the printer by his wife. He continually corrects, revises, and rewrites his proofs. All these are copied out by the Countess. "War and Peace" she copied out from end to end no fewer than six times before the novel assumed the final shape that satisfied the fastidious taste of her husband. His last book, "Life," which is short and metaphysical, she copied out sixteen times in its various versions, besides translating it into French. She was at the same time teaching her children music and English, and superintending the sale, circulation, and distribution of the corrected edition of her husband's writings.

Count Tolstoi is, as it were, an honoured guest in his wife's house. He takes no part in its domestic economy, not even as an adviser. He goes and comes when he chooses. He sits down at meals with the family, although he restricts himself to the simplest fare. He is loved, honoured, almost idolised by those around him; but he can never shake off the conviction that his very shelter under his own roof is an inconsistency, a reluctant compromise between principle and expediency. Nothing but the consciousness that the Countess could, if driven to it, invoke the intervention of the law to prevent the abandonment of all the resources on which the family is maintained has restrained him from making away with the Toula estate, as he has surrendered that which lies further east, and from allowing the booksellers to retain all the profits from the sale of his books.

During my week's sojourn at Yasnaia Poliana, the Count did no manual toil. He had not made any shoes for some time, and although he proposed ploughing the field of a peasant woman whose husband was in gaol for horse-stealing, he did not actually get between the stilts. He really did not seem to have sufficient physical strength to do a long day's hard work. He was ailing, and, as he said, rejoicing in the consciousness that every day brought him nearer to death. We were all much concerned at the evident frailty of his constitution. The previous year, when he had hurt his foot against a cart-wheel, he had been laid up for months. This year he was far from well, but he refused to have any advice from a doctor. Physic and the healing art he held in profound disdain, and it was an attempt to secure the advice of the first physician in Moscow which precipitated his departure from Moscow in the spring of this year. The vegetarian regimen which he has adopted was doing him no good. He was steadily pressing forward along the ascetic path. Until last year he enjoyed the soothing cigarette; now tobacco, like wine and flesh meat, is tabooed. The son smokes, but not the father. Meat is served at dinner and supper, but he contented himself with curds, spinach, or vegetables. He still allowed himself tea, almost the only luxury left. Like General Booth, Count Tolstoi is not yet "saved from tea." But that also will probably speedily follow the rest of the superfluities which have been discarded in the pursuit of the simplification of life.

Life at Yasnaia Poliana was ordered somewhat in this wise. Early in the morning, when the dew was heavy on the fields, the women came to work in the garden long before any one was up and about in the house. Very quiet and still were the early hours when I sat writing all alone before breakfast in the little bedroom library, surrounded by the Count's books on their plain, strong shelves of unvarnished and unpainted wood, the only companions of my solitude. About nine o'clock the English governess would take her seat at the samovar with little Sacha, and tea would be served. We never sat down all together to that morning tea-cup. The small boys would have their glass and then run out and play. The Swiss tutor would drop in, and then after an interval the Count. About 10 or 10.30 the young ladies would appear, and then the room would be cleared for breakfast. The Count would take a long walk through the woods, and at half-past twelve the household would gather for the first time for breakfast. After breakfast they would again disperse, some to read, others to walk or to work. At five dinner would be served, and then between dinner and supper the Count and his daughters, with any guest who might be in the house, would go out for a long stroll, either to the railway station to get letters, or to some neighbouring village, returning at sunset to find the hospitable samovar once more on the table, and tea more or less going on till ten o'clock. After ten, there was conversation or reading, until one by one the household went to bed, and so the day came to a close. A quiet, simple country life, diversified by the occasional arrival of friends and relatives, and sustained and ennobled by a constant sense of the world-wide magnitude of the great problems at which the Count was working—that was what I saw at Yasnaia Poliana. A healthy, human, natural life, amidst books, and children, and flowers, and birds, and bees, and live-stock of all kinds, and simple country folk, that was not a bad environment for a thinker who ever hears through the sighing of the trees the moanings of a troubled world, and yet presses onward, nothing doubting, to the light of a clearer and brighter day.

## CHAPTER II.

### "RESIST NOT EVIL."

THE taste for Russian novels is quite of recent growth in England. A dozen years ago there were only a couple of Turgenieff's inimitable romances to be had in English dress. The exquisitely pathetic story of "Liza," and the deeply interesting "Virgin Soil," were published in London, but they had only a limited vogue. Of other Russian novels there were very few translations. The first English translation of any of Dostoyeffsky's books appeared in 1880, a few weeks before his death. "Prince Serebrenni," by Count Alexei Tolstoi, was translated, and Count Leo Tolstoi's "Cossacks;" but that almost completes the list of English translations of Russian romances up to the death of the late Tzar.

The taste for Russian novels in England set in with the new

reign. It began across the Atlantic years before. You could get nearly all Turgenieff's works in English at Philadelphia years before they were published in London. But when once the Russian novel began to be read, it established its popularity. After Victor Hugo, Turgenieff was the first of European novelists, and when Turgenieff died, the sceptre passed to Count Tolstoi. Few great novelists have written so little. His novels, properly so called, consist of the voluminous "War and Peace," "The Cossacks," and "Anna Karenina." The rest of his writings, excluding shorter sketches and stories, are either biographical, educational, controversial, or religious.

I was much more attracted by Count Tolstoi the religious teacher than by Count Tolstoi the literary artist. His later books, dealing with the profounder problems of existence, are disdained by many who bow before the genius of the author of "Anna Karenina." But it was because of "Ma Confession" and "Ma Religion," excellently translated into English under the title of "Christ's Christianity," that I went pilgriming to Yasnaia Poliana. There is a great charm about "Christ's Christianity." Imagine in the last quarter of the nineteenth century George Fox Redivivus in the garb of a Russian nobleman! The spiritual autobiography of the Count seemed to me as I read it one of the most interesting religious books of this generation. A realist and yet a mystic, a rationalist and yet the disciple of the Nazarene, a Russian count, soldier, novelist, and scholar, preaching the doctrine of absolute non-resistance. Was there ever a greater paradox? For many years I have held that the next great wave of religious revival that would influence European development would take its rise in Russia. Here, in the heart of Russia, has arisen a teacher, who stood at the summit of the culture of his generation, and proclaimed in strange, new accents, the old-world message, "Ecce Homo!" There was a bold, uncompromising logic about his literal interpretation of the words of the Evangel; the whole message was saturated in the Socialist ferment of our time, who could say but that this might be the prophet that was for to come?

I remember well my first meeting with one of Count Tolstoi's disciples. A young Russian, who was on a visit to England, was introduced to me as the translator of "Christ's Christianity." I talked eagerly with him about it, but declared that he seemed to lay an altogether disproportionate stress upon the saying, "Resist not evil." He made that text the cornerstone of the whole Christian faith.

"Now," said I, "if you were going down the street, and a drunken ruffian knocked down and attempted to outrage your little sister, ought he not to be resisted?"

"Only by argument, by persuasion," he replied.

"Yes; but if he were deaf to persuasion, and answered argument by swearing, would you not knock him down to save your sister?"

"Would you?" he asked.

"Yes," I said, hotly, "if I could; wouldn't you?"

"No," he said, "I would not."

"Then you would deserve to be kicked," I burst out roughly; but he stuck to his guns, maintaining that the command was absolute, and that, no matter what the consequences might be, we were bound to make no forcible resistance to evil. Moral suasion was the only agency permitted to moral men. That was the truth of Christ. No one was a Christian who did not recognise and obey that first and most absolute of all the commandments. I wished to have more talk with him, but he refused, and we parted. I sent him some things I had written, setting forth what seemed to me the essential principle of the Christian faith and the ideal of the Christian Church, and received by return a post-card, on which were written these words—"Joy, joy! You are one of ours. Henceforth we have right to count upon you for any service we may need." Although I never met the young disciple again, the ardour with which he hailed me as "one of ours," after having been much prepossessed against me, made me rather anxious to see the master, whose teachings had left so deep an impression on a mind so enthusiastic as Mr. T——'s. Besides, it seemed to me that Count Tolstoi's ideas had by no means arrived at their final stage. He had passed from Atheism to Theism, from Theism to a very fascinating form of literal Christianity—who could say whether or not he has reached the ultimate?

In Petersburg among the more pious I found much less sympathy with Count Tolstoi than I had anticipated. The more orthodox of the Orthodox sniffed at him, the more religious of the Evangelicals bemoaned his heresies much more than they rejoiced over his progress from Atheism to "Christ's Christianity." The literary people were impatient with his theological dissertations. They did not want homilies on the Sermon on the Mount. They wanted another "Anna Karenina;" the literary artist ought to paint pictures for their edification. He should not waste his time in fantastic imaginings of the Kingdom of Heaven, and they flatly refused to take him *au serieux* as a religious teacher and social reformer. At the same time I found among his own disciples a very fervid and very enthusiastic devotion. The young man in charge of the Tolstoian propaganda in Petersburg, whom I subsequently met at Yasnaia Poliana, had finished his university course, abandoned his worldly prospects, donned the peasant's blouse, lived like a workman, and undertook the distribution of the literature of the new faith from Petersburg. A bright, kindly, intelligent youth, he seemed to find great solace in believing. "What would you do if you were suddenly to wake up and find yourself Tzar of Russia?" I asked. "Abdicate instantly," he replied. He was full of all innocent enthusiasms and curious repugnances. Among other things, he said that the Tolstoians objected to railways. They were contrivances of the money-makers, constructed solely to earn dividends, and without any direct desire to benefit the people. Our conversation was somewhat difficult. He only spoke in Russian, and although I had the benefit of an excellent interpreter, the chasm between our mental standpoints was too deep and wide for us to do more than shout across a few words of sympathy and curiosity. I gathered from him that the work of propagandism by colportage was actively prosecuted, and that millions of the neatly printed little tracts with pretty coloured pictures were sold throughout Russia to the peasants. As a prophylactic to Nihilism the propaganda is said to have proved very useful. It affords an outlet for the spirit of divine discontent, which was infinitely nobler than that offered by the party of dynamite—nobler, and at the same time deeper. The number of those who embraced the new doctrine in its entirety, who gave up all that they had and lived by faith, working with their hands, and living and dressing and labouring like the peasants, was not great; but among those who had abandoned all, the new spirit had borne notable fruits in the shape of heroic self-abnegation, and a passionate philanthropy which was sometimes sublime.

All this naturally quickened my desire to see the founder of the new school. The bold and uncompromising logic of the Count in advocating absolute non-resistance had seemed to me to be faulty at only one point. In " Christ's Christianity," he admitted that although it was in his view absolutely forbidden to use force to resist even the foulest and most atrocious wrong-doing—as, for instance, to prevent your wife being carried off to slavery by a horde of obscene savages—it might still be right in certain extreme circumstances to use force to protect a little child from violence. An Englishman who had assisted Mr. T—— in translating " Christ's Christianity," explained to me how this notable exception came to be made—an exception which, it seemed to me, gave up the whole case. He said : " When translating the book, my nature revolted against this doctrine of acquiescence in the vilest outrage; and I put the case through Mr. T—— to Count Tolstoi : Suppose that a man, maddened by drink, attempts to murder my child. Remonstrance has been tried and is useless. I must either restrain the man by force, or permit the child to be murdered. As soon as the man is sober he will bitterly repent the result of his frenzy, but it will be then too late. He will have committed murder, and he will probably be hanged. The child will be dead. Would it not be right for me to do to that man as I would certainly wish to be done by if I were in his position—namely, to employ whatever force might be necessary to prevent him staining his hands with the blood of my child while he was temporarily bereft of his reason by drink?" It was a hard case, and Count Tolstoi gave in.

"Yes," said he; "in such a case force might perhaps be lawful, but in no other." The admission, however, vitiated his whole case. For who can say whether the man or nation which attempts to commit violent wrong is not temporarily bereft of reason, and therefore a fitting object for the restraint of force? Once open the door to the use of force in any circumstances, and the extreme advocate of non-resistance is undone. I wanted to hear from Count Tolstoi how he reconciled his one exception with his imperative veto on all force. Soon after arriving at Yasnaia Poliana I put the case to him. Count Tolstoi was equal to the occasion. He said : " It was a mistake I made. You have no right to use force even to restrain a drunkard from killing a child. It was a fault to have admitted the exception."

The idea that you may use force to repel violence offered by the strong to the weak is, in his opinion, not only unchristian, but grossly inconsistent. "Who are you who propose to repel violence?—you who lived in ceiled houses and fare sumptuously every day—you are a fine set of people to talk of repressing violence; and of preventing wrong. Wash your own hands first: make yourself clean from violence; give up the wealth which you have in excess of that of the labourer, and then perhaps you may talk of resisting the violence of other men." The idea of redressing violence by violence is, he contends, not Christian, but chivalrous, which is a very different thing. Better let a child be killed by a brutal assailant than put yourself in the wrong by smiting him to the ground by violence. I put to him the familiar objection as to what was Christ's meaning when, before going down to Jerusalem, he asked if there were any swords in his little company, and when being told that there were two, replied, "It is enough." Count Tolstoi's answer was certainly not deficient in audacity. "Christ," said he, "certainly asked for swords, and His words seem to me to imply not less certainly that He meant them to be used, probably for repelling the attack of robbers in the defiles through which He had to pass on His way to Jerusalem. But therein He fell, and violated His own precepts. Hence the bitter remorse and penitence of Gethsemane, which was due, in my opinion, to His poignant sorrow at the faithlessness which led Him to contemplate resorting to the sword even in self-defence!"

As for capital punishment, Count Tolstoi roundly told me that if I ever advocated taking a human life, even though it were that of the worst murderer, and the foulest criminal, I was like Peter, who denied his Lord. "'Who art thou that judgest?' You have no right to judge. No, not even the worst of men. If you take your brother's life you are a murderer, no matter under what form of words you cloak your crime. You reply that some men may become like ravenous beasts, and that their destruction may be necessary. But that is just what Christ condemned explicitly when He said that whosoever shall say to his brother 'Raca' shall be in danger of the judgment. As for saying that such a man is a trouble and a nuisance to his neighbours, remember that so have been regarded the best of men. Do you think that Christ was not considered as a great nuisance and a trouble by His brothers? The household went on quietly until He began to make a stir."

The idea of Count Tolstoi seems to be that the use of any force for the restraint of any human action is open to the same arguments which are used against religious persecution. All punishments are in their nature persecution. Murder, robbery, and brutal crime, these, as I understood him, should not be punished any more than the belief in heretical theories of transubstantiation and of the Atonement. To use the sword to repress assassination differs in no whit in principle from the *auto da fé*. You can only punish when you judge, and you have no right to judge. Each man is responsible solely to God. His fellow-men may argue with him and endeavour to constrain him by argument and by passive resistance; but no violence, no force, must be used to give effect to their conclusions.

Count Tolstoi is equally opposed to all taxes. "Taxation can only be collected by force, and all force is forbidden by Christ."

In that case I ventured to suggest there would be no State and no Government.

Count Tolstoi at once rejoined: "And there is no such thing as a State, as a Government. It is a humbug, this State. What you call a Government is mere phantasmagoria. What is a State? Men I know; peasants and villages, these I see; but Governments, nations, States, what are these but fine names invented to conceal the plundering of honest men by dishonest tchinovniks and the murdering of peaceful men under the phrases of mobilisation and war? If men would not be silly as to bow down and worship this false idol, Government, how simple all things would become! All our difficulties come from that. We obey not Christ, but the Government. Everything wrong comes from that. The day when men determine to obey not the Government but Christ, these difficulties will disappear."

"For instance, Russia's difficulty with Poland; England's with Ireland?"

"Our difficulty with Poland only consists in the fact that the peasants are stupid enough to allow themselves to be carried off from their homes, thrust into uniforms, and to shoot dead their brothers who speak Polish and live in Poland. If they refused to leave their village, or to shoulder a rifle or kill their brother at word of command, where would be the Polish difficulty? There would be no Polish difficulty. All difficulties come from disobeying Christ."

Visions of contumacious Quakers who refused to carry arms in the seventeenth century, which I had read in Sunday-school books when a child, flitted before me as he talked, and I asked him whether any Russians refused to serve in the army.

"Sometimes," he said. "There was a friend of mine, a young man, who was drawn for the army, and who refused to take the oath of obedience. 'Swear not at all,' said he, 'is the command of Christ. How can I swear? I will not swear.' So the first thing they did was to put him into a madhouse. Then they sent to him popes and others to argue with him; but they could not argue away the plain words of Christ. They sent him to Odessa to the artillery, but they could make nothing of him. So they sent him to Tashkent, where he spoke to the officers, bearing testimony to Christ's law. They ordered him to put on a sabre, but he refused. So then they sent him to prison, where he remained twelve months. After that they let him go, and he is now free. What he did others can do, and when they all do it, there will be no more wars. In one hundred years, I think, wars will cease from this cause, and we shall look back at war as we now look back at torture, wondering how mankind could be so stupid as to tolerate it." The early Christians, Count Tolstoi maintains, recognised that no Christian could be a soldier; it was only when they ceased to be Christians that they ventured to become soldiers. That is so plain to him that he cannot understand how any one can deny it.

To him, as to Auberon Herbert, the State is a hideous simulacrum, a kind of horrid nightmare, whose influence is only evil. It is due, no doubt, in his case, to the fact that in Russia the life of the people is affected very little by the State, excepting when it takes taxes and makes wars. "My views," said he, "are simply the application of the words of Christ to the things of this life, but they are also the outcome of Russian experience. Our life is in the villages. What would it matter to these peasants if St. Petersburg and Moscow and all that is called Government were suddenly swallowed up by an earthquake? For each of these peasants life would be better, not worse. There is a little story I want to write some day—the experience of a Robinson Crusoe commune—which illustrates that point. A commune emigrated to Siberia as an entire commune. The Government gave what it called assistance and directions, which only made trouble, but *malgré* the Government the emigrants at last crossed the Oural. There they got leave from the Kirghiz to occupy the land and sow rye for one year. They harvested the rye and then moved on. At last they came to some waste land, and they decided to settle there. They sent to the Governor of the district to ask leave. His tchinovniks took bribes, and then it was discovered that some one owned the land on which they had settled, and that they could not stay there. So on they went until they crossed the Russian boundary, and settled in China. They did not know that they were in China, and they sent to tell the Governor that they had chosen a site for their village. The Governor did not know the place, and they were left alone. They remained there for fifteen years, living happily and peacefully without ever hearing a word from the Government, until it was reported to the Governor that they were Russian colonists, and that they ought to be within the Russian frontier. Then taxes were put on, and they had to furnish soldiers. Now wherein was this Robinson Crusoe commune the better off for the Government? Was it not entirely worse off when the Government came to it? So it is with all of us. What is the use of a Government? It is of no use; it is worse than useless."

We crossed as we talked a highway in good repair that ran from Toula to Kieff. "Who made this road?" I asked.

"The Government," he replied.

"Then the Government does at least do some good," I remarked, "if it makes roads?"

"Oh," said he carelessly, "it is always on the look-out to discover or invent a motive for its existence; but in these things, as in railways and agricultural exhibition, and in national education, the Government goes too fast. Why make these things before the people learn the need of them? When they know they need them they will make them without the Government. All this springs from a false idea with which men deceive themselves that they can take short cuts to improvement, and that by violence they can mend each other. They cannot do it. All improvements must begin from the inside. By working the other way from the outside you undo your own work. One of the greatest delusions of the world is that you can by material means help men. It is impossible. It is as if you would lift everything on a table by lifting, not the table, but the table-cloth. To help men, what is that? It is to make them more loving, more kindly, more like Christ. The only true life is to love, and the more we love the more we live. All other things are but semblances which are not, and which will pass away. The only real thing is the love which you have for your fellow-creatures. That alone is. And so certain am I of this, that if you were to offer me a million roubles in one hand, for me to expend in giving more land and building better houses and supplying with library and schools and all advantages every peasant in Yasnaia Poliana, and with the other were to offer to raise the moral standard of the peasants by only one degree, I would accept the latter and discard the former. For the latter would really be good, and by one degree it would make the people happy; but a million roubles might not make them happy: it might even make them more miserable."

The command, "Resist not evil," is to him the key to the whole Christian system, the very corner-stone of the Christian religion. It is this law which unites all Christ's teaching into one indivisible whole; it is the key to open all doors when it is pushed firmly into the lock. The Christian Church is, or ought to be, a Society of Non-resistance. Earthly courts of justice, which judge men, violate Christ's law, and if He thought of these tribunals He must have condemned them. No extremity of evil can justify a resort to force; the Christian who uses force to repel evil merely increases the evil in the world, and passes it on to others. His idea of the duty of Christians is that they should be passive, allowing the force of evil to expend itself upon them without transmitting it to others. Thus, and thus only, can they bring about peace on earth. All active warfare multiplies strife, bitterness, hate. What alone overcomes the world is by suffering all things, bearing all things, and offering a non-conducting medium to the violence of evil men, instead of passing on their violence in new directions.

Most people will reply to this exhortation with the phrase of the apologist for capital punishment who was willing to give it up if the assassins would begin by setting the example. To abandon the use of force seems to the natural man a surrender of the whole game into the hands of the Evil One. How can you expect men to face the martyrdom of passive suffering that would thus be exacted from every Christian? To this Count Tolstoi replies in one of the finest passages in his religious writings, in which he contrasts the martyrdom to which men willingly submit themselves at the bidding of the world, and that from which they shrink when it is ordered by Christ.

> "Let any sincere man review the whole current of his life, and he will see that no suffering came from fulfilling the teaching of Christ; that the greater part of the misfortunes of his life proceeded from his having been led away by the entanglements of the world into opposition to his own impulses.
> 
> "All the hardest moments of my life, from drunkenness and looseness as a student, to duels, war, ill-health, and the unnatural and tormenting conditions under which I now live, all these form a martyrdom in the name of the teaching of the world.
> 
> "Christ says, 'Take up thy cross and follow Me;' that is, bear patiently the lot awarded thee, and obey Me, thy God; yet none obey. But the first worthless man, fitted for nothing but murder, who wears epaulettes, and takes it into his head to say, 'Take not up a cross, but a knapsack and a gun, and follow me to inflict and undergo misery and certain death,' is listened to and obeyed by all. Abandoning family, parents, wives, and children, dressed like buffoons and obeying the will of the first man of higher rank they meet, starving, worn out by long marches, they follow they know not where, like a herd of cattle to the slaughter-house. But they are not cattle—they are men. They cannot but know whither they are driven. With the unanswered question of 'Why?' on their lips, with despair in their hearts, they march to die from cold, and hunger, and disease, from the fire of bullets and cannon balls. They slay and are slain; yet not one of them knows why or wherefore this is so. The Turk roasts them alive, flays them, disembowels them; but the next day again at the call of the trumpet, the survivors march with their eyes open to suffering and death. Yet no one finds any difficulty in obeying such commands. Not only the sufferers themselves, but their fathers and mothers see no difficulty; nay, they even urge their children to obedience. It seems to them that obedience to such commands not only is and must be expedient, but a wise and moral law.
> 
> "We might believe that the teaching of Christ is difficult, terrible, and leads to suffering, were the consequences of the teaching of the world easy, and safe, and agreeable. But in reality the teaching of the world

is more difficult to fulfil, more dangerous, more fraught with suffering than that of Christ.

"There were, it is said, at one time Christian martyrs, but they were exceptions; it has been calculated that their number has reached 330,000 during eighteen hundred years. But if we count the martyrs to the world, for every single martyr to Christ we shall find a thousand martyrs of the world, whose sufferings have been a hundredfold greater. By death in war alone during the present century have fallen thirty millions of men!

"These men were all martyrs to the teaching of the world. Putting the teaching of Christ aside, had they but foreborne to follow that of the world, what sufferings and death would they have escaped."

Granting that a policy of absolute non-resistance involves martyrdom, what of that? Martyrdom is the appointed way by which Christ intended that His kingdom should be established. It is the only effective manner in which His disciples can preach the faith that is in them.

"If a Christian live in the midst of those who are not Christians, and who defend themselves and their property by violence, and he be called upon to take part in this defence, then is the moment for him to fulfil the office of his life. He only knows the truth that he may impart it to others, above all, to those with whom he lives, and who are bound to him by family ties and by friendship; and he cannot show that truth otherwise than by not falling into the error into which they have fallen, by not ranging himself on the side either of the attacking or the defending party, by giving up all to others, by showing practically that he needs nothing but to fulfil the will of God, and that nothing is terrible to him except to fall away from it.

"Therefore, knowing the truth, he cannot but witness to it before men who know it not. The violence, imprisonment, or death to which he may be subjected, are an occasion for him to witness, not by words, but by works."

In discussing the world and all the things that are therein, we naturally came upon the relations between the men and women, the right ordering of which is the foundation of a healthy society. Count Tolstoi holds very strong views on this subject. An anarchist in almost every other sphere of life, he is an inveterate opponent of Free Love. Nothing can exceed the severity of his conception of the binding nature of the marriage tie. One of his chief difficulties in accepting the literal interpretation of the Sermon on the Mount was the apparent sanction which is given to Divorce in case of infidelity to the marriage vow. Canon Liddon gets out of this difficulty by declaring that the invalidating act must have been committed before marriage, otherwise the word adultery would have been used instead of fornication. Nothing that is done after marriage can invalidate a marriage, but a marriage celebrated with one who professes to be what she is not is, *ipso facto*, null and void, as not having possessed the preliminary essentials of the contract. Count Tolstoi escapes by another loophole. He translates the text differently. In our version it stands, "Every one that putteth away his wife, saving for the cause of fornication, maketh her an adulteress." He holds that the correct translation is, "Every one that putteth away his wife, besides the crime of incontinence, obligeth her to be an adulteress." The religious, the grammatical, and the logical meaning of the words of Christ, he maintains, is quite clear. There is no cause justifying divorce. If a man puts away his wife he does it for the cause of incontinence, and obliges, in most cases, the repudiated wife to become an adulteress. But with Count Tolstoi marriage is the union of male and female. When they twain become one flesh it matters not that the Church may never have blessed their union or the law legalised it; they are none the less one, and that which God hath joined let not man put asunder.

"Great, and to be revered also," he writes, "is not so much the human institution of marriage which affords an exterior legality to the union of male and female, which, once consummated, can never again be dissolved without the violation of the will of God." Again he says, "I know that every desertion by man or woman of the one they first lived with is that very divorce which Christ forbids, because those left by the first husband or wife convey incontinence through the world."

Count Tolstoi has not left us to speculate as to the experience through which he passed before he arrived at these convictions. "When quite a youth," he tells us, "my kindhearted aunt, a really good woman, used to say to me that there was one thing above all others which she wished for me—an intrigue with a married woman. *Rien ne forme un jeune homme comme une liaison avec une femme comme il faut.*" For ten years, he tells us, he lived a life of dissipation and debauchery. His chief temptation "arose from my having abandoned the woman with whom I first lived, and from the universal condition of all women so abandoned. I see now that the chief strength of the temptation lay not in my own passions, but in the unnatural position in which I and the women around me were placed." Hence his insistence upon monogamy, which he regards as the natural law of humanity. " I cannot make a difference between unions sanctioned, as it is said, by marriage and those which are not. I can only consider as sacred and binding the communion into which a man can enter but once." I asked him what he would advise in case the other partner to this solely sacred and binding marriage were already married, or had contracted other unions. He replied that when the light of the true doctrine of marriage dawned upon the heart of man, it was his duty to regard as his wedded wife the woman with whom he was at that moment actually cohabiting, and to regard his union with her as indissoluble.

He is no advocate for celibacy. While he declares that " for a man to leave his wife for another woman is not only an unnatural act, but is also cruel and inhuman," he, in the same breath, proclaims that " for a man to remain unmarried after the age of manhood is monstrous and shameful." There is, however, a strong leaning towards asceticism in the later phases of his speculations. He told me with much interest that a community of peasants somewhere east of Toula had, of their own motive, formed themselves into an association, the central principle of which, so far as I could make out from his description, was what may be called married celibacy. " I have much sympathy," he remarked, " with these good people." In reply to some remark of mine about his insistence upon monogamy, he said, " From that I do not think we shall go back. That stage in human development has cost too many sacrifices to be abandoned. We shall go on making further progress in the same direction." " How?" I asked. " First," he said, " in the growth of the conviction that it is shameful for any man to have to do with any woman but her with whom he is united for life. Among our young men, the number who hold this doctrine and practise it is greatly increasing. It is the true doctrine, and it will prevail. Secondly, in the discontinuance of divorce; and thirdly, by much greater continence in the married state." " The rites mysterious of connubial love," which Milton tells us

Eve did not refuse in Paradise, seem to the Russian philosopher more honoured in the breach than in the observance, excepting, of course, when consecrated to the multiplication of the race.

Of Malthus, and the doctrines usually known as Malthusian, Count Tolstoi thought little. A Russian with the half of two continents as his national inheritance cannot be expected to realise the danger of the overcrowding of the world. Besides, he is a diligent student of Henry George's book, and, in a properly organised state of society, he does not think there will ever be more mouths to fill than there is bread with which to fill them.

The views of the Count upon the relations of the sexes really lie at the root of much that is most distinctive in his teaching. When the truth as to exceeding sinfulness of loose living entered his understanding, he tells us it "changed my former appreciation of what is good and great—bad and low in life. What had appeared to me best—a refined, æsthetic life, poetic, passionate loves, sung by all poets and artists—now seemed evil and distasteful. On the other hand, a rude and labouring life, which subdues the passions, seemed good to me. I cannot now desire or seek the physical idleness and sumptuous existence which developed in me an excess of sensuality. I can no longer seek out those amusements which are as fuel to the flame of sensual love—romances, most poems, music, theatres, balls, which in former days not only seemed to me harmless but highly refined pleasures. I can no longer aid the voluptuous lazy existence of others, no longer assist or be a partner in those licentious modes of killing time—romantic literature, theatres, operas, balls, and so forth, which are still stumbling-blocks for me and for others."

A sturdy old Puritan, indeed! No wonder that he is in radical revolt against what he calls an "education worthy of savages, which both physically and mentally nourishes loose desires and justifies them by the highest application of the intellect."

Woman, in Count Tolstoi's ideal, is saved from being the evil temptress who was overwhelmed with the anathemas of the fathers of the Church, by her functions as the bringer forth and the nurse of the new generation. Some who knew him well declare that the ideal woman in his eyes must ever be either nursing an infant or expecting its arrival. He never said any such thing to me, but his wife has not come far short of such an ideal. The Count has no reverence for the ignorance that is often mistaken for innocence. At Moscow there is a story in circulation to the effect that at the birth of one of his children he gravely instructed the whole family assembled round the dinner-table in the physiological phenomena which had preceded and accompanied the advent of the new-comer. An English governess who was present was said to have been speechless with confusion; but the anecdote is probably an ingenious exaggeration, invented in order to illustrate the originality and courage with which the Count applies his principles. It is necessary to be explicit in this world, especially when your daughters may have to spend the next day in the hayfield, amid rustics who are as realistic as nature itself.

Much as the Count admires the peasant, he does not conceal from himself that in the matter of morality the moujik has still much to learn. In his last literary work, the grimly repellent "Power of Darkness," he paints a picture of peasant morals which is quite revolting. Incest, adultery, murder, infanticide constitute the staple of that gruesome drama. Speaking of that play, Count Tolstoi said that it was strange that the public concentrated their attention upon the pornographic detail, and ignored the great lesson of the play, which lesson I take it is the old moral that the love of money is the root of all evil. The play he had intended as a moral lesson for the benefit of the peasants, whereas it had only been performed before the Emperor and in Paris, the two audiences for which it was least adapted. Speaking of this subject, he said that although he did not care for M. Zola for some things, he was the only novelist in France who was doing anything. "The others, what are they doing? Elaborating trifles which may help to spend a fine lady's idle hours. Zola is doing real work. I don't put any count upon his 'Nana,' which is a sketch of a diseased and temporary phase of society. But in 'La Terre' and 'Germinal' we have for the first time authentic pictures of the peasant and the miner. They belong to the permanent elements of humanity. We have been talking about them all our lives. Here is a picture of them as they are. Disagreeable and revolting, perhaps, but it is well to see the facts, and to realise the life our brothers are living. It is a work that has now been done, and done once for all. If any one wishes to see how the majority of these men live, it is there. You can go and look at it when you wish. It is not a picture that you would care to have continually before you."

Yet, notwithstanding this sombre conception of the brutal realities of life among the peasants, they are still Count Tolstoi's source of inspiration even as to the relations of the sexes.

## CHAPTER III.

### "SELL ALL THAT THOU HAST AND GIVE TO THE POOR."

"In thirty years, private property in land will be as much a thing of the past as now is serfdom. England, America, and Russia will be the first to solve the problem. Already the work makes progress. When I was a young man the emancipation of the serf preoccupied the mind of the Russian youth. To-day another work commands the attention of our sons—the destruction of the private ownership of land." So said Count Tolstoi to me in one of the many long and pleasant rambles which we had together over the undulating lands surrounding Yasnaia Poliana. As we strolled under the pleasant shade of the birch-trees, drinking the air laden with the steamy fragrance which rises from spring verdure under the noonday sun, I was constantly reminded of other conversations which I enjoyed years ago, in scenery not dissimilar, with a companion who in cast of mind and habit of thought closely resembled my Russian host. I had but to forget the difference in accent and ignore the dress to imagine that, instead of listening to Count Tolstoi in Yasnaia Poliana, I was being admonished by Auberon Herbert in the New Forest as to the heinous wickedness of all government, the iniquity of all taxation, and the absolute necessity under which we all lay of allowing every one else to do exactly as he pleases. I remember discussing Count Tolstoi's doctrines with Mr. Herbert a couple of years since at Ashley Arnewood, and now that I was discussing them with Count Tolstoi himself I was more than ever struck with the resemblance between the two men. The differences, however, are almost as marked as the points of similarity. It requires a strong effort of imagination to picture Mr. Herbert as a Socialist, and although he is full of the spirit of Christ, our New Forest philosopher has never propounded the doctrine of Count Tolstoi, that the supreme law of humanity is to be found in the literal meaning of the Sermon on the Mount. If you want to know what Count Tolstoi is like, you take Auberon Herbert, Thomas Carlyle, John Ruskin, and George Fox, boil them all down into a single specimen of the human, and you have Count Tolstoi.' Personally he is a most lovable man, full of all tender sympathies and loving-kindness, and vehement conviction, natural, simple, and strong.

I found Count Tolstoi full of Henry George and land nationalisation. " Henry George," he told me, " has formulated the next article in the programme of the progressist Liberals of the world. How I admire his spirit, which is so Christian; his style, which is so clear; and his metaphors, which are so striking ! He has indicated the next step that must be taken. His ideas will spread—nay, they are spreading. During the winter I have at night the peasants to talk with me round the samovar, and we often discussed the future of the land. I found them of two minds. One section would give every adult male an equal portion of land. The other would have the whole land held by the community cultivated and owned in common. But when I explained Henry George's idea they all agreed that this would be the best. Only last week a peasant came nearly forty versts across the country to ask for further explanations about this land nationalisation."

" And what did you tell him ? "

" I told him that under the nationalisation scheme all land would belong to the Government, that there would be probably a reduction of twenty per cent. in the tax they now pay for their land, and that ultimately the reduced land tax would take the place of any other taxes. He was quite satisfied, and he will tell others of the scheme."

" What taxes do the peasants pay ? "

" The direct land tax to which allusion is made is between seven and eight roubles per annum, which they must pay for forty-nine years to repay the State for the advance which it made to the landed proprietors at the time of the Emancipation.

Under George's scheme, instead of paying a terminable seven and a half roubles for forty-nine years, they would pay six roubles in perpetuity. The peasants know this, but they are willing to go on paying the reduced rent to the commune, after the period of repayment is over."

I told Count Tolstoi of the discussions I had held with Henry George in London, and the sore point of the Ten Commandments. "I quite agree with George," said Count Tolstoi, "that the landlords may be expropriated without dishonesty, without compensation as a matter of principle. But as a question of expediency I think compensation might facilitate the necessary change. It will come, I suppose, as the Emancipation came. The idea will spread. A sense of the shamefulness of private ownership will grow. Some one will write an 'Uncle Tom's Cabin' about it; there will be agitation, and then it will come, and many who own land will do as did those who owned serfs, voluntarily give it to their tenants. But for the rest a loan might be arranged so as to prevent the work being stopped by the cry of confiscation."

Count Tolstoi was much interested in hearing of Archbishop Walsh and Lord Ashbourne's Act, and how we hoped to secure the creation of a system of communalisation of the land in Ireland whenever the settlement came.

"Yes," said he, "communalisation is better than nationalisation, although no doubt the nationalisation of land did not answer badly in Turkey; but it is better to vest the land in the commune than in the Central Government. Of course, I do not hold with George about the taxation of the land. If you could get angels from heaven to administer the taxes from the land, you might do justice and prevent mischief. I am against all taxation."

We had been out walking in the cool of the day, and we had come upon a squad of one hundred navvies who were employed at the railway. They were finishing their supper, and were on the point of turning into their sod-built huts, in which they slept, ten on each side, on a rude plank platform, without mattresses, without even straw. Count Tolstoi promised to send them some straw, at which they seemed very pleased. Honest, kindly-looking fellows they were; not so stalwart as our navvies, but full of pleasant courtesy and frank talk. The visit to their huts naturally led to a discussion of the social question.

"We have forgotten Christ," said the Count; "we will not obey Him. And what is the result? There you have a hundred men, each earning fifty copecks a day, without even straw to lie on at night. How can you and I sleep on mattresses and feather beds when these hard-working men have not even straw? If you were Christian you could not. What right have you to too much when your brother has not even enough? The next step in Christianity, the very first step, is for those who have wealth and lands to part with all they have and let it go to the poor."

One of Count Tolstoi's friends and disciples, young Mr. T——, whom I met two years ago in London, at the house of M. Pashkoff, has adopted his views, and is living as a peasant, with his young wife and baby, on his estate at Voronège. But even this absolute identity with the peasants, and literal sharing with them of his entire income, does not satisfy Count Tolstoi. What right have Christians to act as stewards of money which is evil, and solely evil? To assume that you have a right to dispose of your property even by giving it away, is presumption. You have no right to your money—not even enough right to say that this man is more worthy to receive it than that. It is properly not yours at all. It is a stolen hoard which happens to be on your hands, but which the first comer has as much right to as yourself. Hence all that you have to do is to keep your hands off your money, and let any one take it that comes along, and cares to encumber himself with the accursed thing.

"Do you think," said Count Tolstoi, "that the money earned by doctors or lawyers, or editors, is less dishonestly acquired than that taken by a thief or a brigand? It is just the same: all is the result of violence. Take this estate on which we are; how was it acquired? By violence. My great-grandfather was one of Catherine's generals. She took the land from the peasants who worked it, and gave it to him for his services in murdering people in war. That is the origin of one part of it. The other is the result of my writings. That is equally due to violence. Who buy my novels? Rich men. Whence come their riches? Again from violence. There is not enough in the world for any one to have more than his fair share. There is a Russian proverb that says that he who labours honestly can never build a fine house, and it is true. The honest toiler can only get the necessaries. Who gets more is a thief. Whenever you see a big house and luxury, and all that, you see the result of the robbery of the poor. And the result is not only robbery, it is demoralisation. For the thief and the thief's children do not need to work. They become idle, idleness breeds mischief, and their example corrupts and makes discontented the children of those who are too poor to follow their example. If you want to be like Christ you must have no property; you must share all round until you have no more than the others."

If you have money or house or clothes, you must be ready to give them up to the first comer. The result of practising this doctrine, even with the strict limitations imposed by the Countess Tolstoi, has not been very satisfactory. The false poor, the charlatan, the scamp, the drunkard, all swarm to be relieved. The genuine suffering poor remain away. Why the stolen hoard, if it be a stolen hoard, of the rich should be offered as a premium upon impudence, mendacity, and audacious selfishness, I have not yet been able to discern. What would happen if Count Tolstoi carried out his principles to the uttermost is that a score of rascals would possess themselves of his estate, who would spend the rents in vodka instead of in the propagation of temperance principles and the writing of "Anna Karenina."

When I ventured to hint this to the Count, he replied: "You should always choose that which is certainly good in preference to that which is only possibly good. To live in natural relations with my brothers, to till the earth, to grow corn, and to bring myself and my family into harmony with the will of God, which is the law of life revealed by Christ, that is a positive real good. The writing of novels may be only nonsense. There may be some good in them, but perhaps more evil. Who can judge? You say that 'Anna Karenina' may have roused thousands of people to put themselves in more true and loving relations with their kind, but how do I know that it may not have had a different effect on even more thousands? We do not know. And if I could by one word remove all the

80,000 prostitutes from the streets of London, I would not do it if by doing it I had to sacrifice the opportunity of placing myself and my family as tillers of the soil into healthy natural human relationship with my fellows, for the latter is a real good. The other may be or may not."

"I wish," said Count Tolstoi to me one night, "to write a novel, a romance, exposing the conventional illusion of romantic love. I have already written it, but it must be turned upside down and re-written. It is too much of a treatise as it stands, and there is not enough of action in it. In this story my object is to fill the reader with horror at the result of taking romantic love *au sérieux*. The end to which the whole story will lead up will be the murder of a wife by her husband. It will exhibit the depravation of married life by the substitution of romantic love, a fever born of carnal passion, for true Christian love, which is born of identity of sentiment, similarity of ideal, the friendship of the soul. Upon that love—Christian love, the love of brother and sister—if the carnal love can be grafted it is well, but the former, not the latter, is the first condition of happy married life. Herein the peasants teach us a lesson. They regard what we call romantic love as a disease, temporary, and painful, and dangerous. With them no marriage is made under its influence. Anything is better than that. The Herrstaten, who marry by the drawing of lots, are wiser than we. Our system is the worst possible, and the whole of our wedding ceremonial, and the honeymoon, the feasting, and the incitement to carnality are directly calculated to result in the depravation of matrimony. Not in one case out of a hundred does romantic love result in a lifelong happy union. The young people whose lives lie in different orbits are drawn together by this evanescent passion. They marry. For a month they are happy—perhaps even for a year, or two years, never longer, when the only tie is the sensual passion. Then they hate each other for the rest of their lives, spending their time in paying homage to the respectabilities by concealing the truth from their neighbours. It must be so. If Anna Karenina had married Wronsky she must have abandoned him likewise. Romantic love is like opium or hashish; the sensation is overpowering and delightful. But it passes. It is not in human nature not to wish to renew the experience; for this novelty is indispensable. So the wife betrays her husband,

and the husband is false to his wife, and the world becomes one wide brothel. I wish to open the eyes of all to the real nature of the tragic consequences of this substitution of romantic for Christian love. I see it clearly, oh! so clearly; and when you see a thing which no one else seems to see, you feel you must gather all your forces, and devote yourself to setting forth the truth as you see it. This depravation of marriage is all because Christianity has been a word and not a thing. It will, however, be a reality again soon."

"A pleasant belief," I said.

"Yes," said he, "if I did not believe that I should see some advance, however slight, to the coming of the Kingdom of God, I would hang myself. But if I could establish the Kingdom in all its fulness by pressing a button, I should be very miserable, for there would be nothing left for me to do."

## CHAPTER IV.

### THE FIVE COMMANDMENTS OF THE KINGDOM OF HEAVEN.

COUNT TOLSTOI'S views as to the authority of the teachings of Christ are based upon his own conviction of their supreme reasonableness. As light is grateful to the eye, and water to the parched and thirsty traveller, so Christ's teachings commend themselves to his reason and to his heart. They need to be recommended neither by miracles nor by evidences of Christianity. Christ's teachings are their own evidence. They respond to the necessities of our nature, solve the problems of life, and are self-evident, when literally interpreted. The account which he gives of the devious way by which, after long wandering in the wilderness of sin, he was led to see that in Christ alone was salvation, is one of the most deeply interesting pieces of spiritual autobiography that I ever read. At the end of his wanderings he tells us:—

"I, too, like the thief on the cross, believed the teaching of Christ and was saved. And this is no far-reached comparison, but the most exact representation of that mental state of despair and horror at the problem of life and death in which I once found myself, of that condition of peace and happiness in which I live now."

The teaching of Christ, however, was a very different thing from the teaching of the Church about Christ. He declares—

"It is perhaps a terrible thing to say, yet it seems so to me that were it not for the Church's commentaries on this teaching, those who are now called Christians would be much nearer to Christ; they would be much nearer to a reasonable conception of the good in life than they are now."

This is the exact antithesis to the Orthodox teaching, Hear the Church! Anglicans are willing to hear the Church of the first three centuries; Nonconformists only respect the Church of the Apostles; Count Tolstoi is more uncompromising still, and boldly lays the blame for the Church's misunderstanding of Christ's teaching upon the Apostle Paul.

"The separation between the teaching of life and the explanations of life itself began with the preaching of Paul, who was unacquainted with the ethical doctrines expressed in the Gospel of Matthew, and who preached a cabalistic metaphysical theory foreign to Christ's spirit. It became complete in the time of Constantine, when it was found possible to clothe the whole system of pagan life in a Christian dress, and give to it the name of Christianity."

What, then, is the teaching of Christ, according to this Latter Day Christian? Count Tolstoi sums it up under five Commandments, as follows:—

"The first Commandment says, 'Be at peace with all men; consider no man as insignificant or foolish' (Matt. v. 22). If peace be broken, strive to re-establish it with all your strength. The service of God is the destruction of enmity. Be reconciled for the least difference, that you may not lose the true life.

"His second Commandment, 'In spite of physical beauty, resist carnal desires; be a husband to one wife only, a wife to one husband, and quit each other under no pretext.'

"Then comes the temptation to take oaths. 'Know that this is an evil, and swear not at all' (which for him means, do not become a soldier and place your action at the disposal of another).

"The fourth temptation is revenge, miscalled human justice. 'Seek no vengeance, nor justify yourself in that you have been offended, but bear with injuries and render not evil for evil.'

"The fifth temptation is the difference between nationalities, the enmity between races and kingdoms. 'Know that all men are brothers and sons of the one God; break peace with no man under the plea of national aims.' If one of these Commandments be left unfulfilled by men, peace will be broken. If all be fulfilled, then peace shall be in all the world. The fulfilment of these Commandments excludes evil from the life of man."

As there are five Commandments, so there are five evils.

"The first evil he shows me which destroys the good of my life is enmity to other men, my anger against them. Only lately have I understood and believed this, but it has wholly changed my relative estimation of the different orders of men. All that formerly seemed to me fine and noble—honours, fame, education, wealth, all the artificiality and refinement of life, a luxurious household, food, dress, and outward appearance—all this has become to me poor and mean. All that seemed to me poor and mean—the peasantry, and obscure position, poverty, rough manners, simplicity in household arrangements, food, dress, and entertainment—has now become for me fine and noble.

"In my way of life, in food, in dress, and in all outward appearances, I must seek all that tends to bind me more closely to my fellows.

"The second evil is loose living—living, that is to say, not with the woman to whom I am united, but with another.

"The third evil to be guarded against is the taking of oaths.

"The fourth evil is resistance of evil by violence.

"The fifth evil is the distinction which we make between our own nation and foreigners."

As there are five Commandments and five evils, so there are five conditions of happiness in life, all of which are best secured by following the precepts of Christ. He expounds them in this wise, in a passage which reads like a commentary upon the text, How hardly shall a rich man enter into the Kingdom of Heaven.

"One of the first and most generally acknowledged conditions of happiness is a life which does not break the link between man and nature, a life in the open air, and in the light of the sun. It involves an intimate connection with the earth, with its plants and animals.

"Yet look at the life of a worldly man. The greater their success, the farther are they from these conditions of happiness: the greater their worldly happiness, the less they see of the sun, of the fields, and of the woods, and the animals that dwell therein.

"Another indisputable condition of happiness is labour; freely chosen and liked; the physical labour nourishing a good appetite, and sound, restorative sleep.

"A third condition of happiness is a family. Here, again, the greater the worldly success, the less is the happiness possible.

"A fourth condition is a free and living intercourse with all the various classes of mankind.

"There is also a fifth condition of happiness, and that is health and a natural and painless death. Here, once more, the higher a man's position, the less chance he has of these blessings. You will see that the lower the healthier, the higher the more sickly, is true both of men and women."

So Count Tolstoi teaches in works that are not by any means so well known in England as they deserve to be. For no man has ever made so daring an attempt to combine a mode of interpretation severely rational with such unflinching acceptance of the authority of Christ. He rejects almost everything which is associated with the name and teachings of Christ, and yet claims more imperatively than any other one obedience to His commands. Especially does he wage war against the Church. The Church idea, he says, must be destroyed; the Church obscures Christ.

"All by which the world now really lives—socialism, communism, political economy, utilitarianism, the freedom and equality of men and of women, the utmost conception of men, the sacredness of labour, of reason, of science, of art; all that makes the world advance, all that the Church condemns—are parts of the teaching which the Church herself, while striving to hide the teaching of Christ, unconsciously preserved through the ages. In our days the life of the world rolls on its course completely outside the influence of the Church.

"The teaching of Christ, determining life and explaining it, stands now, as it stood eighteen hundred years ago, before the world."

But the Church has outlived the time, and the world has no explanation of its inner life. It cannot but feel its own helplessness; it cannot, therefore, but accept the teaching of Christ.

Christ, in his eyes, was the supreme Rationalist, because He subordinated everything to the inner light—the light that is in you; that is to say, the light of reason. Count Tolstoi says:—

"And He above all things teaches us this, that men should believe in the light while the light is in them. He teaches men to prize above all things this light of reason, that they may live in conformity with it, and no longer do what they themselves think unreasonable."

The teaching of Christ is light. We cannot dispute, cannot disagree about it. It is equally necessary for every man on earth, whatever be his social position. Christ's metaphysical teaching is not new; it is the same doctrine which is written in the hearts of men, and which has been preached by all the sages of the world.

Whatever we may think of this as a legitimate exposition of the Christian faith, it is at least original and in harmony with much that is potent to the spirit of the times. Nor need one greatly lament its shortcomings on the right hand or on the left, if it should be the means of bringing into clearer relief before the eyes of men the teachings and the person of Christ.

Almost the first words which Count Tolstoi addressed to me were devoted to a lamentation over Matthew Arnold. "There is a great friend of mine—my greatest friend—has lately died in England. I was very sorry, very sorry, to hear of his death. He had all my ideas. It is true that he did not see clearly their logical development, but they were there. He would have come to see them in the true light if he had lived. I was so sorry, so very sorry, to hear of his death."

It must not be inferred from his describing Matthew Arnold as a great friend that Count Tolstoi was personally acquainted with the author of "Culture and Anarchy." If they ever met, which I doubt, it was a quarter of a century since, during the Count's only visit to London. It was in the year of the Exhibition, in 1862, that Count Tolstoi came to England. He suffered severely from toothache all the time he was in this country, but he still retains kindly reminiscences of English hospitality, and the club life to which he was introduced at the Athenæum. As Christ said, "Whoso shall do the will of my Father which is in heaven, the same is my brother, my sister, and my mother," so Count Tolstoi's great friends are those who accept the true faith as it is according to Count Tolstoi. No Englishman, he thinks, was more in accord with his views than Matthew Arnold. Hence the lament over his sudden death.

It was strange to find this Russian philosopher, who proclaims so imperiously the duty of accepting, in their literal sense, the teachings of Christ, preferring Mr. Arnold's definition of God to the "My Father which art in heaven" of the Nazarene. Christ might, and did, pray to His Heavenly Father, but in the Tolstoian theory of the Universe, in place of the Heavenly Father to whom the disciples were encouraged to come as little children, there is only Matthew Arnold's "The Eternal, a stream of tendency, not ourselves, which makes for righteousness." That is what seems to him the best definition of the Eternal—a deity as dumb and deaf as the law of gravitation, and as incapable of intelligent communication with the children of men. Yet Count Tolstoi, although unable to recognise a personal God, and opposed to all prayer, repeatedly used the phrase, " I am praying to God." Another time he said, " I am praying constantly for the coming of His Kingdom." Yet when questioned more closely he always said he doubted the possibility of spiritual communion between the soul and God. " Why should I try to look over God's shoulder and jog His elbow as to what He should do ? " " What do you say, then," I asked, " to the Lord's Prayer ? " " That was a *credo* rather than a petition." " But," said I, " Christ prayed to His Father, God, for help and strength, and taught His disciples to pray. Just as your boy might ask you to help him in a sum of arithmetic, so the disciples prayed for Divine guidance." " If my son were to ask me for help," the Count replied, " I would not help him. I would turn him back upon himself, and let him exercise his reason. That is the method of God."

From this springs Count Tolstoi's theory of revelation. While continually appealing to the words of Christ, he disclaims all peculiar and exceptional authority for the Scriptures. Matthew Arnold's definition of Culture supplies him with a formula for his theory of revelation. Reason is the light within whose guidance is God's revelation of His will. The supreme revelation of God's will is to be found in the highest thoughts of human genius. Of these highest thoughts the first place is taken by the words of Christ. " If you would do God's will, obey Christ's teachings." As for Providential guidance vouchsafed to the individual believer, Count Tolstoi will have none of it. There is no one who perfectly obeys Christ's words. He himself, he says, has not fulfilled one eighty-thousandth part. As, therefore, you are disobeying the plain commands of Christ, it is absurd to think that you will receive any other guidance. One of the last things he said to me as I bade him farewell at the railway station was that, until anything had actually happened, you could not speak with confidence as to its being the will of God. Everything is providential that has occurred. But you have no right to regard anything as an indication of God's will either in the present or the future. Providence can only be spoken of in relation to the past.

From Matthew Arnold our first conversation passed, by an odd transition, to the Salvation Army, in which Count Tolstoi was much interested, not altogether sympathetically. The *War Cry* is sent regularly from London to Yasnaia Poliana, and he told me that he had recently deliberately sat down and read one number through from the first column to the last, in order to endeavour to arrive at the soul of this strange movement. He was offended at it not because of its vulgarity, but because of the stress which it laid upon the Atonement, upon human depravity, and upon the punishment of the finally impenitent. He objected also entirely to taking collections for the maintenance of a ministry, even on the exceedingly parsimonious basis of the Salvation Army. "What General Booth and his followers should do," he said, "was not to preach at the expense of other people, but to put themselves in natural relations to the world and its inhabitants by earning their own living by the sweat of their brow." Still, he was attracted greatly by the enthusiasm and self-sacrifice of the Army, its supreme contempt for political and worldly considerations, and its absolute devotion to the saving of souls. "I am beginning to love your Salvation Army," he said once to me after I had been describing some of its leaders and their principles. "But why should they labour only for the next world? All that they say about the importance of saving souls, I say concerning the taking of one step, however short, towards bringing in the Kingdom of Christ here and now."

Of our religious sects he was naturally most attracted by the Quakers. He had the autobiography of George Fox on his bookshelf, but he had not yet read it. He heartily approved of the simplicity of the Society of Friends, of the modesty of their attire, and their use of "thee" and "thou." He was, of course, entirely in accord with their principle of non-resistance. Only in one thing the Friends came short of the Tolstoian ideal: they recognised the right of property.

Count Tolstoi was reluctant to speak of controversial questions. He said, "Christ in His last prayer prayed that all His followers might be one. Hence I always endeavour to discover on what points I can agree with any who follow Christ." It was this craving after the true Catholicity, the essential unity of the Christian Brotherhood, that led him to welcome so heartily a little preface I had written some years ago to "Centres of Spiritual Activity," in which I said that "the Ideal Christian Church at the present time ought to include many professing atheists among its members, for men's definitions of themselves are not free from blunder and self-deception, and many professing atheists are unconscious Christians."

"Always endeavour to find out points of agreement rather than those of antagonism; find out where you sympathise rather than where you are in antipathy, such is the spirit of Christ." Hence Count Tolstoi is reluctant to express opinions upon controverted points, upon the authority of the Scripture, upon miracles, and upon the familiar moot questions which are the battle-ground of fierce polemical debaters. Speaking of human conceptions of God, he said, "What does it matter how we approach Him? I approach Him by the metaphysical road. Yours is the road of the peasant; it suits well the simplicity of the child. It is impossible to me. But why dispute? All these roads are like the spokes of a wheel. They start from different points in the circumference, but they all meet in the centre."

But there are two points which Count Tolstoi would not regard as immaterial. The one is the conception of sin and its punishment, the other the Divinity of Christ. Sin, according to him, consists in conscious failure to abide in the will of God. All violence is sin. All participation in the fruit of violence is sin, for the receiver is as bad as the thief. If the Count takes money for any of his books, and that money has been stolen, he becomes a sinner equally with the thief. As the distribution of the goods of this life is based upon violence, we live in sin, encompassed by it constantly. We must try to live out of it by obeying Christ's laws. But sin is negative purely, and in reality is non-existent. Only the good is. The Orthodox notion of Adam's fall and human depravity Count Tolstoi utterly repudiates. Still, he admits that in the soul, which is of God, there are imperfect elements; diabolic elements which lead it to choose evil rather than the truth. In that choice lies the only judgment. The truth would have made man free. He chooses falsehood, and he is judged, for he remains in bondage, and does not enter into the freedom which he might otherwise have possessed. As for the idea of other punishment for sin, that, he declared, was contrary to reason. "Punishment and God are antagonistic terms. God is love. The whole idea of future punishment is radically false, and contrary to the idea of God." I asked him how he explained the parable of Lazarus. "Oh," said he, promptly, "that is all wrong. It was spoken in order to rebuke the social system which places a yawning chasm between the rich and the poor, and to satirise the idea very prevalent among the rich that the poor are their natural servants, both in this world and the next. The moment Dives sees Lazarus he expects that he will do his bidding. The framework of the satire signifies nothing. Christ constantly took the old Jewish ideas, and worked them into His parables. The idea of Judgment was archaic, it was not Christ's. As for the vision in the Apocalypse, that was of no authority." "But," said I, "what did Christ mean when He said, 'Depart, ye cursed'?"

It was a very hot day; we had had a long walk, and Count Tolstoi changed the subject abruptly by saying he was too tired to talk any longer.

The other point upon which Count Tolstoi insists is the human character of Christ. Christ's Divinity he recognises in a sense. Christ spoke the will of God, and He was God, for all of us have what the peasants call a spark of God in our breast. The great object of all religion is to develop that spark to make man more divine. But Christ was only a man like other men. The story of His birth and of His resurrection seem to Count Tolstoi purely mythical. He died, and He did not rise again. He lived, He sinned, He suffered, and He was crucified, rejoicing in His ability to forgive in death those who injured Him. Of the Atonement he says it has had its day, like torture, and disappears before the truer conception of the nature of God.

It is commonly believed that Count Tolstoi denies the immortality of the soul. This is a mistake. It is to him the best beloved of all his speculative doctrines. We had many long talks about the soul and the future life.

"Until two years ago," said he, "I thought but little of the immortality of the soul. Now I think of it constantly, and I ever think of it more and more."

He believes in the pre-existence as well as the immortality of the soul. Each soul had always existed, and would always exist. Nor would he admit that the soul would not preserve its individuality.

"What is this ego? What is the soul? The consciousness of being? It is not identity of matter. It is not identity of thought. It is like a string on which a continuous series of consciousnesses are strung. It is independent of the body. I will always be I. Life is a cone, cut at the apex by birth, and at the base by death. Existence is the continual broadening of the soul in love, which is the only true life, which is God."

"But," I objected, "there are souls which in life do not broaden, but shrink. What of them?"

"I cannot say," he replied, "for I know not what mysterious change may take place at the moment of death, transforming a loveless nature. Or it is possible it may begin again a new existence on new conditions, in which it may have a new chance to fulfil the law of its being—which is love—which is God. It is with difficulty," he continued, "that I can tear my thoughts away from the next world. I regret every moment in which I do not feel that I am dying. If men could fully realise the truth and nature of the next world, there would be no keeping them in this. I long to depart. But this is wrong—I should be patient, and wait. Yet the thought of death is growing so increasingly pleasant that I need to struggle against the fascination of its approach."

It is interesting to be able to read Count Tolstoi's latest and more matured convictions on this subject, for hitherto most people believed that he denied the immortality of the soul. M. Anatole Leroy-Beaulieu, in his interesting study of Count Tolstoi and religion in Russia,* says, "Tolstoi denies categorically the future life. In becoming Christian, he remains Nihilist. He admits for man no other immortality than that of humanity. According to him, true Christianity knows no other. Jesus, he says, always taught the renunciation of personal life, and the doctrine of individual immortality, which affirms the permanence of personality, is in opposition to that teaching. The survival of the soul after death is like the resurrection of the body—only a superstition opposed to the spirit of the Gospel." This may have been Count Tolstoi's opinion at one time. It is not his

* *Revue des deux Mondes*, Sept. 15, 1888, p. 434.

opinion now. "I will always be I," he declares; and the doctrine of personal immortality has assumed an importance in his conception of life which is utterly at variance with the doctrines imputed to him on the strength of passages in his earlier writings. This change of front in this important Christian doctrine more than ever confirmed me in the opinion that Count Tolstoi's religious ideas are still in the making. This is to a certain extent admitted even by himself, nor is it probable that a thinker, who in less than ten years has traversed the immense expanse which separates absolute Atheism from a Christianity of the very literal description outlined in "Ma Religion," can have already arrived at finality.

There are those who stumble and are offended because of his objections to the miraculous and his rejection of the Orthodox theory of the Incarnation; but these matters of theoretical or polemical speculation seem to me less slight importance than the loyalty and devotion with which he bows before the authority of Christ. We only believe that Christ was God in so far as we recognise practically from day to day in our life and conduct the supreme authority of His words. If we do not as Christ commanded—if we oppose ourselves to what we believe to be His will—we may subscribe the Athanasian Creed morning, noon, and night, but nevertheless we do not really believe it. The practical importance of the doctrine of the Divinity of Christ has always seemed to me to lie in the fact that it invests His teaching with the authority of the Categorical Imperative. If we do not obey we do not believe; the measure of our obedience is the measure of our belief. Hence, from the point of view of the Gospel, Count Tolstoi's uncompromising demand for literal obedience to the precepts of Christ, even though he may be mistaken in his interpretation, seems to afford far more cause for rejoicing than there is reason for lamentation over his hesitation to accept the Orthodox formula as to the Divine nature of Christ. If Christ be God, then is He to be obeyed; and, as no one teaches more unreservedly the duty of obeying Him than Count Tolstoi, he seems to arrive at the same end as the Church, although by a different road.

Wherein his doctrine seems to be most lacking is in the absence of any sense of an unseen intelligence in communion with man. That great void will have to be filled up before "Tolstoism" can hope to satisfy the cravings of the human heart. "A stream of tendency" is but a barren substitute for "Our Father, which art in heaven." A Christ who died and did not rise again is not likely to replace in the heart of humanity the living and risen Redeemer.

But the more confident we are in the reality of these things, the more conscious of the craving which they alone can satisfy, the more must we rejoice when those to whom men listen dedicate the maturity of their powers to proclaim to the world that all the things that are therein are not to be compared to the truth as it is in Jesus. To bring men to Christ even as a man, to teach them to love Him as did the early disciples, is surely the first step in the right road.

## CHAPTER V.

### THE TEACHER AND THE TEACHINGS OF COUNT TOLSTOI.

COUNT TOLSTOI has set forth with great fulness of detail every stage in his mental and spiritual development in his writings. His narrative is, for the most part, metaphysical. He gives little personal detail of his circumstances. I am, therefore, glad to be able to mention one of the accidents which contributed mightily to the change of his views. For many years he had been studying closely the great problem of life. In order to enable him to enter more fully into the spirit of the Gospel, he applied himself after he had passed his fortieth year to the acquisition of Greek. For a long time he wandered in darkness. Then, in his own picturesque phrase, "he discovered a little window through which he could see God." Afterwards he discovered in the words of Christ the nearest guide man has to the will of God. It was about seven years ago, when the Russian census was being taken, that the experience occurred which precipitated the final change of his views. In Moscow, the Government requisitions the University students as census-takers. The Count's eldest son was then at the University, and he took his share with his fellow-students in the work of numbering the people. Count Tolstoi accompanied his son as he went his rounds, penetrating with him into the lowest quarters of the great city. The census is taken in the slums as well as in the palaces, and it was an eventful day on which Count Tolstoi went slumming in Moscow. He came home utterly upset. Up to that time he had lived an easy, egoist, luxurious life. Everything that the heart of man could desire he had to the full: fame, wealth, health, occupation, a large and happy family, and hosts of friends—all were his. He had everything. Now he was suddenly brought face to face with the squalid poverty of those who had nothing. It was as if a vision of the under world had suddenly been revealed to his gaze. He came home a changed man, and from that day he has only had one regret—viz., that his family rendered it impossible for him to abandon all that he had in order to follow the life of those who had nothing. He would have sacrificed all the means by which his family is supported—books, estate, everything; but the family objected to be sacrificed, and the Count yielded to the menace of *force majeure*. Had he attempted to carry out his ideas, an Order of Administration would probably have been issued by the Government, and his property would have been made over to trustees to be administered for the benefit of his wife and family.

His first impulse was to seek salvation by means of the Church. He prayed constantly, and attended all the Church services. Then suddenly he concluded that it was of no use, gave up all Church attendance, and fell back on the teaching of Christ and the five Commandments. In arriving at this result, he says he was most assisted by the teachings of Sutaieff, a peasant of Novgorod, who in the year 1876 had been brought into notoriety by a prosecution instituted against him for refusing to baptise his child until it was old enough to repent of its sins.

Sutaieff, an emancipated serf, who kept a marble-mason's shop at Petersburg, taught himself to read in order to study the Gospel, and by a literal interpretation of its precepts he arrived at the conclusion that commerce was usury, and that the only work without it was the tilling of the fields. Giving effect to this theory he distributed all his savings among the poor, forgave all his debtors their debts, and went to live in his own village. When there he was gradually driven out of

Orthodoxy by the bigotry and intolerance of the priest. When your spiritual pastor responds to an appeal for the explanation of a text bearing on baptism by replying, " What do you want of me, you blackguard? Do you wish me to christen you with this stick?" it is not to be wondered at if you stray into the paths of dissent. When Sutaieff used to argue with the priest, he cut him short by saying that he was the devil. " If I had only known what you would have turned out, I would have drowned you in the baptismal font." After this, in due process of time, Sutaieff became the head of a dissenting congregation that met in his house and read the New Testament. The new Church was based on the doctrine that God is Love, and that all men are brethren. This being so, it followed, according to his logic, that war, usury, commerce, and money were all contrary to the Divine will and the brotherly idea. They tried community of goods, but found that it did not answer, and fell back upon the ancient institution of private property *plus* brotherly assistance in time of need, exchanging labour for labour as much as possible without the intervention of money payments. They tried also to do without locks, bolts, and bars; but they had to give that up also until such time as all accepted the community of goods. A story is told that some peasants from a neighbouring village, hearing that he left his granary unlocked, came to steal his grain. They had carried off all of it but one sack, when Sutaieff appeared. Instead of seizing the thieves, he threw the remaining sack of corn into their cart, saying, " If you are in need of bread, take this also." Such heroic generosity smote the consciences of the thieves, and next day they brought all the grain back, saying, " We have changed our minds." Sutaieff refused to pay taxes unless the officials explained how his money would be spent, for he entertained moral scruples against paying taxes that would be spent in military preparations. Sutaieff's goods were therefore distrained upon just as if he were a Quaker in the olden days, when Church rates were levied in England.*

Sutaieff was the spiritual father of Count Tolstoi, who, as M. Anatole Leroy-Beaulieu has pointed out, has done little more than give a literary dress to the peasant's ideas. Count Tolstoi

* See "The Russian Peasantry," vol. ii., c. 3, and *Revue des Deux Mondes*, Sept. 15, 1888.

would be the first to disclaim any originality for his discoveries. He is the interpreter to the world at large of what the Russian peasants have always known. Nay, he even goes so far in his prostration before the moujik as to declare that the peasants possess as much ability to express their views as any which he can claim.

Some peasant in Siberia had written entirely unaided a pamphlet, which the Count praised very highly, and referred to as an indication that there was plenty of genius among the peasants if only pains were taken to give it opportunity for expression.

Count Tolstoi, like Sutaieff, magnifies labour, and especially manual labour. It is on this ground that men meet in common brotherhood. If any men devote themselves to intellectual toil, they cut themselves off from the masses, and establish an aristocracy. Every day every man ought to do some work with his hands. To plant a tree, to fence a field, to plough, to make boots, that was real work; that was service done for mankind; that placed man in healthy, natural relations with the world and with his fellows.

But most of the so-called intellectual work, what was it? Nothing but illusion. "Tchinovniks sit in offices signing papers, and imagine that they are doing something, that they are governing the country. Ach! what a delusion. It is all a fiction, this Government, a mere hallucination. Of course I do not deny there are men, live men, with pens in their hands, writing on real paper. That is true. Neither do I deny that in yonder church there is a live priest saying masses for the dead. He is doing something, no doubt; he is at least passing his time and making believe that he is employed. But his masses are nothing, and their effect upon the dead is mere nonsense. So it is with Government. It is a chimera. And you who seek to influence Governments and prevent wars by that means, you might as well take your stick and beat the leaves which the wind blows from the trees. There is only one way of obtaining peace and of preventing evil, and that is to refuse yourself to do any act of violence and never, even to prevent evil, do a wrong."

I never could quite master the Count's doctrine of the impotence or non-existence of Governments. He was scornfully contemptuous of the so-called great men—the Napoleons, the Bismarcks, and so forth—who imagine they can make wars and alter the course of history. Bismarck, he said, was like Napoleon; all these statesmen were more or less charlatans, the idols of one hour, the scorn of the next; now lauded to the skies as oracles of wisdom, and then derided as the veriest fools as soon as the spell broke and their power passed. He objected to all political activity, and ridiculed the House of Commons as unsparingly as all other modes of Government.

When the fire broke out in Yasnaia Poliana, he was as energetic as any one in endeavouring to prevent its spreading, but against similar conflagrations in the international field or in domestic politics he opposed an absolute apathetic indifference. I told him that he reminded me of Mr. Carlyle, who advised me only two years before his death to stand aside from politics and to allow things to go from bad to worse, a development which he deemed to be inevitable in a democratic age.

Count Tolstoi heartily concurred. "Yes," said he, "that is right. Take no part in them, having nothing to do with their anti-Christian fiction of Governments. Leave things alone. They must go on from bad to worse before they get better." It was very odd that two men starting from such diametrically opposite standpoints should agree in advising a policy of passivity.

Carlyle's hope was that if democracy were allowed to develop its downward destinies unchecked, it would before long arrive at such a pitch of despair as to hail the strong able man who would rule the people with a rod of iron. Count Tolstoi, on the other hand, looks forward to a coming of the Kingdom of Heaven, in which mankind, cured of the delusion of believing in the hallucination of Governments, and armies, and wars, will live together in Christian brotherhood, in peaceful anarchy. The rival apostles of despotism and anarchy agreed in tendering the same prescription of folded arms.

"If you recognise Property, or Church, or State, there is no future for you," said he on one occasion, "for all these are founded on violence, and violence will not last. Before all those who recognise violence or anything that is based on violence there is no future, only an impassable stone wall. Property, Church, State, Government: these are doomed as was slavery, and all other barbarisms which humanity has left behind." Among other barbarisms which the world must outgrow is the idea of the family and of the nation. I had remarked in the course of one of our conversations that the family was the sacred school of which mankind learned the lessons of love and sympathy, the unit of organisation which society should regard as the ideal, when he sharply interrupted me. "Not so. The family is the great school of selfishness. Why should I care more for my children than for other people's? My children ought to be no more and no less to me than the children of yonder peasant. To love all men equally, whether born in your own family or in that of a total stranger, that is the law of Christ." "If so," remarked the mother of a family to whom I repeated the conversation, "the law of Christ is against the law of nature. If we had not to love our own children more than anybody else's children, the world would die out. Only a mother can rear children, and she can only do it because they are her own. It needs one to be part of yourself to be able to do all for a baby, as it should be done by, without feeling the burden." As Count Tolstoi deprecates the limitation of love to the family, so he sets his face against any national distinctions— colour, rank, nationality—whoso made any distinction between men on those grounds was not truly obeying the law of Christ. Even before his conversion in his unregenerate days he never felt any interest in national distinctions. He marvelled much at the Americans disturbing themselves about the Chinese. "Why should not the Chinese come? What difference did it make that your brother had a yellow skin and was called Chinese? He was still your brother. Why make a distinction which Christ had condemned?" The same argument applied to the objection taken to the influx of Irish and foreign immigrants from the Old World. As for the Mormons, they were polygamous brethren whose mistakes might be remedied by persuasion and arguments, but whose errors ought not to be dealt with by force. Our difficulties with the Irish he would solve in the same off-hand fashion. If no Englishman would consent at the bidding of that anti-Christian fiction, the so-called State, to take a bayonet and therewith murder his Irish brother, there would be trouble about Ireland. The *fons et origo mali* is the ability of the simulacrum called a Government to induce men to kill each other at its bidding. Murder is thus the corner-stone of the organised State, and in forbidding murder Count Tolstoi secures the Christian anarchy which is to him so supreme a desideratum.

"Why not call it murder?" he said to me repeatedly. "We invent fine names to conceal the ugly fact. Christ says, 'Thou shalt not kill,' but the Governments say, 'We say unto you, kill; and we will call it not sin, but duty.' Duty, duty, how I hate that word! It is used to consecrate all crimes. The hangman murders his fellow. His conscience reproaches him. He silences it with the phrase, 'It is my duty.' The soldier kills his neighbour. Again it is his duty; he only obeys orders. There is no such thing as these duties. There is only one duty. That is to obey the law of Christ. It is so clear, so clear; I cannot see how you can ignore it. It is to me only possible by a kind of madness. I had a comrade in the Caucasus who died there, and who seems to me very much to resemble mankind in this respect. He was quite mad, although we never knew it until after his death. He left a pocket-book with his diary behind, and it was this which showed him to be mad. He would make entries quite sensibly for a time, then he would write 'Grupp,' or some such word. Instantly his senses seemed to leave him, and he would write the wildest nonsense. So it seems to me mankind at large has many words like that poor fellow's 'Grupp.' They may talk sensibly enough about other things, but as soon as they say 'State,' 'Government,' 'Mobilisation,' their sense disappears, and they talk like lunatics."

Like many Russians, Count Tolstoi goes almost beside himself at the thought of capital punishment. He wrote to the Emperor on his accession, reminding him of Christ's words, and calling for the pardon of the Nihilists who assassinated his father. M. Pobedonostzeff replied, "You believe in a Christ of weakness and of sentiment, but I believe in a Christ of authority and power." There have been several other executions, every one of which falls upon Count Tolstoi like a red-hot spark on the eyeball. To an Englishman accustomed to at least a score of hangings per annum in England alone, there is something almost incomprehensible in the fierce moral revolt of the cultured Russian against capital punishment. Count Tolstoi, indeed, seems inclined to carry the objection to taking life to almost Buddhistic lengths. He has become a vegetarian, and he quoted with evident sympathy the remark of a peasant, who had shuddered at the human-like cry of a slaughtered pig, " I wonder if its butcher does not think he will have to answer for its life before God." The ordinary objection to capital punishment, that it is often preferable to slow death by prolonged imprisonment, Count Tolstoi gets over by dispensing with all punishment whatever. But when I put to him the question whether the principle of doing as you would be done by did not justify punishment as a preventive measure, he did not make a satisfactory reply. Yet surely it is clear enough that most of us, since the days of Æsop, who made the thief on the gallows bite off his mother's ear because she had not punished his early pilferings, would in our saner moments distinctly prefer that the natural weakness of our good resolutions should be strengthened by the prompt infliction of pains and penalties if we yielded to temptation. Punishment is often considered to imply a certain censoriousness or lack of charity on the part of those who inflict it. Its true basis is such a keen sympathy with those who are tempted as to impel us to erect the most efficacious barrier in our power as a deterrent against yielding to temptations, from which much greater evils would result. A flogging, imprisonment, or even a hanging is but a concrete embodiment of the result of experience, which, in the interest of the tempted, should be pressed home upon the mind by the most effective possible method. As we would choose these for ourselves, so we are warranted by the golden rule in inflicting them upon others.

There was always a great simplicity and candour about Count Tolstoi. Much as he seems to condemn others, he always seems to be strong to fulfil his own favourite precept, and judge not. That he comes, like all of us, far short of his ideal, he has admitted in a very touching passage published by a Russian interviewer, and translated by Mr. Kennan in a recent number of *The Century*:—

" People say to me, ' Well, Lef Nikolaivitch, as far as preaching goes, you preach; but how about your practice?' The question is a perfectly natural one; it is always put to me, and it always shuts my mouth. ' You preach,' it is said, ' but how do you live?' I can only reply that I do not preach—passionately as I desire to do so. I might preach through my actions, but my actions are bad. That which I say is not preaching; it is only my attempt to find out the meaning and the significance of life. People often say to me, 'If you think that there is no reasonable life outside the teachings of Christ, and if you love a reasonable life, why do you not fulfil the Christian precepts?' I am guilty and blameworthy and contemptible because I do not fulfil them; but at the same time I say—not in justification, but in explanation, of my inconsistency—compare my previous life with the life I am now living, and you will see that I am trying to fulfil. I have not, it is true, fulfilled one eighty-thousandth part, and I am to blame for it; but it is not because I do not wish to fulfil all, but because I am unable. Teach me how to extricate myself from the meshes of temptation in which I am entangled—help me—and I will fulfil all. I wish and hope to do it even without he'p. Condemn me if you choose—I do that myself—but condemn me, and not the path which I am following, and which I point out to those who ask me where, in my opinion, the path is. If I know the road home, and if I go along it drunk, and staggering from side to side, does that prove that the road is not the right one? If it is not the right one, show me another. If I stagger and wander, come to my help, and support and guide me in the right path. Do not yourselves confuse and mislead me, and then rejoice over it and cry, 'Look at him! He says he is going home, and he is floundering into the swamp!' You are not evil spirits from the swamp; you are also human beings, and you also are going home. You know that I am alone—you know that I cannot wish or intend to go into the swamp—then help me! My heart is breaking with despair because we have all lost the road; and while I struggle with all my strength to find it and keep in it, you, instead of pitying me when I go astray, cry triumphantly, 'See! He is in the swamp with us!'"

Count Tolstoi was much interested in temperance work. He and his daughters are the centre of a temperance society which has about 1,000 affiliated members all over Russia. The propaganda of teetotalism lay very close to his heart. He took no wine. Kvass, a kind of cross between table beer and barley water, was his ordinary beverage. The Orthodox Church in Russia, I fear, is somewhat indifferent to the Temperance Reformation. Its clergy would be all the better if teetotalism were made a condition of holy orders. This, however, is out of the question. This is chiefly due to the extraordinarily narrow conception of the work of the Church which prevails in the Eastern Communion. When Dr. Alexayeff, of Moscow, returned from Canada full of the enthusiasm of the Temperance Reformation, he sought to rouse the clergy to exert themselves against drunkenness. The Metropolitan of Moscow listened to him patiently, and then said, "What can I do? The work is one of association, and an association pertains to the worldly sphere. I can do nothing. The Church has nothing to do with these things. I can only give you my sympathy." Despairing of succeeding with the clergy, Dr. Alexayeff went to Yasnaia Poliana and appealed to Count Tolstoi, who formed a temperance society there and then of his own household, and has been at work at it ever since.

We made a long excursion one evening to a neighbouring village to inspect a newly-built cottage, the walls of which were made, not of wood, but of puddled loam. The advantage of such a mud hut is that it will not burn. The roof may blaze up and disappear, but the walls stand. As we were fresh from the fire at Yasnaia Poliana, we naturally appreciated the mud walls, and Count Tolstoi determined to rebuild and adopt the new fashion in one of the cottages that had been burnt down. When we reached home, the Count had a warm discussion with a bright and genial young student, who was also a guest, as to the heinousness of taking money for labour, or the products of labour. The student argued, with much shrewdness, that if a man were to be forbidden to sell water from his well he would never sink the well, and the only result of the interdict upon selling water would be that there would be none to sell. The Count was full of compassion for benighted mortals who could be deceived by the old fallacies of Adam Smith, but although he repeated that it was "so clear, so clear," to him, I am afraid he left us unconvinced. It was on the same summer evening that the Count told us a marvellous story of his finding in the Crimea, a year or two before, the last bullet which he had fired when he left besieged Sebastopol, more than thirty years ago. There had only been one shot fired from a new mountain gun which he took with him from Sebastopol to the Caucasus. He had never revisited the scene of his first campaign until the other day, and then, strange to say, he came upon the identical shot which he had fired into the allied lines, sticking into the hill-side as if it had been awaiting his return.

It was a very pleasant week which I passed at Yasnaia Poliana. The weather was fine, and we rambled night and morning in all directions. One thing only in the landscape created a constant sense of pain. There are no enclosed fields in Russia. The pasture adjoins the tilled ground, and the horses and the cattle stray where they please in search of grass. The horses are all so tightly hobbled with a cord at the fetlock of their fore-feet, that it practically reduces them to the use of three legs. It was painful to see the poor things hobbling along in a series of jumps, lifting both the fore-feet together, while their foals frisked naturally around. I suppose it is inevitable, as the horses would otherwise run away from the small boys who are left in charge of them, as the girls are left in charge of the cows; but inevitable or not, it makes you sorry for the horses.

The herds of the peasants browse together on the common land of the village. A remarkable sight it is to come upon such a herd from above, when the animals are lying down chewing the cud in the noonday sun. At a distance it looks as if a large carpet of red and black pattern was spread over the bright green grass. When you come nearer you see that the apparent carpet is due to the odd intermixture of animals lying side by side. There are sometimes hundreds altogether; cows, bullocks, calves, bulls, pigs, and sheep, all intermixed, and lying down so close together that the grass is hardly visible between their bodies. There is room for great improvement in the live stock. The habit of allowing young bulls to run at large among the cows is fatal to any scientific improvement of the breed. Count Tolstoi kept what may be called a pedigree bull in a stall, but he has been very unfortunate. His bulls for two years running killed their keeper, a fact which did not increase the popularity of such high-bred stock in the neighbourhood. Count Tolstoi admits the advantage of improving the breed of cattle, but he is much opposed to agricultural shows—the possibility of a genuine agricultural show by the genuine peasant agriculturists of Russia not yet having been realised by any one. "But how," I asked, "can the improvements made by one be generalised for the use of all except by such means?" "You forget the pilgrims," said Count Tolstoi.

The part which the pilgrims play in the social economy of Russia is quite incredible to those who live in Western lands. The pilgrim in Russia to-day is still what he was to the West in the era before the Crusades—the news-carrier of the world. He is the only popular newspaper of rural Russia. He hears everything, sees everything, repeats everything. He meets at the great shrines—whither pilgrims converge from all points of the compass—strangers from the frozen North and the torrid South. They spend days, weeks, months on the road. They are the popular tourists of Modern Russia. Many of them are habitual tramps, incorrigible vagrants we should call them, who are always on the road. They carry the news from village to village, and share it hospitably with their fellow-pilgrims on the way. If Count Tolstoi imports a new breed of Cochin-China fowl, within a week every village within fifty miles on either side of Yasnaia Poliana will have heard of the strange yellow monsters that lord it in his poultry-yard. For your pilgrim is a good soul, and charitable withal. He takes care that a story loses nothing in the telling, and lest it should perish on the way he sends it forth on its wanderings with ample embellishment and exaggeration. It is these poor folk with the clouted shoon and pilgrim staff who are the real journalists of Muscovy, and like their *confrères* in more artificially organised society, they are among the most potent shuttles which in the loom of life weave the scattered and isolated communities of men into the warp and web of a nation. News, romance, travel, and let us not omit sometimes religious enthusiasm, make the pilgrim one of the bright spots of colour in the somewhat sombre monotony of Russian existence. Never shall I forget the rapt expression of fervent ecstasy in some of the faces of the pilgrim women who were on their knees kissing the floor before the sacred throne of St. Serge, at Troitsa. In some of the pictures of the Crucifixion the old masters have caught that wonderful look of exaltation, the eye radiant with a glory that is not of this world, and which seems to be equally blended of tears and smiles, of intense grief and rapturous joy. But pigments cannot adequately express the emotion that glowed in these women's faces as the solemn music of the chant rose and fell, and the forms of the worshippers bowed in the Holy of Holies of their Russian temple. That look on the upturned face of a peasant girl was one of the most beautiful things I saw in all Russia. Yes, I may say the most beautiful, although I saw the midsummer sun rise over the blue waters of the Neva.

Very pleasant it was to ramble through the woods in the cool of the day, listening to the stories of the country-side and hearing at distant intervals catches of peasant songs, or the liquid melody of the nightingale's song. In the day-time the lark's song was as if it had been in England; the plague of the confusion of tongues did not descend upon the birds. Now and then a great hawk would glide silently over the tree-tops and hover like a feathered death over the copse. Once I saw a snake, some eighteen inches long, whose bite, Count Tolstoi said, was dangerous but not deadly; I had no wish to try the experiment, neither had the snake, for it rustled off rapidly without attempting to bite. The larger animals are becoming extinct. There are some large stags roaming about the woods, and in winter-time the wolves come out of their retreats to prey upon the flocks. All the peasants keep dogs to scare off the unwelcome visitors, who, however, seem to have rather a hard time of it.

A wolf battue is a most popular sport, and from the account given me by the Count's daughters, who had assisted at one the previous winter, the unfortunate wolf has about as much chance as a pheasant in a hot corner in a drive in an English covert. The cold also is often too much for them. Last winter close to Yasnaia Poliana a great grey wolf was found standing erect in the middle of a field, frozen as dead as a stone. A wolf in his healthy condition is an uncanny beast, but a mad wolf is a combination unpleasant to contemplate. Yet this great horror visited Toula quite recently. The patients sent to M. Pasteur to be cured of hydrophobia, who were bitten by mad wolves, came from Toula. The account given of some of these poor people as they were driven along the highway, strapped on the little country carts, was very horrible. As might be imagined from the existence of such a nightmare in the neighbourhood, the alarm of the country-side was great.

A pretty little cottage was pointed out to me near the railway station as the residence of a poor woman who had been the heroine of a very painful story connected with this visitation of the mad wolf. She was a widow who lived with her daughter-in-law and her little grandson. During the time the wolf scare was at its height, a wolf came out of the wood, and attacked one of the widow's dogs. The little lad, thinking the wolf was only a strange dog, picked up a stick, and struck it to make it leave the dog. Instantly the brute left the dog and seized the child. His cries brought out his grandmother, who, seeing him in the mouth of the wolf, ran to extricate him. The wolf dropped the boy and rushed at her. With rare presence of mind the poor woman awaited his approach, and as he came at her open-mouthed she thrust her naked hand down his throat. His jaws closed upon her arm, lacerating it terribly, but, she held her ground notwithstanding all his struggles. Gradually the wolf choked, and she begged the boy to run into the house and bring her a knife with which to cut its throat. The child obeyed, but found his mother temporarily bereft of reason in the house, and it was some time before he could get the knife. At last it was procured, and the animal killed. It was a wolf which had been for some time past the scourge of the neighbourhood. The peasants assembled to see the carcase of their enemy. Suddenly a great fear fell upon them. Perhaps the wolf was mad. If so, the widow woman, who was all weak with pain and loss of blood, might go mad also. Thereupon they seized her and shut her up in an outhouse without attendance, without water, without food or fires. For twenty-four hours she lay there, almost delirious with the fever of her wounds, not knowing but that she had been bitten by a mad wolf. At last she was released. There was no proof that she had hydrophobia, and she was allowed to go at large. But all her dogs were killed; nor were her entreaties attended to when she asked for either a dog or a man to protect her and hers from another attack by the wolves. She recovered, but for months afterwards her house was shunned by the rustics who formerly had frequented it as a traktir or tea-house. "Who knows," they said, "but that she may suddenly go mad and bite us?" Her reward for saving the neighbourhood from the ravages of the wolf was to be badly bitten, to be locked up as mad, to have all her dogs killed, and then when she was released to be boycotted by her former customers, as one who contained within her the seeds of madness.

In the midst of communion with Nature, in all its forms, Count Tolstoi spends his life. For the first twenty years after his marriage he never quitted his estate. Even now he leaves it with reluctance, and always rejoices when the hybernation of winter is at an end. He reads and enjoys Thoreau, with whom he has much in common. Americans are much more in sympathy with Count Tolstoi than the English. His writings were translated in America before they were translated in England, and they seem to find much more enthusiastic readers there than with us.

For one letter which the Count receives from England he receives six from Americans. The admiration is mutual. "Turgenieff," he once said to me, "told me that the Americans wrote nothing worth reading. Therein he was wrong. I like American literature very much—it is very good." He thought William Lloyd Garrison was a little too conscious of his virtue, but he admired his non-resistance principles, and lamented that a Russian translation of his life had been lost in prison. For Emerson he professed great admiration, and also for Theodore Parker's "Bibles of the World."

Of English novels he spoke at some length. Of the more recent he had not heard. "Dr. Jekyll and Mr. Hyde" he had read, but he had not even heard of Walter Besant, whose "All Sorts and Conditions of Men" I sent him after I reached St. Petersburg. The spirit of that novel is Count Tolstoi's in so far as it insists upon personal living among the poor. He was much interested in hearing about Toynbee Hall. Personal service, personal sacrifice, were the notes of his doctrine.

"Do you know," he asked me, "what I liked best in the letter which you wrote from Holloway Gaol about the essence of Christianity being to be a Christ? This: 'Christ did not bribe a superfluous angel by liberal subscriptions in order to be crucified by deputy. Neither can individual Christians be Christs by deputy.'

"That," he said, "is the truth. We must all do the same. We must descend to the level of the men we wish to help and become one of themselves—not as angels from above, but as brothers helping them side by side—that is our duty. Whether we do that or not, is the test whether we are in the Church or not. The real Church consists of those who are united to Christ by obedience to His Commandments. No one has a right to say, 'I am in the Church,' much less 'I am the Church.' All that we dare say is 'I try to be of the Church,' and leave to God and your fellows to say whether or not you succeed."

His idea of Christianity is that of a broad Humanitarianism. Imagine an agricultural Robert Elsmere, with a dash of

Quakerism in his doctrines, and you will be pretty near realising Count Tolstoi. Of our novelists, he spoke most highly of Dickens, who he declared was the most Christian of them all. The best three English novelists, he said, were Thackeray, Dickens, and Trollope – a descending climax. "After Trollope whom have you?"

It was in talking of English authors that Count Tolstoi suddenly exclaimed, "I do not think we have as yet even opened our eyes to the extent to which we can use the press. I have now for some years been thinking out a great project by which we should be able to publish a World's Library at a price and a form which would bring the best thoughts of the best men of all time within the range of the poorest peasant. I was led up to this by the success, the wonderful success, which has attended the sale of cheap tracts in Russia. In the last three years we have begun the circulation by means of the ordinary colporteurs of small tracts written explaining the Commandments of Christ and the duty of man to his neighbour, all of which, of course, are sanctioned by the Censor. They are clearly printed with an illustrative cover, and they are sold wholesale from 1¼ kopecks and upwards. The colporteurs retail them at from two, three, and four kopecks; they are very popular, and we have sold no fewer than eight millions in the last three years; if there is such a demand for such little books, why should we not supply it by bringing the literature of all the world down to the means and capacity of a peasant?"

The following is a list of the publications issued by the Tolstoian Propaganda:—

Two Old Men.  
Three Tales.  
God sees the Truth, but does not at once Reveal it.  
} Approved by the Minister of War for circulation in the army. By Leon Tolstoi.

The Caucasian Prisoner. By Leon Tolstoi.  
What Makes People to Live: a Tale. By Leon Tolstoi.  
The First Brandy-Distiller; or, How the Devil Earned a Crust of Bread a Comedy. By Leon Tolstoi.  
The Power of Darkness: a Drama in Five Acts. By Leon Tolstoi.  
The Candle; or, How the Good Monjik Overcame the Wicked Clerk. By Leon Tolstoi.  
Ivan the Fool and his Two Brothers. By Leon Tolstoi.  
Where Love is, there is God. By Leon Tolstoi.  
Once the Fire is Kindled, it cannot be Extinguished. By Leon Tolstoi.

The Siege of Sevastopol: abbreviated from Stories of the Defence of Sevastopol. By Leon Tolstoi.
The Railway Signal: a Story. By Vsevolod Garshin.
The Bears. By Vsevolod Garshin.
Four Days on the Field of Battle. By Vsevolod Garshin.
Black Ravens, and A Whole Life for Others: Two Tales. By P. V. Zassodimsky.
The Alchemist; or, The Wonderful Stone of the Wise Men: a Tale of the Middle Ages. By P. V. Zassodimsky.
A Child of the "Mir." By P. V. Zassodimsky.
Poverty is no Crime: a Comedy in Three Acts. By A. N. Ostrovsky.
Live not for Yourself, but for God; a Popular Drama in Three Acts. By A. N. Ostrovsky.
Two Brothers: a Peasant Tale. By S. T. Semenov.
In the Town. By S. T. Semenov.
An Unjust Fate: a Tale. By V. T. Savikin.
Grandfather Sofron; or, The Judgment of Man is not that of God. By V. T. Savikin.
A Famine Year: a Peasant Tale. By Ivan Manjuro.
St. Francis of Assisi. By E. Sveshnikov.
Gallia. By O. T. Schmidt.
Christ on a Visit to the Moujik: a Tale. By N. S. Leskov.
A Fellow-Traveller: a Tale. By P. Paverint.
John Huss: a Tale. By A. Erleven.
Mary the Lace-Maker: a Novel. By O. N. Khmelev.
The Thief: a Novel. By A. E. Gololobov.
The Children of Makhmud. By V. N. Nemirovitch Dautchenko.
Ill-Health. By A. Potyekhin.
What can be Seen in the Sky. By T. A. Kleber.
Advice to Mothers on the Nursing of Children. Adapted to peasant life. Compiled from works of Dr. N. F. Mikhalov.
A Woman's Lot: a Peasant Tale.
Fabiola; or, The Early Christians.
Ivan the Warrior: a Tale of the Early Christians.
The Story of the Covetous Moujik Ermil.
A Glorious Deed: an Eastern Tale.
Brother against Brother.
The Travelling Companion: a Tale.
The Division of Property.
King Crœsus and Solon.
The Light of Life.
The Life of St. Paulinus, Bishop of Nolant, and the Sufferings of the Holy Martyrs, Theodore and Nikitin.
Life of St. Peter, the Tax-Gatherer.
Life of the Charitable St. Philarete.
Socrates, the Greek Philosopher.
The Flower-Garden: a Collection of Anecdotes.

The Harp-Player: a Collection of Poems.
Proverbs for Every Day. (An almanack with proverbs for each day.)
A new Short Spelling-Book.
A Christmas Carol. Translated from Charles Dickens.

The volumes are published by T. D. Setin and Co., at Moscow, the great majority at one and a half kopecks. A few of the longer stories are issued at three or five kopecks. As a rule, each volume is from thirty to fifty pages in length, the dramas and comedies being somewhat longer. Most of the volumes have well-drawn illustrations on the paper cover, both back and front; and below, the sentence—" Not in the power of God, but of Truth."

I asked him whether the colporteurs were organised specially for the sale of Tolstoian literature of propaganda.

"No," he replied, "we simply supply the trade. M. Setin of Moscow is at the head of the most extensive colportage in Russia, and all our sale goes through him. Before we began, he used to sell about 2,000,000 a year. He had about 200 different publications, of which he sold on an average 10,000 each. Now we have doubled his business in three years."

"But would Setin be available for your wider project?"

"Certainly, in Russia; but my scheme is not exclusively Russian; it is international. It may only be a dream on my part, but I see the possibility of publishing a Universal Classical Library at not more than five kopecks a volume—that is to say, one penny of your money—which should appear simultaneously in French, German, English, and Russian. To me this is a religious idea; for the best books of the world, what are they? They are the revelation of reason to the mind of man. The mind began in the Infinite—that is, it began in God. It finds expression in all the highest thoughts and classic utterances of human genius."

"Then your Universal Classical Library would be really the collection of the canon of the Scripture of Humanity? Would it not be rather bulky?"

"No. Not if you do that which is indispensable if it is to be brought down to the means and the time of the peasant. That is, if you eliminate all that is accidental, and temporary, and provincial, and leave only that which is eternal and human. When you have eliminated all that divides men, you will find that which unites them is not so unwieldy in dimensions. There is some of it in all classic literature, and it is all in the spirit of Christ. That is all-pervading. You cannot get out of the atmosphere of Christ's teaching. He has solved everything. Try to solve any problem, and you will find when you have solved it that you have been anticipated by Christ."

Between Christ and what is usually denominated Christian, of course, as has been remarked, Count Tolstoi makes a wide distinction. For instance, when we came to discuss what works should find a place in the Penny Universal Classical Library of the World, he said that he would not allow either Milton or Dante a place in the list. Personally he would like to exclude Bunyan also, but, in view of the extreme popularity of the "Pilgrim's Progress" in Russia, he would be neutral. He said that a Frenchman and a Croat were already co-operating with him in the execution of this project, and he would be glad to ascertain what chance there was for the Penny Classical Library in England.

I said that I feared our weekly papers supplied the only reading which the poor cared to buy, and that more might be done by passing the classics through the newspapers than by an independent publication, for which you would, in the first instance, want circulation.

He said that "Marcus Aurelius" was almost ready for the press, and it was purposed to follow it by "Diogenes," "Epictetus," Xenophon's "Memorabilia," Xenophon's "Economica," some eighteen or twenty of Plutarch's "Lives," the "Phædo" and the "Banquet" of Plato, and a very condensed version of the "Iliad" and the "Odyssey." All of these, he thought, would be appreciated and understood by the peasantry in all countries. He objected to include any of the Greek tragedians in the list. If the Library succeeded, after they had published all the classics of the first flight, then they would have a second category, in which Herodotus and Thucydides would have a leading place, but in the first instance Travels and History would be ignored.

Of Latin authors he was very sparing. He rejected Horace and Ovid outright. Parts of Virgil he would allow. Juvenal, Seneca, and Cicero's "De Amicitia," were the others which he mentioned as being in contemplation. The Chinese—Confucius, Mencius, and Laotze—he held in the greatest respect. They would come very near the front; so would a book giving the gist of Buddhism.

We did not, of course, compile an exhaustive catalogue. He mentions with strong approval Pascal and the first part of Thomas à Kempis. Victor Hugo also he put nearly at the front of the French, remarking that "Les Misérables" ought to be read in every language under the sky.

When he came to English authors I was anxious to know whom he would select. Shakespeare, of course, came first. He said that most of his plays were translated into Russian, and some of them were very popular. "Which most?" I asked. "*King Lear*," said he, instantly; "it embodies the experience of every Russian izba. After *King Lear* comes, I think, *Macbeth*, and then *Hamlet*. Milton is very popular, especially among the old peasants, and has long been familiar in an old Russian translation. Bunyan is a great favourite among the Stundists, Molokani, and all the Rationalist Dissenters." "Robinson Crusoe" he would add, of course; also "Gulliver's Travels." He was in doubt about Emerson. But he would publish Bacon's essays, and some of Burke, Theodore Parker, and Matthew Arnold, a good deal of Dickens, some of Scott, and "Felix Holt" and "Adam Bede" of George Eliot.

So the talk went on. I fear it would be difficult to condense "Les Misérables" or "Adam Bede" into the covers of a penny book. Still, the idea has already been partially realised in Germany, and it may yet be realised more completely in England and America. In Russia, where there is the greatest need, Count Tolstoi is already at work.

I could not help marvelling that, with so many projects on hand, Count Tolstoi should attach such exaggerated importance to the need of personal labour in the potato field. To hold up the ideal of Christ's Ethics before the world seems to be more useful labour than wasting his health and strength in ploughing, which any moujik can do better than he. When I begged him to take care of himself, if only that he might live to deliver his message, he shook his head.

"That is propaganda," said he, "and propaganda is the temptation of the devil. My first duty is to live rightly. It may not be my duty to teach; it is my duty to work with my hands."

I will close these desultory reminiscences of many a long and pleasant talk by recalling what Count Tolstoi said as to the political outlook. I put the question to him, "Suppose the Emperor were to ask you what he should do; what would you say?" He was silent for a time, then he said, "I am praying to God to give me wisdom to make the right answer." Then after another pause he said, "If you ask me to imagine such an incredible thing, then I would say—

"Nationalise the land.

"Declare absolute liberty of conscience.

"And establish the liberty of the Press.

"If these three things are done, all the rest would come right."

# INDEX.

Abdul Aziz, Gen. Ignatieff and, 273, 274.
Afghanistan (*see also* CENTRAL ASIA), Russian Policy towards, 115, 116; England's Danger in, 117—120; what England's Policy ought to be, 119; the Frontier Line, 117; Gen. Annenkoff wishes to partition, 150; Gen. Ignatieff on, 300, 301.
Alexander III., Tzar (*see also* RUSSIA), "at Home," 122—129; the Peace-keeper of Europe, 120—129; his Love of Truth, 127, 128; Tribune of all the Russias, 169, 258; the Imperial Shepherd, 194, 258; his Letter-Bag, 198, 208; the Ideal of Authority, 317 — 329; "Stepniak" on, 194, 195.
Alliances, European (*see also* TREATIES) — a so-called Peace League, 2; the true Peace League—Russia, Germany, and England, 64, 90, 126.
Alsace-Lorraine, French Interest in, 10, 15, 16, 31.
Andrassy, Count, and the Annexation of Bosnia, 71.
Annenkoff, Gen., interviewed on the Central Asian Railway, 148—151.
Armenia, the Berlin Treaty violated by Turkey, 70; Gen. Ignatieff's Policy in, 291, 292.
Armies and War Preparations, Conscription proposed for Belgium, 25; Gen. de Brialmont's Belgian Fortifications, 23, 24; Increase of, in Germany, 35, 80, 81, and in Austria, 67—74; the Russian Army, 95, 96; Conscription, 52, 186—188.
Arnold, Matthew, Count Tolstoi on, 430—434.
Art. the Paris Salon, 17, 19, 20.
Austria (*see also* ALLIANCES) as Disturber of the Peace, 65—74, 90; War Preparations of, 67; the Magyars desirous of War, 68, 69; and the Berlin Treaty in Bosnia, 70, 74, 284; in Servia, 72—74; in Bulgaria, 73, 106; German Policy towards, 88; Gen. Ignatieff's Mission in 1877, 284; the Cause of Panslavism, 306—308.
Authority as an Ideal in Russia, 317—329.

Balfour, Mr. A. J., on Ireland in case of War, 5, 6.
Balkan Peninsula. *See* BERLIN TREATY, BULGARIA, &c.
Baltic Provinces, Persecution of Lutherans, 327, 328.
Baptists. *See* RELIGIOUS PERSECUTION.
Battenberg, Prince Alexander of, and Princess Victoria of Germany, 33; and the Throne of Bulgaria, 100; deceived the Tzar, 127, 128.
Beaconsfield, Lord, brought on Russo-Turkish War, 60, 61; Gen. Ignatieff on, 285; Mr. Gladstone on, in Central Asia, 154.
Belgium, Gen. de Brialmont's Fortifications, 23, 24; in next Franco-German War, 23—26.
Berlin the Capital of Prince Bismarck, 27.
Berlin Treaty violated by Turkey in Armenia, Macedonia, &c., 70; fulfilled by Russia, 70; violated by Austria in Bosnia, Bulgaria, and Servia, 70—74, 100—106; Gen. Ignatieff on, 287—290.
Bible Society regarded formerly as revolutionary in Russia, 386.
Bismarck, Count Herbert, 32, 33.
Bismarck, Prince (*see also* GERMANY), worshipped in Germany, 34; his Methods, 32—35, 74—90; and Son, 32, 33; his Objection to Alexander of Battenberg, 33; the Reptile Fund and the Reptile Press, 73—82; as Peace-maker, 83—90; Demon Omnipotens, 84; accused of having poisoned Skobeleff and Gambetta, 85, 86; and German Trade, 145—147.
Black Sea. *See* BOSPHORUS.
Bosnia and Herzegovina annexed by Austria, 70—74, 284.
Bosphorus, The, now in the Hands of Turkey, as Russia's Hall-porter, 108; the Future Custodian of, 108—113; Russian Designs on, 109,

110; Gen. Ignatieff and Russian Annexation, 290, 291.
Boulanger, Gen., in the Ascendant in France, 1, 10, 11—16; interviewed, 11—15; on the Prospects of War, 13—15; M. de Laveleye on, 25; German Opinion of, 31.
Bozo Petrovitch, Candidate for the Bulgarian Throne, 104—106.
Brialmont, Gen. de, fortifies Belgium and Bucharest, 23, 24.
Bulgaria, England and the Liberation of, 60—66; Austrian Interference in, 73—106; the Crux in, 99—106; Prince Ferdinand of Coburg, 73; his Position illegal, 101; English Policy in, in 1876 and 1888, 102; the Russian Official View, 103; suggested Candidates—the Prince of Mingrelia, 104; the Prince of Oldenburg, 104; a Swedish Prince, 104; Bozo Petrovitch, 104—106; Prince Nicholas of Montenegro's Candidature, 104; What Russia demands in, 105; a Military Convention with Russia, 106; the Tzar and Prince Alexander, 127, 128; the Constantinople Conference of 1876-77, 277; the San Stefano Treaty and Gen. Ignatieff's Policy, 286—288; Mr. Gladstone on, 7, 8.

Capital Punishment, Russia and, 224; Tolstoi, Count L., on, 443, 444.
Carlyle on the recognition of "Able Men," 34, 441; M. Pobedonestzeff an Admirer of, 324.
Carnot, President, Portrait of, 17.
Castor and Pollux, or the Siamese Twins, 315—322.
Censorship in Russia. See PRESS, RELIGIOUS PERSECUTION.
Central Asia (see also AFGHANISTAN, INDIA), Russian Advances, 96, 97; England's Real Danger in, 113—120; the Railway to Samarcand, 148—158; Gen. Annenkoff interviewed, 148—151; the Railway opened, 151; Routes from St. Petersburg, 152—154; M. Mestcherin interviewed, 155—158; Mr. Gladstone on, 154; M. de Lesseps on, 154; Gen. Ignatieff's Mission to Khiva and Bokhara, 271, 272.
Channel Tunnel, Mr. Gladstone on, 7.
China, Gen. Ignatieff's Mission, 272, 273; an Incident in Anglo-French War with, 322, 323; a Menace to Russia and England, 306.

Church of Russia. See RELIGION.
Churchill, Lord Randolph, opposed to War, 5, 8.
Clémenceau, M., Editor of *La Justice*, Visit to, 18, 19.
Climate of Russia and Russian Laziness, 320.
Coleridge on England's Responsibilities, 63.
Cologne Cathedral, A Service in, 27.
Commercial Questions in Russia. See FINANCE, SIBERIA.
Conscription, Belgium and, 25; suggested for England by M. de Laveleye, 26; the Curse of the Continent, 52; Russia and, 186—188.
Conservative Party. See SALISBURY, LORD.
Constantinople. See also BOSPHORUS.
Constantinople Conference, Gen. Ignatieff's Reminiscences of, 277—285.
Co-operation, Communal, in Russia, 181, 182.
Concerning Reptiles and Worms, 74.
Crime in Germany since the War of 1871, 55.
Crispi, Signor, on Italy's Alliance with England, 2.
Croatia, Turkish, The Vienna Convention and, 284, 288.

Deputy Tzar, The, of St. Petersburg, 246.
Derby, Lord, on Peace in Europe, 8.
Dog, The, in the Manger, 339.
Duncan, Dr., Chief of the Sanitary Commission of St. Petersburg, 256, 257.

Easter in Russia, 41; Easter Eve in St. Isaac's, 45—47.
Eastern Question. See BERLIN TREATY, BULGARIA, &c.
Education in Russia, 174, 207, 208.
England's Foreign Policy (see AFGHANISTAN, BULGARIA), how England does not do her Duty, 57; England the Mischief-Maker, 60, 61; Duty of, in Fire Brigade of Europe, 64; Natural Allies of, 86, 90, 126; cannot occupy Gallipoli without War, 112; Friendship of, desired by Russia, 125, 126.
Evangelicals in Russia. See RELIGIOUS PERSECUTION.
Eyes and Ears for the Tzar, 204.

Fergusson, Sir James, and an Anglo-Italian Alliance, 2.
Ferry, M., Portrait of, 17; Unpopularity of, 67.

Finance and Trade in Russia (*see also* RAILWAYS, SIBERIA), a Commercial Treaty between Russia and England proposed, 131—142; Gen. Ignatieff on, 131—133; an Opening for British Capital and British Labour, 133—140; the Harvest, 135; Export and Import Trade with Germany and England, 136—138; Fluctuation in the Value of the Rouble, 139, 183; the Case for Reciprocity, 141; the Protective Tariff, 141; Russian Corn taxed in Germany, 142; German Hostility to Russian Commerce, 142—147; German Trade with Finland, 146; Taxation, 188, 189; an Opening for English Commerce in Siberia, and Capt. Wiggins's Enterprise, 159—167 (*see* SIBERIA).

Finland, German Trade with, 146.

Fire Brigades in Russia, 252.

Floquet, M., French Minister of the Interior, Visit to, 17, 18.

Foreign Policy of England. *See* ALLIANCES, SALISBURY, GERMANY, BULGARIA, RUSSIA, CENTRAL ASIA, AFGHANISTAN, &c.

France, and Alsace-Lorraine, 10, 15, 16, 31; State of the Navy of, 10; opposed to War, 10—20, 29, 30; the Ministry of the Interior, 17; the Ministry for Foreign Affairs, 18; Decay of Idealism in, 31; as Disturber of the Peace, 2, 65—67; German Policy towards, 87, 88.

Frankfort, Treaty of, Gen. Ignatieff on, 287.

Frederick III., Emperor of Germany, Death of, 36—38.

Free Trade and Protection. *See* FINANCE.

Freedom, Mr. Gladstone on, 7.

Galkin-Wratzky, M., President of the Russian Prison Board, 224.

George, Mr. Henry, and Land Nationalisation, Count L. Tolstoi on, 421, 422.

Germany (*see also* ALLIANCES, PRINCE BISMARCK) opposed to War, 28—35; more friendly with England, 30; Prince Bismarck's Methods, 32—35, 74—90; War Preparations in, 35; Great Increase of Military Expenditure, 80, 81; Bismarck the Peacemaker, 83—90; the Reptile Press, 73—82; Despotism scientifically organised in, 84; Policy towards France, 87, 88; and towards Austria, 88; What England's Attitude ought to be towards, 89, 90; Gen. Ignatieff on the New Germany, 144; Hostile to Russian Commerce, 142—147; Prince Bismarck's Intelligence Bureau, 214; Gen. Ignatieff's Mission in 1877, 283.

Germany, Emperors of. *See* FREDERICK III. and WILLIAM II.

Gladstone, Mr. (*see also* LIBERAL PARTY), not a non-Interventionist, 7; compared with Gen. Ignatieff, 259—264, 296; calumniated like Ignatieff, 264; Gen. Ignatieff on, 284, 285; on English Alliances, 7; on Freedom, 7; on Bulgaria, 7, 8; on the Channel Tunnel, 7; on a Central Asian Railway in 1873, 154; on the Freedom of the Press, 213; on the Persecution of Catholics in Poland, 326, 327.

Goblet, M., French Minister for Foreign Affairs, Visit to, 18.

Gordon, Gen., Gen. Ignatieff on, 277.

Gortschakoff, Prince, Russian Foreign Minister, 275, 285, 286.

Greschner, M., Governor of House of Correction, 234.

Gresser, Gen., Deputy Tzar of St. Petersburg, 243, 246—258; interviewed, 247—249.

Hartington, Lord, Leader of the Liberal Unionists, 5; Character resembles that of the Tzar, 122.

Haxthausen on Religious Persecution in Russia, 383.

Herat, Projected Railway to, Gen. Annenkoff on, 150; M. Mestcherin against it, 158.

Herbert, Hon. Auberon, compared with Count L. Tolstoi, 420, 421.

Herzegovina. *See* BOSNIA.

Hilton, Mr. Edward, Manager of Col. Pashkoff in Ufa, 344; expelled, 347. 353.

Hilton, Mr. Henry, also expelled, 352. 353; Sir Robert Morier and Sir Edward Thornton on, 352; Col. Pashkoff's Protest, 352.

Hiltons, The Story of the, 35, 344.

Holstein, Herr, Head of Reptile Press Bureau, 76, 77.

Ignatieff, Gen., The Ideas of, 259; the Russian Mr. Gladstone, 259—264, 296, with a dash of Mr.

# INDEX. 461

Labouchere, 262, 269; his Religious Faith, 261, 262; his Nationalism, 263; why called the "Father of Lies," 263—269; and the Strength of the Turkish Army, 1876-77, 267; his Conduct at the Conference of Constantinople, 268; Early Career of, 270—275; came to London as Military Attaché, 270, 276; his Mission to Khiva in 1857, 271; and to Bokhara, 271, 272; his Mission to China, 272, 273; Ambassador at Constantinople, 273—275; proposed as Russian Ambassador in London, 1874, 276; his Reminiscences of Lord Salisbury at Constantinople in 1876, 277—285; opposed to War in the East in 1877, 281; Anecdotes of, and Sir W. White, 282; his Mission to Germany, Austria, and England in 1877, 283 — 285; drafted the Treaty of San Stefano, 286—288; on the Berlin Treaty, 287; on the Cession of Alsace-Lorraine, 287; his Eastern Policy "Hands off," 287; Bulgaria, 288; the Bosphorus, 290; Armenia, 291, 292; no more Annexations, 292; Governor of Nijni Novgorod, 293; re-appointed, 294; Minister of the Interior, 294 —298; his Administrative Reforms, 296; Public Questions dealt with, 297, 298; his Retirement, 298, 302; "at Home" in St. Petersburg, 298—306; and the Parliamentary System, 302; and the Press, 303; his Tolerance, 298, 303; his Policy in Poland, 304; his alleged Oppression of the Jews, 305; and the Chinese, 306; President of the Society of Trade and Commerce, 306; President of the Slavonic Society, 307; Future of, 309—313; suggested Editor of Imperial Newspaper, 222, 309.

India, Lord Lytton as Russian Agent, 114; How Russia endangers, 113; Our True Policy in, 114; our Rule compared to Russia's in Turkestan, 151.

Irish and Russians compared, 40, 335.

Jews in Russia, Gen. Ignatieff and, 297, 305, 306.
Journalism (*see also* PRESS), Government by, 219—223.
Journalists and War, 59.
Juries in Russia, 192.

*Justiciarii errantes* suggested for Russia, 219.

Kennan, Mr. George, on Siberian Prisons, 226—229.
Korff, Count, a Convert to the Pashkoffski. *See* RELIGIOUS PERSECUTION.

Labouchere, Mr. Henry, compared with Gen. Ignatieff, 262, 269.
Land Question in Russia, Peasant Life, 95, 171, 189; Redistribution, 181, 182; Purchase, 189; Nationalisation, Count L. Tolstoi on, 421, 422.
Laud, Archbishop, Redivivus in M. Pobedonostzeff, 324.
Laveleye, M. Emil de, Visit to, 22—26; on the Eastern Question, 23.
Lesseps, M. de, on a Central Asian Railway in 1873, 154.
Liberal Unionists opposed to War, 5.
Liége, Gun Trade of, 22, 23.
Lieven, Princess, and the Evangelicals in Russia, 365.
Liquor Traffic. *See* TEMPERANCE.
Local Government in Russia, the Zemstvo and the Assembly of the Noblesse, 176, 193, 211, 212; the Mir, 175; Judicial Powers, 180; The Socialistic Side of, 180; Taxation, 188, 189; the Police, 191; the Courts of Justice, 192, 193; "Stepniak" on, 177, 178.
London, The Outlook Abroad from, 1888, 4.
Lytton, Lord, as Viceroy of India, 114.

Macedonia, the Danger-Point in Turkish Territory, 107.
Mackenzie, Sir Morell, Visit to, at Charlottenburg, 36, 37.
Maignan's Picture, "The Voices of the Tocsin," 18—20.
Manning, Cardinal, on the Council of Trent, 329.
Mestcherin, M., interviewed on the Central Asian Railway, 155—158.
Mingrelia, Prince of, 104.
Mir in Russia. *See* LOCAL GOVERNMENT.
Molokani in Southern Russia. *See* RELIGIOUS PERSECUTION.
Monopoly, The Effect of, in Religion, 329.
Montenegro, Prince Nicholas's Rule, 105.
Morier, Sir Robert, *Persona grata* at St. Petersburg, 134; obtains

Siberian Concessions for Capt. Wiggins, 165, 166; and the Case of Mr. Henry Hilton, 352.

Navy, French, State of, after the Chinese War, 10.

Nelidoff, M., Russian Ambassador at Constantinople, 110.

Nicholas, Prince of Montenegro, 105.

Nihilism in Russia, 201—204, 293, 359, 360, 366.

Nordenskjöld, Professor, enters the Yenessei, 161.

Novikoff, Mme., on Siberia, 167; pleads for M. Tikhomiroff, 204; dissents from Author's Views on Religion in Russia, 315.

Old Believers or Raskolniks. *See* RELIGIOUS PERSECUTION.

Orjevsky, Gen., and the Evangelicals in Russia, 365.

Panslavism, Meeting of the Slavonic Society, 306; its Aspirations, 307, 308.

Pashkoff, Col., Employer of the Messrs. Hilton, 345—352; on the Expulsion of Mr. Henry Hilton, 352.

Pashkoffski Sect founded by Lord Radstock, 329, 354; The Story of, 353. *See* RELIGIOUS PERSECUTION.

Peace (*see also* ALLIANCES, TREATIES, &c.), The Armed, of Europe, 51; England and, 2, 60—64; Belgium and, 23, 24; Germany and, 28—35, 74—90; France and, 28—35, 65—67; Russia and, 49, 129; Austria and, 65, 74.

Persecution, The Futility of, 380; Naked and Unashamed, 372—380.

Persecution in Russia. *See* RELIGION.

Plea, A, for More Prisons, 223.

Pobedonostzeff, M., *Procureur* of the Holy Synod, Policy of, 318, 321—329, 332—339; the Shadow on the Throne, 323; compared with Archbishop Laud, 324; and the Persecution of the Catholics in Poland, 327; opposed to all but Orthodox Propaganda, 336; and the Case of Mr. Edward Hilton, 347—353; persecutes the Pashkoffski, 358, 391; his Official Memoranda, 373.

Poland, Persecution of Catholics by Russia, 322—328; Mr. Gladstone on, 326, 327; Gen. Ignatieff on, 304, 335; M. Pobedonestzeff on, 327; Count L. Tolstoi on, 410, 411.

Police of Russia, Salaries of, 251, 252; the Village Police, 191; the St. Petersburg Police, 252.

Police Stations in St. Petersburg visited, 249—251; *Police des Mœurs*, the Office in St. Petersburg, 251.

Population of Austria, 68; and of Russia, 93, 95.

Press, Journalists and War, 59; Mr. Gladstone and a Free Press, 213; in Russia, Result of Muzzling the, 213—223; a Russian Editor's Difficulties, 215, 216; M. Suvorin, Editor of the *Novoe Vremya*, 215, 216; a suggested Imperial Newspaper, 219—221; the *Rural Messenger*, 222; Gen. Ignatieff's Ideas on, 222, 303; History of the *Russian Workman*, 339—344; how the Censorship works, 340; Tolstoi utilises the, 452—454.

Prisons in Russia (*see also* POLICE STATIONS), Overcrowding, 223, 226—229, 243, 244; A Plea for More, 223, 245; Reforms in, 224; M. Galkin-Wratzky, President of the Prison Board, 224; Chief Defects of, 225; the Fortress-Prison of Schlüsselburg, 232; an Experimental Imprisonment refused, 232, 233; Mr. Saloman, Secretary of the Prison Board, 234; the St. Petersburg House of Correction described, 234—242; the Prison in Demidoff Pereoulok, 242—244; the New Model Prison, 244, 245; the Arbitrary Imprisonment of Political Suspects, 255; Siberian Prisons (Tiumen and Tomsk), Mr. Kennan on, 226—229.

Protection and Free Trade in Russia. *See* FINANCE.

Radstock, Lord, Founder of the Pashkoffski Sect, 354—360; visited Russia, 1874-76, 357, 358; and forbidden to return, 360. *See also* RELIGION.

Railways in Russia, Slow Increase of, 135, 136; Railway Travelling, 38—41; in Central Asia, 148—158.

Raskolniks or Old Believers. *See* RELIGIOUS PERSECUTION.

Reciprocity, The Case for, with Russia, 141.

Religious Persecution in Russia, the Policy of M. Pobedonostzeff, 318, 321—329, 332; Catholic Poles persecuted, 322—328; Mr. Gladstone on, 326, 327; M. Pobedonostzeff on, 327; Persecution of Lutherans in the Baltic Provinces, 327, 328; the Effect of Monopoly, 329—339; the Peasant's View of the Doctrine of the Trinity, 330; Count L. Tolstoi on, 330, 331; Little Preaching, 332, 333; Opposition to Religious Propaganda, 333—339; the Suppression of the *Russian Workman*, 339—344; the Expulsion of the Messrs. Hilton, 344—353; the Story of the Pashkoffski, 328, 329, 354—363; the Evangelical Conference in St. Petersburg, 1884, 363, 364; M. Pashkoff and Count Korff condemned unheard and banished, 369—372; M. Pobedonostzeff's Official Memoranda, 372—380; Letter of Col. Pashkoff to the Emperor, 390, 391; the Exile and Imprisonment of Pashkoffski, 386, 387; the Stundists and Molokani persecuted, 328, 329, 362, 363, 379, 380, 385; Persecution of the Raskolniks, 380—384; Tardy Concessions, 383, 384; Debates between Missionary Priests and Sectarians, 388; Conferences between Baptists and the Orthodox, 388.

Reptile Press of Prince Bismarck, 73—82.

"Resist not Evil," Count Tolstoi's Central Principle, 404.

Richter, Gen. de, and the Petitions to the Tzar, 208, 209.

Rights, Bill of, suggested for Russia, 218.

Roumania, Agrarian Disturbances, 107.

Russia (*see also* TZAR ALEXANDER, ALLIANCES, ARMIES, JEWS, LOCAL GOVERNMENT, TAXATION, FINANCE, LAND, RAILWAYS, PRISONS AND POLICE STATIONS, POLICE, CAPITAL PUNISHMENT, RELIGION, the PRESS, EDUCATION, TEMPERANCE, GEN. IGNATIEFF, FINLAND, POLAND, CENTRAL ASIA, SIBERIA, BOSPHORUS, &c.), opposed to War, 49 *et seq.*; Alleged Concentration of Troops on Frontier denied, 79, 80; German Policy towards, 88, 89; English Prejudice and English Policy, 90—92; what Russia is, 91, 92; Peasant Life in, 95, 171 (*see also* LOCAL GOVERNMENT); Public Opinion in, 97; Juries, 192; Nihilism, 201—204, 293, 359, 360, 366; the Liberal European and the National Parties, 97; Policy of the Nationalists, 97, 98; the Tzar as Peace-keeper of Europe, 120—129; Foreign Policy, 121 (*see also* ALLIANCES, AUSTRIA, AFGHANISTAN AND CENTRAL ASIA, CHINA, GERMANY, BULGARIA, BERLIN TREATY, CONSTANTINOPLE CONFERENCE, BOSPHORUS, TURKEY); New Fields for British Enterprise, 131; the Commercial Treaties, 131; Imports and Exports, 137; Relation of the Government to the People, 170—193 (*see also* LOCAL GOVERNMENT); an Empire of Villages, 171; the Tzar as Imperial Shepherd, 194—204; the Executive Autocracy, 200; the Bureaucracy, 201; the Tzar, Tribune, 200—204; Private Initiative crushed, 204—206; Cooperation of Capable Citizens in the State Service needed, 207, 208; Gen. de Richter, the Tzar's Secretary, 208; a Consultative Assembly (Zemskie Sobory) proposed, 210, 211; the City Councils of Moscow and St. Petersburg, 211; a Free Press suggested, 213—223; Power of the Tchinovniks, 217; Eyes and Ears for the Tzar, Suggestions, 218—223; why Official Corruption flourishes, 256, 257; the Treaty of San Stefano, 286.

Salisbury, Lord, Foreign Policy of, 2—9; in Bulgaria, 100, 103; at the Constantinople Conference, 277—286; his Subsequent Hostility to Gen. Ignatieff, 280, 281.

Saloman, Mr., Secretary of the Russian Prison Board, 234.

Salon at Paris, 17, 19, 20.

Salvation Army, Count L. Tolstoi on the, 432.

San Stefano, Treaty of, 286; Gen. Ignatieff on, 287, 288.

"Sell all that thou hast, and give to the Poor," 420.

Servia practically annexed to Austria, 72—74.

Shadow, The, on the Throne, 315.

Sheep, The Flock of Little Brown, 169.

Shepherd, The Imperial, 194.

Shepherds and Shearers of the Flock, 187.

Siberia (*see also* PRISONS), Capt. Wiggins's Enterprise, 159—167; an Opening for English Commerce, 159; the Navigation of the Kara

Straits, 160, 161; Capt. Wiggins interviewed, 161—165; the Phœnix Company, 165; Concession granted to English Goods, 166; Accident to the *Phœnix*, 167.

Skobeleff, Gen., said to have been poisoned by Prince Bismarck, 85.

Slavonic Society. *See* PANSLAVISM.

Socialism, the realised Ideal of the Russian Village, 180.

"Stepniak" on the Mir, 177, 178; on the Tzardom, 194, 195.

Stundists. *See* RELIGIOUS PERSECUTION.

Suvorin, M., Editor of the *Novoe Vremya*, 215, 216.

Sutaieff, Count L. Tolstoi's Spiritual Father, 438, 439.

Tariffs. *See* FINANCE.

Taxation in Russia, 188.

Temperance, Gen. Ignatieff's Liquor Commission, 297; Count L. Tolstoi on, 445, 446.

Thornton, Sir Edward, and Mr. Edward Hilton, 347—352.

Tikhomiroff, M., Confessions of a Repentant Nihilist, 204.

Tolstoi, Count Dmitri, Russian Minister of the Interior, 197; and Mr. Edward Hilton, 350—353; and the Pashkoffski, 361.

Tolstoi, Count Leo, Novelist, "at Home" at Yasnaia Poliana, 49, 393—404; his Gospel, 404—457; compared with Hon. Auberon Herbert, 420, 421; his Five Commands and Five Evils, 427—429; Sutaieff, his Spiritual Father, 438, 439; List of his Propagandist Publications, 452—454; on the Doctrine of the Trinity, 330, 331; on Russia's Difficulty with Poland, 410, 411; on the Influence of the State, 410—417, 420—422, 441—443; on the Relations of the Sexes, 417—420, 425, 426; on Henry George and Land Nationalisation, 421, 422; on Matthew Arnold, 430, 431; on the Salvation Army, 432; on the Immortality of the Soul, 434—437; on Capital Punishment, 443, 444; on Temperance, 445, 446; on American and English Literature, 451, 452; on a Universal Classical Library, 454—457.

Trade. *See* FINANCE.

Treaty of Commerce with Russia, 131.

Treaties. *See* BERLIN, SAN STEFANO, FRANKFORT.

Turkey Defaulter in Berlin Treaty in Armenia, Macedonia, &c., 70; Macedonia the Danger-Point, 107; Gen. Ignatieff at Constantinople, 273—275; Abdul Aziz, 273, 274; Constantinople Conference of 1876-77, 277; the New Constitution and Midhat Pasha, 282, 283; the War with Russia in 1877, 283—286; the Treaty of San Stefano, 286.

Tzar. *See* ALEXANDER III.

Ussouri Province ceded to Russia by China, 272, 273.

Victoria, Empress of Germany, 33.

Victoria, Princess, and Prince Alexander of Battenberg, 33.

Vienna Convention, 284, 288.

Village Life and Village Republics in Russia. *See* LOCAL GOVERNMENT.

"War or Peace?" 49, 129.

War Panic and War Preparations (*see also* PEACE, ARMIES, ALLIANCES, AUSTRIA, BELGIUM, FRANCE, GERMANY, RUSSIA, TURKEY), Duration of Recent Wars, 54; the Responsibility of the Press, 59; England's Policy, 60—64.

Waterway, The, to the Russian Australia, 159.

White, Sir William, British Ambassador at Constantinople, 110.

Who is to keep the Keys of the Tzar's House? 167.

Wiggins, Capt. (*see also* SIBERIA), interviewed, 161—165.

William II. ascended the German Throne, 38.

Wischnegradsky, M., Russian Minister of Finance, 132, 139, 189.

Wolseley, Lord, 1, 49, 149, 199.

Worms, Concerning Reptiles and, 74.

Yasnaia Poliana, A Week at, 49, 394.

Zemskie Sobory or Consultative Assembly, 211, 220; Gen. Ignatieff and, 298, 302.

Zemstvo, The, 176, 193, 211, 212.

*Selections from Cassell & Company's Publications.*

## Illustrated, Fine Art, and other Volumes.

**Abbeys and Churches of England and Wales, The:** Descriptive, Historical, Pictorial. 21s.
**After London; or, Wild England.** By the late RICHARD JEFFERIES. *Cheap Edition*, 3s. 6d.
**Along Alaska's Great River.** By Lieut. SCHWATKA. Illustrated. 12s. 6d.
**American Penman, An** By JULIAN HAWTHORNE. Boards, 2s.; cloth, 3s. 6d.
**American Yachts and Yachting.** Illustrated. 6s.
**Animal Painting in Water Colours.** With Eighteen Coloured Plates by FREDERICK TAYLER. 5s.
**Arabian Nights Entertainments (Cassell's).** With about 400 Illustrations. 10s. 6d.
**Architectural Drawing.** By PHENÉ SPIERS. Illustrated. 10s. 6d.
**Art, The Magazine of.** Yearly Volume. With several hundred Engravings, and Twelve Etchings, Photogravures, &c. 16s.
**Behind Time.** By G. P. LATHROP. Illustrated. 2s. 6d.
**Bimetallism, The Theory of.** By D. BARBOUR. 6s.
**Bismarck, Prince.** By C. LOWE, M.A. Two Vols. *Cheap Edition*. 10s. 6d.
**Black Arrow, The.** A Tale of the Two Roses. By R. L. STEVENSON. 5s.
**British Ballads.** 275 Original Illustrations. Two Vols. Cloth, 7s. 6d. each.
**British Battles on Land and Sea.** By the late JAMES GRANT. With about 600 Illustrations. Three Vols., 4to, £1 7s.; Library Edition, £1 10s.
**British Battles, Recent.** Illustrated. 4to, 9s. Library Edition, 10s.
**British Empire, The.** By SIR GEORGE CAMPBELL. 3s.
**Browning, An Introduction to the Study of.** By ARTHUR SYMONS. 2s. 6d.
**Butterflies and Moths, European.** By W. F. KIRBY. With 61 Coloured Plates. Demy 4to, 35s.
**Canaries and Cage-Birds, The Illustrated Book of.** By W. A. BLAKSTON, W. SWAYSLAND, and A. F. WIENER. With 56 Fac-simile Coloured Plates, 35s.
**Cannibals and Convicts.** By JULIAN THOMAS ("The Vagabond"). *Cheap Edition*, 5s.
**Captain Trafalgar.** By WESTALL and LAURIE. Illustrated. 5s.
**Cassell's Family Magazine.** Yearly Vol. Illustrated. 9s.
**Celebrities of the Century:** Being a Dictionary of Men and Women of the Nineteenth Century. 21s.; roxburgh, 25s.
**Changing Year, The.** With Illustrations. 7s. 6d.
**Chess Problem, The.** With Illustrations by C. PLANCK and others. 7s. 6d.
**Children of the Cold, The.** By Lieut. SCHWATKA. 2s. 6d.
**China Painting.** By FLORENCE LEWIS. With Sixteen Coloured Plates, and a selection of Wood Engravings. With full Instructions. 5s.
**Choice Dishes at Small Cost.** By A. G. PAYNE. *Cheap Edition*, 1s.
**Christmas in the Olden Time.** By Sir WALTER SCOTT. With charming Original Illustrations. 7s. 6d.
**Cities of the World.** Three Vols. Illustrated. 7s. 6d. each.
**Civil Service, Guide to Employment in the.** *New and Enlarged Edition*. 3s. 6d.
**Civil Service.—Guide to Female Employment in Government Offices.** Cloth, 1s.
**Clinical Manuals for Practitioners and Students of Medicine.** (*A List of Volumes forwarded post free on application to the Publishers.*)
**Clothing, The Influence of, on Health.** By FREDERICK TREVES, F.R.C.S. 2s.
**Cobden Club, Some Works published for the:—**

Writings of Richard Cobden. 6s.
Local Government and Taxation in the United Kingdom. 5s.
Displacement of Labour and Capital. 3d.
Free Trade versus Fair Trade. 5s.
Free Trade and English Commerce. By A. Mongredien. 6d.
Crown Colonies. 1s.
Popular Fallacies Regarding Trade. 6d.
Western Farmer of America. 3d.
Reform of the English Land System. 3d.
Fair Trade Unmasked. By G. W. Medley. 6d.
Technical Education. By F. C. Montague, M.A. 6d.

Our Land Laws of the Past. 3d.
The Caribbean Confederation. By C. S. Salmon. 1s. 6d.
Pleas for Protection Examined. By A. Mongredien. *New and Revised Edition*, 6d.
What Protection does for the Farmer. By J. S. Leadam, M.A. 6d.
The Old Poor Law and the New Socialism, or, Pauperism and Taxation. By F. C. Montague. 6d.
The Secretary of State for India in Council. 6d.
The National Income and Taxation. By Sir Louis Mallet. 6d.

7 G—8.88.

**Colonies and India, Our: How we Got Them, and Why we Keep Them.** By Prof. C. RANSOME. 1s.
**Colour.** By Prof. A. H. CHURCH. *New and Enlarged Edition*, with Coloured Plates. 3s. 6d.
**Columbus, Christopher, The Life and Voyages of.** By WASHINGTON IRVING. Three Vols. 7s. 6d.
**Commodore Junk.** By G. MANVILLE FENN. 5s.
**Cookery, Cassell's Shilling.** The Largest and Best Work on the Subject ever produced. 1s.
**Cookery, Cassell's Dictionary of.** Containing about Nine Thousand Recipes. 7s. 6d.; roxburgh, 10s. 6d.
**Cookery, A Year's.** By PHYLLIS BROWNE. Cloth gilt or oiled cloth, 3s. 6d.
**Cook Book, Catherine Owen's New.** 4s.
**Co-operators, Working Men : What They have Done, and What They are Doing.** By A. H. DYKE-ACLAND, M.P., and B. JONES. 1s.
**Countries of the World, The.** By ROBERT BROWN, M.A., Ph.D., &c. Complete in Six Vols., with about 750 Illustrations. 4to, 7s. 6d. each.
**Culmshire Folk.** By the Author of " John Orlebar," &c. 3s. 6d.
**Cyclopædia, Cassell's Concise.** With 12,000 subjects, brought down to the latest date. With about 600 Illustrations, 15s.; roxburgh, 18s.
**Cyclopædia, Cassell's Miniature.** Containing 30,000 Subjects. Cloth, 3s. 6d.
**Dairy Farming.** By Prof. J. P. SHELDON. With 25 Fac-simile Coloured Plates, and numerous Wood Engravings. Demy 4to, 21s.
**Dead Man's Rock.** A Romance. By Q. 5s.
**Decisive Events in History.** By THOMAS ARCHER. With Sixteen Illustrations. Boards, 3s. 6d.; cloth, 5s.
**Deserted Village Series, The.** Consisting of *Éditions de luxe* of favourite poems by Standard Authors. Illustrated. Cloth gilt, 2s. 6d.
 Goldsmith's Deserted Village. | Wordsworth's Ode on Immortality,
 Milton's L'Allegro and Il Penseroso. | and Lines on Tintern Abbey.
 Songs from Shakespeare.
**Dickens, Character Sketches from.** FIRST, SECOND, and THIRD SERIES. With Six Original Drawings in each, by FREDERICK BARNARD. In Portfolio, 21s. each.
**Diary of Two Parliaments.** By H. W. LUCY. The Disraeli Parliament, 12s. The Gladstone Parliament, 12s.
**Dog, The.** By IDSTONE. Illustrated. 2s. 6d.
**Dog, Illustrated Book of the.** By VERO SHAW, B.A. With 28 Coloured Plates. Cloth bevelled, 35s.; half-morocco, 45s.
**Dog Stories and Dog Lore.** By Col. THOS. W. KNOX. 6s.
**Domestic Dictionary, The.** An Encyclopædia for the Household. Cloth, 7s. 6d.
**Doré's Dante's Inferno.** Illustrated by GUSTAVE DORÉ. *Popular Edition*, 21s.
**Doré's Dante's Purgatorio and Paradiso.** Illustrated by GUSTAVE DORÉ. *Popular Edition*. 21s.
**Doré's Fairy Tales Told Again.** With 24 Full-page Engravings by DORÉ. 5s.
**Doré Gallery, The.** With 250 Illustrations by GUSTAVE DORÉ. 4to, 42s.
**Doré's Milton's Paradise Lost.** With Full-page Drawings by GUSTAVE DORÉ. 4to, 21s.
**Earth, Our, and Its Story.** By Dr. ROBERT BROWN, F.L.S. Vol. I., with Coloured Plates and numerous Wood Engravings. 9s.
**Edinburgh, Old and New, Cassell's.** With 600 Illustrations. Three Vols., 9s. each; library binding, £1 10s. the set.
**Egypt: Descriptive, Historical, and Picturesque.** By Prof. G. EBERS. Translated by CLARA BELL, with Notes by SAMUEL BIRCH, LL.D., &c. *Popular Edition*, in Two Vols., 42s.
**"89."** A Novel. By EDGAR HENRY. Cloth, 3s. 6d.
**Electricity, Age of, from Amber Soul to Telephone.** By PARK BENJAMIN, Ph.D. 7s. 6d.
**Electricity, Practical.** By Prof. W. E. AYRTON. Illustrated. 7s. 6d.
**Electricity in the Service of Man.** With nearly 850 Illustrations. 21s.
**Encyclopædic Dictionary, The.** A New and Original Work of Reference to all the Words in the English Language. Complete in Fourteen Divisional Vols., 10s. 6d. each; or Seven Vols., half-morocco. 21s. each.
**England, Cassell's Illustrated History of.** With 2,000 Illustrations. Ten Vols., 4to, 9s. each. *New and Revised Edition*. Vols. I. and II., 9s. each.

*Selections from Cassell & Company's Publications.*

**English History, The Dictionary of.** Cloth, 21s.; roxburgh, 25s.
**English Literature, Library of.** By Prof. HENRY MORLEY. Complete in 5 vols., 7s. 6d. each.
 VOL. I.—SHORTER ENGLISH POEMS. | VOL. IV.—SHORTER WORKS IN ENGLISH
 VOL. II.—ILLUSTRATIONS OF ENGLISH | PROSE.
  RELIGION. | VOL. V.—SKETCHES OF LONGER WORKS IN
 VOL. III.—ENGLISH PLAYS. | ENGLISH VERSE AND PROSE.
**English Literature, Morley's First Sketch of.** *Revised Edition*, 7s. 6d.
**English Literature, The Dictionary of.** By W. DAVENPORT ADAMS. *Cheap Edition*, 7s. 6d.; roxburgh, 10s. 6d.
**English Literature, The Story of.** By ANNA BUCKLAND. *New and Cheap Edition.* 3s. 6d.
**English Writers.** An attempt towards a History of English Literature. By HENRY MORLEY, LL.D., Professor of English Literature, University College, London. Vols. I., II., III., and IV., 5s. each.
**Æsop's Fables.** With about 150 Illustrations by E. GRISET. *Cheap Edition*, cloth, 3s. 6d.; levelled boards, gilt edges, 5s.
**Etching : Its Technical Processes, with Remarks on Collections and Collecting.** By S. K. KOEHLER. Illustrated with 30 Full-page Plates. Price £4 4s.
**Etiquette of Good Society.** 1s.; cloth, 1s. 6d.
**Eye, Ear, and Throat, The Management of the.** 3s. 6d.
**Family Physician, The.** By Eminent PHYSICIANS and SURGEONS. *New and Revised Edition.* Cloth, 21s.; roxburgh, 25s.
**Fenn, G. Manville, Works by.** *Popular Editions.* Boards, 2s. each; or cloth, 2s. 6d.
 Dutch the Diver; or, a Man's Mistake. | Poverty Corner.
 My Patients. | The Vicar's People. } In Cloth only.
 The Parson o' Dumford. | Sweet Mace.
**Ferns, European.** By JAMES BRITTEN, F.L.S. With 30 Fac-simile Coloured Plates by D. BLAIR, F.L.S. 21s.
**Field Naturalist's Handbook, The.** By Rev. J. G. WOOD & THEODORE WOOD. 5s.
**Figuier's Popular Scientific Works.** With Several Hundred Illustrations in each. 3s. 6d. each.
 The Human Race. | The Ocean World.
 World Before the Deluge. | The Vegetable World.
 Reptiles and Birds. | The Insect World.
  Mammalia.
**Figure Painting in Water Colours.** With 16 Coloured Plates by BLANCHE MACARTHUR and JENNIE MOORE. With full Instructions. 7s. 6d.
**Fine-Art Library, The.** Edited by JOHN SPARKES, Principal of the South Kensington Art Schools. Each Book contains about 100 Illustrations. 5s. each.
 Tapestry. By Eugène Müntz. Translated by | The Education of the Artist. By Ernest
  Miss L. J. Davis. | Chesneau. Translated by Clara Bell. Non-
 Engraving. By Le Vicomte Henri Delaborde. | illustrated.
  Translated by R. A. M. Stevenson. | Greek Archæology. By Maxime Collignon.
 The English School of Painting. By E. | Translated by Dr. J. H. Wright.
  Chesneau. Translated by L. N. Etherington. | Artistic Anatomy. By Prof. Duval. Translated
  With an Introduction by Prof. Ruskin. | by F. E. Fenton.
 The Flemish School of Painting. By A. J. | The Dutch School of Painting. By Henry
  Wauters. Translated by Mrs. Henry Rossel. | Havard. Translated by G. Powell.
**Five Pound Note, The, and other Stories.** By G. S. JEALOUS. 1s.
**Flower Painting in Water Colours.** First and Second Series. With 20 Fac-simile Coloured Plates in each by F. E. HULME, F.L.S., F.S.A. With Instructions by the Artist. Interleaved. 5s. each.
**Flower Painting, Elementary.** With Eight Coloured Plates. 3s.
**Flowers, and How to Paint Them.** By MAUD NAFTEL. With Coloured Plates. 5s.
**Forging of the Anchor, The.** A Poem. By the late Sir SAMUEL FERGUSON, LL.D. With 20 Original Illustrations. Gilt edges, 5s.
**Fossil Reptiles, A History of British.** By Sir RICHARD OWEN, K.C.B., F.R.S., &c. With 268 Plates. In Four Vols., £12 12s.
**France as It Is.** By ANDRÉ LEBON and PAUL PELET. With Three Maps. Crown 8vo cloth, 7s. 6d.
**Franco-German War, Cassell's History of the.** Two Vols. With 500 Illustrations. 9s. each.
**Fresh-Water Fishes of Europe, The.** By Prof. H. G. SEELEY, F.R.S. *Cheap Edition.* 7s. 6d.
**Garden Flowers, Familiar.** By SHIRLEY HIBBERD. With Coloured Plates by F. E. HULME, F.L.S. Complete in Five Series. Cloth gilt, 12s. 6d. each.
**Gardening, Cassell's Popular.** Illustrated. Complete in 4 Vols., 5s. each.
**Geometrical Drawing for Army Candidates.** By H. T. LILLEY, M.A. 2s.

*Selections from Cassell & Company's Publications.*

Geometry, First Elements of Experimental. By PAUL BERT. 1s. 6d.
Geometry, Practical Solid. By Major ROSS. 2s.
Germany, William of. By ARCHIBALD FORBES. 3s. 6d.
Gladstone, Life of the Rt. Hon. W. E. By G. BARNETT SMITH. With Portrait. 3s.6d.
Gleanings from Popular Authors. Two Vols. With Original Illustrations.
   4to, 9s. each. Two Vols. in One, 15s.
Gold to Grey, From. Being Poems and Pictures of Life and Nature. By MARY
   D. BRINE. Illustrated. 7s. 6d.
Great Bank Robbery, The. A Novel. By JULIAN HAWTHORNE. Boards, 2s.
Great Industries of Great Britain. With 400 Illustrations. 3 Vols., 7s. 6d. each.
Great Northern Railway, The Official Illustrated Guide to the. 1s. ; cloth, 2s.
Great Western Railway, The Official Illustrated Guide to the. 1s. ; cloth, 2s.
Great Painters of Christendom, The, from Cimabue to Wilkie. By JOHN
   FORBES-ROBERTSON. Illustrated throughout. *Popular Edition*, cloth gilt, 12s. 6d.
Gulliver's Travels. With 88 Engravings by MORTEN. *Cheap Edition.* Cloth,
   3s. 6d. ; cloth gilt, 5s.
Gum Boughs and Wattle Bloom. By DONALD MACDONALD. 5s.
Gun and its Development, The. By W. W. GREENER. Illustrated. 10s. 6d.
Guns, Modern Shot. By W. W. GREENER. Illustrated. 5s.
Health at School. By CLEMENT DUKES, M.D., B.S. 7s. 6d. [burgh, 25s.
Health, The Book of. By Eminent Physicians and Surgeons. Cloth, 21s. ; rox-
Health, The Influence of Clothing on. By F. TREVES, F.R.C.S. 2s.
Heavens, The Story of the. By Sir ROBERT STAWELL BALL, LL.D., F.R.S.,
   Royal Astronomer of Ireland. Coloured Plates and Wood Engravings. 31s. 6d.
Heroes of Britain in Peace and War. In Two Vols., with 300 Original Illus-
   trations. 5s. each ; or One Vol., library binding, 10s. 6d.
Holy Land and the Bible, The. By the Rev. CUNNINGHAM GEIKIE, D.D.
   With Map. Two Vols. 24s.
Homes, Our, and How to Make them Healthy. By Eminent Authorities.
   Illustrated. 15s. ; roxburgh, 18s.
Horse-Keeper, The Practical. By GEORGE FLEMING, LL.D., F.R.C.V.S.
   Illustrated. Crown 8vo, cloth, 7s. 6d.
Horse, The Book of the. By SAMUEL SIDNEY. With 28 *fac-simile* Coloured
   Plates. Demy 4to, 35s. ; half-morocco, £2 5s.
Horses, The Simple Ailments of. By W. F. Illustrated. 5s.
Household Guide, Cassell's. With Illustrations and Coloured Plates. *New and
   Revised Edition*, complete in Four Vols., 20s.
How Dante Climbed the Mountain. By ROSE EMILY SELFE. With Eight
   Full-page Engravings by GUSTAVE DORÉ. 2s.
How Women may Earn a Living. By MERCY GROGAN. 1s.
Imperial White Books. In Quarterly Vols. 10s. 6d. per annum, post free ;
   to subscribers separately, 3s. 6d. each.
India, Cassell's History of. By the late JAMES GRANT. With 400 Illustrations. 15s.
India : the Land and the People. By Sir JAMES CAIRD, K.C.B. 10s. 6d.
In-door Amusements, Card Games, and Fireside Fun, Cassell's. 3s. 6d.
Industrial Remuneration Conference. The Report of. 2s. 6d.
Insect Variety: its Propagation and Distribution. By A. H. SWINTON. 7s. 6d.
Irish Parliament, The, What it Was, and What it Did. By J. G. SWIFT
   McNEILL, M.A., M.P. 1s.
Irish Parliament, A Miniature History of the. By J. C. HASLAM. 3d.
Irish Union ; Before and After. By A. K. CONNELL, M.A. 2s. 6d.
John Parmelee's Curse. By JULIAN HAWTHORNE. 2s. 6d.
Kennel Guide, Practical. By Dr. GORDON STABLES. Illustrated. *Cheap Edition*. 1s.
Kidnapped. By R. L. STEVENSON. *Illustrated Edition*. 5s.
King Solomon's Mines. By H. RIDER HAGGARD. *Illustrated Edition*. 5s.
Khiva, A Ride to. By Col. FRED BURNABY. 1s. 6d.
Ladies' Physician, The. By a London Physician. 6s.
Lady Biddy Fane. By FRANK BARRETT. Three Vols. Cloth, 31s. 6d.
Lady's World, The. An Illustrated Magazine of Fashion and Society. Yrly, Vol. 18s.
Land Question, The. By Prof. J. ELLIOT, M.R.A.C. Including the Land Scare
   ' and Production of Cereals. 3s. 6d.
Landscape Painting in Oils, A Course of Lessons in. By A. F. GRACE.
   With Nine Reproductions in Colour. *Cheap Edition*, 25s.

**Law, About Going to.** By A. J. WILLIAMS, M.P. 2s. 6d.
**Laws of Every Day Life, The.** By H. O. ARNOLD-FORSTER. 1s. 6d.
**Letts's Diaries and other Time-saving Publications** are now published exclusively by CASSELL & COMPANY. *(A List sent post free on application.)*
**Local Dual Standards.** By JOHN HENRY NORMAN. Gold and Silver Standard Currencies. 1s.
**Local Government in England and Germany.** By the Rt. Hon. Sir ROBERT MORIER, G.C.B., &c. 1s.
**London, Brighton, and South Coast Railway, The Official Illustrated Guide to the.** 1s.; cloth, 2s.
**London and North Western Railway, The Official Illustrated Guide to the.** 1s.; cloth, 2s.
**London and South Western Railway, The Official Illustrated Guide to the.** 1s.; cloth, 2s.
**London, Greater.** By EDWARD WALFORD. Two Vols. With about 400 Illustrations. 9s. each. *Library Edition.* Two Vols. £1 the set.
**London, Old and New.** By WALTER THORNBURY and EDWARD WALFORD Six Vols., each containing about 200 Illustrations and Maps. Cloth, 9s. each. *Library Edition.* Imitation roxburgh, £3.
**Longfellow, H. W., Choice Poems by.** Illustrated by his Son, ERNEST W LONGFELLOW. 6s.
**Longfellow's Poetical Works.** *Fine-Art Edition.* Illustrated throughout with Original Engravings. Royal 4to, cloth gilt, £3 3s. *Popular Edition.* 16s.
**Luther, Martin: the Man and his Work.** By PETER BAYNE, LL.D. Two Vols., 24s.
**Marine Painting.** By WALTER W. MAY, R.I. With 16 Coloured Plates. Cloth, 5s
**Mechanics, The Practical Dictionary of.** Containing 15,000 Drawings. Four Vols. 21s. each.
**Medicine, Manuals for Students of.** *(A List forwarded post free on application.)*
**Midland Railway, The Official Illustrated Guide to the.** *New and Revised Edition.* 1s.; cloth, 2s.
**Modern Europe, A History of.** By C. A. FYFFE, M.A. Vol. I. From 1792 to 1814. 12s. Vol. II. From 1814 to 1848. 12s.
**Music, Illustrated History of.** By EMIL NAUMANN. Edited by the Rev. Sir F. A. GORE OUSELEY, Bart. Illustrated. Two Vols. 31s. 6d.
**National Library, Cassell's.** In Weekly Volumes, each containing about 192 pages. Paper covers, 3d.; cloth, 6d. *(A List of the Volumes already published sent post free on application.)*
**Natural History, Cassell's Concise.** By E. PERCEVAL WRIGHT, M.A., M.D., F.L.S. With several Hundred Illustrations. 7s. 6d.; roxburgh, 10s. 6d.
**Natural History, Cassell's New.** Edited by Prof. P. MARTIN DUNCAN, M.B., F.R.S., F.G.S. With Contributions by Eminent Scientific Writers. Complete in Six Vols. With about 2,000 high-class Illustrations. Extra crown 4to, cloth, 9s. each.
**Nature, Short Studies from.** Illustrated. *Cheap Edition.* 2s. 6d.
**Neutral Tint, A Course of Painting in.** With Twenty-four Plates by R. P. LEITCH. With full Instructions to the Pupil. 5s.
**Nimrod in the North; or, Hunting and Fishing Adventures in the Arctic Regions.** By Lieut. SCHWATKA. Illustrated. 7s 6d.
**Nursing for the Home and for the Hospital, A Handbook of.** By CATHERINE J. WOOD. *Cheap Edition.* 1s. 6d.; cloth, 2s.
**Oil Painting, A Manual of.** By Hon. JOHN COLLIER. Cloth, 2s. 6d.
**On the Equator.** By H. DE W. Illustrated with Photos. 3s. 6d.
**Orion the Gold Beater.** A Novel. By SYLVANUS COBB, Junr. Cloth, 3s. 6d.
**Our Own Country.** Six Vols. With 1,200 Illustrations. Cloth. 7s. 6d. each.
**Outdoor Sports and Indoor Amusements, Cassell's Book of.** With about 900 Illustrations. *Cheap Edition.* 992 pages, medium 8vo, cloth, 3s. 6d.
**Paris, Cassell's Illustrated Guide to.** Cloth, 1s.
**Parliaments, A Diary of Two.** By H. W. LUCY. The Disraeli Parliament, 1874–1880. 12s. The Gladstone Parliament, 1881–1886. 12s.
**Paxton's Flower Garden.** By Sir JOSEPH PAXTON and Prof. LINDLEY. Revised by THOMAS BAINES, F.R.H.S. Three Vols. With 100 Coloured Plates. £1 1s. each.
**Peoples of the World, The.** By Dr. ROBERT BROWN. Complete in Six Volumes. With Illustrations. 7s. 6d. each.
**Phantom City, The.** By W. WESTALL. 5s.
**Photography for Amateurs.** By T. C. HEPWORTH. Illustrated. 1s.; or cloth, 1s. 6d.

*Selections from Cassell & Company's Publications.*

---

**Phrase and Fable, Dictionary of.** By the Rev. Dr. BREWER. *Cheap Edition, Enlarged*, cloth, 3s. 6d. ; or with leather back, 4s. 6d.
**Picturesque America.** Complete in Four Vols., with 48 Exquisite Steel Plates, and about 800 Original Wood Engravings. £2 2s. each.
**Picturesque Canada.** With about 600 Original Illustrations. Two Vols., £3 3s. each.
**Picturesque Europe.** Complete in Five Vols. Each containing 13 Exquisite Steel Plates, from Original Drawings, and nearly 200 Original Illustrations. £10 10s.; half-morocco, £15 15s. ; morocco gilt, £26 5s. The POPULAR EDITION is now complete in Five Vols., 18s. each.
**Pigeon Keeper, The Practical.** By LEWIS WRIGHT. Illustrated. 3s. 6d.
**Pigeons, The Book of.** By ROBERT FULTON. Edited by LEWIS WRIGHT. With 50 Coloured Plates and numerous Wood Engravings. 31s. 6d. ; half-morocco, £2 2s.
**Pocket Guide to Europe (Cassell's).** Size 5½ in. × 3¾ in. Leather, 6s.
**Poems, Representative of Living Poets, American and English.** Selected by the Poets themselves. 15s.
**Poets, Cassell's Miniature Library of the :—**

- Burns. Two Vols. Cloth, 1s. each; or cloth, gilt edges, 2s. 6d. the set.
- Byron. Two Vols. Cloth, 1s. each; or cloth, gilt edges, 2s. 6d. the set.
- Hood. Two Vols. Cloth, 1s. each; or cloth, gilt edges, 2s. 6d. the set.
- Longfellow. Two Vols. Cloth, 1s. each; or cloth, gilt edges, 2s. 6d. the set.
- Milton. Two Vols. Cloth, 1s. each; or cloth, gilt edges, 2s. 6d. the set.
- Scott. Two Vols. Cloth, 1s. each; or cloth, gilt edges, 2s. 6d. the set.
- Sheridan and Goldsmith. 2 Vols. Cloth, 1s. each; or cloth, gilt edges, 2s. 6d. the set.
- Wordsworth. Two Vols. Cloth, 1s. each; or cloth, gilt edges, 2s. 6d. the set.
- Shakespeare. Twelve Vols., half cloth, in box, 12s.

**Popular Library, Cassell's.** A Series of New and Original Works. Cloth, 1s. each.
- The Russian Empire.
- The Religious Revolution in the Sixteenth Century.
- English Journalism.
- Our Colonial Empire.
- The Young Man in the Battle of Life.
- John Wesley.
- The Story of the English Jacobins.
- Domestic Folk Lore.
- The Rev. Rowland Hill.
- Boswell and Johnson.
- History of the Free-Trade Movement in England.

**Post Office of Fifty Years Ago, The.** 1s.
**Poultry Keeper, The Practical.** By LEWIS WRIGHT. With Coloured Plates and Illustrations. 3s. 6d.
**Poultry, The Book of.** By LEWIS WRIGHT. *Popular Edition*. With Illustrations on Wood. 10s. 6d.
**Poultry, The Illustrated Book of.** By LEWIS WRIGHT. With Fifty Exquisite Coloured Plates, and numerous Wood Engravings. Cloth. 31s. 6d. ; half-morocco, £2 2s.
**Pre-Raphælites (The Italian) in the National Gallery.** By COSMO MONKHOUSE. Illustrated. 1s.
**Printing Machinery and Letterpress Printing, Modern.** By FRED. J. F. WILSON and DOUGLAS GREY. Illustrated. 21s.
**Queen Victoria, The Life and Times of.** By ROBERT WILSON. Complete in 2 Vols. With numerous Illustrations, representing the Chief Events in the Life of the Queen, and Portraits of the Leading Celebrities of her Reign. Extra crown 4to, cloth gilt, 9s. each.
**Queer Race, A.** By W. WESTALL. 5s.
**Rabbit-Keeper, The Practical.** By CUNICULUS. Illustrated. 3s. 6d.
**Red Library of English and American Classics, The.** Stiff covers, 1s. each; cloth, 2s. each.

- People I have Met.
- The Pathfinder.
- Evelina.
- Scott's Poems.
- Last of the Barons.
- Adventures of Mr. Ledbury and his friend Jack Johnson.
- Ivanhoe.
- Oliver Twist.
- Selections from Hood's Works.
- Longfellow's Prose Works.
- Sense and Sensibility.
- Lytton's Plays. [Harte).
- Tales, Poems, and Sketches (Bret
- Martin Chuzzlewit. Two Vols.
- The Prince of the House of David.
- Sheridan's Plays.
- Uncle Tom's Cabin.
- Deerslayer.
- Eugene Aram.
- Jack Hinton, the Guardsman.
- The Talisman.
- Rome and the Early Christians.
- The Trials of Margaret Lyndsay.
- Edgar Allan Poe. Prose and Poetry, Selections from.
- Old Mortality.
- The Hour and the Man.
- Washington Irving's Sketch-Book.
- Last Days of Palmyra.
- Tales of the Borders.
- Pride and Prejudice.
- Last of the Mohicans.
- Heart of Midlothian.
- Last Days of Pompeii.
- Yellowplush Papers
- Handy Andy.
- Selected Plays.
- American Humour.
- Sketches by Boz.
- Macaulay's Lays and Selected Essays.
- Harry Lorrequer.
- Old Curiosity Shop.
- Rienzi.
- Pickwick (Two Vols.).
- Scarlet Letter.

*Selections from Cassell & Company's Publications.*

**Royal River, The: The Thames, from Source to Sea.** With Descriptive Text and a Series of beautiful Engravings. £2 2s.
**Russia.** By Sir DONALD MACKENZIE WALLACE, M.A. 5s.
**Russo-Turkish War, Cassell's History of.** With about 500 Illustrations. Two Vols., 9s. each; library binding, One Vol., 15s.
**Saturday Journal, Cassell's.** Yearly Vols., 7s. 6d.
**Science for All.** Edited by Dr. ROBERT BROWN, M.A., F.L.S., &c. With 1,500 Illustrations. Five Vols., 9s. each.
**Sea, The: Its Stirring Story of Adventure, Peril, and Heroism.** By F. WHYMPER. With 400 Illustrations. Four Vols., 7s. 6d. each.
**Section 558, or the Fatal Letter.** A Novel. By JULIAN HAWTHORNE. Boards, 2s.; cloth, 2s. 6d.
**Sent Back by the Angels.** And other Ballads of Home and Homely Life. By FREDERICK LANGBRIDGE, M.A. 4s. 6d. *Popular Edition*, 1s.
**Sepia Painting, A Course of.** Two Vols., with Twelve Coloured Plates in each, and numerous Engravings. Each, 3s. Also in One Volume, 5s.
**Shaftesbury, The Seventh Earl of, K.G., The Life and Work of.** By EDWIN HODDER. With Portraits. Three Vols., 36s. *Popular Edition*, in One Vol., 7s. 6d.
**Shakspere, The International.** *Édition de luxe.*
 "King Henry IV." Illustrated by Herr EDUARD GRÜTZNER. £3 10s.
 "As You Like It." Illustrated by Mons. EMILE BAYARD. £3 10s.
 "Romeo and Juliet." Illustrated by FRANK DICKSEE, A.R.A. £5 5s.
**Shakspere, The Leopold.** With 400 Illustrations, and an Introduction by F. J. FURNIVALL. Small 4to, cloth gilt, 7s. 6d.; half-morocco, 10s. 6d.; full morocco, £1 1s. *Cheap Edition* 3s. 6d.
**Shakspere, The Royal.** With Exquisite Steel Plates and Wood Engravings. Three Vols. 15s. each.
**Shakespeare, Cassell's Quarto Edition.** Edited by CHARLES and MARY COWDEN CLARKE, and containing about 600 Illustrations by H. C. SELOUS. Complete in Three Vols., cloth gilt, £3 3s.—Also published in Three separate Volumes, in cloth, viz.:—The COMEDIES, 21s.; The HISTORICAL PLAYS, 18s. 6d.; The TRAGEDIES, 25s.
**Shakespeare, Miniature.** Illustrated. In Twelve Vols., in box, 12s.; or in Red Paste Grain (box to match), with spring catch, lettered in gold, 21s.
**Shakespearean Scenes and Characters.** Illustrative of Thirty Plays of Shakespeare. With Thirty Steel Plates and Ten Wood Engravings. The Text written by AUSTIN BRERETON. Royal 4to, 21s.
**Sketching from Nature in Water Colours.** By AARON PENLEY. With Illustrations in Chromo-Lithography. 15s.
**Skin and Hair, The Management of the.** By MALCOLM MORRIS, F.R.C.S. 2s.
**Sonnets and Quatorzains.** By CHRYS, M.A. (Oxon). 5s.
**Standards, Local Dual.** By JOHN HENRY NORMAN. 1s.
**Steam Engine, The Theory and Action of the: for Practical Men.** By W. H. NORTHCOTT, C.E. 3s. 6d.
**Stock Exchange Year-Book, The.** By THOMAS SKINNER. 12s. 6d.
**Summer Tide, Little Folks Holiday Number.** 1s.
**Sunlight and Shade.** With numerous Exquisite Engravings. 7s. 6d.
**Surgery, Memorials of the Craft of, in England.** With an Introduction by Sir JAMES PAGET. 21s.
**Thackeray, Character Sketches from.** Six New and Original Drawings by FREDERICK BARNARD, reproduced in Photogravure. 21s.
**Thorah, The Yoke of the.** A Novel. By SIDNEY LUSKA. Boards, 2s.; cloth, 3s. 6d.
**Three and Sixpenny Library of Standard Tales, &c.** All Illustrated and bound in cloth gilt. Crown 8vo. 3s. 6d. each.

 Jane Austen and her Works.
 Mission Life in Greece and Palestine.
 The Romance of Trade.
 The Three Homes.
 Deepdale Vicarage.
 In Duty Bound.
 The Half Sisters.
 Peggy Oglivie's Inheritance.
 The Family Honour.
 Esther West.
 Working to Win.
 Krilof and his Fables. By W. R. S. Ralston, M.A.
 Fairy Tales. By Prof. Morley.

**Tot Book for all Public Examinations.** By W. S. THOMSON, M.A. 1s.
**Town Holdings.** 1s.

*Selections from Cassell & Company's Publications.*

**Tragedy of Brinkwater, The.** A Novel. By MARTHA L. MOODEY. Boards, 2s.; cloth, 3s. 6d.
**Tragic Mystery, A.** A Novel. By JULIAN HAWTHORNE. Boards, 2s. ; cloth, 3s. 6d.
**Treasure Island.** By R. L. STEVENSON. Illustrated. 5s.
**Tree Painting in Water Colours.** By W. H. J. BOOT. With Eighteen Coloured Plates, and valuable instructions by the Artist. 5s.
**Trees, Familiar.** By G. S. BOULGER, F.L.S., F.G.S. Two Series. With Forty full-page Coloured Plates, from Original Paintings by W. H. J. BOOT. 12s. 6d. each.
**Twenty Photogravures of Pictures in the Salon of 1885,** by the leading French Artists. In Portfolio. Only a limited number of copies have been produced terms for which can be obtained of all Booksellers.
**"Unicode": The Universal Telegraphic Phrase Book.** Pocket and Desk Editions. 2s. 6d. each.
**United States, Cassell's History of the.** By the late EDMUND OLLIER. With 600 Illustrations. Three Vols. 9s. each.
**United States, The Youth's History of.** By EDWARD S. ELLIS. Illustrated. Four Vols. 36s.
**Universal History, Cassell's Illustrated.** With nearly ONE THOUSAND ILLUSTRATIONS. Vol. I. Early and Greek History.—Vol. II. The Roman Period.—Vol. III. The Middle Ages.—Vol. IV. Modern History. 9s. each.
**Vaccination Vindicated.** An Answer to the leading Anti-Vaccinators. By JOHN C. McVAIL, M.D., D.P.H. Camb. 5s.
**Veiled Beyond, The.** A Novel. By S. B. ALEXANDER. Cloth, 3s. 6d.
**Vicar of Wakefield and other Works** by OLIVER GOLDSMITH. Illustrated. 3s. 6d. ; cloth, gilt edges, 5s.
**Water-Colour Painting, A Course of.** With Twenty-four Coloured Plates by R. P. LEITCH, and full Instructions to the Pupil. 5s.
**What Girls Can Do.** By PHYLLIS BROWNE. 2s. 6d.
**Who is John Noman ?** A Novel. By CHARLES HENRY BECKETT. Boards, 2s., Cloth, 3s. 6d.
**Wild Birds, Familiar.** By W. SWAYSLAND. Four Series. With 40 Coloured Plates in each. 12s. 6d. each.
**Wild Flowers, Familiar.** By F. E. HULME, F.L.S., F.S.A. Five Series. With 40 Coloured Plates in each. 12s. 6d. each.
**Wise Woman, The.** By GEORGE MACDONALD. 2s. 6d.
**Woman's World, The.** Yearly Volume. 18s.
**World of Wit and Humour, The.** With 400 Illustrations. Cloth, 7s. 6d. ; cloth gilt, gilt edges, 10s. 6d.
**World of Wonders, The.** Two Vols. With 400 Illustrations. 7s. 6d. each.
**World's Lumber Room, The.** By SELINA GAYE. Illustrated. 2s. 6d.
**Yule Tide.** CASSELL'S CHRISTMAS ANNUAL. 1s.

## ILLUSTRATED MAGAZINES.

*The Quiver*, for Sunday and General Reading. Monthly, 6d.
*Cassell's Family Magazine.* Monthly, 7d.
*"Little Folks" Magazine.* Monthly, 6d.
*The Magazine of Art.* Monthly, 1s.
*The Woman's World.* Monthly, 1s.
*Cassell's Saturday Journal.* Weekly, 1d. ; Monthly, 6d.

*.* *Full particulars of* CASSELL & COMPANY'S **Monthly Serial Publications** *will be found in* CASSELL & COMPANY'S COMPLETE CATALOGUE.

**Catalogues of** CASSELL & COMPANY'S PUBLICATIONS, which may be had at all Booksellers', or will be sent post free on application to the Publishers :—
CASSELL'S COMPLETE CATALOGUE, containing particulars of One Thousand Volumes.
CASSELL'S CLASSIFIED CATALOGUE, in which their Works are arranged according to price, from *Threepence to Twenty-five Guineas.*
CASSELL'S EDUCATIONAL CATALOGUE, containing particulars of CASSELL & COMPANY'S Educational Works and Students' Manuals.

CASSELL & COMPANY, LIMITED, *Ludgate Hill, London.*

*Selections from Cassell & Company's Publications.*

## Bibles and Religious Works.

**Bible, The Crown Illustrated.** With about 1,000 Original Illustrations. With References, &c. 1,248 pages, crown 4to, cloth, 7s. 6d.
**Bible, Cassell's Illustrated Family.** With 900 Illustrations. Leather, gilt edges, £2 10s.; full morocco, £3 10s.
**Bible Dictionary, Cassell's.** With nearly 600 Illustrations. 7s. 6d.; roxburgh, 10s. 6d.
**Bible Educator, The.** Edited by the Very Rev. Dean PLUMPTRE, D.D. With Illustrations, Maps, &c. Four Vols., cloth, 6s. each.
**Bible Work at Home and Abroad.** Yearly Volume, 3s.
**Bible Talks about Bible Pictures.** Illustrated by GUSTAVE DORÉ and others. Large 4to, 5s.
**Bunyan's Pilgrim's Progress (Cassell's Illustrated).** 4to. 7s. 6d.
**Bunyan's Pilgrim's Progress.** With Illustrations. *Popular Edition*, 3s. 6d.
**Child's Life of Christ, The.** Complete in One Handsome Volume, with about 200 Original Illustrations. Demy 4to, gilt edges, 21s.
**Child's Bible, The.** With 200 Illustrations. Demy 4to, 830 pp. *145th Thousand.* *Cheap Edition*, 7s. 6d.
**Commentary, The New Testament, for English Readers.** Edited by the Rt. Rev. C. J. ELLICOTT, D.D., Lord Bishop of Gloucester and Bristol. In Three Volumes, 21s. each.
 Vol. I.—The Four Gospels.
 Vol. II.—The Acts, Romans, Corinthians, Galatians.
 Vol. III.—The remaining Books of the New Testament.
**Commentary, The Old Testament, for English Readers.** Edited by the Rt. Rev. C. J. ELLICOTT, D.D., Lord Bishop of Gloucester and Bristol. Complete in 5 Vols., 21s. each.
 Vol. I.—Genesis to Numbers. | Vol. III.—Kings I. to Esther.
 Vol. II.—Deuteronomy to Samuel II. | Vol. IV.—Job to Isaiah.
 Vol. V.—Jeremiah to Malachi.
**Dictionary of Religion, The.** An Encyclopædia of Christian and other Religious Doctrines, Denominations, Sects, Heresies, Ecclesiastical Terms, History, Biography, &c. &c. By the Rev. WILLIAM BENHAM, B.D. Cloth, 21s.; roxburgh, 25s.
**Doré Bible.** With 230 Illustrations by GUSTAVE DORÉ. *Original Edition.* Two Vols., cloth, £8; best morocco, gilt edges, £15.
**Early Days of Christianity, The.** By the Ven. Archdeacon FARRAR, D.D., F.R.S.
 LIBRARY EDITION. Two Vols., 24s.; morocco, £2 2s.
 POPULAR EDITION. Complete in One Volume, cloth, 6s.; cloth, gilt edges, 7s. 6d.; Persian morocco, 10s. 6d.; tree-calf, 15s.
**Family Prayer-Book, The.** Edited by Rev. Canon GARBETT, M.A., and Rev. S. MARTIN. Extra crown 4to, cloth, 5s.; morocco, 18s.
**Geikie, Cunningham, D.D., Works by:—**
 The Holy Land and the Bible. A Book of Scripture Illustrations gathered in Palestine. With Map. Two Vols. 24s.
 Hours with the Bible. Six Vols. 6s. each
 Entering on Life. 3s. 6d.
 The Precious Promises. 2s. 6d.
 The English Reformation. 5s.
 Old Testament Characters.
 The Life and Words of Christ. Illustrated. Two Vols., cloth, 30s. *Library Edition*, Two Vols., cloth, 30s. *Students' Edition*, Two Vols., 16s. *Cheap Edition*, in One Vol. 7s. 6d.
**Glories of the Man of Sorrows, The.** Sermons preached at St. James's, Piccadilly. By the Rev. H. G. BONAVIA HUNT, Mus.D., F.R.S.Edin. 2s. 6d.
**Gospel of Grace, The.** By a LINDESIE. Cloth, 2s. 6d.
**Helps to Belief.** A Series of Helpful Manuals on the Religious Difficulties of the Day. Edited by the Rev. TEIGNMOUTH SHORE, M.A., Chaplain in Ordinary to the Queen. Cloth, 1s. each.

CREATION. By the Lord Bishop of Carlisle. | THE MORALITY OF THE OLD TESTAMENT. By the Rev. Newman Smyth, D.D.
MIRACLES. By the Rev. Brownlow Maitland, M.A. |
PRAYER. By the Rev. T. Teignmouth Shore, M.A. | THE DIVINITY OF OUR LORD. By the Lord Bishop of Derry.

THE ATONEMENT. By the Lord Bishop of Peterborough.

7 B—8.88.

*Selections from Cassell & Company's Publications.*

---

"**Heart Chords.**" A Series of Works by Eminent Divines. Bound in cloth, red edges, 1s. each.

**My Father.** By the Right Rev. Ashton Oxenden, late Bishop of Montreal.
**My Bible.** By the Rt. Rev. W. Boyd Carpenter, Bishop of Ripon.
**My Work for God.** By the Right Rev. Bishop Cotterill.
**My Object in Life.** By the Ven. Archdeacon Farrar, D.D.
**My Aspirations.** By the Rev. G. Matheson, D.D.
**My Emotional Life.** By the Rev. Preb. Chadwick, D.D.
**My Body.** By the Rev. Prof. W. G. Blaikie, D.D.

**My Soul.** By the Rev. P. B. Power, M.A.
**My Growth in Divine Life.** By the Rev. Prebendary Reynolds, M.A.
**My Hereafter.** By the Very Rev. Dean Bickersteth.
**My Walk with God.** By the Very Rev. Dean Montgomery.
**My Aids to the Divine Life.** By the Very Rev. Dean Boyle.
**My Sources of Strength.** By the Rev. E. E. Jenkins, M.A., Secretary of the Wesleyan Missionary Society.

**Holy Land and the Bible, The.** A Book of Scripture Illustrations gathered in Palestine. By the Rev. CUNNINGHAM GEIKIE, D.D. Two Vols., demy 8vo, 1,120 pages, with Map. Price 24s.

**"I Must."** Short Missionary Bible Readings. By SOPHIA M. NUGENT. Enamelled cover, 6d.; cloth, gilt edges, 1s.

**Life of Christ, The.** By the Ven. Archdeacon FARRAR, D.D., F.R.S., Chaplain in Ordinary to the Queen.
  ILLUSTRATED EDITION, with about 300 Original Illustrations. Extra crown 4to, cloth, gilt edges, 21s.; morocco antique, 42s.
  LIBRARY EDITION. Two Vols. Cloth. 24s.; morocco, 42s.
  POPULAR EDITION, in One Vol. 8vo, cloth, 6s.; cloth, gilt edges, 7s. 6d.; Persian morocco, gilt edges, 10s. 6d.; tree-calf, 15s.

**Luther, Martin: his Life and Times.** By PETER BAYNE, LL.D. Two Vols., demy 8vo, 1,040 pages, cloth, 24s.

**Marriage Ring, The.** By WILLIAM LANDELS, D.D. Bound in white leatherette, gilt edges, in box, 6s.; French morocco, 8s. 6d.

**Moses and Geology; or, The Harmony of the Bible with Science.** By the Rev. SAMUEL KINNS, Ph.D., F.R.A.S. Illustrated. *Cheap Edition.* 6s.

**Protestantism, The History of.** By the Rev. J. A. WYLIE, LL.D. Containing upwards of 600 Original Illustrations. Three Vols., 27s.; Library Edition, 30s.

**Quiver Yearly Volume, The.** With 250 high-class Illustrations. 7s. 6d. Also Monthly, 6d.

**St. George for England;** and other Sermons preached to Children. *Fifth Edition.* By the Rev. T. TEIGNMOUTH SHORE, M.A. 5s.

**St. Paul, The Life and Work of.** By the Ven. Archdeacon FARRAR, D.D., F.R.S., Chaplain in Ordinary to the Queen.
  LIBRARY EDITION. Two Vols., cloth, 24s.; calf, 42s.
  ILLUSTRATED EDITION, complete in One Volume, with about 300 Illustrations, £1 1s.; morocco, £2 2s.
  POPULAR EDITION. One Volume, 8vo, cloth, 6s.; cloth, gilt edges, 7s. 6d.; Persian morocco, 10s. 6d.; tree-calf, 15s.

**Secular Life, The Gospel of the.** Sermons preached at Oxford. By the Hon. W. H. FREMANTLE, Canon of Canterbury. 5s.

**Shall We Know One Another?** By the Rt. Rev. J. C. RYLE, D.D., Bishop of Liverpool. *New and Enlarged Edition.* Cloth limp, 1s.

**Twilight of Life, The. Words of Counsel and Comfort for the Aged.** By JOHN ELLERTON, M.A. 1s. 6d.

**Voice of Time, The.** By JOHN STROUD. Cloth gilt, 1s.

*Selections from Cassell & Company's Publications.*

## Educational Works and Students' Manuals.

**Alphabet, Cassell's Pictorial.** Size, 35 inches by 42½ inches. Mounted on Linen, with rollers. 3s. 6d.
**Arithmetics, The Modern School.** By GEORGE RICKS, B.Sc. Lond. With Test Cards. (*List on application.*)
**Book-Keeping.** By THEODORE JONES. FOR SCHOOLS, 2s. ; or cloth, 3s. FOR THE MILLION, 2s. ; or cloth, 3s. Books for Jones's System, Ruled Sets of, 2s.
**Chemistry, The Public School.** By J. H. ANDERSON, M.A. 2s. 6d.
**Commentary, The New Testament.** Edited by Bishop ELLICOTT. Handy Volume Edition. Suitable for School and general use.

| St. Matthew. 3s. 6d. | Romans. 2s. 6d. | Titus, Philemon, Hebrews, and James. 3s. |
| St. Mark. 3s. | Corinthians I. and II. 3s. | Peter, Jude, and John. 3s. |
| St. Luke. 3s. 6d. | Galatians, Ephesians, and Philippians. 3s. | The Revelation. 3s. |
| St. John. 3s. 6d. | Colossians, Thessalonians, and Timothy. 3s. | An Introduction to the New Testament. 2s. 6d. |
| The Acts of the Apostles. 3s. 6d. | | |

**Commentary, Old Testament.** Edited by Bishop ELLICOTT. Handy Volume Edition. Suitable for School and general use.

| Genesis. 3s. 6d. | Leviticus. 3s. | Deuteronomy. 2s. 6d. |
| Exodus. 3s. | Numbers. 2s. 6d. | |

**Copy-Books, Cassell's Graduated.** Complete in 18 Books. 2d. each.
**Copy-Books, The Modern School.** Complete in 12 Books. 2d. each.
**Drawing Copies, Cassell's "New Standard."** Fourteen Books.
 Books A to F, for Standards I. to IV. .. .. .. .. 2d. each.
 „ G, H, K, L, M, O, for Standards V. to VII. .. .. 3d. each.
 „ N, P, .. .. .. .. .. .. 4d. each.
**Drawing Copies, Cassell's Modern School Freehand.** First Grade, 1s. ; Second Grade, 2s.
**Electricity, Practical.** By Prof. W. E AYRTON. 7s. 6d.
**Energy and Motion: A Text-Book of Elementary Mechanics.** By WILLIAM PAICE, M.A. Illustrated. 1s. 6d.
**English Literature, A First Sketch of,** from the Earliest Period to the Present Time. By Prof. HENRY MORLEY. 7s. 6d.
**Euclid, Cassell's.** Edited by Prof. WALLACE, M.A. 1s.
**Euclid, The First Four Books of.** In paper, 6d. ; cloth, 9d.
**French Reader, Cassell's Public School.** By GUILLAUME S. CONRAD. 2s. 6d.
**French, Cassell's Lessons in.** *New and Revised Edition.* Parts I. and II., each 2s. 6d. ; complete, 4s. 6d. Key, 1s. 6d.
**French-English and English-French Dictionary.** *Entirely New and Enlarged Edition.* 1,150 pages, 8vo, cloth, 3s. 6d.
**Galbraith and Haughton's Scientific Manuals.** By the Rev. Prof. GALBRAITH, M.A., and the Rev. P. f. HAUGHTON, M.D., D.C.L.

| Arithmetic. 3s. 6d. | Natural Philosophy. 3s. 6d. |
| Plane Trigonometry. 2s. 6d. | Optics. 2s. 6d. |
| Euclid. Books I., II., III. 2s. 6d. Books IV., V., VI. 2s. 6d. | Hydrostatics. 3s. 6d. |
| | Astronomy. 5s. |
| Mathematical Tables. 3s. 6d. | Steam Engine. 3s. 6d. |
| Mechanics. 3s. 6d. | Algebra. Part I., cloth, 2s. 6d. Complete, 7s. 6d. |
| Tides and Tidal Currents, with Tidal Cards, 3s. | |

**Geometry, First Elements of Experimental.** By PAUL BERT. Fully Illustrated. 1s. 6d.
**Geometry, Practical Solid.** By Major ROSS, R.E. 2s.
**German of To-Day.** By Dr. HEINEMANN. 1s. 6d.
**German-English and English-German Dictionary.** 3s. 6d.
**German Reading, First Lessons in.** By A. JAGST. Illustrated. 1s.
**Handbook of New Code of Regulations.** By JOHN F. MOSS. 1s. ; cloth, 2s.
**Historical Course for Schools, Cassell's.** Illustrated throughout. I.—Stories from English History, 1s. II.—The Simple Outline of English History, 1s. 3d. III.—The Class History of England, 2s. 6d.
**Historical Cartoons, Cassell's Coloured.** Size 45 in. × 35 in. 2s. each. Mounted on canvas and varnished, with rollers, 5s. each.
**Latin-English Dictionary, Cassell's.** Thoroughly revised and corrected, and in part re-written by J. R. V. MARCHANT, M.A. 3s. 6d.

**Latin-English and English-Latin Dictionary.** By J. R. BEARD, D.D., and C. BEARD, B.A. Crown 8vo, 914 pp., 3s. 6d.
**Latin Primer, The New.** By Prof. J. P. POSTGATE. 2s. 6d.
**Laws of Every-Day Life.** For the Use of Schools. By H. O. ARNOLD-FORSTER. 1s. 6d.
**Lay Texts for the Young, in English and French.** By Mrs. RICHARD STRACHEY. 2s. 6d. [1s. 6d.
**Little Folks' History of England.** By ISA CRAIG-KNOX. With 30 Illustrations.
**Making of the Home, The:** A Book of Domestic Economy for School and Home Use. By Mrs. SAMUEL A. BARNETT. 1s. 6d.
**Marlborough Books.**
   Arithmetic Examples. 3s.   |   French Exercises. 3s. 6d.
   Arithmetic Rules. 1s. 6d.   |   French Grammar. 2s. 6d.
                      German Grammar. 3s. 6d.
**Mechanics and Machine Design, Numerical Examples in Practical.** By R. G. BLAINE, M.E. With Diagrams. Cloth, 2s. 6d.
**Music, An Elementary Manual of.** By HENRY LESLIE. 1s.
**Popular Educator, Cassell's.** *New and Thoroughly Revised Edition.* Illustrated throughout. Complete in Six Vols., 5s. each; or in Three Vols., half calf, 42s. the set.
**Readers, Cassell's "Higher Class":**—"The World's Lumber Room," Illustrated, 2s. 6d.; "Short Studies from Nature," Illustrated, 2s. 6d.; "The World in Pictures." (Ten in Series.) Cloth, 2s. each.
**Readers, Cassell's Readable.** Carefully graduated, extremely interesting, and illustrated throughout. (*List on application.*)
**Readers, Cassell's Historical.** Illustrated throughout, printed on superior paper, and strongly bound in cloth. (*List on application.*)
**Readers for Infant Schools, Coloured.** Three Books. Each containing 48 pages, including 8 pages in colours. 4d. each.
**Reader, The Citizen.** By H. O. ARNOLD-FORSTER. With Preface by the late Rt. Hon. W. E. FORSTER, M.P. 1s. 6d.
**Readers, The Modern Geographical.** Illustrated throughout, and strongly bound in cloth. (*List on application.*)
**Readers, The Modern School.** Illustrated. (*List on application.*)
**Reading and Spelling Book, Cassell's Illustrated.** 1s.
**School Bank Manual, A.** By AGNES LAMBERT. 6d.
**Shakspere Reading Book, The.** By H. COURTHOPE BOWEN, M.A. Illustrated. 3s. 6d. Also issued in Three Books, 1s. each.
**Shakspere's Plays for School Use.** 5 Books. Illustrated. 6d. each.
**"Slöjd," as a means of Teaching the Essential Elements of Education.** By EMILY LORD. 6d.
**Spelling, A Complete Manual of.** By J. D. MORELL, LL.D. 1s.
**Technical Manuals, Cassell's.** Illustrated throughout:—
   Handrailing and Staircasing. 3s. 6d.   |   Machinists & Engineers, Drawing for. 4s. 6d.
   Bricklayers, Drawing for. 3s.   |   Model Drawing. 3s.
   Building Construction. 2s.   |   Orthographical and Isometrical Projection. 2s.
   Cabinet-Makers, Drawing for. 3s.   |  
   Carpenters & Joiners, Drawing for. 3s. 6d.   |   Practical Perspective. 3s.
   Gothic Stonework. 3s.   |   Stonemasons, Drawing for. 3s.
   Linear Drawing & Practical Geometry. 2s.   |   Applied Mechanics. By Sir R. S. Ball, LL.D. 2s.
   Linear Drawing and Projection. The Two Vols. in One, 3s. 6d.   |   Systematic Drawing and Shading. By Charles Ryan. 2s.
   Metal-Plate Workers, Drawing for. 3s.   |  
**Technical Educator, Cassell's.** Illustrated throughout. Popular Edition. Four Vols., 5s. each.
**Technology, Manuals of.** Edited by Prof. AYRTON, F.R.S., and RICHARD WORMELL, D.Sc., M.A. Illustrated throughout.
   The Dyeing of Textile Fabrics. By Prof. Hummel. 5s.   |   Design in Textile Fabrics. By T. R. Ashenhurst. 4s. 6d.
   Watch and Clock Making. By D. Glasgow. 4s. 6d.   |   Practical Mechanics. By Prof. Perry, M.E. 3s. 6d.
   Steel and Iron. By Prof. W. H. Greenwood, F.C.S., M.I.C.E., &c. 5s.   |  
   Spinning Woollen and Worsted. By W. S. McLaren, M.P. 4s. 6d.   |   Cutting Tools Worked by Hand and Machine. By Prof. Smith. 3s. 6d.
                      *A Prospectus on application.*
**Test Cards, Cassell's Combination.** In sets, 1s. each.
**Test Cards, Cassell's Modern School.** In sets, 1s. each.

*A Copy of Cassell and Company's Complete Catalogue will be forwarded post free on application.*

*Selections from Cassell & Company's Publications.*

# Books for Young People.

"**Little Folks**" **Half-Yearly Volume.** With 200 Illustrations, with Pictures in Colour. Boards, 3s. 6d. ; or cloth gilt, 5s.
**Bo-Peep.** A Book for the Little Ones. With Original Stories and Verses. Illustrated throughout. Yearly Volume. Boards, 2s. 6d. ; cloth gilt, 3s. 6d.
**Every-day Heroes.** By LAURA LANE. Illustrated. Cloth, 2s. 6d.
**Legends for Lionel.** New Picture Book by WALTER CRANE. 5s.
**Flora's Feast.** A Masque of Flowers. Penned and Pictured by WALTER CRANE. With 40 pages in Colours. 5s.
**The New Children's Album.** Fcap. 4to, 320 pages. Illustrated throughout. 3s. 6d.
**The Tales of the Sixty Mandarins.** By P. V. RAMASWAMI RAJU. With an Introduction by Prof. HENRY MORLEY. Illustrated. 5s.
**Sunday School Reward Books.** By Popular Authors. With Four Original Illustrations in each. Cloth gilt, 1s. 6d. each.

Seeking a City.
Rhoda's Reward; or, "If Wishes were Horses."
Jack Marston's Anchor.
Frank's Life-Battle; or, The Three Friends.

Rags and Rainbows: a Story of Thanksgiving.
Uncle William's Charge; or, The Broken Trust.
Pretty Pink's Purpose; or, The Little Street Merchants.

"**Golden Mottoes**" **Series, The.** Each Book containing 208 pages, with Four full-page Original Illustrations. Crown 8vo, cloth gilt, 2s. each.

"Nil Desperandum." By the Rev. F. Langbridge, M.A.
"Bear and Forbear." By Sarah Pitt.
"Foremost if I Can." By Helen Atteridge.

"Honour is my Guide." By Jeanie Hering (Mrs. Adams-Acton).
"Aim at a Sure End." By Emily Searchfield.
"He Conquers who Endures." By the Author of "May Cunningham's Trial," &c.

**The "Proverbs" Series.** Consisting of a New and Original Series of Stories by Popular Authors, founded on and illustrating well-known Proverbs. With Four Illustrations in each Book, printed on a tint. Crown 8vo, 160 pages, cloth, 1s. 6d. each.

Fritters; or, "It's a Long Lane that has no Turning." By Sarah Pitt.
Trizy; or, "Those who Live in Glass Houses shouldn't throw Stones." By Maggie Symington.
The Two Hardcastles; or, "A Friend in Need is a Friend Indeed." By Madeline Bonavia Hunt.

Major Monk's Motto; or, "Look Before you Leap." By the Rev. F. Langbridge.
Tim Thomson's Trial; or, "All is not Gold that Glitters." By George Weatherly.
Ursula's Stumbling-Block; or, "Pride comes before a Fall." By Julia Goddard.
Ruth's Life-Work; or, "No Pains, no Gains." By the Rev. Joseph Johnson.

**The "Cross and Crown" Series.** Consisting of Stories founded on incidents which occurred during Religious Persecutions of Past Days. With Illustrations in each Book. 2s. 6d. each.

By Fire and Sword: a Story of the Huguenots. By Thomas Archer.
Adam Hepburn's Vow: a Tale of Kirk and Covenant. By Annie S. Swan.
No. XIII ; or, The Story of the Lost Vestal. A Tale of Early Christian Days. By Emma Marshall.

Strong to Suffer: A Story of the Jews. By E. Wynne.
Heroes of the Indian Empire; or, Stories of Valour and Victory. By Ernest Foster.
In Letters of Flame: A Story of the Waldenses. By C. L. Matéaux.
Through Trial to Triumph. By Madeline B. Hunt.

**The World's Workers.** A Series of New and Original Volumes by Popular Authors. With Portraits printed on a tint as Frontispiece. 1s. each.

The Earl of Shaftesbury. By Henry Frith.
Sarah Robinson, Agnes Weston, and Mrs. Meredith. By E. M. Tomkinson.
Thomas A. Edison and Samuel F. B. Morse. By Dr. Denslow and J. Marsh Parker.
Mrs. Somerville and Mary Carpenter. By Phyllis Browne.
General Gordon. By the Rev S. A Swaine.
Charles Dickens. By his Eldest Daughter.
Sir Titus Salt and George Moore. By J. Burnley.
Florence Nightingale, Catherine Marsh, Frances Ridley Havergal, Mrs. Ranyard ("L. N. R.") By Lizzie Alldridge.

Dr. Guthrie, Father Mathew, Elihu Burritt, Joseph Livesey. By the Rev. J. W. Kirton.
Sir Henry Havelock and Colin Campbell, Lord Clyde. By E. C. Phillips.
Abraham Lincoln. By Ernest Foster.
David Livingstone. By Robert Smiles.
George Muller and Andrew Reed. By E. R. Pitman.
Richard Cobden. By R. Gowing.
Benjamin Franklin. By E. M. Tomkinson.
Handel. By Eliza Clarke.
Turner the Artist. By the Rev. S. A. Swaine.
George and Robert Stephenson. By C. L. Matéaux.

*Selections from Cassell & Company's Publications.*

---

**Five Shilling Books for Young People.** With Original Illustrations. Cloth gilt, 5s. each.

The Palace Beautiful. By L. T. Meade.
"Follow my Leader;" or, the Boys of Templeton. By Talbot Baines Reed.
For Fortune and Glory; a Story of the Soudan War. By Lewis Hough.
Under Bayard's Banner. By Henry Frith.
The Champion of Odin; or, Viking Life in the Days of Old. By J. Fred. Hodgetts.
Bound by a Spell; or, the Hunted Witch of the Forest. By the Hon. Mrs. Greene.
The King's Command. A Story for Girls. By Maggie Symington.
The Romance of Invention. By Jas. Burnley.

**Three and Sixpenny Books for Young People.** With Original Illustrations. Cloth gilt, 3s. 6d. each.

The Cost of a Mistake. By Sarah Pitt.
A World of Girls: A Story of a School. By L. T. Meade.
On Board the "Esmeralda;" or, Martin Leigh's Log. By John C. Hutcheson.
Lost among White Africans: A Boy's Adventures on the Upper Congo. By David Ker.
In Quest of Gold; or, Under the Whanga Falls. By Alfred St. Johnston.
For Queen and King; or, the Loyal 'Prentice. By Henry Frith.
Perils Afloat and Brigands Ashore. By Alfred Elwes.
Freedom's Sword: A Story of the Days of Wallace and Bruce. By Annie S. Swan.

**The "Boy Pioneer" Series.** By EDWARD S. ELLIS. With Four Full-page Illustrations in each Book. Crown 8vo, cloth, 2s. 6d. each.

Ned in the Woods. A Tale of Early Days in the West.
Ned on the River. A Tale of Indian River Warfare.
Ned in the Block House. A Story of Pioneer Life in Kentucky.

**The "Log Cabin" Series.** By EDWARD S. ELLIS. With Four Full-page Illustrations in each. Crown 8vo, cloth, 2s. 6d. each.

The Lost Trail. | Camp-Fire and Wigwam.
Footprints in the Forest.

**The "Great River" Series.** (Uniform with the "Log Cabin" Series.) By EDWARD S. ELLIS. Illustrated. Crown 8vo, cloth, bevelled boards, 2s. 6d. each.

Down the Mississippi. | Lost in the Wilds.
Up the Tapajos; or, Adventures in Brazil.

**The "Chimes" Series.** Each containing 64 pages, with Illustrations on every page, and handsomely bound in cloth, 1s.

Bible Chimes. Contains Bible Verses for Every Day in the Month.
Daily Chimes. Verses from the Poets for Every Day in the Month.
Holy Chimes. Verses for Every Sunday in the Year.
Old World Chimes. Verses from old writers for Every Day in the Month.

**Sixpenny Story Books.** All Illustrated, and containing Interesting Stories by well-known Writers.

The Smuggler's Cave.
Little Lizzie.
The Boat Club.
Luke Barnicott.
Little Bird.
Little Pickles.
The Elchester College Boys.
My First Cruise.
The Little Peacemaker.
The Delft Jug.

**Cassell's Picture Story Books.** Each containing 60 pages of Pictures and Stories, &c. 6d. each.

Little Talks.
Bright Stars.
Nursery Toys.
Pet's Posy.
Tiny Tales.
Daisy's Story Book.
Dot's Story Book.
A Nest of Stories.
Good Night Stories.
Chats for Small Chatterers.
Auntie's Stories.
Birdie's Story Book.
Little Chimes.
A Sheaf of Tales.
Dewdrop Stories.

**Illustrated Books for the Little Ones.** Containing interesting Stories. All Illustrated. 1s. each.

Indoors and Out.
Some Farm Friends.
Those Golden Sands.
Little Mothers and their Children.
Our Pretty Pets.
Our Schoolday Hours.
Creatures Tame.
Creatures Wild.
Up and Down the Garden.
All Sorts of Adventures.
Our Sunday Stories.
Our Holiday Hours.

**Shilling Story Books.** All Illustrated, and containing Interesting Stories.

Seventeen Cats.
Bunty and the Boys.
The Heir of Elmdale.
The Mystery at Shoncliff School.
Claimed at Last, and Roy's Reward.
Thorns and Tangles.
The Cuckoo in the Robin's Nest.
John's Mistake.
Diamonds in the Sand.
Surly Bob.
The History of Five Little Pitchers.
The Giant's Cradle.
Shag and Doll.
Aunt Lucia's Locket.
The Magic Mirror.
The Cost of Revenge.
Clever Frank.
Among the Redskins.
The Ferryman of Brill.
Harry Maxwell.
A Banished Monarch.

*Selections from Cassell & Company's Publications.*

---

**Cassell's Children's Treasuries.** Each Volume contains Stories or Poetry, and is profusely Illustrated. Cloth, 1s. each.

- Cock Robin, and other Nursery Rhymes.
- The Queen of Hearts.
- Old Mother Hubbard.
- Tuneful Lays for Merry Days.
- Cheerful Songs for Young Folks.
- Pretty Poems for Young People.
- The Children's Joy.
- Pretty Pictures and Pleasant Stories.
- Our Picture Book.
- Tales for the Little Ones.
- My Sunday Book of Pictures.
- Sunday Garland of Pictures and Stories.
- Sunday Readings for Little Folks.

---

**"Little Folks" Painting Books.** With Text, and Outline Illustrations for Water-Colour Painting. 1s. each.

- Fruits and Blossoms for "Little Folks" to Paint.
- The "Little Folks" Illuminating Book Pictures to Paint.
- The "Little Folks" Proverb Painting Book.

---

**Eighteenpenny Story Books.** All Illustrated throughout.

- Wee Willie Winkie.
- Ups and Downs of a Donkey's Life.
- Three Wee Ulster Lassies.
- Up the Ladder.
- Dick's Hero; and other Stories.
- The Chip Boy.
- Raggles, Baggles, and the Emperor.
- Roses from Thorns.
- Faith's Father.
- By Land and Sea.
- The Young Berringtons.
- Jeff and Leff.
- Tom Morris's Error.
- Worth more than Gold.
- "Through Flood—Through Fire;" and other Stories.
- The Girl with the Golden Locks.
- Stories of the Olden Time.

---

**The "World in Pictures" Series.** Illustrated throughout. 2s. 6d. each.

- A Ramble Round France.
- All the Russias.
- Chats about Germany.
- The Land of the Pyramids (Egypt).
- Peeps into China.
- The Eastern Wonderland (Japan).
- Glimpses of South America.
- Round Africa.
- The Land of Temples (India)
- The Isles of the Pacific.

---

**Two-Shilling Story Books.** All Illustrated.

- Stories of the Tower.
- Mr. Burke's Nieces.
- May Cunningham's Trial.
- The Top of the Ladder: How to Reach it.
- Little Flotsam.
- Madge and her Friends.
- The Children of the Court.
- A Moonbeam Tangle.
- Maid Marjory.
- The Four Cats of the Tippertons.
- Marion's Two Homes.
- Little Folks' Sunday Book.
- The Magic Flower Pot.
- School Girls.
- Two Fourpenny Bits.
- Poor Nelly.
- Tom Heriot.
- Aunt Tabitha's Waifs.
- In Mischief Again.
- Through Peril to Fortune.
- Peggy, and other Tales.

---

**Half-Crown Books.**

- Little Hinges.
- Margaret's Enemy.
- Pen's Perplexities.
- Notable Shipwrecks.
- Golden Days.
- Wonders of Common Things.
- At the South Pole.
- Truth will Out.
- Pictures of School Life and Boyhood.
- The Young Man in the Battle of Life. By the Rev. Dr. Landels.
- The True Glory of Woman. By the Rev. Dr. Landels.
- The Wise Woman. By George Macdonald.
- Soldier and Patriot (George Washington).

---

**Picture Teaching Series.** Each book Illustrated throughout. Fcap. 4to, cloth gilt, coloured edges, 2s. 6d. each.

- Through Picture-Land.
- Picture Teaching for Young and Old.
- Picture Natural History.
- Scraps of Knowledge for the Little Ones.
- Great Lessons from Little Things.
- Woodland Romances.
- Stories of Girlhood.
- Frisk and his Flock.
- Pussy Tip-Toes' Family.
- The Boy Joiner and Model Maker
- The Children of Holy Scripture.

*Selections from Cassell & Company's Publications.*

---

**Library of Wonders.** Illustrated Gift-books for Boys. Paper, 1s.; cloth, 1s. 6d.

Wonders of Acoustics.
Wonderful Adventures.
Wonders of Animal Instinct.
Wonders of Architecture.
Wonderful Balloon Ascents.
Wonders of Bodily Strength and Skill.
Wonderful Escapes.
Wonders of Water.

---

**The "Home Chat" Series.** All Illustrated throughout. Fcap. 4to. Boards, 3s. 6d. each; cloth, gilt edges, 5s. each.

Home Chat.
Peeps Abroad or Folks at Home.
Decisive Events in History.
Around and About Old England.
Half-Hours with Early Explorers.
Paws and Claws.

---

**Books for the Little Ones.** Fully Illustrated.

A Dozen and One; or, The Boys and Girls of Polly's Ring. By Mary D. Brine. Full of Illustrations. 5s.
The Merry-go-Round. Poems for Children. Illustrated throughout. 5s.
Rhymes for the Young Folk. By William Allingham. Beautifully Illustrated. 3s. 6d.
The Little Doings of some Little Folks. By Chatty Cheerful. Illustrated. 5s.
The Sunday Scrap Book. With One Thousand Scripture Pictures. Boards, 5s.; cloth, 7s. 6d.
Daisy Dimple's Scrap Book. Containing about 1,000 Pictures. Boards, 5s.; cloth gilt, 7s. 6d.
The History Scrap Book. With nearly 1,000 Engravings. 5s.; cloth, 7s. 6d.
The Little Folks' Out and About Book. By Chatty Cheerful. Illustrated. 5s.
Myself and my Friends. By Olive Patch. With numerous Illustrations. Crown 4to. 5s.
A Parcel of Children. By Olive Patch. With numerous Illustrations. Crown 4to. 5s.
Little Folks' Picture Album. With 168 Large Pictures. 5s.
Little Folks' Picture Gallery. With 150 Illustrations. 5s.
The Old Fairy Tales. With Original Illustrations. Boards, 1s.; cloth, 1s. 6d.
My Diary. With Twelve Coloured Plates and 366 Woodcuts. 1s.
Happy Little People. By Olive Patch. With Illustrations. 5s.
"Little Folks" Album of Music, The. Illustrated. 3s. 6d.
Cheerful Clatter. Nearly One Hundred Full-page Pictures. 3s. 6d.
Twilight Fancies. Full of charming Pictures. Boards, 2s. 6d.
Happy Go Luc'y. 2s.
Daisy Blue Eyes. 2s.
Good Times. 1s. 6d.
Jolly Little Stories. 1s. 6d.
Our Little Friends. 1s. 6d.
Daisy Dell's Stories. 1s. 6d.
Little Toddlers. 1s. 6d.
Wee Little Rhymes. 1s. 6d.
Little One's Welcome. 1s. 6d.
Little Gossips. 1s. 6d.
Ding Dong Bell. 1s. 6d.
The Story of Robin Hood. With Coloured Illustrations. 2s. 6d.
The Pilgrim's Progress. With Coloured Illustrations. 2s. 6d.

---

**Books for Boys.**

Commodore Junk. By G. Manville Fenn. 5s.
The Black Arrow. A Tale of the Two Roses. By R. L. Stevenson. 5s.
Dead Man's Rock. A Romance. By Q. 5s.
A Queer Race. By W. Westall. 5s.
Captain Trafalgar. A Story of the Mexican Gulf. By W. Westall. Illustrated. 5s.
Kidnapped. By R. L. Stevenson. Illustrated. 5s.
King Solomon's Mines. By H. Rider Haggard. 5s.
Treasure Island. By R. L. Stevenson. With Full-page Illustrations. 5s.
Ships, Sailors, and the Sea. By R. J. Cornewall-Jones. Illustrated. 5s.
The Phantom City. By W. Westall. 5s.
Famous Sailors of Former Times. History of the Sea Fathers. By Clements Markham. Illustrated. 2s. 6d.
Modern Explorers. By Thomas Frost. Illustrated. 5s.
Wild Adventures in Wild Places. By Dr. Gordon Stables, M.D., R.N. Illustrated. 5s.
Jungle, Peak, and Plain. By Dr. Gordon Stables, R.N. Illustrated. 5s.
O'er Many Lands, on Many Seas. By Gordon Stables, R.N. Illustrated. 5s.
At the South Pole. By W. H. G. Kingston. *New Edition.* Illustrated. 2s. 6d.

---

**Books for all Children.**

Cassell's Robinson Crusoe. With 100 striking Illustrations. Cloth, 3s. 6d.; gilt edges, 5s.
Cassell's Swiss Family Robinson. Illustrated. Cloth, 3s. 6d.; gilt edges, 5s.
Sunny Spain: Its People and Places, with Glimpses of its History. By Olive Patch. Illustrated. 5s.
Rambles Round London Town. By C. L. Mateaux. Illustrated. 5s.
Favorite Album of Fun and Fancy, The. Illustrated. 3s. 6d.
Familiar Friends. By Olive Patch. Illustrated. Cloth gilt, 5s.
Odd Folks at Home. By C. L. Mateaux. With nearly 150 Illustrations. 5s.
Field Friends and Forest Foes. By Olive Patch. Profusely Illustrated. 5s.
Silver Wings and Golden Scales. Illustrated. 5s.
Little Folks' Holiday Album. Illustrated. 3s. 6d.
Tiny Houses and their Builders. Illustrated. 5s.
Children of all Nations. Their Homes, their Schools, their Playgrounds. Illustrated. 5s.
Tim Trumble's "Little Mother." By C. L. Mateaux. Illustrated. 5s.

---

CASSELL & COMPANY, Limited, Ludgate Hill, London, Paris, New York & Melbourne.

www.ingramcontent.com/pod-product-compliance
Lightning Source LLC
Chambersburg PA
CBHW051236300426